INTERNATIONAL
ECONOMICS

Thomas A. Pugel
New York University

Peter H. Lindert
University of California at Davis

Boston   Burr Ridge, IL   Dubuque, IA   Madison, WI   New York   San Francisco   St. Louis
Bangkok   Bogotá   Caracas   Lisbon   London   Madrid
Mexico City   Milan   New Delhi   Seoul   Singapore   Sydney   Taipei   Toronto

McGraw-Hill Higher Education

A Division of The McGraw-Hill Companies

International Economics

Copyright © 2000, 1996, 1991, 1986, 1982, 1978, 1973, 1968, 1963, 1958, 1953 by The McGraw-Hill Companies, Inc. All rights reserved. Printed in the United States of America. Except as permitted under the United States Copyright Act of 1976, no part of this publication may be reproduced or distributed in any form or by any means, or stored in a data base or retrieval system, without the prior written permission of the publisher.

This book is printed on acid-free paper.

1 2 3 4 5 6 7 8 9 0 DOC DOC 9 0 9 8 7 6 5 4 3 2 1 0

ISBN 0-07-290387-2

Vice president/Editor-in-chief: *Michael W. Junior*
Publisher: *Gary Burke*
Senior executive editor: *Paul Shensa*
Development editor: *Shoshannah Flach*
Marketing manager: *Nelson W. Black*
Senior project manager: *Eva Strock*
Senior production supervisor: *Richard DeVitto*
Designers: *Matthew Baldwin; Sabrina Dupont*
Cover designer: *Sabrina Dupont*
Cover illustrator: *Maria Rendon*
Compositor: *Precision Graphics*
Typeface: *Times Roman*
Printer: *RR Donnelley & Sons*

Library of Congress Cataloging-in-Publication Data

Pugel, Thomas A.
    International economics / Thomas A. Pugel, Peter H. Lindert.--[11th ed.]
      p. cm.
    Lindert's name appeared first on earlier ed.
    Includes bibliographical references and index.
    ISBN 0-07-290387-2 (alk. paper)
    1. International economic relations. 2. Commercial policy. 3. Foreign exchange. I.
Lindert, Peter H. II. Title.

HF1411 .L536 2000
337--dc21
                                             99-056092

INTERNATIONAL EDITION ISBN 0-07-116965-2
Copyright © 2000. Exclusive rights by The McGraw-Hill Companies, Inc. for manufacture and export. This book cannot be re-exported from the country to which it is consigned by McGraw-Hill. The International Edition is not available in North America.

http://www.mhhe.com

With this edition, Tom Pugel raises his role. He joined Peter Lindert as coauthor for the tenth edition, and for this eleventh edition Pugel took charge of the revision of the entire book. In recognition, he is now listed as the first author.

As teachers of international economics, we strive to use economic analysis that is rigorous and practical, with a writing style that is concise and readable. We use economic terminology where it enhances the economic logic of the analysis, but we loathe jargon for jargon's sake. We believe that our bicoastal partnership has been highly successful in creating this eleventh edition.

With each year the importance of international economics grows. The world is becoming more integrated, and countries are becoming more interdependent. International trade, direct foreign investments, and international lending and portfolio investments are growing faster than world production. Information and data now spread around the world instantly through the internet and other global electronic media. Increasingly, events and government policy changes in one country affect many other countries. Also increasingly, companies make decisions about production and product development based on global markets.

An enjoyable challenge for a new edition is to incorporate the events that continue to transform the international economy, often as part of the process of globalization (both its upside and its downside). We have gone to great lengths to discuss such important news events as

- The creation of the euro as the new European currency
- Financial crises in Thailand, Indonesia, South Korea, and Russia, as well as the currency crisis in Brazil
- The growing importance of the World Trade Organization as a forum for dispute settlement

- The rise of South America's MERCOSUR as an important regional trade area
- Successful transition by some formerly communist countries in Central and Eastern Europe, but slow or unsuccessful transition by many countries of the former Soviet Union
- The growing debate about immigration into the United States, Canada, and Western Europe

These world events and many others are described and analyzed here as we present applications of the theoretical framework of *International Economics*.

In this edition we also introduce a number of improvements to the overall pedagogical structure of the book.

- We continue to expand the end-of-chapter questions and problems. Each chapter has at least 10, and every odd-numbered question has an answer at the back of the book. (These odd-numbered questions are marked with a diamond as a reminder.)
- Openness to trade can raise a country's growth rate. A new section in Chapter 5 presents the basic concepts, and the relationship of trade policy to growth is taken up again in Chapter 13.
- We enhanced the analysis of product differentiation, monopolistic competition, and trade in Chapter 6. Trade expands the number of varieties of a product available to a buyer, and it tends to lower their prices. Chapter 6 has a new graph showing the determination of the number of varieties and the typical price of a variety.
- The number of countries using antidumping policies has been rising, and the industrialized countries are now both major users and major targets. The discussion of dumping in Chapter 10 is reorganized and sharpened, to explore why exporting firms dump and how the importing country is affected. This analysis leads to a critique of antidumping policy, which is increasingly being used as a protectionist device.
- Chapter 12, "Trade and the Environment," remains unique. It is now more powerful as an analysis of the economics of the interplay between environmental issues and international trade. After exploring whether free trade is anti-environment and whether the World Trade Organization is anti-environment, the chapter builds through the analysis of three types of environmental concerns: purely domestic pollution, transborder pollution, and global environmental problems. We continue to use the specificity rule as a key guide and to explore in depth such battlegrounds as dolphins, sea turtles, extinction of species, overfishing, ozone depletion, and global warming.
- We reorganized the analysis of the political economy of trade policy in Chapter 14, to emphasize the gains and losses of different groups, different types of political activity (voting, lobbying, and contributions),

and the impact of representative democracy. The analysis shows some circumstances in which import protection is unlikely, and others in which it is likely.

- International financial activities have grown rapidly in the past several decades, with the investment managers who control hedge funds becoming important players. We bring this world to life by profiling the best-known global investor, George Soros, in a box in Chapter 17.

- While most countries move toward more flexible exchange rates, some are searching for forms of fixed rates that are more nearly permanent. In Chapter 24 we discuss the growing use of currency boards and the growing interest in "dollarization" (the adoption of another country's currency as the local currency). This leads into an analysis of monetary union as an "international fix." As the most important current example, we explore the advantages and disadvantages of European Monetary Union and the adoption of the euro as the unionwide currency.

- Chapter 26 was substantially rewritten to focus on the financial crises of the 1990s. After presenting a history of international lending to developing countries, we examine the causes of financial crises, the use of rescue packages and debt restructuring to resolve them, and proposals for improving the "international financial architecture" to make them less frequent.

- Multinational firms now produce a substantial part of the world's goods and services. Although we might think that they are replacing international trade, a new section in Chapter 27 shows that direct foreign investment often leads to more international trade, as multinationals exploit comparative advantage when they locate different stages of production in different countries and as their affiliates improve the local marketing of foreign goods produced elsewhere by the multinationals.

We were also careful to retain those stylistic goals—clarity and honesty—that have made *International Economics* an extraordinary success in classrooms around the world. We give the student plenty of quick road signs at the start and end of each chapter, signs that implicitly say "Here's where we're going; here's where we've just been." Similarly, almost every paragraph leads off with its keynote sentence. We are candid about ranking the importance of some tools or facts ahead of others. The undeniable power of some of the economist's tools is applied repeatedly to recent events without apology. Tools that fail to improve on common sense and intuition are not oversold. Some facts are weightier than others, and we tried to order them carefully.

The format of the book is fine-tuned for better teaching. Most (though still not all) exam-worthy **definitions** appear in boldface in the text, and are distinguished from words of *special emphasis,* which appear in italics. For further visual contrast,

Some *key points or results* with a high probability of being covered on the exam are block-indented, like this.

Shaded boxes appear in different type with a different right edge format, unlike the main text. It should be easy to see that they offer extensions and case studies of a different character to be emphasized more or less at the instructor's discretion.

Acknowledgments

We are pleased to pay our respects once again to Charles P. Kindleberger, the author of the first five editions of this textbook.

We offer our deepest thanks to the many people whose advice helped us in our efforts to improve *International Economics* with each edition. We love teaching this material, and we are indebted to our students for many suggestions and insights. We especially thank Pugel's colleagues Jose Campa and Harvey Poniachek for their detailed comments on the tenth edition and suggestions for the eleventh. We also thank A. E. Safarian (University of Toronto) and James Stodder (Hartford Graduate Center) for their written comments and suggestions and Pugel's colleagues Richard Levich and Roy Smith for their help with specific topics in international finance.

We express our gratitude to reviewers whose comments and critiques provided guidance as we wrote the tenth and eleventh editions:

Basudeb Biswas
Utah State University

Donald R. Booth
Chapman University

Francisco Carrada-Bravo
Thunderbird-American Graduate School

Thomas J. Carter
University of Oklahoma

Eleanor D. Craig
University of Delaware

Selahattin Dibooglu
Southern Illinois University–Carbondale

Tom Head
George Fox College

Alan G. Isaac
The American University

Kishore Kulkarni
Metropolitan State College

George H. Lamson
Carleton College

Craig MacPhee
University of Nebraska-Lincoln

Stefan Norrbin
Florida State University

Martin C. Spechler
Indiana University-Indianapolis

Sarah Tinkler
Weber State University

T. Norman Van Cott
Ball State University

Charles H. Wellness
Fitchburg State College and Anna Maria College

Mahmood Yousefi
University of Northern Iowa

We also thank Jiawei Hu and Jin Yoo for their work in compiling data, formatting figures, and gathering other information for the revision.

Thomas A. Pugel
Peter H. Lindert

BRIEF CONTENTS

C O N T E N T S

3   Why Everybody Trades: Comparative Advantage and Factor Proportions   31

4   Who Gains and Who Loses from Trade?   61

PART II

TRADE POLICY 119

10   Pushing Exports   183

11   Trade Blocs and Trade Blocks   213

PART III

Understanding Foreign Exchange   321

15   Payments Among Nations   323

16   The Foreign Exchange Market   343

Thomas A. Pugel is Professor of Economics and International Business at the Stern School of Business, New York University and a Fellow of the Teaching Excellence Program at the Stern School. His research and publications focus on international industrial competition and government policies toward international trade and industry. Professor Pugel has been Visiting Professor at Aoyama Gakuin University in Japan and a member of the U.S. faculty at the National Center for Industrial Science and Technology Management Development in China. He received the university-wide Distinguished Teaching Award at New York University in 1991, and twice he was voted Professor of the Year by the graduate students at the Stern School of Business.

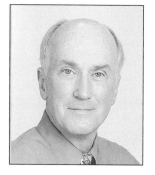

Peter H. Lindert is Professor of Economics and Director, Agricultural History Center, University of California, Davis. His books and journals range widely over modern economic history, international economics, modern inequality trends, government taxes and transfers, human fertility, international debt crisis, international trade competition, land quality, farm policy, and agricultural history. He served as Co-Editor of the *Journal of Economic History*, and was Vice President of the Economic History Association. Professor Lindert was honored with three awards at the University of California, Davis. In 1994 he received the Thomas Mayer Award for Distinguished Teaching in Economics, and in 1995 he was granted the university-wide Distinguished Teaching Award. In 1999 he was awarded the University of California Davis Prize for Undergraduate Teaching and Scholarly Achievement, which recognizes excellence in both teaching and research.

CHAPTER 1

International Economics Is Different

Nations are not like regions or families. They are sovereign, meaning that no central court can enforce its will on them with a global police force. Being sovereign, nations can put up all sorts of barriers between their members and the outside world, and they can be more indifferent to the interests of others. A region or family must deal with the political reality that others within the same nation can outvote it and, therefore, can coerce it or tax it. They have to compromise with others who have political voice. Nations feel less pressure to compromise, and often ignore the interests of foreigners. They use policy tools that are seldom available to regions and never available to families: their own currencies, their own trade barriers, their own fiscal policies, and their own laws of citizenship and residence.

As long as nations exist, international economics will always need a separate body of analysis distinct from the rest of economics. The special nature of international economics makes its study fascinating and sometimes difficult. Future events are sure to keep reminding us of what is special about this field. To see why, let's look at four recent events that have been shaping this book.

Four Events

Trade Blocs, Bananas, and Beef

A trade-bloc revolution culminating in the early 1990s has reshaped international trade. What had been separate nations were increasingly becoming giant multinational trade blocs. Within each large bloc, one could trade with people in the other countries almost as though they were in the same nation.

The West Europeans led the way in the formation of giant economic blocs. Building on progress toward economic integration dating back to the 1950s, the members of the European Union (EU) unified most of the rules of business, trade, and job-holding at the end of 1992. Countries outside the EU found that they had to bargain with an economic unit that had the second-highest gross domestic product of any free-trade unit in the world, larger than that of Japan.

Meanwhile, North America was forging its own formidable economic union. Partly in response to the prospect of tighter unity in Europe, Canada and the United States initiated a free-trade agreement in 1987. For all the debate that the trade pact sparked in Canada, it was quickly eclipsed by the sudden advance of Mexico as a country wanting to join a new North American Free Trade Area (NAFTA). Starting around 1985, Mexico unilaterally started dismantling its high barriers to imports of foreign goods. As part of a larger liberalization and privatization of the economy, the Mexican government pushed hard for the new free-trade area. It was a radical departure in the sense that NAFTA would unify sovereign nations with much wider differences in living standards than in the case of the European Union. Many Mexicans complained that they would lose their jobs to competition from the United States, and many in the United States made exactly the opposite claim. After a bitter fight, NAFTA prevailed in 1993. Over a period of years specified in the agreement, the trade barriers between Mexico and its northern neighbors have been coming down, leaving people on both sides of Mexico's northern border to rethink which goods they should go on selling to, and buying from, their compatriots and which goods they should trade internationally.

By the end of 1994, every nation of significant size had joined a regional trading bloc.[1] Even Japan and China, the last major holdouts, had joined the Asia-Pacific Economic Cooperation (APEC) Forum, which was aimed at lowering trade barriers throughout East Asia and across the Pacific.

Will the new trade blocs define an economic world in which trade is increasingly divided into rival trading blocs? Or will they be a stepping-stone on the journey to a more global economy? The global alternative also got a momentary boost in the early 1990s, as 117 member nations of the World Trade Organization agreed in 1993–94 to partial reductions in the trade barriers between them. This treaty culminated the tense seven-year Uruguay Round of trade negotiations. It reshapes world trade patterns, destroying some jobs and creating others, in ways discussed in Parts I and II of this book.

But it did not take long for fresh fights to break out between the two great trading blocs facing each other across the Atlantic. The biggest fights between North America and the European Union across the 1990s revolved around European imports of bananas and beef.

The great banana war of the 1990s pitted an all-America alliance against an alliance of Europe with its banana-exporting former colonies of the Caribbean and Africa. Ecuador and Central American countries are able to export bananas more cheaply than can the Caribbean and African countries. If there were a global free market in bananas, the exporters in Ecuador and Central America would drive the Caribbean nations out of the banana business.

---

[1]In the case of the formerly communist nations of Eastern Europe, however, the newly formed regional trade groupings are decidedly looser than the Soviet-led Council for Mutual Economic Assistance (CMEA), which dominated East European trade from 1949 to 1991.

Trade-bloc politics has intervened to prevent this competitive outcome. The European Union has long maintained a system of protection favoring Africa and the Caribbean, by imposing tariff duties (taxes) and quotas on the imports of bananas and some other products from outside the community of nations defined by historic ties from the colonial era. At the end of the 1990s, the EU sought to renew this protection while also giving its goods duty-free access to markets in the Caribbean and Africa. The Caribbean and African countries welcomed such protection against cheap bananas from Ecuador and Central America.[2] On the opposing corner stood the United States, whose fruit companies, such as Chiquita Brands and Dole, were the export distributors of those low-cost bananas grown by Ecuadorian and Central American farmers.

If the whole world were a nation, this banana war would have been prevented, or at least settled, long ago. If the laws of the global nation resembled those of the United States, the whole fight would have been left to the marketplace, with no government intervention. Within a nation, it is usually illegal for one region to put a tax on goods from other regions. So Europe's attempt to favor Caribbean and African bananas would have been ruled illegal, and banana sales from Ecuador, Central America, and the U.S. fruit companies would have expanded and taken over the world markets. The Caribbeans and Africans would have cut back on banana production and would have turned to making other things.

Now the world has tried to set up a world trade court, in the form of the World Trade Organization (WTO) based in Geneva.[3] It is a forum for settling trade disputes by saying which trade barriers are allowable as exceptions to the general presumption that nations should trade freely without government barriers. And the WTO has ruled in favor of the Americans a number of times, saying that the European Union's discriminatory barriers in favor of Africa and the Caribbean are a violation of international trade agreements. The EU has been slow to comply with these rulings. In 1999, the WTO took the drastic further step of allowing the Americans to retaliate against the EU by imposing special 100 percent tariffs (or taxes) on imports of as much European exports as the estimated $191 million of bananas from Ecuador and Central America that were unfairly blocked from the European market. The United States began charging a 100 percent tariff on imports of French plastic handbags, German coffee makers, and European lithographs, bed linens, cardboard packing material, and lead-acid storage batteries. These WTO-approved sanctions made it harder, if not impossible, to sell these European products in the United States.

While suffering this defeat in the banana war, the European Union heated up the long-standing beef war in 1999. Americans can produce beef much more cheaply and efficiently than can Europeans, where costs tend to be 30 to 100 percent higher. The EU has maintained high import barriers against most beef from North America, protecting its high-cost domestic beef producers.

---

[2] For the Caribbean nations, however, there is a downside to the continuing protection of their banana exports to Europe. As long as Europe discriminates in favor of their bananas, the North Americans will continue to resist making it easier for Caribbean manufacturers, such as clothing, to enter the North American markets. European discrimination in favor of the Caribbean former colonies will be countered by NAFTA discrimination in favor of clothing and other goods from Mexico, to the disadvantage of the Caribbeans.

[3] For more on the World Trade Organization, see Part II.

With beef, however, the Europeans have a different argument in favor of blocking imports. Much of the beef raised in America (or Australia or some other countries) is given hormones to increase meat production. Starting in the early 1980s, a number of scientific studies raised the possibility that consuming large amounts of these hormones could cause cancer or could cause premature puberty in girls. Other scientific studies denied any such risk, and the scientific debate continues. Different nations reacted differently to this possible risk. While the Americans and Australians continued to allow their residents to consume hormone-augmented beef, the EU forbade its farmers from adding such hormones, and in 1989 added an import ban on hormone-augmented beef. In 1999, the EU heated up the beef war further by preparing to ban all American beef. The United States reacted angrily by threatening retaliatory barriers against European products. So far, the World Trade Organization has sided with the Americans in the beef fight, as it did in the banana war. But both the scientific issue and the political fight remain unresolved.

With beef as with bananas, such fights between regions would not rage in the political arena for so long if the whole world were one country. Its world supreme court would rule one way or the other, and the court's ruling would refer to all beef, not just to beef grown in a certain region. But since nations are sovereign, they have their separate jurisdictions and separate policies. Tariffs and other trade barriers are part of what makes international economics so different.

How Financial Crises Can Spread Around the Globe

Starting in the summer of 1997, the world witnessed a financial crisis that was completely unexpected, even though something like it had happened earlier in the 20th century. The crisis was especially surprising because it started in the part of the world that had generated the greatest success stories about economic "miracles."

From the 1970s to mid-1997, the world had developed a warm glow about "East Asian miracles," "Asian tigers," and "emerging markets" in general. Japan led the way, with supergrowth that doubled incomes within a single decade (the 1960s) and had made Japan the world's largest international lender and banker by the end of the 1980s. True, Japan suffered financial crashes and a recession throughout the 1990s, but the Asian glow continued, as growth accelerated in other East Asian countries. South Korea, Taiwan, Hong Kong, and Singapore became the "Asian tigers," soon joined by Thailand and mainland China. Malaysia and Indonesia looked like they were about to enjoy the same supergrowth. A new Asian model was touted as the key to economic growth, a model involving close cooperation between government and the largest private firms. Led by East Asia, Latin America and even parts of Eastern Europe seemed to be "emerging nations" where one should invest one's savings.

Things suddenly went wrong in the summer of 1997. It was learned that financial institutions in Thailand had overinvested in enterprises and real estate that were unlikely to yield good returns, and that Thailand needed some serious financial reforms to prevent a recurrence of such misinvestment of funds. Both Thais and foreigners who had eagerly lent short-term money in Thailand rushed to pull their money out of Thailand, assuring the kind of financial disaster that they were fearing. With so many trying to unload Thai assets and flee to assets in other currencies, Thailand's currency (the baht) plummeted in its dollar value.

Contagion set in. The idea that supergrowth in Thailand was based on flawed financial institutions and unsound hasty investments spread to the other East Asian economies. Investors began to question the soundness of similar government-backed large firms and banks in Malaysia, Indonesia, South Korea, and even Japan. They rapidly shifted their money out of these economies as well, pushing large financial institutions in these countries toward bankruptcy. Like Thailand's baht, the national currencies of Malaysia (the ringgit), Indonesia (rupiah), and South Korea (won) suddenly dropped in dollar value. By November 1997, Korea was in desperate straits, seeking and receiving huge emergency loans from the International Monetary Fund (IMF), the World Bank, the U.S. government, and others. The long Suharto dictatorship in Indonesia finally came to an end, in the context of this sudden impoverishment and an unrelated ecological disaster (rampant forest fires). The prime minister of Malaysia angrily denounced fickle global speculators, and imposed capital controls to prevent people from moving their money out of Malaysia. Much of East Asia sank into a deep recession that lasted the rest of the decade, though mainland China, Taiwan, and the Philippines were less affected.

The contagion then spread to other areas. Russia's entire financial and monetary system collapsed in August 1998, wiping out ordinary people's savings in an economy already suffering a worse depression than America's famous Great Depression of the 1930s. In early 1999, it was Brazil's turn. Investors doubted the official Brazilian policy of maintaining a fixed dollar value of their national currency (the real). As both Brazilians and foreigners stampeded to get their money out of Brazil in January 1999, the government had to give up and let the real sink in value. Across 1999 some stability returned, but only after lasting economic damage. By this time, the IMF was lending so much emergency funds that, for the first time, it nearly ran out of money.

The odd thing about the contagion was that it was both well founded and poorly founded. It was well founded in the sense that the crisis countries indeed had flaws in their financial and monetary institutions. These flaws had gone unnoticed for too long in the euphoria over "miracles" and "emerging markets." Korea, Thailand, Malaysia, Indonesia, and (to a lesser extent) Japan had too much "cronyism," in which government officials give special breaks to an inner clique of powerful firms that are allowed to make foolish investments. Indonesia's government was particularly corrupt under Suharto, with investment decisions being tied more to his family connections than to the true economic merits of the investment projects. Even worse was Russia's Yeltsin government, or nongovernment, which failed to set up correct government and financial institutions in any sphere. As for Brazil, its monetary, fiscal, and exchange-rate policies were inconsistent, though Brazil was a more soundly structured economy in the late 1990s than it had been earlier.

Yet the contagion was poorly founded in the sense that it spread from information that should have been irrelevant in many cases. Why should financial defects in Thailand have caused a financial crisis in Korea? Why should the meltdown of Russia's economy have caused investors to doubt Brazil all of a sudden, as seemed to have been the case? Or perhaps the contagion of bad news is really a sign of an earlier poorly founded contagion of good news: If investors had seen good news in some emerging economies, such as Thailand, why should their earlier enthusiasm have spread to other countries whose financial institutions were still chaotic, such as Russia?

Surveying the damage, policymakers have hotly debated where the blame should lie. Here are the five leading diagnoses for the financial crisis that started in East Asia:

A. "It's the crisis countries' own fault. Their financial systems are flawed by poor reporting of company accounts and too much cronyism. These countries need thorough *financial reforms,* opening up their financial markets to all investors.

"If many companies fail, let them fail. Every free-market system has bankruptcies, and bankruptcy laws can deal with them. If you help the crisis countries with special bailouts, you will be subsidizing bad behavior."

B. "We need better international *bailouts.* The victims need bigger help in times of crisis. Sudden financial crises cannot be avoided even with the best of policies, and crisis countries need generous emergency loans from international agencies like the International Monetary Fund and the World Bank. They should also be allowed to let their currencies drop in value (depreciate), so that their goods can look cheaper and the extra sales can help their economies recover."

C. "We need international *capital controls.* Excessive freedom of international credit markets causes the instability. Investors can suddenly decide to lend huge amounts to an emerging economy, and then decide to panic and pull out the same huge sums, ruining the financial system of each crisis country. We need new government restrictions on the freedom of international lending and borrowing."

D. "We need international *debt relief* from creditors when things go wrong. Lenders should be more like shareholders and should share in the losses by writing down some of the amounts the debtors owe."

E. "To restore confidence in any national crisis, *tighten the government budget* by raising taxes and/or cutting government spending. That will restore confidence in the country's currency and its whole financial system."

Prominent experts and heads of state disagree over these diagnoses. Diagnosis A, calling for the crisis countries to clean up their own financial messes, was the early front-runner in 1997 and 1998. The IMF and the U.S. government took a particularly hard line in favor of Diagnosis A, demanding tough reforms in Korea and elsewhere as the price of outside aid.

Diagnosis B (we need bailouts) found more favor within the World Bank. The Bank's chief economist Joseph Stiglitz took the unusual step of criticizing the prevailing "Washington consensus" that overemphasized free trade and capital-market liberalization in a time of crisis. This argument brought into the open a long-standing tension between the policy images of those two sister institutions in Washington, the IMF and the World Bank. The IMF is seen as "the stern banker with green eye shade" and the Bank as "the Mother Teresa of lenders." Global speculator and philanthropist George Soros sided with the Bank, calling for much larger international reserve for bailouts in times of crisis.[4]

---

[4]For a sketch of George Soros and his exchange-market activities, see Chapter 17.

Diagnosis C (capital controls) was pushed by Prime Minister Mahathir Mohamad of Malaysia, who blamed fickle speculators for the contagion and for unwarranted pressure on Malaysia's economy. He cited a similar call for capital controls by MIT economist Paul Krugman as a justification for his demands. We touch on capital controls several times in Part III.

Diagnosis D (debt relief) has been demanded both by borrowing countries and by economist Jeffrey Sachs of Harvard. Some debt relief is inevitable in international finance, for reasons explored in Chapter 26.

Diagnosis E (tighter fiscal policy) should not have been advanced as a contender, since it does not fit the situation of the main crisis countries other than Russia. Yet the IMF demanded such tightening even in Thailand and Korea, where it should not have been an issue. Later the IMF conceded its mistake, a mistake that unnecessarily deepened the recessions of Thailand and Korea.

The financial crisis of the late 1990s was not the first one to spread around the globe. There were also the international financial crisis of the 1930s and the international debt crisis of the 1980s. Each of these showed the same kind of contagion. In both cases there were lenders who had earlier thought that if investing in one foreign country was a good bet, then investing in others must be good too. And in both cases, once the investors panicked about investments in one foreign country, they panicked about their investments in many foreign countries, even though conditions were actually different in different countries.

Again we must wonder: Why is there a contagion? Are investors rational in viewing so many foreign countries as similar? Would American investors have reacted to the sudden bankruptcy of Orange County, California, by pulling their money out of lending to any county government anywhere in the United States? Why is *international* finance so different from domestic finance? Why do financial firms keep studying something called "country risk"?

The answer is that international financial crises are different because, again, nations are independent sovereign states. Any lender knows that a loan's value depends on that lender's ability to take a delinquent borrower to court and seize some of the borrower's property. But if the borrower is in another country, there is less assurance that the lender will get his or her money back. So foreign lenders have more to fear. Chapter 26 explores this financial market side of international economics.

The Euro and the Dollar

At the start of 1999, Western Europe created a new international money, something they had dreamed about and debated for a long time. They agreed to shift from their separate national moneys into a common currency called the *euro,* in stages over several years. The group of countries deciding to do so included 11 nations of the 15-nation European Union, a free-trade bloc discussed in Chapter 11. The exceptions were Britain, Denmark, Greece, and Sweden.[5]

---

[5]The 11 nations committed to adopt the euro are Austria, Belgium, Finland, France, Germany, Ireland, Italy, Luxembourg, Netherlands, Portugal, and Spain. Greece desires to join as soon as it qualifies. As the euro came into existence in 1999, the other three EU countries—Britain, Denmark, and Sweden—actively were debating whether or not to join belatedly.

It might seem like a natural choice. If the nations of the European Union want to have a large unified economy like the United States, why shouldn't they have a unified currency like the United States? There are certainly advantages to having nations share a fixed common currency. It's convenient—you don't have to keep changing your money every time you cross a national border, any more than you have to change money when you drive from Kansas to Missouri. It may offer a more reliable unit of value, since the ability of a shared currency to buy goods isn't likely to change as fast as each separate national currency's purchasing power would change. People have long suspected, though it is hard to prove, that having a fixed basis of money exchange between nations would stimulate international trade. So the basic question of this chapter is clearly raised by the issue of the euro: Why should international economics be any different from economic life within a country?

There are reasons why nations have been reluctant to abandon their own national currencies and fix them to an international money. Having your nation's central bank control the national money supply gives it control over national prices, production, and jobs. Do you want to cede control over your nation's money supply to international forces beyond your control? For many countries, including the United States since 1971, the answer has been no. They feel it is important to maintain their monetary sovereignty, basically because they feel they can control their own economy better than any outside institution can. It may turn out that this same basic desire for national monetary sovereignty will weaken countries' commitment to the euro.

In other countries, the answer is actually "Yes, we do want to cede control over our money supply to some foreign institution." The idea of giving up your monetary sovereignty has enjoyed new popularity in countries where disastrous national policies have already ruined their own currencies by oversupplying them until price inflation made each unit of the currency nearly worthless. In such countries there is little confidence that any newly issued national money will keep its value. As a last resort, some of these countries have decided to make some stable foreign currency be the only real money that circulated in their economy. In most cases this has meant *"dollarization"*—accepting the U.S. dollar as the effective national currency, even though the country cannot have any control over the total supply of such money. Panama has done that for several years. In Argentina, Bolivia, Peru, and Uruguay, at least 70 percent of all banking assets and liabilities are now denominated in dollars. Even in urban Russia, despite the wound to national pride, the dollar figures as strongly as the ruble as a currency in which prices are set.

Thus the prospect is that there will be major currency blocs, led by the euro, the dollar, and perhaps the yen, just as there are now major trading blocs such as NAFTA and the EU. There is nothing like this regionalization of currencies and trade policies within a nation. Parts III and IV explore the consequences of this in depth.

The Immigration Fight: Who Is My Neighbor?

On November 8, 1994, the voters of California infuriated many Mexicans. They voted to implement Proposition 187, which would deny education, health, and other public services to the families of those who immigrated into the United

States without proper documentation. While Proposition 187 did not mention any particular nationalities or ethnic groups, many Mexicans took offense. Demonstrators destroyed a McDonald's in Mexico City.

In the United States, Proposition 187 triggered a larger national debate on whether or how to put up new migration barriers along the national borders. In 1996, Congress passed a federal welfare reform law that deprived even "legal" (documented) immigrants of access to public health care benefits and other services. Despite his opposition to this part of the welfare reform bill, President Clinton signed it into law, promising to restore many of those benefits later. In 1997 and 1998, Congress did restore some benefits for legal immigrants, but only for those who had arrived before 1996. Congress continues to debate further changes in its laws affecting immigrants.

America was not alone in having second thoughts about welcoming immigrants in the 1990s. In 1993, Germany revoked its long-standing constitutional provisions guaranteeing safe haven to political and religious refugees from other countries. To most Germans, it seemed there was little choice: Forced to welcome all their new compatriots from East Germany, the nation feared it could not accommodate the pending flood of refugees from the chaos in Eastern Europe. France struggled to calm tensions about its Muslim immigrant population. In Austria, the Freedom Party (despite its name) scored big election gains with the anti-immigrant campaign "Austria for the Austrians." Similar gains were made by the Flemish Nationalist Party in Belgium under the slogan "Our People First." One source of the renewed European fears about immigrants was the rise of unemployment in the early 1990s. Even if immigrants were not to blame for the rise in unemployment (and they were not), it was more natural to target them as scapegoats when jobs were in danger.

There will be fights over immigration as long as there are national borders. Being part of a nation affects most people's answers to the ancient question "Who is my neighbor?" As with the fight over imports, the fact of nationality makes people care less about foreigners than about compatriots, so that they will struggle to keep some people out of the country even though the chance to migrate means more to the migrants than to them. Immigration policy is thus a national prerogative and an explosive issue, one we explore at length in Chapter 25.

Economics and the Nation-State

It should be clear from such events that international economics has to be a separate field of study as long as nations are sovereign. Each nation has its own policies. And for each nation, these policies will always be designed to serve somebody inside that nation. Countries almost never care as much about the interests of foreigners as they do about national interests. Think of any recent debate over restricting cheap imports from other countries—say, Asian and Mexican imports into North America. How loudly have the North Americans spoken out to defend the Asian and Mexican jobs and incomes that would be lost if North American jobs were protected against imports? Conversely, in China, where imports are also often blocked, how much outcry does one hear about how this import barrier might destroy jobs in North America or Thailand? Similarly, immigration policy in a rich country often excludes immigrants without asking what such a policy will do to the well-being of people who want to migrate from the poorer country to the rich country.

The fact that nations have their sovereignty and their separate policies and their separate self-interests means that *nobody is in charge of the whole world economy.* The global economy has no central government, benevolent or otherwise. So if it works well, that is a marvel worth studying. And if it does not work well, the dangers from lack of central control over nations' policies are also worth studying. It is true, as we shall see, that there are international organizations that try to manage the entire globe, particularly the International Monetary Fund, the World Bank, the World Trade Organization, and the United Nations. But most countries have the option to defy or ignore these global institutions if they really want to.

Among the most important policies that each nation can manipulate separately are monetary policy, fiscal policy, and policy toward human migration.

Different Moneys

To many economists, and especially to the average person, the principal difference between domestic and international trade is that the latter involves the use of different moneys. That is, of course, very different from trade within a country, where everybody uses the same currency. You cannot issue your own currency, nor can your roommate, nor can the state of Ohio.

The existence of separate national currencies means that the price ratio between them can change. If a dollar were worth exactly 10 francs for 10 centuries, people would certainly come to think of a franc and the U.S. dime as the same money. Yet, if the price ratio between the two currencies can change, everyone will have to treat them as different moneys. And since the 1970s, the price ratios between major currencies have been fluctuating.

The variability of exchange rates has necessitated a modification of monetary economics, one that has seemed more and more urgent to economists since the 1970s. It is hard to talk about "the money supply" for the whole world in the same way we traditionally use that phrase in basic macroeconomics or in courses on money and banking. If a person in any country could hold any of several currencies whose relative prices can change by the minute, what is the world's money supply? Supply of which currencies? Supplied by whom? Held by whom? Parts III and IV explore the special relationships between national moneys.

Different Fiscal Policies

For each sovereign nation there is not only a separate currency, but also a separate government with its own public spending and power to tax. Differences in national tax policies are as a rule more pronounced than differences between the tax policies of states, provinces, or cities. Thus, in the international arena tax differences can set off massive flows of funds and goods that would not have existed without the tax discrepancies. Banks set up shop in the Bahamas, where their capital gains are less taxed and their books are less scrutinized. Shipping firms register in Liberia or Panama, where registration costs very little and where they are free from other nations' requirements to use higher-paid national maritime workers. Each country's array of export subsidies and duties and import barriers is a separate fiscal policy. The contrasts among the fiscal regimes of states, provinces, and localities are usually not so sharp.

Factor Mobility

In differentiating international from domestic trade, classical economists stressed the behavior of the factors of production. Labor and capital were mobile within a country, they believed, but not internationally. Even land was mobile within a country, if we mean occupationally rather than physically. The same land, for example, could be used alternatively for growing wheat or raising dairy cattle, which gave it a restricted mobility.

The importance of this intranational mobility of the factors of production was that returns to factors tended to equality within countries but not between countries. The wages of French workers of a given training and skill were expected to be more or less equal; but this level of wage bore no necessary relation to the level of comparable workers in Germany or Italy, England or Australia. The same equality of return within a country, but inequality internationally, was believed to be true of land and capital.

This distinction of the classical economists is *partly* valid today. Factors do move internationally, in response to opportunities for economic gain. It is accurate to say that there is a difference of degree in labor mobility interregionally and internationally and that people usually migrate within their own country more readily than they will emigrate abroad. This is true in part because identity of language, customs, and tradition is more likely to exist within countries than between countries. Capital is also more mobile within than between countries. Yet it is partially mobile over both kinds of boundaries. We shall see in Part V what happens when capital moves from country to country.

The Scheme of This Book

This book deals first with international trade theory and trade policy, asking in Part I how trade seems to work and in Part II what policies toward trade would bring benefits and to whom. This essentially microeconomic material precedes the macroeconomic and financial focus of Parts III and IV. In places this approach involves some momentary inconvenience, as when we look at an exchange-rate link between cutting imports and cutting exports. Yet there are gains in logic in proceeding from micro to macro, as in the way that the demand and supply analysis of trade in individual markets sets the stage for the use of the same tools at a more aggregate level in the treatment of international finance. It is in Part III that we enter the world of currencies, examining foreign exchange markets, the balance of payments, and exchange rates. Part IV surveys the policy issue of how nations are affected by, and can best respond to, changing pressures regarding their currencies. Part V examines the special problems raised by the partial international mobility of humans and other assets.

PART I

The Theory of International Trade

CHAPTER 2

The Basic Theory of International Trade

DEMAND AND SUPPLY

For centuries people have been fighting over whether governments should allow trade between countries. There have been, and probably always will be, two sides to the argument. Some argue that just letting everybody trade freely is best for both the country and the world. Others argue that trade with other countries makes it harder for some people to make a good living. Both sides are at least partly right.

International trade matters a lot. Its effects on the economic life of people in a country are enormous. Imagine a world in which your country did not trade at all with other countries. It isn't hard to do. Imagine what kind of job you would be likely to get, and think of what goods you could buy (or not buy) in such a world. For the United States, for example, start by imagining that it lived without its $50 billion a year in imported oil, and cut back on its energy use because the remaining domestic oil (and natural gas and other energy sources) were more expensive. Americans who produce oil and other energy sources might be pleased with such a scenario; but those who work in the auto industry and those who need to heat their homes would not. Similar impacts would be felt by producers and consumers in other parts of the economy suddenly stripped of imports like CD players and clothing. On the export side, suppose that Boeing could sell airplanes, and farmers could sell their crops, only within the United States, and that U.S. universities could admit only domestic students. In each case there are people who gain and people who lose from cutting off international trade. And every one of these differences between less trade and more trade has strong effects on how you choose a career. Little wonder, then, that people are always debating the issue of having less or more trade.

Each side of the trade debate needs a convincing story of just how trade matters and to whom. Yet that story, so useful in the arena of policy debate, requires an even more basic understanding of why people trade as they do when allowed to trade, exporting some products and importing others. If we do not know how people decide what goods and services to trade, it is hard to say what the effects of trade are or whether trade should be restricted by governments.

Four Questions About Trade

This chapter and the rest of Part I tackle the issue of how trade works by comparing two worlds. In one world no trade is allowed. In the other, governments just stand aside and let individual businesses and households trade freely across national borders. We seek answers to four key questions:

1. Why do countries trade? More precisely, what determines which products a country exports and which products it imports?
2. How does trade affect production and consumption in each country?
3. How does trade affect the economic well-being of each country? In what sense can we say that a country gains or loses from trade?
4. How does trade affect the distribution of economic well-being or income among various groups within the country? Can we identify specific groups that gain from trade and other groups that lose because of trade?

A Look Ahead

The chapters in Part I explore these four questions about trade. Our basic theory of trade says that trade usually results from the interaction of competitive demand and supply. This chapter goes straight to the basic picture of demand and supply. It suggests how to measure the gains that trade brings to some people and the losses it brings to others. Chapter 3 launches an exploration of what lies behind the demand and supply curves and discovers the concept of comparative advantage. Countries have different comparative advantages for the fundamental reason that people, and therefore countries, differ from each other in the productive resources they own. Chapter 4 looks at the strong impacts of trade on people who own those productive resources—the human labor and skills, the capital, the land, and other resources. Some ways of making a living are definitely helped by trade, while others are hurt. Chapter 5 shows some key links between trade and economic growth. Chapter 6 examines how actual trade may reflect forces calling for theories that go beyond our basic ideas of demand and supply and of comparative advantage.

Part I explores a diverse set of leading theories. Fortunately, the basic theory of competitive supply and demand serves many purposes fairly well. But the basic theory includes some special cases and some extensions. It also has been challenged by new views, about which economists are still debating.

Part II uses the theories of Part I to explore a broad range of government policy issues. Chapters 7 through 9 set out on a journey to map the border between good trade barriers and bad ones. This journey turns out to be intellectually challenging, calling for careful reasoning. Chapter 10 explores how firms and governments often push for more trade rather than less, promoting exports more than a competitive marketplace would. Chapter 11 switches to the economics of economic blocs like the European Union and the North American Free Trade Area.

Chapter 12 faces the growing debate over how environmental concerns should affect trade policy. Chapter 13 looks at Third World trade and what developing countries can do about it. Chapter 14 examines the politics of international trade policies and tries to explain the special international policy puzzles relating to agricultural trade.

Demand and Supply

Let's review the economics of demand and supply before we apply these tools to examine international trade. The product that we use as an example is motorbikes. We assume that the market for motorbikes is competitive. Although the analysis appears to be only about a single product (here, motorbikes), it actually is broader than this. Demanders make decisions about buying this product instead of other products. Suppliers use resources to produce this product, and the resources used in this production are not available to produce other products. What we are studying is actually one product relative to all other goods and services in the economy.

Demand

What determines how much of a product is demanded? A consumer's problem is to get as much happiness or well-being (in economists' jargon, *utility*) by spending the limited income that the consumer has available. A basic determinant of how much a consumer buys of a product is the person's taste, preferences, or opinions of the product. Given the person's tastes, the price of the product (relative to the price of other products) also has a major influence on how much of the product is purchased. At a higher price for this product, the consumer usually economizes and reduces the quantity purchased. Another major influence is the consumer's income. If the consumer's income increases, the consumer buys more of many products, probably including more of this product. (The consumer buys more if this product is a "normal good." This is not the only possibility—quantity purchased is unchanged if demand is independent of income, and quantity goes down if the product is an "inferior good." In this text we almost always examine only normal goods, as we consider these to be the usual case.)

How much the consumer demands of the product thus depends on a number of influences: tastes, the price of this product, the prices of other products, and income. We would like to be able to picture demand. We do this by focusing on one major determinant, the product's price. After we add up all consumers of the product, we use a market demand curve like the demand curve for motorbikes shown as D in Figure 2.1A.[1] We have a strong presumption that the demand curve slopes downward. An increase in the product's price (say, from $1,000 per motorbike to $2,000) results in a decrease in quantity demanded (from 65,000 to 40,000

---

[1]The equation for this demand curve is $Q_D = 90,000 - 25P$ (or $P = 3,600 - 0.04Q_D$).

FIGURE 2.1

*Demand and
Supply for
Motorbikes*

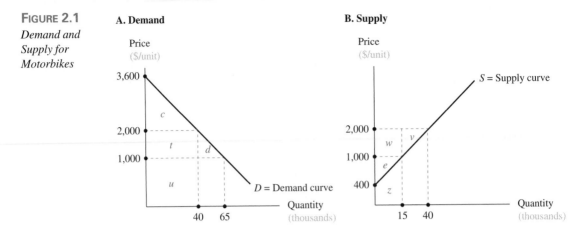

The market demand curve for motorbikes slopes downward. A lower price results in a larger quantity demanded. The market supply curve for motorbikes slopes upward. A higher price results in a larger quantity supplied.

motorbikes purchased per year). This is a movement along the demand curve because of a change in the product's price. The increase in price results in a lower quantity demanded as people (somewhat reluctantly) switch to substitute products (for instance, bicycles) or make do with less of the more expensive product (forgo buying a second motorbike with different features or of a different color).

How responsive is quantity demanded to a change in price? One way to measure responsiveness is by the slope of the demand curve (actually, by the inverse of the slope, because price is on the vertical axis). A steep slope indicates low responsiveness of quantity to a change in price (quantity does not change that much), whereas a flatter slope indicates more responsiveness. The slope is a measure of responsiveness, but it can also be misleading. By altering the units used on the axes, the demand curve can be made to look flat or steep.

A measure of responsiveness that is "unit-free" is **elasticity,** the *percent change in one variable resulting from a 1 percent change in another variable.* The **price elasticity of demand** is the percent change in quantity demanded resulting from a 1 percent increase in price. Quantity falls when price increases (if the demand curve slopes downward), so the price elasticity of demand is a negative number (though we often drop the *negative* when we talk about it). If the price elasticity is a large (negative) number (above 1), then quantity demanded is substantially responsive to a price change—demand is *elastic.* If the price elasticity is a small (negative) number (less than 1), then quantity demanded is not that responsive—demand is *inelastic.*

In drawing the demand curve, we assume that other things that can influence demand—income, other prices, and tastes—are constant. If any of the other influences changes, then the entire demand curve shifts.

Consumer Surplus

The demand curve shows the value that consumers place on extra units of the product, because it indicates the highest price that some consumer is willing to pay for each unit. Because consumers only pay the going market price for these units, using the market increases the economic well-being of all consumers who would have been willing to pay more. Their well-being is increased, and we can measure how much it increases.

To see this, consider first the value that consumers place on the total quantity of the product that they actually purchase. We can measure the value unit by unit. For the first motorbike demanded, the demand curve in Figure 2.1A tells us that somebody would be willing to pay a very high price (about $3,600)—the price just below where the demand curve hits the price axis. The demand curve tells us that somebody is willing to pay a slightly lower price for the second motorbike, and so on down the demand curve for each additional unit. The highest price that someone is willing to pay for each unit of the product reflects the value that the person places on consuming that unit.

By adding up all of the demand curve heights for each unit that is demanded, we see that the whole area under the demand curve (up to the total consumption quantity) measures the total value to consumers from buying this quantity of motorbikes. For instance, for 40,000 motorbikes the total value to consumers is $112 million, equal to area ($c + t + u$). This amount can be calculated as the sum of two areas that are easier to work with: the area of the rectangle ($t + u$) formed by price and quantity, equal to $2,000 × 40,000, plus the area of triangle c above this rectangle, equal to $(1/2) × ($3,600 – $2,000) × 40,000$. (Recall that the area of a triangle like c is equal to one-half of the product of its height and base.) This total value can be measured as a money amount, but it ultimately represents the *willingness* of consumers, if necessary, to forgo consuming other goods and services to buy this product.

The marketplace does not give away motorbikes for free, of course. The buyers must pay the market price (a money amount, but ultimately the value of other goods and services that the buyers must give up to buy this product). For instance, at a price of $2,000 per motorbike, consumers buy 40,000 motorbikes and pay $80 million in total (price times quantity, equal to area $t + u$).

Because many consumers value the product more highly than $2,000 per motorbike, paying the going market price still leaves consumers with a *net gain* in economic well-being. The net gain is the difference between the value that consumers place on the product and the payment that they must make to buy the product. This net gain is called **consumer surplus,** the increase in the economic well-being of consumers who are able to buy the product at a market price lower than the highest price that they are willing and able to pay for the product. For a market price of $2,000 in Figure 2.1A, the consumer surplus is the difference between the total value to consumers (area $c + t + u$) and the total payments to buy the product (area $t + u$). Consumer surplus thus is equal to area c, the area below the demand curve and above the price line. This contribution to the economic well-being of consumers through the use of this market is $32 million, equal to $(1/2) × ($3,600 – $2,000) × 40,000$.

A major use of consumer surplus is to measure the impact on consumers of a change in market price. For instance, what is the effect in our example if the market price of motorbikes is $1,000 instead of $2,000? Consumers are better off—they pay a lower price and decide to buy more. How much better off? Consumer surplus increases from a smaller triangle (extending down to the $2,000 price line) to a larger triangle (extending down to the $1,000 price line). The increase in consumer surplus is area $(t + d)$, which can be calculated as the area of rectangle t, equal to ($2,000 – $1,000) × 40,000, plus the area of triangle d, equal to $(1/2) \times$ ($2,000 – $1,000) × (65,000 – 40,000). The increase in consumer surplus is $52.5 million. The lower market price results in both an increase in economic well-being for consumers who would have bought anyway at the higher price (area t) and an increase in economic well-being for those consumers who are drawn into purchasing by the lower price (area d).

Supply

What determines how much of a product is supplied by a business firm (or other producer) into a market? A firm supplies the product because it is trying to earn a profit on its production and sales activities. One influence on how much a firm supplies is the price that the firm receives for its sales. The other major influence is the cost of producing and selling the product.

For a competitive firm, if the price at which the firm can sell another unit of its product exceeds the extra (or marginal) cost of producing it, then the firm should supply that unit because it makes a profit on it. The firm then will supply units up to the point at which the price received just about equals the extra cost of another unit. The cost of producing another unit depends on two things: the resources or inputs (such as labor, capital, land, and materials) needed to produce the extra unit, and the prices that have to be paid for these inputs.

We would like to be able to picture supply, and we do so by focusing on how the price of the product affects quantity supplied. After we add up all producers of the product, we use a market supply curve like the supply curve S for motorbikes in Figure 2.1B.[2] We usually presume that the supply curve slopes upward. An increase in the product's price (say, from $1,000 per motorbike to $2,000) results in an increase in quantity supplied (from 15,000 to 40,000 motorbikes produced and sold per year). This is a movement along the supply curve. In a competitive industry, an additional motorbike is supplied if the price received covers the extra cost of producing and selling this additional unit. If additional units can be produced only at a rising extra or marginal cost, then a higher price is necessary to draw out additional quantity supplied. The supply curve turns out to be the same as the curve showing the extra cost of producing each unit.

How responsive is quantity supplied to a change in the market price? One way to measure responsiveness is by the slope of the supply curve. Quantity supplied is more responsive if the slope is flatter. A "unit-free" measure is the **price elasticity**

---

[2]The equation for this supply curve is $Q_S = -10,000 + 25P$ (or $P = 400 + 0.04Q_S$).

of supply—the percent increase in quantity supplied resulting from a 1 percent increase in market price. Quantity supplied is not that responsive to price—supply is inelastic—if the price elasticity is less than 1. Quantity supplied is substantially responsive—supply is elastic—if the price elasticity is greater than 1.

In drawing the supply curve, we assume that other things influencing supply are constant. These other things include the conditions of availability of inputs and the technology that determines what inputs are needed to produce extra units of the product. If any of these other influences changes, then the entire supply curve shifts.

Producer Surplus

The supply curve shows the extra costs of producing successive units of the product because it indicates the lowest possible price at which some producer would be willing to supply each unit. Because producers actually receive the going market price for these units, using the market increases the economic well-being of all producers who would have been willing to supply at a lower price. Indeed, we can measure how much their well-being increases.

To see this, consider first the total of the extra costs involved in producing and selling the total quantity that is actually supplied. We can measure this cost unit by unit. For the first motorbike supplied into the market, the supply curve in Figure 2.1B tells us that some producer would be willing to supply this for about $400, the price just above where the supply curve hits the axis. This amount just covers the extra cost of producing and selling this first unit. The supply curve tells us that some producer is willing to supply the second motorbike for a slightly higher price, because the extra cost of the second unit is a little higher, and so on.

By adding up all of the supply curve heights for each unit supplied, we find that the whole area under the supply curve (up to the total quantity supplied) is the total cost of producing and selling this quantity of motorbikes. For instance, the total cost of producing 15,000 motorbikes is equal to area z in Figure 2.1B. This total cost can be measured as a money amount, but for the whole economy it ultimately represents an opportunity cost—the value of other goods and services that are not produced because resources are instead used to produce this product (motorbikes).

The total revenue received by producers is the product of the market price and the quantity sold. For instance, at a price of $1,000 per motorbike, producers sell 15,000 motorbikes, so they receive $15 million in total revenue (equal to area $e + z$).

Because producers would have been willing to supply some motorbikes at a price below $1,000, receiving the going market price for all units results in a *net gain* in economic well-being. The net gain is the difference between the revenues received and the costs incurred. This net gain is called **producer surplus,** the increase in the economic well-being of producers who are able to sell the product at a market price higher than the lowest price that would have drawn out their supply. For a market price of $1,000 in Figure 2.1B, the producer surplus is the difference between total revenues (area $e + z$) and total costs (area z). Producer surplus is thus equal to area e, the area above the supply curve and below the price line. Producer surplus in this case is $4.5 million, equal to $(1/2) \times (\$1,000 - \$400) \times 15,000$.

A major use of producer surplus is to measure the impact on producers of a change in market price. For instance, what is the effect if the market price is $2,000 instead of $1,000? Producers are better off—they receive a higher price and decide to produce and sell more. Producer surplus increases from a smaller triangle (extending up to the $1,000 price line) to a larger triangle (extending up to the $2,000 price line). The increase in producer surplus is equal to area $(w + v)$, or $(\$2,000 - \$1,000) \times 15,000$ plus $(1/2) \times (\$2,000 - \$1,000) \times (40,000 - 15,000)$, which equals $27.5 million. The higher market price results in both an increase in economic well-being for producers who would have supplied anyway at the lower price (area w) and an increase in well-being for producers of the additional units supplied (area v).

A National Market with No Trade

If D in Figure 2.1A represents the *national* demand for the product and S in Figure 2.1B represents the *national* supply, we can combine these into the single picture for the national market for this product, as shown in Figure 2.2. If there is no international trade, then equilibrium occurs at the price at which the market clears domestically, with national quantity demanded equal to national quantity supplied. In Figure 2.2 this no-trade equilibrium occurs at point A, with a price of $2,000 per motorbike, and total quantity supplied and demanded of 40,000 motorbikes. Both consumers and producers benefit from having this market, as

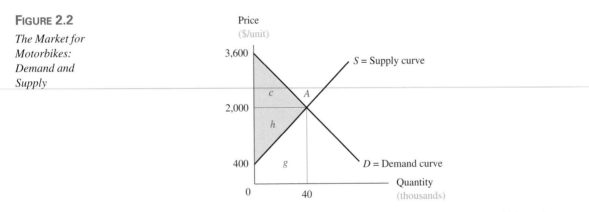

FIGURE 2.2

The Market for Motorbikes: Demand and Supply

The market for motorbikes can be pictured using demand and supply curves. In this example, which may be a national market with no international trade, the market reaches equilibrium at a price of $2,000 per motorbike, with 40,000 motorbikes produced and purchased during the time period (e.g., a year). Under these conditions, consumers get consumer surplus equal to area c and producers get producer surplus equal to area h.

consumer surplus is area c and producer surplus is area h (the same as area $e + w + v$ in Figure 2.1B). In this example, both gain the same amount of surplus, $32 million each. In general, these two areas do not have to be equal, though both will be positive amounts. For instance, consumer surplus will be larger than producer surplus if the demand curve is steeper (more inelastic) or the supply curve is flatter (more elastic) than those shown in Figure 2.2.

Two National Markets and the Opening of Trade

To discuss international trade in motorbikes, we need at least two countries. We will call the country whose national market was shown in Figure 2.2 the United States. This U.S. national market is also shown in the left-hand graph of Figure 2.3; we will add the subscript US to make this clear. We will call the other country the "rest of the world." The "national" market for the rest of the world is shown in the right-hand graph of Figure 2.3. Demand for motorbikes within the rest of the world is D_f, and supply is S_f. With no trade, the market equilibrium in the rest of the world occurs at point H, with a price of $700 per motorbike. To focus on the basic aspects of the situation, we will assume that prices in the two countries are stated in the same monetary units.

Starting from this initial situation of no trade in motorbikes between the two countries, can an observant person profit by initiating some trade? Using the principle of buy low, sell high, the person could profit by buying motorbikes for $700 per motorbike in the rest of the world and selling them for $2,000 per motorbike in the United States, earning profit (before any other expenses) of $1,300 per motorbike. This is called **arbitrage**—buying something in one market and reselling the same thing in another market to profit from a price difference.

Free-Trade Equilibrium

As international trade in motorbikes develops between these two countries, it affects market prices in the countries. The additional supply into the United States, created by imports, reduces the market price in the United States. The additional demand met by exports increases the market price in the rest of the world. In fact, if there are no transport costs or other frictions, free trade results in the two countries having the same price for motorbikes. We will call this free-trade equilibrium price the *international* or *world price*.

What will this free-trade equilibrium price be? We can picture the price by constructing the market for international trade in motorbikes. The U.S. demand for imports can be determined for each possible price at which the United States might import. This demand for imports represents excess demand (quantity demanded minus quantity supplied) for motorbikes within the U.S. national market at that price. For instance, at a price of $2,000 per motorbike, the U.S. national market clears by itself, and there is neither excess demand nor demand for imports. If the price in the U.S. market is $1,000 per motorbike, then there is

FIGURE 2.3   *The Effects of Trade on Production, Consumption, and Price, Shown with Demand and Supply Curves*

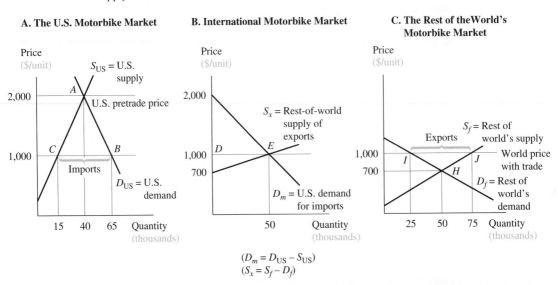

A. The U.S. Motorbike Market   **B. International Motorbike Market**   **C. The Rest of theWorld's Motorbike Market**

$$(D_m = D_{US} - S_{US})$$
$$(S_x = S_f - D_f)$$

In the international market for motorbikes, the desire to trade is the (horizontal) difference between national demand and supply. The difference between U.S. demand and supply, on the left, is graphed in the center diagram as the U.S. demand for imports (the D_m curve). The difference between foreign supply and demand, on the right, is graphed in the center diagram as the foreign supply of exports (the S_x curve). The interactions of demand and supply in both countries determine the world price of motorbikes and the quantities produced, traded, and consumed.

Effects of Trade	*Price*	*Quantity Supplied*	*Quantity Demanded*
United States	Down	Down	Up
Rest of the world	Up	Up	Down

excess demand of distance *CB*, equal to 50,000 units, creating an import demand for 50,000 motorbikes at this price. If excess demands at other prices below $2,000 per motorbike are measured, the curve D_m, representing U.S. demand for imports, can be drawn, as shown in the middle graph of Figure 2.3.

The supply of exports from the rest of the world can be determined in a similar way. This export supply represents excess supply (quantity supplied minus quantity demanded) of motorbikes within the rest-of-the-world market. For instance, at a price of $700 per unit, this market clears by itself, and there is no excess supply and no export supply. If the price in this market is $1,000 per motorbike, then excess supply is distance *IJ*, equal to 50,000 units, creating a supply of exports of 50,000 motorbikes at this price. If excess supplies for other prices above $700 per motorbike are measured, the curve S_x, representing export supply from the rest of the world, can be drawn, as shown in the middle graph of Figure 2.3.

Free-trade equilibrium occurs at the price that clears the international market. In Figure 2.3 this is at point *E*, where quantity demanded of imports equals quantity supplied of exports. The volume of trade (*DE*) is 50,000 motorbikes and the free-trade equilibrium price is $1,000 per motorbike. This equilibrium can also be viewed as balancing total world demand and supply. The international price is also the price in each national market with free trade. At the price of $1,000 per motorbike, total world quantity demanded is 90,000 units (65,000 in the United States and 25,000 in the rest of the world), and total world quantity supplied is also 90,000 units (15,000 plus 75,000). The excess demand within the U.S. market (*CB*) of 50,000 motorbikes is met by the excess supply from the rest-of-the-world market (*IJ*).

What would happen if the world price for some reason was (temporarily) different from $1,000 per motorbike? At a slightly higher price (say, $1,100 per motorbike), the U.S. excess (or import) demand would be less than 50,000 motorbikes, whereas the rest of the world's excess (or export) supply would be above 50,000 units. (These changes occur because in both markets quantity demanded would decrease and quantity supplied would expand.) Because export quantity supplied exceeds import quantity demanded, the imbalance creates pressure for the price to fall back to the equilibrium value of $1,000 per motorbike. Conversely, a price below $1,000 would not last because U.S import quantity demanded would be above the foreign export quantity supplied.

Effects in the Importing Country

Opening trade in motorbikes has effects on economic well-being (in economists' jargon, *welfare*) in both the United States and the rest of the world. We will first examine changes in the importing country, the United States, using Figure 2.4 (page 27), which reproduces Figure 2.3, labeling the areas relevant to consumer and producer surplus.

Effects on Consumers and Producers

For the United States (the importing country), the shift from no trade to free trade lowers the market price. U.S. consumers of the product benefit from this change and increase their quantity consumed. The concept of consumer surplus allows us to quantify what the lower price is worth to consumers. With free trade, consumer surplus is the area below the demand curve and above the international price line of $1,000 per motorbike, equal to area *a* + *b* + *c* + *d* (the same as area *t* + *c* + *d* in Figure 2.1A). Thus, in comparison with the no-trade consumer surplus of area *c*, the opening of trade brings consumers of this product a gain of area *a* + *b* + *d* (equal to $52.5 million, area *t* + *d* in Figure 2.1A). This gain is spread over many people who consume this product (including some who are also producers of this product).

U.S. producers of this product (in their role as producers) are hurt by the shift from no trade to free trade. They receive a lower price for their product and shrink production. Producer surplus decreases from area *e* + *a* with no trade (the same as area *e* + *w* + *v* in Figure 2.1B) to only area *e*. The loss in producer surplus is area *a* (equal to $27.5 million). Area *a* is a loss of producer surplus both on the 15,000 motorbikes still produced in the United States and on the 25,000 that are no longer produced in the United States as imports capture this part of the market.[3]

Net National Gains

If U.S. consumers gain areas $a + b + d$ from the opening of trade and U.S. producers lose area a, what can we say about the net effect of trade on the United States? There is no escaping the basic point that *we cannot compare the welfare effects on different groups without imposing our subjective weights to the economic stakes of each group.* Our analysis allows us to quantify the separate effects on different groups, but it does not tell us how important each group is to us. In our example, how much of the consumer gain does the producer loss of $27.5 million offset in our minds? No theorem or observation of economic behavior can tell us. The result depends entirely on our value judgments.

Economists have tended to resolve the matter by imposing the value judgment that we shall call the *one-dollar, one-vote yardstick* here and throughout this book:

> The **one-dollar, one-vote yardstick** says that the analyst will value any dollar of gain or loss equally, regardless of who experiences it.

The yardstick implies a willingness to judge trade issues on the basis of their effects on aggregate well-being, without regard to their effects on the distribution of well-being. This does not signify a lack of interest in the issue of distribution. It only means that one considers the distribution of well-being to be a matter better handled by compensating those hurt by a change or by using some other non–trade-policy means of redistributing well-being toward those groups (for example, the poor) whose dollars of well-being seem to matter more to us. If the distribution of well-being is handled in one of these ways, trade and trade policies can be judged in terms of simple aggregate gains and losses.

You need not accept this value judgment. You may feel that the stake of, say, motorbike producers matters much more to you, dollar for dollar, than the stake of motorbike consumers. You might feel this way, for example, if you knew that

---

[3]Figure 2.4 does not enable us to identify the "producers" experiencing these losses of producer surplus from the opening of international trade and the new competition from imports. If one views the supply curve as the marginal cost curve facing competitive entrepreneurs who face fixed prices for both outputs and inputs, then it is natural to talk as though whatever changes producer surplus, affects just these entrepreneurs' profits. Taking this approach implicitly assumes that workers and suppliers of capital are completely unaffected by the fortunes of the industry because they can just take their labor and capital elsewhere and earn exactly the same returns. Yet this kind of microeconomic focus is not justified, either by the real world or by the larger model that underlies the demand and supply curves.

Though the present diagrams cannot show the entire model of international trade at once, they are based on a general equilibrium model that shows how trade affects the rates of pay of productive inputs as well as commodity prices and quantities. As we shall see in Chapter 4, anything that changes the relative price of a product also changes the distribution of income within the nation. The issue of how trade affects the distribution of income will be taken up later. Now the key point is simply that as the price of motorbikes drops and the economy moves from point A to point C, the producer surplus being lost is a loss to workers and other input suppliers to the industry, not just a loss to the industry's entrepreneurs. To know how the change in producer surplus is divided among these groups, one would have to consult the full model that will be completed by the end of Chapter 4.

FIGURE 2.4   *The Effects of Trade on Well-Being of Producers, Consumers, and the Nation as a Whole*

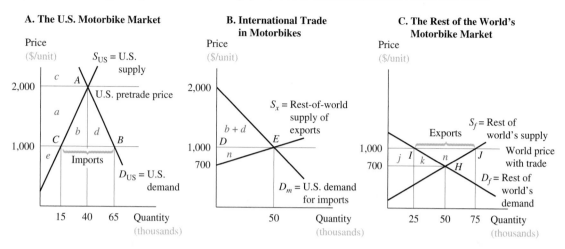

Welfare Effects of Free Trade

	United States			Rest of the World	
Group	*Surplus with Free Trade*	*Surplus with No Trade*	*Net Effect of Trade*	*Group*	*Net Effect of Trade*
Consumers	$a+b+c+d$	c	$a+b+d$	Consumers	$-(j+k)$ [a loss]
Producers	e	$a+e$	$-a$ [a loss]	Producers	$j+k+n$
U.S. as a whole				Rest of the world	
(consumers plus producers)	$a+b+c+d+e$	$c+a+e$	$b+d$	as a whole	n

the producers were, in fact, poor unskilled laborers, whereas the consumers were rich. And you might also feel that there is no politically feasible way to compensate the poor workers for their income losses from the opening of trade. If so, you may wish to say that each dollar lost by producers means five or six times as much to you as each dollar gained by consumers. Taking this stand leads you to conclude that opening trade violates your conception of the national interest. Even in this case, however, you could still find the demand–supply analysis useful as a way of quantifying the separate stakes of groups whose interests you weight unequally.

If the one-dollar, one-vote yardstick is accepted, it gives a clear formula for the net national gains from trade. If motorbike consumers gain area $a + b + d$ and motorbike producers lose area a, the net national gain from trade is area $b + d$, or a triangular area worth $25 million per year [= 1/2 × (65,000 – 15,000 motorbikes) × ($2,000 – $1,000) per motorbike]. It turns out that very little information is needed to measure the net national gain. All that is needed is an estimate of the amount of trade and an estimate of the change in price brought about by trade.

Effects in the Exporting Country

For the rest of the world (the exporting country), the analysis follows a similar path. Here the shift from no trade to free trade increases the market price. The increase in price benefits motorbike producers in the rest of the world, whose producer surplus increases by area $j + k + n$ in Figure 2.4. The increase in price hurts motorbike consumers, whose consumer surplus decreases by area $j + k$. In the exporting country, producers of the product gain and consumers lose. Using the one-dollar, one-vote yardstick, we can say that the rest of the world gains from trade, and that its net gain from trade equals area n.

Which Country Gains More?

This analysis shows that each country gains from international trade, so it is clear that the whole world gains from trade. Trade is a positive-sum activity. At the same time, the gains to the countries generally are not equal—area $b + d$ is generally not equal to area n. These two triangles can be compared rather easily. They both have the same base (equal to 50,000 units, the volume of trade). The height of each triangle is the change in price in the shift from no trade to free trade for each country. Thus, the country that experiences the larger price change has a larger value of the net gains from trade.

To know how the gains from international trade are being divided, one should therefore investigate whose prices were more affected:

> The gains from opening trade are divided in direct proportion to the price changes that trade brings to the two sides. If a nation's price ratio changes x percent (as a percentage of the free-trade price) and the price in the rest of the world changes y percent, then
>
> $$\frac{\text{Nation's gain}}{\text{Rest of world's gains}} = \frac{x}{y}$$
>
> The side with the less elastic (steeper) trade curve (import demand curve or export supply curve) gains more.

In Figure 2.4, the United States gains more. Its gains from trade in this product are $25 million (as its price changes from $2,000 to $1,000, equal to 100 percent of the free-trade price $1,000). The gains from trade for the rest of the world are $7.5 million as its price changes from $700 to $1,000, equal to 30 percent of the free-trade price).

Summary: Early Answers to the Four Trade Questions

Extending the familiar demand–supply framework to international trade has given us useful preliminary answers to the four basic questions about international trade. While the rest of Part I will give fuller answers to these questions by exploring what forces lie behind the demand and supply curves, this chapter's contrasts between no trade and free trade offer these conclusions:

1. Why do countries trade? Demand and supply conditions differ between countries, so prices differ between countries if there is no international trade. Trade begins as someone conducts **arbitrage** to earn profits from the price difference between previously separated markets. A product will be exported from countries where its price was lower without trade to countries where its price was higher.

2. How does trade affect production and consumption in each country? The move from no trade to a free-trade equilibrium changes the product price from its no-trade value to the free-trade equilibrium international or world price. The price change results in changes in quantities consumed and produced. In the country importing the good, trade raises the quantity consumed and lowers the quantity produced of that good. In the exporting country, trade raises the quantity produced and lowers the quantity consumed of the good.

3. Which country gains from trade? Both do. Each country's net national gains are proportional to the change in its price that occurs in the shift from no trade to free trade. The country whose prices are disrupted more by trade gains more.

4. Within each country, who are the gainers and losers from opening trade? The gainers are the consumers of imported goods and the producers of exportable goods. Those who lose are the producers of import-competing goods and the consumers of exportable goods.

Suggested Reading

See the Suggested Reading for Chapter 3.

Questions and Problems

✦1. What is consumer surplus? Using real-world data, what information would you need to measure consumer surplus for a product?

2. What is producer surplus? Using real-world data, what information would you need to measure producer surplus for a product?

✦3. How can a country's supply and demand curves for a product be used to determine the country's supply-of-exports curve? What does the supply-of-exports curve mean?

4. How can a country's supply and demand curves for a product be used to determine the country's demand-for-imports curve? What does the demand-for-imports curve mean?

✦5. A tropical country can produce winter coats, but there is no domestic demand for these coats. Explain how this country can gain from free trade in winter coats.

6. The United States exports a substantial amount of scrap iron and steel to Japan and other countries. Why do some U.S. users of scrap iron and steel support a prohibition on these exports?

✦7. Explain what is wrong with the following statement: "Trade is self-eliminating. Opening up trade opportunities drives prices and costs into equality between countries. But once prices and costs are equalized, there is no longer any reason to trade the product from one country to another, and trade stops."

8. In the mid-1990s, the United States imported about 3 billion barrels of oil per year. Perhaps it would be better for the United States if it could end the billions of dollars of payments to foreigners by not importing this oil. After all, the United States can produce its own oil (or other energy products that substitute for oil). If the United States stopped all oil

imports suddenly, it would be very disruptive. But perhaps the United States could gain if it gradually restricted and then ended oil imports in an orderly transition. If we allow time for adjustments by U.S. consumers and producers of oil, and we perhaps are a bit optimistic about how much adjustment is possible, then the following two equations show domestic demand and supply conditions in the United States:

$$\text{Demand: } P = 42 - 4Q_D$$
$$\text{Supply: } P = 0.6 + 6Q_S$$

where quantity Q is in billions of barrels per year and price P is in dollars per barrel.

a. With free trade and an international price of $18 per barrel, how much oil does the United States produce domestically? How much does it consume? Show the demand and supply curves on a graph and label these points. Indicate on the graph the quantity of U.S. imports of oil.

b. If the United States stopped all imports of oil (in a way that allowed enough time for orderly adjustments as shown by the equations), how much oil would be produced in the United States? How much would be consumed? What would be the price of oil in the United States with no oil imports? Show all of this on your graph.

c. If the United States stopped all oil imports, which group(s) in the United States would gain? Which group(s) would lose? As appropriate, refer to your graph in your answer.

✦ 9. Consider Figure 2.3 showing free trade in motorbikes. Assume that consumers in the United States shift their tastes in favor of motorbikes. What is the effect on the U.S. domestic demand and/or supply curve(s)? What is the effect on the U.S. demand-for-imports curve? What is the effect on the equilibrium international price?

10. Consider again Figure 2.3 showing free trade in motorbikes. Assume that U.S. pro-

ductivity in producing motorcycles increases. What is the effect on the U.S. domestic demand and/or supply curve(s)? What is the effect on the U.S. demand-for-imports curve? What is the effect on the equilibrium international price?

✦ 11. The equation for the demand curve for writing paper in Belgium is

$$Q_D = 350 - (P/2) \text{ (or } P = 700 - 2Q_D)$$

The equation for the supply curve for writing paper in Belgium is

$$Q_S = -200 + 5P \text{ [or } P = 40 + (Q_S/5)]$$

a. What are the equilibrium price and quantity if there is no international trade?

b. What are the equilibrium quantities for Belgium if the nation can trade freely with the rest of the world at a price of 120?

c. What is the effect of the shift from no trade to free trade on Belgian consumer surplus? On Belgian producer surplus? What is the net national gain or loss for Belgium?

12. Country I has the usual demand and supply curves for Murky Way candy bars. Country II has a typical demand curve too, but it cannot produce Murky Way candy bars.

a. Use supply and demand curves for the domestic markets and for the international market to show in a set of graphs the free-trade equilibrium for Murky Way candy bars. Indicate the equilibrium world price. How does this world price compare to the no-trade price in Country I? Indicate how many Murky Ways are traded each time period with free international trade.

b. What are the effects of the shift from no trade to free trade on surpluses in each country? Indicate the net national gain or loss from free trade for each country.

CHAPTER 3

Why Everybody Trades

COMPARATIVE ADVANTAGE AND FACTOR PROPORTIONS

Chapter 2 examined international trade focusing on a single product. That analysis helped answer some major questions about international trade, but only indirectly addressed some others. For an industry with expanding production, where do the additional resources come from? For a shrinking industry, what happens to the resources no longer needed? If consumers increase or decrease the quantity demanded of one product, what effect does this have on demand for other products?

Full analysis of international trade requires consideration of the entire economy. Yet the entire economy is very complex—it consists of thousands of products and the various resources needed to produce them. Fortunately, we can gain major insights by considering an economy composed of just two products. For international trade, one product can be exported and the other imported. This two-product economy thus captures an essential feature of international trade: A country tends to be a net exporter of some products and a net importer of others.

This chapter analyzes the general equilibrium of a two-product economy to address the first of our four basic trade questions: Why do countries trade? In fact, why does everybody—every country as well as every person—find it worthwhile to trade? We proceed in three steps:

1. David Ricardo's principle of comparative advantage allows us to explain trade better than most people's intuition and better than Adam Smith's original explanation of trade patterns.

2. Next, a pair of tools—production-possibility curves and community indifference curves—allows us to perform a number of tasks. They can express Ricardo's principle of comparative advantage and some of Chapter 2's points about the effects of trade; they set the stage for improvements that others made to Ricardo's theory, and they will be used in later chapters, especially Chapter 5.

3. Finally, the Heckscher–Ohlin theory of trade explores some main sources of comparative advantage, some deeper reasons why people trade. This theory emphasizes international differences in the abundance of the "factors of production" (land, labor, skills, capital, and natural resources). These differences in factor abundance turn out to be important because there are also differences in the use of each factor in the production of different products.

This is one of the longer chapters in the book. You may want to read it a few sections at a time. The journey through the chapter is worth it. The chapter as a whole illustrates the flow of how our understanding of comparative advantage has developed.

Adam Smith's Theory of Absolute Advantage

In the late 18th and early 19th centuries, first Adam Smith and then David Ricardo explored the basis for international trade as part of their efforts to make a case for free trade. Their writings were responses to the doctrine of mercantilism prevailing at the time. (See accompanying box.) Their classic theories swayed policymakers for a whole century, even though today we view them as only special cases of a more basic, and more powerful, theory of trade.

In his *Wealth of Nations,* Adam Smith promoted free trade by comparing nations to households. Since every household finds it worthwhile to produce only some of its needs and to buy others with products it can sell, the same should apply to nations:

> It is the maxim of every prudent master of a family, never to attempt to make at home what it will cost . . . more to make than to buy. The tailor does not attempt to make his own shoes, but buys them from the shoemaker. . . .
>
> What is prudence in the conduct of every private family, can scarce be folly in that of a great kingdom. If a foreign country can supply us with a commodity cheaper than we ourselves can make it, better buy it of them with some part of the product of our own industry, employed in a way in which we have some advantage.

Smith's reasoning can be illuminated with a numerical example. Let the two goods in the example be wheat and cloth (perhaps broadly representing agricultural products and manufactured products). To see the effects of trade, begin with a situation in which nations do not trade with each other. Without trade, what would determine the prices of the two goods in each country? Smith thought that all "value" was determined by, and measured in, hours of labor. The opportunity cost of producing a unit of a product was the amount of labor required because this labor was not being used to produce some other product(s). With competitive markets, labor costs then determined the market value or price of that product. In this respect he was imitated by Ricardo and by Karl Marx, who also believed that labor was the basis for all value. Let us suppose that the United States has an **absolute advantage** in producing wheat,

Mercantilism: Older than Smith—and Alive Today

Mercantilism was the philosophy that guided European thinking about international trade in the several centuries before Adam Smith published his *Wealth of Nations* in 1776. Mercantilists viewed international trade as a source of major benefits to a nation. Merchants engaged in trade, especially those selling exports, were good—hence the name *mercantilism*. But mercantilists also maintained that government regulation of trade was necessary to provide the largest national benefits. Trade merchants would serve their own interests and not the national interest, in the absence of government guidance.

A central belief of mercantilism was that national well-being or wealth was based on national holdings of gold and silver (specie or bullion). Given this view of national wealth, exports were viewed as good and imports (except for raw materials not produced at home) were seen as bad. If a country sells (exports) more to foreign buyers than the foreigners sell to the country (the country's imports), then the foreigners have to pay for the excess of their purchases by shipping gold and silver to the country. If the country imports more, then the country must ship gold and silver to foreigners. Imports were also feared because they might not be available to the country in time of war. Gold and silver accruing to the national rulers could be especially valuable in helping to maintain a large military for the country. Based on mercantilist thinking, governments (1) imposed an array of taxes and prohibitions designed to limit imports and (2) subsidized and encouraged exports.

Because of its peculiar emphasis on gold and silver, mercantilism viewed trade as a zero-sum activity—one country's gains come at the expense of some other countries, since a surplus in international trade for one country must be a deficit for some other(s). The focus on promoting exports and limiting imports also provided major benefits for domestic producer interests (in both exporting and import-competing industries).

Adam Smith and economists after him pointed out that the mercantilists' push for more exports and fewer imports turns social priorities upside down. National well-being is based on the ability to consume products (and other "goods" such as leisure time and a clean environment) now and in the future. The importance of national production and exports is only indirect: They provide the income to buy products to consume. Imports are part of the expanding national consumption that a nation seeks, not an evil to be suppressed. Exports are not desirable on their own; rather, exports are useful because they pay for the imports. As the text shows, trade freely transacted between countries can lead to gains for all countries—trade is a positive-sum activity. Indeed, even the goal of acquiring gold and silver can be self-defeating if this acquisition expands the domestic money supply and leads to domestic inflation of product prices—an argument first expounded by David Hume even before Smith did his writing.

Although the propositions of the mercantilists have been refuted, and countries no longer focus on piling up gold and silver, mercantilist thinking is still very much alive today, now with a sharp focus on employment. Exports are good because they create jobs in the country. Imports are bad because they take jobs from the country and give them to foreigners. Once again, trade is depicted as a zero-sum activity. There is no recognition that trade can bring gains to all countries (including mutual gains in employment as prosperity rises throughout the world). Although it does not always win the policy debates, mercantilist thinking pervades discussions of international trade in countries all over the world.

meaning that we can produce it at an absolutely lower labor cost than the rest of the world. And let us suppose that the rest of the world has an absolute advantage in producing cloth. Specifically, we have:

	When Each Country Is Absolutely Better at Making Something = A Case of Absolute Advantage:		
	In the United States		*In the Rest of the World*
Labor required to make:			
1 bushel of wheat	2 hours	<	2.5 hours
1 yard of cloth	4 hours	>	1.0 hour

If there is no trade between nations, the prices of the two goods will be dictated by conditions within each country (calling the rest of the world a country). Smith thought that labor costs alone determined how much wheat it took to buy a yard of cloth, or how much cloth it took to buy a bushel of wheat. People would only trade equal labor values of wheat for cloth. So within the United States, with each bushel of wheat requiring only 2 hours of labor, one would have to give up 2 bushels of wheat, made with 4 hours of labor, to trade for 1 yard of cloth, which also took 4 hours to make. Correspondingly, in the rest of the world, where it takes 2.5 times as much labor to grow a bushel of wheat as it takes to make a yard of cloth, people would have to offer 2.5 yards of cloth to get others to give up a bushel of wheat, which cost the same labor to make. The underlying idea was reasonable: If individual households and businesses had the choice of switching their own labor between growing wheat and making cloth, this choice would tend to dictate the prices at which they were willing to exchange wheat for cloth in their nation's marketplace.

So, because of relative labor costs, it would turn out that people's desire to consume mixtures of wheat and cloth would make these prices prevail in the separate national marketplaces:

	In the United States	*In the Rest of the World*
With no international trade:		
Price of wheat	0.5 yard/bushel	2.5 yards/bushel
Price of cloth	2.0 bushels/yard	0.4 bushel/yard

With no international trade, each nation has its separate price ratio between wheat and cloth. There is really only one ratio in each country, because the price of wheat and the price of cloth are just the reciprocals of each other, just the same thing stated two ways. If you are wondering what happened to prices denominated in money, such as dollars per bushel or dollars per yard, economists tend to put such money prices, or nominal prices, aside when looking at the effects of trade on real values. It's as if we were in a world without money, a world of pure barter between real goods like wheat and cloth.[1]

Now let trade be opened up between the United States and the rest of the world. Somebody will notice the difference between the national prices of the same good and will think of a way to profit from that difference. The first person to notice will think of sending wheat from the United States in exchange for foreign cloth. Consider the profits that person could make on each bushel of American wheat sent abroad in exchange for cloth. Each bushel could be obtained by giving up 0.5 yard of cloth in the United States. But the same bushel would be sold for 2.5 yards of cloth in that other "nation," the rest of the world. Let us assume that the cost of transporting goods between nations is zero.[2] Therefore, with each 0.5 yard of cloth given up, the person can end up with more of the very same good—with 2.5 yards of cloth. Somebody else could profit by starting with a bushel of high-priced wheat in the rest of the world, exchanging it there for cloth, and selling the cloth in the United States in exchange for still more wheat. This person could start with a bushel of wheat and trade it outside the United States for 2.5 yards of cloth, and then ship the cloth to the United States and get 2.5 times 2.0 bushels per yard, or 5.0 bushels of wheat, having started with only one bushel. The principle is simple and universal: As long as prices differ in two places (by more than any cost of transportation between the places), there is a way to profit by arbitrage (buying in one location and selling in another).

The opening of trade would do more than make new exchanges profitable. It would also affect what people decide to produce with their labor. The changes in demand caused by international trade would lead each nation to follow its absolute advantage in deciding what to make. That is, nations would *specialize* in their production. Labor in the United States would be shifted toward making more wheat, which has a higher value when exported abroad, and less cloth, which is cheaper to import from abroad. Meanwhile, in the rest of the world, people would stop making wheat, which is cheaper to import from the United States; instead they would make more cloth, which is getting a higher price when exported to the United States. As long as the unit labor costs stay at the levels

---

[1]We keep money hiding in the wings throughout most of Parts I, II, and V of this book, allowing it to take center stage only in the more macroeconomic Parts III and IV. Money appears briefly in the box later in this chapter titled "What If Trade Doesn't Balance?" and again in Chapter 4, both times to help us think about how exchange rates relate to real prices like the bushels/yard prices used here. Part II switches to what look like ordinary money prices, such as dollars per bicycle in Chapter 7. Even there, however, the prices do not have much to do with money. As in Chapter 2, the dollars are really units of all products other than the one being pictured (e.g., motorbikes).

[2]The assumption of zero transport costs is relatively harmless. Recognizing that transport costs are positive merely reduces the gains from trading but does not reverse any of our major conclusions.

shown above—and Smith's reasoning assumed they would—the United States would keep shifting its labor from cloth to wheat, and the rest of the world would keep shifting its labor from wheat to cloth, until at least one side was completely specialized and could not shift its production anymore.

Thus countries would gain by trading and by specializing according to their absolute advantages, the United States in wheat and the rest of the world in cloth. But where would the shifting stop? At what price would they conduct ongoing trade? Which country would get the greater gains? Smith did not say. In thinking about cases like this one, he was content to show that both nations must be at least as well off as before. The simple labor-cost example hasn't told us how strongly the two nations demand each of the two goods. We know the cost and supply side, but not the demand side; therefore, we can't be sure exactly what price the Americans will get for their wheat and what the rest of the world will get for its cloth in the ongoing trade equilibrium.

We are not completely without information about the equilibrium international price ratio, however. It must lie somewhere between the no-trade price ratios in the United States and the rest of the world, that is, somewhere between 0.5 yard per bushel and 2.5 yards per bushel. To see why, suppose that the United States was asked to consider trading at the ratio of only 0.2 yard of cloth for each bushel of wheat. At 0.2 yard per bushel the United States would offer to export *cloth,* and import wheat, because the price of wheat on the international market is now lower than its cost to produce at home (0.5 yard per bushel). No deal would be made, however. At this low international price of wheat, the rest of the world also wants to export cloth in order to import wheat. No equilibrium is possible. Similar reasoning applies to the other extreme, with a price of wheat higher than 2.5 yards per bushel. In that price range, both the United States and the rest of the world would want to be the exporters of wheat and the importers of cloth. The only way the two sides could agree to have one of them export wheat and the other export cloth is for the international price to settle somewhere in the range where

$$0.5 \leq \text{international price of wheat} \leq 2.5 \text{ (yards/bushel)}$$

that is, where

$$2.0 \geq \text{international price of cloth} \geq 0.4 \text{ (bushel/yard)}$$

Suppose that the strengths of demand, which we examine more closely later in this chapter, are such that the ratio settles at the price of 1 bushel = 1 yard. Then, in the end, both countries end up getting gains (1) from trading and (2) from specialization in their production, just like the gains we started to imagine when thinking about what would happen at first, when the first people began the international trade. The United States gains from the chance to trade at 1.0 yard per bushel. Again, the United States can produce each bushel of wheat by giving up only 0.5 yard of cloth produced, yet trades it internationally for 1.0 yard. The rest of the world makes each extra yard of cloth by only giving up the production of 0.4 bushel of wheat, then trades that extra yard for 1.0 bushel of wheat.

What If Trade Doesn't Balance?

You may be struck by a contradiction between the spirit of the trade theory and recent headlines about international trade.

The theory implies that trade balances. In diagrams like Figure 3.1 (see page 41), the theory seems to imply a perfect balance between the market value of exports and the market value of imports (both values calculated using the international price ratio). The balance seems guaranteed by the absence of money from the diagram, as noted in this chapter's footnote 1. As long as countries are just bartering wheat for cloth, they must think U.S. wheat exports have exactly the same market value as U.S. cloth imports. Export value equals import value. Trade must balance.

Yet the news media have been announcing huge U.S. trade deficits every year since 1975. Imports of goods and services keep exceeding exports. (Conversely, Japan, Germany, and France have been running merchandise trade surpluses in most years since that time.) What's going on? How can the basic theory of trade be so silent about the most newsworthy aspect of international trade flows? Isn't the theory wrong in its statements about the reasons for trade or the gains from trade? Maybe Ricardo was too optimistic about every country's having enough comparative advantage to balance its overall trade.

These are valid questions, and they deserve a better answer than simply, "Well, the model assumes balanced trade." In later chapters, we will add details about how trade deficits and surpluses relate to exchange rates, money, and finance. But the real answer is more fundamental: The model is not really wrong in assuming balanced trade, even for a country with a huge trade deficit or trade surplus!

Take the case of the U.S. trade deficit. It looks as though exports are always less than imports. Well, yes and no. Yes, the trade balance (more precisely the "current-account" balance in Chapter 15) has stayed negative for many years. But a country with a current-account deficit pays for it by either piling up debts or giving up assets to foreigners. Such a country is *exporting* paper IOUs, such as bonds, that are a present claim on future goods. The value of these net exports matches the value of the ordinary current-account deficit.

There is no need to add paper bonds to our wheat-and-cloth examples because the bonds are a claim on future wheat and cloth. Today, the United States may be importing more cloth than it is exporting wheat, but this deficit is matched by the expected value of its net exports of extra wheat someday when it pays off the debt. Trade is expected to balance over the very long run. That expectation could prove wrong in the future: Maybe the United States will default on some of its foreign debts, or maybe price inflation (deflation) will make it give up less (more) wheat than expected. But today's transactions are based on the *expectation* that trade will balance.

Smith's reasoning was fundamentally correct, and it helped to persuade some governments to dismantle inefficient barriers to international trade over the 100 years after he wrote *Wealth of Nations.* Yet his argument failed to put to rest a fear that others had already expressed even before he wrote. What if we have no absolute advantage? What if the foreigners are better at producing everything than we are? Will they want to trade? If they do, should we want to? That fear persisted in the minds of many of Smith's English contemporaries, who feared that the Dutch were more efficient than they at making anything. It persists into the 21st century too. In the wake of World War II, many nations thought they could not possibly compete with the efficient Americans at anything and wondered how they could gain from free trade. Today some Americans have the same fear in reverse: Aren't foreigners getting more efficient at making everything that enters international trade, and won't the United States be hurt by free trade? We turn next to the theory that first answered these fears and established a fundamental principle of international trade.

Ricardo's Theory of Comparative Advantage

David Ricardo's main contribution to our understanding of international trade was to show that there is a basis for beneficial trade whether or not countries have any absolute advantage. His writings in the early 19th century demonstrated what has become known as

> the **principle of comparative advantage:** a nation, like a person, gains from trade by exporting the goods or services in which it has its greatest comparative advantage in productivity and importing those in which it has the least comparative advantage.

The key word here is *comparative,* meaning relative and not necessarily absolute. Even if one nation is the most productive at producing everything and another is the least, they both gain by trading with each other and with third countries as long as their (dis)advantages in making different goods are different in any way.

Ricardo drove this point home with a simple numerical example of gains from trading two goods between two countries.[3] Here is a similar illustration, again using wheat and cloth in the United States and the rest of the world:

	Even If One Country Is Absolutely Worse at Producing Everything, We Still Have a Case of Comparative Advantage:		
	In the United States		*In the Rest of the World*
Labor required to make:			
1 bushel of wheat	2 hours	>	1.5 hours
1 yard of cloth	4 hours	>	1.0 hour

Here, as in Ricardo's original illustration, a nation has inferior productivity in both goods: The United States requires more labor hours to produce either wheat or cloth. The United States, in other words, has no absolute advantage. What

---

[3]His famous illustration showed the gains from trading English cloth for Portuguese wine. He assumed that Portugal was relatively better at making both wine and cloth, but especially better at making wine. After a demonstration like that in the text above, he went on to show that adding money to the analysis had no long-run effect on the gains from trade. See David Ricardo, *On the Principles of Political Economy and Taxation* (1817), pp. 133–149 of the 1951 edition of his collected works.

goods will the United States trade, and how do we know that trade will bring net national gains to both sides?

As in the absolute-advantage case, we can begin by imagining the two economies separately with no trade between them. Ricardo, like Smith, felt that labor costs dictated market value and prices, as long as there was no international trade. In the United States, people would buy or make each yard of cloth, worth 4 hours of labor, by giving up 2 bushels of wheat, which would also take 4 hours to make. In the rest of the world, exchanging equal labor values would mean giving up a yard of cloth for each 2/3 bushel (= 1/1.5) of wheat. Thus, within the two isolated economies, national prices would follow the relative labor costs of wheat and cloth:

	In the *United States*	*In the Rest* *of the World*
With no international trade:		
Price of wheat	0.5 yard/bushel	1.5 yards/bushel
Price of cloth	2.0 bushels/yard	0.67 bushel/yard

Opening up trade brings the same opportunities for arbitrage profit as in the case of absolute advantage. Somebody will notice the international price difference and trade profitably. Perhaps they will acquire wheat in the United States by giving up only 0.5 yard of cloth and sell the same wheat abroad for 1.5 yards of cloth, ending up with a yard of cloth in pure gain. Or perhaps they will acquire cloth in the rest of the world, giving up only 0.67 bushel of wheat for each yard, and sell it in the United States in exchange for 2.0 bushels, ending up with 1.33 bushels of wheat in pure gain.

The opening of profitable international trade will start pushing the two separate national price ratios into a new worldwide equilibrium. As people remove wheat from the American market for export, wheat becomes more expensive relative to cloth in the United States. Meanwhile, wheat becomes cheaper in the rest of the world, thanks to the new supply of wheat from the United States. So wheat tends to get more expensive where it was cheap at first, and cheaper where it was more expensive at first. (A similar process is true for cloth.) The tendencies will continue until the two national prices become one world equilibrium price. Again, we cannot say exactly how many yards per bushel that final international price ratio will be when normal trade is being conducted on an ongoing basis, but we do know that it must settle between the two price ratios that prevailed in each country before trade. Why? Because if the cloth/wheat price ratio were outside that range, both countries would want to be exporters of the same good and importers of the same (other) good. This is impossible because the two countries add up to the entire world, and trade must balance for the planet Earth. Thus, the international price ratio will settle somewhere in the range where

$$0.5 \leq \text{international price of wheat} \leq 1.5 \text{ (yards/bushel)}$$

i.e., where

$$2.0 \geq \text{international price of cloth} \geq 0.67 \text{ (bushel/yard)}$$

Let us again suppose that the demand forces bring the international price ratio to rest at that same convenient value of 1 bushel = 1 yard. Both countries gain from trade and from specialization. To see how, repeat the same argument that was given for the absolute-advantage case when the international price ratio had settled at 1.0 bushel per yard.

Comparing the absolute-advantage and comparative-advantage cases reveals a startling fact that Ricardo was trying to emphasize: The two cases show the basis for trade and the gains from trade in exactly the same way. What matters is that before trade the two countries had different price ratios. It does not matter why they differed. The absolute labor costs (or their reciprocals, the labor productivities) are irrelevant to the fact that countries gain from trade. The direction of trade and the gains from trade arise from differences in the **opportunity costs** of each final good—that is, the amount of the other good you give up to get more of this one. What matters is that without international trade, the opportunity cost of a bushel of wheat in the United States (give up 0.5 yard of cloth) differs from its opportunity cost in the rest of the world (give up 2.5 yards in the first example, or 1.5 yards in the second). In this way, Ricardo advanced thinking by laying to rest the fear that trade would work only if everyone had an absolute advantage in something.[4]

Ricardo's Constant Costs and the Production-Possibility Curve

Ricardo's numerical illustration succeeded in proving the principle of comparative advantage. We can also show Ricardo's comparative advantage using a diagram representing what whole nations can produce and consume.

Figure 3.1 portrays comparative advantage at the level of whole nations. Each nation can produce only so much because its labor force and productivity are limited. To show what a nation is capable of producing requires more than a single number. It requires a whole curve. For example, consider that the United States has 100 billion hours of labor available during the year, and that labor productivities are as shown in the Ricardian numerical example (2 hours to produce 1 bushel of wheat, and 4 hours to produce 1 yard of cloth). Then, the United States can make 50 billion bushels of wheat a year if it only produces wheat—or it can make 25 billion yards of cloth a year if it makes only cloth. The United States can also produce a mix of wheat and cloth, say, 20 billion bushels of wheat and 15 billion yards of cloth. The curve showing all the combinations of wheat

---

[4]Comparative advantage indicates which country is the relatively low-cost producer, so it determines the trade pattern, and trade brings gains to both high-productivity countries (the rest of the world in our example) and low-productivity countries (the United States). While a country cannot have a comparative advantage in all products, absolute advantage does still matter. Having an absolute advantage in all products means that the country is more productive than other countries. High-productivity countries have high real wages and are rich countries. Low-productivity countries have low real wages and are poor countries. But trade is neither a cause nor an effect of this absolute productivity difference.

FIGURE 3.1

The Gains from Trade, Shown for Ricardo's Constant-Cost Case

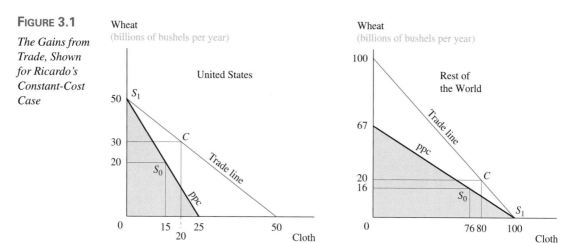

The solid lines are the production-possibility curves (ppc's), showing what each nation can produce. With no trade, each country's consumption is limited by its ability to produce so that consumption occurs at a point like S_0 in each country. With free trade, each country specializes in producing only one good, at S_1. Each country can reach its desirable levels of consumption (consuming at a point like C) by trading along the colored trade line.

Result: Both sides gain from trade. For each country, specializing and trading make it possible to consume more of both goods at C, relative to a no-trade point like S_0 on the ppc.

and cloth that the United States can produce if it uses all its resources at maximum efficiency is a curve often used in economics:

> The **production-possibility curve** (ppc) shows all the combinations of outputs of different goods that an economy can produce with full employment of resources and maximum productivity.

The solid lines in Figure 3.1 are the ppc's for the United States and the rest of the world (assuming that the rest of the world also has 100 billion hours of labor available annually). Note that each is a straight line with a constant slope (steepness). This slope is the cost of extra cloth, the number of bushels of wheat each country would have to give up to make each extra yard of cloth. In this case, the cost is always $50/25 = 2$ bushels per yard for the United States, the same marginal cost of cloth as in the numerical example. With no trade and competitive markets, this cost is also the relative price of cloth in the United States. For the rest of the world the cost of extra cloth is $67/100 = 2/3$. This is also the relative price of cloth in the rest of the world with competitive markets and no trade. The ppc's in Figure 3.1 are drawn as straight lines to reflect Ricardo's belief that the marginal or opportunity cost of each good is constant in each country.

To set the stage for the more modern portrayals of the basis for trade, let us use Figure 3.1 to restate the gains from trade and specialization. If neither country traded, each could only consume and enjoy combinations of wheat and cloth that are on (or below) its ppc, combinations like those shown as S_0 in Figure 3.1.

When trade is opened, each nation can trade at a price between 2/3 and 2 bushels per yard. Again, let us suppose that demand conditions make the free-trade price equal 1 bushel per yard. Each country then specializes in producing only the good in which it has a comparative advantage, at point S_1. To show how each nation gains from trade at this price, we need to consider how trade should be drawn on the diagram. When a nation sells its exports to get imports, it ends up consuming a different set of goods. How different? In a diagram such as Figure 3.1, the line connecting where a nation produces and where it consumes is a line along which wheat trades for cloth at the world price ratio, 1 bushel per yard. Two trade (or price) lines are shown in Figure 3.1.

If the United States specializes in making only wheat, at S_1, it can export wheat for cloth imports at the world price ratio, moving along the trade line. Giving up wheat and gaining cloth imports means moving southeast along the trade line. The United States could consume anywhere along this colored line. Clearly, this is a better set of consumption options than if the United States did not trade. For each point like S_0, where the nation consumes what it produces, there are better consumption points like C, where it can end up consuming more of everything by specializing and trading. The United States gains from trade. It is equally clear that the rest of the world also gains from specializing in cloth production (at S_1) and trading some of that cloth for wheat, moving northwest along its trade line to consume at some point like C. Thus, Figure 3.1 is a different way to view the workings of comparative advantage with Ricardian constant costs.

Later writers challenged Ricardo's simple assumption of constant marginal costs. First, they noted empirically that many industries seem to be characterized by rising, rather than constant, marginal costs, so that more and more of other goods have to be given up to produce each succeeding extra unit of one good. Second, they thought of some good reasons for expecting that marginal costs would rise when one industry expands at the expense of others. One obvious possibility is that each individual industry, contrary to the assumption of Ricardo's trade example, may itself have diminishing returns or rising costs. Even if every industry has constant returns to scale, the shift from one industry to another may involve increasing marginal costs because of subtle effects stemming from the fact that different goods use resource inputs in different proportions.

Perhaps the most damaging objection to the assumption of constant marginal costs is that it implies something that fails to fit the facts of international trade and production patterns. The constancy of marginal costs in Figure 3.1 leads us to conclude that each country would maximize its gain by specializing its production completely in its comparative-advantage good.[5]

The real world fails to show total specialization. In Ricardo's day, it may have been reasonable for him to assume that England grew no wine grapes and

---

[5]With constant costs one of the two trading countries can fail to specialize completely only in the special case in which the international price ratio settles at the same price ratio prevailing in that country with no trade. In this case the country whose price ratio does not change is a "large" country and the other country is a "small" country. The large country continues to produce both goods with free trade because the small country cannot export enough to satisfy all demand for this product in the large country. Figure 3.1 assumes that the countries are of sufficiently similar "size" that both completely specialize in production.

relied on foreign grapes and wines, but even with cloth imports from England, the other country in his example, Portugal, made most of its own cloth. Complete specialization is no more common today. The United States and Canada continue to produce some of their domestic consumption of goods they partially import— textiles, cars, and furniture, for example.

Increasing Marginal Costs

In the modern theory of international trade, economists replace the constant-cost assumption used in the Ricardian approach with a more realistic assumption about marginal costs that is likely to hold in most cases. They assume **increasing marginal costs:** As one industry expands at the expense of others, increasing amounts of the other goods must be given up to get each extra unit of the expanding output. Figure 3.2 shows a case of increasing marginal costs. This can be seen

FIGURE 3.2

Production Possibilities Under Increasing Costs

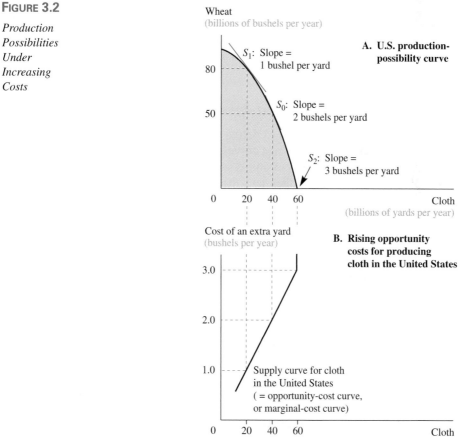

Increasing opportunity costs can be shown in either of two equivalent ways: as changing slopes along a convex production-possibility curve or as a rising supply (or marginal-cost) curve.

by following what happens to the marginal cost of producing an extra yard of cloth as we shift more and more resources from wheat production to cloth production. When the economy is producing only 20 billion yards of cloth, the slope of the production-possibility curve at point S_1 tells us that one extra yard could be made each year by giving up 1 bushel of wheat. When 40 billion yards are being made each year, getting the resources to make another yard a year means giving up 2 bushels of wheat, as shown at point S_0. To push cloth production up to 60 billion yards per year requires giving up wheat in amounts that rise to 3 bushels for the last yard of cloth. These increasing costs of extra cloth also can be interpreted as increasing costs of producing extra wheat: When one starts from a cloth-only economy at point S_2 and shifts increasing amounts of resources into growing wheat, the costs of an extra bushel mount (from 1/3 yard at S_2 to 1/2 yard at S_0, 1 yard at S_1, and so forth).

The increasing marginal costs reappear in a familiar form in the lower half of Figure 3.2. Here the vertical axis plots the marginal costs of extra cloth, which were the slopes in the upper half of the figure. The resulting curve is a supply curve for cloth (such as we used in Chapter 2). The marginal costs of producing extra cloth are the marginal costs that a set of competitive U.S. cloth suppliers would equate to the market price they receive when selling the cloth. This re-expression shows the link between the two-product analysis of this chapter and the one-product focus of Chapter 2.

What's Behind the Bowed-Out Production-Possibility Curve?

What information do we need to derive the production-possibility curve of each country? Why are increasing-cost curves (bowed-out in shape) so likely to occur?

A country's production-possibility curve is derived from information on both total factor (resource) supplies and the production functions that relate factor inputs to output in various industries. In Appendix B we show how the production-possibility curves are derived under several common assumptions about production functions in individual industries.

We can sketch the explanation for the prevalence of increasing costs (and the bowed-out shape) even without a rigorous demonstration. The key point is that different products use factor inputs in different proportions. To stay with our wheat-and-cloth example for a moment, wheat uses relatively more land and less labor than cloth, whether the yarn for the cloth comes from synthetic fibers or from natural fibers such as cotton or silk. This basic variation in input proportions can set up an increasing-cost (bowed-out) production-possibility curve even if constant returns to scale exist in each industry. When resources are released from cloth production and are shifted into wheat production, they will be released in proportions different from those initially prevailing in wheat production. The cloth industry will release a lot of labor and not much land relative to the labor and land use pattern in wheat. To employ these factors, the wheat industry must shift toward using more labor-intensive techniques. The effect is close to that of the law of diminishing returns (which, strictly speaking, refers to the case of adding more of one factor to fixed amounts of the others): Adding so much labor to slowly changing amounts of land causes the gains in wheat production to decline as more and more resources, mainly labor, are released from cloth production. Thus, fewer and fewer extra bushels of wheat production are gained by each extra yard of lost cloth production.

What Production Combination Is Actually Chosen?

Out of all the possible production points along the production-possibility curve, which one point does the nation select? That depends on the price ratio that competitive firms face. Suppose that the price of cloth in terms of wheat is two bushels per yard. If you are a competitive firm vying with other firms around you, you will see one of these three conditions at any production point:

- If the opportunity cost of producing another yard of cloth is *less* than the 2 bushels per yard that you can sell it for, then try to make more cloth (and take resources away from wheat). Firms would react this way at a point like S_1 in Figure 3.2, where the opportunity cost is less (the slope of the ppc is flatter) than 2 bushels per yard.
- If the opportunity cost of producing another yard of cloth is *more* than the 2 bushels you can sell it for, then try to make less cloth (and shift resources into growing wheat). Firms would react this way at a point like S_2, where the opportunity cost is greater (the slope of the ppc is steeper) than 2 bushels per yard.
- If the opportunity cost of producing another yard of cloth is *equal* to the 2 bushels you can sell it for, then you are producing the right amount. There is no reason to shift any production between cloth and wheat. Firms would react this way at point S_0.

By choosing to produce at S_0 (40 billion yards of cloth and 50 billion bushels of wheat) when the price is 2 bushels per yard, firms end up maximizing the value of national production. The price is represented by a price line whose slope is 2 bushels per yard, and the price line with this slope is tangent to the ppc at S_0. Where the two are tangent, you cannot increase the value of national production, measured in either yards or bushels, by moving to any other point on the production-possibility curve.[6]

What happens if the relative price of cloth declines to 1 bushel per yard? With a lower price of cloth, we expect that cloth production will decrease. The resources released as cloth production decreases are shifted into wheat production, and wheat output increases. After a period of transition, during which resources are shifted from the cloth industry to the wheat industry, the production point chosen by the country will shift to point S_1. The tangent line at S_1 has a

---

[6]This can be seen by extending the two-bushels-per-yard price line from point S_0 to touch either axis in Figure 3.2. The point where the extended line hits the horizontal axis is the value of the whole national production of wheat plus cloth, expressed as the amount of cloth that it could be traded for. Similarly, the point where the extended line hits the vertical axis is the value of the same national production, expressed in bushels of wheat. You can see that this value is greater when the nation produces at S_0 than when it produces at any other point on the ppc, as long as the price (and the slope of a price line through this other point) is 2 bushels per yard.

slope of 1 bushel per yard and represents a new price line. The production combination chosen has less cloth (20) and more wheat (80).

Community Indifference Curves

The production-possibility curve pictures the production side of a country's economy. To complete the picture of the economy, we need a way to depict the determinants of demand for two products simultaneously.

For an individual, economists typically begin with the notion that each individual derives well-being (or happiness or utility) from consuming various goods and services. Figure 3.3 shows the usual way of relating an individual's utility to amounts of two goods, again wheat and cloth, that the individual consumes. Instead of drawing utility in a third dimension rising out of the printed page, economists draw contours called *indifference curves*. An **indifference curve** shows all the consumption points at which utility equals some constant. For example, the indifference curve I_0 shows that the individual is *indifferent* between points *A, B,* and *C,* each of which gives the same utility. Any consumption point below and to the left of I_0 is worse than *A* or *B* or *C* in the eyes of this individual. Points above and to the right of I_0 are better. For example, point *D,* on the better indifference curve I_1, yields a higher level of utility than *A* or *B* or *C*. Point *E*, on I_2, is even more preferred.

Each indifference curve is typically presumed to have a bowed shape as shown in the figure. The individual has an infinite number (a complete map) of indifference curves, representing infinitesimally small differences in utility, and

FIGURE 3.3

Indifference Curves Relating an Individual's Utility Levels to Consumption of Two Goods

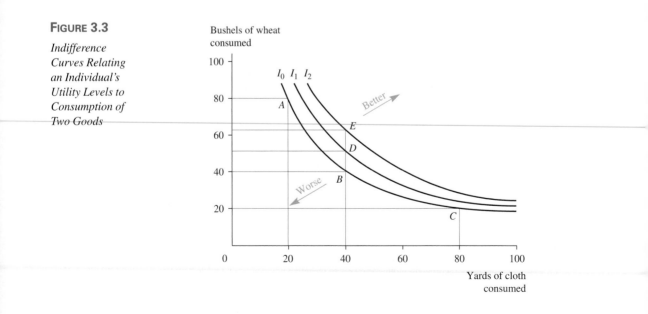

showing the person's preferences regarding various combinations of the products. Our diagrams typically show only a small number of indifference curves from this complete map.

The actual consumption point chosen by the individual depends on the budget constraint facing the person—the income that the individual has available to spend on these products and the prices of the products. The budget constraint is $Y = P_W \cdot Q_W + P_C \cdot Q_C$, assuming that the individual spends all his income Y on the two products wheat (W) and cloth (C). For given income and prices, the equation is a straight line showing combinations of cloth and wheat that the individual is able to purchase with this income: $Q_W = (Y/P_W) - (P_C/P_W) \cdot Q_C$. The slope of this budget constraint is the (negative of the) price ratio P_C/P_W, the relative price of cloth, so we usually refer to this budget constraint as a price line. Given the budget constraint or price line, the individual chooses consumption to be as well off as possible—to reach the highest feasible indifference curve. This is the indifference curve that is just tangent to the price line.

When exploring trade issues, we want to portray how the entire nation, not just one individual, decides on consumption quantities and what this decision implies for the economic well-being (welfare or utility) of the nation as a whole. Can we portray a large group of people (like a country) as having a set of indifference curves? Although there are problems with this portrayal, a single set of indifference curves for a group of people is remarkably useful as a tool for our analysis. We will utilize **community indifference curves,** which purport to show how the economic well-being of a whole group depends on the whole group's consumption of wheat and cloth. In what follows, we look at sets of indifference curves like those in Figure 3.3 as if they were community indifference curves for millions or billions of people. We will use community indifference curves, along with the price line representing the national budget (or income) constraint, as the basis for the choice of national quantities demanded and consumed of the two products.

Nonetheless, we must keep in mind that economic theory raises difficult questions about community indifference curves. First, the shapes of individual indifference curves differ so there is no completely clear way in which to "add up" individuals' indifference curves to obtain community indifference curves. Second, the concept of national utility or welfare is not well defined. How can we say whether the community is better off with an average of 40 bushels less and 40 yards more? Some members of the community may lose, while others gain. Who can say that the increase in satisfaction of the one is greater than the decrease in satisfaction of the other? Levels of satisfaction or welfare cannot be compared from one person to another.

These are real difficulties. We will use community indifference curves because they are convenient and neat. They are reasonable for depicting the basis for national demand patterns for two products simultaneously. Under certain assumptions they provide information on national well-being or welfare, but some caution is needed in using them in this way. Higher national welfare, as shown by community indifference curves, does not mean that each person is actually better off.

Production and Consumption Together

Figure 3.4 summarizes information on the U.S. economy. The production capabilities of the United States are shown by the bowed-out (increasing-cost) production-possibility curve, and U.S. consumption preferences are shown by a map of community indifference curves, of which three are shown.

Without Trade

With no trade the United States must be self-sufficient and must find the combination of domestically produced wheat and cloth that will maximize community well-being. Of all the points at which the United States can produce, only S_0 can reach the indifference curve I_1. A point such as S_1 can only yield a lower indifference curve, such as I_0. At S_1 either consumers or producers or both will find the prevailing price ratio allows them to be better off by moving toward S_0. If the price ratio is temporarily tangent to the production-possibility curve at S_1, consumers will find that this makes cloth look so cheap that they would rather buy more cloth than 20 billion yards and less wheat than 80 billion bushels. Their shift in demand will cause producers to follow suit and shift more resources into cloth production and out of wheat. The tendency to alter production will persist until the economy produces and consumes, at S_0, 40 billion yards of cloth and 50 billion bushels of wheat.

FIGURE 3.4

Indifference Curves and Production Possibilities Without Trade

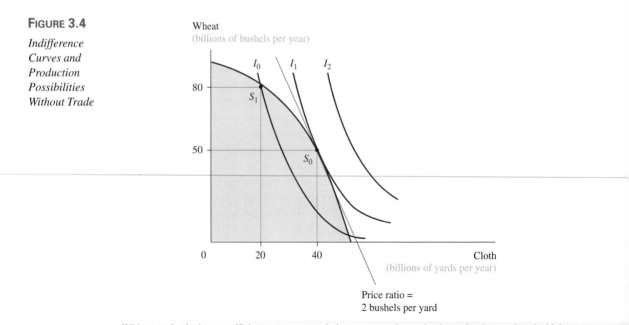

Without trade, the best an efficient economy can do is to move to the production point that touches the highest consumption indifference curve, just as an individual does. This best no-trade point is S_0, where the nation both produces and consumes, reaching indifference curve I_1.

For the shapes of the curves shown, there is one and only one such optimizing point. The no-trade (or autarky) equilibrium point is S_0, where a community indifference curve (I_1) is tangent to the production-possibility curve. The slope of the straight line tangent to both of these at point S_0 shows the no-trade equilibrium relative price of cloth for the United States, equal to 2 bushels per yard.

With Trade

To show the effects of opening the world to international trade, we examine the economies of both countries. The left side of Figure 3.5A shows the U.S. economy (the same as in Figure 3.4), and the right side shows the economy of the rest of the world. The no-trade equilibrium in each country is at point S_0. With no trade the U.S. relative price of cloth would be 2 bushels per yard, while the relative price in the rest of the world would be 0.67 bushel per yard.

As in previous examples, the difference in price ratios with no trade provides the immediate basis for trade. With free trade the United States imports cloth from the rest of the world and exports wheat to the rest of the world. This trade tends to decrease the relative price of cloth in the United States and increase the relative price of cloth in the rest of the world. With free trade (and assuming no transport costs), trade results in an equilibrium international price ratio in the range of 0.67 to 2 bushels per yard. The price ratio for this free-trade equilibrium is the price that results in the quantity of wheat exported by the United States being equal to the quantity of wheat imported by the rest of the world, and the quantity of cloth exported by the rest of the world being equal to the quantity of cloth imported by the United States.

For the conditions in each country shown by their ppc's and community indifference curves, the free-trade equilibrium occurs at a price ratio of 1 bushel per yard. In the shift from no trade to free trade, producers in the United States respond to the lower relative price of cloth (and thus higher relative price of wheat) by reducing production of cloth and increasing production of wheat, shifting production from point S_0 to S_1. With production at S_1, the United States can trade wheat for cloth with the rest of the world at the price of 1 bushel per yard, so that consumption can be at any point along the price line through S_1 corresponding to the price ratio of 1 bushel per yard (that is, with a slope of 1). Given this price line, the United States will consume at point C_1, the tangent point with the highest achievable community indifference curve I_2.

In the rest of the world, the shift from no trade to free trade increases the relative price of cloth, so producers respond by increasing production of cloth and decreasing production of wheat from point S_0 to S_1. The rest of the world can trade away from their production point at the international equilibrium price ratio so consumption can be at any point along the price line through S_1 corresponding to this price ratio (slope of 1). Given this price line, the rest of the world will consume at point C_1.

At the international price ratio of 1 bushel per yard, the United States is willing to export 40 billion bushels of wheat, the difference between the 80 produced

FIGURE 3.5

*Two Views of
Free Trade and
Its Effects*

A. With indifference curves and production-possibility curves

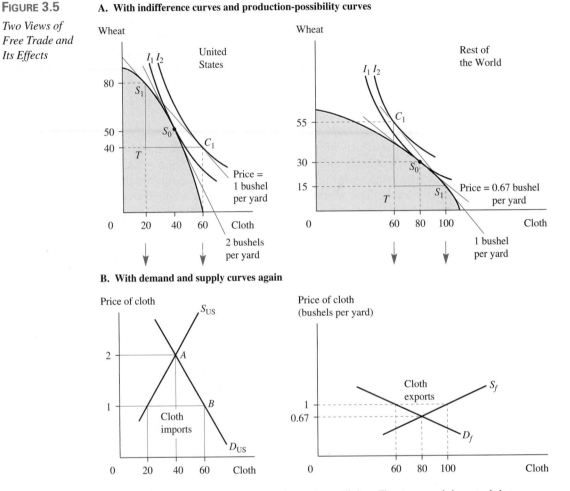

There are two convenient ways to portray a free-trade equilibrium. The upper panel shows trade between two countries for two products, with each country producing at its point S_1 and consuming at its point C_1. The lower panel shows the same thing using supply and demand curves that focus on one product (cloth), the approach discussed in Chapter 2.

domestically at point S_1 and the 40 consumed domestically at point C_1. The rest of the world wants to import 40 billion bushels of wheat, equal to the difference between the 55 consumed domestically and the 15 produced domestically. At this price ratio, the United States wants to import 40 billion yards of cloth (60 consumed minus 20 produced domestically). The rest of the world is willing to export 40 billion yards (100 produced minus 60 consumed domestically). Thus, the international trade markets for both products are in equilibrium, confirming that the price ratio of 1 bushel per yard is the international equilibrium price ratio. The export–import quantities in each country can be summarized by the "trade triangles" that show these quantities. The trade triangle for the United States is shown by the right triangle $S_1 T C_1$, and that for the rest of the world $C_1 T S_1$. International equilibrium is achieved when these two trade triangles are the same size so that both sides agree on the amounts traded.

We will generally assume that there is only one free-trade equilibrium international price ratio for a given set of supply and demand conditions in each country. To see why a price ratio other than 1 bushel per yard generally will not be an international equilibrium, consider a price line flatter (making cloth even cheaper) than the price of 1 bushel per yard. The United States would respond to such a price by producing above and to the left of point S_1 and trading large volumes of wheat for cloth in order to consume out beyond C_1. The catch, however, is that the rest of the world would not want to trade so much at a price ratio that makes its cloth cheaper than 1 bushel per yard. This can be seen by finding the tangency of the new flat price line to the rest of the world's production-possibility and indifference curves on the right side of Figure 3.5A. The result of a price ratio making cloth cheaper than 1 bushel per yard is closer to S_0, the no-trade point. With the rest of the world wanting so little trade at such a price, the large demand for imported cloth by the United States would increase the relative price of cloth. The price would return to the equilibrium unitary price shown in Figure 3.5.

Demand and Supply Curves Again

The community indifference curves also can be combined with the production-possibility curves to plot out demand curves for cloth or wheat. A demand curve for cloth shows how the quantity of cloth demanded responds to its price. To derive the U.S. demand curve for cloth, start in Figure 3.5A with a price ratio and find how much cloth the United States would be willing and able to consume at that price. At 2 bushels per yard, the United States is willing and able to consume 40 billion yards a year (at S_0). At 1 bushel per yard, the United States would consume 60 billion yards (at C_1). These demand points could be replotted in Figure 3.5B, with the prices on the vertical axis. Point S_0 above becomes point A below; point C_1 above becomes point B below; and so forth. The same could be done for the rest of the world. (The demand-curve derivation is like that found in ordinary price-theory textbooks, except that the nation's income constraint slides along a production-possibility surface instead of rotating on a fixed-income point.) In this way the handy demand–supply framework can be derived from community indifference curves plus production-possibility curves. The international equilibrium focusing on a single product (the approach discussed in Chapter 2 and shown in Figure 3.5B) is therefore consistent with the general equilibrium approach using two products.[7]

---

[7]The theoretical literature on international trade often uses the indifference and production-possibility curves to derive an *offer curve*. An offer curve is a way of showing how a nation's offer of exports for imports from the rest of the world depends on the international price ratio. A nation's offer curve shows the same information as its export supply or import demand curve. Appendix C discusses how an offer curve can be derived and used.

The Opening of Trade and China's Shift Out of Agriculture

The real world does in fact reveal the behavior portrayed in the diagrams and discussion of this chapter. Countries do react to the opening of trade in the ways predicted by diagrams like those in Figure 3.5.

A good example still in progress is China's response to becoming a major trading nation after the near-total isolation and self-sufficiency that Chairman Mao imposed between 1958 (at the start of the Great Leap Forward) and 1976 (the year of Mao's death and the end of the Great Proletarian Cultural Revolution). Though China covers a huge geographic area, it is not a land-abundant country. Rather, it is labor-abundant and land-scarce. True to the ancient Chinese saying "Many people, little land," the country has over one-fifth of the world's population but only ½th of its farmable land. For such a labor-abundant country, this chapter's theories would predict the following responses to the chance to open up trade.

- China should export labor-intensive products like clothing and import land-intensive products like wheat.
- China should shift resources out of producing land-intensive products like wheat and into

producing labor-intensive products like clothing.

- China's production specialization should be incomplete. The country should go on producing some land-intensive products, though these should be a lower-share of production than before.
- China should be a more prosperous country with trade than without trade. The theory even allows for the possibility that China could consume more of all goods, including both wheat and clothing.

All these predictions have been coming true in China since 1976. The trade pattern is what we would expect: China has become a strong exporter of all sorts of manufactured products, including clothing, that take advantage of the country's abundant labor supply. China has also turned to imports for a rising share of its consumption of land-abundant products, including wheat.

All over China, people have noticed the shift of production out of agriculture and into export-oriented industry. For example, in the crowded coun-

The Gains from Trade

There are two ways to use a figure like Figure 3.5A to show that each nation gains from international trade. First, trade allows each country to consume at a point (C_1) that lies beyond its ability to produce (its production-possibility curve). This is a gain from trade as long as we view more consumption as desirable. It is the same demonstration of the gains from trade that we used for the Ricardian approach earlier in the chapter. Second, trade allows each country to achieve a higher community indifference curve (I_2 rather than I_1 with no trade). However, the use of community indifference curves to show national gains from trade may hide the fact that opening trade actually hurts some groups while bringing gains to others. We take up this issue of the distribution of gains and losses in the next chapter.

How much each country gains from trade depends on the international price ratio in the ongoing international trade equilibrium. As individuals we benefit

tryside of Shandong province, villages that once struggled with poor soil to grow wheat and corn for cities like Tianjin or Beijing have abandoned farming and now make furniture and pharmaceuticals. Even the relatively fertile villages of Jiangsu province, near the mouth of the Yangtse River, make textiles, steel, and other industrial goods. Similarly, in the south, Guangdong province used to send its rice far north to Beijing. Now Guangdong, a leader in China's rapid industrialization, consumes more rice than it produces, supplementing local crops with rice imports from Thailand.

Both public opinion and the available statistics agree that the great majority of China's population have gained purchasing power. People naturally worry about the relative decline of China's own food production, and voice fears about being dependent on imports. These fears seem to be greater in the government than in the population at large. The government in the 1990s has decided to channel a larger share of taxpayers' money into promoting agricultural production, to retard the shift away from being self-sufficient in food. Yet many are less worried. Wu Xiedong, leader of one of those Jiangsu villages that switched from growing grain to making textiles and steel, is optimistic about the shift. As he put it in 1995, "As long as the present policy that allows farmers to go into industry doesn't change, we will con-

tinue to grow very fast." As for relying on imported food, Wu says, "America has lots of grain, right? If America buys my steel, I'll buy America's grain. Then we can all get rich."* So far, so good. China's food consumption per capita has risen faster than China's food production per capita (which has also risen, thanks to reforms that have raised the country's productivity on all fronts).

China's experience mirrors what happened earlier to Japan, Korea, Taiwan, and Hong Kong. All of these labor-abundant and land-scarce areas reacted to the opening of trade by shifting into labor-intensive industry and out of land-intensive agriculture, and all of them prospered. As for the fear of dependence on food imports, which officials in all these countries still express, Chapter 14 will explore alternative ways of addressing the risks.

---

*Note the "if" part of this statement. If U.S. policy blocked imports of industrial products from China, using tools like those we discuss in Part II, the Chinese would reduce imports from the United States, and the gains from trade would be cut.

Source: Reprinted by permission of *The Wall Street Journal,* © 1995. Dow Jones & Company, Inc. All Rights Reserved Worldwide.

from receiving high prices for the things that we sell (such as our labor services) and paying low prices for the things that we buy. A similar principle applies to countries. A country gains more from trade if it receives a higher price for its exports relative to the price that it pays for its imports. For each country, the gains from trade depend on the country's terms of trade.

> A country's **terms of trade** are the price of its export good(s) relative to the price of its import good(s).

In our example, the rest of the world exports cloth and imports wheat, so the terms of trade for the rest of the world are the relative price of cloth. In Figure 3.5A we can show that the rest of the world would gain more from trade if its terms of trade were better—if the international relative price of cloth were higher. Then the international price line would be steeper than the line through S_1 and C_1, and the rest of the world could reach a community indifference curve higher than I_2. For the United States, its terms of trade are the relative price of wheat, its export good. The United States would gain more from trade if the relative price of wheat were higher, resulting in a flatter international price line than the line through S_1 and C_1. Then the United States could reach a community indifference curve higher than I_2.

Trade Affects Production and Consumption

Figure 3.5A shows that there are substantial effects on production quantities when trade is opened. The opening has two types of implications for production. First, *within each country* output expands for the product in which the country has a comparative advantage—more wheat in the United States and more cloth in the rest of the world. In each country, the growing industry expands by acquiring factor resources from the other industry in the economy. The import-competing industry reduces its domestic production—cloth in the United States and wheat in the rest of the world. Although production shifts in each country, the countries do not (necessarily) specialize completely in producing their export good if the production-possibility curve is bowed-out because of increasing costs.

Second, the shift from no trade to free trade results in more efficient *world* production as each country expands output of the product in which it is initially the lower-cost producer. In the particular case shown in Figure 3.5A, the efficiency gains show up as an increase in world production of wheat (from 50 + 30 = 80 with no trade to 80 + 15 = 95 with trade), while world cloth production is unchanged at 120.

In each country, opening to trade also alters the quantities consumed of each good, as the consumption point shifts from S_0 with no trade to C_1 with free trade. Consumer theory indicates that the quantity consumed of the importable product in each country will increase. The relative price of the importable product declines in each country so consumers in the country buy more of it (a positive substitution effect). Meanwhile, real income rises in each country (as a result of the gains from trade) so consumers buy even more (a positive income effect). The quantity consumed of the exportable product in each country could increase, stay the same, or decrease because of opposing pressures from a negative substitution effect (resulting from the higher relative price of the exportable good) and a positive income effect (as real income rises). In the particular case shown in Figure 3.5A, the quantities consumed of the exportable product actually decrease (50 to 40 for wheat in the United States and 80 to 60 for cloth in the rest of world), but other outcomes for these two consumption quantities are possible.

What Determines the Trade Pattern?

Our general view of national economies engaged in international trade is shown in Figure 3.5A. The immediate basis for the pattern of international trade that we see here is that relative product prices would differ between the two countries if there was no trade. But why would relative product prices differ with no trade? They can differ either because production conditions differ—the relative shapes of the production-possibility curves differ between the countries—or because consumption conditions differ—the relative shapes and positions of the community indifference curves differ between the countries—or because of some combination of these two differences.

In our example the basis for the United States to import cloth could be that the United States has a high demand for cloth, perhaps due to a harsh climate or fashion consciousness. Although this kind of explanation may apply to a few products, most analysis focuses on production-side differences as the basis for no-trade price differences, assuming that demand patterns are similar for the countries.

Production-side differences can be a basis for the international trade pattern when the relative shapes of the production-possibility curves differ, with the ppc for one country skewed toward producing wheat and the ppc for the other country skewed toward producing cloth. For instance, in Figure 3.5A, the ppc for the United States is skewed toward production of wheat, and the ppc for the rest of the world is skewed toward production of cloth. Why do we see these production-side differences? There are two basic reasons.

First, the production technologies or resource productivities may differ between countries. For instance, the United States may have superior technology to produce wheat and somehow keep its secret from the rest of the world. The better technology results in relatively high resource productivity in U.S. wheat production. This will skew the U.S. production-possibility curve toward producing larger amounts of wheat, resulting in a comparative advantage for the United States to produce and export wheat. This type of comparative advantage was the basis for trade in the Ricardian approach. Although this can be a production-side basis for comparative advantage, for the remainder of this chapter and in Chapter 4 we assume that it is not. Instead, we assume that both countries have access to the same technologies for production and are capable of achieving similar levels of resource productivity. This assumption is plausible if technology spreads internationally because it is difficult for a country to keep its technology secret. (Issues related to technology will be taken up in Chapters 5 and 6.)

The second reason that the relative shapes of the production-possibility curves can differ is more subtle but has become the basis for the orthodox modern theory of comparative advantage. It is the Heckscher–Ohlin theory based on (1) differences across countries in the availability of factor resources and (2) differences across products in the use of these factors in producing the products.

The Heckscher–Ohlin (H–O) Theory: Factor Proportions Are Key

The leading theory of what determines nations' trade patterns emerged in Sweden. Eli Heckscher, the noted Swedish economic historian, developed the core idea in a brief article in 1919. A clear overall explanation was developed and publicized in the 1930s by Heckscher's student Bertil Ohlin. Ohlin, like Keynes, managed to combine a distinguished academic career—professor at Stockholm and later a Nobel laureate—with political office (Riksdag member, party leader, and government official during World War II). Ohlin's persuasive narrative of the theory and the evidence that seemed to support it were later reinforced by another Nobel laureate, Paul Samuelson, who derived mathematical conditions under which the Heckscher–Ohlin (H–O) prediction was strictly correct.[8]

The Heckscher–Ohlin theory of trade patterns says, in Ohlin's own words,

> Commodities requiring for their production much of [abundant factors of production] and little of [scarce factors] are exported in exchange for goods that call for factors in the opposite proportions. Thus indirectly, factors in abundant supply are exported and factors in scanty supply are imported. (Ohlin, 1933, p. 92)

Or, more succinctly,

> **The H–O theory predicts that countries export the products that use their abundant factors intensively** (and import the products using their scarce factors intensively).

To judge this plausible and testable argument more easily, we need definitions of factor abundance and factor-use intensity:

> A country is relatively **labor-abundant** if it has a higher ratio of labor to other factors than does the rest of the world.

> A product is relatively **labor-intensive** if labor costs are a greater share of its value than they are of the value of other products.

The Heckscher–Ohlin explanation of trade patterns begins with a specific hunch as to why product prices might differ between countries before they open trade. Heckscher and Ohlin predicted that the key to comparative costs lies in factor proportions. If cloth costs 2 bushels a yard in the United States and less than a bushel a yard elsewhere, it must be primarily because the United States has relatively more of the factors that wheat uses intensively, and relatively less of the factors that cloth uses intensively, than does the rest of the world. Let *land* be the factor that wheat uses more intensively and *labor* be the factor that cloth uses more intensively. Let all costs be decomposable into land and labor costs (e.g., it takes certain amounts of land and labor to make fertilizer for growing wheat and certain other amounts of land and labor to make cotton inputs for cloth making). Therefore, the H–O theory predicts that the United States exports wheat and imports cloth because wheat is land-intensive and cloth is labor-intensive and

$$\frac{\text{(U.S. land supply)}}{\text{(U.S. labor supply)}} > \frac{\text{(rest of world's land supply)}}{\text{(rest of world's labor supply)}}$$

---

[8]Ohlin backed the H–O theory with real-world observation and appeals to intuition. Samuelson took the mathematical road, adding assumptions that allowed a strict proof of the theory's main prediction. Samuelson assumed (1) that there are two countries, two goods, and two factors (the frequent "2 × 2 × 2" simplification); (2) that factor supplies are fixed for each country, fully employed, and mobile between sectors within each country, but immobile between countries; (3) that the consumption patterns of the two countries are identical; and (4) that both countries share the same constant-returns-to-scale technology. The H–O predictions follow logically in Samuelson's narrow case and seem broadly accurate in the real world. Our analysis in the text is based on Samuelson's depiction of the theory.

Under these conditions[9] with no international trade, land should rent more cheaply in the United States than elsewhere, and labor should command a higher wage rate in the United States than elsewhere. The cheapness of land cuts costs more in wheat farming than in cloth making. Conversely, the scarcity of labor should make cloth relatively expensive in the United States. This, according to H–O, is why product prices differ in the direction they do before trade begins. And, the theory predicts, it is the difference in relative factor endowments and the pattern of factor intensities that make the United States export wheat instead of cloth (and import cloth instead of wheat) when trade opens up.

---

[9]Take care not to misread the relative factor endowment inequality. It does not say the United States has more land than the rest of the world. Nor does it say that the United States has less labor. In fact, the United States really has less of both. Nor does it say the United States has more land than it has labor—a meaningless statement in any case. (How many acres are "more than" how many hours of labor?)

Rather it is an inequality between *relative* endowments. Here are two correct ways of stating it: (1) There is more land per laborer in the United States than in the rest of the world and (2) the U.S. share of the world's land is greater than its share of the world's labor.

Summary

International trade occurs because product prices would differ if there was no trade. This chapter focuses on theories emphasizing production-side differences between countries as the reason for product prices to differ without trade. Three variants emphasizing the supply side are Adam Smith's **theory of absolute advantage,** David Ricardo's **principle of comparative advantage,** and the **Heckscher–Ohlin (H–O) theory** stressing factor proportions.

The principle of **comparative advantage** says that it will pay the country to produce more of those goods in which it is relatively more efficient and to export them in return for goods in which its relative advantage is least. Trade is not a zero-sum game in which one side gains only what the other loses. The whole world gains from trade, and each side is at least as well off with free trade as with no trade. A country can gain from trade even if it is worse at everything, or better at everything, than the rest of the world.

The principle of comparative advantage, as first successfully argued by Ricardo in the early 19th century, assumed constant marginal costs. Dropping his constant-cost assumption to allow for increasing marginal costs makes it easier to explain why countries do not specialize completely in producing only one product. It does not overturn the principle of comparative advantage, however.

International differences in the shape of the **production-possibility curves** (ppc's) stem largely from the facts that (1) different goods use the factors of production in different proportions and (2) nations differ in their relative factor endowments. Building on these two facts, the **Heckscher–Ohlin (H–O)** explanation of trade patterns predicts that nations will tend to export the goods that use their relatively abundant factors more intensively in exchange for imports of goods that use their scarce factors more intensively.

The gains from trade for each country can be demonstrated in two ways. First, trade allows the country to consume beyond its ability to produce—it allows consumption outside of its production-possibility curve. Second, trade allows the country to reach a higher **community indifference curve,** indicating that the country reaches a higher level of national economic well-being or welfare.

Suggested Reading (for Chapters 2 and 3)

Irwin (1996) provides a good survey of thoughts about the advantages and disadvantages of free trade, starting with the ancient Greeks and continuing through mercantilists, Smith, Ricardo, and recent economic analysis. The technical literature on free trade is vast and cannot be cited at length here. For advanced technical surveys, see Chapters 1–3, 7, and 8 of Jones and Kenen, Vol. I (1984).

Roy Ruffin (1988) has improved the Ricardian model of comparative advantage so that it generates the predictions of the Heckscher–Ohlin model. He does so by interpreting productivity differences in the one-factor Ricardian approach as differences in relative factor endowments.

Questions and Problems

✦ 1. "According to Ricardo's analysis, a country exports any good whose production requires fewer labor hours per unit than the labor hours per unit needed to produce the good in the foreign country. That is, the country exports any good in which its labor productivity is higher than the labor productivity for this good in the foreign country." Do you agree or disagree? Why?

2. "For my country, imports are the good thing about international trade, whereas exports are more like the necessary evil." Do you agree or disagree? Why?

✦ 3. The country of Pugelovia has an endowment (total supply) of 20 units of labor and 3 units of land, whereas the rest of the world has 80 units of labor and 7 units of land. Is Pugelovia labor-abundant? Is Pugelovia land-abundant? If wheat is land-intensive and cloth is labor-intensive, what is the Heckscher–Ohlin prediction for the pattern of trade between Pugelovia and the rest of the world?

4. Explain how a supply curve can be obtained or derived from an increasing-cost production-possibility curve. Use Figure 3.4 to derive the supply curve for cloth. For a bit more challenge, use Figure 3.4 to derive the supply curve for wheat.

✦ 5. In your answer to this question, use a diagram like Figure 3.4, making it large enough so that you can see the curves and quantities clearly. The no-trade point is as shown in Figure 3.4, a price ratio of 2 (bushels per yard) and 40 units of cloth demanded. Sketch the derivation of the portion of the country's cloth demand curve for cloth prices of 2 and below. (To do this, examine a price of about 1.5, then 1.0, and then 0.5. In your analysis you will need to show additional community indifference curves—ones that exist but are not shown explicitly in Figure 3.4.)

6. Return to your answer for question 5. For prices below 2, which good does the country export? Which good does it import? How does the quantity (demanded or needed) of imports change as the price changes? What is happening to the country's terms of trade as the price declines? What is happening to the country's well-being or welfare as the price declines?

✦ 7. You are given the information shown in the table about production relationships in Lindertania and the rest of the world.

You make several Ricardian assumptions: These are the only two commodities, there

	Inputs per Bushel of Rice Output	Inputs per Yard of Cloth Output
Lindertania	75	100
Rest of the world	50	50

are constant ratios of input to output whatever the level of output of rice and cloth, and competition prevails in all markets.

a. Does Lindertania have an absolute advantage in producing rice? Cloth?

b. Does Lindertania have a comparative advantage in producing rice? Cloth?

c. If no international trade is allowed, what price ratio would prevail between rice and cloth within Lindertania?

d. If free international trade is opened up, what are the limits for the equilibrium international price ratio? What product will Lindertania export? Import?

8. Consider another Ricardian example, using standard Ricardian assumptions:

	Labor Hours per Bottle of Wine	Labor Hours per Kilogram of Cheese
Vintland	15	10
Moonited Republic	10	4

Vintland has 30 million hours of labor in total per year. Moonited Republic has 20 million hours of labor per year.

a. Which country has an absolute advantage in wine? In cheese?

b. Which country has a comparative advantage in wine? In cheese?

c. Graph each country's production-possibility curve. Using community indifference curves, show the no-trade equilibrium for each country (assuming

that with no trade, Vintland consumes 1.5 million kilos of cheese and Moonited Republic consumes 3 million kilos of cheese).

d. When trade is opened, which country exports which good? If the equilibrium international price ratio is ½ bottle of wine per kilo of cheese, what happens to production in each country?

e. In this free-trade equilibrium, 2 million kilos of cheese and 1 million bottles of wine are traded. What is the consumption point in each country with free trade? Show this graphically using community indifference curves.

f. Does each country gain from trade? Explain, referring to your graphs as is appropriate.

◆9. The real wage is the purchasing power of 1 hour of labor. That is, for each product it is the number of units of the product that a worker can buy with his earnings from 1 hour of work. In a Ricardian model, for any product actually produced by the worker, the worker is simply paid according to her productivity (units of output per hour, the inverse of the labor hours per unit of output). This is then her real wage in terms of this product. In your answer to this question, use the numerical example from the section on Ricardo's theory of comparative advantage.

a. With no trade, what is the real wage of labor with respect to each good in the United States? In the rest of the world? Which country's labor has the higher "average" real wage?

b. With free trade and an equilibrium price ratio of 1 bushel per yard, each country completely specializes. What is the real wage with respect to wheat in the United States? By using international trade to obtain cloth, what is the new value of the real wage with respect to cloth in the

United States? What does this tell us about gains from trade for the United States? What is the real wage with respect to cloth in the rest of the world? By using international trade to obtain wheat, what is the new value of the real wage with respect to wheat in the rest of the world? What does this tell us about the gains from trade for the rest of the world?

   c. With free trade, which country's labor has the higher "average" real wage? In what sense does absolute advantage matter?

10. In your answer to this question, use the numerical example from the section on Ricardo's theory of comparative advantage. What is the effect on the pattern of trade predicted by the Ricardian analysis if the number of labor hours required to make a unit of wheat in the United States is reduced by half (that is, if its productivity doubles)? Now return to the initial numbers. What is the effect on the pattern of trade if instead the number of hours required to make a unit of cloth in the United States is reduced by half (productivity doubles)?

◆ 11. Extending what you know about production-possibility curves, try to draw the production-possibility curve (ppc) for a nation consisting of four individuals who work separately. The four individuals have these different abilities:

Person A can make 1 unit of cloth or 2 units of wheat or any combination in between (e.g., can make 0.5 cloth and 1 wheat by spending half time on each).

Person B can make 2 cloth or 1 wheat or any combination in between.

Person C can make 1 cloth or 1 wheat or any combination in between.

Person D can make 2 cloth or 3 wheat or any combination in between.

What is the best they can all produce? That is, draw the ppc for the four of them. Try it in these stages:

   a. What is the most wheat they could grow if they spent all of their time growing wheat only? Plot that point on a cloth–wheat graph.

   b. What is the most cloth they could make? Plot that point.

   c. Now here's the tricky part. Find the best combinations they could produce when producing some of both, where *best* means they could make that combination but could not make more of one good without giving up some of the other.

12. In your answer to this question, use a diagram like Figure 3.4 and start from a no-trade point like S_0 with a no-trade price ratio of 2 bushels per yard. Now trade is opened and the country can trade whatever it wants at an international price ratio of 1 bushel per yard. (In your answers, you will need to picture additional community indifference curves that exist but are not shown explicitly in Figure 3.4.)

   a. Show that the country can gain from trade even if the country does not change its production point. (Production stays at point S_0.) (*Hint:* The price line with slope of 1 will go through point S_0 but will not be tangent to the production-possibility curve.)

   b. Show that the country can gain even more from trade if it also adjusts the production point to its optimal position (given the price ratio of 1).

   c. What happens to the volume of trade as the country's position shifts from that shown in part *a* to that shown in part *b*?

CHAPTER 4

Who Gains and Who Loses from Trade?

If it seems so likely that nations gain from opening trade, why should free-trade policies have so many opponents year in and year out? We shall return to this question repeatedly here and in Part II. The answer does not lie mainly in public ignorance about the effects of trade. Trade *does* typically hurt large groups within any country, and many opponents of freer trade probably perceive this point correctly. To make our analysis of trade an effective policy guide, we must show just who stands to be hurt by freer trade.

A virtue of the Heckscher–Ohlin (H–O) theory of trade patterns is that it offers realistic predictions of how trade affects the income of groups representing different factors of production (e.g., landlords, workers). In each country international trade is almost sure to divide society into gainers from trade and losers from trade because changes in relative product prices are likely to raise the rewards of some factors and lower the rewards of others. A key purpose of this chapter is to show the implications of the Heckscher–Ohlin theory for the income received by the different factors of production.

The Heckscher–Ohlin theory claims to provide powerful insights into the basis for trade and the effects of trade, including the gains and losses for different production factors. But how well does it actually fit the world's trade? A second key purpose of the chapter is to examine the empirical evidence on Heckscher–Ohlin, including its ability to explain actual trade patterns, and the identity in specific countries of the factors that gain and lose from trade.

Who Gains and Who Loses Within a Country

According to the Heckscher–Ohlin approach, trade arises from differences in the availability of factor inputs in different countries and differences in the proportions in which these factors are used in producing different products. Opening to trade alters domestic production (for instance, from S_0 to S_1 in Figure 3.5A in the previous chapter). There is expansion in the export-oriented sector (the one using the country's abundant factor intensively in production), while there is contraction in the import-competing sector (the one using the country's scarce factor intensively). The changes in production have one set of effects on incomes in the short run, but another in the long run.

Short-Run Effects of Opening Trade

In the short run, when laborers, plots of land, and other inputs are still tied to their current lines of production, the demand for these factors, and therefore the incomes or returns that they earn, depend on the sector in which they are employed. Some people will enjoy higher demand for the factors they have to offer, because their factors are employed in the sector that is attempting to expand its production. U.S. landlords in wheat-growing areas can charge higher rents because their land is in strong demand. U.S. farm workers in wheat-growing areas are likely to get (temporarily) higher wages. Foreign clothworkers can also demand and get higher wage rates. Foreign landlords in the areas raising cotton and wool and other fabrics for clothmaking can also get higher rents.

Meanwhile, the sellers of factors to the declining industries—U.S. clothworkers, U.S. landlords in areas supplying the cloth-making industry, foreign wheat-area landlords and farmhands—lose income through reduced demand and therefore reduced prices for their services.

For the short run, then, gains and losses divide by output sector: All groups tied to rising sectors gain, and all groups tied to declining sectors lose. One would expect employers, landlords, and workers in the declining sectors to unite in protest.

The Long-Run Factor-Price Response

In the longer run, factors can move between sectors in response to differences in returns. Sellers of the same factors will eventually respond to the gaps that have been opened up in the short run. Some U.S. clothworkers will find better-paying jobs in the wheat sector, bidding wages back down in the wheat sector while bidding them back up in the cloth-making sector. Some U.S. cotton- and wool-raising land will also get better rents by converting to wheat-related production, bringing rents in different areas back in line. Similarly, foreign farmhands and landlords will find the pay better in the cloth-related sector, bringing down cloth-related pay and bringing up wheat-related pay. The full process of the effects of opening trade on factor prices in the long run is summarized in Figure 4.1.

When the factors respond by moving to the better-paying sectors, will all wages and rents be bid back to their pretrade levels? No, they will not. In the long run, wage rates end up lower for all U.S. workers and higher for all foreign workers, while land rents end up higher everywhere in the United States and lower in the rest of the world (each relative to its level with no trade).

What drives this crucial result is the imbalance in the changes in factor demand. Wheat is more land-intensive and less labor-intensive than cloth making. Therefore, the amounts of each factor being hired in the expanding sector will fail to match the amounts being released in the other sector—until factor

FIGURE 4.1

*How Free Trade
Affects Income
Distribution in
the Long Run:
The Whole
Chain of
Infuence*

	In the United States	**In the Rest of the World**
Initial prices:	Wheat cheap, cloth expensive	Wheat expensive, cloth cheap
	Trade opens: —— wheat ⟶ ◀— cloth ——	
Prices respond to trade.	P_{wheat} up, P_{cloth} down	P_{wheat} down, P_{cloth} up
Production responds to prices.*	Produce more wheat. Produce less cloth.	Produce less wheat. Produce more cloth.
Crucial step— Factor demands change.	For each yard of cloth sacrificed, many workers and few acres laid off; extra wheat demands few workers and much land.	For each bushel of wheat sacrificed, much land and few workers laid off; extra cloth demands many workers and little land.
Factor prices respond.	Wage rates fall and rents rise (in both sectors).	Wage rates rise and rents fall (in both sectors).
Long-run results:	Prices equalized between countries. Countries specialize more. Net gains for both countries. Winners: U.S. landowners, foreign workers. Losers: U.S. workers, foreign landowners.	

*At this point, the short-run effects come into play, but the economy continues to move toward the longer-run effects shown in the rest of this figure.

prices adjust. In the United States, for example, expanding wheat production will create demand for a lot of land and very few workers, whereas cutting cloth production will unemploy a lot of workers and not so much land.[1] Something has to give. The only way the employment of labor and land can adjust to the available national supplies is for factor prices to change. The shift toward land-intensive, labor-sparing wheat will raise rents and cut wages *throughout* the United States in the long run. The rise in rents and the fall in wages will continue until producers come up with more land-saving and labor-using ways of making wheat and cloth. Once they do, rents and wages will stabilize—but U.S. rents still end up higher and wages lower than before trade opened up. The same kind of reasoning makes the opposite results hold for the rest of the world.

Trade, then, makes some people absolutely better off and others absolutely worse off in each of the trading countries. The gainers and losers in the short run

---

[1]This passage uses convenient shorthand that is quantitatively vague: "a lot of" land, "very few" workers, and so on. These should give the right impressions with a minimum of verbiage. For more precision about the implied inequalities, see the numerical example in the box "A Factor-Ratio Paradox."

FIGURE 4.2

Winners and Losers: Short Run Versus Long Run

Effects of free trade in the short run
(After product prices change and production attempts to respond, but before factors move between sectors)

	In the United States		In the Rest of the World	
	On Landowners	*On Laborers*	*On Landowners*	*On Laborers*
In wheat	Gain	Gain	Lose	Lose
In cloth	Lose	Lose	Gain	Gain

Effects of free trade in the long run
(After factors move between sectors in response to changes in factor demands, as shown in Figure 4.1)

	In the United States		In the Rest of the World	
	On Landowners	*On Laborers*	*On Landowners*	*On Laborers*
In wheat	Gain	Lose	Lose	Gain
In cloth	Gain	Lose	Lose	Gain

Reminder: The gains and losses to the different classes do not cancel out leaving zero net gain. In the long run, both countries get net gains. In the short run, net national gains or losses depend partly on the severity of the unemployment of displaced factors.

are somewhat different from those in the long run, because more adjustment can occur in the long run. Our discussion of winners and losers in the short and long runs is summarized in Figure 4.2.

Three Implications of the H–O Theory

The Heckscher–Ohlin model has three major implications for factor incomes. These implications follow from the sort of analysis done in the previous section.

The Stolper–Samuelson Theorem

The conclusion that opening to trade splits a country into specific gainers and losers in the long run is an application of a general relationship—the general **Stolper–Samuelson theorem:**[2]

---

[2]Four important conditions and assumptions are needed for the Stolper–Samuelson theorem: (1) The country produces positive amounts of two goods (e.g., wheat and cloth) with two factors of production (e.g., land and labor) used in producing each good. One good (wheat) is relatively land-intensive; the other (cloth) is relatively labor-intensive. (2) Factors are mobile between sectors and fully employed overall in the economy. In addition, it is often assumed that total factor supplies (factor endowment sizes) are fixed, though this can be relaxed somewhat. (3) Competition prevails in all markets. (4) Production technology involves constant returns to scale (e.g., if all factors used in producing a product double, then output of the product doubles).

A Factor-Ratio Paradox

The effects of trade on factor use have their paradoxical side. By assumption, the same fixed factor supplies get reemployed in the long run. But everything else about factor use changes. To deepen understanding of several subtleties that help explain how trade makes gainers and losers, this box poses a paradox:

> In one country, trade makes the land/labor ratio fall in both industries—but this ratio stays the same for the country as a whole. In the rest of the world, the same kind of paradox holds in the other direction: Trade makes the land/labor ratio rise in both industries—but this ratio again stays the same overall.

How, in one country, could something that falls in both industries stay the same for the two industries together? How, in the rest of the world, could it rise in both yet stay the same for the two together?

The explanation hinges on a tug-of-war that is only hinted at in the main text of this chapter. Here is what the tug-of-war looks like for the United States in our ongoing example: Trade shifts both land and labor toward the land-intensive wheat sector, yet rising rents and falling wages induce both sectors to come up with more labor-intensive ways of producing. The two effects just offset each other and remain consistent with the same fixed total factor supplies.

Let's look at a set of numbers illustrating how our wheat–cloth trade might plausibly change factor-use ratios in the United States and the rest of the world:

Sector	United States Before (with No Trade)				Rest of the World Before (with No Trade)			
	Output	Land Use	Labor Use	Land/Labor Ratio	Output	Land Use	Labor Use	Land/Labor Ratio
Wheat	50	35	35	1.000	30	16	32	0.500
Cloth	40	18	65	0.277	80	18	160	0.113
Whole economy		53	100	0.530		34	192	0.177

Sector	After (with Free Trade)				After (with Free Trade)			
	Output	Land Use	Labor Use	Land/Labor Ratio	Output	Land Use	Labor Use	Land/Labor Ratio
Wheat	80	48	64	0.750 (down)	15	9	12	0.750 (up)
Cloth	20	5	36	0.139 (down)	100	25	180	0.139 (up)
Whole economy		53	100	0.530 (same)		34	192	0.177 (same)

Here we have both the factor-ratio paradox and its explanation. In the United States the change in factor prices has induced both wheat producers and cloth producers to come up with production methods having lower land/labor ratios (more labor-intensive techniques). Yet the same fixed factor supplies are employed.

One can see that the key is the shift of U.S. output toward land-intensive wheat. If it had been the only change, the aggregate land/labor ratio would have risen. This is what induced the rise in rents and the fall in wages, and they in turn induced the shift toward labor-intensive techniques in both industries. (The same point again applies in mirror image for the rest of the world.)

Given certain conditions and assumptions, an event that changes product prices in a country unambiguously raises the real returns to the factor used intensively in the rising-price industry and lowers the real returns to the factor used intensively in the falling-price industry in the long run, regardless of which goods the sellers of the two factors prefer to consume.

A shift from no trade to free trade is an event that changes product prices. For instance, in our example, the opening of trade increases the relative price of wheat in the United States. The Stolper–Samuelson theorem then predicts a rise in the real income of the owners of land (the factor used intensively in producing wheat) and a decline in the real income of the providers of labor (the factor used intensively in producing cloth). In the rest of the world, the real income of labor increases and the real income of landowners decreases.

Stolper and Samuelson showed that this result does not depend at all on which goods are consumed by the households of landowners and laborers. The result clashed with an intuition many economists had shared. It seemed, for instance, that if U.S. laborers spent a very large share of their incomes on cloth, they might possibly gain from free trade by having cheaper cloth. Not so, according to the theorem. Opening trade must enable one of the two factors to buy more of either good, and it will make the other factor poorer in its ability to buy either good.

Let's try to see why. Under competition, the price of each good must equal its marginal cost. In our wheat–cloth economy, price must equal the marginal land and labor costs in each sector:

$$P_{wheat} = \text{marginal cost of wheat} = ar + bw$$

and

$$P_{cloth} = \text{marginal cost of cloth} = cr + dw$$

where the product prices are measured in the same units (e.g., units of a commodity, or dollars), r is the rental rate earned on land, and w is the wage rate paid to labor. The coefficients a, b, c, and d are physical input/output ratios. These indicate how much land (a and c) or labor (b and d) is required to produce 1 unit of each good. The easiest case to consider is one where these coefficients are constant.

Suppose that the price of wheat rises 10 percent and the price of cloth stays the same. The higher price of wheat (and the resulting expansion of wheat production) will bid up the return to at least one factor. In fact, it is likely to raise the rental rate for land, since growing wheat uses land intensively. So r rises. Now look at the equation for the cloth sector. If r rises and the price of cloth stays the same, then the wage rate w must fall absolutely. The contraction of cloth production drives down the wage rate. Next take the fall of w back to the equation for the wheat sector. If w is falling and P_{wheat} is rising 10 percent, then r must be rising *more* than 10 percent to keep the equation valid. So if wheat is the land-intensive sector,

$$P_{wheat} \uparrow \text{ by } 10\% \text{ and } P_{cloth} \text{ steady means } r \uparrow \text{ more than } 10\% \text{ and } w \downarrow.$$

Thus a shift in relative product prices brings an even more magnified response in factor prices: A factor more closely associated with the rising-price sector will have its market reward (e.g., *r* in our example) rise even faster than the product price rise. Therefore, its real return (its purchasing power with respect to either product) rises. A factor more closely associated with other sectors will have its real purchasing power cut. In our example, the lower wage rate means workers lose purchasing power with respect to both the higher-priced wheat and the stable-priced cloth. The real wage rate decreases.

The same principle emerges no matter how we change the example (e.g., even if we let the price of wheat stay the same and increase the price of cloth instead, so that the real wage rate rises and the real rental rate declines, or even if we let producers change the input/output coefficients *a, b, c,* and *d* in response to changes in *r* and *w*).[3] The principle really just follows from the fact that price must equal marginal cost under competition, both before and after trade (or some other event) has changed the price ratio between wheat and cloth.

The Specialized-Factor Pattern

The Stolper–Samuelson theorem applied to the opening of international trade is a special case using only two factors and two commodities. Its results are part of a broader pattern, one that tends to hold for any number of factors and commodities:

> The more a factor is specialized, or concentrated, into the production of exports, the more it stands to gain from trade. Conversely, the more a factor is concentrated into the production of the importable good, the more it stands to lose from trade.

This pattern should seem plausible. You may wonder whether it is meant as a pattern for the short run, when factors are immobile, or for the long run. The answer is both. The longer a factor continues to be associated with producing exportables, the greater its stake in freer trade. The longer it is associated with production threatened by imports, the more it gains from limits on trade. In the extreme case, a factor that can be used only in one sector has a lifelong or permanent stake in the price of that sector's product. A good example of such an immobile factor is farmland, which is hard to convert to other uses. There is little difference between the short run and the long run when it comes to farmland. If the land is of a type that will always be good for growing import-competing crops, there is nothing subtle about the landowner's stake in policies that keep out imports of those crops.

---

[3]For a numerical example, let both prices start at 100, let *r* and *w* both start at 1, and let $a = 40$, $b = 60$, $c = 25$, and $d = 75$. Let the price of wheat rise by 10 percent to 110. Your task is to deduce what values of *r* and *w* could satisfy the new wheat equation $110 = 40 r + 60 w$, while still satisfying the cloth equation $100 = 25 r + 75 w$. You should get that *r* rises to 1.5 and *w* falls to 5/6.

The text says that the result still holds even if *a, b, c,* and *d* change. To be more precise, the result still holds if *a* or *c* falls when *r* rises, or if *b* or *d* falls when *w* rises. These are the economically plausible directions of response, so the result holds in all plausible cases.

The Factor-Price Equalization Theorem

The same basic trade model that predicts the Stolper–Samuelson result also makes an even more surprising prediction about the effects of trade on factor prices in different countries. Beginning with a proof by Paul Samuelson in the late 1940s, the **factor-price equalization theorem** was established about the effect of trade on international differences in factor prices:[4]

> *The factor-price equalization theorem:* Given certain conditions and assumptions, free trade will equalize not only commodity prices but also the prices of individual factors between the two countries, so that all laborers will earn the same wage rate and all units of land will earn the same rental return in both countries even if factors cannot migrate between countries.

This is a remarkable conclusion. It follows from the effects of opening trade on factor prices in each country. With no trade, workers in the United States, the labor-scarce country, earn a high wage rate, and workers in the rest of the world (labor-abundant) earn a low wage rate. The opening of trade results in a lowering of the wage rate in the United States and a rise of the wage rate in the rest of the world (recall Figure 4.1). If product prices are the same in the two countries with free trade, if production technologies are the same, and if both countries produce both products (among other necessary conditions), then the wage rate is also the same for the two countries with free trade. (You might try to develop similar reasoning for land rents.)

The factor-price equalization theorem implies that laborers will end up earning the same wage rate in all countries, even if labor migration between countries is not allowed. Trade makes this possible, within the assumptions of the model, because the factors that cannot migrate between countries end up being implicitly shipped between countries in commodity form. Trade makes the United States export wheat and import cloth. Since wheat is land-intensive and cloth is labor-intensive, trade is in effect sending a land-rich commodity to the rest of the world in exchange for labor-rich cloth. It is as though each factor were migrating toward the country in which it was scarcer before trade.

Does Heckscher–Ohlin Explain Actual Trade Patterns?

The Heckscher–Ohlin approach to trade provides important insights, in theory, about the gains from trade, the effects of trade on production and consumption, and the effects of trade on the incomes of production factors both within each country and internationally. These insights are based on the hunch by Heckscher

---

[4]The important conditions and assumptions needed for the factor-price equalization theorem include all four of those for the Stolper–Samuelson theorem (see footnote 2) and the following additional ones: (5) Both countries produce positive amounts of both goods with free trade. (Both are incompletely specialized in production.) (6) Trade is free of government restrictions or barriers to trade (like tariffs). (7) There are no transport costs. (8) The technologies available (or the production functions) are the same for both countries. (9) There are no factor-intensity reversals. (If wheat is the relatively land-intensive good in one country, then it is also the relatively land-intensive good in the other country.)

and Ohlin about the basis for trade—why countries export some products and import others. To know if the Heckscher–Ohlin theory actually is useful, we must consider whether this hunch is right. Does it help to explain real-world trade patterns?

The first formal efforts to test the H–O theory used the simple model of two factors of production and U.S. trade data. These tests failed to confirm the H–O theory. (See the box "The Leontief Paradox" on page 71.) More recent tests recognize that more than two types of production factors are relevant to the H–O explanation of trade patterns.

Economists have tested the H–O theory in several ways. Complete tests require information on the factor endowments of different countries, international trade for various products, and the factor proportions used in producing these products. The upshot of these tests can be seen through a look at factor endowments and trade patterns.

Factor Endowments

Figure 4.3 shows the shares of several countries in the "world" endowments of certain factors of production. To recognize the patterns of relative abundance and scarcity here, a country's share of the world endowment of one factor should be compared to that country's shares of the world endowments of other factors. Physical (or nonhuman) capital is relatively abundant in the industrialized countries, including the United States and the five other countries shown specifically in the figure. Highly skilled labor, represented here by professional and technical workers, is also abundant in the industrialized countries. This category includes scientists and engineers, a key input into the research and development (R&D) that influences international competition in high technology goods. Indeed, most scientists and engineers engaged in R&D in the world work in the United States, Japan, Germany, France, and Britain.

Unskilled labor, represented here by the lowest-skilled stratum (illiterate labor), is relatively scarce in the developed countries. The opposite pattern of abundance and scarcity for physical capital, highly skilled labor, and unskilled labor is found for the developing countries. For medium-skilled labor (the nonscientific skilled and semiskilled workers), the international contrasts are not nearly so sharp. Countries have them in shares that tend to be in the middle of the abundance–scarcity spectrum.

Figure 4.3 confirms what we know about the distribution of the world's arable (farmable) land and forestland. These types of land are relatively concentrated in North America and certain other developed and developing countries (e.g., Australia, Argentina). Europe and Japan are poorly endowed with arable land and forestland. If there were convenient world data on *other natural resources*—minerals, metal ores, and fishing rights—these data would show slightly different patterns. Canada would again be relatively abundantly endowed, though the United States would not. Other leading resource-abundant countries are the oil producers and the metal ore producers (Australia, Bolivia, Chile, Jamaica, Zambia).

FIGURE 4.3

Shares of the "World's" Factor Endowments, Early 1990s

Country	Physical Capital	Highly Skilled Labor[a]	Medium-Skilled Labor[b]	Unskilled Labor[c]	Arable Land	Forestland
United States	25.8%	28.5%	13.6%	0.5%	24.1%	15.8%
Canada	3.6	5.8	1.3	0.1	6.0	27.3
Japan	15.0	10.4	7.2	0.3	0.5	1.4
Germany	9.3	4.6	4.5	0.2	1.5	0.6
France	5.6	3.4	2.9	0.1	2.4	0.8
United Kingdom	3.6	6.5	3.0	0.1	0.8	0.1
Other industrialized countries	19.5	14.2	13.1	0.9	13.7	14.2
Developing countries	17.6	26.6	54.4	97.8	51.0	39.8
	100%	100%	100%	100%	100%	100%

Note: All figures are approximations. The "world" refers to 60 countries (25 industrialized countries and 35 developing countries) for which reasonable data are available. Physical capital is for 1992, the labor categories are for 1994, and the land categories are for 1993.

[a]Workers in professional and technical occupations.

[b]Literate workers who do not belong to the professional and technical category.

[c]Illiterate workers.

Source: Data on physical capital from Penn-World Tables (available at http://nber.org). Data on labor from World Bank, *World Development Report 1994,* 1994, Table 25, and *World Development Report 1996,* 1996, Table 4; and International Labor Office, *Yearbook of Labor Statistics,* various years and tables. Data on literacy and on land from United Nations Development Programme, *Human Development Report 1997,* 1997, Tables 1, 24, and 43.

International Trade

If Heckscher and Ohlin have given us the right prediction, the unequal distribution of factors should be mirrored in the patterns of trade, with each country exporting those goods and services that use its abundant factors relatively intensively.

International trade patterns broadly confirm the H–O prediction that nations tend to export the products using their abundant factors intensively. Consider first the United States. U.S. exports and imports for selected goods are shown in Figure 4.4 (page 72). The United States is relatively abundant in arable land, and tends to be a net exporter (exports exceed imports) of temperate-zone agricultural products, such as wheat, corn, and soybeans. The United States has abundant endowments of some natural resources, such as coal, and tends to be a net exporter of these resource products, while it is a net importer (imports exceed exports) of many other natural resource products, such as petroleum, which are found more abundantly in some other countries. The United States is relatively abundant in skilled labor, including scientists and engineers employed in R&D, and tends to be a net exporter of products that are skilled-labor–intensive or technology-intensive, including chemicals, aircraft, and precision instruments (e.g., scientific and medical instruments). Less-skilled labor is relatively scarce in the United States, so the country is a net importer of less-skilled-labor–intensive products like clothing and shoes. (The United States is also a major net exporter of business services—for instance, marketing, management, accounting, and consulting—reflecting the abundance of skilled labor that is important in producing these services.)

The Leontief Paradox

What we now know about the mixtures of productive factors that make up the exports and imports of leading nations has been learned largely because Wassily Leontief was puzzled in the 1950s. Leontief, who was later awarded the Nobel Prize in economics, set off a generation of fruitful debate by following the soundest of scientific instincts: testing whether the predictions of a theory really fit the facts.

What Leontief decided to test was the Heckscher–Ohlin theory that countries will export products whose production requires more of the country's abundant factors and import products whose production relies more on the country's scarce factors. He assumed that the U.S. economy at that time was capital-abundant (and labor-scarce) relative to the countries with which it traded.

Leontief's *K/L* Test

Leontief computed the ratios of capital stocks to numbers of workers in the U.S. export and import-competing industries in 1947. This computation required figuring out not only how much capital and labor were used directly in each of these several dozen industries but also how much capital and labor were used in producing the materials purchased from other industries. As the main pioneer in input-output analysis, he had the advantage of knowing just how to multiply the input-output matrix of the U.S. economy by vectors of capital and labor inputs, export values, and import values to derive the desired estimates of capital-labor ratios in exports and import-competing production. So the test was set: If the H–O

prediction was correct, and the United States was more capital-abundant, then the U.S. export bundle should embody a higher capital–labor ratio (K_x/L_x), when all the contributions of input industries were also included, than the capital–labor ratio embodied in the U.S. production that competed with imports (K_m/L_m).

Leontief's results posed a paradox that puzzled him and others: In 1947, the United States was exporting labor-intensive goods to the rest of the world in exchange for relatively capital-intensive imports! The key ratio $(K_x/L_x)/(K_m/L_m)$ was only 0.77 when H–O said it should be well above unity. Other studies confirmed the bothersome Leontief paradox for the United States between World War II and 1970.

Broader and Better Tests

The most fruitful response to the paradox was to introduce other factors of production besides just capital and labor. Perhaps, reasoned many economists (including Leontief himself), we should make use of the fact that there are different kinds of labor, different kinds of natural resources, different kinds of capital, and so forth. Broader calculations of factor content have paid off in extra insights into the basis for U.S. trade. True, the United States was somewhat capital-abundant, yet it failed to export more capital services than it imported. But the post-Leontief studies showed that the United States was also abundant in farmland and highly skilled labor. And the United States is indeed a net exporter of products that use these factors intensively, as H–O predicts.

The pattern of U.S. trade in some other goods appears to be inconsistent with H–O. Three of these are shown in Figure 4.4. The United States is a net importer of steel and motor vehicles (automobiles). The United States both exports and imports large amounts of computers. Factor proportions do not seem to be able to explain U.S. trade patterns for these products. In Chapter 6 we will examine other theories that may explain them.

The trade pattern of Japan is also broadly consistent with H–O. Arable land and natural resources are scarce in Japan, which is crucially dependent on imports

FIGURE 4.4

*U.S.
International
Trade in
Selected
Products, 1995
(billions of $)*

A. Products Whose Trade Is Consistent with H–O Theory

Product	U.S. Exports	U.S. Imports
Wheat (041)	5.2	Small
Corn (044)	7.5	Small
Soybeans (2222)	5.4	Small
Coal (322)	3.6	Small
Petroleum and petroleum products (33)	6.2	56.1
Chemicals (5)	60.2	41.3
Aircraft (792)	25.6	6.2
Precision instruments (87)	19.4	11.9
Clothing and accessories (84)	6.7	41.6
Shoes and other footwear (85)	Small	12.2

B. Products Whose Trade Appears to Be Inconsistent with H–O Theory

Product	U.S. Exports	U.S. Imports
Iron and steel (67)	6.2	15.6
Computers (752)	23.1	35.4
Motor vehicles (78)	49.2	102.6

Note: Commodity numbers from the Standard International Trade Classification are
shown in parentheses.

Source: United Nations, *Yearbook of International Trade Statistics, Volume 1, 1995,*
1996.

of agricultural, fishing, forestry, and mineral products. Without trade, Japan would
be a far poorer country. Japan has relatively abundant skilled labor (including scientists and engineers), and tends to export skilled-labor–intensive manufactured
products. Although Japan several decades ago was a net exporter of less-skilled-
labor–intensive products, the country now is a net importer of these products, a
pattern consistent with its current relative scarcity in less-skilled labor.

Canada is relatively abundant in natural resources and tends to export primary products. Even its exports of manufactures tend to be intensive in natural
resources, including petrochemicals, metals, wood products, and paper. Ohlin
was not surprised by the Canadian trade pattern, and neither are we.

The comparative-advantage patterns for West European countries are more
muted. They have comparative advantages rather like those of Japan, but their
trade patterns are not so extreme, with more balance in export–import ratios for
various products.

In general, trade patterns fit the H–O theory reasonably well but certainly not
perfectly.[5]

---

[5]A comprehensive test by Bowen, Leamer, and Sveikauskas (1987) measured the ability of factor endowments and U.S. input–output patterns to predict the net factor flows through trade in 1967. Out of 324 cases,
defined by 12 factors and 27 countries, H–O correctly predicted the sign of net exports in 61 percent of the
cases. This share was better than a coin flip, but only modestly so. The results of more recent testing by Trefler (1995) indicate that all three of the bases for trade noted in Chapter 3 may be important for explaining
actual trade—namely, factor endowment differences, technology differences, and a bias toward consuming
domestically produced products.

What Are the Export-Oriented and Import-Competing Factors?

The link of factor endowments to international trade patterns emphasized in the H–O theory also suggests, through the logic of the Stolper–Samuelson theorem, the effects of trade on factor groups' incomes and purchasing power. National policymakers need to know which factor groups are likely to gain and lose from liberalizing trade in order to anticipate their views on trade or plan ahead for ways to compensate them, if society wishes to do so.

The U.S. Pattern

Figure 4.5 shows the factor content of U.S. exports and of U.S. imports competing with domestic production. Overall, labor incomes account for a greater share of the value of U.S. exports than of the value of U.S. imports. This reflects partly the fact that there are slightly more jobs associated with U.S. exports than with an equal value of imports. (See the box "U.S. Jobs and Foreign Trade.") It is also due in part to the greater average skill and pay levels on the export side. In fact, it seems wise to divide labor into at least two types—skilled and unskilled—as in Figure 4.5. Skilled labor in the United States is an export-oriented factor, while unskilled labor is an import-competing factor. Farmland is another export-oriented factor, while physical capital (as suggested by the Leontief paradox) and mineral rights generally are import-competing factors.

FIGURE 4.5

A Schematic View of the Factor Content of U.S. Exports and Competing Imports

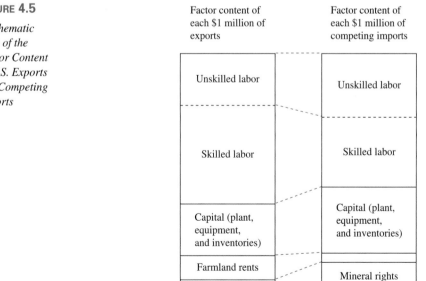

Note: Vertical distances are meant to give rough impressions of factor-content proportions in U.S. exports and the set of outputs that would replace the U.S. imports that compete with domestic products. The estimates must be rough since we lack correct calculations of the returns earned by farmland, mineral depletion, and physical capital.

The Canadian Pattern

Canada, by contrast, implicitly exports and imports the factor mixtures sketched in Figure 4.6. About the only similarity to the U.S. pattern is that both countries are net exporters of the services of farmland through their positions as major grain exporters. Otherwise, the export–import patterns of the United States are reversed in Canada, in large part because the heavy bilateral trade between the two countries casts them in complementary roles. Canada is a net importer of labor, much of it embodied in U.S. exports to Canada. It is a slight net exporter of nonhuman capital (some of it owned, however, by U.S. subsidiaries in Canada). Finally, Canada is a heavy net exporter of mineral-rights services through its exports of mineral products.

Patterns in Other Countries

The patterns of factor content have also been roughly measured for other countries. Two such results deserve quick mention here.

The factor content of *oil-exporting countries* is not surprising. They explicitly export mineral rights in large amounts, of course. The less populous oil exporters, particularly the oil nations of the Arabian peninsula, also export capital services through the interest and dividends they earn (the "lending services" they provide) on their foreign wealth. The same countries implicitly import just about every other factor: all human factors and farmland.

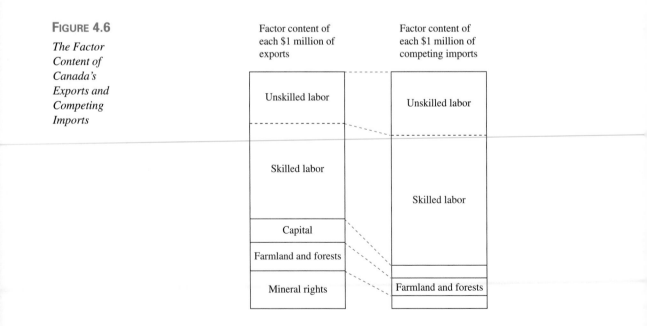

FIGURE **4.6**

The Factor Content of Canada's Exports and Competing Imports

The *oil-importing developing countries* implicitly import capital and human skills as well as oil. They export unskilled labor, the services of agricultural land, and minerals other than oil. Here lies an important comment on the distributional effects of trade in the Third World. For many developing countries, lower-income groups selling unskilled labor or working small farm plots have the greatest positive stake in foreign trade since their products are the exportable ones. Protection against trade often widens the income gaps between rich and poor in developing countries. We return to this pattern, noting exceptions and complications, in Chapter 13.

Do Factor Prices Equalize Internationally?

Perhaps the most remarkable conclusion of the Heckscher–Ohlin theory is that trade can equalize the price of each factor of production across countries. The factor-price equalization theorem is more than just remarkable. It is also clearly wrong in the strong form in which it is stated. Even the most casual glance at the real world shows that factor prices are not fully equalized across countries. For example, the same labor skill does not earn the same real pay in all countries. Machine operators do not earn the same pay in Mexico or India as in the United States or Canada. Neither do hair stylists. Given the large number of assumptions—some of them not realistic—that are necessary to prove the strong form of the factor-price equalization theorem, it is not surprising that the real world is not fully consistent with the theorem. For instance, in the real world governments do impose barriers to free trade, and technologies (or production functions) are not exactly the same in all countries.

An interesting question, representing a weaker form of the theorem, is whether trade tends to make factor prices more similar across countries than they would be with no trade. In our ongoing example, with no trade the return to land (the abundant factor) in the United States would be low, and the return to land (the scarce factor) in the rest of the world would be high. Opening to trade increases the return to land in the United States and reduces the return to land in the rest of the world—an example of a tendency toward international factor-price equalization. That is exactly what happened before World War I: As Europe expanded its trade with land-rich America and Australia, the high land rents in Europe tended to stagnate while the low land rents of America and Australia shot up, reducing the global inequality of land rent. Another real-world example of the tendency toward equalization is the rise in real wage rates in the industrializing countries of Asia (such as Singapore) as these countries have strongly integrated themselves into world trade. Wage rates in these countries are approaching wage rates in the Western industrialized countries for comparable types (skills) of workers. Although we still do not see full factor-price equalization in the real world, there appear to be tendencies toward equalization.

U.S. Jobs and Foreign Trade

The U.S. Congress has often come close to passing comprehensive bills to slash U.S. imports through tariffs or other barriers. These attempts have been defended as necessary to protect U.S. jobs. Does more trade mean fewer U.S. jobs? Does less trade mean more U.S. jobs? Economists have developed a relatively clear and surprising answer.

Consider general restrictions that reduce U.S. imports across the board. Such restrictions are likely to result in no more, and possibly fewer, U.S. jobs at given wage rates! This is because (1) reducing U.S. imports also tends to reduce U.S. exports and (2) the average jobs content of U.S. exports is at least as high as that of U.S. imports.

There are four reasons to think that reducing imports reduces exports. First, exports use importable inputs. If these imports are not so readily available, U.S. exports become less competitive. Second, foreigners who lose sales to us cannot buy so much from us. As foreigners lose income from exports to us, they buy less of many things, including less of our exports. Third, foreign governments may retaliate by increasing their own protection against imports. U.S. exports decline as they face additional foreign barriers.

Fourth, cutting our imports may create pressures for changes in exchange rates. We will discuss exchange rates further in Parts III and IV. Here we depart briefly from barter trade to recognize that most trade is paid for with national currencies. Reducing demand for imports also reduces demand for foreign currencies used to pay for the imports. If the foreign currencies then lose value—thus increasing the exchange-rate value of the U.S. dollar—the higher dollar value tends to make U.S. goods appear to be more expensive to foreign buyers. In response they buy less of our exports.

The combination of these four effects results in roughly a dollar-for-dollar cut in exports if imports are cut. If both exports and imports are cut, the effect on U.S. jobs then depends on whether more jobs are created in the expanding import-competing industries than are lost in the declining-export industries. A number of studies indicate that the jobs content of U.S. exports is similar to that of U.S. imports—

indeed, if anything, the jobs content of U.S. exports is slightly higher.[1] (In addition, the average wage rate tends to be higher in export industries.)

If a sweeping cut in imports would probably not increase jobs but might end up costing jobs, why would labor groups favor such import cuts? The largest lobbyist for protection against imports is the AFL–CIO. The goods-sector membership of this organization is concentrated in industries that are more affected by import competition than is the economy (or labor) as a whole. It is practical for the AFL–CIO to lobby for protectionist bills that would defend the jobs of AFL–CIO members and their wages even if these bills would cost many jobs and wages outside of this labor group. To understand who is pushing for protection, it is important to know whose incomes are most tied to competition against imports.

This discussion refers to a general restriction against U.S. imports. Selective barriers against specific imports would alter the net effect on U.S. jobs. For instance, studies of existing U.S. barriers, which are selective, show that they are most restrictive on goods having a higher-than-average jobs content, especially in less-skilled jobs categories. Thus, existing U.S. import barriers bring a slight increase in U.S. jobs, even though raising new barriers against all imports might reduce U.S. jobs.

We conclude by noting that the validity of focusing on jobs gained and lost through trade is itself debatable. Jobs gained or lost through changes in international trade are themselves a small part of overall changes in jobs in the economy brought about by many different types of adjustments, including shifts in demand and changes in technologies. A well-functioning economy is dynamic—employment shifts between sectors to reallocate workers (and other resources) to their highest-value uses. While there are disruptions in the short run, the reallocations are crucial to economic growth.

---

[1]For instance, the U.S. International Trade Commission (1986) concluded that in 1984 there were 25,100 jobs per $1 billion of U.S. exports and 23,100 jobs per $1 billion of import replacement.

Summary: Fuller Answers to the Four Trade Questions

With the help of this chapter's exploration of the effects of trade on income distribution and the basic view of trade offered in Chapters 2 and 3, we can summarize by remeasuring our progress in answering the four basic questions about trade introduced at the start of Chapter 2.

1. Why do countries trade? Supply and demand conditions differ between countries because production conditions and tastes differ. The main theories emphasize differences in production conditions rather than in tastes. Ricardo argued that trade is profitable because countries have different comparative advantages in producing different goods. His examples stressed differences in resource productivities. The Heckscher–Ohlin theory agrees that comparative advantages in production are the basis for trade, but H–O explains comparative advantage in terms of underlying differences in factor proportions. Each country tends to export those goods that intensively use its relatively abundant factors of production. The evidence is that the Heckscher–Ohlin theory explains a good part of the world's actual trade patterns reasonably well, but that some important aspects of trade patterns do not square easily with H–O.

2. How does trade affect production and consumption in each country? In the country importing a good, it will raise consumption and lower production of that good. In the exporting country, it will raise production of that good, but in the general case we cannot say for sure what happens to the quantity consumed of that good. With the exception of the latter conclusion, these answers are unchanged since Chapter 2.

3. Which country gains from trade? Both sides gain. Each side's net national gains are proportional to the change in its price from its no-trade value, so that the country whose prices are disrupted more by trade gains more. This conclusion stands as it did in Chapter 2: Trade makes every nation better off in the net national sense defined in Chapter 2. (Later chapters will show how an already-trading nation can be made worse off by trading more, but some trade is better than no trade at all.)

4. Within each country, who are the gainers and losers from opening trade? This chapter has concentrated on this fourth question, and its answers go well beyond those summarized at the end of Chapter 2.

In the short run, with factors unable to move much between sectors, the gainers and losers are defined by the product sector, not by what factors of production the people are selling. The gainers are those who consume imported goods and produce exportable goods. Those who lose are the producers of import-competing goods and consumers of exportable goods. So far, the answer remains close to the answer given at the end of Chapter 2.

In the long run, when factors can move between sectors and the economy achieves full employment, the division between gainers and losers looks different. The Stolper–Samuelson theorem shows that

- If you make your living selling a factor that is more abundant in your country than it is in other countries, you gain from trade (by receiving a higher real income), regardless of what sector you work in or what goods you consume. Examples are scientists and grain-area landowners in the United States, and less-skilled laborers in China.

- If you make your living selling a factor that is relatively scarce in your country, you lose from trade (by receiving a lower real income), regardless of what sector you work in or what goods you consume. Examples are less-skilled laborers in the United States, and scientists and grain-area landowners in China.

A corollary of these long-run effects on different groups' fortunes is that trade can reduce international differences in how well a given factor of production is paid. A factor of production (for instance, less-skilled labor) tends to lose its high reward in countries where it was scarce before trade and to gain in countries where it was abundant before trade. Under certain conditions the **factor-price equalization theorem** holds: Free trade will equalize a factor's rate of pay in all countries, even if the factor itself is not free to move between countries. Those conditions for perfect equalization are not often met in the real world, but there is real-world evidence that opening trade tends to make factor prices less unequal between countries.

Suggested Reading

The contrast between factors' short-run and long-run fortunes from expanded trade was explicitly derived by Mussa (1974).

   For excellent surveys of empirical tests of trade theories, see Deardorff (1984), and Leamer and Levinsohn (1995). Tough tests of the Heckscher–Ohlin theory appear in Leamer (1984), Bowen, Leamer, and Sveikauskas (1987), and Trefler (1993, 1995). For a sampling from the vast literature on the factor content of U.S. foreign trade, see Leamer (1980), Stern and Maskus (1981), Brecher and Choudhri (1982), and Maskus (1985). On Canada's foreign trade, see Postner (1975).

Questions and Problems

✦ 1. As a result of the North American Free Trade Area (NAFTA), the United States and Canada are shifting toward free trade with Mexico. According to the Stolper–Samuelson theorem, how will this shift affect the real wage of unskilled labor in Mexico? In the United States or Canada? How will it affect the real wage of skilled labor in Mexico? In the United States or Canada?

2. "The factor-price equalization theorem indicates that with free trade, the real wage earned by labor becomes equal to the real rental rate earned by landowners." Is this correct or not? Why?

✦ 3. "Opening up free trade does hurt people in import-competing industries in the short run. But in the long run, when people and resources can move between industries, everybody ends up gaining from free trade." Do you agree or disagree? Explain.

4. One of your relatives suggests to you that our country should stop trading with other countries because imports take away jobs and lower our national well-being. How would you try to convince him that this is probably not the right way to look at international trade and its effects on the country?

✦ 5. The empirical results that Leontief found in his tests are viewed as a paradox. Why?

6. Consider our standard model of the economy, with two goods (wheat and cloth) and two factors (land and labor). A decrease now occurs in the relative price of wheat. What are the short-run and long-run effects on the earnings of each of the following: Labor employed in the wheat industry? Labor in the cloth industry? Land used in the wheat industry? Land in the cloth industry?

✦ 7. In the long run in a perfectly competitive industry, price equals marginal cost and firms earn no economic profits. The following two equations describe this long-run situation for prices and costs, where the numbers indicate the amounts of each input (labor and land) needed to produce a unit of each product (wheat and cloth):

$$P_{\text{wheat}} = 60w + 40r$$
$$P_{\text{cloth}} = 75w + 25r$$

   a. If the price of wheat is initially 100 and the price of cloth is initially 100, what are the values for the wage rate w and the rental rate r? What is the labor cost per unit of wheat output? Per unit of cloth? What is rental cost per unit of wheat? Per unit of cloth?

b. The price of cloth now increases to 120. What are the new values for w and r (after adjustment to the new long-run situation)?

c. What is the change in the real wage (purchasing power of labor income) with respect to each good? Is the real wage higher or lower "on average"? What is the change in the real rental rate (purchasing power of land income) with respect to each good? Is the real rental rate higher or lower "on average"?

d. Relate your conclusions in part c to the Stolper–Samuelson theorem.

8. You are given the following input cost shares in the wheat and cloth industries for the country of Pugelovia:

	For Each Dollar of		
	Wheat Output	Cloth Output	Overall National Income
Total labor input	$0.60	$0.59	$0.60
Total land input	0.15	0.06	0.10
Total capital input	0.25	0.35	0.30
	$1.00	$1.00	$1.00

Suppose that a change in demand conditions in the rest of the world raises the price of wheat relative to cloth, so producers in Pugelovia try to expand production of wheat in order to export more wheat.

a. If all factors are *immobile* between the wheat and cloth sectors, who gains from this change? Who loses?

b. If all factors are freely *mobile* between the wheat and cloth sectors, who gains from this change? Who loses?

✦ 9. From the following information calculate the total input shares of labor and capital in each dollar of cloth output:

	For Each Dollar of		
	Cloth Output	Synthetic Fiber Output	Cotton Fiber Output
Direct labor input	$0.50	$0.30	$0.60
Direct capital input	0.20	0.70	0.40
Synthetic fiber input	0.10	0.00	0.00
Cotton fiber input	0.20	0.00	0.00
All inputs	$1.00	$1.00	$1.00

Cloth is the only product that this country exports. The total input share of labor in producing $1.00 of import substitutes in this country is $0.55, and the total input share of capital is $0.45. Is this trade pattern consistent with the fact that this country is relatively labor-abundant and capital-scarce?

10. Consider the following data on some of Japan's exports and imports in 1995, measured in billions of U.S. dollars:

Product	Japanese Exports	Japanese Imports
Food (0)	2	46
Metal ores (28)	Small	9
Petroleum and petroleum products (33)	2	36
Chemicals (5)	29	24
Iron and steel (67)	18	6
Computers (752)	17	10
Motor vehicles (78)	78	13
Aircraft (792)	Small	3
Clothing and accessories (84)	Small	19
Shoes and other footwear (85)	Small	3
Precision instruments (87)	12	6

Note: Commodity numbers from the Standard International Trade Classification are shown in parentheses.

For which of these products do Japan's exports and imports appear to be consistent with the predictions of the Heckscher–Ohlin theory? Which appear to be inconsistent?

CHAPTER 5   Growth and Trade

The world keeps changing, and trade responds. Real investments expand countries' stocks of physical capital. Population growth adds new members to the labor force. Education and training expand labor skills. Discoveries of resource deposits change our estimates of countries' endowments of natural resources. Land reclamation and other shifts in land use can alter the amount of land available for production. New technologies improve capabilities to produce goods and services. Consumer tastes change, altering demands for various products. Each of these forces affects trade patterns.

The Heckscher–Ohlin theory, introduced in Chapter 3, is a snapshot of the international economy during a period of time. We can also use the H–O model to show the effects of changes over time. In a way we have already done this in previous chapters—the shift from no trade to free trade is an example of one kind of change that can occur over time.

This chapter focuses on changes in productive capacity that can occur in the economy over time. These production-side changes are usually called *economic growth* (although we can also consider cases of decline). There are two fundamental sources of capacity growth: increases in countries' endowments of production factors (e.g., physical capital, labor, and land) and improvements in production technologies.

In this chapter we will analyze the implications of growth, especially the implications for international trade flows and national economic well-being or welfare. Our analysis focuses on "before" and "after" pictures, with the after picture showing the economy after it fully adjusts (in the long run) to the growth that we are analyzing.

Some of the growth effects explored here will agree with common intuition, but some will not. In particular, we will discover two odd effects of growth in a nation's resources (its factor endowments) for producing a good that it already exports. First, merely getting more of a resource that is used intensively in producing exports actually causes other industries in the economy to decline. This result, known among economists by the daunting name the *Rybczynski theorem,* lies behind today's fears that acquiring more natural resources, such as discovering new oil, can retard development through what is better known as the *Dutch disease.* Second, expanding our ability to make the goods that we export can actually make us worse off as a nation, a perverse outcome known as *immiserizing growth.*

These paradoxes are part of this chapter's tour of the variety of ways in which economic growth can affect trade and national well-being. The chapter also examines links between technology and trade, including technology differences as a basis for comparative advantage, the cycle of innovation of new technologies and diffusion of these technologies internationally, and the impact that openness to international trade can have on economic growth.

Balanced Versus Biased Growth

Growth in a country's production capabilities, whether from endowment increases or technology improvements, shifts the country's production-possibility curve outward. As the ppc shifts out, we are interested in knowing the effects on the production quantities for the different products. For instance, if product prices remain unchanged at their initial pregrowth values, how will production respond?

The three basic types of growth in Figure 5.1 represent different possibilities for growth experienced by the United States. The first case, Figure 5.1A, is **balanced growth,** in which the ppc shifts out proportionately so that its relative shape is the same. In this case, growth would result in the same proportionate increase in production of all products if product prices remain the same. Before the growth, production is at point S_1, 80 wheat and 20 cloth, and the relative price of cloth is 1 bushel per yard. As a result of growth the ppc shifts out. At the same relative price (implying another price line parallel to the one through S_1), the country would produce, for instance, at point S_2, 112 wheat and 28 cloth. Balanced growth could be the result of increases in the country's endowments of all factors by the same proportion. Or it could be the result of technology improvements of a similar magnitude in both industries.

Growth can also be biased toward producing more of one of the products, with the output of the other product increasing by proportionately less, staying the same, or declining. In this case the shift in the production-possibility curve will be skewed toward the faster-growing product. Figure 5.1B shows growth that is biased toward producing more cloth. If the relative product price remains unchanged, production quantities do not change proportionately. For instance, with production initially at point S_1, growth biased toward cloth shifts production to a point like S_3 if the relative price remains at 1 bushel per yard. Cloth production increases from 20 to 40 units. Wheat production in this case remains unchanged at 80. Other examples of this type of **biased growth** could have wheat production either growing somewhat (but by less than the percent increase in cloth production) or decreasing below 80.

Figure 5.1C shows growth that is biased toward wheat production. The ppc shift is skewed toward wheat. At the relative price of 1 bushel per yard, the produc-

FIGURE 5.1   *Balanced and Biased Growth*

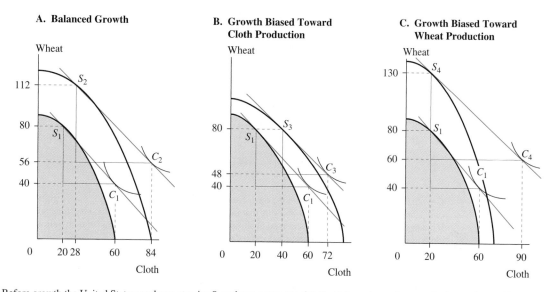

Before growth the United States produces at point S_1 and consumes at point C_1. Balanced growth expands the ppc in a uniform or neutral way. Biased growth expands the ppc in a way skewed toward one good or the other. If the price ratio remains unchanged, then production growth (to points S_2, S_3, S_4) increases national income and increases consumption of both goods (points C_2, C_3, C_4). By altering production and consumption, growth may change the country's willingness to trade (the size of its trade triangle). For balanced growth and for growth biased toward wheat, the case of increased willingness to trade is shown. For growth biased toward cloth, the case of less willingness to trade is shown.

tion point would shift from S_1 to a point like S_4. In this example, wheat production increases from 80 to 130 and cloth production remains unchanged. In other specific examples of growth biased toward wheat, cloth production might either (1) increase by a lesser percentage than wheat production increases or (2) decrease.

Biased growth arises when the country's endowments of different factors grow at different rates, or when improvements in production technologies are larger in one of the industries than in the other. A specific example of unbalanced growth in factor endowments is the situation in which one factor grows, but the other factor is unchanged. A specific example of different rates of technology improvement is the situation in which technology in one industry is improving but technology in the other industry is not changing.[1]

---

[1]The case in which technology in one industry is improving but no other production-side growth is occurring actually looks a little different from the graphs in Figures 5.1B and 5.1C. For instance, growth biased toward cloth could occur if only cloth production technology is improving. In this case the ppc shifts out in a manner that is skewed toward cloth, *and the ppc intercept with the wheat axis does not change.* This wheat intercept shows no production of cloth so the better cloth technology does not expand the production capability. The rest of the ppc shifts out, as any cloth production benefits from the improved cloth technology. A similar reasoning applies to an improvement only in wheat technology. In this case the ppc intercept with the cloth axis does not change, but the rest of the ppc shifts out.

FIGURE 5.2

*Single-Factor
Growth: The
Rybczynski
Theorem*

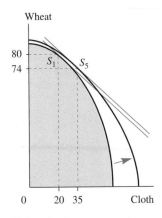

Growth in one production factor, with the other factor not growing, results in strongly biased growth. If only labor grows, the ppc shifts out in a way that is biased toward more cloth production. If the price ratio remains the same, the actual production point shifts from S_1 to S_5. The Rybczynski theorem indicates that cloth production increases and wheat production decreases.

Growth in Only One Factor

The case in which only one factor is growing has important implications, summarized in the **Rybczynski theorem:**

> In a two-good world, and assuming that product prices are constant, growth in the country's endowment of one factor of production, with the other factor unchanged, results in an increase in the output of the good that uses the growing factor intensively, and a *decrease in the output of the other good.*[2]

To see the logic behind this theorem, consider the case in which only labor is growing. The most obvious place in which to put the extra labor to work is in the labor-intensive industry—cloth in our ongoing example. Thus, it is not surprising that cloth production increases.

However, with the production techniques in use, increasing cloth production requires not only extra labor but also some amount of extra land, the factor whose overall supply did not grow. During a period of transition, the cloth sector obtains this extra land from the wheat sector so that wheat production decreases. (In addition, as wheat production declines, it releases both land and labor, all of which must be reemployed into cloth production. Therefore, the proportionate expansion of cloth production will actually be larger that the proportion by which the overall labor endowment grows.)

Figure 5.2 shows the effects of this growth in the labor endowment. As a result of the growth, the ppc shifts out at all points. Even if the country only pro-

---

[2]The other important conditions and assumptions include (1) the country produces positive amounts of both goods before and after growth, with both factors used in producing each good; (2) factors are mobile between sectors and fully employed; and (3) the technology of production is unchanged. Rybczynski (1955) also explored the changes in the terms of trade that are likely to accompany factor growth, as we will do subsequently in this chapter. (You may abbreviate his name as "Ryb" when answering exam questions.)

The "Dutch Disease" and Deindustrialization

Developing a new exportable resource can cause problems. One, discussed later in this chapter, is the problem of "immiserizing growth": If you are already exporting and your export expansion lowers the world price of your exports, you could end up worse off. Another problem has been called the *Dutch disease,* after a situation perceived by the Netherlands following the development of new natural gas fields under the North Sea.

It seemed that the more the Netherlands developed its natural gas production, the more depressed its manufacturers of traded goods became. Even the windfall price increases that the two oil shocks offered the Netherlands (all fuel prices skyrocketed, including that for natural gas) seemed to add to industry's slump. The Dutch disease has been thought to have spread to Britain, Norway, Australia, Mexico, and other countries that have newly developed natural resources.

The main premise of this fear is correct: Under many realistic conditions, the windfall of a new natural resource does indeed erode profits and production in the traded industrial-goods sector. Deindustrialization occurs for the same reason that underlies the Rybczynski theorem introduced in this chapter: The new sector draws resources away from the industrial sector. Specifically, to develop production of the natural resource, the sector must hire labor away from the industrial sector, and it must obtain capital that otherwise would have been invested in the industrial sector. Thus, the industrial sector contracts.

Journalistic coverage of the apparent link between natural resource development and deindustrialization tends to discover the basic Rybczynski effect in a very different way. The press tends to notice that the development of the exportable natural resource causes the nation's currency to rise in value on foreign exchange markets, by letting the nation earn more foreign exchange. A higher value of the nation's currency makes it harder for international customers to buy the whole range of the nation's tradable goods and services. To the industrial sector this feels like a drop in demand, and the sector contracts. The foreign exchange market, in gravitating back toward the original balance of trade, is simply producing the same result we would get from a barter trade model: If you export more of a good, you'll end up either exporting less of another good or importing more. Something has to give so that trade will return to the same balance as before.

So far, it looks as though the disease really does imply deindustrialization. That seems realistic to economists who have studied this issue. We should note, though, two ways in which industry could actually expand. First, if the price of the natural resource does drop, contrary to the terms of the example just presented, and the resource is a major industrial input (such as oil), then profits and production in the industrial sector could be raised instead of cut. Second, the new natural resources could be taxed and the tax proceeds given out to industrial producers in such a way as to bring net stimulus to industry (e.g., as direct output subsidies or as generous tax breaks for such things as real industrial investment or export sales).

We should also note that merely shifting resources away from industry into natural resources is not necessarily bad, despite a rich folklore assuming that industrial expansion is somehow key to prosperity. But bad or not, it is a very likely side effect of gaining new natural resources.

duced wheat, the extra labor presumably could be employed in wheat production to generate some extra wheat output. However, the outward shift in the ppc is biased toward more cloth production, the industry in which labor is the more important production factor. If the relative price is initially 1 bushel per yard and remains unchanged, then growth shifts production from point S_1 to a point like S_5 on the new ppc. Cloth production increases from 20 to 35, and wheat production decreases from 80 to 74.

The Rybczynski result suggests that development of a new natural resource, such as oil or gas in Canada or Britain, may retard development of other lines of production, such as manufactures. (See the box "The 'Dutch Disease' and Deindustrialization.") Conversely, rapid accumulation of new capital and skills in a fast-growing trading country can cause a decline in domestic production of natural resource products and make the country more reliant on imported materials. This happened to the United States, which was transformed from a net exporter to a net importer of minerals as it grew relative to the rest of the world, perhaps partly because of the accumulation of skills and capital.

Changes in the Country's Willingness to Trade

Growth alters a country's capabilities in supplying products. Growth also alters the country's demand for products, for instance, by changing the income that people in the country have to spend. As production and consumption change with growth, a country's willingness or interest in engaging in international trade can change. That is, even if the relative price between two products stays constant, the country could increase its willingness to trade (it could want to export and import more) or decrease its willingness to trade (it could want to export and import less). To analyze this further, we assume as usual that both goods are normal goods so that an increase in income (with product prices unchanged) increases the quantities demanded of both goods.[3]

We can examine changes in the country's willingness to trade in each of the three cases of growth shown in Figure 5.1. In each graph the change in willingness can be shown by changes in the size of the trade triangle for each equilibrium because the trade triangle shows the country's export and import quantities. Before the growth occurs we presume that the country was at a free-trade equilibrium with production at S_1 and consumption at C_1. The trade triangle connecting S_1 and C_1 shows exports of 40 wheat and imports of 40 cloth.

Consider first the case of balanced supply-side growth, Figure 5.1A. As we showed previously, production shifts to S_2 with growth. Proportionate expansion of production means that wheat production increases by 32 and cloth by 8. With the relative price constant, the price line shifts out. The country has more income and expands its consumption quantities for both goods. However, this by itself is not enough to indicate the change in the country's willingness to trade. If the consumption of wheat increases by less than 32, then the quantity of wheat available for export will increase—the size of the trade triangle and the country's willingness to trade will increase. If the consumption of wheat expands by more than 32, then the quantity of wheat available for export will decrease—the size of the trade triangle and the country's willingness to trade

---

[3]An alternative assumption is that one of the two goods is inferior so that quantity demanded of this inferior good would decrease as income increases. While this case is possible, it would complicate the discussion without adding major insights.

will decrease.[4] The changes in the consumption quantities depend on the tastes of the consumers in the country, summarized by the shapes of the community indifference curves and the specific community indifference curve that is tangent to the new postgrowth price line. The case actually shown in Figure 5.1A has the new community indifference curve tangent to the new price line at point C_2, so that the quantities consumed expand proportionately to 56 wheat and 84 cloth. In this case, the increase in wheat consumption (16) is less than the increase in wheat production (32) so the trade triangle and the country's willingness to trade expand.

Suppose next that growth is biased toward cloth, as shown in Figure 5.1B. Production shifts to S_3 with growth, raising cloth production with no change in wheat production. More wheat is consumed (as the consumption point shifts to a point like C_3), so there is less wheat available for export. In this case, the trade triangle and the country's willingness to trade shrink. A similar analysis applies to the growth shown in Figure 5.2, growth even more biased toward cloth production.[5]

When growth is biased toward wheat, as shown in Figure 5.1C, our demand for cloth increases as consumption shifts to a point like C_4 so we want to import more. The strong growth of wheat production also increases the amount available for export. The trade triangle expands, showing the country's greater willingness to trade.

Effects on the Country's Terms of Trade

Changes in a country's willingness to trade can alter the country's terms of trade if the country is large enough for its trade to have an impact on the international equilibrium. In turn, any change in the country's terms of trade affects the well-being or welfare of the country, thus having an impact on the extent to which the country benefits from its growth. In this section we first examine the case of a **small country,** one whose trade does not affect the international price ratio. We then examine the case of the **large country,** one whose trade can have an impact on the relative international price ratio (that is, an effect on the price the country receives for its exports, the price it pays for its imports, or both).

---

[4]We could also reach the same conclusions by focusing on changes in the quantities of cloth produced and consumed. In the order presented in the paragraph, consumption of cloth would increase by more than production increases so that desired imports increase; or consumption would rise by less so that desired imports would decline. Of course, it is also possible that the quantities produced and consumed of cloth would increase by equal amounts (as would those for wheat), in which case the trade triangle and the country's willingness to trade would not change.

[5]If the growth is sufficiently biased toward producing more of the good that is initially imported, the country's pattern of trade could reverse itself, making the country an exporter of cloth and an importer of wheat. This case was noted for the United States at the end of the previous section. There is nothing immutable about the trade pattern—comparative advantage and disadvantage can reverse over time.

Small Country

If a country is "small" (that is, a price-taker in world markets), then its trade has no impact on the international price ratio (the country's terms of trade). The graphs shown in Figure 5.1 represent the full analysis of growth by the country. In each of these cases the country gains from its growth in the sense that it reaches a higher community indifference curve (at point C_2, C_3, or C_4, depending on the type of growth).

Large Country

If a country is large, a change in its willingness to trade affects the equilibrium international price ratio. Consider first the case in which growth reduces the country's willingness to trade at any given price, as shown in Figure 5.3 (which reproduces the ppc shift of Figure 5.1B). The reduction in the country's demand for imports reduces the relative price of the import good (or the reduction in the country's supply of exports increases the relative price of the export good). This change in the equilibrium international price is an improvement in the country's terms of trade. In this case, the country gets two benefits from growth: (1) the production benefit from growth as the ppc shifts out and (2) the benefit from improved terms of trade as it receives a better price for its exports relative to the price that it has to pay for its imports. In Figure 5.3 the improved terms of trade are shown in a flatter price line (a lower relative price of cloth, the import good). In response, the country shifts its production point to S_6 on the new ppc and decides to consume at a point C_6. With this ppc growth and no change in the

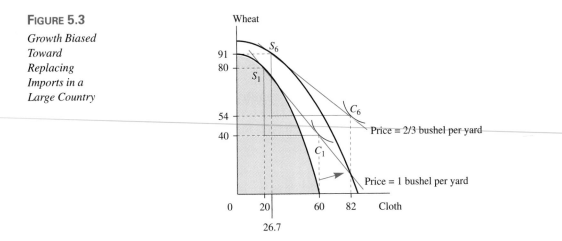

FIGURE 5.3

Growth Biased Toward Replacing Imports in a Large Country

A large country can gain in two ways from an expanding ability to produce the import-competing good—here, cloth. In addition to the gains from being able to produce more (already shown in Figure 5.1B), it can improve its terms of trade. By demanding fewer imports (a decreased willingness to trade), it makes cloth cheaper on world markets. After growth, the relative price of cloth declines to 2/3 bushel per yard in the example shown. The country's remaining imports cost less. Thus, the country gains more from growth, as consumption shifts from C_1 to C_6, because the price line becomes flatter.

terms of trade, the country would reach the welfare level associated with the community indifference curve through C_3 (48 wheat and 72 cloth) in Figure 5.1B. The improvement in the terms of trade permits the country to reach the higher welfare level associated with the community indifference curve through C_6 (54 wheat and 82 cloth) in Figure 5.3.

Consider next the case in which growth increases the country's willingness to trade. The increase in the country's demand for imports increases the relative price of the import good (or the increase in the country's supply of exports reduces the relative price of the export good). This change in the equilibrium international price ratio is a deterioration in the country's terms of trade. In this case the effect on the country's well-being or welfare is not clear. Growth brings a production benefit, but the country is hurt by the subsequent decline in its terms of trade. (It receives a lower price for its export goods relative to the price that it pays for its import goods.)

If the terms of trade do not decline by too much, then the country gains overall from growth, but not by as much as it would if the terms of trade did not change. However, if the adverse movement is not small, a surprising consequence is possible.

Immiserizing Growth

What happens if the terms of trade decline a great deal in response to growth in the country's ability to produce its export good? If the terms of trade decline substantially, the country's well-being or welfare could fall as a result of growth in the country (or, in the in-between case, the country's well-being could essentially be unchanged). The possibility of a decline in well-being is shown in Figure 5.4, in which a large improvement in wheat-production technology results in a shift in the ppc that is strongly skewed toward expanding wheat production. For a relatively steep price line (showing a large decline in the country's terms of trade), the country's production is at point S_7 on the new ppc and its consumption at point C_7. The welfare level for C_7 is less than that for point C_1 before growth. This possibility is a remarkable result, first analyzed carefully by Jagdish Bhagwati. It is called the possibility of **immiserizing growth:**

> Growth that expands the country's willingness to trade can result in such a large decline in the country's terms of trade that the country is worse off.

Three conditions seem crucial for immiserizing growth to occur:

1. The country's growth must be strongly biased toward expanding the country's supply of exports (increasing its willingness to trade), and the increase in export supply must be large enough to have a noticeable impact on world prices.
2. The foreign demand for the country's exports must be price inelastic so that an expansion in the country's export supply leads to a large drop in the international price of the export good.

FIGURE 5.4

*Immiserizing
Growth in a
Large Country*

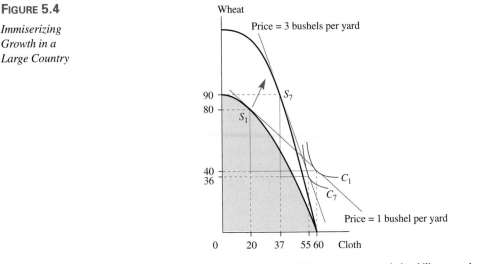

A large country actually could be made worse off by an improvement in its ability to produce the goods it exports. Such a perverse case of immiserizing growth is shown here. By expanding its ability to produce wheat, its export good, the large country increases its supply of exports (expands its willingness to trade). This drives down the relative price of wheat in world markets. Looked at the other way, this causes an increase (here a tripling) of the relative price that it must pay for its imports of cloth. The decline in the country's terms of trade is so bad, in this case, that it outweighs the benefits of the extra ability to produce. Consumer enjoyment is lower at C_7 than at the initial consumption point C_1.

3. Before the growth, the country must be heavily engaged in trade so that the welfare loss from the decline in the terms of trade is great enough to offset the gains from being able to produce more.

Countries that export a diversified selection of export goods do not seem to be at much risk of experiencing immiserizing growth. A developing country that relies on one or a few primary products (agricultural or mineral products) is more at risk. For example, consider a country like Zambia that relies on a mineral ore (e.g., copper) for nearly all its export revenues. A discovery that leads to the opening of several new large mines would increase its ore exports and greatly reduce the international price of this ore. As a result of the decline in the price, the country could be worse off. For instance, the money value of Zambia's exports of copper ore could decline (if the price falls more than the export quantity increases), and Zambia then could not afford to import as much as before the growth.

It may seem foolish for a nation to undergo an expansion that makes itself worse off. But remember that the expansion would be undertaken, both in the model and in the real world, by individual competitive firms, each of which might profit individually from its own expansion. Individual rationality can add up to collective irrationality.

The possibility of immiserizing growth offers large countries a policy lesson that transcends the cases in which it actually occurs. By itself, the case of immiserizing growth is probably just a curious rarity. Even for large countries the necessary conditions listed above are not likely to be met very often. Yet a larger point emerges from Figures 5.3 and 5.4. Notice that *any* effect of growth in the national economy on the terms of trade affects the returns from encouraging that growth. Suppose that the government is debating which industries to favor with tax breaks or subsidies, and has to choose between encouraging import-replacing industries and encouraging export-expanding ones. In Figure 5.3 we found that the country reaped greater benefits if its expansion of import-competing capabilities causes a drop in the price of imports. By contrast, in Figure 5.4, expanding export industries is less beneficial because it lowers the relative price of exports. This is true whether or not the bad terms-of-trade effect is big enough to outweigh the gains from being more productive. So a large country has reason to favor import-replacing industries over export industries: *If* other things are truly equal, why not favor industries that turn world prices in your favor rather than against you?[6] We return to this point when discussing trade policy for developing countries in Chapter 13.

Technology and Trade

This chapter's discussion of biased growth can be linked to the general discussion of the basis for comparative advantage presented in Chapter 3. As we noted there, comparative advantage skews countries' capabilities for producing various goods. In presenting the Heckscher–Ohlin theory, we spent much time discussing differences in factor endowments as the basis for comparative advantage.

Another basis for comparative advantage is differences in production technologies available in the various countries. Technology differences tend to skew production in each country toward producing the good(s) in which the country has the relatively better technology (that is, the technology of greatest advantage or least disadvantage).

Technology-based comparative advantage can arise over time as technological change occurs at different rates in different sectors and countries. For instance, in our ongoing example, improvements in the production technology used in the wheat industry in the United States over time would skew U.S. production capabilities toward producing larger amounts of wheat—the U.S. ppc would shift out in a way biased toward wheat production (as in Figure 5.1C). These technology improvements could include improved farming practices or better seed varieties. If the technology for wheat production is not improving in a comparable manner in the rest of the world, then the United States can develop a comparative advantage in wheat based on its relative technology advantage in wheat.

In some ways this technology-based explanation is an alternative that competes with the H–O theory. Technology differences can become an important

---

[6]Remember, however, that the whole reason for favoring import replacement here relates to turning international prices in this nation's favor. For the world as a whole, there can be no such gain and no immiserizing growth: One country's gains (losses) from changes in the terms of trade equal another country's losses (gains).

cause (sometimes the dominant cause) of the pattern of trade in specific products. For instance, the fact that the United States has become a net importer of steel products can be explained in part by the adoption of newer production technologies for steel in Japan and other countries.

In other ways technology differences can be consistent with an H–O view of the world, at least one using an extended and dynamic H–O approach. To see this, we must consider the question of where the technological improvements come from.

Some technological improvement happens by chance or through the unusual efforts of individuals. However, most industrially useful new technology now comes from organized efforts that we call *research and development (R&D)*. This R&D is done largely by businesses and focuses on improvements in production technologies for existing products and on new product and production technologies for new or improved products. Products or industries in which R&D is relatively important, such as aircraft, semiconductors, and pharmaceuticals, are usually called *high technology*. Ongoing (and costly) R&D within these high tech industries can create an ongoing stream of new and improved technology over time.

The most obvious link to the H–O theory is the national location of R&D itself. R&D is a production activity that is intensive in highly skilled labor—scientists and engineers in particular. Most of the world's R&D is done in the few advanced countries with an abundance of this type of labor, especially the United States, Germany, Japan, France, and the United Kingdom. Another factor of importance is capital willing to take the substantial risks involved in financing R&D investments. The relative abundance of *venture capital* (outsiders' purchase of ownership in new ventures) in the United States is the basis for a U.S. advantage, while other countries like Japan depend more on internal funding of R&D within its large corporations.

The national location of production of goods using the new technology, which is what is shown explicitly in our ppc graph, is not so clear-cut. It seems reasonable that the first use in production could be in the same country in which the R&D was done. However, technology can spread internationally. This international "trade" in technology is called *diffusion*. New technology is difficult to keep secret, and other countries have an incentive to obtain the technology improvements. Indeed, the creator of the new technology has the incentive to apply it in production in the national location(s) in which the new technology is most suitable (and therefore most profitable). H–O theory suggests that the suitable location fits the factor proportions of production using the new technology to the factor endowments of the national locations.

Individual Products and the Product Cycle

One effort to find a pattern in these technology activities is the **product cycle hypothesis** first advanced by Raymond Vernon. When a product is first invented (born), it still must be perfected. Additional R&D is needed, and production is often in small amounts by skilled workers. In addition, the major demand is mostly in the high-income countries since most new products are luxuries in the economist's sense. Close communication is needed between the R&D, production, and marketing people in the producing firm. All this suggests that both R&D and initial production are likely to be in an advanced developed country. Over time, the product and its production technology become more standardized and familiar (mature). Factor intensity tends to shift away from skilled labor and toward less-skilled labor. The technology diffuses and production locations shift into other countries, eventually into developing countries that are abundant in less-skilled labor. Trade patterns change in a manner consistent with shifting production locations. The innovating country is initially the exporter of the new product, but it eventually becomes an importer. Although it is dynamic and emphasizes additional considerations like demand and communication, many aspects of this product cycle hypothesis are consistent with H–O theory.

The product cycle hypothesis does fit the experience of products in many industries in the past century. Pocket (or hand-held) calculators are an example. These were pioneered by Texas Instruments and Hewlett-Packard in the United States in the early 1970s. Soon Sharp and other Japanese consumer electronics firms began to dominate a product whose characteristics had begun to stabilize. More recently, assembly production has shifted into the developing countries.

Nonetheless, the usefulness of the product cycle hypothesis is limited for several reasons. These have to do with the unpredictable lengths or progression of the phases of the cycle. In many industries—especially high tech industries—product and production technologies are continually evolving because of ongoing R&D. Rejuvenation or replenished youthfulness is important. In addition, international diffusion often occurs within multinational (or "global") corporations. In this case, the cycle can essentially disappear. New technology developed by a multinational corporation in one of its research facilities in a leading developed country can be transferred within the corporation for its first production use in affiliates in other countries, including those in developing countries.

Openness to Trade Affects Growth

So far, most of the discussion in this chapter has looked at how growth in production capabilities can affect international trade. Clearly, growth can have a major impact on international trade. There is also likely to be an impact in the other direction, from trade to growth. Openness to international trade can have an impact on how fast a country's economy can grow—how fast its production capabilities are growing over time.

We can gain major insights into this question by considering how openness to trade can affect the technologies that the country can utilize. As we noted

Trade, Technology, and U.S. Wages

Americans have reason to worry about trends in real wages since the early 1970s. One major trend has been a rising gap between the wages of relatively skilled workers and the wages of less-skilled workers. For instance, from the mid-1970s to the mid-1990s, the ratio of the average wage of college graduates to that of high school graduates increased by 15 percent. Many less-skilled workers have seen their wages decline in real (purchasing power) terms. Meanwhile, the importance of international trade increased dramatically for the United States. The ratio of the sum of exports and imports to total national production (GDP) approximately doubled from about 12 percent in the early 1970s to about 23 percent in the mid-1990s. Do we see here the effects on U.S. wages of a "race to the bottom" driven by rising imports? More precisely, is this the Stolper–Samuelson theorem at work, as rising trade alters the returns to scarce and abundant factors in the United States?

Given the political implications of the trend toward greater wage inequality, economists have studied it carefully. While increasing trade presumably has had some effect on wage rates through the Stolper–Samuelson effect, economists have generally concluded that trade has not been the main culprit.

For the Stolper–Samuelson theorem to be the main culprit—the predominant effect—at least two other things should be true. First, the changes in factor prices should result from changes in product prices. Specifically, a decline in the relative price of less-skilled-labor–intensive goods should be behind the decline in the relative wages of less-skilled workers. Second, and more subtly, the change in the relative wage should induce industries to become more intensive in their use of the now cheaper less-skilled labor. (See the "A Factor-Ratio Paradox" box in Chapter 4, page 65.)

Research by Lawrence and Slaughter (1993) shows that neither of these two things appears to have occurred. They examine data on U.S. manufacturing industries and equate skilled labor with nonproduction workers and less-skilled labor with production workers (a reasonable if not perfect scheme). They find no evidence that the relative international price of manufactured goods that use less-skilled labor intensively declined during the 1980s—in fact, the relative price of less-skilled-labor–intensive goods appears to have risen somewhat. They also find that most manufacturing industries became more intensive in their use of skilled labor and less intensive in less-skilled labor.

These changes are not consistent with the Stolper–Samuelson theorem, and they conclude that changes in international trade prices are not the predominant cause of the rising wage inequality. Other economists have concluded similarly that changes in the trade flows themselves (imports and exports) are not the predominant cause.

If not trade, then what? Most researchers have concluded that the major driving force changing demands for skilled and unskilled labor has been technological change. In fact, technological change may be exerting two effects. First, technological progress has been faster in industries that are more intensive in skilled labor. As the cost and prices of these skill-intensive products decline, and the quality of these products is improved, demand for the products increases. As demand shifts toward skill-intensive products and their production increases, the demand for skilled labor expands, increasing the relative wage of skilled labor. Second, the technological progress that has occurred within individual industries appears to be biased in favor of using more skilled labor. This bias increases demand for skilled labor even more, reinforcing the pressure for an increase in wage inequality. We see this bias in the shift toward greater use of computers generally and in the shift toward computer-controlled flexible manufacturing systems in manufacturing specifically.

In Western Europe these effects seem to have played themselves out somewhat differently. High minimum wages have prevented wage rates for less-skilled workers from declining so much. Instead, unemployment has increased since the early 1970s and has remained high. While inequality of earnings has not increased so much in Western Europe, unemployment, especially among the less skilled, has become a serious problem.

previously in the discussion of product life cycle, there are two sources of new technology for a country: technology developed domestically and technology imported from foreign countries. If a country closes itself to international trade, it probably cuts itself off from this second source of new technology. Looked at in the other way, countries that are open to international trade (and international exchanges more generally) tend to grow faster. Let's consider more closely the reasons for this relationship. (We might also note that the relationship is actually complex, so that none of these reasons is completely straightforward. We will focus on generally positive effects, without providing the caveats that may apply.)

Trade provides access to new and improved products. For our production-side analysis, capital goods are an important type of input into production that can be imported. Trade allows a country to import new and improved capital goods, which thus "embody" better technology that can be used in production to raise productivity. The foreign exporters can also enhance the process, for instance, by advising the importing firm on the best ways to use the new capital goods. More generally, openness to international activities generally leads the firms and people of the country to have more contact with technology developed in other countries. This greater awareness makes it more likely that the country will gain the use of the new technology, through purchase of capital goods or through licensing or imitation of the technology.

Openness to international trade can also have an impact on the incentive to innovate. Trade can provide additional competitive pressure on the country's firms, driving them to seek better technology to raise their productivity in order to build their international competitiveness. Trade provides a larger market in which to earn returns to innovation. If sales into foreign markets provide additional returns, then the incentive to innovate increases, and firms devote more resources to R&D activities.

Openness to international trade thus can enhance the technology that a country can use, both by facilitating the diffusion of foreign-developed technology into the country and by accelerating the domestic development of technology. Furthermore, these increases in the current technology base can be used to develop additional innovations in the future. This is a key insight of the "new growth theory," which posits that economic policies and activities influence the growth rate. The current technology base provides a source of increasing returns over time to ongoing innovation activities. The growth rate for the country's economy (and for the whole world) increases in the long run.

In conclusion, openness to trade can accelerate long-run economic growth. This indicates an additional source of gains from international trade (or from openness to international activities more generally). Empirically, there is a strong positive correlation between the growth rate of a country and its international openness. This is not proof of causation, but it is consistent with the theoretical analysis that suggests why openness can raise growth. We take up this issue again in Chapter 13, when we discuss developing countries.

Summary

Growth in a country's production capabilities results from increases in the country's endowments of factors of production or from technological improvements. **Balanced growth** shifts the country's production-possibility curve outward in a proportionate manner. If the product price ratio is unchanged, production of each product increases proportionately. Consumption of both goods also increases. This alters the country's trade triangle and its willingness to trade unless the increases in quantities produced and consumed are equal. For instance, if the growth in production quantity of the exportable good exceeds the growth in its consumption quantity, then the trade triangle and the willingness to trade increase.

Biased growth shifts the ppc outward in a manner that is skewed toward one good. If the product price ratio is unchanged, production of this good expands, but production of the other good increases by a lesser proportion, stays the same, or declines. If growth is biased toward producing more of the import-competing good, the country's trade triangle and its willingness to trade tend to shrink. If growth is biased toward producing more of the exportable good, the country's trade triangle and its willingness to trade tend to expand.

The trade of a **small country** has no impact on international prices. The analysis of growth in a small country is straightforward because its growth does not alter its terms of trade.

The trade of a **large country** does have an impact on international prices. If growth results in a large country becoming less willing to trade, then the relative price of the country's export good increases. In this case, growth benefits the country both through expansion of its production capabilities and by improvement of its terms of trade.

If growth results in a large country becoming more willing to trade, then the relative price of its export good decreases. This deterioration in the terms of trade reduces the benefits to the country of growing productive capabilities. Indeed, it is possible that, if the terms of trade decline substantially, the country could be worse off after growing—a possibility called **immiserizing growth.**

The relationship of technology to the shape of the ppc indicates that differences in technology between countries can be a basis for trade. In some ways, this technology explanation competes with the Heckscher–Ohlin explanation in that countries export products in which they have relative technology advantages. In other ways, technology differences can be linked to H–O. For instance, the research and development that leads to new technologies tends to be located in countries that are well endowed with the highly skilled labor like scientists and engineers that are needed to conduct the R&D. The **product cycle hypothesis** is an attempt to offer a dynamic theory of technology and trade by emphasizing that the location of production of a good is likely to shift from the leading developed countries to developing countries as the product moves from its introduction to maturity and standardization.

Openness to international trade can also influence the rate of economic growth by affecting the rate at which the country's production technology is improving. With international openness, diffusion of new foreign technology into the country increases, because of imports of capital goods that embody the foreign technology, or licensing or imitation of the foreign technology. Innovation by domestic firms increases, because of competitive pressure and the greater returns available through foreign sales. Empirically, there is a significant positive relationship between the international openness of a country and the economic growth of that country.

Suggested Reading

A classic theoretical study of the effects of technological progress on a country's economy and trade (using techniques similar to those presented in Appendix B) is Findlay and Grubert (1959). The product cycle hypothesis of trade is put forth in Vernon (1966), but doubts are voiced by Vernon himself (1979). Cline (1997), Johnson (1997), Lawrence (1996), and Freeman (1995) each survey the effects of trade and other influences on rising wage inequality.

Grossman and Helpman (1995) provide a technical survey of economic theories of the relationships between technology and trade. Romer (1994) and Rivera-Batiz and Romer (1991) present technical discussions of the effects of trade openness on growth.

When you feel that you are nearing mastery of the theoretical material in Chapters 2 through 5, give yourself a test by looking at the first 10 paradoxes in Magee (1979). First look at Magee's listing of the paradoxes on his pages 92–93; then try to prove or explain them before looking at the answers.

Questions and Problems

✦ 1. Pugelovia's growth has been oriented toward expansion of its export industries. How do you think Pugelovia's terms of trade have been changing during this time period?

2. "According to the Rybczynski theorem, an increase in the country's labor force will result in an increase in the quantity produced of the labor-intensive good, with no change in the quantity produced of the other good." Do you agree or disagree? Why?

✦ 3. A number of Latin American countries export coffee and import other goods. A long-term drought now reduces coffee production in the countries of this region. Assume that they remain exporters of coffee. Explain why the long-term drought in the region might lead to an increase in the region's well-being or welfare. What would make this gain in welfare more likely?

4. "A country whose trade has almost no impact on world prices is at great risk of immiserizing growth." Do you agree or disagree? Why?

✦ 5. Why does the Heckscher–Ohlin theory predict that most research and development (R&D) activity is done in the industrialized countries?

6. If every new product goes through a product cycle, will the technological initiator (e.g., the United States or Japan) develop chronic overall "trade deficits"?

✦ 7. Explain the effect of each of these on the shape and position of the country's production-possibility curve:

   a. A proportionate increase in the total supplies (endowments) of all factors of production.

   b. New management practices that can be used in all industries to improve productivity by about the same amount in all industries.

   c. New production technology that improves productivity in the wheat industry, with no effect on productivity in the cloth industry.

8. Which of the following can lead to a *reversal* of the country's trade pattern (that is, a

shift in which a previously exported good becomes an imported good, or a previously imported good becomes an export good)? Consider each separately. Explain each.

  a. Growth in the country's total supply (endowment) of the factor that is initially scarce in the country.

  b. International diffusion of technology.

  c. Shifting tastes of the country's consumers.

✦9. A free-trade equilibrium exists in which the United States exports machinery and imports clothing from the rest of the world. The goods are produced with two factors: capital and labor. An increase now occurs in the U.S. endowment of capital, its abundant factor.

  a. What is the effect on the shape and position of the U.S. production-possibility curve?

  b. What is the effect on the actual production quantities in the United States if the product price ratio is unchanged? Explain.

  c. What is the effect on the U.S. willingness to trade?

  d. Assuming that the U.S. growth does affect the international equilibrium price ratio, what is the change in this price ratio?

  e. Is it possible that U.S. national well-being or welfare declines as a result of the endowment growth and the resulting change in the international price ratio? Explain.

10. A free-trade equilibrium exists in a two-region, two-product world. The United States exports food and imports clothing. A long-term drought now occurs in East Asia.

  a. What is the effect on East Asia's willingness to trade?

  b. Assuming that each region is large enough to influence international prices, how does East Asia's drought affect the equilibrium international price ratio?

  c. Show on a graph and explain the effect of all this on the following *in the United States:* (1) Quantities produced of food and clothing. (2) Quantities consumed of food and clothing. (3) U.S. well-being or welfare.

  d. Which group in the United States is likely to gain real income in the long run as a result of all this? Which group in the United States is likely to lose real income?

✦11. A free-trade equilibrium exists in which the United States exports food and imports clothing. U.S. engineers now invent a new process for producing clothing at a lower cost. This process cannot be used in the rest of the world.

  a. What is the effect on the U.S. production-possibility curve?

  b. What is the effect on the U.S. willingness to trade? (Assume that the United States remains an importer of clothing.)

  c. Assuming that the change in the United States is large enough to affect international prices, will the equilibrium international price of clothing rise or will it fall?

12. Continue with the scenario of question 11—the new process in the United States and the effect on the international equilibrium price ratio. Focus now on effects in the rest of the world.

  a. Show graphically and explain the effect on quantities produced, quantities consumed, and well-being or welfare in the rest of the world.

  b. Explain as precisely as possible why well-being or welfare changes in the rest of the world.

CHAPTER 6

Alternative Theories of Trade

When the facts change, theories often need to change with them. The facts of international trade seem to be moving in directions that force us either to expand on the standard theory of Chapters 2 through 5 or to replace it with new theories. Here we explore facts about world trade and the leading theories that try to explain the aspects that are not consistent with the standard theory.

One key fact is the importance of two-way trade in very similar products—both exporting and importing products in the same industry. Another key fact is the dominance of a few large firms in some world industries. These facts point us toward considering theories based on types of market structure different from the perfectly competitive markets of standard trade theory. We will examine three major alternatives: monopolistic competition (with its emphasis on product differentiation), global oligopoly, and industries that concentrate in a few places because of scale economies that arise from interactions among the firms located within each area.

Trade Facts in Search of Better Theory

According to trade theory based on comparative advantage, nations should trade with each other to exploit their production-side differences. We would expect that industrialized countries (like the United States, Japan, and Germany) would trade with the developing countries, and indeed this part of the trade pattern is generally well explained by comparative-advantage theory.

According to comparative-advantage theory, nations that are similar in their production-side capabilities (and in their general demand patterns) should trade little with each other. Industrialized countries are similar in many aspects of their factor endowments (physical capital, skilled labor, and unskilled labor) and also in their technologies and technological capabilities. Comparative-advantage theory predicts that these countries should trade rather little with each other, except for some trade based in primary products (for instance, food products and minerals) resulting from differences in endowments of arable land and natural resources.

In fact, industrialized countries trade extensively with each other. Trade between industrialized countries is about half of all world trade. Over 70 percent of the exports of industrialized countries go to other industrialized countries, and about four-fifths of these exports are nonfood manufactured products. These facts appear to be inconsistent with comparative-advantage theory.

The Rise of Intra-Industry Trade

Perhaps there is still some comparative-advantage basis for production specialization across industries among the industrialized countries. That is, perhaps each industrialized country specializes in and exports products in a particular range of industries, exploiting some subtle production-side comparative advantage. A close look at the data suggests that this is not true. Much trade in manufactured goods between industrialized countries is **intra-industry trade**—two-way trade (exports and imports) of the same or very similar goods (goods in the same industry). Economists coined this term in the 1970s to describe such trade as Hondas for Volkswagens, French wine for Italian wine, or Boeing airplanes for Airbus airplanes.

To describe the phenomenon more carefully, specialists divide a country's trade in an industry's products into the part that is net trade (or interindustry trade) and the part that is intra-industry trade. Net trade is the value of the difference between exports and imports for the industry. Net trade is positive (net exports) if the country's exports are larger; it is negative (net imports) if imports are larger.

Intra-industry trade is the part of total trade that is not net trade—the part that is matched exports and imports. For instance, in Figure 4.4 we noted that the United States exported $23.1 billion of computers and imported $35.4 billion of computers in 1995. The magnitude of net, or interindustry, trade in computers was $12.3 billion. Intra-industry trade was $46.2 billion ($23.1 billion of exports matched by the same amount of imports). Intra-industry trade in computers was most (79 percent) of total U.S. trade in computers ($58.5 billion). (Note that in calculating the amount of intra-industry trade, we care only about the magnitude of any net trade, not whether the net trade is positive or negative.)

The importance of intra-industry trade in a country's overall trade (in total or for a broad class of industries such as manufacturing) can be calculated as an index using information on the exports (X) and imports (M) of each constituent industry:

$$\text{Intra-industry trade (IIT) share} = 1 - \left(\frac{\text{sum of } |X - M|}{\text{sum of } X + M} \right)$$

The absolute values of $(X - M)$ is the magnitude of net trade for each constituent industry. The IIT share is also equal to 1 minus the share of net or interindustry trade in the country's overall trade. The IIT share is a number between 0 and 1 (or

FIGURE 6.1   *Intra-Industry Trade (IIT) as a Percentage of Trade in Nonfood Manufactured Goods with Other Industrialized Countries*

Country	1970	1987
United States	45.3	51.0
Canada	44.8	55.7
Japan	23.6	22.2
West Germany	58.9	65.5
France	65.5	72.3
United Kingdom	57.8	68.8

For trade in nonfood manufactured goods (SITC 5 through 8) with other industrialized countries, intra-industry trade has been increasing and is more than half of overall trade for most industrialized countries. The estimates are based on nearly 1,000 different individual industries (the five-digit level of the SITC) and refer to trade among 14 industrialized countries (the 6 shown and 8 other European countries).

Source: Vona (1990).

100 percent). If all trade is between industries, like the trade of wheat for cloth in Chapters 3 and 4, then for each industry either exports (X) or imports (M) is 0. In this extreme case, all trade is interindustry, and the IIT share is 0. On the other hand, if all trade involves matched exports and imports $(X = M)$ for each industry, the IIT share is 1 (or 100 percent). If some trade is net trade and some trade is intra-industry trade, the IIT share will have a value between 0 and 1, with its size indicating the importance of the part that is intra-industry trade.

Figure 6.1 reports information on the importance of intra-industry trade in the trade of nonfood manufactured products among industrialized countries. The estimates are based on dividing this sector into almost 1,000 different industries so that they presumably are not biased by a failure to disaggregate the sector's products into meaningful, narrowly defined industries.[1] For five of the six countries shown, by 1987 IIT was more than half of the country's overall trade in these products with other industrialized countries. Japan is the exception. (Some have blamed Japanese government policies for making Japan different in its dearth of intra-industry trade, but this has not been proved or disproved decisively.) In addition, the importance of intra-industry trade has tended to rise over time. This is true of all the countries shown in Figure 6.1 except Japan.

We also know from other studies that IIT is more prevalent where trade barriers and transport costs are low, such as within free-trade areas like the European Union (formerly the European Community). In Figure 6.1 the IIT shares are

---

[1]In the analysis of intra-industry trade, a well-defined industry would consist of products viewed as close substitutes by consumers and produced using very similar factor intensities. The latter is needed to conform to the definition of an industry stressed in the factor-proportions theory. Although we cannot prove that each of these nearly 1,000 industries meets this definition, it seems unlikely that the industries are too aggregated. If the industry definition is too aggregated, estimates of the IIT share tend to be biased upward because some interindustry trade (measured at the correct level of individual industries) can appear to be intra-industry trade when several industries are incorrectly added up into a single too-broad "industry."

particularly high for the three European countries. Furthermore, IIT is more characteristic of the (high-income) industrialized countries, and IIT shares tend to be lower for the (low-income) developing countries.

Intra-industry trade seems to call for a different kind of analysis from the standard trade models of Chapters 3 and 4. While there are several reasons that we might observe or measure intra-industry trade, the major explanation focuses on the role of **product differentiation**—consumers view the products of an industry as close but not perfect substitutes for each other. If IIT is based on two-way trade in varieties of the same basic product, then growth in IIT over time and higher IIT for higher-income countries can be understood partly from the demand side. Income growth shifts demand toward luxuries, and product variety is a luxury. The higher the incomes of consumers, the more consumers can seek variety in the products that they buy. Thus, affluent people vary their choices of wines, beers, automobiles, music, clothing, travel experiences, and so on. Some varieties will be imported, while the varieties produced in the country can be exported to consumers in other countries. IIT results.

Yet, demand effects cannot be the whole story. Why are products produced in only a limited number of varieties, rather than in the nearly infinite number of varieties that would be appropriate to match precisely the tastes of each individual consumer in the world? That is, why are differentiated products generally not produced to be fully customized to the specific demand of each individual? Something on the supply side limits the actual number of varieties offered on the market. Full customization (with each variety produced at a small individual scale) would be too costly. Scale economies in some aspect of production (or distribution) encourage larger production for each variety. Thus, scale economies limit the number of different varieties offered into the market.

Global Industries Dominated by a Few Large Firms

One major set of facts about modern trade that may require theory beyond comparative advantage is the substantial trade among industrialized countries, much of which involves exchanges of very similar products (intra-industry trade). The second major set of facts about modern trade that challenges the standard theory involves a departure from the assumption of highly competitive international markets.

Some important industries in the world are dominated by a few large firms. Production of commercial aircraft is dominated by two firms: Boeing and Airbus. Production of microprocessors is dominated by Intel and Motorola. In such industries as steel, five firms account for half or more of world sales.

Analysis of these industries using our standard model may not be appropriate. The assumption of perfect competition may not be suitable; rather, these industries are global oligopolies. In the latter part of this chapter we will discuss some aspects of international competition in this type of industry. One key departure from the standard theory is the importance of scale economies in the production activities of the firm. Exploiting substantial scale economies is an explanation of why a few firms come to dominate some industries.

Economies of Scale

Our standard theory of international trade assumed constant returns to scale for each firm. The major alternative theories of international trade use the existence of economies of scale as a major departure. The discussion of the basis for intra-industry trade and the discussion of global oligopolies both suggested a key role for scale economies. **Economies of scale** or increasing returns to scale exist if increasing expenditures on all inputs (with input prices constant) increase the output quantity by a larger percentage so that the average cost of producing each unit of output declines. For instance, economies of scale exist if doubling all input amounts (labor, capital, and so forth) more than doubles output. Economies of scale are often not easy to measure precisely, but they appear to be of some importance in many industries.

In discussing scale economies, several distinctions are important. First, scale economies can be internal to each firm, or they can be external to the individual firm. Scale economies are **internal** if the expansion of the size of the firm itself is the basis for the decline in its average cost. Larger firms may be able to reduce average cost through greater use of specialization by their workers, use of more specialized machines, or the spreading of fixed costs, such as research and development or production set-up costs, over more units of output.

Scale economies **external** to the individual firm relate to the size of the entire industry within a specific geographic area. The average cost of the typical firm declines as the output of the industry within this area is larger. External scale economies can arise if concentrating the industry geographically gives rise to better input markets, including specialized services for the industry or specialized kinds of labor required by the industry. External economies can also result as new knowledge about product and production technology diffuses quickly among firms in the area, through direct contacts among the firms or as skilled labor transfers from firm to firm. External scale economies appear to explain the clustering of some industries—high technology semiconductor, computer, and related producers in Silicon Valley, banking and finance in New York City, stylish clothing, shoes, and accessories in Italy, or watches in Switzerland. We will discuss the relationship of external scale economies to international trade in the last section of this chapter.

A second major distinction is the size or extent of scale economies, especially for economies that are internal to the firm. How much does average cost decline as output expands? How large must a firm be to exploit all (or most) economies of scale? The answers to these questions matter a lot for the type of structure that arises on the seller side of the market.

If scale economies are modest or moderate, then there is room in the industry for a large number of firms. If, in addition, products are differentiated, then we have a mild form of imperfect competition called **monopolistic competition,** a type of market structure in which a large number of firms compete vigorously with each other in producing and selling varieties of the basic product. Because each firm's product is somewhat different, each firm has some control over the price that it charges for its product. This contrasts with the perfectly competitive market structure used in standard trade theory. With perfect competition, each of the many small firms takes the market price as given and believes that it has no direct control or influence on this market price.

If scale economies are substantial over a large range of output, then it is likely that a few firms will grow to be large in order to reap the scale economies. If a few large firms dominate the global industry, perhaps because of substantial scale economies, then we have an **oligopoly.** The large firms in an oligopoly know that they can control or influence prices. A key issue in an oligopoly is how actively these large firms compete. If they do not compete too aggressively, then it is possible for the firms to earn economic (or pure) profit, profit greater than the normal return to invested capital. In the extreme, the industry could be a global **monopoly,** in which one firm dominates the world industry.

Monopolistic Competition and Trade

International trade with product differentiation and monopolistic competition has been analyzed in the past two decades by Paul Krugman, Elhanan Helpman, and others. To set the stage for this type of analysis, we turn first to monopolistic competition within a closed national economy, using a model pioneered by Edward Chamberlin in the 1930s. As the hybrid name suggests, monopolistic competition is somewhat like monopoly and somewhat like competition. It is like monopoly in that the individual firm has some control over the price that it charges, because it produces a unique differentiated good that consumers consider to be somewhat different from the varieties offered by other firms in the industry. The firm faces a downward-sloping demand curve for its product. It is like competition in that the entry and exit of firms eventually push each firm toward zero pure profit. Although some scale economies exist that are internal to the firm, they are moderate so entry is fairly easy and a large number of firms compete in the overall market. The firm's product competes so closely with the other varieties that the firm cannot extract pure profits above all costs, at least not for very long.

Figure 6.2 imagines a firm, say, Honda, facing monopolistic competition in Japan's national market for compact cars. Like a monopolist, Honda bases its profit-maximizing decision on its marginal revenue curve (MR_1) because it is aware that expanding its own production and sales requires lowering its price, which eats into its total revenue. It will only expand its production out to a point where the marginal revenue it gets from extra cars, taking the price cutting into account, just covers the marginal cost of making and selling them. That point, where profits are maximized, is the output of 4 million cars a year, where marginal revenue equals marginal cost at point C. To get that many cars sold, it charges "what the traffic will bear," the price of 1.9 million yen dictated by the demand curve at point A.

So far our description of Honda's situation sounds like the pure monopoly case from a basic course in microeconomics. Honda could indeed be a pure

FIGURE 6.2

A Monopolistic-Competitive Firm in a Market Before Trade Opens

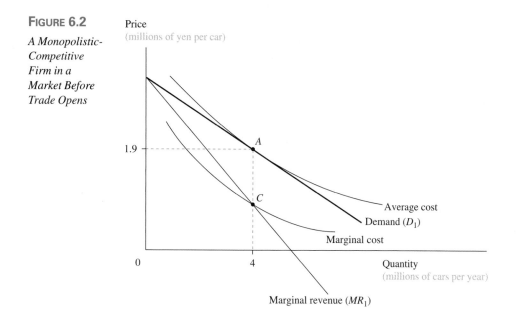

Price (millions of yen per car)

1.9

A

C

Average cost

Demand (D_1)

Marginal cost

0   4   Quantity (millions of cars per year)

Marginal revenue (MR_1)

monopolist for a while, after first entering a market where its unique product had some advantages. After a while, though, there will be indirect competition from competing cars even if they are not identical to Honda's compact car. Honda may continue to find its maximum profits at optimal points like C, but eventually the entry of new firms into the compact auto industry will drive Honda's pure profits down to zero. Figure 6.2 therefore shows an equilibrium in which entry, or even just the threat of entry, by new competing firms has pushed Honda's demand curve down so that it just touches the average cost curve. At point A, with output at 4 million cars per year, price just equals average cost, leaving the firm with no pure profits.[2] Point A's equilibrium is on the downward slope of the average cost curve, because auto production benefits from some economies scale.

Opening to Trade

If this closed national market for automobiles is now opened to trade, two things will happen. First, Honda (and other Japanese producers) can now export to consumers in foreign markets that prefer the Japanese car models. Second, Honda (and other Japanese producers) will face some additional competition from

---

[2]One might wonder how we know that the equilibrium at point A (price = average cost) occurs at exactly the same output as the optimization at point C (marginal revenue = marginal cost), as drawn in Figure 6.2. One can use differential calculus to prove that both outputs must be the same. At point A we know not only that price equals average cost, but also that the demand curve and the average cost curve are tangent to each other. These two pieces of information are enough to prove that marginal cost must equal marginal revenue at that same output.

imports of car models produced by foreign firms like Volkswagen. In the short run after trade is opened, Honda may earn some pure profits if foreign demand is large, or it may suffer some economic losses if the import competition is severe. Honda and other firms in the world industry must make adjustments. Some firms in the industry may exit, or new firms may enter. When the transition to a new long-run equilibrium is complete, Honda (assuming it does not exit) will again find its price just equal to its average cost level, but the situation has probably changed somewhat. Figure 6.3 shows the initial equilibrium before trade was opened at point *A* (the same point *A* as in Figure 6.2). It also shows final equilibrium at point *B,* after trade is opened and further competitive adjustments occur. The final demand curve facing Honda (home plus foreign demand) is D_2. We presume that demand in this large world market, with more competitors offering more different models, is more elastic than the initial home-only demand, resulting in a flatter D_2 demand curve. The net result of the opening of trade is that Honda's output is greater and its price is lower.

So far we have focused on a single firm (Honda) selling in the market. We can also picture the entire market. Figure 6.4 shows what is happening for the overall market. It resembles a supply-and-demand diagram, but the interpretation is a bit different. The price curve *P* shows the relationship between the number of varieties (or different models) available in the market and the price that a firm can charge for its variety. As the number of varieties increases, the price decreases, because the demand for each variety becomes more elastic (the demand curve facing each firm becomes flatter). The unit cost curve *UC* shows the relationship between the unit (or average) cost level for each variety and the number of varieties produced. Given the size of the market, unit cost increases as the number of varieties increases, because the production level for each variety declines as more varieties crowd into the market. (The market *UC* curve is different from the individual firm's *AC* curve.

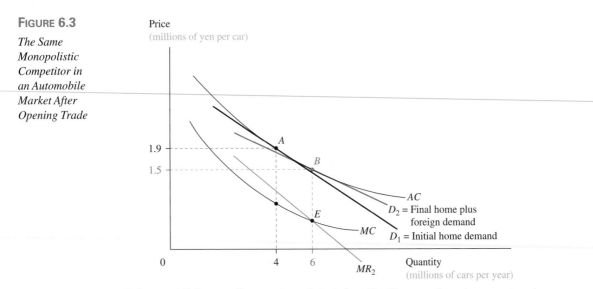

FIGURE 6.3

The Same Monopolistic Competitor in an Automobile Market After Opening Trade

Under monopolistic competition, opening trade leads firms like this one to a lower home-country price.

FIGURE 6.4

The Automobile Market, with No Trade and with Free Trade

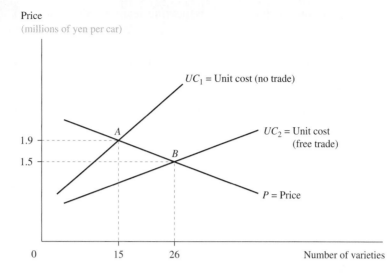

Under monopolistic competition, opening trade leads to a lower price and larger number of varieties available to consumers.

The UC curve keeps track of the entire market by focusing on the number of varieties, and using this to infer the cost level achieved by each individual firm.)

The equilibrium for the overall market is at the intersection of the two curves. We can see this by considering what happens if the number of varieties is different from that shown by the intersection. If the number of varieties is less, then price would be above average cost, and firms earn supernormal profits, so new firms enter the market offering new varieties. If the number of varieties instead is greater, then firms earn losses and some varieties disappear (exit) from the market.

With no trade, the size of the market is limited to the domestic market, and the unit cost curve is UC_1. The market equilibrium is at point A, with 15 different models (Honda Civic, Toyota Corolla, and so forth) produced and offered for sale in the national market, each at a price of 1.9 million yen. When international trade in this type of product becomes possible, the size of the market increases (to the entire world market). As the size of the market increases, the unit cost curve shifts down to UC_2. With a larger market, more varieties can be produced with no cost penalty. (The price curve does not shift, because it does not depend on the size of the market.) With free trade, the equilibrium shifts to point B. The price of a compact is competed down to 1.5 million yen, and 26 different models will be offered for sale to consumers. Some of these 26 models will be produced domestically, and some will be imported. Some of the domestic production will be exported to foreign consumers.

Basis for Trade

What is the basis for Honda (and other Japanese producers) to export automobiles? At first glance, it appears to be scale economies. But the downward-sloping average cost (AC) curve presumably is not special to Honda. Internal scale economies stem from engineering realities common to all auto producers. Other firms, including non-Japanese producers, have similar downward-sloping average cost curves, so there may be no comparative advantage.

Rather, the basis for exporting is the production of a unique model demanded by some consumers in foreign markets. Product differentiation is also the basis for some amount of auto imports into Japan. The result is intra-industry trade. The role of scale economies is that firms in each country produce only a limited number of models (or varieties) of the basic product. These models can be exported, but the country also imports other models (or varieties) from foreign producers. Economies of scale encourage production specialization for different varieties within the same industry. Intra-industry trade in differentiated products can be large, even between countries that are similar in their general production capabilities.

In addition to intra-industry trade, this industry may also have some net trade—that is, Japan may be either a net exporter or a net importer of automobiles. The basis for the net trade can be comparative advantage. For instance, if autos are capital-intensive and Japan is capital-abundant, then Japan will tend to be a net exporter of autos. The Heckscher–Ohlin theory can explain the part of trade that is net trade, even though there is also substantial intra-industry trade.

Once we recognize product differentiation and the competitive marketing activities that go with it (for instance, styling, advertising, and service), net trade in an industry's products can also reflect other differences between countries and their firms. Net trade in a product can be the result of differences in international marketing capabilities. Or, it can reflect shifting consumer tastes given the history of choices of which specific varieties are produced by each country. For instance, Japanese firms focused on smaller car models, and they benefited from a consumer shift toward smaller cars in the United States following the oil price shocks of the 1970s. Japanese auto producers also marketed their cars skillfully and developed a reputation for high quality at reasonable prices. Japan developed large net exports in automobile trade with the United States during the 1970s and 1980s. Some of this was the result of comparative cost advantages, but another part was the result of focusing on smaller cars at the right time and skillful marketing.

Gains from Trade

Product differentiation, monopolistic competition, and intra-industry trade add major insights into the national gains from trade and the effects of trade on the well-being or welfare of different groups in the country. A major additional source of national gains from trade is the increase in varieties of products that become available to consumers through imports, when the country opens to trade. For instance, the economic well-being of consumers increases when they can choose to purchase an automobile not only from the domestic models such as Honda but also from imported foreign models such as Volkswagen, because some may prefer the Volkswagen. Another source of gains from trade arises from the international competition that can lower the prices of domestic varieties, as shown in Figure 6.4, bringing additional gains to home consumers.

These national gains from trade accrue to consumers generally. They can be added to trade's other effects on the well-being or welfare of different groups within the country. Two major insights result. First, the opening (or expansion) of trade has little impact on the domestic distribution of factor income if the (additional) trade is intra-industry. Because extra exports occur as imports take part of the domestic market, the total output of the domestic industry is not changed much. There is little of the interindustry shifts in production that put pressures on factor prices. In this case, all groups can gain from the (additional) trade because of gains from additional product variety. Second, gains from greater variety can offset any losses in factor income resulting from interindustry shifts in production that do occur. Groups that appear to lose real income as a result of Stolper–Samuelson effects will not lose as much; and they could actually believe that their well-being is enhanced overall if they value the access to greater product variety that trade brings.

A good example of these types of effects is the expansion of trade in manufactured goods within Western Europe during the past four decades, much of it intra-industry trade. This expansion of trade has led to few political complaints, both because there has been little pressure for redistribution of factor income domestically as this trade has expanded, and because Europeans generally have gained from access to a greater variety of products.

Oligopoly and International Trade

Oligopoly exists when a few firms supply much of the market. Global oligopoly could occur, for instance, if substantial scale economies internal to each firm give large firms a cost advantage over any smaller rival firms.

Each large firm in an oligopoly knows that it is competing with a few other large firms. It knows that any action that it takes (such as lowering its price, increasing its advertising, or introducing a new product) is likely to provoke reactions from its rivals. Modeling this interdependence among oligopoly firms as a game has led to insights. Consider a simple example that illustrates this kind of application of game theory. Picture competition between two dominant large firms as a choice of competition strategy by each. Each firm can choose either to compete aggressively (for instance, setting low prices or using a lot of advertising) or to restrain its competition (setting higher prices or using advertising moderately). The outcome of the game depends on which strategy each firm chooses. The best outcome for both firms together is usually for both to restrain their competition, in which case they both earn substantial economic profits. However, if they cannot cooperate with each other, then the play of the game may result in both competing aggressively. If one firm decides to restrain its competition, then the other often can earn even higher profits by competing aggressively to gain a large market share. In this case the first firm may well suffer losses rather than earn profits. Both know that the other is likely to act in this way, so neither is willing to restrain its competition—both compete aggressively and earn low profits. They are caught in what is called a *prisoners' dilemma*. The solution, of course, is for the two firms to find some way to cooperate in restraining their competition so that they both earn substantial profits (rather than both earning low profits).

The cooperation may be by formal agreement (although this is illegal in the United States and many other countries). The cooperation may be tacit or implicit, based on recognition of mutual interests and patterns of behavior established over time.

Unfortunately, there is no one "best" way for firms to play more complex, dynamic oligopoly games that are more realistic than this simple two-firm game, so the application of game theory to oligopoly has its limits. Nonetheless, game theory does highlight that cooperating with rivals is possible (though not assured) in an oligopoly. Firms in an oligopoly can earn economic profits, and these can be substantial if competition is restrained.

We offer several observations in lieu of a full theory of oligopoly and trade. If substantial scale economies exist, production tends to be concentrated in a few countries in order to take advantage of the scale economies. These countries will then tend to be net exporters of the product, while other countries are importers.

How does this trade pattern get established? History matters. Firms initially chose these production locations for a number of reasons. One prominent reason presumably was that comparative advantage indicated low-cost production with access to required factor inputs at these locations. However, even if the location initially was consistent with comparative advantage, this can change over time. Once the production locations are chosen and high-volume production achieves scale economies in these locations, the pattern of production and trade can persist even if other countries could potentially produce the good more cheaply. Production may not develop at a potentially lower-cost location because production volume there must be high enough to achieve the available scale economies. A smaller scale of production would result in higher average cost that can cancel out any other cost advantages to the location. Achieving high production volume in the new location means that the new producer must gain a large share of the market. This may not be possible without an extended period of losses for the entrant because (1) the increase in supply lowers prices or (2) previously established firms may fight the entrant using other competitive reactions. Thus, production in this lower-cost location may fail to develop. This problem for the potential entrant firm and country is an example of an infant-industry situation, which we will discuss further in Chapter 9.

Does it matter in which countries the production is located (or, perhaps more precisely, which countries own the oligopoly firms)? The answer is that it can matter to national well-being or welfare, especially if the oligopoly firms earn economic (or pure) profit on their export sales. (This same point applies to the national location or ownership of a global monopoly.) These pure profits arise from the ability to charge high export prices to foreign buyers, thus enhancing the country's terms of trade. (The pure profits can also be seen simply as an addition to national income that comes from foreign buyers.)

Putting all of this together, we see that the current pattern of national locations for a global oligopoly is somewhat arbitrary, and the small number of countries that have the industry's production obtain additional gains from trade if the firms earn pure profits on their exports. The national gain from having high-profit oligopoly firms in a country is the basis for national governments to use various policies to influence the location decisions (or the global market shares) of the oligopoly firms in favor of domestic production. These issues are taken up further in the discussion of strategic trade policy in Chapter 10.

External Scale Economies and Trade

A final case worth examining is an industry that benefits from substantial external scale economies. External economies exist when the expansion of the entire industry's production within a geographic area lowers the average cost in the long run for each firm in the industry in the area. If there are no or only modest internal scale economies, then a large number of firms can exist in the industry. We have a case in which substantial (external) scale economies coexist with a (perfectly) competitive industry.

If an expansion of an industry lowers costs for each firm, then new export opportunities (or any other source of demand growth) can have a dramatic effect. Figure 6.5 imagines that a national semiconductor industry is competitive, but characterized by external economies of scale. There is an initial equilibrium at point *A,* with many firms competing to sell 40 million units at $19 a unit. Here the usual short-run supply and demand curves (S_1 and D_1) intersect in the usual way. What is new in the diagram is the coexistence of the upward-sloping supply curve S_1 with the downward-sloping long-run average cost curve. The upward-sloping supply curve is the sum of small individual firms' views of the market. Each firm

FIGURE 6.5

External Economies Magnify an Expansion in a Competitive Industry

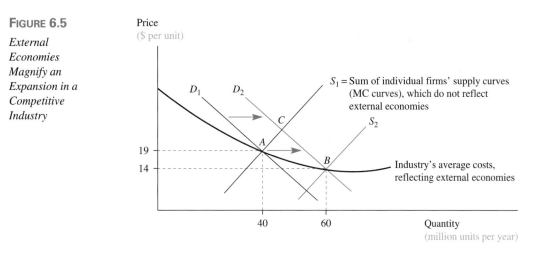

Results:
- In industries that can reap external economies (e.g., knowledge spillovers from firm to firm), a rise in demand triggers a great expansion of supply and lowers costs and price.
- Therefore expanding trade brings gains to all consumers (home-country and foreign alike) as well as to the exporting producers.
- Corollary: Among nations having the same initial factor endowments, cost curves, and demand curves, whichever nation moved first to capture its export market would gain a cost advantage in this product.

operates at given levels of industry production, which it cannot affect very much. It reacts to a change in price according to its own upward-sloping supply curve, and the sum of these supply curves is shown as S_1.

The industry's downward-sloping average cost curve comes into play when demand shifts. To bring out points about international trade, let us imagine that opening up a new export market shifts demand from D_1 to D_2. Each firm would respond to the stronger demand by raising output. If each firm were acting alone and affected only itself, the extra demand would push us up the supply curve S_1 to a point like C. Yet the new export business raises the whole industry's output and employment, bringing additional external economies. For instance, there could be more development and exchange of useful information, which raises productivity and cuts costs throughout the industry. This means, in effect, a sustained rightward movement of the industry supply curve. To portray the cost-cutting more conveniently than with multiple shifts of the supply curve, Figure 6.5 shows the average cost curve reflecting external economies, a curve that could in principle be measured from economic behavior. The external economies lead to a decline in average cost as industry output expands. As Figure 6.5 is drawn, we imagine that demand and supply expansion catch up with each other at point B, a new equilibrium.

What are the welfare effects of the opening of trade for an industry with external economies? Producers of the product in an exporting country tend to gain producer surplus as a result of the expansion of industry output, although the decline in price will mitigate the gain. Producers in importing countries lose producer surplus. Consumers in the importing countries gain consumer surplus as price declines and their consumption increases. Consumers in the exporting country also gain consumer surplus as price declines and consumption quantity increases. Here is a definite contrast to the standard case (e.g., Figure 2.4), where buyers suffer from price rises on goods that become exportable with the opening of trade.

What explains the pattern of trade that emerges in industries subject to external scale economies? Many of the issues are similar to those raised with respect to substantial internal scale economies. Production tends to be concentrated in a small number of locations. If trade is opened, some locations, such as that shown in Figure 6.5, will expand and export, while other nations shrink or cease production and rely on imports. It is not easy to predict which locations will expand and which will shrink or cease production. The size of the domestic market with no trade may be important if the larger domestic market permits domestic firms to be low-cost producers when trade is opened. Historical luck or a push from government policy may be important if the first countries to capture export markets become the low-cost producers. The outcome is analogous to the production of pearls. Which oysters produce pearls depends on luck or outside human intervention. An oyster gets its pearl from the accidental deposit of a grain of sand or from a human's introducing a grain of sand to cultivate a pearl. The external economies case is one in which a lasting production advantage is acquired by luck or policy even if there are no differences in nations' initial comparative advantages. The production locations and pattern of trade tend to persist even if other locations are potentially lower-cost. Other locations cannot easily overcome the scale advantages of established locations. These other locations may view this as an infant-industry problem.

Summary: How Does Trade Really Work?

This chapter examined several theories that have broadened our answers to the four major questions about trade. The alternative theories focus on **product differentiation** and monopolistic competition, substantial **internal scale economies** and global oligopoly, and **external scale economies.**

According to the standard trade theory emphasizing comparative advantage, the similarity of industrialized countries in factor endowments and technological capabilities suggests little reason for trade among them. Yet we observe the opposite. Trade among industrialized countries represents about half of world trade. Furthermore, an increasing share of world trade consists of **intra-industry trade (IIT),** two-way trade within industry categories. A challenge for trade theory is to explain (1) why we have so much IIT and (2) whether the standard model's conclusions about the gains from trade and the effects of trade still hold.

Much IIT involves trade in differentiated products—exports and imports of different varieties of the same basic product. Part of the reason that we have rising intra-industry trade is that product variety is a luxury in a prospering world. Rising per capita incomes cause an even faster rise in demand for luxuries. Yet, by itself increasing demand does not explain intra-industry trade. To put intra-industry trade in proper perspective, we need to consider features on the producers' side of the same expanding markets.

Moderate internal economies of scale and **monopolistic competition** are important to understanding intra-industry trade. Firms competing using differentiated products are able to export to some consumers in foreign markets even as they face competition from imports of varieties produced by foreign firms. Net trade in these differentiated products may still be based on comparative advantage.

Another major fact is that some industries are dominated by a few large firms. Global **oligopoly** can arise when there are substantial scale economies internal to each firm. These large firms choose production locations to maximize their profits, and comparative advantages are likely to be prominent in such location decisions. Over time, conditions may change, but the production locations and the trade pattern do not necessarily change, because of the scale advantages of the established locations.

Some other industries, while competitively populated by a large number of firms, also tend to concentrate in a few production locations because of scale economies that are external to the individual firm and instead depend on the size of the entire industry in the location. It can be difficult to predict or explain which production locations prosper—home market size, history, luck, and government policy may affect which country locations capitalize on the external economies.

Thinking about imperfect competition and economies of scale also adds to our understanding of the gains from trade and the effects of trade on different groups. It does not contradict the main conclusions of the standard competitive-market analysis of Chapters 2 through 5. Rather, it broadens the set of conditions under which we see gains from trade, with some changes in how any gains or losses are distributed among the groups. Figure 6.6 summarizes gains and losses for three kinds of trade: the standard competitive trade of Chapters 2 through 5 plus two of the three kinds of trade analyzed in this chapter. Oligopoly is not included because we do not have a single generally accepted model.

Relative to standard competitive trade, both trade based on monopolistic competition and trade based on external economies provide additional benefits to consumers, especially consumers of exportable products. In the case of monopolistic competition, the additional gains come from (1) access to greater product variety and (2) a tendency for additional competition to lower product prices. In the case of external economies, gains to consumers in the exporting country arise from the decline in the price for the good as the local industry expands and achieves greater external economies so that cost and price decline. Relative to standard competitive trade, trade based on monopolistic competition has less of an impact on producing firms and factor incomes, because firms under pressure from import competition also have the opportunity to export into foreign markets.

Although not portrayed fully in Figure 6.6, global oligopoly (or monopoly) also has implications for well-being or welfare. Trade allows firms to concentrate production in a few locations, achieving scale economies that lower costs and can reduce prices charged to consumers. Furthermore, a global oligopolist (or monopolist) firm can earn pure profits on its export sales. In comparison with standard competitive trade, these pure profits on exports add to both the gains to export producers and the national gains from trade for the exporting country.

Where does the theory of trade patterns stand?

The standard model of Chapters 2 through 5, complete with both demand and supply

sides, has the virtue of breadth. We can use it to explain most trade patterns as long as we equip it with a long list of explanatory variables. Its weakness lies in that same breadth, that same ability to expand to explain any case: The problem is that we *need* to equip it with a long list of explanatory variables to explain all the real-world trade patterns. That gets cumbersome. For example, to explain why Toyota Corporation developed an advantage in exporting automobiles to the whole world, we have to start with the personal entrepreneurial vision of Eishi Toyota and call it a "factor endowment" of Toyota Corporation and of Japan. This is a valid way to use our standard model in explaining Toyota's success, but it does not give us any predictive power, any ability to forecast.

The Heckscher–Ohlin variant of the standard model makes the stronger assertion that the way to explain who exports what to whom is to look at factor proportions alone, concentrating on a few main factors of production. That has the scientific virtue of giving more testable and falsifiable predictions than the broadest standard model (of which it is a special case). But, as we saw in Chapter 4, the tests of the Heckscher–Ohlin model give it only a

FIGURE 6.6   *Summary of Gains and Losses from Opening Up Trade in Three Cases*

	Kind of Trade		
Group	*Standard Competition (Chapters 2–5)*	*Monopolistic Competition (IIT)* (This Chapter)*	*External Economies (This Chapter)*
Exporting country	Gain	Gain	Gain
Export producers	Gain	*	Gain
Export consumers	Lose	Gain	Gain
Importing country	Gain	Gain	Gain
Import-competing producers	Lose	*	Lose
Import consumers	Gain	Gain	Gain
Whole world	Gain	Gain	Gain

* In monopolistic competition that results in intra-industry trade (IIT), producers are both exporters and import-competing at the same time. If trade is mostly or completely IIT, then the effects on producers as a group tend to be small.

Note: The gains and losses to producers in all cases refer to changes in producer surplus in the short run. In the long run, these gains and losses shift to the factors most closely tied to the export or import-competing industries (according to the Stolper–Samuelson theorem).

middling grade. It predicts the correct direction of trade better than a coin flip, but only modestly better.

Our ability to predict (explain) trade patterns is improved somewhat if we add technology differences and models based on scale economies and imperfect competition. Technology differences can be a basis for comparative advantage. In the modern world, most new technology is developed through research and development (R&D). The location of R&D is largely determined by factor endowments. The location of the initial production of products using the new technologies is somewhat linked to the location of the R&D, but the technology is also transferred to or diffuses to other countries, often rapidly.

The monopolistic competition model suggests that product differentiation can be a basis for successful exporting, although it does not predict which specific varieties of a differentiated product will be produced by which countries. The models based on substantial scale economies (internal or external) indicate that production tends to be concentrated at a small number of locations, but they do not precisely identify which specific countries will be the production locations. History, luck, and perhaps early government policy can have a major impact on the actual production locations.

The most promising directions for improving the predictive power of our trade theories lie in (1) developing a better theory of how new technologies, and new knowledge in general, arise and (2) giving the theory a historical dynamic so we can be more systematic about how the past determines current production locations.

Suggested Reading

Intra-industry trade is measured and interpreted in Grubel and Lloyd (1975), Tharakan (1983), Greenaway and Tharakan (1986), Greenaway and Milner (1988), and Vona (1990 and 1991).

The economies-of-scale and imperfect-competition models of trade were launched independently by Dixit and Norman (1980),

Krugman (1979), and Lancaster (1980). A readable summary of this work is found in Krugman (1983); a more technical survey appears in Helpman (1990). Technical presentations of both monopolistic competition and global oligopoly models of trade are in Helpman and Krugman (1985).

Questions and Problems

✦1. "According to the Heckscher–Ohlin theory, countries should engage in a lot of intra-industry trade." Do you agree or disagree? Why?

2. Economies of scale are important in markets that are not perfectly competitive. What is the key role of economies of scale in the analysis of markets that are monopolistically competitive? What is the key role in oligopoly?

✦3. "Once we recognize that product differentiation is the basis for much international trade,

there are likely to be more winners and fewer losers in a country when the country shifts from no trade to free trade." There may be several reasons why this statement is true. What are the reasons? Explain each briefly.

4. A country is the only production site in the world for hyperhoney infinite pasta, a wonderful product produced using a delicate, highly perishable extract obtainable from some trees that grow only in this country. Furthermore, there is no domestic demand for

this product in the country, so all production will be exported. The country's government has the choice of forming the pasta-producing industry either as a monopoly or as a large number of small pasta producers that will act as perfect competitors. What is your advice to the country's government about which market structure to choose for the pasta industry?

✦5. Production of a good is characterized by external economies of scale. Currently there is no trade in the product, and the product is produced in two countries. If trade is opened in this product, all production will be driven to occur in only one country.

   a. With free trade, why would production only occur in one country?

   b. Does opening trade bring gains to both countries? Explain.

6. The world market for large passenger jet airplanes is an oligopoly dominated by two firms: Boeing in the United States and Airbus in Europe.

   a. Explain why the market equilibrium might involve either a low price for airplanes or a high price for airplanes.

   b. From the perspective of the well-being or welfare of the United States (or Europe), why might a high-price equilibrium be desirable?

   c. What price outcome is desirable for Japan or Brazil? Why?

   d. If the outcome is the high-price equilibrium, does Japan or Brazil still gain from importing airplanes? Explain.

✦7. A monopolistically competitive industry exists in both Pugelovia and the rest of the world, but there has been no trade in this type of product. Trade in this type of product is now opened.

   a. Explain how opening trade affects domestic consumers of this type of product in Pugelovia.

   b. Explain how opening trade affects domestic producers of this type of product in Pugelovia.

8. Measurement of intra-industry trade can be understood more firmly with a numerical example. In your answer to this question, use the data on U.S. and Japanese exports and imports shown in Figure 4.4 and question 10 from Chapter 4. Use only the data on the eight manufactured products (chemicals, iron and steel, computers, motor vehicles, aircraft, clothing, shoes, and precision instruments). Use zero for any value called *small*.

   a. What is the intra-industry trade share for these eight products for the United States?

   b. What is the intra-industry trade share for these eight products for Japan?

   c. For these eight products, which country engages in relatively more intra-industry trade?

✦9. For major product categories, North–South trade between the industrial countries and the rest of the world in 1994 looked something like this (in billions of dollars):

Product Category	Exports (X) by the Industrial Countries to the Rest of the World	Imports (M) into the Industrial Countries from the Rest of the World
Food, beverages, and tobacco	$ 60	$ 74
Petroleum and other fuels	18	130
Chemicals	84	25
Machinery and transport equipment	389	194
Clothing and footwear	10	78

   a. Calculate the intra-industry trade share for each individual product category. Calculate the net trade for each product category as a percentage of total trade $(X + M)$ in the category.

b. Which product categories have the highest intra-industry trade share. Why might this be?

c. What might explain the pattern of net trade (net exports or net imports) across the categories that show substantial net trade as a percentage of total trade?

10. You are an adviser to the Indian government. Until now, government policy in India has been to severely limit imports into India, resulting also in a low level of Indian exports. The government is considering a policy shift to much freer trade.

a. What are the three strongest arguments that you can offer to the Indian government about why the policy shift to freer trade is desirable for India?

b. Which groups in India will be the supporters of the policy shift toward freer trade? Which groups will be the opponents?

PART II

Trade Policy

CHAPTER 7

The Basic Analysis of a Tariff

Most economists favor letting nations trade freely, with few tariffs or other barriers to trade. Indeed, economists have tended to be even more critical of trade barriers than have other groups in society, even though economists have taken great care to list the exceptional cases in which they feel trade barriers can be justified. Such agreement among economists is rare. Why should they agree on this one issue?

The striking consensus in favor of free trade is based primarily on a body of economic analysis demonstrating that there are usually net gains from freer trade, both for nations and for the world. Chapter 2 showed, with demand and supply curves, that free trade brings greater aggregate well-being than no trade. The main task of this chapter and the following chapters of Part II is to compare free-trade policies with a wide range of trade barriers, barriers that do not necessarily shut out all international trade. It is mainly on this more detailed analysis of trade policies that economists have based their view that free trade is generally better than partial restrictions on trade, with a list of exceptions. This analysis makes it easier to understand what divides the majority of economists from groups calling for restrictions on trade.

To see what is lost or gained by putting up barriers to international trade, let us take a close look at the effects of the classic kind of trade barrier, a tariff on an imported good. This chapter spells out who is likely to gain and who is likely to lose from a tariff, and explains conditions under which a nation could end up better off from a tariff. Chapters 8 through 10 will extend the basic story told here.

A **tariff,** as the term is used in international trade, is a tax on importing a good or service into a country, usually collected by customs officials at the place of entry. Tariffs come in two main types. A **specific tariff** is stipulated as a money amount per physical unit of import, such as dollars per ton of steel bars, or dollars per eight-cylinder two-door sports car. An **ad valorem** (on the value) tariff is a percentage of the estimated market value of the goods when they reach the importing country. We will not pay much attention to this distinction, because it makes almost no difference to our conclusions.

For the industrialized countries, tariff rates on most products have decreased to relatively low levels in the process of liberalization that began in the 1930s. In 1996, tariff rates averaged 4 to 6 percent on imports into the United States, Canada, the European Union, and Japan. But tariffs on some products are much higher, up to 48 percent in the United States, 28 percent in Canada, 103 percent in the European Union, and 52 percent in Japan. Average tariff rates are higher in most developing countries. For instance, the average tariff rate on imports into Mexico was about 14 percent in 1996, with tariffs ranging up to 260 percent.

A Preview of Conclusions

Our exploration of the pros and cons of a tariff will be detailed enough to warrant listing its main conclusions here at the outset. This chapter and Chapters 8 and 9 will discuss how

- A tariff almost always lowers world well-being.
- A tariff usually lowers the well-being of each nation, including the nation imposing the tariff.
- As a general rule, whatever a tariff can do for the nation, something else can do better.
- There are exceptions to the case for free trade, as we shall see later:
    - *a.* The first exception is the "nationally optimal" tariff discussed near the end of this chapter. When a nation can affect the prices at which it trades with foreigners, it can gain from its own tariff. (The world as a whole loses, however.)
    - *b.* Chapter 9 presents some "second-best" arguments for a tariff: In cases where other incurable distortions exist in the economy, imposing a tariff may be better than doing nothing.
    - *c.* In a narrow range of cases with distortions that are specific to international trade itself, a tariff can be better than any other policy, and not just better than doing nothing.
- A tariff absolutely helps those groups tied closely to the production of import substitutes, even when the tariff is bad for the nation as a whole.

You may wish to review these overall conclusions after we have completed the analysis of import barriers in this and the next two chapters.

The Effect of a Tariff on Producers

Intuition suggests that domestic producers which compete against imports will benefit from a tariff. If the government places a tax on imports of the product, the domestic price of the imported product will rise. Domestic producers can then expand their own production and sales, or raise the price they charge, or both.

The tariff, by taxing imports to make imports less competitive in the domestic market, should make domestic producers better off.

The demand and supply analysis of a tariff agrees with our intuition. It goes beyond intuition, though, by allowing us to calculate just how much a tariff benefits producers.

We begin with a demand–supply view of the U.S. market for bicycles without any tariff. For most of this chapter, we deal with the simple case in which our nation is a competitive "price-taker" in the world markets for the goods we import, taking the world price—the price that we must pay foreign exporters for the product—as given. Economists also call this case of a price-taking country the **small-country case.**

In the free-trade situation shown in Figure 7.1, bicycles are imported freely at the given world price of $300, an equilibrium price determined by competition between foreign bikes and comparable domestic bikes. At this price consumers buy S_0 bikes a year from domestic suppliers and import M_0 bikes a year, buying a total of $D_0 = S_0 + M_0$ bikes. To use illustrative numbers, let's say that consumers buy $D_0 = 1.6$ (million bikes a year), domestic producers make $S_0 = 0.6$, and the remaining $M_0 = 1.0$ are imported.

Recall from Chapter 2 that producer surplus is the amount that producers gain from being able to sell bikes at the going market price. Graphically, producer surplus is the area above the supply curve and below the market price line. Let's review why this is producer surplus.

The supply curve tells us, for each possible quantity supplied, the lowest price that will draw out another bike produced and supplied. This is true because the supply curve indicates the marginal cost of each additional unit, and a

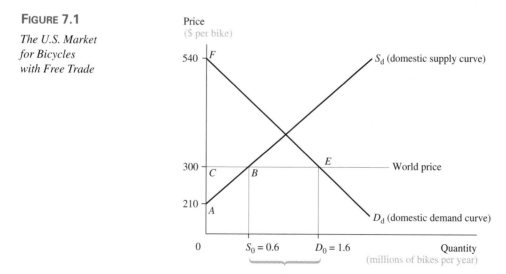

competitive producer will supply an additional unit as long as the price (the extra revenue) covers the marginal (or extra) cost. Thus, according to the supply curve S_d in Figure 7.1, some firm is willing to supply the very first bike for $210 (at point A). This firm receives the market price of $300, bringing a net gain (producer surplus) of $90 on this first unit. Similarly, as we go up the supply curve from point A toward point B, we find that the vertical distance between the supply curve and the price of $300 show the gains that producers are getting on each additional unit. By summing the gain on each unit supplied, we see that producers receive the area of triangle CBA as producer surplus—the amount by which the price exceeds the incremental costs, unit by unit. We might immediately think that this is a measure of profit, and much or all of it could be profit. But it is possible that other resources used in production may also share in the producer surplus. For instance, the expansion of quantity produced could drive up wage rates for the type of labor used in the industry, because the industry increases its demand for this labor.

Now imagine a tariff of 10 percent on imported bikes.[1] Because this is a small country, foreign exporters insist on continuing to receive $300 for each bike they export. So the 10 percent tariff is $30 per bike, *and* this amount is passed on to consumers. The domestic price of imported bikes rises to $330.

When the tariff is imposed, domestic producers can also raise the price that they charge for their bikes. If domestic and imported bikes are perfect (or very close) substitutes, then domestic producers raise their price to $330. When the tariff drives the domestic market price to $330, domestic firms respond by raising their output and sales, as long as the higher price exceeds the marginal cost of supplying the extra units.

Figure 7.2 shows the same bicycle market introduced in Figure 7.1. When the tariff is imposed, domestic producers expand output from S_0 to S_1. At output S_1 their costs of producing each extra bike, shown by the supply curve, rise as high as the tariff-ridden market price of $330. It is not profitable for them to raise their output any higher because doing so would raise their marginal costs above $330, the price they receive when selling bikes in competition with foreign firms in the domestic market.

With the tariff in place, domestic producer surplus is area $g + a$, the area below the new $330 price line and the above domestic supply curve. As a result of the tariff, domestic producer surplus increases by area a, which equals $21 million per year. We can think of this as composed of two pieces. First the rectangular part of area a covering the first 0.6 million bikes reflects the higher price received on units that are supplied even if there is no tariff. Second, the triangle at the right-hand end of area a reflects the additional producer surplus earned on the extra 0.2 million bikes supplied.

---

[1]The U.S. bicycle example is realistic. The Bicycle Manufacturers Association at times has lobbied Congress for higher bicycle tariffs to stem import competition, which have claimed about half of the U.S. market.

FIGURE 7.2

The Effect of a Tariff on Producers

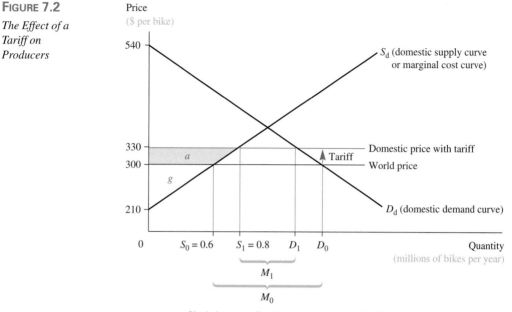

Shaded area a = Producer's gain from tariff = $21 million

The $30 bike tariff gives domestic producers extra surplus on all the bikes they would have produced even without the tariff (an extra $30 × S_0) plus smaller net gains on additional sales [gain equaling $1/2$ × $30 × $(S_1 − S_0)$].

The Effect of a Tariff on Consumers

Intuition also suggests that buyers of a good imported from abroad will be hurt by a tariff. Consumers end up paying a higher price, or buying less of the product, or both. Again, we can use demand and supply analysis to calculate the consumer loss.

First, let's return to the free-trade situation (before the tariff is imposed) shown in Figure 7.1. With free trade domestic consumers buy D_0 bikes at the world price of $300. Recall from Chapter 2 that consumer surplus is the amount that consumers gain from being able to buy bikes at the going market price. Graphically, consumer surplus is the area below the demand curve and above market price line. To see this, recall that the demand curve tells us the highest price that some consumer is willing to pay for each additional bike. Thus, according to the demand curve in Figure 7.1, some consumer is willing to pay $540 for the first bike (at point F). This consumer can buy the bike at the market price of $300, so the consumer receives a net gain (consumer surplus) of $240 on that first unit. As we go down the demand curve from point F to point E, we find that the vertical distances between the demand curve and the world price of $300 show us the bargains that these consumers are getting, by paying less for bikes than the maximum amount they would have been willing to pay. So summing up the entire area (*FEC*) between the demand curve and the $300 price line tells us the amount of consumer surplus, the amount by which what consumers would have been willing to pay exceeds what they actually pay for the bikes.

Now the government imposes a tariff of 10 percent on imported bikes. Figure 7.3 shows the consumers' view of the bicycle market with the tariff. The tariff raises the price that consumers must pay for bikes (both imported and domestically produced) to $330.

By raising the price to $330, the tariff forces some consumers to give up an extra $30 per bike to get the same $D_1 = 1.4$ million bikes they would rather have bought at $300, while it makes other consumers decide that a bike is not worth $330 to them, so the quantity demanded drops back from D_0 to D_1. The net loss to consumers from the tariff is the total shaded area, $a + b + c + d$. This is the amount that consumers lose by having their consumer surplus from bicycle purchases cut from triangle *FEC* to triangle *FGH*. In our numerical example, it equals $45 million a year (the rectangular area $a + b + c$ plus the triangular area d).

What domestic consumers lose from the tariff (here $45 million) is larger than what domestic producers gain ($21 million). The reason is straightforward: Producers gain the price markup on only the domestic output, while consumers are forced to pay the same price markup on both domestic output and imports. Figures 7.2 and 7.3 bring this out clearly for the bicycle example. The tariff

FIGURE 7.3

*The Effect of a
Tariff on
Consumers*

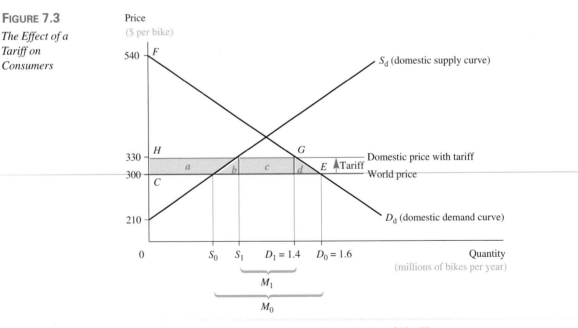

Shaded area = Cost of the tariff to consumers = $45 million

An import tariff of $30 raises the price consumers must pay for either imported or domestic bikes. This costs them the full $30 on every bike they continue to buy (D_1) plus smaller net enjoyment (area d) on bikes they would have bought at the lower tariff-free price but will not buy at the higher price including the tariff.

brought bicycle producers only area a in gains, but cost consumers this same area a plus areas $b + c + d$. As far as the effects on bicycle consumers and bicycle producers alone are concerned, the tariff is definitely a net loss.

The Tariff as Government Revenue

The effects of a tariff on the well-being of consumers and producers do not exhaust its effects on the importing nation. As long as the tariff is not so high as to prohibit all imports, it also brings revenue to the government. This revenue equals the unit amount of the tariff times the volume of imports with the tariff—area c in Figure 7.3.

The tariff revenue is a definite gain for the nation's government. This gain could take any of several forms. It could become extra government spending on socially worthwhile projects. It could be matched by an equal cut in some other tax, such as the income tax. Or it could just become extra income for greedy government officials. Although what form the tariff takes can certainly matter, the central point is that this revenue accrues to somebody within the country so that it counts as an element of national gain to be weighed in with the consumer losses and producer gains from the tariff. The government's gain equals the tariff of $30 times imports of $M_1 = 0.6$ million, or $18 million a year.[2]

The Net National Loss from a Tariff

By combining the effects of the tariff on consumers, producers, and the government, we can determine the net effect of the tariff on the importing nation as a whole.

The first key step is to impose a social value judgment. How much do you really care about each group's gains or losses? If one group gains and another loses, how big must the gain be to outweigh the other group's loss? To make any overall judgment, you must first decide how to weigh each dollar of effect on each group. That is unavoidable. Indeed, anybody who expresses an opinion on whether a tariff is good or bad necessarily does so on the basis of a personal value judgment about how important each group is.

The basic analysis starts out by using the **one-dollar–one-vote welfare measure:** *Every dollar of gain or loss is just as important as every other dollar of gain or loss, regardless of who the gainers or losers are.* Let's use this welfare yardstick here just as we did in Chapter 2. Later we discuss what difference it would make if we choose to weigh one group's dollar stakes more heavily than those of other groups.

If the one-dollar–one-vote yardstick is applied, then a tariff like the one graphed in Figures 7.2 and 7.3 brings a clear net loss to the importing nation as well as to the world as a whole. This can be seen by studying Figure 7.4 (page 130),

---

[2]We note a possible exception. Part of the tariff may be used up as real resource cost of administering and enforcing the tariff, so that this amount does not represent a national gain.

The Effective Rate of Protection

To gain more understanding of how much protection is given to producers by a country's tariffs, we need to take a closer look at how products are produced. We are interested in how tariffs affect "value added" in an industry. Value added is the amount that is available to make payments to the primary production factors in the industry. That is, value added is the sum of wages paid to labor, the rents paid to landowners, and the profits and other returns to the owners and providers of capital.

In addition to these primary factors, firms also use various kinds of components and material inputs in production. This is more important than it sounds, because it means that many tariffs matter to the industry, not just the tariff on the good it produces. Specifically, firms in a given industry are affected by tariffs on their purchased inputs as well as by the tariff on the product they sell. Firms selling bicycles, for example, would be hurt by tariffs on steel or rubber. This complicates the task of measuring the effect of the whole set of tariffs on an individual industry's firms.

To give these points their due requires a more detailed portrayal of supply–demand interactions in many markets at once. To cut down on the elaborate details, economists have developed a simpler measure that does part of the job. The measure quantifies the effects of the whole tariff structure on one industry's value added per unit of output without trying to estimate how much its output, or other outputs and prices, would change.

> The **effective rate of protection** of an individual industry is defined as the percentage by which the entire set of a nation's trade barriers raises the industry's value added per unit of output.

The effective rate of protection for the industry can be quite different from the percent tariff paid by consumers on its output (the "nominal" rate of protection). This difference is brought out clearly by the example on the facing page.

What are the effects of a 10 percent tariff on bicycle imports and a 5 percent tariff on imports of steel, rubber, and all other material inputs into the bicycle industry? The 10 percent tariff on bicycles by itself raises their price and the value added by the bicycle industry by $30 per bike, as before. The 5 percent tariff on bicycle inputs costs the bicycle industry $11 per bike by raising the prices of inputs. The two sets of tariffs together would raise the industry's unit value added by only $19 per bike. But this extra $19 represents a protection of value added (incomes) in the bicycle industry of 23.8 percent of value added, not just 10 percent

which shows the same bicycle example. We have seen that the dollar value of the consumer losses exceeds the dollar value of the producer gains from the tariff. We have also seen that the government collects some tariff revenue, an element of national gain. The left side of Figure 7.4 makes it clear that the dollar value of what the consumers lose exceeds even the sum of the producer gains and the government tariff revenues.

The same net national loss can be shown in another way, just as we saw in Chapter 2. The right side of Figure 7.4 shows the market for imports of bicycles. Our demand curve for imports of bicycles is a curve showing the amount by which our demand for bicycles exceeds our domestic supply of bicycles at each price. It is thus a curve derived by subtracting our domestic supply curve from our domestic demand curve for bicycles at each price (horizontally) since imports equal demand minus domestic supply. This allows us to show the net national loss (area *b* + *d*) on the right side of Figure 7.4 as well as on the left. Since area *b*

Illustrative Calculation of an Effective Rate of Protection

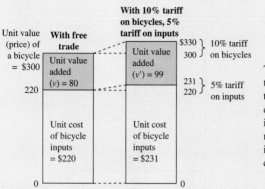

Effective rate
of protection for = $\dfrac{v' - v}{v} = \dfrac{\$99 - \$80}{\$80} = 23.8\%$
bicycle industry

To see who is getting protected by trade barriers, it helps (1) to distinguish an industry and its suppliers and (2) to look at the effects of the whole set of barriers, not just the one directly protecting the industry. In this case, the bicycle industry's 10 percent tariff raises its value added per bike by more than 10 percent. On the other hand, the tariffs on the inputs the bicycle industry buys hurt it. The net result in this case is an "effective rate of protection" of 23.8 percent.

or less, as one might have thought from a casual look at the nominal tariff rates themselves.

This example illustrates two of the basic points brought out by the concept of effective rate of protection: A given industry's incomes, or value added, will be affected by trade barriers on its inputs as well as trade barriers on its output, and the effective rate of protection will be greater than the nominal rate when the industry's output is protected by a higher duty than the tariff duties on its inputs.

We might add three other insights. First, if the tariff rates on the inputs are the same as the tariff rate on the output, then this rate is also the effective rate of protection. (Try this by modifying our example by using a 5 percent tariff on bicycles.) Second, the effective rate of protection can be negative—the tariff structure can penalize value added in the industry. (Try this using a 2 percent tariff on bicycles.) Third, export producers are penalized with something like negative effective protection if their costs are increased by tariffs on the inputs they use in production.

and area *d* have the same tariff height and relate, respectively, to the net shift from imports to domestic supply and the total decline in demand, area *b* + *d* is a triangle with the tariff as its height and the total cut in imports as its base, as shown in the right-hand side.

The net national loss from the tariff shown in Figure 7.4 is not hard to estimate empirically. The key information we need consists only of the height of the tariff itself and the estimated volume by which the tariff reduces imports, ΔM. The usual way of arriving at this information is to find out the percent price markup the tariff represents, the initial dollar value of imports, and the percent elasticity, or responsiveness, of import quantities to price changes. It is handy, and perhaps surprising, that the net national loss from the tariff can be estimated just using information on imports, as on the right side of Figure 7.4, without even knowing the domestic demand and supply curves. In our domestic example, the net loss *b* + *d* equals $6 million.

FIGURE 7.4   *The Net National Loss from a Tariff in Two Equivalent Diagrams*

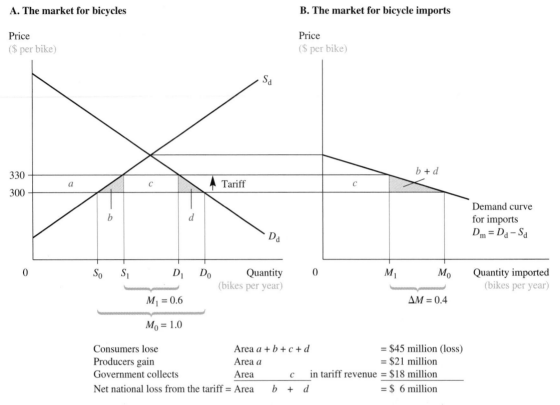

A. The market for bicycles

B. The market for bicycle imports

Consumers lose	Area $a + b + c + d$		= \$45 million (loss)
Producers gain	Area a		= \$21 million
Government collects	Area	c in tariff revenue	= \$18 million
Net national loss from the tariff = Area	$b + d$		= \$ 6 million

Under the assumptions of this chapter, a tariff brings a net national loss. What it costs consumers is greater than what it brings producers plus the government's tariff revenue. The two reasons for the net loss are summarized in areas b and d. Area b (the production effect) represents the loss from making at higher marginal cost what could have been bought for less abroad. Area d (the consumption effect) represents the loss from discouraging import consumption that was worth more than what it cost the nation.

Why is there a net loss? What logic lies behind the geometric finding that the net national loss equals areas $b + d$? With a little reflection, we can see that these areas represent gains from international trade and specialization that are lost because of the tariff. **Area d,** sometimes called the **consumption effect** of the tariff, shows the loss to consumers in the importing nation that corresponds to their being induced to cut their total consumption of bicycles. They would have been willing to pay prices up to \$330 to get the extra foreign bicycles lost in area d. The extra bicycles would have cost the nation only \$300 a bike in payments to foreign sellers. Yet the tariff discourages them from buying these bicycles. What the consumers lose in area d, nobody else gains. Area d is a "deadweight" loss, an element of overall inefficiency caused by the tariff.

Area b is a welfare loss tied to the fact that some consumer demand is shifted from imports to more expensive domestic production. The tariff is raising domestic production from S_0 to S_1 at the expense of imports. The domestic supply curve, or the marginal cost curve, is assumed to be upward sloping, so that each extra bicycle costs more and more to produce, rising from a resource cost of $300 up to a cost of $330. The domestic resource cost of producing these bicycles is more than the $300 price at which the bicycles are available abroad. This extra cost of shifting to more expensive home production, sometimes called the **production effect** of the tariff, is represented by area b. Like area d, it is a deadweight loss. It is part of what consumers pay, but neither the government nor bicycle producers gain it. It is the amount by which the cost of drawing domestic resources away from other uses exceeds the savings from not paying foreigners to sell us the extra units $(S_1 - S_0)$. Thus, the gains from trade lost by the tariff come in two forms: the consumption effect of area d plus the production effect of area b.

The basic analysis of a tariff identifies areas b and d as the net national loss from a tariff only if certain assumptions are granted. One key assumption is that the one-dollar–one-vote yardstick is an appropriate measure of different groups' interest. Use of this yardstick implies that consumers' losing areas a and c were exactly offset, dollar for dollar, by producers' gaining area a and the government's collecting area c. That is what produced $(b + d)$ as the net loss for the nation. Suppose that you personally reject this yardstick. Suppose, for example, that you think that each dollar of gain for the bicycle producers is somehow more important to you than each dollar of consumer loss, perhaps because you see the bicycle consumers as a group society has pampered too much. If that is your view, you will not want to accept areas b and d as the net national loss from the tariff. The same basic analysis of the tariff is still useful to you, however. You can stipulate how much more weight you put on each dollar of effect on bicycle producers than on each dollar for consumers, and you can apply your own differential weights to each group's dollar stake to see whether the net effect of the tariff is still negative.

The Terms-of-Trade Effect and a Nationally Optimal Tariff

It is time to relax a key assumption we have been making. So far, this chapter has made the small-country assumption: We have assumed that the importing nation, here the United States, cannot affect the world price of the imported good. In particular, the tariff on bicycle imports did not affect the world price of bicycles, which stood fixed at $300, tariff or no tariff.

The small-country assumption is often valid. Many individual nations as importers have small shares of world markets for individual commodities. Thus, in many cases an importing nation cannot force foreign suppliers to sell for less by trying to strike a tougher bargain. If Canada tried to demand a lower import price for bicycles by taxing foreign sales of bicycles to Canada, foreign suppliers might simply decide to avoid sales to Canada altogether and sell elsewhere at the same world price. Similarly, Singapore could not expect to force foreign sellers of rice to supply it more cheaply. Any attempt to do so would simply prove that Singapore was a price taker on the world market by causing rice exporters to avoid Singapore altogether, with little effect on the world rice price.

Yet in some cases a nation has a large enough share of the world market for one of its imports to be able to affect the world price unilaterally. A nation can have this **monopsony power** even in cases in which no individual firm within the nation has it. For example, the United States looms large enough in the world auto market to be able to force foreign exporters like Toyota to sell cars to the United States at a lower price by putting a tariff on foreign autos. The United States probably has the same monopsony power to some extent in the world markets for many other goods.

A nation with such power over foreign selling prices could exploit this advantage with a tariff on imports, even though no competitive individual business within the nation could do so. Let's look at a case in which a large buying country could affect the whole world price of a good it imports, just by imposing a tariff. In the economist's jargon, we say there is a **terms-of-trade effect** because a large country's tariff affects the terms of trade, which Part I defined as the ratio of the international prices of our exports to the international prices of our imports.

Suppose that the United States were to impose a small tariff on bicycles. Imposing the tariff markup would make the price paid by U.S. consumers exceed the price paid to foreign suppliers. Now, however, the markup is likely to lower the foreign price as well as raise the domestic price a bit. As long as they can produce and sell to the United States smaller amounts at a lower marginal cost, foreign suppliers are likely to prefer to cut their price to the United States a bit to limit the drop in their sales to the United States. Why? Because before the tariff, under free trade, they were selling an amount of bicycles to the United States that just brought their marginal cost up to the world price, say $300, which was also the price in the United States. If the U.S. government imposed a tariff on each bike, the foreign bicycle exporters would face a tough choice. They might try to insist that they be paid the same old $300 on each bicycle. But if they did, the price to U.S. buyers would now equal $300 plus the tariff, and U.S. customers would buy fewer bikes. For each competing foreign exporter, that means losing some sales at their $300 price. But the marginal cost is now less than $300 at the lower rate of production and sales. Each of them would be better off shaving the world price a bit below $300 as long as the price is still above the now-lower marginal cost. The United States succeeds in paying a lower price to foreigners on every imported bike, even though the tariff-including price to U.S. consumers is higher than $300.

This is what makes it possible for the United States to gain as a nation from its own tariff. To be sure, there is still a loss in economic efficiency—what economists call a *deadweight loss*—both for the United States and for the world. By discouraging some imports that would have been worth more to buyers than the price being paid to cover the foreign seller's costs—and by shifting some production to higher-cost domestic producers—the tariff still has its costs. But as long as the tariff is small, those costs are outweighed for the United States by the gains from continuing most of the previous imports at a lower price paid to foreign exporters. So, for tariff rates that are not too high, the United States as a nation is better off than with free trade.

This point can be made more fully using the illustration in Figure 7.5, which shows the same diagram of the market for bicycle imports as in Figure 7.4B, except that now the foreign supply curve slopes upward instead of being flat at a fixed world price. Suppose again that the United States imposes a very small tariff, say $3, on bicycles. The tariff drives a wedge of $3 between the price that exporters receive and the price (including the tariff) that importers pay. Even with this tariff wedge, the market still must clear—the quantity of exports (from the supply-of-exports curve) must equal the quantity of imports (from the demand-for-imports curve).

For the curves shown in Figure 7.5A, the $3 tariff drives up the domestic price of imports to $301.50, and lowers the price charged by foreign exporters to $298.50. The quantity traded declines to 0.98 million bikes. Figure 7.5A shows that the United States loses a bit on the 0.02 million bicycles that consumers decide not to buy each year now that they must pay the extra $1.50. The loss is very small, however. It is easily outweighed by the gain reaped by the United States at the expense of foreign suppliers on the remaining 0.98 million bicycles

FIGURE 7.5   *National Gains from a Tariff that Affects Foreigners' Selling Price*

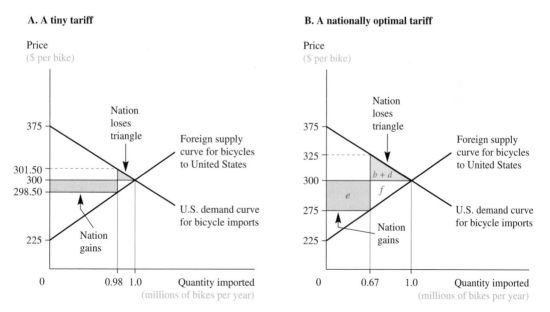

If the foreign supply curve slopes up, an importing nation has some power over the price it pays foreigners for imports even if individual importers have no such power. The importing nation can exploit this national monopsony power. In the left panel (A), it imposes a slight ($3) tariff and gains slightly because competition makes foreign suppliers pay part of the $3. It can gain more by raising the tariff further—up to a point. The right panel (B) shows the nationally optimal use (or abuse) of this power in which the maximum national gains have been squeezed, with a tariff of $50 (= $325 – $275).

imported each year. By getting the foreigners to sell those bicycles at $1.50 less, the United States has made them pay for part of the tariff. This national gain ($1.50 × 0.98 million bikes a year) easily outweighs the small triangle of dead-weight loss on discouraged imports.

If a tiny tariff works for the nation with power over prices, higher tariffs work even better—but only up to a point. To see the limits to a nation's market power, we can start by noting that *a prohibitive tariff cannot be optimal.* Suppose that the United States were to put a tariff on bicycle imports that was so high as to make all imports unprofitable, as would a tariff of over $150 a bike in Figure 7.5, driving the price received by foreign suppliers below $225. So stiff a tariff would not be successful in getting the foreigners to supply the United States at low prices since they would decide not to sell any bicycles to the United States at all. Lacking any revenues earned partly at the expense of foreign suppliers, the United States would find itself saddled with nothing but the loss of all gains from international trade in bicycles. The optimal tariff—the tariff rate that creates the largest net gain for the country imposing it—must be somewhere in between no tariff and a prohibitively high one.

The optimal tariff can be derived in the same way as the optimal price mark-down for any monopsonist, any buyer with market power. Appendix D derives the formula for the optimum tariff rate. It turns out that the optimal tariff rate, as a fraction of the price paid to foreigners, equals the reciprocal of the price elasticity of foreign supply of our imports.

It makes sense that the lower the foreign supply elasticity, the higher our optimum tariff rate: The more inelastically foreigners keep to supplying a nearly fixed amount to us, the more we can get away with exploiting them. Conversely, if their supply is infinitely elastic (the small-country case), facing us with a fixed world price, then we cannot get them to accept lower prices. If their supply elasticity is infinite, our own tariffs hurt only us, and the optimal tariff is zero.

Figure 7.5B shows an optimal tariff for a large country. The nation gains the markdown on foreign bicycle imports, represented by area *e*, which considerably exceeds what the nation loses as a net consumer of bicycles in area *b + d*. The national gain, *e − b − d*, is greater than the national gain at any other tariff rate.[3]

For the world as a whole, however, the nationally optimal tariff is still unambiguously bad. What the nation gains is less than what foreigners lose from our tariff. Figure 7.5B shows this. The United States gained area *e* only at the expense of foreign suppliers, dollar for dollar, leaving no net effect on the world from this redistribution of income through price. But foreign suppliers suffered more than that. They also lost area *f* in additional producer surplus on the exports discouraged by the tariff. Therefore, the world loses areas *b + d* and *f*, which would have been the gains from trade caused by the fact that U.S. consumers value foreign bicycles more highly below the level of imports of 1.0 million a year than it costs

---

[3]As Figure 7.5B is drawn, the tariff rate does fit the optimal-tariff formula. The rate equals ($50/$275) or about 18.2 percent. The elasticity of foreign supply works out to be 5.5 at this point on the foreign supply curve, so the tariff rate of about 18.2 percent is the reciprocal of 5.5. This would not be true for any other tariff rate.

foreign suppliers to make and sell them. The tariff may be nationally optimal, but it still means a net loss to the world.

Even for a large nation facing inelastic foreign supply curves, it might be unwise to levy what looks like an optimal tariff. Even if individual foreign suppliers cannot fight back, their governments can. Foreign governments may retaliate by putting up new tariff barriers against our exports. Knowing this, even large countries like the United States restrain the use of their power in individual import markets. Yet the optimal tariff is still an important concept.

Summary

A tariff redistributes well-being from domestic consumers of the product to domestic producers and the government, which collects the tariff revenue. For a small country (one that cannot affect world prices), a tariff on imports clearly lowers national well-being. It costs consumers more than it benefits producers and the government.

To reinforce your understanding of these basic welfare effects of a tariff, imagine how you might describe each of them to legislators who are considering a tariff law. Remember what this performance in the policy arena requires. You have to speak in language that is clear to a wide audience. You can't use any diagram or equation—no legislator will be impressed by such abstractions. You can, however, use the following concise verbal descriptions to explain each of the key effects shown by lettered areas in Figures 7.2 through 7.4:

1. "By raising the price on strictly domestic sales, a tariff redistributes incomes from consumers to producers. The amount redistributed is the price markup times the average quantity of domestic sales." (This describes area a.)

2. "A tariff shifts some purchases from foreign goods to home goods. This costs more resources to make at home than to buy abroad." (This describes area b, the production effect.)

3. "A tariff makes consumers pay tax revenue directly to the government." (This describes area c.)

4. "A tariff discourages some purchases that were worth more than they cost the nation." (This describes area d, the consumption effect.)

5. "Both by shifting some purchases toward costly home goods and by discouraging some purchases worth more than they cost the nation, the tariff costs the nation as a whole. The cost equals one-half the price markup times the drop in our imports." (This describes area $b + d$, the net national loss.)

The effects of tariffs on producer interests are further clarified by the concept of the effective rate of protection, which measures the percent effect of the entire tariff structure on the value added per unit of output in each industry. This concept incorporates the point that incomes in any one industry are affected by the tariffs on many products.

When a nation as a whole can affect the price at which foreigners supply imports, a positive tariff can be nationally optimal. The nationally optimal tariff rate equals the reciprocal of the foreign supply elasticity. If the foreign supply curve is infinitely elastic, so that the world price is fixed for the nation, the optimal tariff rate is zero. The less elastic the foreign supply, the higher the optimal tariff rate. As we shall note in Chapter 9, however, the tariff is only optimal if foreign governments do not retaliate with tariffs on our exports. With or without retaliation, the nationally optimal tariff is still bad for the world as a whole.

Suggested Reading

For a good example of practical estimates of the welfare effects of recent trade barriers, see the estimates for 21 imported products in Hufbauer and Elliott (1994).

Questions and Problems

✦ 1. What is the minimum quantitative information you would need to calculate the net national loss from a tariff in a small price-taking country?

2. "A tariff on imports of a product hurts domestic consumers of this product more than it benefits domestic producers of the product." Do you agree or disagree? Why?

✦ 3. What is the production effect of a tariff? How would you describe it in words, without reference to any diagram or numbers? How would you show it on a diagram, and how would you compute its value?

4. What is the consumption effect of a tariff? How would you describe it in words, without reference to any diagram or numbers? How would you show it on a diagram, and how would you compute its value?

✦ 5. You have been asked to quantify the welfare effects of the U.S. sugar duty. The hard part of the work is already done: Somebody has estimated how many pounds of sugar would be produced, consumed, and imported by the United States if there were no sugar duty. You are given the information shown in the table.
Calculate the following measures:
 a. The U.S. consumers' gain from removing the tariff
 b. The U.S. producers' losses from removing the tariff
 c. The U.S. government tariff revenue loss
 d. The net effect on U.S. national well-being

6. Suppose that the United States produces 1.4 million bicycles a year and imports another 1 million; there is no tariff or other import barrier. Bicycles sell for $400 each. Congress is considering a $40 tariff on bicycles like the one portrayed in Figures 7.2 through 7.4. What is the maximum net national welfare loss that this could cause the United States? What is the minimum national welfare loss if ours is a small country that cannot affect world price? (*Hint:* Draw a diagram like Figure 7.4 and put the numbers given here on it. Next, imagine the possible positions of the relevant curves.)

	Situation with Import Tariff	Estimated Situation without Tariff
World price (delivered in New York)	$0.10 per pound	$0.10 per pound
Tariff (duty)	$0.02 per pound	0
Domestic price	$0.12 per pound	$0.10 per pound
U.S. consumption (billions of pounds per year)	20	22
U.S. production (billions of pounds per year)	8	6
U.S. imports (billions of pounds per year)	12	16

✦ 7. As in question 5, you have been asked to quantify the welfare effects of removing an import duty; somebody has already estimated the effects on U.S. production, consumption, and imports. This time the facts are different. The import duty in question is a 5 percent tariff on imported motorcycles. You are given the information shown in the table.

Calculate the following:

a. The U.S. consumer gain from removing the duty

b. The U.S. producer loss from removing the duty

c. The U.S. government tariff revenue loss

d. The net welfare effect on the United States as a whole

Why does the net effect on the nation as a whole differ from the result in question 5?

8. For the international trade market for bicycles shown in Figure 7.5, demonstrate that a rather large tariff, for instance, a tariff which resulted in imports of 0.33 million bicycles, would not be an optimal tariff for the importing country.

✦9. This problem concerns the effective rate of protection. With free trade, each dollar of value added in the cloth-making industry is divided as follows: 40 cents value added, 30 cents for cotton yarn, and 30 cents for other fibers. Suppose that a 25 percent ad valorem tariff is placed on cloth imports and a 1/6 tariff (16.7 percent) goes on cotton yarn imports. Work out the division of the tariff-ridden unit value of $1.25 (the old dollar plus the cloth tariff) into value added, payments for cotton, and payments for other fibers. Then calculate the effective rate of protection.

10. What is the formula for the nationally optimal tariff? How great is the optimal tariff if the foreign supply of our imports is infinitely elastic?

	Current Situation with 5 Percent Tariff	*Estimated Situation Without Tariff*
World price of motorcycles (landed in San Francisco)	$2,000 per cycle	$2,050 per cycle
Tariff at 5 percent	$100 per cycle	0
U.S. domestic price	$2,100 per cycle	$2,050 per cycle
Number of cycles bought in U.S. per year	100,000	105,000
Number of cycles made in U.S. per year	40,000	35,000
Number of cycles imported by U.S. per year	60,000	70,000

CHAPTER 8

Nontariff Barriers to Imports

Protecting domestic producers against import competition

- Clearly helps those producers.
- Probably hurts the importing nation as a whole.
- Almost surely hurts the world as a whole.

So it is with a typical tariff barrier, as suggested in Chapter 7, and so it is with other kinds of barriers against imports. Knowing this, you might expect that protectionist interests will have most sway at the national or even local level, while the interests of consumers and the world as a whole will be better defended at the global level. That is the case. In fact, for half a century now, the world interest has been defended mainly by global agreements to liberalize trade, and by a superpower with a stake in global prosperity. Those agreements have succeeded in cutting tariffs, the subject of Chapter 7. They have failed to make nearly so much progress against nontariff import barriers, the subject of this chapter.

WTO: Tariff Success Versus the Rising Nontariff Challenge

Since 1995, the **World Trade Organization (WTO)** has overseen the global rules of government policy toward international trade. As of mid-1998, the WTO had 132 member countries that agreed to its rules and dispute settlement procedures, with a number of countries waiting to be accepted into membership. Its headquarters is in Geneva.

The WTO subsumed and expanded on the **General Agreement on Tariffs and Trade (GATT)**, a "provisional" agreement signed by 23 countries in 1947. The WTO, as did the GATT before it, codifies three major principles: (1) liberalization of trade, (2) nondiscrimination—the most favored nation (MFN) principle, and (3) no unfair encouragement for exports.

The Uruguay Round, 1986–1993:
A Difficult Step Toward Free Trade

The Battle of Geneva went right down to the deadline in 1993. Trade officials from 117 nations had fought over every word, every comma, of a proposed trade liberalization agreement that they first began to hammer out when negotiations opened in Uruguay back in 1986. In fact, the initial deadline for easy ratification of the agreement by the United States and other governments was not met, and it looked as though the whole seven years would be a wasted effort.

Yet somehow the negotiators managed to cheat the clock, setting a new deadline and reaching agreement at what could be called the 13th hour. Every single member country was unhappy about something in the proposed agreement. Yet when it was clear that the whole agreement really was about to die, all the major parties gave up on things they were fighting for, convinced at last that an imperfect agreement was better than none. The most bitter fights were not over conventional tariffs, but over a host of issues in the thorny thickets at the trade-policy frontier. Here is a summary of the achievements, nonachievements, and lingering disputes that are the historical legacy of the Uruguay Round they eventually signed at Marrakesh, Morocco, in April 1994:

- *Tariffs.* The 117 nations agreed to cut their tariffs by one-third. As part of this general reduction, the industrialized countries agreed to eliminate a range of tariffs, including tariffs on most steel products, pharmaceuticals, wood and wood products, and farm and construction machinery.
- *Import quotas.* As introduced in this chapter, these are limits on the quantity of imports, such as limits on the tons of sugar or peanut imports into the United States. The Uruguay Round replaced many agricultural quotas (and other

NTBs) with new tariffs that should allow about the same amount of imports. The gain from this switch from quotas to tariffs is indirect: Tariffs may prove easier to liberalize in future international negotiations. The Japanese and Korean governments reluctantly agreed to remove their bans on rice imports.

- *Voluntary export restraints (VERs).* Another NTB introduced in this chapter, these are limits on exports imposed at the insistence of the importing country. Trade in clothing and textiles is constrained by a global web of VERs under the Multifiber Arrangement. As a result of the Uruguay Round, these will be eliminated by the year 2005. In addition, other use of VERs is prohibited, and other VERs in existence must be phased out by 1999.
- *Domestic content requirements.* The rules are getting tougher with countries that try to limit imports through the domestic content requirements described in this chapter. It will be harder to demand that firms in a country have to sell products that have most of their value produced by people from the country.
- *Dumping.* Dumping means selling abroad at a price that is "too low" according to definitions that will be presented in Chapter 10. GATT rules oppose dumping. The United States and the EU are the world leaders in complaining about other countries' dumping exports at prices that are "too low." Many developing countries feel that the United States and Europe have abused the right to put up tariffs against imports of products that are allegedly being dumped. The United States and the EU won on this issue at the Uruguay Round with little new

restraint on their ability to impose antidumping tariffs.

- *Subsidies.* Agricultural trade is distorted by both import barriers and production and export subsidies. In addition to the alteration in import barriers noted above, the industrialized countries agreed to reduce their domestic production subsidies by 20 percent and their export subsidies by 36 percent, as well as reducing the volume of subsidized exports by 21 percent. Developing countries agreed to make lesser reductions. Outside of agriculture, there were some improvements in the code covering the use of subsidies and the policies that importing countries can adopt, a topic that we take up in Chapter 10.

- *Intellectual property.* The new agreement will eventually require that all countries honor other countries' patents, copyrights, and trademarks. It attacks the widespread practice of copying ("pirating") innovating firms' products without getting, and paying for, a license to use their innovations. As noted in this chapter, this tough requirement represents a victory for the United States and other technological leaders. It is a step toward what many would consider "fair trade," not a step toward free trade as such.

- *Services.* Many countries block international trade in services with outright bans on foreign suppliers and with legal red tape. The Uruguay Round established a General Agreement on Trade in Services. This agreement itself contains little in way of liberalization, but it provides a framework for future negotiations for liberalization. In 1997, negotiations reached agreements to open up national markets for telecommunications services and financial services. For telecommunications, 68 countries reached firm commitments to remove restrictions in local and long-distance telephone and wireless communications. Because a number of these have state monopolies, the potential effects are huge, including large decreases in prices. For financial services, 102 countries agreed to remove restrictions in banking, securities, and insurance.

- *Audiovisual services.* As we will discuss in Chapter 11, the European Union protects European makers of films, television shows, and audio recordings against the highly competitive U.S. productions. Various nontariff tools have been put to protectionist use, and taxes on movie tickets and blank cassettes are used to subsidize Europe's film producers. The failure to reach any agreement on this sector was a major defeat for the United States.

- *World Trade Organization.* The Uruguay Round established the World Trade Organization as the permanent body to administer the agreements of the Round, as well as the General Agreement on Tariffs and Trade. Among other improvements, the WTO has a much stronger dispute settlement procedure than the GATT had. If disputes between member countries cannot be resolved by discussion, a panel of experts examines the case and reaches a decision. A country can appeal a decision, but it cannot block it just by objecting. Retaliation is authorized in the absence of settlement of the dispute.

The Uruguay Round is a complex set of agreements. Economists nonetheless have fearlessly attempted to estimate the effects of the Round. These studies suggest that the Round can bring welfare gains of about 1 percent of world GDP (about $200 billion per year) by the early 2000s. Most of the gains come from the reduction of agricultural subsidies, the opening of the Japanese and Korean rice markets, and the elimination of VERs in textiles and clothing. Most of the gains go to the industrialized countries, because they are making most of the liberalizations.

Under the GATT, its member countries pursued rounds of negotiations to lower governmental barriers to trade. These negotiations have been very successful in reducing tariffs so that the world as a whole can benefit from more efficient specialization. Tariff barriers among the industrial countries have been greatly reduced in eight rounds of multilateral negotiations: Geneva 1947, Annecy 1949, Torquay 1951, Geneva 1956, the Dillon Round 1960–1961, the Kennedy Round 1964–1967, the Tokyo Round 1973–1979, and the Uruguay Round 1986–1993.

It wasn't easy. From the start, the agreements had to excuse some of the least reformable trade barriers to lend credibility to its pressure for removal of others. Agricultural protection and subsidies have been left largely intact, though serious efforts to reform agricultural trade have gained momentum in the Uruguay Round. Developing countries are also allowed to be heavily protectionist, though some have unilaterally liberalized their trade in the 1980s and 1990s. Still, the average tariffs of industrial countries, which were about 40 percent of import value in the 1940s, will be about 3 percent after the Uruguay Round takes full effect. Part of the credit for this liberalization goes to the negotiating procedures set up under GATT. Each nation's government is able to defend its tariff-cutting "concessions" against its domestic protectionists as a price it must pay to give its exporters better access to other markets, even though imports are something a country gains and exports are something it gives up.

The negotiations have had less success, however, in attacking nontariff barriers (NTBs). The NTBs take many forms—import quotas, product standards, domestic content requirements, state monopolies on foreign trade, buy-at-home rules for government purchases, administrative red tape to harass foreign sellers, complicated exchange controls, and so forth. In the manufacturing sector, NTBs are used frequently to provide protection to local producers of food products, beverages, textiles and clothing, footwear, iron and steel, and transport equipment. These industries are often considered "sensitive" in North America and Europe because of rising competition from new exporters. (We will examine several of these industries in more depth in Chapter 10.)

The protective effects of nontariff barriers are harder to measure than those of a tariff. As a result, it is harder to get international agreement on what constitutes an exchange of "comparable" NTB reductions. And perhaps because these barriers are harder to measure and compare, protectionism has increasingly taken refuge behind nontariff barriers since the 1970s. In fact, the striking contrast between GATT's success against tariffs and its frustration with nontariff barriers may reflect an underlying causal connection: Maybe governments were willing to cut their tariffs because they knew they could just replace many tariff barriers with their nontariff equivalents.

Just how far GATT has been able to come, and the continuing struggle that focuses on nontariff barriers, can be seen by looking at the achievements of the Uruguay Round of negotiations from 1986 through 1993. As summarized in the accompanying box, the Uruguay Round made major cuts in the remaining tariffs. Its progress was only mixed on the many nontariff fronts, however.

This chapter examines some of the main ways that governments keep out imports without using a tariff. Fortunately, the tools we used in Chapter 7 can be used again here with slight modifications. We start with import quotas, the classic nontariff barrier to imports. After that we turn to some other NTBs, concluding with a look at how much protection and how much damage recent import barriers have brought.

The Import Quota

The best-known nontariff trade barrier is the import quota, a limit on the total quantity of imports allowed into a country each year. One way or another, the government gives out a limited number of licenses to import items legally and prohibits importing without a license. As long as the quantity of licensed imports is less than the quantity that people would want to import without the quota, the quota not only cuts the quantity imported but also drives the domestic price of the good up above the world price at which the license holders buy the good abroad.

Reasons for Quotas

There are several reasons why governments have often chosen to use quotas rather than tariffs as a way of limiting imports. The first is as insurance against further increases in import competition (protectionist insurance) and import spending (balance-of-payment insurance). Quotas help ensure that the quantity of imports is strictly limited. If, for instance, increasing foreign competitiveness lowers the world price of imports, a quota will simply hasten the reduction in the total amount spent on imports. A tariff, by contrast, allows later foreign price cuts to raise both import quantities and (if our demand for imports is elastic) import values, thus complicating any official forecasts of the balance of payments.

Quotas are also chosen in part because they give government officials greater administrative flexibility and power in dealing with domestic firms. As we shall discuss below, these officials usually have discretionary authority over who gets the import licenses under a quota system, and they can use this power to their advantage (e.g., by taking bribes). For their part, protectionist interests also see a quota system as an opportunity to lobby for special license privileges, whereas a tariff is a source of government revenue to which they do not have easy access.

These are some common reasons why government officials and protectionist industries often prefer quotas. Note that these are not arguments showing that quotas are in the interest of the nation as a whole.

Quota Versus Tariff with Competition

When we analyze the welfare effects of an import quota, we find that the quota is no better, and in some cases it is worse, than a tariff for the nation as a whole. To compare the two, let us compare an import quota with an equivalent tariff—that is, a tariff just high enough to make the quantity of imports equal to the amount allowed by the quota if the quota is used.

The effects of a quota on bicycles are portrayed in Figure 8.1. Here we continue with some convenient assumptions we made in Chapter 7. We assume (a) that the domestic bicycle industry is competitive and not monopolized with or without the quota and (b) that the quota is so restrictive as to be less than what people would want to import at the world price. We further assume (c) that the world price is fixed by an infinitely elastic foreign supply of imports. (This is the small-country case from Chapter 7.)

Domestic buyers as a group face a total (domestic plus import) supply curve that equals the domestic supply curve plus the fixed quota quantity (Q_Q) of imports at all prices above the world price. Their inability to buy as much as they want at the world price drives up the domestic price of bicycles, in this case to $330. At the price of $330, the domestic market clears—the quantity supplied by domestic producers (S_1, read off the S_d curve), plus the quota quantity imported (Q_Q), equals the quantity demanded (D_1).

FIGURE 8.1   *The Effects of an Import Quota under Competitive Conditions*

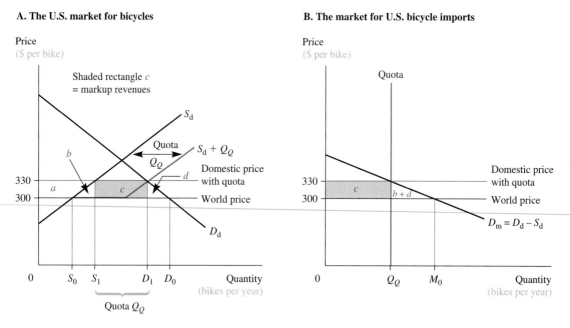

A quota cuts off the supply of imports by placing an absolute limit (Q_Q) on what can be bought from abroad.

Under the competitive conditions shown here, the effects of an import quota are the same as those of a tariff that cuts imports just as much. The quota shown here has the same effects on everybody as the $30 tariff shown in Figure 7.4, as long as the government turns over the revenue from selling import licenses (area *c* in either half of the diagram) to the same residents as those that would get the tariff revenues.

The welfare effects of the quota are equivalent to those of a tariff under competitive conditions. The quota in Figure 8.1 has induced domestic producers to raise their production from S_0 to S_1, costing the nation area b by having bicycles produced at home at marginal costs rising up to \$330 when they could have been bought abroad for \$300 each without the quota. At the same time, consumers lose area d without its being a gain to anyone else. The price markup on the allowed imports (rectangle c), is an internal redistribution from consumers to whoever commands the licenses since the license holders can import bikes by paying foreign exporters only \$300 and then sell them at the higher home price of \$330. So the net national loss is again areas b and d. This is the same set of results that we got with a \$30 tariff (back in Figure 7.4), the tariff that let in the same amount of imports as the quota.

The import quota looks best—or looks least bad—under these competitive conditions, which make it no better or worse than the equivalent tariff. The quota looks worse than the tariff under either of two sets of conditions: (1) if the quota creates monopoly power or (2) if the licenses to import are allocated inefficiently. Let us look at these two situations in order.

Quota Versus Tariff with Monopoly Power

The import quota turns out to cost the nation more than the equivalent tariff if the quota creates a domestic monopoly. It may do so. A dominant domestic firm cannot get much monopoly power from a nonprohibitive tariff because it faces an elastic competing import supply at the world price plus the tariff. With a quota, however, the domestic firm knows that no matter how high it raises its price, competing imports cannot exceed the quota. So a quota gives the dominant domestic firm a better chance of facing a sloping demand curve and, thus, a better chance to reap monopoly profits with higher prices. Therefore, with the monopoly-creating quota we get even higher prices, lower output, and greater national losses than from a tariff that would give us the same amount of imports. Appendix E presents this result geometrically, and it shows how to quantify the extra losses from a monopoly-creating import quota.

Ways to Allocate Import Licenses

The welfare effects of an import quota further depend on how the government allocates legal rights to import. Whoever gets these rights without paying for them captures the gains represented by area c in Figure 8.1 at the expense of consumers. Here are the main ways of allocating import licenses:

1. Competitive auctions (the best and rarest way)
2. Fixed favoritism (the most arbitrary way)
3. Resource-using application procedures (the least efficient way)

The government can run an **import-license auction,** selling off import licenses on a competitive basis, either publicly or under the table. The public auction might work as follows. Every three months the government announces that licenses to import so many tons of steel or so many bicycles or whatever will be auctioned off at a certain time and place. Such a public announcement is likely to evoke a large enough number of bidders for the bidding to be competitive, especially if bid rigging is a punishable crime. The auction is likely to yield a price for the import licenses that approximately equals the difference between the foreign price of the imports and the highest home price at which the licensed imports can be sold (assuming that the transactions costs of preparing and submitting bids is negligible).

Returning to Figure 8.1, we can see that such an auction would tend to yield a price of $30 per imported-bicycle license, since that is the price markup at which all competitive license holders can resell imported bicycles in the home market. In this case of a public auction, the quota system does not cost the nation any more than an equivalent tariff. The proceeds of the quota (area *c* in Figure 8.1) amount to a redistribution of income within the country. Bicycle consumers implicitly pay for the proceeds in the higher home price of bicycles, and the government collects the proceeds as auction revenues and then uses them to cut some other kind of tax or to spend on public goods worth this amount to society. The public auction revenues are essentially just tariff revenues under another name. The public auction, although the least costly way to allocate import licenses, is seldom used in the real world.[1]

Some use is made of a variant on the competitive auction, however. Government officials can be corrupt and do a thriving business of auctioning import licenses under the table to whoever pays them the highest bribes. This variant entails some obvious social costs. Such blatant and persistent corruption can cause talented persons to become bribe-harvesting officials instead of pursuing productive careers. Public awareness of such corruption also raises social tensions by advertising injustice in high places.

Import licenses adding up to the legal quota can also be allocated on the basis of **fixed favoritism,** with the government simply assigning fixed shares to firms without competition, applications, or negotiations. One common way of fixing license shares is to give established firms the same shares they had of total imports before the quotas were imposed. This is how the U.S. government ran its oil import quotas between 1959 and 1973. Licenses to import, worth a few billion dollars a year in price markups, were simply given free of charge to oil companies on the basis of the amount of foreign oil they had imported before 1959. This device served the political purpose of compensating the oil companies that were dependent on imports for their cutbacks in allowed import volumes, so that they would not lobby against the import quotas. Income was redistributed, of course, toward oil companies and away from the rest of the United States, which could have benefited from the proceeds of a public auctioning of import licenses instead of this fixed distribution of free licenses.

---

[1]Robert Feenstra has estimated that auctioning off the U.S. import quota rights to steel, textiles, apparel, machine tools, sugar, and dairy products could have brought the government about $5 billion a year around 1987 (Feenstra, 1989, p. 246).

The final way of allocating import licenses is by **resource-using application** procedures. Instead of holding an auction, the government can insist that people compete for licenses in a nonprice way. One messy way is to give import licenses on a first-come, first-served basis each month or each quarter. This ties up many people's time in standing in line, time that they could have put to some productive use. Another common device for rationing imports of industrial input goods is to give them to firms on the basis of how much productive capacity they have waiting for the imported inputs. This policy also tends to foster resource waste because it causes firms to overinvest in idle capacity in the hope of being granted more import licenses. Any application procedure forcing firms or individuals to demonstrate the merit of their claim to import licenses will also cause them to use time and money lobbying with government officials. Add to this the cost of hiring extra government officials to process applications.

Anne Krueger has estimated that import-rationing procedures once cost the economies of Turkey and India large shares of their gross national product (7.3 percent for India in 1964, 15 percent for Turkey in 1968). As a rough rule of thumb, she suggests that the resource cost will approximate the amount of potential economic rents being fought for, or something like area c in Figure 8.1. This will tend to be the result since firms will use more resources in expediting their applications for import licenses up to the point where these resource costs match the expected economic rents from the licenses, or area c. Note that this is quite different from the result of the public auction. The auction caused area c to be redistributed within society, from consumers of the importable good through the government to the beneficiaries of the government's auction revenues—presumably with almost no real cost of resources used in the process. The application procedures tend to convert area c into a loss to all of society by wasting resources in red tape and expensive rent seeking. Resource-using application procedures emerge as the most costly way of administering an import quota system.

Voluntary Export Restraints (VERs)

A quantitative limit can also harm the nation more than a tariff by giving monopoly power to foreign exporters. This odd result has occurred in the case of the **voluntary export restraints** (**VERs**), which are arrangements by which the government of an importing country coerces foreign exporters to agree "voluntarily" to restrict their exports into that country. Yes, that's right—the importing country actually gives *foreigners* monopoly power, *forces* them to take it, and calls their compliance "voluntary"!

VERs are used by large, powerful countries as a rear-guard action to protect their industries that are having trouble competing against a rising tide of imports. The United States has forced VERs on Asian and other foreign suppliers of U.S. imports since the early 1960s. First in clothing and textiles, and later in steel, automobiles, and other products, the U.S. government found itself seeking strict import limits in order to ease protectionist lobbying pressures. Yet the U.S. government wanted to avoid the embarrassment of imposing import quotas itself, in violation of GATT, while still professing to lead the world march toward free trade. It thus pressured foreign suppliers into agreeing to limit the quantity of exports to the U.S. market.

A clear example of the political chemistry that mixes protectionism with a desire to save face by not imposing outright quotas came in 1981, when sales of Japanese cars were capturing a rapidly growing share of the U.S. auto market. American autoworkers were losing their jobs, and the auto companies were running low on profits. Congress was ready to respond to the protectionist pressure and impose stiff import quotas if necessary. As president of the nation that was supposed to lead global progress toward freer trade, Ronald Reagan had a problem. In March 1981, his cabinet was having a key debate over quotas on Japanese auto imports. Reagan's autobiography later explained his thinking at that moment:

> As I listened to the debate, I wondered if there might be a way in which we could maintain the integrity of our position in favor of free trade while at the same time doing something to help Detroit and ease the plight of thousands of laid-off assembly workers.
>
> The Japanese weren't playing fair in the trade game. But I knew what quotas might lead to; I didn't want to start an all-out trade war, so I asked if anyone had any suggestions for striking a balance between the two positions. [Then–Vice President] George Bush spoke up:
>
> "We're *all* for free enterprise, but would any of us find fault if Japan announced without any request from us that they were going to *voluntarily* reduce their exports of autos to America?"
>
> I knew the Japanese read our newspapers and must know about the sentiment building up in Congress for quotas on their cars; I also knew there must be some apprehension in Tokyo that, once Congress imposed quotas on automobiles, there was a good possibility it might try to limit imports of other Japanese products.
>
> I liked George's idea and told the cabinet I'd heard enough and would make a decision, but didn't tell them what it was. After the meeting, I [arranged an extra meeting during the already-scheduled visit of Japanese Foreign Minister Masayoshi Ito to Washington]. . . .
>
> Foreign Minister Ito . . . was brought into the Oval Office for a brief meeting. . . . I told him that our Republican administration firmly opposed import quotas but that strong sentiment was building in Congress among Democrats to impose them.
>
> "I don't know whether I'll be able to stop them," I said, "But I think if you *voluntarily* set a limit on your automobile exports to the country, it would probably head off the bills pending in Congress and there wouldn't be any mandatory quotas."[2]

Japan agreed, and its auto firms "voluntarily" limited their exports from Japan to the United States. The automobile VERs were quite restrictive until 1987, by which time America demanded fewer auto imports because of the recovery of the domestic industry and the opening of "transplant" Japanese factories in the United States.

In addition to the United States, the European Union and Canada have used VERs as a major form of import restriction. The countries most often forced to restrict their exports have been Japan, Korea, and the transition countries of Cen-

---

[2]Ronald Reagan (1990), pp. 253–255, as quoted in Low (1993), pp. 114–115. Emphasis in the original.

tral and Eastern Europe; and the products most often restricted are textiles and clothing, agricultural products, steel, footwear, electronics, automobiles, and machine tools. The global Uruguay Round agreement struck a blow against VERs by calling for their eventual elimination.

Figure 8.2 shows the welfare effects of a voluntary export restraint in two similar pictures. In Figure 8.2A, limiting imports does not affect the world price outside of the importing country, whereas in Figure 8.2B, it does affect that world price. To take an example, let us say that the importing country is the United States and the product in question is autos from Japan and Korea. Figure 8.2 allows us to compare a VER with (1) an outright quota on imports and (2) free trade. Both the VER and the import quota impose the rigid quantitative limit represented by the "quota" M_1, and free trade is represented by the supply–demand equilibrium at price P_0.

VER Versus Import Quota.   Among other things, Figure 8.2 shows us how much more a VER might cost an importing nation, relative to an import quota. If the government of the importing country, the United States, administers an import quota of M_1, it will get the goods at the world price and somehow allocate the shaded price-markup gains among domestic residents. That is, it keeps the price markup revenues of area c within the country, and also captures some terms-of-trade gains (area e) if its import quota can force down the world price. But if the M_1 limit is enforced by the foreign exporters as a VER by their agreeing on fixed shares of this country's import market, the foreign exporters no longer compete among themselves to expand their sales to this market. Faced with this limited but prearranged import demand, they as exporters charge the highest price the traffic will bear on M_1 of imports—the high price P_1. The importing country loses all the shaded price markup by letting foreign exporters limit this country's imports instead of having a regular official import quota. Correspondingly, foreign exporters find a pure gain in the VER, relative to being shut out by an import quota. These exporters, not somebody in the importing country, gain the whole price-markup profit (area c in Figure 8.2A or area $c + e$ in Figure 8.2B). For the world as a whole, the VER and the import quota look equally bad in this analysis. Both of them restrict trade to M_1, and both cost the world the triangle $(b + d)$ and, in the large-country case, triangle f.[3]

---

[3]In the long run, a VER arrangement tends to wear down in a way that an import quota might not. It is, in effect, a cartel among the exporting firms. Like any cartel, its very success in getting a higher markup attracts other suppliers. Take the VERs for textiles and apparel, for example. When they were formed, they did not include potential suppliers who could later become competitive. In particular, the textile and apparel agreements initially left out the People's Republic of China, which had isolated itself in the 1960s. Later, when China became competitive, the VER arrangement either had to let China compete openly in the U.S. market, which would have erased the price markup, or had to take some VER export allotments from other suppliers and give them to China. As more and more new suppliers arrive on the scene, looking for a share of the U.S. market, prices tend to decline toward free-trade prices like P_0 in Figure 8.2, unless the VER can be expanded to include the new suppliers and tightened to limit the expansion of the total quantity imported.

FIGURE 8.2   *Welfare Effects of VERs Versus Quotas Versus Free Trade*

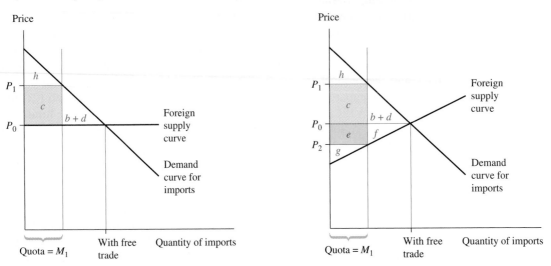

A. When limiting imports does not affect the world price (small-country case)

B. When limiting imports affects the world price (large-country case)

This view of an import market subject to voluntary export restraint allows us to compare the net national, foreign, and world welfare effects of the VER with either free trade or an import quota enforced by the government of the importing country.

	If the importing country is a price-taking (small) country, as in Figure 8.2A:		
	Importing Country	*Foreign Exporters*	*World as a Whole*
Net Gains from Trade			
With free trade	$c + (b + d) + h$	zero	$c + (b + d) + h$
Import quota	$c + h$	zero	$c + h$
With VER	h	c	$c + h$
Net Gains from VER Versus Two Alternatives			
VER versus free trade	$-c - (b + d)$	c	$-(b + d)$
VER versus quota	$-c$	c	zero

	If restricting trade affects the world price, as in Figure 8.2B:		
	Importing Country	*Foreign Exporters*	*World as a Whole*
Net Gains from Trade			
Free trade	$c + (b + d) + h$	$e + f + g$	$c + (b + d) + e + f + g + h$
Import quota	$c + e + h$	g	$c + e + g + h$
VER	h	$c + e + g$	$c + e + g + h$
Net Gains from VER Versus Two Alternatives			
VER versus free trade	$-c - (b + d)$	$c - f$	$-(b + d) - f$
VER versus quota	$-c - e$	$c + e$	zero

VER Versus Free Trade. For the importing country, the VER is very expensive relative to free trade. That country loses the triangle ($b + d$) on the prevented imports, and it also loses the price markup, as just mentioned. For the foreign exporters, the VER's effects can be bad, good, or neutral relative to free trade. If the foreigners' export supply curve is perfectly flat (as in Figure 8.2A), the VER simply gives them area *c*. If the importing country is a "large country," the foreign exporters experience two opposing effects. On the one hand, they are shut out of part of the U.S. market, cutting their gains from trade. (That is, they lose area *f*.) On the other hand, each firm adhering to the VER agreement gets to charge a higher markup on its remaining exports to the United States. (This gain is area *c*.)

Thus, as shown in Figure 8.2, the overall gains and losses from VERs depend on what they are being compared with. To summarize, if a VER arrangement is set up

	Instead of Free Trade	*Instead of Import Quotas*
The importing country	loses (by choice)	loses (by choice)
Foreign exporters	could gain or lose	gain
The world as a whole	loses	breaks even (with the same loss relative to free trade)

There is another important effect of a VER. For many products, foreign exporters can adjust the mix of varieties or models of the product that they export, while remaining within the overall quantitative limit, to increase the profit that they earn. Usually, the profit margin on higher-quality varieties is larger, so the exporters shift toward these varieties (a process called "quality upgrading"). When the Japanese firms implemented the VER on their auto exports to the United States, one part of their strategy was to shift the mix of models away from basic subcompact cars (like the Honda Civic) and toward larger models (like the Honda Accord and eventually the Acura line).

Other Nontariff Barriers

In addition to quotas and VERs, there are many other kinds of nontariff import barriers today. Indeed, we should be impressed with governments' creativity in coming up with new ways to discriminate against imports whenever they need to disguise their protectionism.

NTBs reduce imports by operating through one or more of three channels:

- Direct limit on the quantity of imports
- Increasing the cost of getting imports into the market

- Creating uncertainty about the conditions under which imports will be permitted

Quotas and VERs are examples of the first channel. Government procurement that requires the government to purchase domestic products is another. Import licensing requirements can operate through the second and third channels. The application process adds to the cost of importing, and the possibility that the license will be denied creates uncertainty that deters importing.

Let's look more closely at two other NTBs from the vast toolkit used against imports.

Product Standards

If you are looking for rich variety and imagination in import barriers, try the panoply of restrictive laws and regulations pertaining to product quality, including those enforced in the name of health, sanitation, safety, and the environment. Such standards can be noble efforts to enhance society's well-being, and they need not discriminate against imports. But, if a government is determined to protect local producers, it can always write rules that can be met only by local products. The United States has in the past tried to find hidden health hazards in the way beef cattle are raised in Argentina, in a transparent attempt to protect domestic ranchers. Japan and Europe have similarly found fault with the hormones and tight living space that American ranchers and poultry raisers give their animals. Similarly, Germany has passed a beer bottle law requiring that breweries selling in Germany take back a certain share of their bottles to be reused in the same plants where they were first filled; this is not too burdensome *if* that plant happens to be in Germany rather than overseas.

Quality standards do not raise tariff or tax revenues for the importing country's government. On the contrary, enforcing these rules with border inspections uses up government resources. From the viewpoint of the world as a whole, the quality standards may bring a gain to the extent that they truly protect health and safety. Yet it is easy for governments to disguise costly protectionism in virtuous clothing.

Domestic Content Requirements

Domestic content requirements mandate that a product assembled or produced in the country must have a specified amount of domestic value, in the form of wages paid to local workers or materials and components sourced from domestic producers. Domestic content requirements thus limit the import of materials and components that otherwise would have been used in making the product. For instance, local content requirements for automobiles can be used to force the auto manufacturers to use more locally produced automobile components and parts. If set high enough, the domestic content requirements can force domestic production of such expensive parts as engines or transmissions.

A closely related NTB, sometimes called a *mixing requirement,* stipulates that an importer must buy a certain percentage of the product locally. For example,

Carrots Are Fruit, Snails Are Fish, and Cows Need Passports

Governments have shown perhaps their greatest trade-policy ingenuity when deciding in what categories different imported goods and services belong. Their decisions are by no means academic. Economic stakes are high because an import that falls into one category can be allowed into a country duty-free, whereas the same import defined as falling into a related category may be subject to a high tariff or banned altogether.

You can bet that if definitions matter so much to trade policy, there will be intense lobbying over each commodity's official definition. Protectionists will insist that an imported commodity be defined as belonging to the class with the high import barrier, but importing firms will demand that it be put in the duty-free category. Where such strong pressures are brought on government, don't always expect logic in the official definitions.

Some of the resulting rules are bizarre. While examples can be found in any country's trade classifications, health codes, and the like, a particularly striking array of regulations was passed by the European Union (EU) in 1994:

- Carrots are a fruit, the EU officials have ruled, which allows Portugal to go on selling its carrot jam throughout Western Europe without high duties.
- The land snail, famously served in French restaurants, is officially a fish. Therefore European snail farmers can collect fish farm subsidies, allowing them to remain more competitive against other food products.
- Cattle must have individual passports to prevent their being taken from one EU country to another in search of better subsidies or easier health-code enforcement. The numbers on the new passports are not the same as the 14-digit numbers already stamped on their ear tags.

The United States has similarly bent the rules, modifying the definition of a car versus a passenger van versus a truck to reflect different pressures in protectionist debates. With even greater ingenuity, private firms have changed the look and the names of their products to get around each set of official definitions. For instance, a VER on down-filled ski parkas led to the innovation of two new products. One was a down-filled ski vest that had one side of a zipper on each armhole. The other was a matched pair of sleeves, each with one side of a zipper at the top of the sleeve. Once the two products were imported, the distributor knew what to do.

Such games have also been played with great frequency over the definitions of *foreign* and *domestic products* whenever domestic content rules are applied. As long as definitions mean money gained or lost, products will be defined in funny ways.

Source: Scripps Howard News Service, December 20, 1994.

Colombia once allowed the free import of the world's best steel, but only if the buyer showed that it had also bought finished steel from Colombian mills. Such mixing requirements have also been used to restrict imports of foreign entertainment. Canada has often imposed "Canada time" requirements on radio and TV stations, forcing them to give a certain share of their air time to songs and shows recorded in Canada. Similarly, as we shall see again in Chapter 11, the EU, led by France, has waged a sustained war against American entertainment, partly by stipulating that at least a certain percentage of entertainment must be from domestic studios.

Like quality standards, domestic content and mixing requirements do not generate any tariff or tax revenue for the government. The gains on the implicit price markups are captured by the protected home-country sellers of the protected products. The world as a whole suffers the usual deadweight loss because the local products are either less desired or more costly to produce.

America's "Section 301": Raising Import Barriers to Lower Them?

Sometimes import barriers are defined by the conditions under which they are imposed, not by the actual form of the barrier itself. A controversial example is a U.S. policy that could take the form of either a tariff or a nontariff barrier.

Since 1974, the United States has had a policy of threatening new barriers against imports based on whether it feels its own *ex*porters are being treated unfairly by *other* countries' government policies. Section 301 of the Trade Act of 1974 gave the president power to impose barriers against imports from a country using "unfair trade practices" to shut out imports from the United States and other countries.

What are the effects of the U.S. government's threatening other countries with retaliation under Section 301? That depends on whether the threatened country gives in and removes the practices that the United States says are unfair. Let's take a case in which the other country gave in to U.S. demands; then we will consider what happens if it does not.

One case in which U.S. threats to use Section 301 succeeded in forcing another country to give up unfair trade practices occurred in early 1995. Chinese firms had been making and selling copies of American-designed products without paying the designers for the use of their *intellectual property rights.* Instead of paying a license fee to the American owners of the international patents or copyrights, Chinese producers competed directly against those owners in the markets for computer software, pharmaceuticals, agricultural and chemical products, books and periodicals, and audiovisual products such as compact discs and movies. The WTO's rules backed the Americans, especially after the Uruguay Round agreement demanded that intellectual property rights be honored. The United States threatened to use Section 301 to slap high tariffs on Chinese goods if China did not start honoring U.S. intellectual property rights within a few weeks.

In this case, the threat of trade war seemed to work. China agreed to start enforcing foreign patents and copyrights, imposing penalties on Chinese firms found to be in violation. While success depends on continued enforcement by the government of China, it appears that this case resulted in better U.S. access to the Chinese market.

What if the other country refuses to change the practices the United States objects to? The United States can then retaliate by giving import protection to an arbitrary set of domestic industries—industries that may have nothing to do with the industries in which the foreign countries were alleged to have been unfair to

U.S. exporters. For example, in 1985 the EU decided to ban imports of cattle treated with growth hormones, responding to public concerns, even though there was no scientific evidence of any health risks. After negotiations between the governments failed, the EU implemented the ban in 1989, and the United States retaliated by imposing tariffs on imports from the EU of various food products, including beef, hams, tomatoes, certain beverages, and pet food. In this type of case, Section 301 is just another protectionist device and can be analyzed like a tariff, quota, or VER. Carrying out the retaliation against another country's goods is likely to reduce the well-being of both sides.

There is a real danger that using Section 301 will backfire in this way. Other countries have been irked by the self-righteous tone with which the United States has written and used 301. They detect protectionist hypocrisy on the part of the Americans. They also rightly point out that 301 allows the United States to conduct its own unilateral "trade crimes" trials, deciding by itself what is "unfair."

Since 1974, there have been about 100 Section 301 cases. The major foreign targets have been the European Union (especially for agricultural products) and Japan (especially for manufactured products), with Korea, Taiwan, Canada, and Brazil also being frequent targets. A careful recent study concluded that in about half of these cases the United States succeeded at least partially in achieving its objectives (improved market access, reduced foreign subsidies, or improved protection of intellectual property), with 11 cases judged to be largely or wholly successful. Even for the successes, increases in U.S. exports usually were small (with the exception of large increases in U.S. exports of cigarettes, beef, and semiconductors to Japan, following negotiated resolutions of Section 301 complaints).

Generally, there has been a drop-off in Section 301 cases since 1991. The WTO has a binding dispute settlement process, a major improvement over the weak process available under the GATT, so that U.S. complaints are now more likely to be sent to and resolved by the WTO. For instance, Kodak's 1995 complaint about barriers into the Japanese film market was shifted from Section 301 to the WTO in 1996. Kodak complained that its low share of the Japanese market (about 10 percent) was due to Japanese government support of Fuji's domination of distribution channels. In 1998, the WTO ruled against the complaint, citing insufficient evidence. In this case the decision was against the U.S. charge, but most other WTO rulings have been in favor of U.S. complaints. Another change brought by the WTO is a limit on the U.S. ability to retaliate unilaterally using Section 301, because foreign countries can complain to the WTO about the retaliation.

How Big Are the Costs of Protection?

Now that we see the kinds of effects that tariff and nontariff barriers have, their importance needs to be weighed. Are the costs large or small? Large or small relative to what? Are they larger for nontariff barriers than for tariffs? Would raising new barriers make a big difference?

As a Percentage of GDP

One popular way of weighing the importance of any economic cost or benefit is to see whether it looks like a big share of gross domestic product. The debate over this question was launched by a simple demonstration that seemed to show that costs of protection had to be small. Let's start with that simple demonstration.

Since the late 1950s, several economists have tried to estimate the net national welfare losses from tariffs and other trade barriers in the real world. Basically their procedure has been to estimate the sizes of areas $b + d$ in Figures 7.4 and 8.2 for several internationally traded commodities. They have used information on the extent of imports and the height of the tariff or other price-raising import barrier, and an estimate of the price elasticity of import demand for each product.

As far back as 1960, Harry G. Johnson argued that the value of the loss from tariffs had to be a very small share of a nation's gross domestic product (GDP). Using a diagram like Figure 7.4B, Johnson noted that for any commodity, area $b + d$ as a share of GDP can be reexpressed as

$$\frac{\text{Net national loss from the tariff}}{\text{GDP}} = \frac{1}{2} \times \text{tariff rate} \times \frac{\text{percent change in import quantity}}{\text{import quantity}} \times \frac{\text{import value}}{\text{GDP}}$$

By studying these fractions, Johnson showed how this kind of measure of net loss from a tariff might easily look like a small fraction of GDP. Suppose, for example, that a nation's import tariffs were all 10 percent tariffs and that they caused a 20 percent reduction in import quantities. Suppose the total imports of all commodities were 10 percent of GDP. In this realistic case, the net national loss from all tariffs on imports equals $1/2 \times 0.10 \times 0.20 \times 0.10$, or only 0.1 percent of GDP! Johnson thus argued that the net national loss from tariffs is not likely to be great, at least for a country that is not very dependent on foreign trade, such as the United States.

Other empirical studies more or less confirmed Johnson's hunch. The first wave, like Johnson, estimated triangles of net national loss like those shown in Figures 7.4 and 8.2. These stand in the tradition that economists call (*Marshallian*) *partial-equilibrium analysis,* because it looks only at a single market without exploring economywide effects of a trade barrier. Then, from the mid-1970s on, more complex *computable general equilibrium (CGE)* methods were applied to the same task of welfare estimation. The CGE estimates were based on large computer-solved models of the economy that can pick up subtle income and price repercussions that are hidden by diagrams like those in this chapter. With either method, Marshallian or CGE, the range of welfare gains from freer trade was less than 10 percent of GDP. The authors of the studies usually concluded that the effects they measured were "small" shares of GDP.

Yet there are several ways in which these studies underestimate the costs of protection as a share of GDP. Here are five ways in which the true cost is a bigger share of GDP than such numbers might imply:

- *Foreign retaliation.* If our country were to introduce new import barriers, other governments would retaliate by putting up new barriers against our exports. The true costs would be greater than any shown in the diagrams above or in Harry Johnson's simple equation, especially if a trade war breaks out, in which each side counterretaliates with still higher import barriers.

- *Enforcement costs.* Any trade barrier has to be enforced by government officials. That is costly since the people enforcing the trade barrier could have been usefully employed elsewhere. To this extent, part of the revenues collected by the government (area *c* in our diagrams) is not just a pure redistribution from consumers to the government, as we have assumed so far, but a waste of some of society's resources.

- *Rent-seeking costs.* Firms seeking protection may use techniques such as lobbying that also use resources. If this is the case, then part of the producer surplus created by protection (area *a* in our diagrams) is not a pure redistribution (from consumers to producers), but instead a waste of resources. In addition, firms and individuals may use resources to attempt to claim the tariff revenues or rents on the quota quantity of imports, another reason that some of area *c* could be a resource waste.

- *Innovation.* Protection can mute the incentive to innovate new technology, because there is less competitive pressure. In addition, protection can cause a loss because it reduces the number of varieties of products available in the domestic market. (Recall the discussion in Chapter 6.)

- *New barriers cost much more than existing ones.* Notice that all the estimates discussed so far, such as Johnson's calculation, quantify the costs of *existing* trade barriers. These may look small simply because governments have cooperated to lower their trade barriers so much over the last half-century. Yet most of the debate over trade barriers is over new ones that could more than double the percent price gap caused by tariffs, quotas, and the like. So the debate is over proposals that would impose much bigger costs than the existing ones.

Furthermore, moving to higher barriers has an accelerating, nonlinear cost to it. If you study the net-loss triangles again, you will see that they take the form

$$\text{Net loss} = (1/2) \times (\% \text{ tariff}) \times (\% \text{ cut in imports})$$

Since the percent cut in imports equals the percent tariff rate times some import-demand elasticity, the formula could be restated as

$$\text{Net loss} = (1/2) \times (\% \text{ tariff})^2 \times (\text{import-demand elasticity})$$

Note that the tariff (or price markup from a quota or VER) has a *squared* effect. This means that doubling today's tariffs or other trade barriers would quadruple their net cost, and tripling them would make their net cost nine times as great as with the existing barriers. Thus a lot is at stake in debates over new trade barriers, even if the current ones seem to have a low cost.

As a Share of the Protection Given

In a different perspective, the costs of import barriers look larger than they look as a share of GDP. The usual political reason for import barriers is to protect the incomes of a threatened domestic industry. Even if that industry is not a large share of GDP, society should know how much it costs for each dollar of protection given. If each dollar of income help to a threatened industry costs the rest of society only $1.03, it would not be so expensive to provide assistance to a group that might need to be helped one way or another (e.g., with unemployment compensation and tax relief) if it is driven out of business. Yet if it costs the rest of society $2 for every dollar of income protected, that would strike most observers as expensive.

To get a quick idea of how different this perspective looks, let's return to Harry Johnson's classic example of import barriers that cost only 0.1 percent of GDP. In this case, the tariffs gave domestic producers a 10 percent hike in the price they received for their product. If that threatened industry was itself as big as 10 percent of our GDP, then its gain in producer surplus (area *a* in our diagrams) was something close to 10 percent of 10 percent, or 1.0 percent of GDP. The net national loss of 0.1 percent of GDP therefore equals 10 percent (0.1/1.0) of the income protection it provides. In other words, every dollar of income protected costs all of society an extra 10 cents. Since the protected group is part of society, each dollar of its protection costs the rest of society $1.10, even in Johnson's example.

In the real world, the costs often loom larger than in this hypothetical case. Figure 8.3 shows us the net losses and gains from selected U.S. import barriers in 1990, first as millions of dollars per year and then as losses or gains per dollar of income that is protected against imports. These calculations are based on diagrams like Figures 7.4, 7.5, and 8.2.

The upper panel of numbers reminds us quickly that even small shares of GDP can equal billions of dollars, something worth fighting over.

In the lower panel, we see the costs to other groups of each dollar of income protected. For each dollar of protected producer income, consumers lose more than $2 on average for the 23 cases. And the United States as a whole loses $0.49 for each dollar of protected income. That is, other Americans lose $1.49 for each $1.00 gained by the protected U.S. industries. Out of the $0.49 in net national loss, $0.26 is a pure deadweight loss, while the rest is a loss of price markup to foreigners on VERs. There is ample reason for consumers and other groups to fight against proposals to protect domestic industries against imports.

The world as a whole loses more, for each dollar protected, than the $0.26 of deadweight loss experienced by the United States. Foreigners lose nine cents, per dollar of protection, on lost exports to the United States. So the world as a whole bears a net loss of $0.35. In other words, each dollar of protected income is more than offset by $1.35 of losses to all other groups.

There is an interesting contrast in the net losses and gains between industries protected by tariffs and those protected by quotas or, especially, VERs. U.S. tariff protection seems to cost less. It costs the world only 15 cents per dollar of protec-

FIGURE 8.3 *Losses and Gains from U.S. Import Protection, Selected Products, 1990*

	Protected Producers' Gain (Area a)	Consumer Loss (Area a+b+c+d)	U.S. Terms-of-Trade Gain (Area e)*	U.S. Deadweight Loss (Area b + d)	U.S. Net National Gain (Area e* – b – d)	Foreign Deadweight Loss (Area f)	Net World Loss (Area b+d+f)
In Millions of Dollars							
Tariffs in 14 sectors[a]	710	1,999	465	70	395	39	109
Quotas in 4 sectors[b]	2,538	3,623	171	686	–515	94	780
5 sectors with VERs[c]	9,587	22,918	–3,575	2,539	–6,114	1,018	3,556
All 23 sectors	12,835	28,540	–2,939	3,295	–6,234	1,151	4,446
Per Dollar of Protected Income							
Tariffs in 14 sectors[a]	$1.00	$2.81	$0.65	$0.10	$0.56	$0.05	$0.15
Quotas in 4 sectors[b]	$1.00	$1.43	$0.07	$0.27	–$0.20	$0.04	$0.31
5 sectors with VERs[c]	$1.00	$2.39	–$0.37	$0.26	–$0.64	$0.11	$0.37
All 23 sectors	$1.00	$2.22	–$0.23	$0.26	–$0.49	$0.09	$0.35

Note: "Areas" refer to areas marked in Figures 7.4, 7.5, and 8.2.

*Except for VERs, where this is not *e* but the markup lost, relative to free trade, on area *c*.

[a]The 14 tariff-protected sectors are ball bearings, benzenoid chemicals, canned tuna, ceramic articles, ceramic tiles, costume jewelry, frozen concentrated orange juice, glassware, luggage, polyethylene resins, rubber footwear, softwood lumber, women's nonathletic footwear, and women's handbags.

[b]The four sectors protected by import quotas are dairy products, peanuts, sugar, and coastal shipping.

[c]The five sectors protected by VERs are apparel, textiles, machine tools, steel, and autos. The estimates for steel and autos capture only the effects of their modest tariffs. The VER arrangements remained in effect, but after 1987 import demand had fallen below the set limits, making the VERs redundant.

Source: Hufbauer and Elliott (1994).

tion and actually brings a net gain of $0.56 to the United States. How does a tariff bring a net national gain? As it happens, the United States, as a large country, gets "terms-of-trade" gains because other nations must cut their export prices to the United States to minimize their losses from U.S. tariffs. These terms-of-trade gains were discussed when Chapter 7 introduced the idea of a nationally optimal tariff. Smaller nations, which must take world prices as given, cannot reap such gains at the expense of the rest of the world.

Another reason that tariff protection looks less costly than nontariff barriers in practice is that the big threats lead, politically, to tough measures, usually in the form of new quotas and voluntary export restraint agreements. Those industries protected by tariffs are ones whose protection is ancient and slowly declining, as negotiations chip away at tariff barriers. The really tough cases of major import protection are the quota and VER sectors, especially dairy products, sugar, coastal shipping services, apparel, and textiles. The political process protects such industries heavily, even at big cost per dollar of income protected. In the case of apparel and textiles, the United States uses VERs that give away large price markups to foreign exporters, as we saw when looking at area *c* in Figure 8.2. This is why studying the rows in Figure 8.3 shows higher costs for the quota and VER sectors.

Summary

Nontariff policies affecting international trade have emerged as the more important kind of trade distortion. Tariffs have been gradually lowered by GATT negotiations in the postwar era, while import quotas and other nontariff barriers (NTBs) have been rising. The Tokyo Round and the Uruguay Round included some efforts to limit and reduce NTBs, but the World Trade Organization, a new international organization that, in 1995, subsumed the GATT, continues to struggle to liberalize NTBs.

Government officials in a country have many reasons for turning to import quotas and other nontariff barriers. Economic efficiency apparently is not a valid reason for this choice. The basic analysis of the main nontariff barrier to trade, an import quota, indicates that it is at least as bad as a tariff. It is more costly than the tariff if it creates domestic monopoly power or if resources are used up in the private pursuit of licenses to import items legally.

A formal protection that became important in the 1980s, especially in the United States and the EU, is the voluntary export restraint (VER) arrangement. Here the importing country threatens foreign exporters with stiff quotas if they do not agree to restrict exports by themselves. Under a negotiated VER arrangement, the main foreign exporters form a cartel among themselves, agreeing to cut export quantities. At the same time, they are allowed to charge the full markup on their limited sales to the importing country, where the product has become more expensive. A curious result is that the importing country, which insisted on the VER in the first place, loses even more than if it had collected a tariff or quota markup itself.

Other important nontariff barriers include domestic content requirements, mixing requirements, government procurement favoring domestic products, import licensing requirements, and a host of quality and safety standards that have protectionist effects. In addition, the United States uses the threat of imposing new tariff on nontariff barriers, under Section 301 of the U.S. trade law, in an effort to force foreign-country governments to remove allegedly unfair policies that limit the access of U.S. exports to these countries.

The net costs of import barriers, both tariff and nontariff, look small from some perspectives but large from others. They look small as a share of GDP when calculated in terms of the ordinary triangles. Yet this analysis overlooks foreign retaliation, enforcement costs, rent-seeking, and other considerations that make import barriers look more expensive, both in relation to GDP and in relation to the protection provided.

Suggested Reading

U.S. policy and its conflicts with the WTO are neatly summarized by Destler (1995) and Low (1993). Schott (1994) and Whalley and Hamilton (1996) survey the accomplishments and shortcomings of the Uruguay Round. Hoekman and Kostecki (1995) examine the history of the WTO and the GATT.

On the different ways to allocate import quota licenses, the analysis of resource-using application procedures is given by Krueger (1974). Feenstra (1989) looks at the practicalities of auctioning off import licenses.

The costs of U.S. protectionism are quantified by Hufbauer and Elliott (1994). The meaning of such costs, with extra treatment of the effects on foreign exporters, is interpreted by Feenstra (1992). Hufbauer (1996) provides a survey of similar studies for other countries. Feenstra (1995) provides a technical survey of work estimating the effects of protection.

Jones (1994) examines the rise of VERs. Bayard and Elliott (1994) provide an in-depth analysis of Section 301, and Elliott and Richardson (1997) update some of this analy- sis. A critical review of the U.S. use of Sec- tion 301 as a trade weapon is "Gunboat Diplomacy," *The Economist,* March 12, 1994, pp. 71–73.

Questions and Problems

✦ 1. What are import quotas? Why do many gov- ernments use them instead of just using tar- iffs to restrict imports by the same amounts? Is it because quotas bring a bigger national gain than tariffs?

2. What are voluntary export restraint (VER) agreements? Why do many governments force foreign exporters into them instead of just using quotas or tariffs to restrict imports by the same amounts? Is it because VERs bring the importing country a bigger national gain than quotas or tariffs?

✦ 3. Under what conditions could an import quota and a tariff have exactly the same effect on price, and bring the same gains and losses (given a tariff level that restricts imports just as much as the quota would)?

4. Define each of the following import policies, and describe its likely effects on the welfare of the importing country as a whole: (a) product standards and (b) domes- tic content requirements.

✦ 5. To protect Kodak jobs, the United States might decide to cut its imports of photographic film by 60 percent. It could do so by either (a) imposing a tariff high enough to cut film imports by 60 percent or (b) persuading Fuji and other foreign film makers to set up a VER arrangement to cut their exports of film to the United States by 60 percent. Which of these two policies would be less damaging to the United States? Which would be less damaging to the world as a whole? Explain.

6. The United States is considering adopting a regulation that foreign apples can be imported only if they are grown and

harvested using the same techniques that are used in the United States. These methods are used in the United States to meet various government standards about worker safety and product quality.

a. As a representative of the U.S. government, you are asked to defend the new import regulation before the WTO. What will you say?

b. As a representative of foreign apple growers, you are asked to present the case that this regulation is an unfair restriction on trade. What will you say?

✦ 7. Suppose that the U.S. government is under heavy pressure from the Rollerblade and K2 companies to put the brakes on imports of Bauer in-line skates from Canada. The pro- tectionists demand that the price of a $200 pair of in-line skates must be raised to $250 if their incomes are to be safe. The U.S. government has three choices: (1) free trade with no protection; (2) a special tariff on in- line skates backed by vague claims that Canada is using unfair trade practices (citing Section 301 of the Trade Act of 1974), and (3) forcing Bauer to agree to a voluntary export restraint. The three choices would lead to these prices and annual quantities:

	With Free Trade	With an $80 Tariff	With a VER
Domestic U.S. price per pair	$200	$250	$250
World price per pair	$200	$170	$170
Imports of in-line skates (millions pairs)	10	6	6

Note that the $80 tariff restricts imports by 4 million pairs a year, the same restriction that the VER arrangement would enforce.

a. Calculate the U.S. net national gains or losses from the tariff, and the U.S. gains or losses from the VER, relative to free trade. Which of the three choices looks best for the United States as a whole? Which looks worst?

b. Calculate the net national gains or losses for Canada, the exporting country, from the tariff and the VER. Which of the three U.S. choices harms Canada most? Which harms Canada least?

c. Which of the three choices is best for the world as a whole?

8. A small country's protectionism can be summarized: The typical tariff rate is 50 percent, the (absolute value of the) price elasticity of demand for imports is 1, imports would be 20 percent of the country's GDP with free trade, and the protected industries represent 15 percent of GDP. Using our triangle analysis, what is the approximate magnitude of the economic costs of the tariff protection, as a percentage of the country's GDP? As a percentage of the gain of producer surplus in the protected sectors?

♦ 9. For a small country, consider a quota and an equivalent tariff that permit the same initial level of imports. The market is competitive, and the government uses fixed favoritism to allocate the quota permits, with no resources expended in the process. There is now an increase in domestic demand (the domestic demand curve D_d shifts to the right). If the tariff rate is unchanged, and the quota quantity is unchanged, are the two still equivalent? Show this using a graph. Be sure to discuss the effects on domestic price, production quantity, and consumption quantity, on import quantity, and on producer surplus, consumer surplus, deadweight losses, and government revenue or its equivalent for the quota.

10. A Japanese friend asks you to explain and defend American use of Section 301. What will you say?

CHAPTER 9

Arguments For and Against Protection

Our search for the boundary that divides good import barriers from bad barriers continues. Up until now, Chapters 7 and 8 found only bad barriers, ones that brought net harm to the world economy. Of the ones we explored, only the "nationally optimal tariff" was good for the nation that imposed it, but it too was bad for the world as a whole. We have yet to find the borderland where import barriers start to look good for the nation and for the world. Where is that border? Is the land beyond the border—the realm of good import barriers—tiny or huge?

One reason why all import barriers have looked bad so far is that Chapters 7 and 8 posed tests that give A's to the free-trade arguments and F's to the arguments for protection against imports. Our analysis stayed in a Garden of Eden, that is, a perfect world in which a new import barrier was the Original Sin. The world of Chapters 7 and 8 worked perfectly until the import barrier was introduced.

It is time to put the free-trade argument to a tougher test, a test that gives protectionist arguments more chance to prevail. To set up the test, we turn our attention away from that perfect world, toward worlds that already have economic flaws, to see whether a trade barrier might help cure those flaws.

In shifting from perfect worlds to worlds in which economic incentives are already distorted against the best interest of society, we shift our view in other ways too. No longer do we compare the import barrier just with free trade, but also with other options. And instead of seeking numbers that quantify how much net gain a trade barrier brings, we will often be content to know just whether that net effect is positive or negative. We shall establish some of the policy conclusions previewed at the start of Chapter 7: There are valid "second-best" arguments for protection, yet some other policy is usually better than barriers to imports in the second-best cases. It turns out that the valid arguments for protection are quite different from its usual defenses.

The Troubled World of Second Best

To locate the boundaries to the free-trade argument, we must go beyond a key simplifying assumption made in Chapters 7 and 8. So far we have been assuming that any demand or supply curve could do double duty, representing both private and social benefits or costs. Our demand curve was supposed to represent not only marginal benefits of an extra bicycle to the private buyer but also the extra benefits of another bicycle to society as a whole. Our supply curve was supposed to represent not only the marginal cost to private producers of producing another bicycle at home but also the marginal cost to society as a whole.

As far as economic incentives were concerned, free trade was a beautiful world: Everybody expanded an activity (e.g., buying or supplying bicycles) until all incentives were in perfect balance. Suppliers supplied more until the marginal cost to them, which was also the marginal cost to society of supplying an extra bike, just met the price they were paid for the bike. They expanded their supply up to the point where *both they and all society* just broke even on the last bike. Buyers did something similar. They bought more bicycles up to the point that the value of an extra bicycle, *both for them and for all society,* no longer exceeded the private and social cost of supplying the extra bicycle. That is the beauty of an ideal price system.

Distortions

We have assumed, in other words, that under free trade there were no incentive **distortions,** which are gaps between the private and social benefits or costs of an activity. The tariff in Chapter 7 introduced a distortion between the marginal cost of a bicycle to consumers (the tariff-including domestic price) and the marginal cost to society of buying another bicycle abroad (the world price). Private incentives (the tariff-including domestic price) no longer reflected social costs at the margin.

To get a firm grip on what incentive distortions mean, let us begin by returning briefly to the world that does not have any. The first row in Figure 9.1 summarizes what the economist means by a "first-best" world, a world free of any distortions. The market price (P) acts as a signal to consumers and producers. Consumers buy the product up to the point where the price they are willing to pay, representing the extra benefits (MB) they receive from another unit, just equals the price they must pay, and the extra benefit to society (SMB) is just the extra benefit that the consumer gets. Producers supply the product up to the point where the price they receive just covers the extra costs (MC) of producing the product, and the extra costs to society (SMC) are just the extra costs that the individual firm incurs. That is, all five marginal values are equal: Price (P) = buyers' private marginal benefit (MB) = social marginal benefit (SMB) = sellers' private marginal cost (MC) = social marginal cost (SMC). Incentives are perfectly balanced.

It is often unrealistic to assume that the distortions in our domestic economy either are zero or happen to cancel each other out. Distortions exist, and they pose some of the most intriguing policy problems of economics. Distortions include the wide range of effects that economists have also called **externalities** or **spillover effects** (net effects on parties other than those agreeing to buy and sell in a marketplace).

The first example of an externality in Figure 9.1 is the classic case of river pollution, an example we will explore at more length in Chapter 12. The sellers of paper products do not reckon the damage done by the paper mills' river pollution into the cost of their production, so the pollution costs are not incorporated into the price of paper, unless special action is taken. Nor do the buyers of petroleum fuels reckon that the social cost of pollution from consuming those fuels is part of the price of the fuels. Such distortions between the interests of private parties and the net interests of society as a whole occur in other spheres as well for a host of reasons. We live in a **"second-best" world,** one that includes gaps between private and social benefits or costs. As long as these gaps exist, private actions will not lead to a social optimum.

Our second second-best example supposes that jobs in a certain import-competing domestic sector will generate greater returns for society than are perceived by the people who are deciding whether to take those jobs. This can happen if the sector is a modern one in which jobs bring gains in knowledge and skills plus changes in attitudes, benefiting persons other than the workers and employers in that sector (SMB > P, which is the wage rate). Or perhaps short-run costs of moving to jobs in a high-paying sector seem higher to the workers

FIGURE 9.1

Incentive Distortions and Their Effects

Situation	Incentives at the Margin	Effects
First-best world	P = MB = MC = SMB = SMC	Exactly the right amount is supplied and demanded. Social rewards and private rewards are the same.
Second-best worlds:		
External costs	SMC > P	Too much is supplied because suppliers make and sell extra units for which the social costs exceed the price, which equals MC and MB and SMB. (Example: production that pollutes air or water.)
External benefits	SMB > P	Not enough is demanded because demanders receive only P, not SMB. (Example: training or education brings extra gains in attitudes or team skills.)
Distorting tax	P with tax > SMC	Not enough is supplied because the tax makes the price to buyers exceed the price received by suppliers.
Monopoly power	P > SMC	Not enough is demanded because the monopolist sets the price too high.
Monopsony power (a case not developed in this textbook)	P < SMB	Not enough is supplied because the monopsonist sets its buying price too low. (Example: A single firm dominates a labor market and sets wages too low.)

P = Price

MB = Private marginal benefit of an activity (to those who demand it)

MC = Private marginal cost of an activity (to those who supply it)

SMB = Social marginal benefit of the activity (to everybody affected)

SMC = Social marginal cost of the activity (to everybody affected)

outside this sector than they do to society as a whole. In this case, the social cost of attracting workers into this sector may be a lot lower than the wage rate the firms in the sector would pay their workers. For either of these reasons, there is a case for policy devices to attract additional workers to the sector.

How should a society try to fix its distortions? There are two basic policy approaches. One is optimistic about government's ability to cure distortions, while the other is pessimistic. In this chapter we follow the optimistic approach, the tax-or-subsidy approach developed by British economist A. C. Pigou. The other approach, the property-rights approach that builds on the ideas of Nobel Prize winner Ronald Coase, is more pessimistic about using government subsidies and taxes. It suggests that creating new private-property institutions is better than using taxes or subsidies.[1] Here we set aside the property-rights approach and follow the tax-subsidy approach because the trade policy debate is usually over taxes and subsidies (e.g., a tariff is a tax). While we explore how government taxes and subsidies, at their best, *can* cure distortions, remember that there is reason to debate whether such government interventions *will* work that well in practice.[2] The idea here is to explore the best possible cases for government interference with trade, without assuming that these are the most likely real-world outcomes.

The tax-or-subsidy approach, as pioneered by Pigou, says we should spot distortions in people's private incentives and have a wise government eliminate them with taxes or subsidies. If marginal social costs exceed private incentives and prices (SMC > MC = P = MB = SMB), as in the pollution case, let the government levy a tax of SMC – SMB to bring the two in line by raising the price. If social benefits of something exceed private incentives (SMB > MB = P = MC = SMC), as in the training case, let the government pay a subsidy of SMB – SMC so that consumers in the marketplace get the full social returns.

Could trade barriers help to cure distortions in the domestic economy? Even before we get to specific trade-policy examples, it should not be difficult to see how distortions and the tax-subsidy approach can relate to the debate over import barriers. If there is a distortion in our economy, perhaps cutting imports could help. A quick example is the worker-training case already mentioned. If the social benefit of having workers get training in a certain industry is greater than their current market wage, isn't it possible that we could reap net social gains by protecting their jobs and their new skills against foreign competition? This is the kind of issue we turn to repeatedly in this chapter.

---

[1]For example, the property-rights approach says that if there is a problem of polluting a river, we can make private incentives equal social effects by making the river somebody's private property: Either let the downstream river users own it and charge the paper mill for any pollution, or let the paper mill own it and demand compensation for cleaning it up. Choose between these two property-rights assignments by choosing the one that costs less to implement and enforce. The property-rights approach will resurface in Chapter 12's treatment of international environmental issues.

[2]We can see this more broadly and also clear up a possible confusion. In Figure 9.1, a tax is listed as a possible source of a distortion. That is, if the market otherwise gets to the first-best solution (because there is no other distortion), then introducing a tax causes a distortion. If, instead, a distortion already exists, then the market will not get to the first-best outcome by itself. Then an appropriate tax (or subsidy) can improve the market outcome. But the wrong tax (or subsidy) will make things even worse.

The Specificity Rule

Externalities and other incentive distortions complicate the task of judging whether a trade barrier is good or bad for the nation as a whole. Realizing this, some scholars have stressed that there is no cure-all prescription for trade policy problems in a second-best world. Once you realize that domestic distortions exist, each case must be judged on its own merits.

Yet we are not cast totally adrift in this world of distortions. We do not have to shrug and just say "Every case is different. It all depends." There is a useful rule that works well in most cases. Let's learn the logic of that rule first, before applying it to the cases considered in the rest of this chapter.

Here is a rough rule that serves well for policy making in a distortion-riddled economy:

> The **specificity rule:** Intervene at the source of the problem. It is usually more efficient to use the policy tool that acts as directly as possible on the source of the distortion separating private and social benefits or costs.

The specificity rule applies to all sorts of policy issues. Let's illustrate it first by using some examples removed from international trade. Suppose that the most serious distortion to be attacked is crime, which creates fear among third parties as well as direct harm to victims. Since crime is caused by people, we might consider combating crime by reducing the whole population through compulsory sterilization laws or taxes on children. But such actions are obviously very inefficient ways of attacking crime since less social friction would be generated (per crime averted) if we fought crime more directly through greater law enforcement and programs to reduce unemployment, a major contributor to crime.

A less extreme example of the specificity rule brings us back to those paper mills polluting rivers. To attack this problem, we could tax all production of paper products or we could subsidize the installation of a particular waste treatment device where the mills' pipes meet the river. But the specificity rule cautions us to make sure that we are as close as possible to the source of the problem. Taxing all paper products is likely to be too broad an instrument since it discourages the production of all paper without regard to the extent of pollution. The paper manufacturers would get the signal that society wants them to make less paper, but not the signal to look for less polluting ways of making paper. On the other hand, subsidizing the installation of a waste treatment device may be too narrow an instrument. Nothing assures us that the waste treatment approach is the cheapest way to reduce pollution. Perhaps a change in the internal production processes of the paper mills could cut down on the load of waste needing any pipeline treatment more cheaply than the cost of the waste treatment equipment. The problem arose from the failure to provide the paper manufacturers with incentives for cutting pollution, not from their failure to adopt a particular method. The specificity rule thus directs us to look at incentive policies geared to the act of pollution itself—such policies as taxes or quantitative limits on the amount of pollution discharged (effluent charges and environmental quality standards).

As we will see in the cases we now turn to, the specificity rule tends to cut against import barriers. Although a barrier against imports can be better than doing nothing in a second-best world, the rule shows us that some other policy instrument is usually more efficient than a trade barrier in dealing with a domestic distortion. To see how, let us begin with the domestic target at which import barriers are most often aimed.

A Tariff to Promote Domestic Production

Debates over trade policy often come up with reasons for giving special encouragement to the domestic production of a commodity that is currently being imported. These reasons are varied. In fact, most popular second-best arguments for protection can be viewed as variations on the theme of favoring a particular import-competing industry. Each argument stresses that there are social benefits to domestic production in this particular import-competing industry that cannot be captured by the domestic industry unless it is protected. Let us turn first to the general pros and cons of a tariff to promote domestic production, setting aside for the moment the reasons why there might be side benefits to society from domestic production. We consider the case of a small country (whose trade has no impact on world prices), so that our analysis is not complicated by any effects on the international terms of trade.

A nation might want to encourage domestic production of bicycles, perhaps because it thinks the experience of producing this manufactured good generates modern skills and attitudes or simply because it takes pride in producing its own modern bikes. It could foster this objective by putting a $30 tariff on imported bicycles, as shown in the diagram of the national bicycle market in Figure 9.2A. The tariff brings the nation the same elements of net loss that it did back in Chapter 7 (and Figure 7.4A): The nation loses area b by producing at greater expense what could be bought for less abroad, and it loses area d by discouraging purchases that would have brought more enjoyment to consumers than the world price of a bicycle. But now something is added: The lower part of the diagram portrays some social side benefits from home production, benefits that are not captured by the domestic bicycle producers. That is, we suppose that the marginal social side benefits of making our own bicycles can be represented by the MSSB curve at the bottom. By raising the domestic price of bicycles, the tariff has encouraged more production of bicycles. This increase in domestic production, from S_0 to S_1, has brought area g in extra gains to the nation.

Compared with doing nothing, levying the tariff in Figure 9.2A could be good or bad for the nation, all things considered. The net outcome depends on whether area g is larger or smaller than the areas b and d. To find out, we would have to develop empirical estimates reflecting the realities of the bicycle industry. We would want to estimate the dollar value of the annual side benefits to society and also the slopes of the domestic supply and demand curves. The net national gain $(g - b - d)$ might turn out to be positive or negative. Until we know the specific numbers involved, all that we can say, so far, is that the tariff might prove to be better or worse than doing nothing.

FIGURE 9.2   *Two Ways to Promote Import-Competing Production*

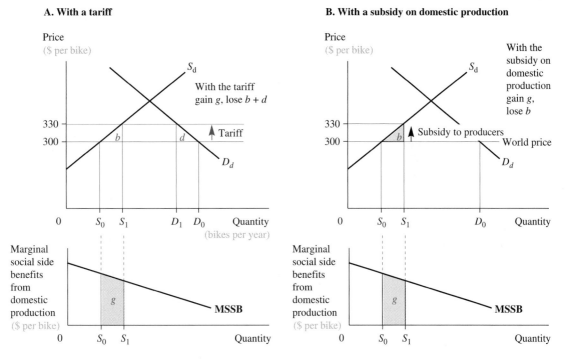

Compare the side effects of two ways of getting the same increase in domestic output ($S_0 - S_1$) and in domestic jobs. Both the $30 tariff and the $30 subsidy to domestic production encourage the same change in domestic production. But the tariff also need-lessly discourages some consumption of imports (the amount $D_1 - D_0$) that was worth more to the buyers than the $300 each unit of imports would have cost the nation. The production subsidy is better than the tariff because it strikes more directly at the task of raising domestic production of this good.

We should use our institutional imagination, however, and look for other pol-icy tools. The specificity rule prods us to do so. The locus of the problem is domestic production, not imports as such. What society wants to encourage is more domestic production of this good, not less consumption or less imports of it. Why not encourage the domestic production directly by rewarding firms on the basis of the amount of this beneficial good they produce?

Society could directly subsidize the domestic production of bicycles by hav-ing the government pay bicycle firms a fixed amount for each bicycle produced and sold. This would probably encourage them to produce more bicycles. Any increase in production that a given tariff could coax out of domestic firms could also be yielded by a production subsidy. Figure 9.2B shows such a subsidy, namely, a $30 subsidy per bicycle. The subsidy increases the revenue per unit sold to $330 ($300 paid by consumers and $30 paid by the government). This subsidy is just as good for bicycle firms as the extra $30 in selling price that the tariff made possible. Either tool gets the firms to raise their annual production from S_0 to S_1, giving society the same side benefits.

The $30 production subsidy in Figure 9.2B is definitely better than the $30 tariff in Figure 9.2A. Both generate the same social side benefits, and both cause domestic firms to produce $(S_1 - S_0)$ extra bicycles each year at a higher direct cost than the price at which the nation could buy foreign bicycles. (In both cases this extra cost is area b.) Yet the subsidy does not discourage the total consumption of bicycles by raising the price above $300. Consumers continue to pay $300 for each bicycle, equal to the world price of obtaining an imported bicycle, and they continue to consume D_0 bicycles. Consumers do not lose the additional area d. This is a clear advantage of the $30 production subsidy over the $30 tariff.

What made the production subsidy better was its conformity to the specificity rule: Since the locus of the problem was domestic production, it was less costly to attack it in a way that did not also affect the price at which consumers bought from foreigners.[3]

If our concern is with expanding jobs, rather than output, in the import-competing industry, the same results hold with a slight modification. A production subsidy would still be preferable to the tariff since it still achieves any given expansion in both bicycle production and bicycle jobs at lower social cost. We could come up with even better alternatives, however. If the locus of the problem is really the number of jobs in the bicycle industry, it would be even more efficient to use a policy tool that not only encouraged production but also encouraged firms to come up with ways of creating more jobs per dollar of bicycle output. A subsidy tied to the number of workers employed is better than a subsidy tied to output. (Alternatively, if the object is to create jobs and cure unemployment throughout the entire domestic economy, then it is logical to look first to economywide expansionary policies, such as fiscal policy or monetary policy, and not to policy fixes in any one industry.)[4]

---

[3]Although this conclusion is broadly valid, a special assumption was needed to make the net advantage of the production subsidy exactly equal area d. It has been assumed here that no other distortions between private and social incentives result when the government comes up with the revenues to pay the production subsidies to the bicycle firms. That is, it has been assumed that there is no net social loss from having the government either raise additional taxes or cancel some spending to pay this subsidy to bicycle producers.

This assumption is strictly valid if the tax revenues going into the subsidy come from a head tax, a tax on people's existence, which should only redistribute income and not affect production and consumption incentives. Yet head taxes are rare, and the more realistic case of financing the production subsidy by, say, raising income taxes or cutting other government spending programs is somewhat murkier. Raising the income tax might or might not affect people's incentives to earn income through effort. Or if the government spending reallocated to the production subsidy had previously been providing some other public goods worth more than their marginal cost, there is again an extra loss that can attend the production subsidy. These possible source-of-subsidy distortions would have to be considered in policy making. Yet it seems reasonable to presume that they are less important than the distorting of consumption represented by area d.

[4]So why do governments so often use import barriers instead of direct production subsidies that are less costly to the economy? Once an industry's political lobby is strong enough to get government help, it uses its influence to get a kind of help that is sheltered from political counterattacks. The production subsidy favored here provides no such shelter. The subsidy is a highly visible target for fiscal budget cutters. Every year it has to be defended again when the government budget is under review. A tariff or other import barrier, however, gives much better shelter to the industry that seeks government help year after year. Once it is written into the law, it goes on propping up domestic prices without being reviewed. In fact, it might even generate government revenue (e.g., tariff revenue), giving it more political appeal.

The Infant Industry Argument

The analysis of the use of a tariff to promote domestic production helps us judge the merits of many of the most popular and time-honored arguments for protection. Of all the protectionist arguments, the one that has always enjoyed the most prestige among both economists and policy makers is the **infant industry argument,** which asserts that a temporary tariff is justified because it cuts down on imports while the infant domestic industry learns how to produce at low enough costs to compete without the help of a tariff. The argument stresses that industries learn by doing and that their cost curves will fall if they can gain experience. Tariff protection gives them this chance by keeping competition from countries with established industries at bay while the domestic firms incur the high initial costs of getting started. The infant industry argument differs from the optimal tariff argument in that it claims that in the long run the tariff protection will be good for the world as well as the nation. It differs from most other tariff arguments in being explicitly dynamic, arguing that the protection is needed only for a while.

The infant industry argument has been popular with aspiring countries at least since Alexander Hamilton used it in his Report on Manufacturers in 1791. The United States followed Hamilton's protectionist formula, especially after the Civil War, setting up high tariff walls to encourage production of textiles, ferrous metals, and other goods still struggling to become competitive against Britain. Similarly, Friedrich List reapplied Hamilton's infant industry ideas to the cause of shielding nascent German manufacturing industries against British competition in the early 19th century. The government of Japan has believed strongly in infant industry protection—sometimes, but not always, in the form of import protection. In the 1950s and 1960s in particular, Japan protected its steel, automobile, shipbuilding, and electronics industries before they became tough competitors and the import barriers were removed.

The infant industry argument will continue to deserve attention because there will always be infant industries. The development of new products with new technologies will continue to contribute a growing share of world production and trade so nations will have to consider time and again what to do about the development of new industries in which other countries currently have a comparative advantage. Similarly, as we will see in the next section, the same kind of argument can be used for protecting the redevelopment efforts of a threatened old industry as well as for nurturing a new one.

How strong is the infant industry argument? Three conclusions emerge in most cases:

1. There can be a case for some sort of government encouragement.
2. A tariff may or may not help.
3. Some other form of help is a better infant industry policy than the tariff.

To the extent that infant industry concerns call for encouraging current domestic production, the analysis of the previous section applies. If nurturing the infant home industry will bring side benefits by causing the labor force and other industries to develop new capabilities, subsidizing production can achieve this more cheaply than can taxing imports. If the extra foreseen benefits take the form of future cost reductions for the same industry, through "learning by doing," then there is a better alternative than either the tariff or the production subsidy. If an industry's current high costs are outweighed by the later cost cutting that experience will allow, then the industry can borrow against its own future profits to make it through the initial period in which costs are higher than the market price. Our bicycle industry, for example, could survive its youth by borrowing and then repaying the loan out of the profits it will make as a healthy competitor later on. Also, if defects in lending markets prevent such action, the government could advance loans to new industries—still not using the tariff.

If the role of help is truly temporary, there is another argument against using the tariff to protect the infant. Tariffs are not easily removed once they are written into law, and there is the danger that an infant that never becomes efficient will use part of its tariff-bred profits to sway policymakers to make a bad tariff immortal.[5] A production subsidy, by contrast, has the economic advantage of being subject to more frequent public review as part of the government's ordinary budget review process. It can be removed in cases in which the earlier help to an infant industry has proved to be a mistake.

More sophisticated versions of the infant industry argument give more complicated defenses, yet each of these is better viewed as a defense of some policy other than protection against imports. Consider, for example, the correct point that workers trained in modern manufacturing skills in a firm struggling to compete against imports may leave that firm and take their skills to a competing firm. This threat might make new firms underinvest in training their workers. A tariff to protect modernized firms is not quite on target, though, since the tariff will not keep workers from leaving the firms that trained them. More appropriate is a subsidy on training itself, compensating the firm giving the training for benefits that would otherwise accrue largely to others. (Or the private firms could simply take more care to keep the wage lower during training, with a commitment to paying much higher wages for workers who stay with the same firm after training.) Again, the specificity rule cuts against the tariff: Although protecting an infant industry and its skill creation with a tariff on imports may be better than doing nothing, some other method can get at the problem more efficiently than the tariff.

This line of reasoning can be applied to the case of computer manufacture and computer services as an infant industry. Should the governments of Brazil or Japan protect their computer industries against competition from U.S. firms? If so, how? There is abundant evidence that the benefits of an expanding computer sector spill over to many industries and are not fully appropriated by computer firms. (Remember the external economies argument of Chapter 6.) These side benefits in the form of new productive knowledge are generated both by the industry that produces computers and by the industries that use computer services. The gains and losses from any one policy can be quantified only through a detailed investigation of the alternatives for developing these industries in Brazil and Japan.

---

[5]In a study of Turkish protection, Krueger and Tuncer (1982) found no evidence that protected industries cut costs faster than unprotected ones.

Yet, the tariff is likely to be especially inferior to direct subsidies to production, training, and research in a technologically complex industry like computers, where many of the gains in knowledge occur in the consuming industries. If the encouragement is to be extended to the total use of computer services as well as to the domestic production of computers, it will not help to retard the purchase of computers with a tariff. This point seems reflected in the approach of Japan's Ministry of International Trade and Industry, commonly known by its English acronym, MITI. MITI has indeed protected the Japanese computer industry against imports, but it has leaned increasingly on other forms of assistance: loans, patents, tax breaks, and so forth.

The Dying Industry Argument and Adjustment Assistance

The same issues and results that arose in the infant industry debate also arise in debates about saving dying industries from import competition. Once again, protection against imports might or might not be better than doing nothing. And once again, doing something else is better than blocking imports.

There will always be firms and industries whose whole livelihood is threatened by the continued invasion of competing imports. Time and again society faces a choice: Should they be allowed to go out of business, or should they be protected? If we are in a "first-best" world, the answer is clear. Since the social value of anything is already reflected in private incentives, ordinary demand and supply curves are already leading us to the right choice without any government intervention. If rising import competition is driving domestic producers out of business, so be it. Adjustment out of the industry is necessary, so that the nation can enjoy the net gains from increasing trade. As long as we take a one-dollar–one-vote approach to measuring the national interest, as in Chapters 2 through 8, the pleas and demands of those going out of business are less important than the gains that the extra trade offers the rest of society.

There are ways, however, in which we could reject the rosy "first-best" view of a world. One way to overturn the free-trade view that nothing is wrong here is to rethink the supply curves we have been using so far. We have usually assumed that a domestic supply curve, which is also the marginal-cost (MC) curve, accurately reflects what continued domestic production would cost society. That marginal-cost concept relies on the notion that MC reflects all opportunity costs. In other words, we have usually assumed that if some marginal home production is lost to extra import competition, the resources used in that home production are released into other uses that are *just as good as* employment in this industry. That's the implicit logic behind assuming that the marginal cost of home production equals the world price under free trade: Cut that production, save that marginal cost for some other equally good use.

A protectionist would often be right in insisting that the resources do *not* have some other equally profitable use that they can easily turn to if they leave the import-threatened industry. There is the danger that they would suffer a big loss in income by having to find their next-best alternative. Bicycle-making firms don't just decide to sell all their plant and equipment for the full amount of its recent bicycle-making value, and take that capital into an expanding industry. Bicycle workers don't just decide to start new careers as electronic workers next Monday for the same pay in the same town. Leaving an industry is costly. In the extreme case, suppose that the threatened people have so fully committed themselves to the bicycle industry that their earning power is zero in all other sectors. In this case, the full amount of future income that imports threaten to take away from them are a solid capital loss to society as well as to them. Wouldn't it be better for society to intervene, and wouldn't blocking the imports be better than standing by and doing nothing while the bicycle industry dies?

This protectionist argument about a dying industry is just as valid as the arguments we examined in the past two subsections ("A Tariff to Promote Domestic Production" and "The Infant Industry Argument"). Its validity also has the same limits as before. In fact, it is the very same argument, but in a different setting. The argument that businesses and workers do not have equally good opportunities outside the threatened industry can be recast in terms of Figure 9.2. The opportunity cost of leaving the bicycle industry can be represented by area g in Figure 9.2, the marginal social side benefit of continuing extra production. Area g's extra benefits from home production exist, in this case, because part or all of the area under the supply curve S_d does *not* represent a true cost of staying in this industry, as our first look at a supply curve like S_d usually assumes. So it might be true that protecting a dying industry against imports is better than doing nothing. The choice depends, again, on whether area g is greater than areas $b + d$ in Figure 9.2.

However, there is some other policy that works better than putting up import barriers. The specificity rule reminds us to look at the core of the problem. The argument about poor opportunities in other industries, if it is valid, argues for encouraging production and jobs, not for discouraging imports. There is, again, no reason to make imports more expensive to consumers as long as one can help producers directly. Here the menu of better options is exactly the same as with infant industries. If the threat can be overcome with some new investments in skills and equipment, lend the bicycle industry the money it needs to make those investments. If the bicycle workers and managers can be more productive only if retrained for other jobs, let society consider subsidizing their retraining. And, most simply, if there is really a social advantage in keeping up bicycle production, return to the lesson of Figure 9.2: The production subsidy is better than the import barrier.

In fact, governments have often seen the wisdom of helping out industries that need not die, and helping them with something other than import protection. One good example was the U.S. government's bailout loans to Chrysler at the end of the 1970s. Here was a case in which the firm's retooling problems were truly temporary, and it could afford to repay generous loans on time. Chrysler did repay its debts to the government and has survived in the same industry, and would have even without the protection of those binding VERs on Japanese automobiles from 1981 to 1987. (Of course, not all bailouts work so well. Many just end up being a continual drain on the taxpayers.)

Similarly, since the early 1960s, the U.S. government has offered workers in import-threatened industries payments of **adjustment assistance,** including government financial aid to relocate and retrain workers (and managers of firms) for re-employment in other sectors. In principle, adjustment assistance can work very well. In practice, it remains a good idea, though as much for its political wisdom as for its economic wisdom.

To see both its limits and its wisdom, let us consider how the idea of adjustment assistance has been attacked from two sides. First, those U.S. labor groups who originally backed it have felt betrayed because, in practice, it has provided so little support. In the first decade after President Kennedy's Trade Expansion Act of 1962 set up an adjustment assistance program, the official standards for eligibility for assistance were so stringent that nobody received any aid. The standards were loosened up somewhat through the Trade Act of 1974, in response to complaints by labor groups, but even today it provides only limited assistance. Furthermore, even for those who qualify for assistance, these groups believe that it mainly provides temporary compensation (for instance, in the form of extended unemployment benefits), and that the retraining is rather ineffective—the retraining often does not result in new skills and good alternative employment.

From a different side, defenders of the free marketplace question the whole concept of adjustment assistance for import-competing industries. They ask why society should single out this particular group for aid. Why don't we give equally generous aid to those whose incomes are lowered by technological change, government rerouting of highways, bad weather, or shifts in consumer tastes? If we care about people who suffer income losses, why not cushion the fall of all incomes regardless of the cause? What is so special about those people who are hurt by import competition? These are valid questions. Some countries, most notably Sweden, indeed apply their income maintenance and personnel retraining programs across the board without singling out those people injured by trade changes.

There remains the delicate problem of preserving the incentive to move out of an industry with a bad future. On the one hand, adjustment assistance programs support retraining and relocation. But there is a perverse incentive in the promise of getting such aid if you are hurt by imports: Firms and workers may be implicitly encouraged to gamble on import-vulnerable industries if they know that relief will be given should things work out badly. Here is the classic social insurance dilemma: the desire to be there with help if an activity works out badly, versus the desire to discourage people from getting into, or staying with, such activities. The social insurance dilemma plagues adjustment assistance policy just as it plagues farm support policy, other welfare programs, and disaster relief (e.g., helping flood victims versus discouraging them from settling in flood-prone lowlands).

Yet, in many countries there may be a practical political case for tying adjustment to import injury. Where foreign trade is involved, free-trade advocacy is weakened because many of its main beneficiaries, being foreigners, have no votes in national politics. With no votes for foreign workers or firms, there is extra danger that uncompensated injured workers and firms in the importing country will join lobbying alliances for more sweeping protectionist legislation. More generous adjustment assistance for import-competing groups than for others might be one effective political step to forestall more protectionist policies.

The Developing Government (Public Revenue) Argument

Import tariffs can still be justified by another second-best argument relating to conditions in less developed countries. In a poor nation, the tariff as a source of revenue may be beneficial and even better than any alternative policy, *both for the nation and for the world as a whole.*

For a developing nation with low living standards, the most serious "domestic distortions" may relate to the government's inability to provide an adequate supply of public goods. A low-income nation like Mauritania would receive large social benefits if it expanded such basic public services as the control of infectious diseases, water control for agriculture, and primary schooling. Yet, the administrative resources of many poor nations are not great enough to capture these social gains. (Others, of course, have the necessary administrative resources and use them inefficiently.)

In such nations the import tariff becomes a crucial source, not of industrial protection but of public revenue. With severe limits on the supply of literate civil servants, Mauritania will find tariffs efficient. Revenue can be raised more cheaply by simply guarding key ports and border crossings with a few customs officials who tax imports and exports than revenue can be raised with more elaborate kinds of taxes. Production, consumption, income, and property cannot be effectively taxed or subsidized when they cannot be measured and monitored.

The developing government argument is a valid reason why many low-income countries receive between one-quarter and three-fifths of their government revenue from customs duties, a higher dependence on customs than is found in equally trade-oriented high-income countries such as Canada. (On average for industrialized countries, taxes on international trade are about 2 percent of government revenues.) In principle, a developing-country government can use the tariff to maximize social gains, gains that may even make the world as a whole benefit from tariffs in low-income countries. This is not to say that every government that heavily taxes foreign trade is using the money to fund socially worthy investments. Foreign trade has also been heavily taxed by corrupt and wasteful governments, like those ruled by Bokassa (Central African Empire, now a Republic), Louis XIV (17th-century France), Marcos (Philippines), Ceausescu (Romania), and Mobuto (Zaire).

Other Arguments

The other leading arguments for tariff protection relate to the national pursuit of "noneconomic" goals. Although aggressive economists may insist that nothing lies outside their field, these arguments do relate to points that are not usually thought of as part of standard economic analysis. The potential range of such arguments is limitless, but the view that man does not live by imported bread alone usually focuses on three other goals: national pride, income distribution, and national defense. Fortunately, a modified version of the specificity rule applies to a country pursuing some noneconomic objective. To achieve the noneconomic objective with the least economic cost to the nation, use a policy that acts as directly as possible on the specific objective.

National Pride

Nations desire symbols as much as individuals do, and knowing that some good is produced within our own country can be as legitimate an object of national pride as having cleaned up a previous urban blight or winning Olympic medals. As long as the pride can be generated only by something collective and nation-wide, something not purchased by individuals in the marketplace, there is a case for policy intervention. If the pride is generated by domestic production itself, then the appropriate policy tool is a domestic production subsidy, not an import barrier (setting aside the developing government cases). Only if the pride comes from self-sufficiency itself is blocking imports the best policy approach.

Income Redistribution

A second, less economic objective to which trade policy might be addressed is the distribution of income within the nation. Often one of the most sensitive issues in national politics is either "What does it do to the poor?" or "What effect does it have on different regions or ethnic groups?" A tariff might be defended on the grounds that it restores equity by favoring some wrongly disadvantaged group, even though it may reduce the overall size of the pie to be distributed among groups. It is certainly important to know the effects of trade policy on the distribution of income within a country, a subject already treated in Chapter 4 and one to which we return in Chapter 14.

If the issue is inequity in how income is distributed within our country, why should trade policy be the means of redressing the inequity? Why not attack the problem directly? If, for example, greater income equality is the objective, it is less costly to equalize incomes directly, through taxes and transfer payments, than to try to equalize them indirectly by manipulating the tariff structure. Only if political constraints were somehow so binding that the income distribution could be adjusted only through import policy would import barriers be justified on this ground.

National Defense

The national defense argument says that import barriers would help the nation accumulate more stockpiles or capacity to produce goods that would be important in a future military emergency.

It has a rich history and several interesting twists to its analysis. English mercantilists in the 17th century used the national defense argument to justify restrictions on the use of foreign ships and shipping services: If we force ourselves to buy English ships and shipping, we will foster the growth of a shipbuilding industry and a merchant marine that will be vital in time of war. Even Adam Smith departed from his otherwise scathing attacks on trade barriers to sanction the restrictive Navigation Acts where shipping and other defense industries were involved. The national defense argument remains a favorite with producers who need a social excuse for protection. In 1984, the president of the Footwear Industry of America, with a straight face, told the Armed Services Committee of Congress,

> In the event of war or other national emergency, it is highly unlikely that the domestic footwear industry could provide sufficient footwear for the military and civilian population. . . . We won't be able to wait for ships to deliver shoes from Taiwan, or Korea or Brazil or Eastern Europe. . . . [I]mproper footwear can lead to needless casualties and turn sure victory into possible defeat.[6]

The same aroma pervaded the U.S. oil industry's national defense argument used to justify oil import limits from 1959 through 1973.

The importance of having strategic reserves on hand for emergencies is clear. Yet a little reflection shows that none of the popular variants of the national defense argument succeeds in making a good case for an import barrier. That is, the popular national defense arguments fail to follow the specificity rule. For instance, if the objective is to maintain domestic production capacity for a product that is crucial to the national defense, then a production subsidy is the policy that has the lower cost to the nation.

The possibilities of storage and depletion also argue against the use of a tariff to create defense capability. If the crucial goods can be stored inexpensively, the cheapest way to prepare for the emergency is to buy them up from foreigners at low world prices during peace. Thus, the United States could stockpile low-cost imported footwear instead of producing it domestically at greater cost. And if the crucial goods are depletable mineral resources, such as oil, the case for the tariff is even weaker. Restricting imports of oil when there is no foreign embargo causes us to use up our own reserves faster, cutting the amount we can draw on when an embargo or blockade is imposed. It is better to stockpile imports at relatively low peacetime cost, as the United States has done with its Strategic Petroleum Reserve since the mid-1970s. To believe that restricting imports would increase our untapped reserves, we would have to accept two doubtful propositions: (1) Protecting domestic oil producers makes them discover extra reserves faster than it makes them sell extra oil for peacetime consumption and (2) there is no more direct way to encourage further oil exploration within the country.[7]

---

[6]As quoted in *Far Eastern Economic Review,* October 25, 1984, p. 70.

[7]We will take a closer look at the case against using import barriers to prepare for national emergencies in Chapter 14's section "The Food Security Issue."

Summary

There are valid arguments for import barriers, though they are quite different from those usually given. One way or another, all valid defenses of import barriers lean on the existence of relevant distortions, or gaps between private and social costs or benefits.

In a second-best world where there are **distortions** in the domestic economy, imposing a tariff may be better than doing nothing. Whether or not it is better will depend on detailed empirical information. Yet, when imposing the tariff is better than doing nothing, something else is still often better than the tariff. The **specificity rule** is a rough guideline that says: Use the policy tool that is closest to the locus of the distorting gap between private and social incentives. This rule cuts against import barriers, which are usually only indirectly related to the source of the

distortion. Thus, many of the main arguments for blocking imports—such as the infant industry argument and national defense argument—fall short of showing that import barriers are better than other policy tools. Although blocking imports is sometimes better than doing nothing, it is usually inferior to some other policy tool.[8]

The case for a tariff is most secure in the developing government setting, in which the country is so poor and its government so underdeveloped that the tariff is a vital source of government revenue to finance basic public investments and services.

Where, then, are the borders that separate good trade barriers from bad ones? Figure 9.3 maps those borders by summarizing the policy results of the main cases surveyed in this chapter plus Chapter 7's nationally optimal tariff

FIGURE 9.3

Can an Import Barrier Be Better Than Doing Nothing, and Is It the Best Policy?

A Summary of Verdicts[a]

Goal to Be Promoted	Can an Import Barrier Be Better Than Doing Nothing?	Is an Import Barrier the Best Policy Tool?
Domestic production	Yes, it can.	No.
Domestic jobs	Yes, it can.	No.
An infant industry	Yes, it can.	No.
A dying industry	Yes, it can.	No.
A developing government	Yes, it can.	Yes, it can be.
National pride	Yes, it can.	No, unless *only* self-sufficiency can make the nation proud.
A fairer income distribution	Yes, it can.	No.
National defense	Yes, it can.	No.
National monopsony power (large country)	Yes, it can.	For nation, yes; for world, no (Chapter 7's nationally optimal tariff).
Antidumping (Chapter 10)	In some cases.	For nation, in some cases; for world, no.
Counter a foreign export subsidy (Chapter 10)	Yes, it can.	For nation, no; for world, yes.

Note: Remember that "Yes, it can" does not mean "Yes, it is." To see what separates situations when the import barrier is better than nothing from situations when it is worse, review the text of this chapter.

[a]In all verdicts except that for national monopsony power, the conclusions refer to a small country, so that the conclusions are not confounded by the possibility of optimum-tariff effects on the terms of trade.

[8]At this point you may wish to review Chapter 7's section "A Preview of Conclusions," noting how each case discussed in Chapter 9 fits that preview.

CHAPTER 10

Pushing Exports

Controversy over export behavior and export policy has begun to rival the perennial fights over import barriers. On the export side, however, the fight takes on a somewhat different form. Here the fight usually centers on the artificial *promotion* of trade rather than on trade barriers. This chapter explores how both businesses and governments push for more exports than their country would sell under ordinary competition. The underlying policy questions are: Can a country export too much for its own good or for the good of the world? Is that happening today? If so, what should an importing country do about another country's excessive exports?

These questions do not arise in a vacuum. Real governments, pressured by real business and labor lobbies, have long fought over what producers in importing countries consider artificial and excessive exports from other countries. The heat of debate on this issue intensified during the past two decades. U.S. and European producers charged that Japan, Korea, Brazil, and other rapidly growing industrial powers were engaging in "unfair trade," violating both the rules of ordinary competition and the trade rules of the World Trade Organization with unfair export pushing. Others have chosen to imitate rather than to condemn. Many Americans and Europeans argue that their countries need to adopt the strategy of "industrial targeting" (or "industrial policy") that seems to have been practiced in Japan and other countries. **Industrial targeting** means having the government and industry agree far in advance on just which industrial lines need the most encouragement and subsidy, grooming them as future export specialties.

We address the debate over "unfair trade" and "industrial targeting" here. We turn first to dumping, the most important way in which private firms artificially export more than competitive supply and demand would lead us to expect. Then we explore how governments push exports, both with outright subsidies and with subtler export-promotion policies.

Dumping

Dumping is selling exports at a price that is too low—less than "normal" value (or "fair market value," as it is often called in the United States). There are two meanings of *normal value*. The long-standing definition is the price charged to domestic buyers in the home market (or to buyers in other markets). Under this traditional definition, dumping is international price discrimination favoring buyers of exports. The second definition of normal value arose in the 1970s. It is cost-based—the average cost of producing the product, including profit and overhead costs. Under this second standard, dumping is selling exports at a price that is less than the full average cost of the product.

Why would an exporting firm engage in dumping? Why would it sell exports at a price lower than the price it charges for its product in its home market, or lower than its average cost? There are several reasons. In order to judge whether dumping is good or bad, it is important to understand the full range of reasons that dumping occurs.

Predatory dumping occurs when the firm temporarily charges a low price in the foreign export market, with the purpose of driving its competitors out of business. Once the rivals are gone, the firm will use its monopoly power to raise prices and earn high profits.

Cyclical dumping occurs during periods of recession. During the part of the business cycle when demand is low, a firm makes export sales that are lower than its average costs. If these low prices gain export sales, then the firm can use more of its production capacity and provide work for its labor.

Seasonal dumping is intended to sell off excess inventories of a product, often without lowering the price in the main market (usually the home market). For instance, toward the end of a fashion season, U.S. clothing companies may decide to sell off remaining stock of swimsuits at very low prices in Canada. Prices in the major U.S. market are kept more stable, with the Canadian market absorbing the extra supply. Similarly, dumping can be a technique for promoting new products in new markets, the equivalent of an introductory sale, especially when an exporting firm is attempting to establish its product in the foreign market.

Persistent dumping occurs because firms with market power use *price discrimination* between markets to increase their total profits. A firm will maximize profits by charging a lower price to foreign buyers if it has greater monopoly power (less competition) in its home market than abroad and if buyers in the home country cannot avoid the high home prices by buying the good abroad and importing it cheaply. When these conditions hold, the firm can make home-country buyers pay a higher price and thus earn a higher total profit. This is not predatory; it is not intended to drive any other firms out of business. And it can persist for a long time—as long as these market differences continue.

Figure 10.1 shows such a case of profitable price discrimination under the simplifying assumption that the firm faces a constant marginal cost of production. (In addition, the marginal production cost is the same regardless of whether the product is sold in the home market or exported, assuming that essentially the same product is sold in both places.) The illustration is based on a real case that

FIGURE 10.1

Dumping

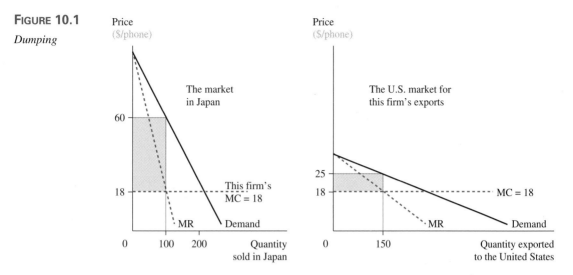

The price-discriminating monopolist maximizes profits in two markets by pricing so that the marginal revenue (MR) from extra sales in each market just matches marginal cost (MC). To make this happen, the firm charges a higher price in the market where the demand curve it faces is less elastic (steeper). In this case, that is the home market in Japan, perhaps because it is protected from competition there. In the more demand-elastic competitive U.S. market, the firm charges less. In this way, it maximizes the total profits shown in the two shaded areas. The firm can get away with such discrimination only if there is no way for buyers in the high-price country to be served with output from the other country, and if policy makers do not retaliate against the dumping.

surfaced in 1989. The U.S. government determined that firms in Japan, Korea, and Taiwan were all guilty of dumping telephones in the U.S. market, causing injury to AT&T (the plaintiff) and other U.S. firms.[1] We illustrate with the case of a single Japanese firm (e.g., Matsushita).

What makes persistent dumping profitable is that the firm faces a less elastic (steeper) demand curve in its home market than in the more competitive foreign market. That is, home-country buyers would not change the quantity they buy very much in response to price, whereas foreign buyers would quickly abandon this firm's product if the firm raised its price much. Sensing this, the firm maximizes profits by equating marginal cost and marginal revenue in each market. In the U.S. market the profit-maximizing price is $25, which makes U.S. consumers buy 150 telephones a year, at which level marginal revenue just equals the marginal cost of $18. In Japan's home market, where consumers see fewer substitutes for the major Japanese brands, the profit-maximizing price is $60, which causes consumers to buy 100 phones a year, again equating marginal costs and revenues.

---

[1]The actual dumping case involved phone equipment for small businesses, although here we illustrate with the case of personal phones from Japan. The U.S. International Trade Commission estimated dumping margins (home-market price above price on sales to the United States) of 120 to 180 percent for major firms in Japan and Taiwan, but only a trivial difference for Korean firms. The Asian exporters had raised their share of the U.S. phone market for small businesses to 60 percent by 1989.

This price discrimination is more profitable for the firm than charging the same price in both markets, which would yield lower marginal revenues in Japan than in the United States. As long as transport costs and import barriers in Japan make it uneconomical for Japanese consumers to import Japanese-made telephones back from the United States, the firm continues to make greater profits by charging a higher price in the Japanese market. Often government policy is what keeps the two markets separate by protecting the dumper against foreign competition in the higher-priced home market (Japan, in this example).

Reacting to Dumping: What Should a Dumpee Think?

Domestic firms competing against exports dumped into their market are likely to complain loudly to their government, charging that this is unfair. How should the importing country view dumping? What should be its government policy toward dumping?

The free-trader's first instinct is to welcome dumping and thank the exporting country. After all, we do not usually argue when someone tries to sell us something at a low price. This instinct seems clearly correct for persistent dumping. Compared to the high price in the exporting country, the importing country gets the gains from additional trade at the low export price. The importing country's terms of trade are better, and the benefits to consumers are larger than the losses to the import-competing producers. To see this, consider what will happen to the importing country if it imposes a tariff on the dumped imports, to force the tariff-inclusive price up to about the level in the exporting country. In Figure 10.1, the duty would be 140 percent $(= 60 - 25)/25)$. This duty is prohibitive: The Japanese firm ceases all exports to the United States, and the United States thus loses all gains from trade in this product. Through similar logic, the importing country generally should welcome seasonal and introductory-price dumping.

Cyclical dumping raises an additional issue for the importing country. If the foreign exporter is particularly aggressive, then it will gain export sales that permit it to maintain production and employment. Since the import-competing firms lose sales, the exporting country is in effect "exporting unemployment." The importing country is harmed temporarily, and there may be a case for temporary government policies to fight cyclical dumping.

However, viewed in another way, the case of cyclical dumping is not so clear-cut. Much of the time cyclical dumping is not an aggressive strategy to export unemployment, but rather the normal working of a competitive marketplace. When there is a temporary downturn in demand, price falls in a competitive market, and firms move down their supply curves. For a competitive industry, price will fall below full average cost in this situation, because firms will continue to produce and sell as long as the market price is above average variable cost. This is exactly what we want to happen when there is a recession in demand, so there is little economic basis for the importing country's government to fight cyclical dumping if it reflects the normal working of competitive markets.

Predatory dumping is the most troubling type of dumping for the importing country. Although the importing country gains from low-priced imports in the short run, it will lose because of high-priced imports once the exporting firm succeeds in establishing its monopoly power. A key question is how frequently foreign firms use predatory dumping. Predatory dumping of manufacturing goods was widely alleged during the international chaos of the 1920s and 1930s. In truth, there is no clear evidence that widespread predatory dumping has been practiced, despite a rich folklore about it. Predatory dumping is likely to be rare in modern markets. The firm considering predatory dumping must weigh the losses from low prices that are certain in the short run against the possible but uncertain profits in the more distant future. Indeed, even if the firm drives out its current competitors in the importing country, it may find that, once it raises prices, new firms, including new exporters from other countries, enter as competitors. Recent research suggests that no more than 5 percent of all cases of alleged dumping in the United States and the European Union show even a moderate possibility for predation (and it is possible that none of these cases involves predation).

Actual Antidumping Policies: What Is Unfair?

For the country importing the dumped exports, our discussion suggests that dumping is often good for the country, but that two types of dumping—predatory dumping and aggressive cyclical dumping—can be bad for the country. The implication is that the country's government policy toward dumping (its antidumping policy) should examine each case and consider benefits and costs before imposing antidumping duties or other restrictions on dumped imports. In fact, actual government policies are not at all like this.

The WTO, and the GATT before it, permit countries to retaliate against dumping. Antidumping cases increased rapidly beginning in the 1970s. Prior to the late 1980s, the United States, the European Union, Canada, and Australia were the importing countries that accounted for over 90 percent of antidumping cases, and most countries had no antidumping policies. Since then, a large number of countries have begun to use antidumping policy. Figure 10.2 shows the countries that have been most active in antidumping cases during the 1990s. A number of developing countries now use antidumping frequently. Worldwide, the countries whose exporters are most frequently charged with dumping are the United States, China, Japan, the European Union, Korea, Taiwan, and Brazil. The products most often involved are chemicals, metals, machinery, textiles and apparel, consumer electronics, and cement.

Let's look more carefully at U.S. antidumping policy. A case usually begins with a complaint from U.S. producers. The U.S. Department of Commerce examines whether dumping has actually occurred, and the U.S. International Trade Commission examines whether U.S. firms have been injured. In addition, negotiations may occur with foreign exporters. If they agree to raise prices or to limit their exports, then the case can be terminated or suspended. (This type of outcome has been common in cases involving steel and chemicals.)

FIGURE 10.2	Importing Country	Average Annual Number of Cases Initiatied, 1991–1995	Average Antidumping Duty Imposed 1991–1995	Antidumping Orders in Effect End of 1995	Average Age (Years) of Orders in Effect End of 1995
Top 10 Initiators of Antidumping Cases	United States	49	57%	294	7
	Australia	43	26	75	3
	European Union	32	29	133	4
	Mexico	23	104	81	2
	Argentina	23	na	20	1
	South Africa	20[a]	na	15	3
	Canada	16	36	98	6
	Brazil	14	34	23	3
	Turkey	11	19	37	3
	New Zealand	8	32	25	4

Note: na = not available.

[a]For 1994–1995 only.

Source: Congressional Budget Office, "Antidumping Action in the United States and Around the World: An Analysis of International Data," *CBO Papers,* June 1998, Tables B-1, B-2, B-5, and B-7.

The Department of Commerce usually finds some amount of dumping—the law and the procedures are biased to make showing dumping easy. In more than half of the cases full average cost is the basis for calculating normal value. The injury standard is not strict, but injury is usually the key to the outcome of the case. If both dumping and injury are found, customs officials are instructed to levy an extra import duty equal to the discrepancy (the margin) between the actual export price and the normal value. More than half of the cases brought in the United States result in antidumping duties or an exporter agreement to restrain their export prices or volumes.

Recent research shows some clear patterns of effects of all this. Shortly after the complaint is filed, the prices of the exporters charged with dumping increase, probably to try to reduce the final dumping margin, and export quantities decrease, because of the higher price and because of the uncertainty about the outcome of the case. If antidumping duties are imposed, the export quantities decrease further, often to zero (as we noted for the case shown in Figure 10.1). The effect on export prices varies from case to case, because exporters face a mix of incentives and because market conditions differ. The exporter has some incentive to lower its export price further, to absorb some of the duty, so that the duty-inclusive price in the import country does not increase by as much. But, it is then at risk of higher antidumping duties in the future. The exporter instead has some incentive to increase its export price, to show that it is no longer dumping, so that the duties will be removed.

Under current antidumping policies in the United States and a growing number of other countries, we get the following results:

1. The procedure is biased toward finding dumping.
2. The injury test considers only import-competing producers. There is no consideration of whether predation or some other source of harm to the country is involved.

3. Overall, the process is biased toward imposing antidumping duties, even though this probably usually lowers the well-being of the importing country. Antidumping duties also generally lower world welfare.

Antidumping policy starts out sounding like it is about unfair exports. But a closer examination indicates that something else is going on here. Antidumping policy has become a major way for import-competing producers in a growing number of countries to gain new protection against imports, with the usual dead-weight costs to the world and to the importing country. As shown in Figure 10.2, the average antidumping duties imposed against foreign exporters are very high, much higher than most regular tariffs, so the deadweight losses can be large. And, as shown in Figure 10.2, the antidumping duties continue for years (the oldest U.S. antidumping duty still in effect at the end of 1995 was 29 years old). There is also the cost of arguing the cases and gathering the data to prove or disprove dumping and injury. In addition, import-competing firms use the threat of a dumping complaint to prod exporters to raise their prices and restrain their competition—the harassment effect—even if no complaint is actually filed.

Thus, the WTO-approved practice of countries retaliating against dumping is generally bad for the world, and it is usually bad for the importing nation.[2]

Export Subsidies

Exports are actually subsidized more often than they are taxed. Patrick Low has estimated that in 1988 subsidies to producers of exported goods amounted to 0.6 percent of GDP in the United States, 0.9 percent in Japan, and 2.5 percent in the European Communities.[3]

This is curious and controversial. It is curious for at least two reasons. First, why would a country want to discriminate in favor of selling exports instead of giving just as good a bargain to its own residents? That is, why should a government want its home buyers to pay more than foreign buyers? Second, it is curious that the same export-subsidizing countries restrict their imports, without seeming

---

[2]There is a case in which retaliation against persistent dumping could bring gains to the whole world. If the "convicted" dumper ceases all price discrimination, continues to serve both markets, and is rewarded by getting the duty removed again, the world could end up better off from the temporary punitive use of the duty. The world is better off in the sense that output is redirected to the home-country buyers who valued the good more highly at the margin. One example of this kind of gain is the outcome of the U.S. dumping case against Korean consumer electronics producers, which led to a lowering of the higher prices Korean consumers paid for these products.

Recall that this is only one of a number of possible outcomes, and the others are usually bad for the world. For instance, the dumpers may move their export-market production to the importing country at some extra expense of world resources. Or they might abandon the controversial foreign market as not worth the bother if it is spoiled by an antidumping duty. The issue of dumping is complex. The text gives the welfare results that seem most likely, however.

[3]Patrick Low (1993), pp. 75–76. In the United States, it is not surprising that export subsidies exceed export taxes because the U.S. Constitution prohibits the taxing of exports.

to notice that subsidizing exports implicitly subsidizes imports. As we saw in Chapter 4, more exports and more imports go together. The export subsidy, by giving the country more foreign-exchange earnings and raising the exchange-rate value of the home currency, makes it easier for others in the home country to buy foreign goods that compete against home goods.

Export subsidies are controversial because they violate international ethics. One provision of the WTO rules proscribes export subsidies as "unfair competition" and allows importing countries to retaliate with protectionist "countervailing duties." Our analysis of export subsidies will broadly agree with the WTO: Export subsidies are bad from a world point of view. The international division of gains and losses turns out to be very different from what you would expect just by listening to who favors export subsidies and who complains about them: Export subsidies are bad for the countries that use them, but are good for the countries that complain about them!

Governments subsidize exports in many ways, even though they do so quietly to escape indictment under the WTO. They use taxpayers' money to give low-interest loans to either exporters or their foreign customers. An example is the U.S. Export–Import Bank, or Eximbank. Founded in the 1930s, it has compromised its name by giving easy credit to U.S. exporters and their foreign customers but not to U.S. importers or their foreign suppliers. Governments also engage in direct promotional expenditures on behalf of exporters, advertising their products abroad and supplying cheap information on export market possibilities. Income tax rules are also twisted to give tax relief based on the value of goods or services each firm exports.

Export subsidies are small on average, but they loom large in certain products and for certain companies. Most Eximbank loans have been channeled toward a few large U.S. firms and their customers. Boeing, in particular, has been helped to extra foreign aircraft orders by cheap Eximbank credit. The biggest percent export subsidies apply to agricultural products. All major countries have committed themselves to government programs that raise farmers' incomes by artificially using tax money to buy up (and to pay farmers not to plant) "surplus" farm products. To cut taxpayers' losses on these accumulated surpluses, the governments of Western Europe and North America sell the extra products at a loss abroad, sometimes with additional subsidies, offering a bargain to other nations who are able to buy at the relatively low world price. The Uruguay Round agreement promised to reduce agricultural subsidies around the world.

Countervailing Duties

If a foreign government is subsidizing exports into your national market, should you enjoy the bargain on imports or should you retaliate by imposing countervailing import duties protecting the domestic industry in a way sanctioned by the WTO? Officials may make up their minds on this issue partly with an eye to politics. Officials feeling intense lobbying pressure from the threatened domestic industry are more likely to seize the chance to impose duties, with fanfare about defending the industry from unfair foreign competition, whereas officials who are sensitive to consumer interests may avoid imposing the duty.

At the end of 1995, the WTO reported that there were 108 countervailing duty measures in effect around the world (for comparison, the global total of antidumping orders then in effect was 817). Retaliation against export subsidies has been a specialty of the United States, with 72 of these 108. Australia, Mexico, Canada, and Brazil also make some use of countervailing duties. The U.S. countervailing duties apply to exports from a wide range of countries, with steel and textiles and clothing as the products most frequently involved.

The economic pros and cons of countervailing duties against subsidized exports can be shown with the help of Figure 10.3, which can serve as a rough portrayal of the market for imported Korean steel shapes on the West Coast of either Canada or the United States. With free trade and no subsidy, the market tends toward equilibrium at point A. As usual, this maximizes world gains from trade in this market, since the marginal value of an extra ton, represented by the height of the demand curve, just matches the price P_0, which represents the marginal resource cost of supplying an extra ton of Korean steel.

The Korean government's export subsidy artificially lowers the supply curve (here assumed to be perfectly elastic) to P_1 and raises West Coast imports to M_1. From a world point of view, this is too much trade. North American firms are being encouraged to use Korean steel up to point C, where the value to them of the last ton is only P_1, yet it costs the world P_0 in Korean resources to supply the last ton. This *excess trade* costs the world as a whole the shaded area ABC in the form of wasted resources. For the importing country, however, this is a bargain. Area $ACEF$ represents the importing country's net gain from the cheaper steel imports. At the same time, the subsidy of $(P_1 - P_0)$ per unit exported costs the Korean government area $BCEF$, which is also the loss to Korea on the decline in its terms of trade.

Now suppose that the United States or Canada were to put a countervailing duty on Korean steel, one just large enough to offset Korea's export subsidy. We would return to the same price (P_0) and volume of trade (M_0) as with free trade and no subsidy at point A. This makes good sense in terms of world efficiency since it eliminates that waste represented by area ABC. For the world, the countervailing duty in Figure 10.3 represents a successful use of Chapter 9's specificity rule. In this case the problem was indeed excess exports from Korea to North America and the countervailing duty taxes exactly that activity to the extent of the distorting subsidy.

The net result of the subsidy plus the countervailing duty together is interesting. Trade ends up being unaffected (still at point A), but Korean taxpayers unknowingly send invisible checks to North American taxpayers, to the tune of the area $ADEF$, each year. Yet the importing country would be serving the world interest at its own expense since it would lose area ACD by denying steel-using firms the better bargain. Export subsidies thus create a curious division of national and world welfare stakes.

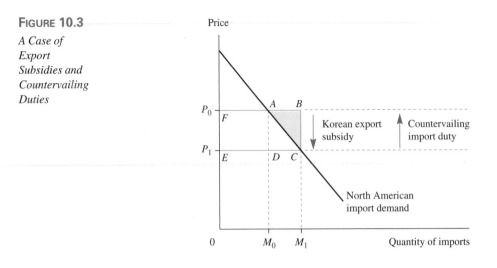

FIGURE **10.3**

*A Case of
Export
Subsidies and
Countervailing
Duties*

This diagram gives the effect of (*a*) a Korean export subsidy on steel to North America (either Canada or United States, say); (*b*) a North American countervailing duty against Korean steel, as allowed by the WTO; and (*c*) the two together. An odd pattern results: Each policy brings net losses to the country adopting it (so why do they do it?), yet for the world as a whole the countervailing duty undoes the harm done by the Korean export subsidy.

To harvest these results from the diagram trace these steps and results:

	Moves Equilibrium		Welfare Effects on		
Policy	*From Point*	*To Point*	*North America*	*Korea*	*Both ("World")*
Korea's export subsidy	*A* → *C*		gains *ACEF*	loses *BCEF*	lose *ABC*
North America's countervailing duty	*C* → *A*		loses *ACD*	gains *ABCD**	gain *ABC*
Both together	*A* back to *A*		gain *ADEF*	lose *ADEF*	zero
			(Korean taxpayers implicitly pay North American taxes.)		

* There are less exports to waste the subsidy on.

If export subsidies are bad for the world as a whole, and retaliating against them is good for the world as a whole, then the WTO shows wisdom in allowing the importing countries to use the countervailing-duty weapon. This is a clear and useful conclusion.

Next to every silver lining, though, there is a cloud. In this case, two clouds prevent the clear analysis above from being a final judgment on the costs and benefits of export subsidies and countervailing duties.

The first cloud is similar to the one that hangs over antidumping. Import-competing firms have an incentive to complain about foreign subsidies to exports, in an effort to gain protection against imports. A number of policies and programs of foreign governments could have the effect of subsidizing exports, although they are not given out strictly in proportion to exports. For instance, governments sometimes decide to promote a rising industry's production and employment. They will give subsidies, tax breaks, and cheap loans to that industry on the basis of its new investments, its new output, and its new jobs. In antisubsidy cases, it is usually possible for the complaining firms to establish that some kind of foreign subsidy is present that might benefit exports. Then they can gain the protection of countervailing duties, if they can show that they have been injured by these "subsidized" exports. Thus, at times, the antisubsidy procedures can become a tool of protection rather than a response to unfair exports. Nonetheless, this seems to happen less frequently for antisubsidy cases than for antidumping cases, and the duties are smaller (U.S. countervailing duties average about 10 percent).

The second cloud is that the usual analysis may be wrong in assuming competitive supply and demand, and this does matter to the results. Suppose that the real-world market in question features the clash of two giant firms, each of which could supply the whole market. This is not a case of competitive supply and demand, and it is a plausible case that leads to a very different conclusion. Let us turn to a two-firm game in which either firm's home government can help both its own country and the world by using an export subsidy.

Strategic Export Subsidies Could Be Good

The economics of an export subsidy looks very different if international competition in some industry departs from the laws of supply and demand, and consists of an oligopolistic duel between two giant firms for the global market. (Recall our discussion of oligopoly and trade in Chapter 6.) In this duel of giants, an export subsidy can be either good or bad, both for the exporting country and for the world.

To see the possibility of a good export subsidy, let us imagine a simplified case inspired by the continuing real-world competition between Boeing and Europe's Airbus Industrie. Suppose that it becomes technologically possible for them to build a new kind of passenger plane. To keep a clear focus on the key points, let us say that there is no difference between Airbus and Boeing in the cost of making the new plane. Aircraft manufacture is an industry having "economies of scale"—that is, as the firm expands all inputs in proportion, its outputs go up at an even faster rate so that the cost of making any one unit drops as the output rises. Therefore, either firm is capable of supplying the whole world market at a low cost. If only one firm captures the whole world market, it will reap some monopoly profits. If both firms produce, they will bid down the price to their low variable costs, and make no operating profits.

Figure 10.4 sets the stage by considering what might happen if Airbus and Boeing simultaneously faced a decision about whether to make the new plane. For either of them, it is a tough decision. Let's look at it from Airbus' viewpoint.

FIGURE 10.4

*A Two-Firm
Competitive
Game with No
Government
Subsidies:
Airbus Versus
Boeing*

Payoff matrix, with no subsidies:

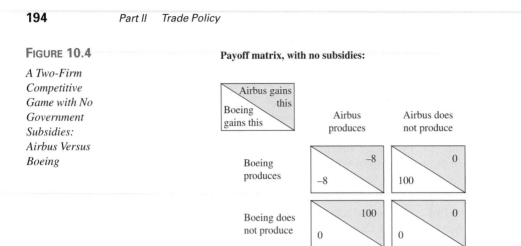

When two competing firms face each other with identical choices and no government help, the result depends on whether one decides to produce or they both decide to produce. If one goes ahead and the other holds back, the first-mover wins 100. But if they both produce, they both lose 8, as in the upper left box here.

Should it choose to invest 8 and produce the new planes (left column), or should it not invest and not produce (right column)? Well, that all depends on what Boeing does. If Airbus could be sure Boeing would stay out, it should definitely invest the 8 and produce, making the profits of 100 shown in the lower left box. But what if Boeing does produce? Then the two of them would have a price war and get no profits to offset their initial investments of 8.

So choosing to enter the market looks risky for Airbus. It looks similarly risky for Boeing. As you can see by studying the payoffs for the two rows, Boeing would want to produce only if it could be sure that Airbus won't produce (upper right box). But in a noncooperative game like this, neither firm can choose the outcome—each can only choose a strategy (column or row). They might react to the threat of competition by producing nothing, leaving the world in the lower right box—with no new planes.

Either government could break through the uncertainty by offering a subsidy to its producer, one that covers all the producer's initial costs. Again, let's take the European viewpoint. The governments of Britain, France, Germany, and Spain could agree (as they have in the past) to give subsidies to Airbus. If they give Airbus a start-up subsidy of 10, which more than covers its fixed initial costs of 8, we could have the situation shown in panel A in Figure 10.5. Looking down the left column of possibilities, Airbus can see that it should definitely produce—either it gains only 2 (invest 8, get 10 back in subsidies) in the face of competition from Boeing, or it gains a full 110 if Boeing is frightened off. Airbus gains, the world's consumers gain (an amount not shown here). Even Europe as a whole gains if Airbus makes the 110 in profits, because after subtracting the subsidy of 10, the net gain to Europe is still 100. So here is a case of an export subsidy that is good for the world as a whole, and good for the exporting country (the European Union) as well.

FIGURE 10.5

*A Two-Firm
Competitive
Game with
Government
Subsidies:
Airbus Versus
Boeing*

A. Payoff matrix, with European government subsidies to Airbus:

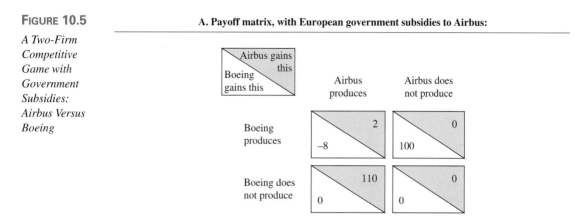

If the European governments give Airbus a subsidy of 10, to ensure the firm a gain of 2 even with full competition, Airbus will choose to produce. Boeing probably will not produce. Airbus wins 110, consumers benefit, and the world as a whole gains. So in this case, the subsidy to an exporter looks good.

B. Payoff matrix, with government subsidies to both firms:

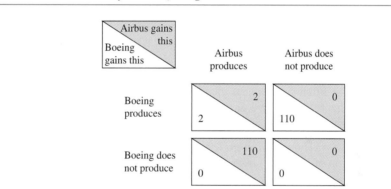

But in this case, with both governments offering subsidies, the two nations will both lose. We'd get the upper left result. The gain of 2 to each firm is based on a loss of 10 to each government.

It's not so easy, though. Suppose that the U.S. government decides to subsidize Boeing's market entry in the same way that the EU subsidizes Airbus. Then we have the problem shown in panel B of Figure 10.5. Each firm sees a green light and decides to produce since each firm makes a positive profit regardless of whether or not the other produces. This is fine for the firms, but each government is losing 10. So *as nations,* the EU and the United States are each losing 8 (for each, this equals the 2 of profits that the firm shows minus the 10 of subsidy cost to the government). The only good news in panel B is hidden from view: The world's consumers gain. But if most of those consumers are outside the EU and the United States, these two nations may choose to give up after a while or else see the danger and decide never to subsidize or produce in the first place.

These simple examples bring out the two key points about an export subsidy in a duel between two exporting giants: (1) The export subsidy *might* be a good thing, as shown in panel A in Figure 10.5, but (2) the case for giving the subsidy is very fragile, depending on too many conditions to be a reliable policy.

What Role Has Government Played with the Rising Exporters?

The dominant controversy within the debate over "unfair trade" is the role of governments in artificially encouraging export invasions of other countries' markets. Americans and Europeans have insisted that they need protection against imports because the governments of Japan and the newly industrializing countries have been equally unwilling to play by the rules of free-market competition. You can't have free trade without fair trade, says the slogan.

How big a role has government intervention played in the recent invasions of exports from newly rising industrial powers into the established markets of North America and Europe? In which industries, and in which exporting countries, has its role been greatest? Are there lessons that other governments should learn about how to launch export drives? The rest of this chapter turns to these issues, weaving evidence from a few leading industrial sectors into some tentative lessons.

First, however, a clear warning is in order: The issue changes at this mid-chapter point. We are turning from the key welfare question to a more popular and more easily answered question. Here is the contrast:

• The question no longer addressed in what follows is the key welfare question of whether government export-pushing is good or bad for that nation, for the importing nations, or for the world as a whole. We have made good progress on that question already, especially with the analysis of dumping and export subsidies we have just completed.

• The question now addressed is whether government export promotion, for better or worse, actually had the effect of raising exports enough to explain the big changes in international competition that have occurred over the past quarter century. That is, we look at cases in which new exporters tried to capture major shares of the market in the United States and other industrial countries, asking (a) whether they "succeeded" and (b) whether government assistance to exporters played a key role in such market captures. To repeat, we have narrowed the definition of *success* drastically to get firmer answers to a question asked more often. Here *success* means only that your exporters raise their share of a foreign market—which could bring a net welfare *loss* to your own country and the world, as in Figure 10.3's analysis of export subsidies. This is a limited and dangerous concept of success, but it is one that can be measured, and one that dominates public discussion of the issue of unfair trade. As it turns out, the results differ from what is popularly imagined.

Steel

Over the first half of the 20th century, the U.S. steel industry was the unquestionable world leader in productivity and output. Yet between the 1950s and the 1980s, U.S. steel firms lost most of their export markets and much of the domestic U.S. market for basic steel products. Their share of world output dropped from 45 percent to 14 percent. The loss of markets was experienced mainly by large integrated mills producing basic shapes. Japan overtook the United States in both exports and production, though more recently Japan's own steel industry is having its mettle tested by the heat of increased foreign competition. After the mid-1980s, a downsized U.S. steel industry finally achieved stability producing specialty high-grade steel. With so great a decline in so classic and strategic an industry, many in the United States have tried to diagnose what went wrong.

In particular, there have been detailed investigations into whether the decline in American competitiveness was a credit to the government of Japan, a fault of the U.S. government, or both.[4] The best answer seems to be neither. It is true that the government of Japan did use import barriers to reserve much of the home market for Japan's own steelmakers before the 1970s. That allowed them to charge higher prices in the home market than in export markets. Yet this home-market protection apparently played little role in explaining how they managed to forge ahead as exporters. And the Japanese government provided some help in the form of subsidies and tax breaks in the 1950s, but these then declined to less than one-quarter of 1 percent of total steel costs in the 1970s. Furthermore, it is not true, as the U.S. steel industry complained, that Japan let its firms pollute more and clean up less, giving them a cost advantage in international competition. Steel industry pollution control costs were actually higher in Japan than in the United States from 1972 to 1976, and only slightly lower than the U.S. level in the early 1980s. Meanwhile, on the American side, government did not impose any particularly high costs on steel firms. It did scrutinize their pricing policies and threaten them with antitrust investigations from time to time, but these supervisions seem unrelated to the dramatic fall of the industry's market share.

If government policies played only a small role in the rise of Japan's steel exports to the United States, what other forces explain that historic rise? Here we have the benefit of detailed studies of the relative cost of producing steel in the two countries. Perhaps the most important factor was the relative decline in the productivity performance of the American steel industry. As of 1956, the U.S. industry was clearly more productive in its use of resources than Japan's steel

---

[4]Notice that we focus only on Japan's exports to the United States here. If we were pursuing the broader question of how so many other countries' steel industries also grew faster than those of the United States and Western Europe, we would get a somewhat different answer about the role of government. Many governments, especially the Soviet Union before 1991, lavished aid on their steel industries and gave them protection in home markets. This chapter, however, concentrates on the promotion of exports. While many countries have subsidized steel exports, as in our example of Korean steel above, the main story has been the rise of Japan's exports to North America and Europe between the 1950s and the 1980s. In this, the front-page story of postwar international trade in steel, the role of government was tiny, as the text argues.

industry. By 1976, that contrast had reversed, with America's industry 15 percent less efficient than the Japanese. Managers of the largest U.S. steel firms were slower than others to innovate with new techniques, and even built new plants with obsolescent designs. A second factor was noncompetitive wage rates. The American steel industry had yielded so much to the union power of the United Steel Workers that wage rates were 10 to 20 percent above what we would predict from the nature of the work and the attributes of the steel workers. The wage premium enjoyed by the United Steel Workers rose to its highest level ever in the early 1980s, at the very time that the industry was in full retreat. Japan's steel workers enjoyed no such premium over wage rates paid in other industries. A final factor was that the Japanese firms had been more aggressive in seeking out new low-cost supplies of iron ore, particularly in Australia and Brazil.

In other words, there are good reasons why Japan was able to invade the American steel market so extensively between the late 1950s and the early 1980s, but the role of government was not one of these reasons. Japanese firms outinnovated and outmanaged the major U.S. firms, and U.S. steel workers were overpaid.

Autos

Like the American steel industry, the American auto industry achieved global dominance for half a century. Like steel, too, it has been forced to retreat since the 1960s in the face of foreign, especially Japanese, competition in the U.S. market. Two reasons for the reversal are also similar in the two industries: high American wage rates and productivity failure. The main difference between the two cases is that the auto industry in the United States kept a larger market share than the domestic steel industry. At its peak in 1950, the U.S. auto industry produced three-quarters of the world's automobiles, and a large share of the remainder was produced by U.S. subsidiaries in other countries. Its productivity—the ratio of real outputs to real inputs—was much higher than Germany's or Britain's. America had an even greater advantage in productivity and product quality over Japan, whose cars simply could not compete. In the 1950s, the Governor of the Bank of Japan urged his compatriots to bow to America's permanent comparative advantage:

> Efforts to foster an automobile industry in Japan are meaningless. This is a period of international specialization. Since America can produce cheap, high quality cars, should we not depend on America for automobiles?[5]

Yet in Japan and elsewhere, this belief in a static comparative advantage lost out to the infant industry argument. Across the 1950s, Europe and Japan rebuilt their auto industries with the help of protection against imports. Also in the 1950s, Detroit's performance started to skid, with declining durability and fuel efficiency of its cars. The first import invasion into the U.S. auto market was led by the famous Volkswagen "beetles" in the late 1950s. In the 1960s, Japan shifted from a strategy of mere knockdown car assembly under foreign license to a thor-

---

[5] As quoted in Duncan (1973), p. 74.

oughly reorganized system of production aimed at long-run penetration of the North American market. The number of defects per car, initially very high, became quite low by the mid-1970s, allowing Japanese firms to build a reputation for economy and reliability before shifting into the fast-lane market for sports cars and luxury cars. By 1980–1982, Japanese cars had captured 22 percent of the U.S. market.

Government aid to automakers in Japan seems to have played only a minor role in the rise of Japan's auto industry. It is true that high import barriers protected Japan's automakers when they were getting established in the 1950s and 1960s. These were removed as soon as Japan's own export drive shifted into high gear. One might argue that by securing the home-market profit base, government protection became a vehicle for delivering cheap capital to the auto industry. Yet capital could hardly have been cheaper for them than it was for General Motors. As for the frequent argument that Japan's Ministry of International Trade and Industry played a key role in encouraging the automakers to develop export plans, such an argument is rarely valid—as rarely as the number of times that games are won by cheerleaders on the sidelines rather than by players.

Government aid in America was at least as generous as government help in Japan from the late 1960s on. The U.S. government bailed out Chrysler Corporation in 1978 with a set of loans that, unlike most bail-out loans, were actually repaid on time by a rejuvenated Chrysler. And from 1981 to 1987, the government jump-started the auto industry's recovery by imposing "voluntary" export restraints on Japan, as described in Chapter 8.

If Japan's invasion of the U.S. auto market was not due to more generous government backing, what did cause it? As with steel, Japan's export invasion into the American market up to the early 1980s featured the development of superior Japanese production techniques, a dip in American efficiency, and excessive rates of pay in the American auto industry. By 1980, at the height of the "car wars" crisis, Japan had developed the ability to produce an average car with 17 percent less real input. In addition, the quality of the average car had climbed in Japan, but had dipped in America, as revealed by measurements of fuel efficiency, repair needs, and overall consumer satisfaction. There is consensus, even among top management in the auto industry, that the U.S. industry had some key organizational defects that did not plague Japanese auto firms. In particular, American practice up to the 1980s undervalued teamwork and relied too much on separation of different job functions. Each stage of design or manufacture would work in relative isolation and then "throw it over the wall" to the next stage, whereas in major Japanese firms the designers, engineers, and line workers would communicate more on each stage of design and production.

In addition to falling behind in efficiency, the U.S. auto industry was overpaid. For one thing, in the auto industry even more than in most others, top executives received a much higher premium in the United States than in Japan and other countries. Graef Crystal has estimated that in the 1980s top U.S. auto executives were paid about 10 times what their Japanese counterparts received, a difference that is hard to reconcile with the differences in managerial performance. For another, the United Auto Workers, like the United Steel Workers in the steel sector, were paid wages and salaries that were well above those of comparable workers in other sectors of the economy. Alan Krueger and Larry Summers estimated that in 1984, after the import invasion had peaked, members of the United Auto Workers received 24.4 percent more pay than their skills and the nature of the work could explain. This union pay premium could have accounted for almost half the cost difference between Japanese and American cars.

After the early 1980s, the U.S. auto industry regrouped and stopped losing ground. The import share of the American auto market stabilized and even dropped a bit, as did Japan's share of world production. The price and quality differences between Japanese and U.S. cars narrowed, and Detroit's Big Three stopped losing money.

The way in which American autos managed to shift from reverse to neutral across the 1980s gives us clues on how to allocate blame for the earlier import invasion. If the main culprit had been a drop in the inherent quality of American workers across the 1970s, a main response of the 1980s would have been a mass shutdown of U.S. plants. U.S. production would have dropped, while U.S. *firms* would have kept the same share of world production, thanks to expansion of their production in other countries. That was not the dominant trend, however. In the 1980s, new plants opened up in the United States as fast as other plants closed, with relatively little exodus of U.S. firms to other countries. It was not a case of superior U.S. management fleeing inferior U.S. workers.

The key trends in the U.S. auto industry in the 1980s were changes of ownership, management, and type of contract within the United States, not an emigration of jobs and output. Within the United States, the net loss of auto plants run by U.S. firms was offset by the opening of eight new U.S. auto and truck plants under Japanese and joint Japanese–American ownership. Something similar happened in Europe. On the pay front, the high pay packages negotiated with the United Auto Workers were replaced with initially lower wage rates, mostly with non-UAW work forces. Auto industry currents in the 1980s suggested that the real problems had been specific to U.S. managers' ability to manage operations in the United States, especially the interaction of U.S. firms with the UAW, not a problem shared by all auto production in America.

Apparel

Throughout the 20th century, Asian manufacturers of apparel have captured a larger and larger share of the North American and European markets. The sector has demanded and received heavy protection in America and Europe, including protection by voluntary export restraint (VER) agreements (see Chapter 8) since 1962. Yet Asian exports take an ever higher share of a slowly growing market.[6]

---

[6]This section refers to the apparel (clothing) sector, but not to the textile sector producing fiber and yarn. In the textile sector, the Americans have continued to enjoy export success. Their productivity, based on relatively high technology and capital-intensity, sets the world standard, and their labor force does not receive any pay premium over what we would predict given their skills and the nature of the work.

Governments in the exporting countries did not tailor this success in the export of apparel. They basically just let it happen, especially in Hong Kong, Taiwan, and Singapore. Rather, the only major role of government was to retard this development, as the governments of importing countries raised the trade barriers higher and higher.

The success of Asian apparel exports has a relatively straightforward explanation. There has been no great productivity failure in America and Europe. Nor has the apparel sector paid excessively high wage rates. Rather, the problem facing the American and European apparel sector is a basic fact beyond their control: Apparel is a sector that uses unskilled labor relatively intensively. Being in countries where unskilled labor is relatively scarce, they are at a cost disadvantage even when producing as efficiently as possible. The rise of Asian exports is caused by Asia's elimination of earlier institutional backwardness, allowing the region's technology and productivity to converge toward American and European levels in apparel manufacture. As the productivity gap closes, comparative advantage is dictated more and more by the relative abundance of unskilled labor. In other words, the apparel story is one that fits the Heckscher–Ohlin model of Chapters 3 through 5 more and more closely.

Aircraft

So far we have looked at cases in which the rise of some countries' exports have little or nothing to do with help from their governments. Aircraft is different. In this case government has played a key role in encouraging the take-off of aircraft exports. What is striking about this success story of export-pushing by government is that it worked first where it was an accident instead of where it was intended. Government aid launched the dominant exporters of commercial aircraft in a high-income country that believes in minimal government, namely the United States, rather than in that country's main economic rivals, whose governments speak more openly about promoting and subsidizing export drives. Let's turn first to the role of government in the American success. Then let's look at government aid to the aircraft sector in the EU.

For a half-century the United States lavished massive government assistance on Boeing, Lockheed, and McDonnell Douglas to ensure itself of the best military aircraft in the world. Such solid backing is crucial to any company that wants to become efficient in either military or commercial aircraft. For a new company to become an efficient low-cost producer of modern jets takes, conservatively, 10 to 14 years without showing profits plus eventual sales of 500 planes a year. No company will dare to enter into the uncertainties of such a long-run strategy without solid assurance of cheap credit and at least some assured sales. The military priorities of the U.S. government gave that assurance. Backed so firmly on the military front, private firms could either become lazy and dependent on subsidies or become efficient and competitive. For whatever reasons, Boeing and the other top U.S. aircraft producers took off on the more efficient runway. Once they became strong exporters of commercial as well as military aircraft, they (especially Boeing) lobbied ever more effectively for export subsidies, like the Eximbank subsidies mentioned earlier in this chapter.[7] The U.S. industry—now consolidated into Boeing after mergers—remains highly competitive and successful.

Given America's long head start, it was difficult for other countries to catch up in an industry with such high start-up costs. For instance, for decades the Japanese government has offered substantial support to Japanese firms to promote commercial aircraft production, with little to show for it.

Governments in the EU also attempted to use heavy subsidies to develop a commercial aircraft industry. The opening venture did not work well. Britain and France cooperated to produce the supersonic Concorde, which took in tremendous subsidies without ever being able to repay the government's investment. The EU then shifted to nurturing Airbus in the mid-1970s. By the early 1990s, Airbus had established itself as a viable producer, competing aggressively with Boeing over a range of aircraft sizes (but not in the largest, jumbo jets, in which the Boeing 747 has a monopoly position). In the late 1990s, Airbus accounts for about one-third of global aircraft sales. We can now declare Airbus to be reasonably successful. In aircraft, heavy government aid to an exporter has worked twice: first in the United States, a leading opponent of long-range government planning, and then in the EU.

Television

In the various electronics sectors—radio, television, video, computers, computer supplies, and so on—there is a curious time path to the fortunes of the main international competitors. Up to 1960, it seemed clear that the United States was beyond challenge as the leader in virtually all electronics sectors. The main lesson to be learned was how to be like the United States. Between 1960 and 1990, the U.S. share of everything electronic declined sharply, and the apparent lesson was to learn from Japan. Since 1990, Japanese leadership in technology and trade has suffered some setbacks, and the lessons have to be reconsidered once again. Here we illustrate with the cases of television and semiconductors.

The switch from American to Japanese leadership in designing and selling TV sets was dramatic. In the 1950s, U.S. firms controlled almost all the American market and exported to some extent. By the late 1980s, only Zenith among the U.S. firms continued to produce television sets within the United States (along with several of Japan's giants). The rest of U.S. firms' production had migrated abroad, but still could not match the market share of the Japanese firms—even in North America.

The rapid displacement of U.S. firms by imports, mostly from Japan, may have been due in part to the role of government. One government slightly encour-

---

[7]The only blemish on this record of successful, although accidental, export-pushing was the U.S. government's characteristic refusal to intervene in the late 1960s and early 1970s when McDonnell Douglas and Lockheed had a dogfight over the long-range trijet market. Laura Tyson (1992, pp. 176–191) argues that if the government had directed one of the two companies to stay out of this indivisible market niche, and had produced smaller passenger jets instead, it could have prevented the birth of Europe's Airbus Industrie altogether.

aged the industry while another obstructed it. On the private front, there was a performance gap, but it should be thought of as exceptionally good performance by Japanese firms rather than as any fault of American firms or workers. While there are signs that the American consumer electronics firms made organizational mistakes like those of U.S. auto firms, the signs are not strong. Nor did workers in consumer electronics plants get an inflated noncompetitive wage rate.

Japan's Ministry of International Trade and Industry (MITI) helped Japanese firms use a protected market as a base for financing export expansion of television sets and related consumer electronics goods. Like steel and autos, consumer electronics were protected against imports. The government also permitted domestic cartel-like collusion among the seven electronic giants: Hitachi, Matsushita (Panasonic), Mitsubishi, Sanyo, Sharp, Sony, and Toshiba. Japan's labyrinthine distribution system also systematically excluded U.S. electronic goods. Dividing the protected domestic market among themselves, the seven firms attracted enormous investments and launched their export drive.

American government policy slightly hindered American firms in the new international competition. The American tradition of stern antitrust policies kept large American firms from launching drives that would have brought a large share of the U.S. television market under the control of one or two efficient U.S. giants. The Sherman (Antitrust) Act of 1890 and the Clayton Act of 1914 threaten to prosecute colluding groups of firms or large individual firms that unfairly exploit a dominant market position. That threat restrained the market aggression of the top U.S. electronic giants before the 1970s. What U.S. antitrust policy could not do was prosecute the seven Japanese giants for colluding in their home market in Japan, generating profits that helped them export competitively. Thus the seven giant Japanese firms could pursue markets in a way that might have raised antitrust problems if pursued by a large American firm. Similarly, giant foreign firms were allowed to buy up U.S. companies, whereas domestic U.S. takeovers would have been prohibited by antitrust policy. Partly because of this bias in U.S. antitrust policy, Japan won the race to finance R&D and expanded production.

Instead of seeking political support for outright import protection, the U.S. firms maintained that only unfair Japanese trade practices needed to be stopped. They pressed antidumping and antitrust cases against Japan, with only minor success in the television sector. A major "positive finding" (guilty verdict) was returned in 1970, for example, when Sony was found guilty of dumping televisions in the U.S. market at an f.o.b. factory price of $180 versus the $333 then charged on sets bound for the domestic market. Sony's response was not to eliminate the price discrepancy, but to replace exports to the American market with a new production subsidiary in San Diego. In the end, litigation proved slow and therefore costly for Zenith, Motorola, and other plaintiffs, so they sold off U.S. plants to Japanese buyers and set up production abroad. By the 1980s, Japan had won out in the global television markets. The lesson seemed to be that there are gains from having government coordinate a whole industry's research and development.

The story did not stop there, however. The early 1990s brought a stunning setback for the whole idea of government-led coordination of research and market planning. Japan lost in its gambles on a particular new TV technology, a specific version of high-definition television (HDTV). As far back as the 1960s, Japan's government and the Japan Broadcasting Corporation (NHK) targeted the development of HDTV, with its CD-quality sound and movie-quality pictures, as a top national priority. As of 1990–1991, Japan seemed poised for victory, when it became the first nation to have actual transmission to HDTV sets. Japan's main competitor was in Europe, against a team led by Phillips of Holland, Robert Bosch of Germany, and Thomson S.A. of France. It seemed as though the global HDTV market would fall to one of these far-sighted government-backed alliances, and not to any American firms, which had no grand alliance and got no subsidies from the U.S. government.

Since 1991, the currents have reversed. The specific HDTV design of the Japanese and EU consortiums suddenly became obsolete. They made big investments in analog, instead of digital, designs for transmission of image information. By the end of 1991, it became clear that digital systems could soon deliver better image information more cheaply. The teams ready to develop the digital system were predominantly American, not Japanese or European. The U.S. Federal Communications Commission (FCC) has coordinated a standard in the United States, based largely on the technology of the Zenith research group. But it is still not clear that this version of HDTV will gain market acceptance. Cable TV systems have not adopted the FCC standards, and broadcast systems are wary of the cost of shifting to HDTV. In the meantime, a rival European effort has developed its own version of digital HDTV.

The lessons of the TV experience need to be interpreted with care. By actively encouraging the major Japanese electronic companies to collude and cooperate, the government probably did play some role in Japan's export success. Japanese firms remain the global leaders generally, now based on their private capabilities in high-quality production and a continuing flow of innovations in related products like VCRs and digital video disks. The sudden demise of Japan's long-run plans in HDTV gives a clear warning about government policy. The collective approach of having government and all major firms agree on the same long-range plans can backfire. A group can make a big collective mistake, just as it can achieve a collective success. Perhaps it is not that grand planning is inherently better or worse—perhaps it is just that a bigger gamble means more is either won or lost on one gamble.

Semiconductors

With semiconductor devices for computers, as with television sets, America's fortunes swung from world leadership before the 1960s to serious jeopardy in the mid-1980s to clear resurgence after 1990.

As with most electronic products, the pioneering inventions were American. So was the early stage of product development, centered in Silicon Valley. At its peak around 1977, the American semiconductor industry served 95 percent of the U.S. market, half the European market, and 57 percent of the entire world market. Significantly, it served only a quarter of the Japanese market, where—again—

formidable barriers blocked imports. By 1987, the United States had become a net importer of semiconductors, with a quarter of its demand supplied by Japan. The U.S. share of world production had dropped from 57 percent to 40 percent, Europe's share had dropped from 15 percent to 10 percent, and Japan's share had risen from 28 percent to 50 percent.

The two leading nations have very different semiconductor industries. The U.S. industry featured small venture capital innovating firms, some of which later became giants. In Japan semiconductors are but one product in the operations of giant conglomerates like Fujitsu, Hitachi, NEC, and Toshiba. The specialized American firms have their advantage in the business of pioneering invention, while the Japanese industry excels in production. The question to ask is, Why don't American giants like AT&T or IBM, heavy users of semiconductors, dominate over their counterparts in Japan? Again, as with televisions, U.S. antitrust policy seems to have canceled the hunt for large market shares. An antitrust settlement in 1956 forced AT&T to license out its patented semiconductors in the 1950s, and the threat of antitrust suits would have plagued any pursuit of a dominant market share by either AT&T or IBM. Large U.S. firms accordingly left the semiconductor industry to the small venture capitalists, who seemed threatened by Japan's giants. In Japan, the government organized and subsidized a key joint research project in the late 1970s, through which the Japanese firms achieved major improvements in their abilities to produce the most advanced chips.

Yet again, as with television, the pendulum swung back from Japan to America in semiconductors in the early 1990s. Led by a young firm (Intel) and two resurgent giants (Motorola and IBM), the U.S. semiconductor industry rose to the dominant position in the key market for microprocessors. At the same time, Japanese firms saw their dominance in memory chips eroded by the rise of Korean and Taiwanese producers, who emulated the Japanese strategy to build their positions in the industry. Thus, after a quarter-century of coordinated planning in Japan and an unplanned free-for-all in America, U.S. firms regained the edge in production and exports of semiconductors, through innovative and profitable chips like microprocessors.

Overall Patterns

From experiences like these, we should try to see an overall pattern—if only because journalists and politicians will try to draw their own patterns anyway. Figure 10.6 summarizes what seem to have been the roles played by government versus other forces. The pattern is clearest for the first three sectors and subtler for the next three.

In the first three sectors, government clearly played little role. In steel and autos, the rise of Japan as a successful exporter stemmed largely from private organizational improvements in Japan plus America's productivity failures and uncompetitively high rates of pay. In apparel, there is nobody to blame for the rise of Asian and low-income countries as exporters to America and Europe. It is only natural that a sector that intensively uses less-skilled labor would fit the comparative advantage of countries that were abundant in that kind of labor. The

FIGURE 10.6   *Government Aid to Export-Oriented Industries Versus Other Explanations of Recent Shifts in Trade Competition*

Sector and Competitors	Role of Government Aid to Exporters	Other Explanations for the Competitive Shift
Steel—Japan into U.S. market since 1956	Small.	Flawed management and productivity shortfall in large U.S. firms; union power in U.S.; better ore supply for Japan.
Autos—Japan into U.S. market since 1970	Negligible.	Flawed management and productivity shortfall in large U.S. firms; union power in U.S.
Apparel—Asian exports invade America and Europe	None.	Factor proportions—apparel uses less-skilled labor intensively, favoring newly industrializing economies.
Aircraft—U.S. versus EU	Heavy aid on both sides.	Government aid and getting a head start are indeed the key. Good results for United States; reasonable success for the EU (and none yet for Japan).
Television—Japan into the U.S. market	Small influence. MITI protected the home market of the seven giant exporting firms. U.S. antitrust policy allowed takeovers by foreign, but not U.S., giant firms.	General success, but a setback for planning in HDTV in the early 1990s. Extraordinarily strong managerial performance by Japanese firms.
Semiconductors—Japan into the U.S. market	Some MITI help to Japanese firms' R&D versus government antitrust threat to large U.S. firms before 1980s.	Again general success, but a retreat in the early 1990s. Japanese firms develop temporarily superior technology.

only real question is why that hadn't happened earlier. The answer seems to be that those countries had serious institutional problems that had to be solved first.

In the latter three sectors, the role of government export-pushing is a more open question. Ironically, the case in which successful market dominance owed most to government (U.S. aircraft) was in the leading country that believed least in government planning. For other cases, a positive role of government can again be argued, especially before 1990, but the record is mixed even in these high technology sectors where the case for export-pushing has had its best chance to show strength.

Does Japan Really Push Exports?

If government help in pushing Japanese exports does not show up very dramatically in the six sectors we just surveyed, where is Japan's famous "industrial targeting"? Are there other sectors in which the government of Japan has done more to promote exports and rapid growth? If so, which sectors?

In fact, Japan does *not* "push exports" in the sense of giving greater subsidies and other government help to export-oriented sectors. Japan does not even have a coherent industrial targeting policy of favoring futuristic industries, those with the greatest growth potential. On the contrary, government policy in Japan gives greatest help to those sectors that are in the most trouble, those most destined to decline.

Some myths die hard, so it is important to measure the effects of Japanese government policy on different sectors as carefully as possible. A study by Richard Beason and David E. Weinstein did that. For each sector of Japan's economy, Beason and Weinstein measured output growth, productivity growth, and the potential for the "economies of scale" we discussed in Chapter 6. They then compared each of these measures with each of four kinds of government policy aimed at helping producers in a particular sector of the economy: direct subsidies, income tax breaks, protection against imports, and cheap low-interest loans from the official Japan Development Bank. In most cases the relationship between success and help from the government is negative, not positive.

Figure 10.7 shows how one particular success measure, namely, output growth, relates to government policy when we compare different sectors of Japan's economy. Panel A ranks sectors from top to bottom according to their growth rates. Those at the top, such as electrical machinery, grew fastest. They also were the most export-oriented. Those at the bottom, such as textiles, grew slowest and were generally threatened by import competition. If the government of Japan really backed the winners, as MITI claims and most people think, then the sectors at the top of the table should rank as the most helped (ranks 1, 2, 3, . . .), and those at the bottom should be given little help (ranks 13, 12, 11, . . .) so that they give up more resources to faster-growing sectors. This is not the case. The correlation between government help and sectoral growth was negative, a fact summarized by the correlation coefficients in panel B. As shown there, the negative relationship prevails for all four policy tools, regardless of whether we look at the pre-1973 and post-1973 eras separately. In fact, the results would look even more dramatic if we included Japan's farm sector, which belongs at the bottom of the table in panel A. Farm output grew no faster than 1 percent a year over this period. Yet, as we shall see again in Chapter 14, protection for Japan's farmers is more generous than protection for any other sector in Japan, and more generous than government supports for farmers in most other countries. The heavy farm supports have drained resources away from the faster-growing sectors.

What this means is that the back-the-winners strategy usually called *industrial targeting* was not really practiced by Japan, the nation most famous for having such a strategy. Japan's government policy was in fact a crude response to intense political lobbying from endangered declining sectors—just like the sectoral policies of the United States and most other industrial-country governments. It might even have reduced Japan's exports by bidding resources away from export lines into the protected sectors.

Why have most people thought that Japan practiced a coherent strategy of industrial targeting? One possible factor is that it was in MITI's interest to have people believe that Japan's government policies deserve credit for the industrial export victories in electronics and autos. Another is that observers in North America and Europe gave too much credence to the role of government policy in

FIGURE 10.7

*Government
Help Versus
Sectoral Growth
in Japan,
1955–1990*

A. How the sectors ranked, 1955–1990

Sector	Growth of Output per Year	Government Help Ranking (1 = Most helped by government; 13 = Least helped)			
		Net Subsidies	*Tax Relief*	*Protection vs. Imports*	*Cheap Loans*
Electrical machinery	12.2%	9	8	8	8
General machinery	11.4	4	8	11	12
Transport equipment	10.8	11	8	4	7
Fabricated metal	10.1	6	7	12	10
Oil and coal	9.8	13	3	7	2
Precision instruments	9.3	10	8	6	13
Ceramics, stone, glass	8.7	8	3	9	5
Pulp and paper	7.7	5	13	10	6
Chemicals	7.6	7	3	5	3
Basic metals	7.2	2	6	3	4
Processed food	6.3	12	12	1	9
Mining	3.8	1	1	13	1
Textiles	2.7	3	2	2	11

B. Coefficients of correlation between output growth and government help

Type of Government Help	1955–1990 (as Above)	1955–1973 Only	1973–1990 Only
Net subsidies	–0.13	–0.05	–0.34
Tax relief	–0.55	–0.47	–0.77
Protection against imports	–0.31	–0.11	–0.14
Cheap loans	–0.31	–0.48	–0.07

Result: For each type of government aid in each time period, government help was negatively, not positively, correlated with the sector's output growth. Far from favoring the fast-growth sectors, the government was trying to check the decline of Japan's relatively declining, and less exporting, sectors.

Note: "Cheap loans" refers to subsidized loans from the Japan Development Bank.
Source: Richard Beason and David E. Weinstein (1996).

Japan's success in the 1970s and 1980s. Perhaps they succumbed to the crude idea that if Japan is very successful, then anything that *looks* distinctively Japanese must be a key to economic growth. The evidence for the importance of industrial targeting, it turns out, was anecdotal and weak.

If Japan did not really practice industrial targeting very much, how do we know whether real industrial targeting would work well? One possibility is to look back at specific policies that really were targeted at successful exporters instead of viewing the overall policy mix surveyed in Figure 10.7. We did that earlier in this chapter by noting that targeting may have worked well in (1) U.S. and EU aircraft, (2) Japanese television before the HDTV setback, and (3) Japanese semiconductors before the United States rallied back in the 1990s.

The other way to see whether real targeting works is to find a country that practiced it more faithfully than did Japan. Korea did that. In the 1970s, the government of Korea gave very cheap loans to fast-expanding firms in steel, chemicals, transport equipment, and shipbuilding. These did indeed become export-oriented sectors and achieved faster-than-average productivity gains. While the Korean government's heavy protection of agriculture probably held back industrial expansion, its policy within manufacturing apparently backed winners. Targeting can work, though there is no guarantee that it will.

Summary

Dumping is selling exports at a price lower than the price in the home market or lower than the full average cost of production. Exporters may engage in dumping to drive foreign competitors out of business (predatory dumping), during recessions in industry demand (cyclical dumping), to unload excess inventory (seasonal dumping), or to increase profits through price discrimination (persistent dumping). The importing country benefits from the dumped exports, because it pays a lower price for its imports. But the importing country could be hurt by cyclical dumping (importing unemployment) or by predatory dumping (higher prices in the future).

The WTO permits the importing country to retaliate with an antidumping duty. It appears that the process of imposing antidumping duties has become a major source of new protection for import-competing producers, because the process is biased to find dumping and impose duties.

Export subsidies are condemned by the WTO. By causing excessive trade, they bring losses to the country making the subsidy and to the world as a whole. A **countervailing duty** against subsidized exports brings a loss to the country levying it but brings a gain to the world as a whole by offsetting the export subsidy. The combination of an export subsidy and an equal countervailing duty would leave world welfare unchanged, with taxpayers of the export-subsidizing country implicitly making payments to taxpayers of the importing country.

It is at least possible that export subsidies could be good for the exporting nation and for the world as a whole. If export competition takes the form of an oligopoly game between two giant producers, each of which could dominate the market alone (e.g., Boeing versus Airbus), then the government that is first to subsidize its exporter can capture the global market and bring gains both to the exporting nation and to the world as a whole. We do not know that such a case has arisen, but it is possible.

How well do export-promoting policies, and industrial targeting policies in general, really work? This chapter explores this issue by looking at recent experience in six industrial sectors (steel, autos, apparel, aircraft, televisions, and semiconductors). For the first three sectors, it is not true that governments in the exporting countries have played any great role. For steel and autos, the private industry's own productivity performance and rates of pay are more relevant. For apparel, the rise of Asian exports into America and Europe is just a natural catching-up with a comparative advantage that should have existed even earlier. For three relatively high tech sectors (aircraft, television, and semiconductors), there is arguably a more significant role for export promotion by governments. Government help was key in the cases of U.S. and EU commercial aircraft and perhaps was important in some of Japan's export successes in the electronics sectors.

The conventional wisdom is wrong about industrial targeting by the government of Japan. It is not true that overall government policy has tipped economic incentives in favor of the industries with the greatest growth potential. While one famous part of Japan's government, the Ministry of International Trade and Industry (MITI), does try to push exports in the fastest-growing sectors, its effect is slight, as suggested by our survey of six sectors. Even this slight encouragement to exporting fast-growers has been more than canceled by official Japanese assistance to sectors whose share of the economy is destined to drop, such as textiles and agriculture. Japan, like other countries, gives its greatest government help to sectors in trouble, not to likely successes.

Suggested Reading

Stiglitz (1997) provides a critique of U.S. antidumping and antisubsidy policies. Ethier (1982) presents the basic theory of dumping. Tharakan (1991), Finger (1993), Hindley and Messerlin (1996), and Prusa (1997) discuss actual antidumping policies. Brander (1995) provides a technical survey of strategic trade policy.

The experiences of the six industrial sectors surveyed in this chapter are detailed in Eichengreen (1988) and Lindert (forthcoming).

A superb survey of America's competitive position in manufactures is *Made in America* by the MIT Commission on Industrial Productivity (Dertouzos, Lester, and Solow, 1989).

Flamm (1996) presents the historical development of U.S.–Japanese competition and government policies in the semiconductor industry. Sophisticated studies of competitive currents in the auto and semiconductor sectors are presented in Feenstra (1988). On aircraft and semiconductors, see also Tyson (1992).

For a critical view of the practice of strategic industrial policy in Japan, see Johnson (1982), Yamamura (1986), and Prestowitz (1988), as well as Beason and Weinstein (1996). The industrial targeting policies of Korea are enthusiastically surveyed by Amsden (1989) and carefully judged by Zeile (1993).

Questions and Problems

✦ 1. What are the two official definitions of dumping?

2. You have been asked to propose key provisions that should be the basis for revision of U.S. antidumping policy, to make the policy more likely to contribute to enhanced U.S. well-being. What will you propose?

✦ 3. Which of the following three beverage exporters is guilty of dumping in the U.S. market?

	Banzai Breweries (Japan)	Tipper Laurie, Ltd. (UK)	Bigg Redd, Inc. (Canada)
Average unit cost	$10	$10	$10
Price charged at brewery for domestic sales	$10	$12	$9
Price charged at brewery for export sales	$11	$11	$9
Price when delivered to United States	$12	$13	$10

4. What is a countervailing duty?

✦5. What would happen to world welfare if the United States paid exporters a subsidy of $5 for every pair of blue jeans they sold to Canada, but Canada charged a $5 countervailing tariff on every pair imported into Canada? Would the United States gain from the combination of the export subsidy and import tariff? Would Canada? Explain.

6. Consider the case of an export subsidy for an importing country that has some monopsony power—that is, the case in which the foreign supply-of-exports curve is upward-sloping. Use a graph like that in Figure 10.3.

   a. In comparison with free trade, what is the effect of the export subsidy on the international price and the quantity traded?

   b. The importing country now imposes a countervailing duty that returns the market to the initial free-trade quantity traded. In comparison with the market with just the export subsidy, explain why the countervailing duty is good for the world. Explain why the countervailing duty can also increase the well-being of the importing country.

✦ 7. In the Airbus-versus-Boeing example in Figure 10.4, what strategy should the EU government follow if the upper left box (*a*) gives Airbus and Boeing each a sure gain of +5 or (*b*) gives Boeing a gain of +5 and Airbus a gain of zero? Should the EU offer a subsidy to Airbus? Explain.

8. Has the government of Japan followed a policy of industrial targeting, with greater government help for those parts of the economy that develop more successful growth of output and exports?

✦ 9. You have been hired to write a defense of the idea of having government plan and subsidize the expansion of an export-oriented industry, taking resources away from the rest of the economy in the short run. Briefly describe how you would defend such an industrial targeting strategy as good for the nation as a whole. Which of the industrial experiences surveyed in this chapter best supports your case? Explain.

10. You have been hired to discredit the argument you just presented in answering Question 9. Give a strong case against getting the government into the export-pushing business. Which of the industrial experiences surveyed in this chapter best supports your case? Explain.

CHAPTER 11

Trade Blocs and Trade Blocks

Chapters 7 though 9 looked at equal-opportunity import barriers, ones that tax or restrict all imports regardless of country of origin. But some import barriers are meant to discriminate. They tax goods, services, or assets from some countries more than those from other countries. The analysis of Chapters 7 through 9 can now be modified to explain the effects of today's trade discrimination.

We look at two kinds of trade barriers that are designed to discriminate:

1. **Trade blocs,** which allow imports into each member country from other member countries freely, or at least cheaply, while imposing barriers against imports from outside countries. The European Union (EU) has done that, allowing free trade between members while restricting imports from other countries.

2. **Trade embargoes,** or what the chapter title calls "trade blocks." Some countries discriminate completely against certain other countries, usually because of a policy dispute. They deny the outflow of goods, services, or assets to a particular country while allowing export to other countries, or discriminate against imports from the targeted country, or block both exports to and imports from the target.

Types of Economic Blocs

Some international groupings discriminate in trade alone, while others discriminate between insiders and outsiders on all fronts, becoming almost like unified nations. To grasp what is happening in Western Europe and North America and may happen elsewhere, we should first distinguish among the main types of economic blocs. Figure 11.1 and the following definitions show the progression of economic blocs toward increasing integration:

FIGURE 11.1

*Types of
Economic Blocs*

| | **Features of Bloc** | | | |
Type of Bloc	*Free Trade Among the Members*	*Common External Tariffs*	*Free Movement of Factors of Production*	*Harmonization* of All Economic Policies (Fiscal, Monetary, Etc.)*
Free-trade area	√			
Customs union	√	√		
Common market	√	√	√	
Economic union	√	√	√	√

*If the policies are not just harmonized by separate governments, but actually decided by a unified government with binding commitments on all members, then the bloc amounts to full economic nationhood. Some authors call this *full economic integration.*

1. A **free-trade area,** in which members remove trade barriers among themselves, but keep their separate national barriers against trade with the outside world. One example of a free-trade area, true to its name, is the European Free Trade Area formed in 1960. (See the chronology given later in this chapter.) Another is the North American Free Trade Area (NAFTA), which formally began at the start of 1994.

2. A **customs union,** in which members again remove all barriers to trade among themselves and also adopt a common set of external barriers. The European Economic Community (EEC) from 1957 to 1992 included a customs union along with some other agreements. The Southern Common Market (MERCO-SUR), formed by Argentina, Brazil, Paraguay, and Uruguay in 1991, is actually a customs union.

3. A **common market,** in which members allow full freedom of factor flows (migration of labor or capital) among themselves in addition to having a customs union. Despite its name, the European Common Market (EEC, which became the European Community, EC, and is now the European Union, EU) was not a common market up through the 1980s because it still had substantial barriers to the international movement of labor and capital. The EU became a true common market, and more, at the end of 1992.

4. Full **economic union,** in which member countries unify all their economic policies, including monetary, fiscal, and welfare policies as well as policies toward trade and factor migration. Most nations are economic unions. Belgium and Luxembourg have had such a union since 1921. The EU is on a path toward full unity.

The first two types of economic bloc are simply **trade blocs** (i.e., they have removed all explicit trade barriers but have kept their national barriers to the flow of labor and capital and their national fiscal and monetary autonomy). Trade blocs have proved easier to form than common markets or full unions among sovereign nations, and they are the subject of this chapter. Freedom of factor flows within a bloc is touched on only briefly here—we return to it in Part V. The monetary side of union enters in Part III.

Is Trade Discrimination Good or Bad?

How good or how bad is trade discrimination? It depends, first, on what you compare it to. Compared to a free-trade policy, putting up new barriers discriminating against imports from some countries is generally bad, like the simple tariff of Chapters 7 through 9. But the issue of trade discrimination usually comes to us from a different angle: Beginning with uniform tariffs (the same tariff regardless of country of origin), what are the gains and losses from removing barriers only between certain countries? That is, what happens when a trade bloc like the EU or NAFTA gets formed?

Two opposing ideas come to mind. One instinct is that forming a customs union or free-trade area must be good because it is a move toward free trade. If you start from a uniform set of trade barriers in each nation, having a group of them remove trade barriers among themselves clearly means lower trade barriers in some sense. Since that idea is closer to free trade, and Chapters 7 through 10 found free trade better with only carefully limited exceptions, it seems reasonable that forming a trade bloc allows more trade and raises world welfare. After all, forming a nation out of smaller regions brings economic gains, doesn't it?

On the other hand, we can think of reasons why forming a free-trading bloc can be bad, even starting from uniform barriers to all international trade. First, forming the trade bloc may encourage people to buy from higher-cost partner suppliers. The bloc would encourage costly production within the bloc if it kept a high tariff on goods from the cheapest source outside the bloc and no tariff on goods from a more costly source within the bloc. By contrast, a uniform tariff on all imports has the virtue that customers would still do a lot of their buying from the cheapest source. Second, the whole idea of trade discrimination smacks of the bilateralism of the 1930s, that is, when separate deals with individual nations destroyed much of the gains from global trade. Third, forming blocs may cause international friction simply because letting someone into the bloc will shut others out.

For all these reasons, World Trade Organization (WTO) rules are opposed to trade discrimination in principle. A basic WTO principle is that trade barriers should be lowered equally and without discrimination for all foreign trading partners. That is, the WTO espouses the **most favored nation (MFN) principle.** The MFN, dating back to the mid-19th-century wave of free trade led by Britain, stipulates that any concession given to any foreign nation must be given to all nations having MFN status, and the WTO says that all contracting parties are entitled to that status.

However, other parts of WTO rules permit deviations from MFN under specific conditions. One deviation is special treatment for developing countries. Another deviation permits trade blocs if the trade bloc removes tariffs and other trade restrictions on most of the trade among its members, and if its trade barriers against nonmembers do not increase on average. The WTO, and the GATT before it, have looked like a "paper mouse" when it comes to nondiscrimination, because these rules have been applied loosely, and no trade bloc has ever been ruled in violation. By the late 1990s, nearly half of world trade occurred within functioning trade blocs, including the 15 countries of the EU, the 4 remaining countries of EFTA, the preferential trade agreements that the EU has with 26 other (mostly European) countries (including the EFTA countries), the 3 countries of NAFTA, the Israel–U.S. Free Trade Area, the 4 countries of MERCOSUR and its trade agreements with Chile and Bolivia, and the Closer Economic Relations agreement between Australia and New Zealand.

The Basic Theory of Customs Unions: Trade Creation and Trade Diversion

Trade discrimination can indeed be either good or bad. We can give an example of this and, in the process, discover what conditions separate the good from the bad cases.

It may seem paradoxical that the formation of a customs union (or a free-trade area) can either raise or lower welfare since removing barriers among member nations looks like a step toward free trade. Yet, the analysis of a customs union is another example of the not-so-simple theory of the second best, which we discussed in Chapter 9.

The welfare effects of eliminating trade barriers between partners are illustrated in Figure 11.2, which is patterned after Britain's entry into the EC (now the EU) in 1973. To simplify the diagram greatly, all supply curves are assumed to be perfectly flat.[1] We consider two cases. In one, forming the trade bloc is costly because too much trade is diverted from lower-cost to higher-cost suppliers. In the other, forming the trade bloc is beneficial because it creates more low-cost trade.

In Figure 11.2A, the British could buy Japanese cars at £5,000 if there were no tariff. The next cheapest alternative is to buy German cars delivered at £5,500. If there were free trade, at point *C,* Britain would import only Japanese cars and none from Germany.

Before its entry, however, Britain did not have free trade in automobiles. It had a uniform tariff, imagined here to be £1,000, which marks up the cost of imported Japanese cars from £5,000 to £6,000 in Figure 11.2. No Britons buy the identical German cars because they would cost £6,500. The starting point for our discussion is thus the tariff-ridden point *A,* with the British government collecting (£1,000 times 10,000 = £10 million) in tariff revenues.

Now let Britain join the EU, as it did in 1973, removing all tariffs on goods from the EU while leaving the same old tariffs on goods from outside the EU. Under the simplifying assumptions made here, German cars now cost only

---

[1]There is an alternative analysis assuming upward-sloping supply curves for all three countries, with similar but more widely applicable results (e.g., Harry G. Johnson, 1962). One point revealed by the upward-sloping supply analysis is that trade diversion may bring terms-of-trade gains to the bloc partners at the expense of the rest of the world. Diverting demand away from outside suppliers may force them to cut their export prices (i.e., the bloc's import prices). On the export side, diverting bloc sales toward bloc customers and away from outside customers may raise the bloc's export-price index. Thus, the bloc may gain from a higher terms-of-trade ratio (= export price/import price), a possibility assumed away by the flat outside-world supply curve in Figure 11.2.

The flat–supply-curve case is used here because its diagram (or its algebra) makes the basic points more clearly.

FIGURE 11.2   *Trade Diversion Versus Trade Creation in Joining a Customs Union: UK Market for Imported Compact Cars*

A. Trade Diversion Dominates, Bringing a Net Loss

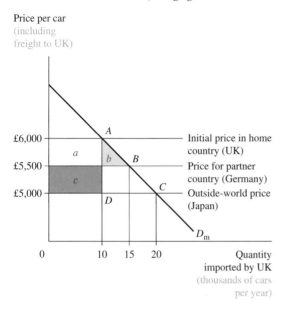

B. Trade Creation Dominates, Bringing a Net Gain

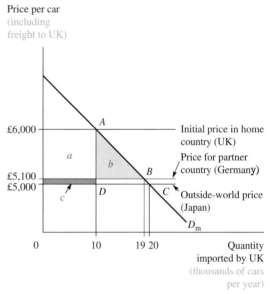

Starting from a uniform tariff on all compact cars (at point A), Britain joins the EU customs union, removing tariffs on imports from EU partners like Germany, but not on imports from the cheapest outside source, Japan. With the flat supply curves assumed here, all the original imports of 10,000 cars from the cheapest outside source are replaced with imports from new partner countries (e.g., Germany). The shift from A to B creates 5,000 extra imports, bringing national gains for the UK (area b). But it also diverts those 10,000 cars from the cheapest foreign supplier to the partner country, imposing extra costs (area c). In this case, the loss exceeds the gain, bringing a net loss:

Gain area $b = (1/2)(6,000 - 5,500)(15,000 - 10,000) =$
    Gain of £1.25 million

Loss area $c = (5,500 - 5,000)(10,000) =$ Loss of £5 million

    Net loss = £3.75 million

In this case, Germany's price is not much greater than that quoted by Japanese suppliers. Removing the tariff on German (and other EU) cars creates 9,000 new imports of cars, yielding the trade-creation gain shown as area b. Another 10,000 cars are again diverted from the cheapest supplier (Japan), but this trade diversion costs less than in Figure 11.2A. So

Gain area $b = (1/2)(6,000 - 5,100)(19,000 - 10,000) =$
    Gain of £4.05 million

Loss area $c = (5,100 - 5,000)(10,000) =$ Loss of £1.00 million

    Net gain = £3.05 million

£5,500 in Britain (instead of that plus the £1,000 tariff), while the price of Japanese cars in Britain remains £6,000 because they still incur the tariff. British purchasers of imported cars switch to buying only German cars. In addition, seeing the price of imported cars fall to £5,500 in Britain, they buy more (at point B). Clearly, British car buyers have something to cheer about. They gain the areas a and b in consumer surplus, thanks to the bargain. But the British government loses all its previous tariff revenue, the area $a + c$ (again, £10 million). So, after we cancel out the gain and loss of a, Britain ends up with two welfare effects:

1.   A welfare gain from trade creation (in this case, from the extra 5,000 cars). **Trade creation** is the net volume of new trade created by forming the trade bloc. It causes the national gain shown as area *b* in Figure 11.2. Area *b* represents two kinds of gain in the British economy: gains on extra consumption of the product, and gains on replacement of higher-cost British production by lower-cost partner production.

2.   A welfare loss from trade diversion (in this case, from the 10,000 cars). **Trade diversion** is the volume of trade diverted from low-cost outside exporters to higher-cost bloc-partner exporters. It causes the national loss shown as area *c*.

This is the general result: The gains from a customs union are tied to trade creation, and the losses are tied to trade diversion.

The net welfare effect, the trade-creation gain minus the trade-diversion loss, could be positive or negative. In the first case, Case A in Figure 11.2, the loss on trade diversion happens to dominate. The gain from trade creation would dominate, however, if the new customs union partners, such as Germany, were almost the lowest-cost suppliers in the world, as assumed in Case B of Figure 11.2. If they can supply cars almost as cheaply as the Japanese, then there won't be much cost from diverting Britain's customers away from Japanese compact cars. Case B assumes that the trade-diversion cost is only £100 on each of the diverted 10,000 cars. At the same time, there is a lot of trade creation in Case B. Removing the £1,000 tariff on German cars cuts the price of imports from the old £6,000 on Japanese cars with tariff to £5,100 on German cars without tariff, resulting in a substantial gain. In the specific case shown in Figure 11.2, Case B, there is a net national (and world) gain from the effects of the customs union on trade in this kind of automobile.[2]

Reflecting the one-good cases in Figure 11.2, you can figure out what conditions dictate whether the gains outweigh the losses. Here are three tendencies that make for greater gains from a customs union:

a. The greater the difference between the home-country and partner-country costs (supply curves), the greater the gains.

b. The smaller the difference between the partner-country and outside-world costs (supply curves), the greater the gains.

c. The more elastic the import demand, the greater the gains.

So the best trade-creating case is one with high preunion tariffs [allowing bigger cost differences in (*a*)], costs that are almost as low somewhere within the union as in the outside world [keeping the difference in (*b*) small], and highly elastic demands for imports. Conversely, the worst trade-diverting case is one with inelastic import demands and high costs throughout the new customs union.

---

[2]To imagine a case of pure trade creation, with no trade diversion at all, just switch the words *Germany* and *Japan* in either half of Figure 11.2. With Germany now the cheapest supplier, nobody in Britain would buy Japanese cars with or without the EU customs union. Forming the union expands trade from point *A* to point *C*, bringing the net gain *ACD.*

The EU Experience

The formation of the EU's customs union has provided an experiment in the effects of trade integration. Numerous studies in the 1960s and 1970s tended to conclude that the net gains from forming the EU (then the EEC) were small but positive. For example, net welfare gains on trade in manufactured goods calculated by Balassa (1975, p. 115) were a little under one-tenth of 1 percent of members' total GNP. That tiny positive estimate overlooks some losses from the EU, but also overlooks some likely gains. By concentrating on trade in manufactured goods, the literature generally overlooked the significant social losses from the EU's Common Agricultural Policy. This policy protects and subsidizes agriculture so heavily as to bring serious social losses of the sort described in Chapter 14.[3] On the other hand, the studies of the 1960s and 1970s generally confined their measurements to static welfare effects like those in Figure 11.2, omitting possible dynamic gains from economies of scale or improved productivity incentives. Here, unfortunately, is a research frontier still unsettled: We know that economies of scale and better productivity performance are key possible outcomes of economic union, but we still lack good estimates of them. For now, the empirical judgment is threefold: (1) On manufactured goods, the EU has brought enough trade creation to suggest small positive net welfare gains. (2) The static gains on manufactures have probably been smaller than the losses on the Common Agricultural Policy. (3) But the net judgment still depends on what we believe about the unmeasured dynamic gains from economies of scale and productivity stimuli.

The formation of a truly common market in 1992 probably brought some net gains. To put numbers on those gains requires more imagination beyond the basic trade effects of Figure 11.2. The 1992 unification involved removing all sorts of nontariff trade barriers:

- No longer are truckers irked by thousands of trade barriers within the EU, such as frontier checkpoint delays, paperwork, and freight-hauling restrictions.
- The change brought an end to product "quality" codes that were thinly disguised devices for protecting higher-cost domestic producers. Examples include German beer purity regulations, Italian pasta protection laws, Belgian chocolate content restrictions, and Greek ice cream

---

[3]Trade diversion on agricultural products is one reason why empirical studies find that joining the EC in 1973 may have cost Britain dearly. The Common Agricultural Policy meant that British consumers had to lose cheap access to their traditional Commonwealth food suppliers (Australia, Canada, and New Zealand). They had to buy the more expensive EU food products and also had to pay taxes on their remaining imports from the Commonwealth, taxes that were turned over to French, Danish, and Irish farmers as subsidies. This cost Britain an estimated 1.8 percent of GDP in the 1970s, versus a static-analysis gain of less than 0.2 percent of GDP on manufactured goods (Miller and Spencer, 1977). The Thatcher government later bargained for a fairer sharing of the burdens of farm subsidies.

specifications.[4] Some standards were harmonized, but in most cases countries mutually recognized the validity of each other's standards.

- Capital is now free to flow anywhere in the EU countries.
- Workers from any of the EU countries can now practice their trades and professions anywhere.

How much benefit might such a miscellany of measures bring to the EU? It is hard to say, given the difficulty of measuring such key determinants as economies of scale. Despite the difficulty, the EU published a bold set of estimates of the gains to be expected. The welfare estimates from the "official" 1988 Cecchini Report run around 5 to 6 percent of the EU's gross domestic product. Half of the forecast gain relates to economies of scale and the benefits of increasing competition, two kinds of effects that are notoriously hard to quantify. These EU estimates should be considered more enthusiastic than scientific. Recent studies conclude that gains are probably 1 percent or less of GDP.

North America Becomes a Bloc

The Canada–U.S. Free-Trade Area

The idea of a free-trade area between Canada and the United States has been debated since the 19th century, but has only recently been enacted. As late as 1986, when the two countries had a minor trade war over lumber and corn plus another tiff over Arctic navigational rights, there seemed little chance of a free-trade area. But in 1987–1988 the mood swung around and a pact was signed after all. Do the effects show more trade creation than trade diversion? Does Canada or the United States gain more?

Economists tend to expect greater absolute effects on Canada than on the United States. The basic reasoning surfaced back in Chapter 2, where we reasoned that the absolute net national gains should be distributed in proportion to the two nations' price changes caused by the opening of new trade. We expect that Canada's import-demand and export-supply curves are less elastic than the U.S. curves. Therefore, opening new trade should shift Canadian prices more than U.S. prices. If so, the net national gains should be absolutely greater for Canada. So should the relative-price shock to different parts of the economy. Import-competing producers are likely to be hurt more, and consumers and exporters helped more, in Canada than in the United States, even in absolute dollar terms.

---

[4]The EU has been fashioning controversial new quality codes regulating the entertainment industry after 1992. In effect, the EU has put a quota on TV and film imports from the United States and other outside suppliers. EU viewers face a world with tighter restrictions on such programs as, in France, "Les Flintstones," "Beverly Hills 90210," and "Deux flics de Miami." The cultural effects are debatable: U.S. shows sometimes have been replaced by imitative EU "original" productions along the lines of the quiz shows "La roue de la fortune" and "Le juste prix."

Postwar Trade Integration in Western Europe

1950–1952: Following the Schuman Plan, "the Six" (Belgium, France, West Germany, Italy, The Netherlands, and Luxembourg) set up the European Coal and Steel Community. Meanwhile, Benelux is formed by Belgium, The Netherlands, and Luxembourg. Both formations provide instructive early examples of integration.

1957–1958: The Six sign the Treaty of Rome setting up the European Economic Community (EEC or "Common Market"). Import duties among them are dismantled and their external barriers are unified in stages between the end of 1958 and mid-1968. Trade preferences are given to a host of developing countries, most of them former colonies of EEC members.

1960: The Stockholm Convention creates the European Free Trade Area (EFTA) among seven nations: Austria, Denmark, Norway, Portugal, Sweden, Switzerland, and the United Kingdom. Barriers among these nations are removed in stages, 1960–1966. Finland joins EFTA as an associate member in 1961. Iceland becomes a member in 1970, and Finland becomes a full member in 1986.

1967: The European Community (EC) is formed by the merger of the EEC, the European Atomic Energy Commission, and the European Coal and Steel Community.

1972–1973: Denmark, Ireland, and the United Kingdom join the EC, converting the six into nine. Denmark and the United Kingdom leave EFTA. The United Kingdom agrees to abandon many of its Commonwealth trade preferences. Also, *Ode to Joy* from Beethoven's Ninth Symphony chosen as EC's anthem.

1973–1977: Trade barriers are removed in stages, both among the nine EC members and between them and the remaining EFTA nations. Meanwhile, the EC reaches trade preference agreements with most nonmember Mediterranean

countries along the lines of earlier agreements with Greece (1961), Turkey (1964), Spain (1970), and Malta (1970).

1979: European Monetary System begins to operate based on the European Currency Unit. The European Parliament first elected by direct popular vote.

1981: Greece joins the EC as its 10th full member.

1986: The admission of Portugal and Spain brings to 12 the number of full members in the EC.

1986–1987: Member governments approve and enact the Single European Act, calling for a fully unified market by 1992 and for weighted voting rules that no longer require unanimity in the European Council.

1989–1990: The collapse of the East German government brings a sudden expansion of Germany and therefore of the EC. Unemployment is initially high in the East Germany, but labor and capital start to flow in large volumes between East and West Germany. East Germans are given generous entitlements to the social programs of Germany and the EC.

1991–1995: Seven countries from Central Europe establish Association Agreements.

End of 1992: The Single European Act takes effect, integrating labor and capital markets throughout the EC.

1993: The Maastricht Treaty is approved, making the EC into the European Union (EU), which calls for unification of foreign policy, for cooperation in fighting crime, and for monetary union.

1995: Following votes with majority approval in each country, Austria, Sweden, and Finland join the EU, bringing the number to 15. As it had done in 1972, Norway rejected membership in its 1994 vote.

1999: Eleven EU countries establish the euro as a common currency, initially existing along with each country's own currency.

Suspecting as much, most studies of the Canada–U.S. free-trade area focused on Canada's stake in it. Some studies concluded that Canada would gain 1 to 2.5 percent of its GDP. A few studies concluded that Canada could gain much more—its GDP could increase by 8 to 10 percent thanks to the free-trade pact, a far larger gain than any EU country has ever gotten from the Common Market so far. In these high estimates more than half of Canada's gain comes from the opening of U.S. markets, rather than from Canada's own removal of trade barriers. Better access to U.S. markets seems especially important in studies that reckon there are economies of scale to be reaped by Canadian industry when faced with a much bigger market. The importance of access to U.S. markets seems like a reasonable justification for Canada's making a separate deal with the United States: Global liberalization through multilateral negotiations would have done much less to give Canada foreign markets, given the dominant importance of selling to the United States.

Mexico's Liberalization and NAFTA

Starting in 1985, the Mexican government became increasingly determined to break down its own barriers to a freer, more privatized Mexican economy. A series of reforms deregulated business and knocked down barriers to imports of goods and services from other countries. The culmination of this economic liberalization drive was the 1993 signing of an agreement with the United States and Canada to form the **North American Free Trade Area (NAFTA).** NAFTA eliminates tariffs and some nontariff barriers on trade within the area, with some liberalizations phased in over 5- to 15-year periods. It removes barriers to cross-border business investments within the area, and Mexico must phase out performance requirements, including local content requirements and export requirements, that the Mexican government had imposed on foreign businesses operating in Mexico. NAFTA requires open trade and investment in most service industries (including banking and other financial services). Supplemental agreements call for better enforcement of labor and environmental standards, but these have had little effect as of mid-1998. NAFTA does not, however, call for free human migration between these countries, nor does it denationalize Pemex, Mexico's huge government oil monopoly.

NAFTA was controversial, especially in Mexico and the United States, from the moment it became a strong political possibility in 1990. Critics in Mexico sounded the alarm that Mexican jobs would be wiped out, widening the already enormous gaps between rich and poor in Mexico. They also warned that the huge United States would use NAFTA to force Mexico to make many changes in its policies, weakening Mexican sovereignty. American labor groups were convinced that they would lose their jobs to Mexicans, whose wage rates were only a tiny fraction of those paid in the United States. This concern was dramatized by H. Ross Perot's famous claim in 1992 that NAFTA would cause a "great sucking sound" as American jobs were instantly sucked down into Mexico. Critics in the United States also decried that NAFTA rewarded and strengthened a corrupt political system in Mexico. In addition, environmentalists in both countries feared that NAFTA would lead to an expansion of the already serious pollution in Mexico, especially in the *maquiladora* industrial towns along the U.S.–Mexican border.

Reuters/Bettmann

Proponents in Mexico hoped to use NAFTA to have some influence on U.S. trade policies like antidumping, a goal that the Canadians also had for the Canada–U.S. Free Trade Area. They also expected Mexico to attract more investments into Mexico from foreign businesses using Mexico as a base for North American production. Proponents in the United States hoped to solidify the market-oriented reforms in Mexico, making Mexico a more dependable economic and political ally. But proponents of NAFTA were also extravagant in some of their claims, particularly when asserting that defeating NAFTA would send the Mexican economy into a giant depression, forcing an unemployed army to march over the U.S. border in search of jobs.

Concerns over jobs and the environment were so severe within the United States and Canada that they nearly defeated NAFTA. Yet in the end, the proponents prevailed, and NAFTA became official at the beginning of 1994.

To get an idea of what is happening as NAFTA frees up trade between Mexico and its neighbors to the north, we can start by looking at actual experience in the years just before NAFTA. Mexico in fact began slashing import barriers as early as 1985 in a bold campaign to bring more competition and efficiency to the Mexican economy. Mexico's tariffs had always been high, and were raised even higher after the debt crisis forced Mexico to tighten its belt in 1982. By 1992 they were slashed to an average tariff of only 10 percent on goods from the United States. Meanwhile, U.S. tariffs on goods from Mexico averaged only about 4 percent by 1992. There was more liberalization of trade *before* NAFTA than the hotly debated NAFTA itself could add. During this pre-NAFTA liberalization, incomes and jobs grew both in Mexico and in the United States and Canada, though this basic point went unnoticed by those who foresaw economic doom in NAFTA.

Trying to estimate the effects of NAFTA almost became a new industry in itself. Consulting firms, government economists, and academics produced a variety of forecasts comparing the NAFTA world with a non-NAFTA world. The carefully conducted studies agree in their guarded optimism about the net national effects: All three countries will be slight net gainers, and the rest of the world will suffer only negligible damage if any. Figure 11.3 shows a set of estimates that typify the results of the most extensive studies. According to the multisectoral "computable general equilibrium model" of Drusilla Brown, Alan Deardorff, and Robert Stern, Mexico would be the biggest gainer in percent terms, especially in the part of the estimates that adds in the effects of the likely acceleration of foreign investment in Mexico. Canada's predicted gains come in second as a share of the initial levels of national income or wages (though the absolute size of any effect on Canada is probably the smallest of the three countries' absolute effects). The United States is the least affected in percent terms, basically because the U.S. economy is by far the largest of the three, and because most U.S. import barriers removed by NAFTA were already low. Other investigations generally agree with this verdict that NAFTA will raise national incomes and even the demand for labor, though some talk about creating extra jobs instead of about raising wage rates.

Is NAFTA really likely to help everybody? Is there no major group that is hurt by this movement to freer trade? Yes, somebody is hurt. The best guess about NAFTA is that it corresponds to the kind of result we kept finding in earlier chapters: Freer trade (in this case, NAFTA's discriminatory freeing of trade) absolutely hurts import-competing groups even though the net effect on whole nations or the whole world is positive. Who is hurt in the United States? The main sectors where U.S. incomes and jobs will be lost to Mexican competition are apparel (clothing), field crops (e.g., tomatoes, sugar), furniture, and autos. On the other hand, Mexico will buy more U.S. financial services, chemicals, plastics, and high tech equipment.

There is a pattern here. The kinds of sectors where U.S. incomes and jobs will be jeopardized most by Mexican competition are those that involve less-

---

FIGURE 11.3

Estimates of the Effects of the North American Free Trade Area on National Incomes and Wage Rates

Percent Changes over a World Without NAFTA as Predicted by the Brown–Deardorff–Stern "Computable General Equilibrium Model"

	In Mexico	*In United States*	*In Canada*	*In the Rest of the World*
Effects of Removing Trade Barriers Within NAFTA, with No Effects of Capital Flows				
Real national income	1.6	0.1	0.7	–0.0
Real average wage rate	0.7	0.2	0.4	–0.1
Effects of Removing Trade Barriers Within NAFTA, with Induced Capital Flows into Mexico				
Real national income	5.0	0.3	0.7	–0.0
Real average wage rate	9.3	0.2	0.5	–0.0

Source: Drusilla K. Brown, Alan V. Deardorff, and Robert M. Stern (1992), as cited in Nora Lustig, Barry Bosworth, and Robert Z. Lawrence (1992), pp. 44–47, 220.

skilled labor. NAFTA would allow Mexico's low-skilled apparel workers, for example, the easy access to the U.S. market that they and their Asian competitors have long been denied. Jobs will almost surely be lost in some U.S. apparel establishments as some of the U.S. clothing firms "out-source" these tasks to Mexico. Foreseeing such a likelihood, the U.S. legislation approving NAFTA called for retraining and other adjustment assistance to import-damaged producers such as those in the apparel sector. Yet the magnitudes of such job losses seem small in aggregate national perspective. In Mexico too there would be job and wage-rate losses, but they would be localized and overshadowed by job and wage-rate gains.

The other group likely to be hurt slightly by NAFTA are those outside world producers of goods in which Mexico's trade with its northern neighbors will expand the most. NAFTA will probably cause some trade diversion from Asia. Asian makers of cars, clothing, furniture, financial services, and high tech equipment will probably suffer losses. These losses usually are not large, however, as implied by the low figures in the far-right column in Figure 11.3.

One other seemingly technical feature of NAFTA has received a surprising amount of attention. Because each member of a free-trade area maintains its own barriers against imports from outside the area, a member country must still police its borders, to tax or prohibit imports that might otherwise avoid its higher external barriers by entering through a lower-barrier partner country. Its customs officials must enforce *rules of origin* that determine which products have been produced within the free-trade area, so that they are traded freely within the area, and which products have not been produced within the area. These rules guard against a firm's ruse of doing minimal processing within the area and then claiming that the product is locally produced.

The NAFTA rules of origin are incredibly complex, covering over 200 pages with thousands of different rules for different products. Analysis of these rules has concluded that many of them are protectionist, acting like regional local content requirements. Here is another, more subtle reason for producers from the rest of the world to lose. For instance, the rules of origin for automobiles indicate that autos can trade between NAFTA countries freely only if they have at least 62.5 percent value from North American parts and production. This rule benefits U.S. auto companies and hurts foreign auto companies, even if the latter have production facilities in North America, and it also reduces world well-being and probably also North American well-being.

Free-Trade Areas Among Developing Countries

In several less developed settings in the 1960s and 1970s, a different idea of gains from economic union took shape. The infant industry argument held sway. It was easy to imagine that forming a customs union or free-trade area among developing countries would give the union a market large enough to support a large-scale producer in each modern manufacturing sector without letting in manufacturers from the highly industrialized countries. The new firms could eventually cut their costs through economies of scale and learning by doing until they could compete internationally, perhaps even without protection.

For all the appeal of the idea, its practice "has been littered with failures," as Pomfret has put it, and the life expectancy of this type of trade bloc was short. The Latin American Free Trade Area (Mexico and all the South American republics) lacked binding commitment to free internal trade even at its creation in 1960, and by 1969 it had effectively split into small groups with minimal bilateral agreements. The Central American Common Market, also created in 1960, scored some small victories for a decade, but fell apart in the 1970s. Other short-lived unions with only minimal concessions by their members included a chain of Caribbean unions, the East African Community (Kenya, Tanzania, and Uganda) disbanded in 1977, and several other African attempts. One centrifugal force was the inherent inequality of benefits from the new import-substituting industries. If economies of scale were to be reaped, the new industrial gains would inevitably be concentrated into one or a few industrial centers. Every member wanted to be the group's new industrial leader, and none wanted to remain more agricultural. No formula for gains-sharing could be worked out. Even the Association of Southeast Asian Nations (ASEAN), with its broader industrial base, was unable to reach stable agreements about comparative advantage when this was tried in the late 1970s and early 1980s. Mindful of this experience, most experts became skeptical about the chances for great gains from most developing-country free-trade areas.

Yet the same institution can succeed later, even after earlier setbacks, especially if economic and political conditions have changed. As we have seen, the idea of a free-trade area between Canada and the United States failed to get launched for about a century before its time arrived.

The key change in the trade policies since the 1970s, as we will examine in more depth in the next chapter, has been a shift in development philosophy, toward an outward, pro-trade (or at least pro-export) orientation. As in the case of Mexico, many developing countries have pursued economic reforms to liberalize government policies toward trade and business activity more generally. Forming a trade bloc can be part of this thrust to liberalize (although, as we have seen, it is actually liberalizing internal trade while discriminating against external trade).

There is already one major case of Latin American success (so far) despite earlier failures. In 1991, Argentina, Brazil, Paraguay, and Uruguay formed MERCOSUR, and by 1995 it had established internal free trade and common external tariffs (averaging 12 percent) for most products, with the rest to be completed by 2006. In 1996, Chile became an associate member and established a free-trade area with the MERCOSUR countries, and Bolivia also established an associate agreement. Trade among MERCOSUR countries has increased rapidly since 1991. One study of the effects of MERCOSUR concluded that it will increase real national incomes by 1 to 2 percent, with much of the gain coming from economies of scale and the benefits of increasing competition among firms from different MERCOSUR countries. However, other observers are more cautious, because trade within MERCOSUR has increased most rapidly in capital-intensive products like automobiles and machinery, products that are not consistent with the member countries' global comparative advantage. It is likely that substantial trade diversion is occurring in these products, and the losses from trade diversion must be set against other gains. MERCOSUR is a success in terms of survival and increasing internal trade, but its net effects on the well-being of its member countries are not yet clear.

Trade Embargoes

Trade discrimination can be more belligerent—a trade block, instead of a trade bloc. A nation or group of nations can keep ordinary barriers on its trade with most countries, but insist on making trade with a particular country or countries difficult or impossible. To wage economic warfare, nations have often imposed economic sanctions, embargoes, or boycotts. The term *sanctions* is the most general, referring either to discriminatory restrictions or to complete bans on economic exchange. Embargoes and boycotts both refer to complete bans. What is being restricted or banned can be ordinary trade, or it can be trade in services or assets, as in the case of a ban on loans to a particular country.

Waging economic warfare with trade embargoes and other economic sanctions dates back at least to the fifth century BC. The American colonists boycotted English goods in the 1760s as a protest against the infamous Stamp Act and Townshend Acts. In this case, the boycott succeeded—Parliament responded by repealing those acts. The practice of economic sanctions has been more frequent in the latter half of the 20th century than in any earlier peacetime era, and the use of sanctions increased during the 1990s. The United States practices economic warfare more readily than any other country. In 1998, over 75 foreign countries were the target of some form of economic sanction imposed by a U.S. governmental unit (federal, state, or local). One estimate indicated that up to $15 billion of U.S. exports per year were blocked by sanctions in the mid-1990s.

The effects of banning economic exchanges are easy to imagine. A country's refusal to trade with a "target" country hurts both of them economically, and it creates opportunities for third countries. But who gets hurt the most? The least? Magnitudes matter because they determine whether the damage to the target rewards the initiating country enough to compensate for its own losses on the prohibited trade.

To discover basic determinants of the success or failure of economic sanctions, let us consider a particular kind: a total embargo (prohibition) on exports to the target country.[5] Figure 11.4 imagines a total embargo on exports to Iraq. The example portrays one side of the restrictions imposed on Iraq by many countries since 1990, when Iraq first invaded Kuwait. In addition to these restrictions on exports to Iraq, the countries applying sanctions also refused to import oil or other goods from Iraq or to lend to Iraq. The sanctions were mandated under a

---

[5]The case of an embargo on imports from the target country is symmetrical to the export case studied here. In standard trade models, the symmetry is exact. As we noted in Part I, the net gains and losses on the export side and those on the import side are the same thing in two guises. As an exercise at the end of this chapter, you are invited to diagram the import embargo case and to identify the gains and losses and what makes them large or small.

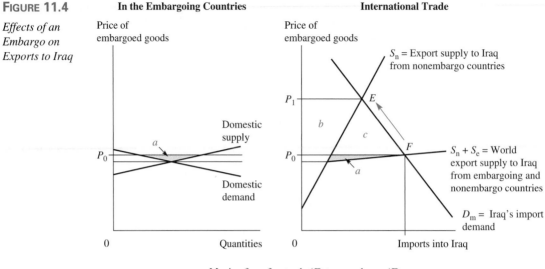

FIGURE 11.4

Effects of an Embargo on Exports to Iraq

In the Embargoing Countries

International Trade

Moving from free trade (F) to an embargo (E) means

Embargoing countries lose	a
Iraq loses	$b + c$
Other countries gain	b
World as a whole loses	$\dfrac{}{a + c}$

United Nations resolution, and most major powers participated in this action against Iraq. Still, Jordan, Iran, and some other nations were more sympathetic to Iraq and allowed some trade to continue.

Free-trade equilibrium is represented by point F in Figure 11.4. Here Iraq's import demand is balanced by the rest of the world's export supply at the price index P_0. For any exporting nation, the supply curve of exports is just the difference between its domestic supply curve and its domestic demand curve, as shown on the left side of Figure 11.4.

When some countries decide to put an embargo on exports to Iraq, part of the world export supply to Iraq vanishes. Figure 11.4 shows the disappearance of the embargoing countries' supply S_e, meaning that the combined supply curve $S_n + S_e$ is replaced by the S_n curve alone. With their imports thus restricted, Iraqis find importable goods more scarce, as represented by the price rise from P_0 to P_1, which accompanies the movement from the free-trade equilibrium F to the embargo equilibrium E. The new scarcity costs Iraq as a nation the area $b + c$ for reasons already described in Chapters 2 and 7 through 9. It also has its economic costs for the countries enforcing the embargo, however. They lose area a. The loss a is shown in two equivalent ways: on the left as a difference between producer losses and consumer gains, and on the right as a loss of surplus on exports. Meanwhile, countries not participating in the embargo gain area b on extra sales to Iraq at a higher price. What the world as a whole loses is therefore area $a + c$, the loss of efficient world trade.

Within countries on the two sides of the embargo, different groups will be affected differently. In the embargoing countries (e.g., Canada, the United Kingdom, the United States), the embargo lowers the price below P_0, slightly helping some consumers while hurting producers. Within Iraq, there might be a similar division (not graphed in Figure 11.4), with some import-competing producers benefiting from the removal of foreign competition, while other groups are damaged to a greater extent.

If the embargo brings economic costs to both sides, why do it? Clearly, the countries imposing the embargo have decided to sacrifice area *a,* the net gains on trade with Iraq, for some other goal, such as preventing Iraq's aggression against its neighbors, forcing Iraq to reveal and destroy germ and other weapons, or forcing the Iraqi government to respect the human rights of minorities. By their actions the embargoing governments imply that putting the pressure on Iraq is worth more than area *a.* The lost area *a* is presumably not a measure of economic irrationality but, rather, a willing sacrifice for other goals, like the income sacrifices each of us makes for other goals ranging from simple leisure to moral principles. As Figure 11.4 is drawn, the hypothetical export embargo is imagined to cause Iraq more economic damage, measured by area *b + c,* than the embargoers' loss represented by area *a.*[6]

Embargoes can also fail, of course. In a study of sanctions imposed between 1945 and 1983, Gary Hufbauer and Jeffrey Schott concluded that sanctions failed to affect the policies of the target country in about half the cases. There are two ways in which trade embargoes fail: political failure and economic failure.

Political failure of an embargo occurs when the target country's national decision makers have so much stake in the policy that provoked the embargoes that they will stick with that policy even if the economic cost to their nation becomes extreme. Such political stubbornness is very likely if the target country is a dictatorship and the dictatorship would be jeopardized by retreating from the policy that provoked the embargo. In such a case, the dictatorship will refuse to budge even as the economic costs mount.

---

[6]In the real-world debate over sanctions, critics consistently argue that the sanctions would harm large numbers of innocent civilians, whose right to a better government is a political outcome that sanctions are supposed to bring about. Thus in the case of worldwide sanctions against South Africa (1986–1993), critics argued that the sanctions would lower incomes of "nonwhite" South Africans, the very groups the sanctions were supposed to help liberate. It has similarly been argued that sanctions against Iraq have harmed mainly children and minorities. This may be correct in the short run, as all sides of the debate have long known.

To judge whether the sanctions are in the best interests of the oppressed within the target country, the best guide would be their own majority opinion. That opinion is not easily weighed in a context of disenfranchisement, press censorship, and tight police controls. The foreign governments imposing sanctions clearly imply that the policy gains are worth more than their own loss of area *a* plus the short-run losses that they believe that oppressed parties in the target country are willing to sustain for the cause.

If the targeted regime holds firm to its policy (or its whim), despite the economic losses, then the regime's part of the losses is a lower-bound measure of what it thought the controversial policies are worth to it. If the regime changes the policies as demanded, then the policies were worth less to it than the implied costs.

What the economic analysis of the embargo adds is (1) reminders of the economic stakes involved plus (2) measures suggesting how the conflicting parties value the policies that are the target of the embargo.

An example of political failure of economically "successful" sanctions was Saddam Hussein's refusal to retreat from Kuwait or, after Iraq was driven from Kuwait, to step down from power. Defenders of the idea of pressuring Saddam Hussein with sanctions were right in asserting that sanctions would bring greater damage to the economy of Iraq than to the embargoing countries. Yet Saddam Hussein's grip on power was so firm in the early 1990s that he could not be removed from power, or be forced to make a major change in certain policies, even if a majority of Iraqi citizens suffered great hardship. A counterexample was the UN-based sanctions imposed on South Africa in 1986, which succeeded in hastening the end of apartheid and the minority-rule police state.

The second kind of failure is **economic failure of an embargo,** in which the embargo inflicts little damage on the target country, but possibly even great damage on the imposing country. The basic economics of embargoes can contribute to our explanation of why some attempts succeed while others fail. Figure 11.5 leads us to the key points by showing two kinds of (export) embargoes that fail economically. In both cases, elasticities of supply and demand are the key.

In Figure 11.5A, the countries imposing the embargo have a very inelastic export supply curve, implying that their producers really depend on their export business in the target country. Banning such exports and erasing the supply curve S_e from the marketplace costs the embargoing nation(s) a large area a. The target country, by contrast, has a very elastic import demand curve D_m. It cuts its demand greatly when the price goes up even slightly, from P_0 to P_1. Apparently, it can do fairly well with supplies from nonembargoing countries (the S_n curve alone). Accordingly, it loses only the small areas $b + c$. Any nation considering an embargo in such a case must contemplate sustaining the large loss a, in pursuit of only a small damage ($b + c$) to the target country. What works against the embargo in Figure 11.5A is the low elasticity of the embargoing country itself and the high elasticity of either the target country's import demand or its access to competing nonembargo supplies.

Figure 11.5B shows a case in which the embargo "fails" in the milder sense of having little economic effect on either side. Here the embargoing country is fortunate to have an elastic curve of its own (S_e) so that doing without the extra trade costs it only a slight area a. On the other hand, the target country also has the elastic demand curve D_m and access to the elastic competing supplies S_n. Therefore it sustains only the slight damage $b + c$, and presumably can defy the embargo for a long time.

So, embargoes and other economic sanctions apply stronger pressure when the embargoing country or countries have high elasticities and the target countries have low ones. When is this likely to be true? Our simple analysis offers suggestions that seem to show up in the real world:

1. Big countries pick on small ones. A country (or group of countries) with a large share of world trade can impose sanctions on a small one without feeling much effect. In economic terms, the big country is likely to have highly elastic trade curves (like S_e in the examples here) because it can deal with much larger markets outside the target country. A small target country, on the other hand, may depend heavily on its trade with the large country or countries. Its economic vul-

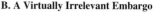

FIGURE 11.5

Two Kinds of Economically Unsuccessful Embargoes

A. An Embargo That Backfires

The cost to the embargoers, *a*, is much larger than the damage, *b + c*, to the target country.

B. A Virtually Irrelevant Embargo

The costs to both sides are negligible because elasticities are so high.

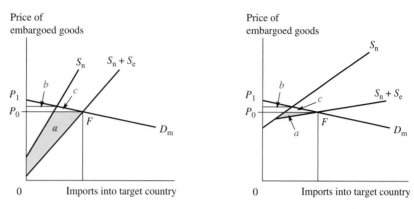

nerability is summarized by low elasticities for trade curves like D_m and S_n. Little wonder that the typical postwar embargo is one imposed by the United States on smaller-trading nations like Cuba, Iran, Nicaragua, and Nigeria.

2.   Sanctions have more chance of success if they are extreme and sudden when first imposed. Recall that the damage $b + c$ is larger, the lower the target country's trade elasticities. Elasticities are lower in the short run than in the long run, and they are lower when a massive share of national product is involved. The more time the target country has to adjust, the more it can learn to conserve on the embargoed products and develop alternative supplies. Of course, quick and sudden action also raises the damage to the initiating country itself (area a), so success must be premised on the embargoing country's having alternatives set up in advance, alternatives that raise its elasticities and shrink area a.

3.   As suggested by the definition and example of political failure, embargoes have more chance of changing a target government's policies when the citizens hurt by the embargo can apply political pressure on the stubborn head(s) of state, as in a democracy. In a strict dictatorship, the dictator can survive the economic damage to citizens and can hold out longer.

The first of these three points provides insight into why the effectiveness of unilateral sanctions imposed only by the United States has changed over time. In the 1950s, when the United States was predominant, its own sanctions could have some effect on countries like Iran and even Britain and France (in the Suez Canal dispute). With the growth of other countries and their economies, unilateral U.S. sanctions have become much less effective, because S_n (from the rest of the world) has expanded and become more elastic.

One U.S. response has been to push for UN mandates for sanctions that direct all countries to participate. Before 1990, the only UN-mandated sanctions were against South Africa and Rhodesia (now Zimbabwe). Since 1990, the UN has established sanctions against Iraq, Serbia, Somalia, Libya, Liberia, Haiti, and Angola.

Another U.S. response has been much more controversial—the use of secondary sanctions to compel other countries to join the U.S. sanctions. For instance, the Helms–Burton Act threatens sanctions to stop foreign firms from making new investments in oil and gas production in Iran and Libya. Foreign countries strongly object to such pressures on their firms. The president has delayed enforcing these laws, but they remain dangerous—they threaten to turn (potential) allies into enemies.

Summary

The trade bloc revolution of the late 1980s and 1990s has raised the importance of trade discrimination. The European Union has developed a true common market with uniformity of virtually all regulations and taxes on trade and factor movements, and the EU is progressing toward its stated goal of economic union, in which all economic policies are unified. From the Treaty of Rome in 1957 to 1992, the EU had adopted the less binding kind of economic bloc called a customs union, in which member countries adopt a uniform external tariff and remove all tariffs and quotas on trade among themselves.

The basic three-country model of a customs union shows that its welfare benefits for the partner countries and the world depend on its trade creation, the amount by which it raises the total volume of world trade. Its costs depend on its trade diversion, the volume of trade it diverts from lower-cost outside suppliers to higher-cost partner-country suppliers. Whether a customs union is good or bad overall depends on the difference between its trade creation effect and its trade diversion effect. In the case of the EU, for manufactured products, most economists think that its trade creation has slightly outweighed its trade diversion up through the 1980s. EU enthusiasts expect larger gains from the 1992 market integration.

A lesser form of trade bloc is the free-trade area in which member countries remove all tariffs and quotas on trade among themselves, but keep their separate barriers on trade with nonmember countries. In this case, member countries must use rules of origin and maintain customs administration on the borders between themselves to keep outside products from entering the high-barrier countries cheaply by way of their low-barrier partners. Three examples of free-trade areas are the European Free Trade Area created in 1960, the Canada–U.S. Free Trade Area that began to take effect in 1989, and the North American Free Trade Agreement (NAFTA) signed in 1993. Of all the participants in recent trade blocs, the ones predicted to gain the largest share of GDP from bloc membership are Canada and Mexico.

Efforts by developing countries to form trade blocs failed in the 1960s and 1970s, but they have become more successful in the 1990s. Trade among the MERCOSUR countries in South America has expanded rapidly since the bloc was formed in 1991, but some of this expanded intrabloc trade is trade diversion.

Another form of trade discrimination is economic sanctions, such as a trade embargo. Our basic analysis of an export embargo (which has effects symmetrical with those of an import embargo) reveals how the success or failure of such economic warfare depends on trade elasticities. Success is more likely when the embargoing countries have high trade elasticities, meaning that they can easily do without the extra trade. Success is also more likely when the target country has low trade elasticities, meaning that it cannot easily do without trading with the embargoing countries. As the simple theory implies, embargoes are typically imposed by large trading countries on smaller ones, and success is more likely the quicker and more extreme the sanctions.

Suggested Reading

The customs union literature is usefully surveyed in Pomfret (1997). Baldwin and Venables (1995) present a technical survey. On the economics of the European Union, see El-Agraa (1990) and Neal and Barbezat (1998). On the 1992 changes, see Cecchini (1988) and Flam (1992).

The likely effects of the North American Free Trade Area are well summarized by Lustig, Bosworth, and Lawrence (1992) and by Hufbauer and Schott (1993). The larger liberal-ization of the Mexican economy is analyzed by Lustig (1992). On Canada's stake in trade liberalization, see Wonnacott and Wonnacott (1967, 1982) and Morici (1991). Weintraub (1997) looks at NAFTA's first several years. Flores (1997) provides an analysis of MERCOSUR.

The economics and the foreign policy effects of trade embargoes are well analyzed in Hufbauer and Schott (1983, 1985). Judgment on sanctions against South Africa was rendered by Hayes (1987).

Questions and Problems

✦ 1. What is the difference between a free-trade area and a customs union?

2. What is the most favored nation principle?

✦ 3. How are trade creation and trade diversion defined, and what roles do they play in the world gains and losses from a customs union?

4. Why are rules of origin needed for a free-trade area? How might they be protectionist?

✦ 5. Homeland is about to join Furrinerland in a free-trade area. Before the union, Homeland imports 10 million transistor radios from the outside world market at $100 and adds a tariff of $30 on each radio. It takes $110 to produce each transistor radio in Furrinerland.

   a. Once the free-trade area is formed, what will be the cost to Homeland of the transistor radio trade diverted to Furrinerland?

   b. How much extra imports would have to be generated in Homeland to offset this trade-diversion welfare cost?

6. Which countries are likely to gain, and which are likely to lose, from the North American Free Trade Area? How are the gains and losses likely to be distributed across occupations and sectors of the Mexican economy? The U.S. economy?

✦ 7. Suppose that the United States currently imports 1.0 million pairs of shoes from China at $20 each. With a 50 percent tariff, the consumer price in the United States is $30. The price of shoes in Mexico is $25. Suppose that as a result of NAFTA, the United States imports 1.2 million pairs of shoes from Mexico and none from China. Describe the likely gains and losses to U.S. consumers, U.S. producers, the U.S. government, and the world as a whole.

8. What kinds of countries tend to use economic embargoes? Do embargoes have a greater chance of succeeding if they are applied gradually rather than suddenly?

✦ 9. Which of the following trade policy moves is most certain to bring gains to the world as a whole: (*a*) imposing a countervailing duty against an existing foreign export subsidy, (*b*) forming a customs union in place of a uniform tariff on imports from all countries, or (*c*) levying an antidumping import tariff? (This question draws on material from Chapters 8 and 10 as well as from this chapter.)

10. Draw the diagram corresponding to Figure 11.4 for an embargo on imports from the target country. Identify the losses and gains to the embargoing countries, the target country, and other countries. Describe what values of elasticities are more likely to give power to the embargo effort and what values of elasticities are more likely to weaken it.

CHAPTER 12

Trade and the Environment

As nations interact more and more with each other, they have more and more effect on each other's environments. Often the international environmental effects are negative, as when activity in one nation pollutes other nations' air and water, or when it uses up natural resources on which other nations depend. These environmental concerns have become irreversibly global, and are a growing source of international friction.

Inevitably, international trade has been drawn into the environmental spotlight, both as an alleged culprit in environmental damage and as a hostage to be taken in international environmental disputes. This chapter addresses the rising debate over the proper role of government policies in attacking environmental problems when the problems and policies have international effects.

Is Free Trade Anti-Environment?

One attack on international trade is that it makes environmental problems worse. There are at least three reasons why this might be true. First, it may be the case that free trade simply promotes production or consumption of products that tend to cause large amounts of pollution. It is difficult to evaluate such a broad claim as this. But it is easy to find cases of the opposite, where government policies that limit or distort trade result in environmental damage. For instance, in the early 1980s, the United States forced Japan to limit its exports of autos to the United States. As a result, U.S. consumers tended to buy U.S. cars that were less fuel-efficient than the Japanese cars they could no longer buy, probably resulting in more pollution. Another well-researched case is the environmental effects of government policies that protect domestic agriculture. The web of import limits and export and production subsidies leads to excessive use of pesticides and fertilizers as protected farmers strive to expand production. Free trade would lead to farming that is more friendly to the environment.

A second possible reason is that free trade permits production to be shifted to countries that have lax environmental standards. Exports from these "pollution havens" then serve demand in countries with tighter standards, with the result that total world pollution is higher. However, research on relocation of production in response to differences in environmental standards finds that the effects are small. The costs to firms of meeting environmental protection regulations are usually small (less than 1 or 2 percent of sales revenues), even in the most stringent countries, so the incentive to relocate is usually small.

A third possible reason follows from the gains from international trade. Free trade raises world incomes.

Will higher average incomes make humans pollute more or pollute less? Will it make them use up hard-to-renew resources faster or slower? There are tendencies in both directions. Higher incomes mean more production and consumption, and these activities tend to pollute. On the other hand, higher incomes also raise people's commitment to environmental cleanup and to conservation. In the language of the economist, caring about the environment is a "luxury good," one with a high income elasticity. As incomes go up, so does the share of resources that people devote to preventing environmental degradation.

To judge how the growth of incomes is likely to affect the environment, and to shed light on recent environmental debates between rich and poor nations, Figure 12.1 sketches how some leading kinds of environmental degradation relate to a nation's per capita income. The income patterns are strikingly diverse. Starting at the top of Figure 12.1, we are reminded that sanitation improves as countries prosper, both in cities and in the countryside. Economic growth improves basic sanitation. Similarly, dust and soot and other particulates pollute the urban air less and less as a nation's average income rises above $300 per capita. By contrast, sulfur dioxide (SO_2) attacks the lungs of city dwellers more aggressively as nations develop from the poorest ranks (e.g., Bangladesh) to average incomes around $5,000 (as in Mexico). By itself, the downslope of the SO_2 curve beyond the $5,000 income level might suggest that growth cleans up city air. However, it still may not remove SO_2 from a *whole nation's* air if urbanization continues, since the urban SO_2 levels shown here are higher than those in the countryside that people abandon for the growing cities. Some problems clearly grow as nations become richer, as shown by the bottom pair of curves. Richer nations have more solid waste to dispose of, and they emit more carbon dioxide (CO_2) and other "greenhouse gases," potentially altering the earth's climate. We see that income growth has conflicting effects on pollution—a richer country has better sanitation and less soot, but more solid waste and more greenhouse-gas emissions.

In summary, free trade is not inherently anti-environment. Relocation of production to avoid stringent environmental standards seems to be small. Free trade does raise incomes, but it is not clear whether higher incomes raise or lower overall pollution.

FIGURE 12.1

Pollution Problems by Income Level, 1991

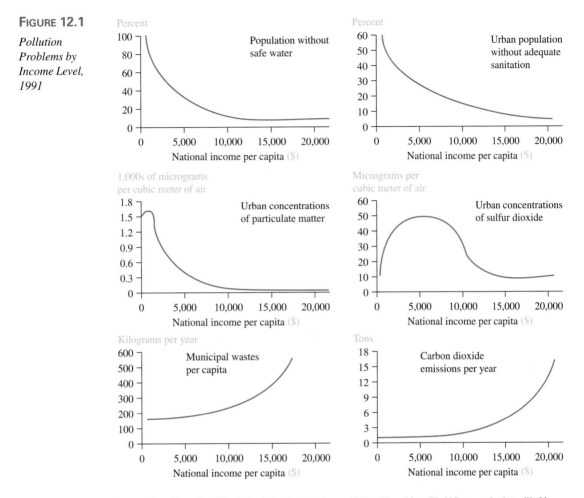

Source: Adapted from World Bank, *World Development Report*, 1992, p. 11, and from World Resource Institute, *World Resources 1992–93*. The figures for particulates and sulfur dioxide refer to concentrations on the 95th-percentile worst days of the year, and are based on 1991 estimates by Alan Krueger and Gene Grossman. Those for carbon dioxide have been arbitrarily raised for low-income countries from the World Bank curve, which referred only to emissions from the burning of fossil fuels.

Is the WTO Anti-Environment?

Even if free trade is not itself anti-environment, environmentalists often complain that the global rules of the trading system, the rules of the World Trade Organization (WTO), prevent governments from pursuing strong environmental protection policies. There are some things that are not in doubt. Most important, a government can take actions to control environmental damage caused by its own firms' production. Beyond this, there are questions.

The main preoccupation of the WTO (and the GATT before it) is with liberalizing trade, but the rules also make special mention of environmental concerns. Article XX lists general exceptions to its free-trade approach. While Article XX begins by repeating the signing governments' fear that any exceptions are subject to abuse by protectionists, it does admit exceptional arguments for trade barriers. Two of those arguments are environmental exceptions to the case for free trade:

> Subject to the requirement that such measures are not applied in a manner which would constitute a means of arbitrary or unjustifiable discrimination between countries where the same conditions prevail, or a disguised restriction on international trade, nothing in this Agreement shall be construed to prevent the adoption or enforcement by any contracting party of measures:
>
> . . . (b) necessary to protect human, animal, or plant life or health;
>
> . . . (g) relating to the conservation of exhaustible natural resources if such measures are made effective in conjunction with restrictions on domestic production or consumption.

There is an obvious tension here. The signing parties conceded that environmental concerns might conceivably justify trade barriers, but they were suspicious that such concerns would be a mere facade, an excuse for protectionists to shut out foreign goods.

There are three important types of policies that may qualify for environmental exceptions. First, consumption of products can cause damage. WTO rulings make it clear that a country generally can impose product standards or other limits on consumption to protect the country's health, safety, or the environment, even though such a policy will limit imports. A key is that the policy applies to all consumption, not just to imports. But the WTO is also vigilant against disguised protectionism. As a result of the Uruguay Round, policies that impose product standards to protect health or safety must have a scientific basis. This requirement tries to prevent a government from inventing standards that are written to limit imports. More controversially, it also may prevent a government from responding to public perceptions of risks, such as concern about genetically altered foods, if there is little scientific evidence supporting the public fears.

Second, production in foreign countries can cause environmental damage. Can a government limit imports of a foreign product produced using methods that violate the country's own environmental standards? In several recent rulings (discussed in the box "Dolphins, Turtles, and the WTO," page 250), the WTO indicated that the environmental exception does not permit a country to limit imports based on production methods used by firms in other countries. Essentially, the WTO is unwilling to let a country use its trade policy to punish another country for having a different environmental policy toward production processes.

Third, there are some environmental problems that are global in scope and that may require global solutions negotiated among many governments. Can a multilateral environmental agreement use controls on international trade to implement the agreement, or sanctions on a country's trade to enforce the agreement? Two important multilateral agreements discussed later in this chapter, the

Convention on International Trade in Endangered Species and the Montreal Protocol, use trade bans, even for trade with countries that have not signed the agreements. The WTO has not been asked to rule on these agreements. The WTO seems to be comfortable with this multilateral approach to well-defined environmental problems, but it has not actually issued any rulings endorsing them.

The Specificity Rule Again

To get a better grip on the links between trade and the environment, we must first revisit some key points of microeconomics. Environmental effects such as pollution call for special policies or institutional changes if, and only if, they are what economists call externalities. Recall from Chapter 9 that externalities are spillovers:

> An **externality** exists when somebody's activity brings direct costs or benefits to anybody who is not part of the marketplace decision to undertake the activity.[1] If your activity imposes a direct cost on somebody who has no impact on your buying or selling, they bear an external cost. If your activity brings them a direct benefit without their participation, they receive an external benefit.

Also recall that whenever an externality exists, there is a distortion, caused by a gap between private and social costs or benefits. Where there are distortions, a competitive market, in the absence of government policy, results in either too much or too little of the activity, because people see only the private costs and benefits of their actions, not the full social costs and benefits.

Pollution is an externality that imposes an external cost on people who did not have any say over the pollution. Depletion of a hard-to-renew resource can also involve an externality, but only if somebody who would pay for conserving that resource is not given the chance to do so.

Because an externality leads to sub-par performance of a market, there is a role for government policies to enhance the efficiency of the market. As we saw in Chapter 9, the specificity rule is a useful policy guide:

> The **specificity rule:** Intervene at the source of the problem. It is usually more efficient to use the policy tool that is specific to the distortion that makes private costs and benefits differ from social costs and benefits.

If, for example, an industry is causing acid rain by discharging sulfurous compounds into the air, the best approach is a policy that restrains the discharge of the

---

[1]The definition refers only to "direct" effects on others so as to exclude effects transmitted through prices. If people decide to smoke fewer cigarettes, their not polluting the public air reduces an externality—the external cost to those whose pleasure and health might be hurt by the smoke. But if the switch to nonsmoking drops the price of cigarettes, we will not call the implications of that price drop *externalities*. So externalities do not include the income losses to tobacco companies, the possibly lower wages for tobacco workers, the lower land values in tobacco-raising areas, and so on. Those are just market-price effects, not (direct) externalities. (We stick to this definition even though Alfred Marshall tried to confuse us by calling such market-price effects *pecuniary externalities*.)

sulfur compounds themselves. That is usually better than, say, taxing electrical power, because this latter approach would not send the electric companies the signal that the problem is their emissions of sulfurous compounds. Even worse would be more indirect measures like cutting down on all economic growth or all population growth to reduce the emissions.

There are several ways for a government to attack the externality directly. The two leading strategies to be explored here represent opposing sets of beliefs about the proper role of government in our lives:

- Use of *government taxes and subsidies.* The government could tax private parties to make them recognize the external costs that their actions (e.g., pollution) impose on others. (Correspondingly, it could pay them subsidies to get them to recognize the external benefits their actions give to others.)
- Changing *property rights* so that all relevant resources are somebody's private property. If somebody owns a resource, including even the right to pollute it, then what they decide to do with it depends on what others offer for that resource. If they choose to pollute (or to deplete the resource), it is because they were not offered enough by others to avoid pollution (or depletion). There is a new market for the private property, a market whose absence caused the externality in the first place.

Different as these two approaches are, they are both valid ways to attack an externality. Sometimes one is more practical, sometimes the other. In our discussions, we will often use the tax-and-subsidy approach, but we should keep in mind that the same efficiency-enhancing outcome could sometimes be achieved using the property-rights approach.

A Preview of Policy Prescriptions

Following the specificity rule, we can develop general guidelines for solutions to international externalities. If we could choose any kind of policy measure whatsoever, the specificity rule would take us on the most direct route: If the externality is pollution in some place, make the pollution itself more expensive; if resource depletion is excessive, make the depletor pay more. Often, though, we cannot hit the exact target, the externality itself. Often the only workable choices are policies toward some economic flow near the target, such as production, consumption, or trade in products related to the externality. What then?

When we have to choose between doing nothing and intervening in product markets *related to* externalities, as a substitute for controlling the externalities directly, we should follow guidelines like those summarized in Figure 12.2.

The table contains two sets of best-feasible prescriptions: One for the whole world acting as one government, and one for a single nation unable to get cooperation from other governments. These represent the two extremes in international negotiations over issues like pollution or natural-resource depletion: The greater the scope for international cooperation, the more relevant is the column of pre-

FIGURE 12.2 *Types of Externalities and Product-Market Prescriptions*

Source of External Costs (e.g., Pollution) Harming Our Nation	Examples	If the Whole World Had Only One Government, Its Best Product-Market Policy Would Be	Best Product-Market Policy for Our Nation Acting Alone
Just our own production	Chemicals	Tax our production	Tax our production (as in Figure 12.3)
Just foreign production	Acid rain across borders; tuna and dolphins; ivory	Tax foreign production	Tax our imports
World production	CO_2 buildup from fossil fuels; CFCs	Tax world production (or consumption)	Tax our production and imports
Just our own consumption	Fossil fuels, tobacco, narcotics	Tax our consumption	Tax our consumption
Just foreign consumption	Fossil fuels, tobacco, narcotics	Tax foreign consumption	Tax our exports
World consumption	Fossil fuels, tobacco, narcotics	Tax world consumption (or production)	Tax our consumption and exports

Note: Tax here means "impose government restrictions." These could be taxes, quantitative quotas, or outright prohibitions.

Remember that only "best product-market policy" interventions are considered here. In many cases, a more direct approach would tax an input or specific technology (e.g., use of high-sulfur coal or fuel-inefficient automobiles) rather than the final product (e.g., electricity from power plants or road transportation). And in other cases, an optimal policy might manipulate more than one product market at once.

scriptions for a world with a single government. The more hopeless it is to gain cooperation, the more we must settle on the single-nation prescriptions in the right column.

Note that if nations cooperate, as if they formed a single world government, there would be essentially no role for international trade policy. In the best of worlds, government would devise a way to tax the activity of pollution itself, to translate its concern about pollution into direct incentives. In the one-world-government column of Figure 12.2, the recommended policies are one step away from taxing pollution itself, taking the form of taxes on production or consumption. Note that they are not taxes on exports or imports.[2] This is because pollution and other externalities seldom arise from trade as such. The specificity rule accordingly calls for taxes near the source of the pollution, and taxes on production or consumption are closer to that target than taxes on international trade.

If one nation must act alone, trade barriers could be an appropriate second-best solution. That would happen if our nation suffered from transborder pollution, either from foreign production (e.g., foreign producers of our steel causing acid rain in our country) or from foreign consumption (e.g., foreign cars burning our exported gasoline upwind from our nation). In this situation, the only way in which our nation can discourage the foreign pollution is by taxing imports of the

---

[2]It may seem suspicious that Figure 12.2 mentions raising taxes, but not lowering them or giving out subsidies. The reason is simply that the cases listed here are all cases of negative externalities, the kind that do harm and must be reduced by taxing the polluting activities. If Figure 12.2 had dealt with the mirror-image cases, in which there are external benefits rather than costs, it would have recommended lower taxes or subsidies.

products made by a polluting process (e.g., foreign steel) or by taxing exports of products that generate pollution when consumed (e.g., gasoline).

The rest of the chapter takes up discussion of each of three types of sources of external costs noted in Figure 12.2. First we look at issues when the external costs are ones we impose on ourselves—domestic pollution and similar national externalities. Then we analyze cases in which the activity of another country imposes an external cost on our country—transborder pollution and similar cross-country externalities. Finally, we examine the challenges of global external costs—global pollution and similar worldwide externalities.

Trade and Domestic Pollution

Economic activities sometimes produce significant amounts of domestic pollution (or similar environmental degradation). That is, the costs of the pollution fall only (or almost completely) on people within the country. If there are no policies that force internalization of these external costs, then we reach two surprising conclusions about trade with domestic pollution. First, free trade can reduce the well-being of the country. Second, the country can end up exporting the wrong products; it exports products that it should import, for instance.

To see this, consider the case of an industry whose production activity creates substantial water pollution, in which the local rivers, lakes, and groundwater are polluted. For instance, consider the paper-making industry in a country like Canada. It is very convenient for paper companies to dump their chemical wastes into the local lakes, and the firms view this as a free activity (if the Canadian government has no policy limiting this kind of pollution). The Canadian companies are happy that the lakes are there, and the firms' operations thrive, producing profits, good incomes for their workers, and good products for their customers at reasonable prices.

Other Canadians have a different view, of course. Having the lakes turn brown with chemical waste spoils the scenery, the swimming, the fishing, and other services that they get from their lakes. The dumping of wastes into the lakes imposes an external cost on other users of the lakes.

The top half of Figure 12.3 shows the Canadian market for paper, with the domestic supply curve reflecting the private marginal cost of production, and the domestic demand curve reflecting the private marginal benefits of paper consumption (which are also the social marginal benefits if there are no external benefits). The bottom half of Figure 12.3 shows the additional costs imposed on the country by the pollution that results from production of paper in the country. We keep track of this negative externality using the marginal social side costs (MSSC) of the pollution. (This figure is the analog of Figure 9.2, which showed the case of external benefits.) To keep the analysis simple, we assume that the external cost of the pollution is constant at $0.30 per ream of paper.

With no international trade (and no government policies limiting pollution), the paper market clears at a price of $1 per ream, with 2 billion reams produced and consumed per year. Because there is no recognition in the market of the cost of the pollution, this is overproduction of paper.

FIGURE 12.3

When Domestic Production Causes Domestic Pollution

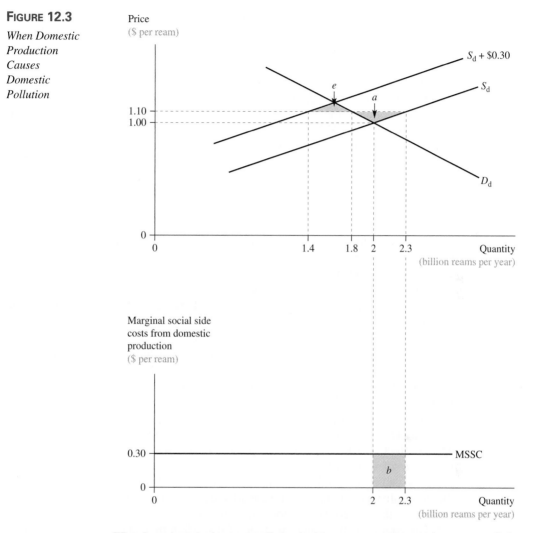

When domestic production causes pollution that imposes an external cost on the country, we find several surprising results about trade. If the government has no policy limiting this pollution, then domestic firms ignore the marginal social side costs (MSSC) of their pollution, and operate along the supply curve S_d. If the world price is $1.10, then the country exports 0.5 billion reams of paper. In comparison with no trade, the country may be worse off, as it is here (gain of the shaded triangle *a* in the top of the figure, but loss of the shaded rectangle *b* in the bottom).

The country may also export the wrong products. Here it would be best if the country actually imported 0.4 billion reams. That would happen if a $0.30 tax, equal to the MSSC, made domestic producers operate along the supply curve $S_d + $0.30, which reflects all social costs.

Consider the shift to free trade, with an international price of $1.10 per ream (and still no government policies limiting pollution). Domestic production expands to 2.3 billion reams, domestic consumption declines to 1.8 billion, and 0.5 billion reams are exported. For the case shown in Figure 12.3, free trade unfortunately makes the country worse off. The usual gain from trade is shown by the shaded triangle *a* in the upper graph, a gain of $25 million. But the extra production brings pollution that has an extra cost of the shaded area *b* in the lower graph, a social side cost of $90 million ($0.30 per ream on the additional 300 million reams produced). Free trade reduces the well-being of the country by $65 million.

The country's government could avoid this loss by prohibiting exports of paper. But we know from the specificity rule that this is not the best government policy. The best policy attacks pollution directly, for instance by placing a tax on pollution from paper production. If there is no way to reduce pollution per ream produced, then the tax will add $0.30 per ream to the firms' cost of production. The tax forces the firms to recognize the cost of pollution, and it alters their behavior. The domestic supply shifts up by the amount of the tax, to S_d + $0.30. This new supply curve now reflects all social costs, both the private production costs and the external pollution costs.

If this government policy is in place, what happens with free trade? Domestic consumers still buy 1.8 billion reams of paper, but now domestic producers supply only 1.4 billion reams. As shown, it is actually best for the country to import paper, not export it. Because the new supply curve includes the cost of pollution, we can read the effects of trade on the country from the top half of Figure 12.3, without referring to the bottom half. We find the usual triangle of gains from importing, the shaded triangle *e*.

From this example we see that pollution that imposes costs only on the local economy can still have a major impact on how we think about international trade and its effects. *With no government policy limiting pollution,* the country can end up worse off with free trade, and the trade pattern can be wrong. In the case of pollution caused by production that we examined, the country exported a product that it should instead import. (If, instead, the pollution cost is not so high, then the problem is that the country exports too much.)[3]

The country can correct this type of distortion by using a policy that forces polluters to recognize the external cost of their pollution. In our paper example, the government used a pollution tax, but instead it could establish property rights. For instance, people could be given the right to the water. Polluting firms then must pay the owners for the right to pollute. Or a limited number of rights to pollute could be created by the government, so that firms need to buy these rights if they want to pollute.

If domestic firms must pay the pollution tax (or pay for the right to pollute), they probably will not be happy. The pollution tax raises their production costs,

---

[3]What can happen if pollution is caused by consumption, not production? In this case the country tends to consume too much of the product, so the country could import a product that it should instead export (or, at least, it imports too much of the product).

and they produce and sell less. In addition, they face competition from imports at the world price of $1.10. Even if they accept the reason for the pollution tax, they may still complain about the imports. If other countries do not impose a similar pollution tax on their producers, then the domestic firms often complain that the imports are unfair. They claim that the lack of foreign pollution controls is a form of implicit subsidy, or that the foreign firms are engaged in "eco-dumping" based on lax foreign government policies.

What are we to make of these complaints? Should the country impose countervailing duties on imports from a country with different pollution policies? From the national perspective of the importing country, the answer is generally no. Foreign production may create pollution in the foreign country, but this has no impact on the importing country if the costs of this foreign pollution affect only foreigners. As with many other complaints about unfair exports, the best policy for the importing country is simply to enjoy the low-price imports. Indeed, under the rules of the World Trade Organization, lax foreign pollution policies are not a legitimate reason for imposing countervailing duties.

From the perspective of the whole world, it depends on why the foreign pollution policies are different from those of the importing country. It may be efficient for the foreign country to have different, and perhaps more lax, pollution policies. The pollution caused by foreign production may not be so costly, because the foreign production itself creates less pollution, because the foreign environment is not so badly affected, or because foreigners place less value on the environment. In our paper example, the production process or the raw materials used in foreign production may create less pollution. Or the foreign country may have larger water resources or rainfall, so that the pollution is not so damaging because the foreign environment has a larger "assimilative capacity." Or the foreign country may assign a high value to producing income to purchase basic goods, because its people are poor, so that they are willing to accept some extra pollution more readily.

On the other hand, the foreign country may simply have policies that are too lax. From the point of view of the foreign country and the world, it would be better if it had tougher pollution policies. As a type of second-best approach, import limits by other countries could improve things. But these limits will not make the importing country better off, even though they might raise world well-being.

Transborder Pollution

In the previous section we considered pollution that had costs only to the country doing the pollution. While we reached some surprising conclusions about free trade in the absence of government policies limiting pollution, we also had a ready solution. The government should implement some form of policy addressing pollution that is occurring in its country. If each country's government addresses its own local pollution problems, then each can enhance its own national well-being, and in the process, world well-being is also raised.

However, many types of pollution have transborder effects—effects not just on the country doing the pollution but also on other countries. Transborder pollution raises major new issues for government policies toward pollution.

Suppose that a German paper company builds a new paper mill on the Danube River, just to the west of where it flows into Austria. It is very convenient for the paper company to dump its chemical wastes into the river, and it views this as a free activity (if the German government has no policy limiting this kind of pollution). Austrians have a different view. The dumping of wastes into the German Danube imposes an external cost on the Austrians and others (Slovaks, Hungarians, Serbs, Romanians, and Bulgarians) downstream.

The Right Solution

Figure 12.4 shows how we can determine the "right" amount of pollution, the amount that brings the greatest net gain to the world as a whole.[4] The figure focuses directly on pollution, without also showing the supply and demand for paper. It portrays Germany's benefits and Austria's costs from different rates of dumping waste into the Danube by the German paper mill. If left to itself, the German mill dumps as much as it wants into the Danube, ignoring the costs to Austria (and other nations). It will pollute until there is no more that it wants to dump at zero cost. That will be at point *A*, with the paper company dumping 180 million tons of waste per year. Point *A* is a disaster in Austria, where the river damage rises along the marginal cost curve in Figure 12.4.

Point *A* is also inefficient from a world perspective. Any pollution beyond 80 million tons is inefficient—it does more damage than it benefits the paper company. In the figure any waste dumping above 80 million tons has marginal costs that are above the marginal benefits. For instance, while the last few tons dumped bring the German firm almost no extra benefits (perhaps because these would be easy to avoid or clean up), these last few tons cost the Austrians about 700 marks per ton.

But, looking at it from the other side, we see that a total ban on dumping into the Danube would also be a mistake in this situation. The total ban, if effectively enforced, would force the paper mill to point *D*. Downstream users would be delighted, of course, to have the river clean. But the complete cleanup costs more than it is worth. That is, allowing the first ton of pollution each year would be worth 720 marks to the paper company (perhaps because it is very costly to capture the last small amounts of waste for alternative disposal). Yet downstream users lose only 60 marks of extra enjoyment and income (at point *C*). The downstream cost of the first ton of pollution is not that high, probably because the river can assimilate this small amount of pollution without much damage. From a

---

[4]Here, as in other chapters, the interest of the "world as a whole" is the sum of net gains to all parties, with each dollar (or mark) of gain or loss worth the same regardless of whose gain or loss it is. That is, we continue to follow the one-dollar–one-vote yardstick introduced in Chapter 2. To reject it, we would have to have another set of welfare weights, considering a dollar or mark of gain to the German firm to have a different value from the same value of gain to Austrians.

FIGURE 12.4

A Classic Case of International Pollution with an Ideal Policy Solution

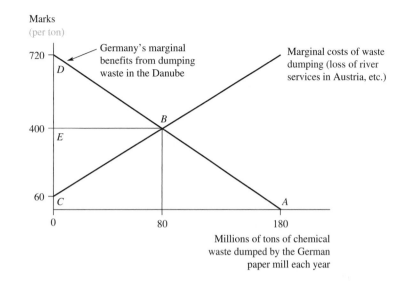

world viewpoint, the first ton of pollution should be allowed. In fact, if Figure 12.4 correctly portrays the marginal benefits and costs, pollution up to 80 million tons adds to world well-being, because the benefit to Germany from using the Danube for its waste is greater than the costs imposed on Austria. The paper company should be allowed to dump waste up to 80 tons per year, but no more than that. At point *B*, the benefits of using the river as a drain for wastes stop exceeding the costs of doing that. However offensive the idea may be to those who love clean water and don't buy much paper, the economist insists that 80 million tons, not zero tons (or 180 million tons), is the "optimal amount of pollution" in this situation.[5]

To get the right solution, something must be done to make the paper company recognize the costs of its pollution, so that it reduces the pollution, and this something cannot be too drastic. The specificity rule indicates that the best government policy is one that acts directly on the problem. A government could use the tax/subsidy approach to guide the use of the Danube to the optimal point *B*, if the government has good estimates of the marginal costs and benefits of the pollution. For instance, the government could tax the paper company 400 marks for every ton it dumps into the river. The company will respond by dumping 80 million tons a year (at point *B*), since up to that 80 millionth ton the company's gain from putting each extra ton of waste in the river exceeds the 400-mark tax. An efficient balance would be struck between the competing uses of the river.

A pollution tax like the one just described might well happen if "the government" were the Austrian government. But here the problem becomes international. Austria has no direct tax power over a paper mill in Germany, except to the

---

[5]At point *B*, allowing 80 million tons of pollution brings the world a net gain of area *BCD*, or $(1/2) \times (720 - 60) \times 80 = 26.4$ billion marks per year.

extent that the mill happens to do business in Austria. More likely, the tax/subsidy option is in the hands of the German government since the paper mill is on the German side of the border. Germany might not tax the paper mill at all. Dumping 180 tons a year (at point *A* again) brings greater national gains to Germany than the world-efficient pollution tax at point *B*.

The likelihood that one country would decide to go on imposing an external cost on the rest of the world is a setback for the economist seeking global efficiency. To the efficiency-minded economist, it would not matter how we got to point *B* as long as we got there. But the German government has no incentive to tax the German company for its pollution.

We can imagine another way, assigning property rights, to try to get the efficient solution. A World Court could rule that the Danube is the property of the German paper company (or the German government), and Austria must pay the German company to reduce its pollution. Or the World Court could rule that the Danube belongs to Austria, and the German company must buy the right to pollute for each ton it dumps. The Nobel Prize–winning economist Ronald Coase pointed out that *either* court ruling could result in the same amount of pollution, as long as the property rights can be enforced. If the German company owned the river, the Austrian users would be willing to pay 400 marks per ton to reduce pollution to 80 million tons, and the German firm would agree to reduce its pollution to this level. If Austria owned the river, the German firm would be willing to pay 400 marks per ton for the right to dump 80 million tons, and the Austrians would accept this offer. Who gets the money depends on who owns the river, but in either case the same amount of pollution results.

This private-property approach has a major problem, however, when it comes to international disputes. There is no supreme world court that can enforce a property claim of one country's residents in another country. Austrians have no real legal recourse if the German paper mill insists on discharging all its wastes into the Danube. The Austrian government could threaten to take retaliatory actions against Germany. But it is unlikely that Austria would hold the right kind of power to force Germany to cooperate on the specific issue of the paper mill and the Danube, if the Germans did not want to cooperate. The result is likely to be inefficient.[6]

We therefore get the same striking results for either the tax/subsidy approach or the property-rights approach. The good news is that any of several arrangements *could* give us the efficient compromise solution to the transborder pollution problem (at point *B*). The bad news is that the two sides probably would not

---

[6]As it happens, the German–Austrian case is relatively benign in real life because Germany does care greatly about good relations with Austria, and both are members of the European Union. Yet the question, Whose river is it, anyway?, is destined to arise more and more often. Here are some examples: (1) Turkey has upstream control of the Euphrates, a vital resource for Syria and Iraq. (2) Now that they are separate nations, Russia, Belarus, and the Ukraine will struggle over the headwaters of the Dnieper. (3) If the eight upstream nations use the Nile more intensively, there will be consequences for Egypt. (4) The Zambezi River, where irrigation has recently begun (in Zimbabwe), will be the focus of major disputes when upstream countries start to pump great volumes. (5) Several drought-prone nations, most notably Mali and Niger, compete for the waters of the Niger River upstream from Nigeria.

reach that efficient solution. More likely, negotiations would break down and each side would do as it pleased in its own territory. The result could be costly rampant pollution, as at point *A*, if the polluting firms can do as they please.

A Next-Best Solution

If international negotiations fail, the Austrian government must still consider what it can do on its own. If an international agreement is not possible, what can the government of the country that is being harmed by the other country's pollution do? It cannot tax or restrict the pollution-creating activity in the other country directly. But it may be able to have some influence by adopting policies toward international trade.

In our example, let's say that Austria imports paper from Germany, and that Austrian paper production does not create much pollution (or this pollution is controlled by appropriate Austrian government policies). The Austrian government could attempt to reduce the dumping of waste into the Danube by limiting its imports from Germany (or, if possible, from the specific firm whose factory is responsible for the pollution). The decline in German paper exports reduces German paper production, and this also reduces the amount of waste that is dumped into the Danube. Austria gives up some of the gains from importing paper—that is, Austria suffers the usual deadweight losses from restricting imports. But Austria can still be better off if the gain from reducing the costs of the river pollution exceeds these usual deadweight costs. If instead Austria exports paper to Germany, then the Austrian government should consider subsidizing paper exports to Germany. The increase in Austrian exports can reduce German import-competing paper production, again leading to less dumping of waste.

There is a major problem with this indirect approach to addressing transborder pollution. The rules of the WTO generally prohibit the Austrian government from increasing its import tariffs or subsidizing its exports. Although, as we have seen, the rules also offer exceptions for measures intended to protect the environment, the WTO interprets this exception narrowly (see the box "Dolphins, Turtles, and the WTO"). So the WTO might not permit Austrian use of trade policy in response to lax German environmental policies.

NAFTA and the Environment

Environmental problems along the Mexico–U.S. border provide a real case of the challenges of transborder pollution. This issue was prominent in the fight over approving the North American Free Trade Agreement (NAFTA), adding to the concerns already discussed in Chapter 11, and it remains important in evaluations of the effects of NAFTA.

Mexico has a strong set of environmental protection laws and regulations on the books, comparable to those of the United States. But Mexican enforcement of these is weak. Weak enforcement is not surprising, and it is not only the result of limited administrative resources. As we saw in Figure 12.1, popular demand for clean air and water is a luxury good, one that nations feel they can afford only when

Dolphins, Turtles, and the WTO

Dolphins have long had a special appeal to humans because of their intelligence and seeming playfulness. The sympathy for dolphins, like the sympathy for all large animals, grows with income. It was inevitable that any threat to dolphins, even though they are not an endangered species, would mobilize a strong defense in the industrialized countries. This threat came from methods used to catch tuna in the Eastern Tropical Pacific Ocean.

Most tuna are caught by methods that do not harm dolphins. But, for unknown reasons, large schools of tuna choose to swim beneath herds of dolphins in the Eastern Tropical Pacific. Before 1960, this posed no threat to dolphins. Fishing crews used hooks to catch tuna, and dolphins' sonar allowed them to avoid the hooks. However, the 1960s brought a new method for catching tuna, purse-seine fishing, in which speedboats and helicopters effectively herd the dolphins and tuna into limited areas, where vast nets encircle large schools of tuna. As the nets draw tight underwater, the dolphins, being mammals, drown. Six million dolphins have died this way since 1960.

The United States tried to stop this purse-seine netting with the Marine Mammals Protection Act of 1972, but with limited effect. The law can prohibit use of this method in U.S. waters, out to the 200-mile limit, and use of this method by U.S. ships anywhere in the world. Fishing fleets responded to the 1972 law by reflagging as ships registered outside the United States. Between 1978 and 1990, the share of U.S. boats in the Eastern Pacific tuna fleet dropped from 62 percent to less than 10 percent.

The United States still had some economic weapons at its disposal. The government pressured the three main tuna-packing and tuna-retailing firms (Star-Kist, Bumble Bee, and Chicken of the Sea) to refuse to buy tuna taken with dolphin-unsafe methods. While there have been charges that at least one of the firms packed dolphin-unsafe tuna under its dolphin-safe label, the dolphin-safe scheme does appear to have had some success. Through this and other forms of pressure, the estimated dolphin mortality in tuna fishing dropped from 130,000 in 1986 to 25,000 in 1991.

The United States did not let the matter rest there, however. In 1991, the U.S. government banned tuna imports from Mexico and four other countries. Mexico immediately protested to the GATT, where a dispute resolution panel handed down a preliminary ruling that the U.S. import ban was an unfair trade practice, a protectionist act against Mexico. The GATT panel ruled that the United States cannot restrict imports based on production methods used by firms in other countries. The EU also challenged the U.S. legislation as a violation of the GATT, because it included a "secondary boycott" against tuna imports from any country importing dolphin-unsafe tuna from countries like Mexico that use this fishing method. In 1994, a GATT panel again ruled against the United States.

These rulings indicate that the WTO (which incorporates the GATT) will interpret the environmental exceptions narrowly. That is, the WTO will not endorse efforts by one country to use trade policy to impose its environmental policies outside of its borders, or to force other countries to change their environmental policies. Environmentalists are furious, because they believe that the WTO places its principles of trade policy ahead of environmental safeguards.

Within these constraints, what can the United States do if it wishes to save more dolphins? One

GDP per capita has reached high levels. Mexico has sacrificed air and water quality for economic development. Mexico City's smog is as bad as any in the world.

For the United States a major concern is the pollution emanating from the Mexican side of the Mexico–U.S. border. In the 1960s, the governments of Mexico and the United States encouraged growth of industry just south of the border, where businesses could assemble goods for reentry into the United States without

possibility would be a tax or ban on U.S. consumption of dolphin-unsafe tuna. As a domestic measure it might pass WTO scrutiny, although affected foreign producing countries could complain that it was a disguised form of illegitimate import restriction. The major problem probably would be implementing the consumption policy: How does one identify only tuna that is caught with dolphin-unsafe methods? A more fruitful possibility is to negotiate with other countries to get them to alter the methods that they use to catch tuna, perhaps by offering other benefits in exchange. In 1995, six countries (including Mexico) agreed to adopt dolphin-friendly fishing. However, some fishing fleets could just reflag to yet other countries, so the best solution probably would be a global multilateral agreement on tuna fishing.

Sea turtles, a species threatened with extinction, present a very similar case. Some shrimp are caught with nets that trap and kill sea turtles. A U.S. law passed in 1989 requires shrimpers in U.S. waters to alter their nets with turtle-excluder devices, and it prohibits shrimp imports from countries that fail to protect sea turtles from deadly entrapment in nets. Four Asian countries filed a complaint with the WTO in 1997, and the WTO issued a ruling against the United States, stating the United States was not permitted to use trade policy to force other countries to adopt environmental polices, even to protect an endangered species. With this negative ruling, the United States has the choice of dropping these import policies or keeping them and facing some penalties from the complaining countries. At the same time, the U.S. government negotiated and reached agreements with some foreign countries. The foreign countries agreed to use nets with turtle-excluder devices, and the United States provides money and training in how to use the modified nets.

©Dion Ogust, The Image Works

the usual tariffs and quotas. The arid border is not a forgiving place for a large industrial population. The absence of infrastructure for the several thousand *maquiladora* firms producing there, and the millions of people attracted by the jobs available, became all too obvious. U.S. critics can point to unmanaged hazardous wastes, soil erosion, air pollution, raw sewage and other water pollution, and natural resource depletion from Tijuana to the mouth of the Rio Grande.

While the pollution is most severe on the Mexican side of the border, major damage also affects the American side. Coal-fired power plants in northern Mexico cause serious air pollution in Texas, and Mexican water pollution is fouling the Rio Grande, a prime source of water for many U.S. towns.

Critics of NAFTA argued that freer trade would yield more environmental damage in the trade-oriented *maquiladora* zone, and they recommended rejecting NAFTA. In response to these criticisms, a side agreement on environmental issues was attached to NAFTA. It established a commission to investigate complaints about failure to enforce national environmental laws. It set up a bank to fund cleanup projects using billions of dollars obtained with governmental backing. Mexico also promised to enforce its environmental standards more effectively. With these additional provisions, environmental lobbying groups were actually divided about the final version of NAFTA. The Sierra Club and Friends of the Earth strongly opposed NAFTA on environmental grounds, while the Audubon Society, the Environmental Defense Fund, the National Wildlife Federation, and the Natural Resources Defense Council gave qualified support to NAFTA with the added environmental provisions.

However, even with these provisions in NAFTA and the general spirit of cooperation it has engendered, progress has been very slow. The commission can investigate, but it has no power to mandate enforcement. It appears to have had little impact on Mexican enforcement of its environmental laws, which remains weak. As of 1998, the bank had not received the amount of government funding that was promised, and it has been slow to approve and fund projects. So far the environmental problems along the Mexico–U.S. border show how difficult it can be to address transborder pollution, especially when the two countries do not share the same views about the importance of environmental quality.

Global Environmental Challenges

Our discussion of transborder pollution focused on cases in which one country's activities impose external costs on another country. Things become even more controversial when the whole world's economic activities impose external costs on the whole world. Two important global environmental challenges are depletion of the ozone layer and global warming resulting from the buildup of greenhouse gases. Other challenges also have a global dimension, especially those that involve extinction of species or depletion of common resources such as fish stocks. We begin with an overview of important concepts and then examine specific applications.

Global Problems Need Global Solutions

Consider a global environmental problem like the depletion of the ozone layer caused by human release of chemicals. As we will see when we look at this in more detail, many types of activities release these chemicals, and the total of the global release causes the depletion. The harm of ozone depletion has global effects, with some countries more affected than others.

What would each country do if it set its own policy toward this problem? From the purely national viewpoint, each country would recognize that chemical releases have some negative effect on its people, and it might use a policy to limit releases if it thought the national harm was large enough. But, for the whole world, total releases would be much too large. Each country would ignore the harm that its own releases did to other countries, so it would not be sufficiently stringent with its own environmental policy.

To get closer to the best global policy, the countries would need to find some way to cooperate. Each would need to tighten its standards compared to what it would do on its own. If each country does this, the whole world is better off. Many, but perhaps not all, of the countries will also each be better off. Each country incurs some costs in tightening its standards, but each also derives benefits from the reduction of the environmental damage.

Still, it may be very difficult to reach this global agreement. One problem is that there may be disagreement about the costs of the environmental damage or the costs of tightening standards. Science is unlikely to provide a definitive accounting, and countries differ in their willingness to take environmental risks. Even if this problem is not so large, others are likely to arise. Countries that suffer net losses from tightening may be unwilling to take part, unless they receive some other kind of compensation. Even countries that gain from the global agreement have a perverse incentive. A country can gain even more by free-riding. That is, it can gain most of the benefits if other countries abide by the agreement to tighten standards, even if this country does not, and it avoids the costs of tightening its own standards.

Because of the problem of free-riding, a global agreement needs some method of enforcement, to get "reluctant" countries to agree in the first place, and to assure that they abide by the agreement after it is established. There is no global organization that can provide these enforcement services. Countries can establish an enforcement mechanism as part of the global agreement, but it is not clear what it should be. It is generally not possible to impose fines directly. One possible penalty is some kind of trade sanctions, to reduce the offending country's gains from trade. As we saw in Chapter 11, such sanctions also have costs for the countries imposing the sanctions, and in any case they often do not work.

This is a sobering analysis. When an environmental problem causes only domestic costs, it is up to the government of the country to address it. When the problem is transborder but regional among a small number of countries, it is more difficult but still may be solvable by negotiations. When the problem is global, a global (or nearly global) multilateral agreement is needed, but negotiating and enforcing this agreement may prove to be very difficult or impossible. To gain more insight, let's turn to four problems that are global in nature. We begin with a fairly effective global agreement to use trade policy to prevent the extinction of endangered species. We then turn to depletion of ocean fishing stocks, and the lack of any effective solutions to this global inefficiency. Then we portray a successful, nearly global agreement to reverse ozone depletion. We conclude with the most daunting of global environmental issues, greenhouse gases and global warming.

Extinction of Species

Extinction of species is a natural process. Still, within the past half century the specific role of human activity in causing extinction has become recognized and controversial. It is reckoned that human activities eliminated only 8 mammal species and 24 birds in the 18th century, then 29 mammals and 61 birds in the 19th century, and 52 mammals and 70 birds from 1900 to 1987. There is a general belief that there is a loss when a species becomes extinct, perhaps because there may be future uses for the species (for instance, as a source of medicinal products). Thus, a global effort to prevent extinction of species can be economically sensible.

Human activities contributing to extinction include destruction of habitat, introduction of predators, and pollution. In addition, excessive hunting and harvesting can also cause extinction. The specificity rule indicates that the best global policy to preserve species would be a policy that promotes the species through such direct means as protected parks and wild areas; ranching, cultivation, and similar management intended to earn profits from the ongoing existence of the species; and zoos and gardens to maintain species in captivity. While there is no global agreement specifically to promote these best solutions, there is a global agreement that attempts to control the pressure of international demand as a source of incentives for excessive hunting and harvesting.

In 1973, over 100 nations signed the Convention on International Trade in Endangered Species of Wild Fauna and Flora (**CITES**). With 138 member countries by 1997, CITES establishes international cooperation to prevent international trade from endangering the survival of species. An international scientific authority decides which species are endangered. Commercial trade is usually banned for species threatened with extinction—about 900 species, including elephants, gray whales, and sea turtles. To export these products for noncommercial purposes, a nation must obtain an export permit from the central authority, and it must have a copy of an import permit from a suitable buyer in a country that signed CITES. Commercial trade is limited for an additional 29,000 species because free trade could lead to the threat of extinction.

No species with a trade ban has become extinct. Some, including the rhino and the tiger, continue to decline, but CITES has probably slowed the declines. Generally, CITES seems to be fairly effective. This is impressive in that most member countries have incomplete national legislation, poor enforcement, and weak penalties for violating the trade bans or controls.

Much of the conflict over endangered species naturally centers on Africa, with its unique biodiversity and its fragile ecosystems. The biggest fight so far has been over the fate of the African elephant, which is hunted for its ivory tusks.

The human slaughter of elephants accelerated at an alarming rate in the 1970s and 1980s. The African elephant population was cut in half within a span of only eight years in the 1980s. The problem was most severe in eastern Africa, north of the Zambezi River. The governments of Kenya, Tanzania, and Zambia, while ostensibly committed to protecting elephants, were not preventing killing by poachers. The threat to elephants was weaker in southern Africa, south of the

Zambezi, for three reasons: The governments of Zimbabwe, Botswana, and Namibia enforced conservation more aggressively, agriculture was less of a threat to the wild animal population, and some elephants of Botswana and Zimbabwe had tusks of poor commercial quality.

In 1977, the African elephant was placed on the list of species with controlled trade. Public pressure from affluent countries to save the elephants became intense by the late 1980s. Although the African elephant did not fully meet the official definition, in 1989 it was moved to the list of endangered species. Also in 1989, most of the CITES countries signed a complete ban on exporting or importing ivory. The drastic reduction in demand, especially demand from the affluent countries, caused ivory prices to plummet, from $100 per kilogram to only $3 or $4 per kilogram. Poaching decreased (mostly a movement down the poachers' supply curve) and elephant populations stabilized or even increased.

The bans on trade in African elephants and their ivory appear to be successful. Especially in eastern Africa, it has greatly reduced poaching. However, by itself it may not be a long-run solution. Africa's human population growth will bring more crop cultivation, and cultivation is simply inconsistent with a roaming elephant population. Where crops come, the elephant will go. Even in dry southern Africa, irrigation will eventually bring crops.

Fortunately, there have been further developments. In 1997, Zimbabwe, Botswana, and Namibia asked CITES to end the bans for their elephants. They argued that elephants were not endangered in their countries—in fact, they had too many elephants. They argued that they needed some economic use of elephants to justify the costs of managing the herds. Based on the principle of "sustainable use" that it had previously adopted in 1992, CITES permitted limited hunting of elephants for these three countries. By adopting a role for sustainable use, CITES recognizes that the profit of commercial trade can deter other pressures toward extinction. But CITES now must face the challenge of evaluating claims of sustainable use, rather than simply using its precautionary bans. For many species the ultimate success of CITES probably depends less on its bans and, paradoxically, more on its ability to encourage economic management for commercial uses.

Overfishing

The oceans and the fish and other animals and plants that live in them are one of the great global resources. However, major problems can develop because no one actually owns these resources. About a quarter of the 200 main fish stocks in the world are in decline, and another quarter are on the verge of decline. For most fish species, this is not a threat of extinction but, rather, that populations are becoming smaller than they should be. Why are we squandering this resource? What can we do?

We have here an example of the "tragedy of the commons." With open access to fishing and no ownership, the incentive of each fishing firm is to catch as many fish as possible. There is no incentive to conserve. Even if one fishing firm did restrain its catch to maintain the fish stock, others would simply increase their catch. So all fish too much, and the fish stock declines. Rather than limiting their fishing industries, governments often make matters worse by subsidizing them. The result is severe overcapacity of fishing boats.

With good management of fishing stocks, the world catch of fish could be 10 to 20 percent larger than it is now. But even single nations have trouble managing their fishing activities. The fishing industry, with its overcapacity, pushes for lesser limits, even if this is only helpful in the short run. When government policy imposes a limit, another kind of inefficiency often arises. The fishing firms race to take the limited amount. A full year's take of Alaska sable is caught in less than a week, and fishing then ceases for the rest of the year. This is wasteful of resources, it is dangerous for the fishing boats, and it is value-destroying, because consumers consider frozen fish to be inferior to fresh.

Global or multilateral agreements could enhance global fishing. But given the difficulty of negotiating and enforcing such agreements, effective ones are rare. We pay a global cost, in the form of less fish at a higher price.

CFCs and Ozone

The 1940s brought new technologies for using chlorofluorocarbon compounds (CFCs) in several industries. About 30 percent of CFCs came to be used in refrigeration, air conditioning, and heat pumps; about 28 percent in foam blowing; about 27 percent in aerosol propellants; and about 15 percent in dry cleaning and other industrial cleaning and degreasing. By the early 1970s, evidence had accumulated showing that CFCs and the halons used in fire extinguishers, while not directly toxic, were depleting ozone in the upper atmosphere. The chemical process is slow and complex. It takes 7 to 10 years for released CFCs to drift to the stratosphere, where their chlorine compounds interact with different climatic conditions to remove ozone. By 1985, the now-famous ozone holes were clearly detected in the stratosphere near the North and South Poles. Unfortunately, stratospheric ozone is an important absorber of ultraviolet rays from the sun, and its removal raises dangers of skin cancer, reduced farm yields, and climatic change.

In 1987 over 50 nations signed the **Montreal Protocol** on Substances that Deplete the Ozone Layer.[7] The signing parties agreed to ban exports and imports of CFCs and halons. After more scientific evidence accumulated, most signatory nations agreed in 1990 to phase out their own production of these chemicals by 2000, with later deadlines and interim production limits for developing countries.

Note that the protocol called for outright bans and other quantitative limits, not a pollution tax or polluting-product tax like those discussed in Figures 12.2 through 12.4. The reason is that the scientific evidence suggested a steeply rising social-cost curve for CFC emissions into the atmosphere. With the cost curve so vertical, it did not make sense to use tax rates on a trial-and-error basis in the hope of achieving the large cut in pollution. It was better to legislate the bans and

---

[7]The signatories were 18 industrial OECD nations, Argentina, Brazil, Mexico, Egypt, Kenya, South Africa, Zambia, Malaysia, Thailand, the (former) Soviet Union, Bulgaria, (former) Czechoslovakia, Hungary, and 25 other developing countries. By 1997, the number of signatories had risen to 163 countries.

limits from the start, without waiting several years to see if some tax schedule had the right effects.

The Montreal Protocol is achieving much of the economic and environmental effect it was supposed to have. The rate of atmospheric buildup of chlorofluorocarbon-11 and chlorofluorocarbon-12 dropped more than 50 percent between 1988 and 1992, a faster drop than what cautious industry estimates had predicted. Some warnings are still in effect, however. First, the ozone holes will remain for a long time; concentrations in the stratosphere will not return to normal levels until the end of the 21st century. Second, the CFC protocol allows developing countries a 10-year delay in their phaseout of CFCs. Fortunately, refrigerator manufacturers in a number of developing countries, including China and Brazil, have made major progress in replacing CFCs with less harmful alternatives. Third, continued production in developing countries has led to substantial smuggling of CFCs into industrialized countries. Nonetheless, dramatic progress has been made over the situation since the Montreal Protocol was signed, and the end of the net atmospheric buildup should occur in the early 2000s.

Why the success in this case? Why didn't nations try to "free-ride" and refuse to comply while demanding that others do so, as so often happens? Experts point to several factors that eased the signing and enforcement of the Montreal Protocol:

- The scientific evidence was clearer about CFCs and ozone than it is about other possible human threats to the atmospheric balance.
- A small group of products was involved, for which substitutes appear to be technologically feasible with limited cost increases.
- Production of CFCs was concentrated in the United States and the EU, and in a few large publicity-conscious firms (mainly DuPont) so that agreement could be easily reached and enforced.
- The same higher-income countries that dominated production and use of these chemicals were also closer to the North and South Pole, and would thus expect to suffer most of the environmental damage themselves.

Greenhouse Gases and Global Warming

Finally, we turn to the most daunting environmental problem of all. It is feared that human activity, especially the burning of fossil fuels, is raising the concentration of carbon dioxide (CO_2) in the earth's atmosphere, and that the rise of CO_2 will cause a pronounced warming of the earth's climate through a "greenhouse effect." The warming could bring desertification of vast areas, and could flood major coastal cities and farm areas when it has melted much of the polar ice caps. It is hard to imagine a solution as clean and workable as the Montreal Protocol's phaseout of chlorofluorocarbons. The activities that release carbon dioxide, methane, and other greenhouse gases into the atmosphere are harder to do without than were CFC refrigerants and sprays. In addition, the damage from adverse climatic change would be spread around the globe unpredictably and unevenly.

To see the available options, we should first clear the air, so to speak, by noting some limits on the choices available. Three main points must be made at the outset: (1) The scientific facts are in doubt, (2) three palatable solutions will fall short of arresting the CO_2 buildup, and (3) international trade is not the cause or the cure.

First, the scientific facts about the greenhouse effect are far less certain than the facts about CFCs and stratospheric ozone. We do know that atmospheric concentrations of CO_2 have risen since the 1960s and are still rising. Human activity is probably the main source of the buildup, though the magnitudes are still being debated. The effects of the CO_2 buildup cannot be predicted precisely. We do know that there is a greenhouse effect—in fact, it is crucial to keeping the earth's surface and lower atmosphere warm. The prevailing theory is that the buildup of greenhouse gases will raise temperatures, but there is controversy over how much. A typical forecast is an increase in average temperatures of about two degrees centigrade by the year 2100, but there is also a wide variance in forecasts. While there has been some warming during the past century, swings in average temperatures are normal in earth's history. Even if the earth is getting warmer and CO_2 buildup is the main reason, the climatic changes and economic damages are also difficult to predict. Some countries would gain from the warming, some would lose; and we are unsure about which countries to list in the gaining and losing columns.

This scientific uncertainty argues for a middle policy path that we could call an "insurance" path. Given the risks, it would be foolish to do nothing. It would also be foolish to risk wrecking the world economy with radical changes. Better to start leaning gently in the direction of cutting greenhouse-gas emissions, while knowledge accumulates.

Second, it must be understood that three relatively palatable policy changes will fall far short of stopping the CO_2 buildup.

1. One desirable option is known as the "no-regrets" option. Let's just remove all those unwarranted *subsidies* to energy use that should have been removed anyway. Removing bad old energy subsidies in Eastern Europe and the former Soviet Union would probably cut global CO_2 emissions by 6 to 7 percent. Doing the same in developing countries would cut global emissions by another 4 percent. But these add up to only 10 to 11 percent of the emissions, and the net global buildup of CO_2 would continue.

2. A second option would be to take CO_2 out of the atmosphere with afforestation, that is, by stopping deforestation and reforesting previously cleared land. Unfortunately, the popular press has overrated and misdirected this solution. The overrating has taken the form of undue emphasis on mature forests, especially in the tropics. Contrary to widespread belief, a mature forest does not absorb CO_2 from the atmosphere. It has achieved an equilibrium in which the absorption of atmospheric CO_2 by plant growth is approximately canceled by the release of CO_2 from decaying plant matter. Only growth of new forests absorbs CO_2 in significant degree. It would take perpetual growth of new forests equal in area to all current U.S. forests to cut the CO_2 buildup by 20 to 25 percent. Even for this to happen, that reforestation would have to be done in the temperate zone, not in the tropics featured in the media. The absorption of CO_2 by new growth is

actually less effective in the tropics than in the temperate zone. Tropical forests sequester only about half as much CO_2 per hectare as temperate-zone forests. On atmospheric grounds, the call for reforestation would be better directed at Wisconsin than at a Wisconsin-sized area in the Amazon. Forests play much less role in the greenhouse-gas balance than does the burning of fossil fuels.

3. A third option that doesn't work is to wait for depletion of the earth's fossil fuels to push up the price of energy to a point where we stop raising the global CO_2 levels. Finite as planet Earth may be, there is no prospect of exhaustion, or even severe scarcity, of fossil fuels in the next few decades. This fact is often obscured by popular measures of how many years of energy consumption the global fuel reserves can supply. Thirty years ago, for example, it was shown that known reserves of liquid fuels could only support the then-current rate of consumption for another 30 years.[8] Since then, energy consumption roughly tripled the old rate, implying that we ran out of fuel some years ago. After this rapid exhaustion of our reserves, how many years' reserves do we have left? Actually, more than 40 years' worth at the new higher rates of consumption! The truth is that Earth contains so much oil and other fossil fuels, and our exploration for them has been so incomplete, that our current fuel habits may exhaust our good air long before they exhaust our cheap fuel supplies. To clean up the air, we must artificially raise the price of fuel long before geology will do the job for us.

A third initial point is that international trade policy cannot be the best tool. If we are to attack greenhouse-gas emissions near their source, we must attack either total consumption or total production of fossil fuels, the main human source of greenhouse-gas emissions. International trade in fuels is large, but well below half the total fuel consumption. If we were to tax international trade as such, there would still be too much substitution of one source for another to achieve a great global reduction in emissions. If we relied on taxing international trade in fuels, fuel-importing countries like the United States would substitute home supplies for imports, and fuel-exporting countries like Mexico would divert their fuel from exports to home use.

Thus far, we have limited the search for solutions in three ways. First, sheer scientific uncertainty urges a gradual "insurance" approach, somewhere in between doing nothing and taking radical steps. Second, some hopes—the easy "no-regrets" reforms, afforestation, and naturally rising fuel scarcity—prove to fall short as cures for the CO_2 buildup. Finally, trying to cut emissions by cutting international trade leaves too many options for substituting home fuel use for traded fuel.

We are left to consider the direct approach: tax consumption or production of fossil fuels on a near-global scale. What effects would such a global tax have on world income? Many economists have tried to estimate the effects of greenhouse-gas abatement. Figure 12.5 shows the gist of most studies, drawing on some 1991 estimates by John Whalley and Randall Wigle. In this case, the tax is levied on

---

[8]For all fuels, as opposed to liquid fuels, reserves equaled 46 years' consumption around 1965, and about 66 years' consumption today. See World Bank (1992), Table A.10.

Figure 12.5   *Welfare Effects of Carbon Taxes on Various Regions of the World*

	A Tax on the Carbon Content of Fossil Fuel Production, Collected by the Producers' Governments	*A Tax on the Carbon Content of Fossil Fuel Consumption, Collected by the Consumers' Governments*	*A Tax on the Carbon Content of Either Consumption or Production, Rebated on a Global per Capita Basis*
Average tax rate ($/ton of carbon)	$448	$448	$448
Welfare Change by 2030 (% of GDP)			
Whole world	−4.4%	−4.4%	−4.2%
European Union	−4.0	−1.0	−3.8
U.S. and Canada	−4.3	−3.6	−9.8
Japan	−3.7	+0.5	−0.9
Other industrial market economies	−2.3	−2.1	−4.4
Oil exporters	+4.5	−18.7	−13.0
Rest of the world	−7.1	−6.8	+1.8

Source: Anderson and Blackhurst (1992), p. 103, citing Whalley and Wigle. For further detailed estimates, see the chapters by Winters and by Piggott, Whalley, and Wigle in Anderson and Blackhurst.

each unit of carbon content, to aim as directly as possible at greenhouse-gas emissions. Presuming that we learn that global warming is a serious problem that requires a fairly aggressive approach, the tax is set at a dollar rate that aims to cut emissions in half from 1990 to 2030.

Any variant of the global carbon tax would cut world income (world GDP) by something over 4 percent by the year 2030, according to the first row of numbers in Figure 12.5. That is a significant price to pay for better climate, though it is limited by economies' (estimated) ability to conserve on fossil fuels in response to the tax.

When we look at how the cost is distributed across the major economic regions of the world, we see big differences that would surely spark a heated debate in any world conference over such a tax. In the first column, the tax is levied on fuel producers and the tax revenues are rebated by their governments to the populations of those fuel-producing countries. That brings a huge 4.5 percent windfall gain to the oil-exporting countries, from a system that taxes the rest of the world heavily. This solution seems unlikely unless there is a sudden revival in the waning power of the Organization of Petroleum Exporting Countries (OPEC), discussed in Chapter 13.

Alternatively, suppose that the tax is collected on fuel consumption by governments where the fuel is consumed. While that might seem a greater hardship on fuel consumers than the production tax, it is not. On the contrary, if the tax is global and uniform, the share of it that is paid by fuel consumers (as opposed to producers) is the same whether the tax falls directly on consumers or directly on producers. Regardless of who directly pays the tax, the slopes of demand and supply curves will dictate how the tax burden is split between consumers and producers. Actually, having the tax collected in the consuming countries is a boon to them inasmuch as the revenue is collected and domestically rebated by their own governments, as in the middle column of estimates in Figure 12.5. In this case, the industrial countries suffer much less than with the production tax (Japan actually gains on the deal), and the oil-exporting countries take a beating from the loss of world demand.

Finally, if the tax on either fuel production or fuel consumption is distributed around the world so that everybody gets the same tax-revenue rebate per person, the welfare effects would be distributed according to the right column in Figure 12.5. Poor countries, represented by the "rest of the world" category, would receive a net gain because their tax receipts exceed the cost of fuel scarcity. To the extent that the global policy intends to equalize incomes around the world, this approach would have appeal. The larger point, though, is that the differences in how the tax revenues are distributed have such huge welfare consequences that any world negotiations over the carbon tax would surely be acrimonious.

Actual world negotiations over global warming have indeed been difficult and unproductive so far. Industrial countries committed in Rio de Janeiro in 1992 to keep their CO_2 emissions at 1990 levels, but they have not done so. For instance, U.S. emissions will be over 10 percent larger in 2000 than they were in 1990.

A new agreement was reached in Kyoto in late 1997. Industrial nations, which account for about three-fifths of global greenhouse-gas emissions, agreed to cut their emissions of greenhouse gases to 6 to 8 percent below their 1990 levels by the years 2008–2012 and then to continue reductions. Developing countries refused to make any commitments, however. They argued that they are not the major source of current emissions, and that they should not slow their economic growth.

The Kyoto agreement includes some trading among countries of credits for emission reductions. This approach is conceptually very attractive—creating a market for the right to emit—and it could be the basis for expanding the agreement in the future. It encourages emission reductions where they can be achieved at lowest cost, so it enhances economic efficiency. (A carbon tax would do this as well, by encouraging reductions to avoid paying the tax.) In addition, the initial allocations of rights could be used to induce developing countries to become part of an expanded agreement in the future, by giving them more than their current share of global emissions.

However, the Kyoto agreement itself is not likely to meet its objectives. Because there are no commitments by developing countries, the U.S. Congress is unlikely to enact legislation to implement it. Indeed, the United States has long taxed fuel much less than other industrial countries, and any efforts to raise fuel prices or limit fuel use would be very difficult politically. The United States accounts for about one-fifth of global greenhouse-gas emissions. Without U.S. participation, the agreement cannot accomplish much. We remain well short of a global approach to global warming.

Summary

International trade is not inherently anti-environment, and the best solution to environmental problems is seldom one that involves trade policy. The rules of the WTO are generally consistent with this application of the specificity rule. They permit countries to impose environmental standards on domestic production activities and on domestic consumption activities (including environment-based product standards). The WTO also offers the possibility of an environmental exception to its free-trade thrust. But the WTO has usually ruled against a single country that attempts to use trade policy to punish what the country views as environmentally damaging production activities in other countries. The WTO seems to view trade limits that are part of multilateral environmental agreements more favorably.

Because environmental problems like pollution involve an externality, government policies are usually needed to get markets to be efficient. In fact, if a country's government fails to implement a policy to limit pollution, free trade may make a country worse off, and the country may end up exporting the wrong products.

Transborder pollution is an example of an international externality, in which production (or consumption) activities in one country impose external costs on other countries. As with all external costs, the best solution is one that addresses the pollution directly, by imposing a tax on the pollution, or by establishing property rights (to water or whatever is being polluted, or as limited rights to pollute). However, it is often challenging for the government of the country hurt by the pollution to gain the cooperation of the government of the country doing the pollution. For instance, little progress has been made in reducing environmental problems along the Mexico–U.S. border, even though a side agreement to NAFTA established a commission and a bank for this purpose.

In some cases the environmental problem is global: Global production or consumption is imposing a worldwide external cost. The best approach to a global environmental problem is a global cooperative agreement, but achieving this is usually difficult. Often, there are differences of opinion about the size of the external costs or the appropriate policies to adopt. Countries that suffer little or no harm have little incentive to cooperate and impose costs on themselves. More generally, countries have an incentive to free-ride on the efforts of others. Often an agreement has no real enforcement mechanism. Trade sanctions provide a possible threat against countries that do not abide by an agreement, but, as we saw in Chapter 11, sanctions often do not work.

The chapter concluded with four examples of global environmental problems. Two have been addressed by successful global agreements. An agreement on using trade limits and trade bans to prevent the extinction of species has been fairly effective. But the ultimate solution may well involve creating economic incentives for "sustainable use" (the propagation and management of the previously endangered species), as the discussion of elephants and ivory suggested. The global agreement on CFCs has also been effective and should reverse the ozone damage over time. Success here seems to be based on clear scientific evidence, the rather small number of CFC producers, the availability of substitutes at reasonable cost, and the fact that the major producing countries were also those likely to suffer the most damage.

Two problems have not been addressed successfully. Because no one owns the oceans and their resources, overfishing has led to declines in fish stocks. The large number of fishing firms and their political activity to resist limits have prevented effective global agreements. Global warming as a result of the atmospheric buildup of CO_2 and other greenhouse gases is the most daunting global environmental problem. Science does not provide clear guidance on the magnitude of the problem and its likely effects on different countries. All countries contribute to global emissions of greenhouse gases. Most developing countries prefer to pursue growth and rising incomes and are not willing to constrain their development by taking actions to reduce their emissions. The true commitment of industrialized countries, especially the United States, is also questionable.

Suggested Reading

Esty (1994), Uimonen and Whalley (1997), and Anderson and Blackhurst (1992) provide excellent surveys of trade and environment issues, and Esty includes discussion of the major legal cases. The chapters by Bhagwati and Srinivasan and by Levinson in Bhagwati and Hudec (1996), as well as Subramanian (1992), focus on specific issues.

For a series of appraisals of global environmental problems, see World Resources Institute, *World Resources 1992/93* and later years. A similar global tour, with more emphasis on economic solutions, is the World Bank's *World Development Report 1992.*

Numerous works provide individual case studies. On CFCs, see the chapter by Enders and Porges in Anderson and Blackhurst. On NAFTA and the environment, see Hufbauer and Schott (1993) and U.S. Office of Technology Assessment, *US–Mexico Trade: Pulling Together or Pulling Apart?* (1992). On dolphins and tuna, see Boreman (1992). On elephants and ivory, see Bonner (1993). On greenhouse gases, see Anderson and Blackhurst, as well as Cline (1992), the special symposium in the Fall 1993 issue of *The Journal of Economic Perspectives,* and a host of studies cited there.

Questions and Problems

✦ 1. Does a rise in national income per capita tend to worsen or improve air pollution, water pollution, and sanitation? Explain.

2. "One of the benefits of free trade is that it corrects the distortion caused by pollution." Do you agree or disagree? Why?

✦ 3. Which of the following probably violate the rules of the WTO?

   a. A country's government places a tax on domestic production to reduce pollution caused by this production.

   b. A country's government restricts imports of goods produced using production methods that would violate the importing country's environmental protection laws.

   c. A country's government places a tax on domestic consumption of goods (both imported and domestically produced) to reduce pollution caused by this consumption.

   d. A country's government restricts imports of a good, to reduce pollution caused by consumption of this good.

4. Mining of metallic ores often causes harm to the environment in the area around the mines. Some countries impose strict policies to limit the environmental damage caused by this mining, but others do not. The mining companies in the strict countries complain that this is unfair, and ask for limits on imports of ores and

metals from the lax countries. As a government official interested in advancing the national interest in a strict country, how would you evaluate the request of your mining companies?

✦ 5. Oil spills from ocean-going tankers are rare but bring huge damages to coastlines when they occur within 200 miles of shore. Unfortunately, most tanker spills do occur on or near coasts. Rank the following alternatives according to how efficient they are in responding to the threat of oil spills. Explain your ranking.

   a. Each nation with an endangered coastline should impose a tax on all imported oil, a tax that raises enough revenue to compensate for any oil spill damages.

   b. Each coastal nation should impose a tax on all domestically purchased oil, a tax that raises enough revenue to compensate for any oil spill damages.

   c. Oil-carrying companies should be legally liable for all damages, in the courts of the countries whose national waters are polluted by the spills.

   d. Each coastal nation should intercept all oil tankers in national waters and charge them a fee that will cover the estimated costs of future oil spills.

   e. We might as well save ourselves the expense of trying to prevent spills. They are just accidents beyond the control of the shipping companies; they are part of the cost of having coasts.

6. Consider the example of domestic pollution shown in Figure 12.3. Suppose that the marginal social side cost of the pollution is $0.05 per ream produced (instead of $0.30).

   a. With this different MSSC, does free trade make the country better off or worse off?

   b. To gain the most from trade, should the country export or import paper? How much?

✦ 7. Which of the following would do most to cut the global buildup of carbon dioxide over the next 20 years?

   a. Eliminating all subsidies to energy use in Eastern Europe and in other developing countries.

   b. Restoring the original tropical rain forest.

   c. Restoring the original temperate-zone rain forest.

   d. A tax of $448 per ton of emitted carbon, as described in this chapter.

   e. A trend toward rising fuel scarcity, caused by exhausting the world's reserves of fossil fuels.

8. Assume that the production of cement also produces a substantial amount of air pollution and that a technology is available that can lower the pollution but with somewhat higher production costs for the cement. Because of the availability of raw materials in Lindertania, it produces large amounts of cement, and its exports supply most demand in Pugelovia. But the air pollution from Lindertania's production blows into Pugelovia, causing a noticeable deterioration in Pugelovia's air quality. Although Lindertania suffers some harm itself from this air pollution, it does not now have any policy to reduce the pollution. The Pugelovian government wants to address this air pollution problem.

   a. If the two countries' governments cooperate, what is the best solution to address the problem? Explain.

   b. If Pugelovia must come up with a solution on its own, what should the Pugelovian government do? Explain.

✦ 9. Use your no. 2 pencil to write down your views on this trade-and-environment debate:

   According to the Rainforest Action Network (RAN), a rain forest wood called *jelutong* is being logged at a dangerous rate in Indonesia. The reason is that pencil makers recently shifted about 15 percent of their production from the more expensive cedar wood to jelutong, saving $1 on every dozen pencils. The Incense Cedar Institute, which represents three major companies growing cedar in the United States, echoes the concerns of RAN about the threat to tropical rain forests. Speaking for the pencil makers, executives of Dixon Ticonderoga explain that the jelutong wood in Indonesia is not gathered from rain forests, but is planted and harvested on plantations.

What should be done about the use of jelutong wood in making pencils? Should the government of Indonesia block the export of jelutong wood? Should the government of the United States tax or prohibit jelutong imports? Defend your view. If you feel you need more information than is given here, what extra information would be decisive?

10. Why did the Montreal Protocol succeed in limiting global emissions of chlorofluoro-carbons (CFCs), whereas the world has been unable to limit the emission of CO_2? What differences between the two cases explain the difference in outcome?

CHAPTER 13

Trade Policies for Developing and Transition Countries

Much of the world's attention focuses on the high-income economies—the United States, Japan, and the industrialized countries of Western Europe. The attention is not surprising, given that these areas produce 70 percent of world output and an even greater share of the supply of media services. Yet, over five-sixths of the world's population lives in countries that are considered developing countries. One surprise is how widely the fortunes of these developing countries vary. Some have succeeded in developing, and have experienced high growth rates. Others have experienced serious economic declines.

Figure 13.1 summarizes the best available measures of growth rates in real gross domestic product (GDP) per person for broad regions and for selected individual countries. The first point shown by Figure 13.1 is that the "developing countries" have not been catching up to the high-income ("developed") countries.[1] On the contrary, their average product per person has grown more slowly than it has in the developed economies.

The most striking pattern shown in Figure 13.1, however, is the wide disparity in growth rates among the "developing" countries. Some are achieving supergrowth, while some have suffered declining income levels during the past decade or more. Incomes have tended to grow fastest in East Asia. The "Four Tigers"

---

[1]Following the global convention, we use the term *developing countries* as a synonym for what the World Bank also calls *low- and middle-income countries*. In 1997, that meant every place with a per capita national income at or below the general standard set by Chile, the Czech Republic, and Malaysia.

The choice of terms to describe countries with low income levels has changed constantly over the past century. The general pattern of evolution has been toward increasingly optimistic, or even euphemistic, terminology in official international discourse. At midcentury commentators could still speak of rich and poor countries. Soon, however, neither the high-income nor the low-income countries would abide such a stark contrast. From the mid-1950s to the mid-1960s, it was generally acceptable to speak of *underdeveloped countries* or *less developed countries (LDCs)*. With time, however, even terms like these were viewed as condescending.

(South Korea, Taiwan, Singapore, and Hong Kong) have grown so quickly over the past two decades that they have joined the league of high-income countries. Several other countries in East Asia also achieved high growth rates, including Thailand, Indonesia, and China. At the rate achieved in 1990–1997, China's per capita income will double in about 6½ years. The Asian crisis beginning in 1997 has set many of these countries back, but for most the downturns during this crisis have not erased the growth gains of the previous years.

However, in over 40 percent of the "developing" countries for which we have data, income per person in fact declined between 1990 and 1997. Most of these were countries in Africa and countries in Central and Eastern Europe and Central Asia that are making a transition from central planning to a market-based economy. The gaps in growth rates are much wider among developing countries than among high-income countries.

Why are the fortunes of developing countries so different, with some joining the high-income club while others stay poor? Do differences in their trade policies play a role? Are there lessons about trade policy to be learned by studying what the supergrowing *newly industrializing countries (NICs)* did that countries with stagnating or declining incomes did not? And what role do trade policies play in a successful transition from central planning to a market economy? This chapter reveals some clear answers and some still-unresolved questions about the trade-policy options for developing and transition countries.

Which Trade Policy for Developing Countries?

What should the government of, say, Ghana do about imports and exports if it is determined to reverse the economic stagnation that has held down the living standards of its people? To supplement the greater task of reforming its whole economy, Ghana has these basic trade-policy choices:

1. A free-trade policy that accepts and exploits the country's comparative advantages. For Ghana, this means continuing to export cocoa, coffee, and other primary products without taxing either exports or imports very much.

From the 1960s through the 1980s, another attractive alternative presented itself. The *Third World* was a handy and relatively judgment-free way to contrast the low- and middle-income countries of the non-communist world with the high-income market economies (First World) and the communist bloc (Second World). But in 1989–1991 the Second World vanished with the breakup of the communist bloc and the Soviet Union. Without a Second World, what does *Third World* mean? These formerly communist countries became the *transition economies,* and they are now part of the set of developing countries.

Diplomatic practice has retreated to the relatively benign term *developing country.* Few are bothered by two curious implications of this term: (1) that the high-income "developed" countries are no longer developing and (2) that countries whose incomes are dropping are "developing" if and only if their incomes are already low. Another name for developing and transition countries is *emerging economies,* used especially for their emerging financial markets.

	Annual Growth Rate in Per Capita GDP, 1990–1997	Per Capita GDP, 1997 (at International Dollar Prices)
FIGURE 13.1 *Growth Rates, 1990–1997, and Levels of Income per Capita, 1997*	*Region or Nation*		
27 High-Income Countries	**1.4%**	**$22,770**
Singapore (fastest growing)	6.6	29,000
United States	1.5	28,740
Hong Kong	3.4	24,540
Japan	1.1	23,400
Canada	0.9	21,860
United Kingdom	1.6	20,520
Australia	2.5	20,170
United Arab Emirates (worst decline)	−1.5	16,470*
South Korea	6.2	13,500
106 Low- and Middle-Income Countries	**1.2**	**3,230**
21 Latin American and Caribbean	1.6	6,660
25 European and Central Asian	−5.5	4,390
10 Middle Eastern and North African	0.1	4,580
10 East Asian and Pacific Rim	8.6	3,560
5 South Asian	3.8	1,580
35 Sub-Saharan African	−0.6	1,470
Selected Low- and Middle-Income Countries		
Chile (richest of these 106 countries)	5.6	12,080
Argentina	3.2	9,950
Mexico	0.0	8,120
South Africa	−0.2	7,490
Hungary	−0.1	7,000
Thailand	6.3	6,590
Poland	3.7	6,380
Brazil	1.7	6,240
Namibia	1.5	5,440
Russia	−8.9	4,190
Philippines	1.0	3,670
China (fastest growing)	10.8	3,570
Indonesia	5.8	3,450
Ukraine	−13.2	2,170
Georgia (worst decline)	−26.1	1,980
Ghana	1.6	1,790
India	4.1	1,650
Pakistan	1.5	1,590
Bangladesh	2.9	1,050
Nigeria	−0.2	880
Sierra Leone (poorest of these 106 countries)	−5.8	510

Note: Measures of gross domestic product per capita adjusted for purchasing power parity (at international dollar prices) are better than the often-cited estimates of average dollar incomes based on exchange-rate conversions. The purchasing power parity estimates reflect the ability to buy a broad range of goods and services at the prices prevailing in each country, whereas using exchange rates to convert other-currency values into U.S. dollars misleads by reflecting only the international prices of goods that are heavily traded between countries. As a rule, comparisons based on exchange-rate conversions overstate the relative poverty of low-income countries by failing to reflect the cheapness of their nontraded services. For more on purchasing power parity, see Chapter 18.

*Value for 1995; 1997 value not available.

Source: World Bank, *World Development Report, 1998/99* (1998, Tables 1, 3, and 11).

2. A policy that taxes its traditional exports to raise funds for the development of other sectors of the economy. The country could tax such exports either unilaterally or as part of an international cartel of countries exporting the same products. For Ghana, this means taxing exports of cocoa and coffee.

3. A policy that taxes and restricts imports to protect and subsidize new industries serving the domestic market. For Ghana, this might mean forcing Ghanaians to buy more expensive domestic steel, televisions, and airline services.

4. A policy to favor new export lines, particularly in manufactured goods. Any government subsidies to new export sectors could come from taxing other foreign trade or from taxes not related to trade. Ghana might subsidize exporters of clothing or electrical machinery, for example.

A developing country today does indeed face this choice alone, for the most part, without much international help. In the 1960s and 1970s, there was a movement to raise the incomes of developing countries by negotiating a global agreement establishing a New International Economic Order (NIEO). This movement urged three main global policy actions: (1) global agreements to raise the prices of primary products exported by developing nations; (2) global cooperation to stabilize those same prices; and (3) opening industrial-country markets for manufactures exported by the developing countries. The institutional base was UNCTAD, the United Nations Conference on Trade and Development, set up in 1964 and still operating from headquarters in Geneva. The NIEO movement represented an intermediate phase in the retreat from global assistance over the second half of the 20th century. The generous foreign aid of the 1950s was declining, and NIEO was conceived as a way to give aid to developing countries through generous prices in world markets. In the altered climate of the 1980s and 1990s, the NIEO idea yielded to the conviction that individual countries had to set their own policies unilaterally, with no global help other than negotiated trade liberalizations like NAFTA or the Uruguay Round.

In choosing a trade policy, should a developing country just follow the trade-policy guidelines laid out in Chapters 7 through 10? Or are developing countries so different that they need a separate trade policy analysis? The basic answer is that the trade policy conclusions of Chapters 7 through 10 do apply to all countries, whether "developed" or "developing." The pros and cons of restricting or subsidizing trade are the same, and the specificity rule still compels us to consider alternatives to trade policy when trade is not the source of the development problem. All that is different in this chapter is the degree of emphasis put on certain points.

Developing countries are different in that they face certain challenges that are less formidable, though still present, in a developed economy. These challenges fall into three categories:

1. *Factor endowments are different in developing countries.* They have less nonhuman capital and fewer human skills per person in the labor force. Some of them also control most of the world's oil reserves, and others have the right conditions for growing tropical crops.

2. *Capital markets work less efficiently in developing countries.* A defining characteristic of a lower-income country is that there are more barriers to the lending of money to the most productive uses. As a result, good projects must overcome a higher cost of capital (interest rate) than the rate at which capital is available to less promising sectors. One underlying reason is that property rights are less clearly defined, holding back the willingness to invest in new assets.

3. Similarly, *labor markets work less efficiently in developing countries.* The wage gaps between expanding and declining sectors are greater than in higher-income countries. The wider wage gaps are an indirect clue that some labor is being kept from moving to its most productive use.

These differences imply some special tasks for the government of a developing country. There is a case for considering which sectors to protect or subsidize or give cheap loans to, if the government cannot quickly eliminate the barriers to efficient capital and labor markets. The government must also decide whether it is realistic to try to change the nation's comparative advantage, so that its exports increasingly use its growing endowments of human skills or physical capital.

We explore the alternatives to free trade for a developing country, starting with (1) the popular idea of shutting out imports to nurture new industries producing for domestic markets. After that, we turn to (2) some special considerations about the export market for primary products, and then look at (3) the alternative strategy of developing exports of manufactures.

Import-Substituting Industrialization (ISI)

It is natural to think that industrialization is the surer way to overall economic improvements. After all, most high-income countries have industrialized. To develop, officials from many countries have argued, they must cut their reliance on exporting primary products and must adopt government policies allowing industry to grow at the expense of the agricultural and mining sectors. Can this emphasis on industrialization be justified? If so, should it be carried out by restricting imports of manufactures?

The Great Depression caused many countries to turn toward import-substituting industrialization (ISI). Across the 1930s world price ratios turned severely against most primary-product–exporting countries. Although this decline in the terms of trade did not prove that primary exporters were suffering more than industrial countries, it was common to suspect that this was so. Several primary-product–exporting countries, among them Brazil and Australia, launched industrialization at the expense of industrial imports in the 1930s.

The ISI strategy gained additional prestige among newly independent nations in the 1950s and 1960s. This approach soon prevailed in most developing countries whose barriers against manufactured imports came to match those of the most protectionist prewar industrializers. Though many countries have switched toward more pro-trade and export-oriented policies since the mid-1960s, ISI remains an important policy for developing countries.

ISI at Its Best

To see the state of knowledge about the merits and drawbacks of ISI, let us begin by noting the four main arguments in its favor. If ISI could be fine-tuned to make the most of these arguments, it would be a fine policy indeed.

1. The *infant industry argument* from Chapter 9 returns, with its legitimate emphasis on large economic and social side benefits from industrialization. These side benefits were reviewed in Chapter 9: gains in technological knowledge and worker skills transcending the individual firm, new attitudes more conducive to growth and national pride. As we saw in Chapter 9, the economist can imagine other tools more suitable to each of these tasks than import barriers. But in an imperfect world these better options may not be at hand, and protection for an infant modern-manufacturing sector could bring gains.

2. The *developing government argument* from Chapter 9 lends further support to ISI. Suppose that the only way that a government can raise revenues for any kind of economic development is to tax imports and exports. Such taxation could bring great gains to a nation whose government cannot mobilize resources for health, education, and so on without taxing trade. ISI would be a by-product of such taxation of foreign trade.

3. For a large country, or a large organization of countries, replacing imports can bring better *terms-of-trade effects* than expansion of export industries. Here we return to a theme sounded first in the discussion of "immiserizing growth" in Chapter 5 and again during Chapter 7's discussion of the nationally optimal tariff.

The country's own actions could affect the prices of its exports and imports on world markets. Expanding exports might lead to some decline in export prices, as illustrated with the extreme case of export growth that is absolutely immiserizing.[2] By contrast, replacing imports with domestic production will, if it has any effect at all on the price of the continuing imports, tend to lower these prices (excluding the tariff or other import charge) and offer the nation a better bargain. If you can affect the prices at which you trade, wouldn't it be better to expand your supply of import-competing industries, forcing foreigners to sell you the remaining imports at a lower price?

This terms-of-trade argument works best for large developing countries such as Brazil. It is for these that the chances of affecting the terms of trade are the greatest. Large countries also face greater danger of importing-country protectionist backlash when pushing new export lines. And large countries can manufacture in plants large enough to take advantage of economies of scale, even without exporting. Alternatively, the terms-of-trade argument can support the idea of forming an international export cartel, to which we turn later in this chapter.

4. Replacing imports of manufactures is a way of using *cheap and convenient market information*. A developing country may lack the expertise to judge just which of the thousands of heterogeneous industrial goods it could best mar-

---

[2]One variant on the "immiserizing growth" theme is the fear that successful development of new export lines can be sabotaged by protectionist backlash in the main importing countries, as has happened to some Asian manufactures in the markets of North America and Europe.

ket abroad. But government officials (and private industrialists) have an easy way to find which modern manufactures would sell in their own markets. They need only look at the import figures. Here is a handy menu of goods with proven markets. If the problems of cost and product quality can be conquered by new domestic producers, there is a clear basis for a protected industry (though protection still brings the costs described in Chapter 9).

Experience with ISI

History and recent economic studies offer four kinds of evidence on the merits of ISI. Casual historical evidence suggests a slightly charitable view, while three kinds of detailed tests support a negative verdict.

In support of ISI, it can be said that today's leading industrial countries protected their industry against import competition earlier, when their growth was first accelerating. The United States, for example, practiced ISI from the Civil War until the end of World War II, when most American firms no longer needed protection against imports. Japan, in the 1950s, launched its drive for leadership in steel, automobiles, and electronics with heavy government protection against imports. When these industries were able to compete securely in export markets, Japan removed its redundant protection against imports into Japan.

Such a casual reading of history is at least correct in its premise: The industrialized countries did at times give import protection to industries that became their export strengths. But as we saw in Chapter 10, it is wrong to infer that most cases of industrial protection nurtured sectors that responded with strong productivity gains. On the contrary, even Japan, like the United States and most other industrialized countries, gave its strongest protection to sectors whose decline was long-lasting. In all likelihood, ISI in the earlier history of these countries probably slowed down their economic growth. Most of the infant industries, in other words, never grew up or were already aging badly.

In contrast to the weaknesses of the evidence for ISI, the evidence against it takes three forms that in combination add up to a strong case. The first kind of test casting serious doubt on the merits of ISI is the estimation of its static welfare costs, using the methods introduced in Chapter 7. A series of detailed country studies quantified the welfare effects of a host of developing-country trade barriers in the 1960s and early 1970s, many of which were designed to promote industrialization. The barriers imposed significant costs on Argentina, Chile, Colombia, Egypt, Ghana, India, Israel, Mexico, Pakistan, the Philippines, South Korea, Taiwan, and Turkey. Only in Malaysia did the import barriers bring a slight gain, here because of a favorable terms-of-trade effect.[3]

By themselves, these standard calculations of welfare costs of trade barriers are vulnerable to the charge of assuming, not proving, that ISI is bad. Such calculations assume that all the relevant effects are captured by measures of consumer and producer surplus, without allowing protection any chance to lower cost curves as it is imagined to do in the infant industry case. It would be fair to demand firmer proof.

---

[3]See Bela Balassa (1971), Jagdish Bhagwati and Anne Krueger (1973–1976), and A. Choksi et al. (1991).

FIGURE 13.2

Trade-Policy Orientation and Average Annual Growth in Real GDP per Capita for 41 Developing Countries, 1963–1992

Trade-Policy Orientation	1963–1973	1973–1985	1980–1992
Strongly outward	6.9%	5.9%	6.4%
Moderately outward	4.9	1.6	2.3
Moderately inward	4.0	1.7	–0.2
Strongly inward	1.6	–0.1	–0.4

Note: Outward means that the government had low trade barriers and some export subsidies. *Inward* means reliance on trade barriers. The three strongly outward economies in all periods were Hong Kong, South Korea, and Singapore. In 1963–1973 the 16 strongly inward (antitrade) regimes in the sample were Argentina, Bangladesh, Burundi, Chile, Dominican Republic, Ethiopia, Ghana, India, Pakistan, Peru, Sri Lanka, Sudan, Tanzania, Turkey, Uruguay, and Zambia. For 1973–1985 and 1980–1992 the 14 strongly inward countries were the previous 16 plus Bolivia, Madagascar, and Nigeria, but minus Chile, Pakistan, Sri Lanka, Turkey, and Uruguay.

Source: World Bank, *World Development Reports* for 1987 and 1994.

A second kind of test looks at what happens when a country changes its trade-policy orientation. Here there were two dramatic early cases. Until the late 1950s, Taiwan used ISI but then switched to a policy that encouraged exports, and it subsequently achieved growth rates of about 10 percent per year. South Korea used ISI until policy refoms in the early 1960s increased its incentives for exports and lowered its import barriers. Its growth rate increased to about 10 percent per year. Hong Kong and Singapore also used policies that encouraged exports and achieved high growth rates. Other countries have achieved substantial effects. In the case of Ghana, the ISI strategy was part of a larger heavy hand of government that turned early growth into a 42 percent decline of Ghana's living standards over the decade 1974–1984. The country was saddled with costly industrial white elephants that never became efficient. Only thereafter, after partial reforms that included a partial liberalization of trade policy, did Ghana regain positive economic growth.

A third kind of test compares growth rates of countries practicing ISI with growth rates of countries using policies that emphasize exporting. Figure 13.2 makes such comparisons for 41 countries grouped according to the orientation of their trade policies, first during the faster worldwide growth of 1963–1973, then during the oil and debt crises of 1973–1985, and finally in 1980–1992. In all periods, the three countries with strongly outward-oriented trade policies (Hong Kong, South Korea, and Singapore) grew fastest, and the many countries with strongly inward orientation grew slowest.[4]

Such direct comparisons of freer-trade regimes with regimes that practiced a variant on ISI have the virtue of simplicity: They look directly at the two variables of interest (trade policies and economic growth). Yet here, as always, correlation cannot prove causation. By itself, this kind of evidence against ISI is subject to the suspicion that maybe some other force caused economic growth to be correlated

---

[4]In practice, the two kinds of policy were applied in very different dosages. What the World Bank calls *strongly outward* orientation should be thought of not as policies of aggressive subsidies to trade but as policies closer to free trade than the opposite *strongly inward* policies. For example, the government of outward-oriented South Korea paid less in export subsidies than it collected in import tariffs from 1965 on, and removed most of both the subsidies and the tariffs by the mid-1980s. The text can thus talk of the outward-oriented policies as something closer to free trade and laissez-faire.

with freer trade policies. Or perhaps the causation ran the opposite way—perhaps successful growth itself brings freer trade policies, even though policies departing from free trade helped promote growth. While it is not possible to answer these concerns fully, economists have conducted more complicated tests of the statistical significance of trade policy. After allowing for the effects of other variables such as investment, initial income, and education, this research tends to confirm that ISI-type trade barriers are a negative influence on economic growth.

If theory suggests that ISI can work well, why does experience make it look like a bad idea? There is no direct contradiction because theory only asserted that ISI *can* be better than free trade under certain conditions. It just so happens that those conditions did not hold as far as we can read in the record book since the early 1960s. The theory failed, above all, in the assumption that an informed government tried to maximize national income. Real-world governments are ill-informed, and they lack the power to stop protecting industries that turn out to be inefficient. Worse, many governments have their own self-interest, which conflicts with the goal of maximizing national well-being. Embarking on a policy of ISI has so far not turned any economy into a supergrower like South Korea. South Korea itself has followed a relatively free-trade economy (aside from heavy protection for its farmers). More often, the ISI route is the road that turns a South Korea into a North Korea. ISI often results in industries in which domestic firms have high costs and domestic monopoly power, and produce products of low quality.

Outward-oriented policies encourage domestic firms to make use of the country's abundant resources, and the firms can use sales into international markets to achieve scale economies. The efforts to succeed in foreign markets also mean that domestic firms face international competitive pressure, so that they are driven to raise product quality and resource productivity. The country can use its rising exports to pay for its rising imports. At the same time, an outward-oriented policy is not enough by itself to produce high growth rates. It must be part of a set of policies that minimize distortions in the economy, that nurture high rates of investment, and that provide such infrastructure as ports, airports, electricity, and communications.

Still, doubts persist. Can exports really help developing countries succeed? We turn now to two areas of concern. One is pessimism about the prices of primary products that developing countries export. The second is pessimism about exports of manufactured products.

Are the Long-Run Price Trends Against Primary Producers?

A recurring idea is that developing countries' growth is held back by relying on exports of primary products (agriculture, forestry, and minerals). Here we explore first whether primary-product exports have a bleak future. Then we examine the prospects for taxing these exports as part of an international cartel among exporting countries.

In the 1950s, Raul Prebisch and others argued that developing countries are hurt by a downward trend (and also an instability) in primary-product prices.

International markets, ran the argument, distributed income unfairly, trapping the exporters of primary products into worsening trends in their terms of trade (the price of their exports divided by the price of their imports, or P_x/P_m). And since the developing countries were net exporters of primary products, the alleged downward trend in their earning power was seen as a force widening the income gap between the world's rich and the world's poor.[5]

Does the fear of falling prices sound reasonable? Should the government of a developing country discourage farming, forestry, and mining, and give people an incentive to move to industry and the service sector? Economists have studied the issue for over a century. It is clear that there are at least two major forces depressing, and at least two forces raising, the trend in the prices of primaries relative to manufactures.

The relative price of primary products is depressed by Engel's law and synthetic substitutes.

1. *Engel's law.* In the long run, per capita incomes rise. As they rise, demand shifts toward luxuries—goods for which the income elasticity of demand (percent rise in quantity demanded/percent rise in income causing the change in demand) is greater than 1. At the same time, the world's demand shifts away from staples—goods for which the income elasticity of demand is less than 1. The 19th-century German economist Ernst Engel (not Friedrich Engels) discovered what has become known as Engel's law: The income elasticity of demand for food is less than 1 (i.e., food is a staple). Engel's law is the most durable law in economics that does not follow from definitions or axioms. It means trouble for food producers in a prospering world. If the world's supply expanded at the exact same rate for all products, the relative price of foods would go on dropping because Engel's law says that demand would keep shifting (relatively) away from food toward luxuries.

2. *Synthetic substitutes.* Another force depressing the relative prices of primary products is the development of new human-made substitutes for these natural materials. The more technology advances, the more we are likely to discover ways to replace crops, minerals, and other raw materials that were needed in centuries past. The most dramatic case is the development of synthetic rubber around the time of World War I, which ruined the incomes of rubber producers in Brazil, Malaysia, and other countries. Another case is the development of synthetic fibers, which have lowered demand for cotton and wool.

On the other hand, two other basic forces tend to raise the relative prices of primary products:

---

[5]Be careful not to assume, as many discussions imply, that there is a tight link between being a developing country and being an exporter of primary products. On average, the developing countries are only slight net exporters of primary products, and import significant amounts of them from North America, Australia, and New Zealand. And their comparative advantage in primary products varies greatly. Some developing countries export only primary products (e.g., Saudi Arabia), while others export almost no primary products and are heavily dependent on importing them (e.g., South Korea).

1. *Nature's limits.* Primary products use land, water, mineral deposits, and other nonrenewable resources. As population and incomes expand, the natural inputs become increasingly scarce, other things being equal. Nature's scarcity eventually raises the relative price of primary products, which use natural resources more intensively than do manufactures.

2. *Relatively slow productivity growth in the primary sector.* Over most historical experience, productivity has advanced more slowly in agriculture, mining, and other primary sectors than in manufacturing. This lack of speed translates into a slower relative advance of supply curves in primary-product markets than in manufacturing markets, and therefore a rising relative price of primaries (or a falling relative price of manufactures), other things being equal. One reason for this tendency is, again, the greater relevance of nature's limits in primary production. Another reason is the tendency for cost-cutting breakthroughs in knowledge to be more important in manufacturing than in primaries (though exceptions to this rule are increasingly frequent in the age of biotechnology).

So, we have two tendencies that depress the terms of trade for primary producers, and we have two that raise them. How does the tug-of-war work out in the long run? Figure 13.3 summarizes 20th-century experience.

It depends on when you look at the data and how far back into history you look. Studying Figure 13.3, we can understand why the fear of falling relative primary prices was greatest in the 1930s, the 1950s (when Prebisch's argument achieved popularity), and the 1980s. Those were periods of falling or depressed primary prices. On the other hand, little was written about falling primary prices just before World War I, the historical heyday of high prices for farm products and other raw materials. Nor was there much discussion of depressed prices during World War II, the Korean War of 1950–1953, or the OPEC-led speculative boom in primary-product prices around 1973–1974. During such times, many writers revived the old Malthusian arguments about the limits to planet Earth.

To stand back from the volatile swings in the terms of trade, let's look over as long a period as possible. For Figure 13.3, it is convenient to scan the period 1900–1986, though following some price series back to 1870 or forward to the 1990s would tell a similar story. The overall change is clear. By 1986, relative primary-product prices were about half of what they were in 1900. The trend has indeed been downward. Somehow, Engel's law and the technological biases toward replacing primary products have outrun nature's limits and the relative slowness of productivity growth in primary sectors. (Or, in shorthand, Prebisch outran Malthus.) Cutting the relative price in half over 87 years means a downward trend of 0.8 percent a year. Although that is not a rapid trend, it helps argue in favor of shifting resources into industry if we expect the same trend to continue.

Some commodities have declined in price more seriously than others. The price of rubber snapped downward between 1910 and 1920 and has never really bounced back since. Significant price declines have also been the rule for cocoa, sugar, copper, tin, wheat, and rice. Only wool and coffee showed significantly upward trends between 1900 and 1982, and the price of coffee weakened after 1982. Even fuels like oil and coal have lacked a net upward price trend over the

FIGURE 13.3

*The Terms of
Trade for
Primary
Products,
1900–1986*

$(P_x/P_m) = $ Dollar-price index for primary-product exports/Dollar-price index for exports of manufactures

A. Overall indexes

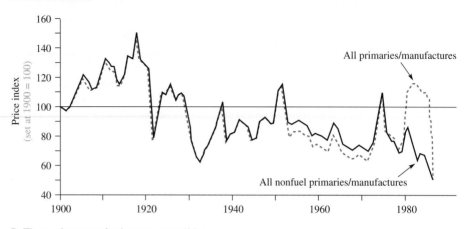

B. Three subgroups of primary commodities

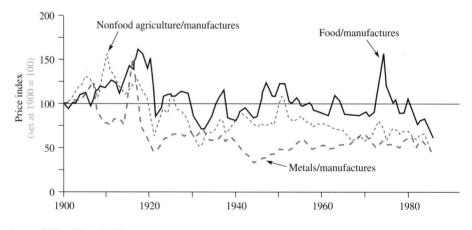

Source: Grilli and Yang (1988).

20th century to date, despite the resounding price flare-ups of 1973–1974 and 1979–1980.

While the net downward trend in primary prices stands as a tentative conclusion, there are three downward-trend biases in the available measures, measures like those presented in Figure 13.3.

1. *The fall in transport costs.* The available data tend to be gathered at markets in the industrial countries. Yet technological improvements in transportation have been great enough to reduce the share of transport costs in those final prices in London, New York, or Tokyo. That has left more and more of the final price

back in the hands of the primary-product exporters. Quantifying this known change would tilt the trend in the prices received by producers toward a flatter, less downward trend.

2. *Faster unmeasured quality change in manufactures.* Often, we have to deal with long runs of price data on products that have been getting better in unknown degree. Hidden quality improvements are thought to have been more impressive in manufactures (and services) than in primary products. So what might look like a rise in the relative price of manufactures might be just a rise in their relative quality, with no trend in the terms of trade for given quality. This data problem is potentially serious, given that many 20th-century data have, for example, followed the prices of machinery exports per ton of exports, as if a ton of today's computers were the same thing as a ton of old electric motors.

3. *Price cuts on new products are often unmeasured.* When a new product appears, its price typically drops rapidly before stabilizing. Officials gathering price data have a hard time incorporating the price data on the new products into their overall price indexes until the product has aged and its price has already dropped a great deal. Since new products are much more important in the manufacturing sector than in the primary sector, such measurement lags hide much of the relative drop in the prices of manufactures, overstating the relative fall of primary-product prices.

When all is said and done, the relative price of primary products may have declined as much as 0.8 percent a year since 1900 (as in Figure 13.3), or there could have been no trend. It is unlikely that the three measurement biases have been so strong that the true trend was upward (i.e., in favor of primaries). There is a weak case for worrying about being a producer of agricultural or extractive products on price-trend grounds.

International Cartels to Raise Primary-Product Prices

The OPEC Victories

History records many attempts at international cartels (international agreements to restrict selling competition). The greatest seizure of monopoly power in world history was the price-raising triumph of the Organization of Petroleum Exporting Countries (OPEC)[6] in 1973–1974 and again in 1979–1980.

A chain of events in late 1973 revolutionized the world oil economy. In a few months' time, the 13 members of OPEC effectively quadrupled the dollar price of crude oil, from $2.59 to $11.65 a barrel. Oil-exporting countries became rich almost overnight. The industrial oil-consuming countries sank into their deepest

---

[6]OPEC was created by a treaty among five countries—Iran, Iraq, Kuwait, Saudi Arabia, and Venezuela—in Baghdad in 1960. Since that time, the following countries joined: Qatar (1961), Indonesia and Libya (1962), United Arab Emirates (1967), Algeria (1969), Nigeria (1971), and Ecuador and Gabon (1973).

depression since the 1930s. The "real" price of oil (what the price of a barrel of oil could buy in terms of manufactured exports from industrial nations) tripled.

The sequel was a plateau of OPEC prosperity, a further jump, and finally growing signs of weakness. From 1974 to 1978, the real price of oil dipped by about a sixth, but stayed much higher than it had been at any time before 1973. Next came the second wave of OPEC price hikes, the second "oil shock," in 1979–1980. Led by the Iranian Revolution and growing panic among oil buyers, the oil price more than doubled. In the mid-1980s, however, OPEC weakened. The real price of oil dropped suddenly in 1985, from 4 to 5 times the old (pre-1973) real price in 1980–1984 to only 1.84 times the old price for 1985–1989. By 1998, the real price of oil in world markets had fallen to a level only a little above the real price back in 1972. Here, then, were two dramatic cartel victories and a subsequent retreat. The victories and the retreat both need explanation.

The oil shocks of 1973–1974 and 1979–1980 were not the result of a failure of supply or exhaustion of earth's available resources. The world's "proved reserves" of known and usable oil have grown even faster than world oil consumption. Nor were the costs of oil extraction rising much.

The 1973–1974 and 1979–1980 oil price jumps were human-made. The key was that world demand was growing far faster than *non-OPEC* supplies. Postwar oil discoveries have been very unevenly distributed among countries. The share of OPEC countries in world crude oil production rose to over 50 percent by 1972. Furthermore, OPEC's share of proved reserves—roughly, its share of future production—is over two-thirds. Ample oil reserves are still being discovered the world over, but they happen to be concentrated increasingly in the Middle East, forcing importing nations into greater dependence on OPEC nations.

And by the early 1970s, the United States was for the first time becoming vulnerable to pressure from oil-exporting countries. Largely immune to oil threats in earlier Middle East crises, the United States found itself importing a third of its oil consumption, part of it from Arab countries, by 1973. Today imports are an even higher share, about half, of U.S. oil consumption, and the United States consumes about a quarter of the world's oil. It is still true that the United States, with its huge economy and its cheap-oil policy, plays a leading role in determining the world price of oil.

With their growing importance in world production, and with growing U.S. reliance on oil imports, OPEC countries were able to create a scramble among buyers to pay higher prices for oil in 1973 and again in 1979.

Classic Monopoly as an Extreme Model for Cartels

How big could the cartel opportunity be? That is, if a group of nations or firms were to form a cartel, as OPEC did, what is the greatest amount of gain they could reap at the expense of their buyers and world efficiency? If all of the cartel members could agree on simply maximizing their collective gain, they would behave as though they were a perfectly unified profit-maximizing monopolist. They would find the price level that would maximize the gap between their total export sales revenues and their total costs of producing exports. When cutting

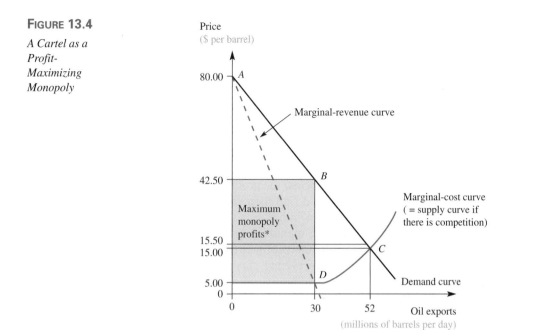

FIGURE 13.4

A Cartel as a Profit-Maximizing Monopoly

*Including some fixed costs.

If a cartel were so tightly disciplined as to be a pure monopoly, it would maximize profits according to the familiar monopoly model. It would not keep prices so low and output so high as to behave like a competitive industry, out at point C. Why not? Because the slightest price increase, starting at point C, would give them net gains. Instead the cartel would set price as high, with demand and output as low, as shown at point B. At this level of output (30 million barrels a day), profit is maximized because the marginal revenue gained from a bit more output raising and price cutting just balances the marginal cost of the extra output.

output back to the level of demand yielded by their optimal price, they would take care to shut down their most costly production units (e.g., oil wells) and keep in operation only those with the lowest operating costs.

Figure 13.4 portrays a monopoly or cartel that has managed to extract maximum profits from its buyers. To understand what price and output yield that highest level of profits, and what limits those profits, we must first understand that the optimal price lies above the price that perfect competition would yield, yet below the price that would discourage all sales. Let us analyze the cartel's self-interest in the same way we looked at the optimal import tariff in Chapter 7.

If perfect competition reigned in the world oil market, the marginal-cost curve in Figure 13.4 would also be the supply curve for oil exports. Competitive equilibrium would be at point C, where the marginal cost of raising oil exports has risen to meet $15, the amount that extra oil is worth to buyers (as shown by the demand curve). Point C is not the optimal point for the set of producers. If they were to agree to raise prices a tiny bit, say, to $15.50 a barrel, they would surely gain. The quantity would be cut only slightly, costing sellers little business. At the same time, they would get a 50-cent markup on all of the nearly 52 million barrels that they would continue to sell. The markup on the 52 million barrels would easily outweigh the profits lost on the small amount of lost sales, making a slight positive price increase and export reduction better than competitive pricing.

Yet, the negative slope of the demand curve for the cartel's product limits how high its members could push their common price. This point is clear enough if we just consider the extreme case of a prohibitive price markup. If the cartel were foolish enough to push the price to $80 a barrel in Figure 13.4, it would lose all of its export business, as shown at point A. The handsome markup to $80 would be worthless, since nobody would be paying it to the cartel. Thus, the cartel's best price must be well below the prohibitive price.

The cartel members could find their most profitable price through trial and error, trying out several prices in between the competitive and prohibitive limits to see what price seemed to maximize profits. The basic model of monopoly shows that the highest possible profits are those corresponding to the level of sales at which the marginal-revenue curve intersects the marginal-cost curve. These maximum profits would be reaped at point B in Figure 13.4, with a price set at $42.50 a barrel, yielding 30 million barrels of export sales a day and monopoly profits of ($42.50 − $5) × 30 million barrels = $1,125 million a day. If the cartel had not been formed, competition would have limited the profits of its members to the area below the $15 price line and above the marginal-cost curve (minus some fixed costs not shown in the diagram). Given the demand curve and the marginal-cost curve, the profits gained by pushing price and quantity to point B is the best the cartel can do.

The cartel price that is optimal for its members is not optimal for the world, of course. For the 30 million barrels per day, the extra cartel profits above the $15 price line are just a redistribution of income from buying countries to the cartel, with no net gain for the world. Furthermore, the cartel causes net world losses by curtailing oil exports that would be worth more to buyers around the world than those exports cost the cartel members themselves to produce. The world net loss from the cartel is represented in Figure 13.4 by the area BCD (which would equal a little over $412.5 million a day as drawn in Figure 13.4). This area shows that what the cartel is costing the world as a whole is the gap between what buyers would have willingly paid for the extra 22 million barrels a day, as shown by the height of the demand curve, and the height of the marginal-cost curve between 30 million barrels and 52 million barrels.

The Limits to Cartel Power

The theory of cartel policy can identify several constraints on cartel success in addition to the practical constraints posed by international politics. Let us look first at the limits to cartel market power in the extreme case in which the cartel members succeed in behaving just like the unified monopoly in Figure 13.4. We then note some theoretical reasons for expecting cartel success to fade away with time and compare these theoretical hunches with actual OPEC experience.

The Optimal Markup

The basic theory of monopoly stresses that the elasticity of demand limits the power of any monopoly. More specifically, the formula for the optimal monopoly markup is (as explained in Appendix D)

$$t^* = \frac{\text{optimal price} - \text{marginal cost}}{\text{price}} = \frac{1}{|d_c|}$$

where $|d_c|$ is the absolute value of the elasticity of demand for the cartel's sales (here, the elasticity of export demand if the cartel members do not charge the same high price within their own countries). This formula applies equally to pure private domestic monopolies and to international cartels behaving like monopolies. It shows that the more (less) elastic the demand for the cartel's sales over the relevant range of prices, the lower (higher) is the optimal monopoly markup. In the extreme case in which the cartel faces an infinite elasticity of demand at a given world price, the optimal markup is zero, and the cartel might as well be dissolved.

If the cartel controls only part of the total world supply, then the elasticity of demand facing the cartel (d_c) depends on three other parameters:

1. The elasticity of world demand for the product (d).
2. The elasticity of competing noncartel supply of the product (s_0).
3. The cartel's share of the world market (c).

The importance of each factor is easy to see. A highly elastic world demand for the product (a highly negative d) means that buyers find it easy to find other ways of spending their money if the price of the product rises much, so that the cartel has very limited power to raise profits by raising prices. A cartel's chances for continued high profits also depend on the elasticity of supply from other countries (s_0) in the obvious direction: The harder it is for other countries to step up their competing output and sales when the cartel posts its high prices, the better are the cartel's chances of success. That is, a low s_0 enhances cartel power in the world market. Finally, the higher the cartel's current share of world sales (c), the better the cartel's prospects.

The dependence of the cartel's success on these three factors can be summarized in a single convenient formula. As shown in the middle of Appendix D, the demand elasticity facing the cartel is related by definition to the other three parameters:

$$d_c = \frac{|d - s_0(1 - c)|}{c}$$

and the optimal cartel markup rate, as a fraction of price, is

$$t^* = \frac{c}{|d - s_0(1 - c)|}$$

To see how the formula works, consider two examples. The first is a case in which cartel members control half of world exports when their cartel is set up

($c = \frac{1}{2}$) and they face a world elasticity of export demand of only -2 ($d = -2$) and an equal positive elasticity of competing supply ($s_0 = 2$). In this case, the formula implies that the optimal cartel markup can be as high as one-sixth of price so that marginal costs are only five-sixths of price.

Alternatively, consider a different cartel that commands only a quarter of world export sales ($c = \frac{1}{4}$) and faces a world demand for exports of the product of -6 and a supply elasticity from other countries of 8 ($d = -6$, $s_0 = 8$). Then the formula implies that the optimal markup is only $\frac{1}{48}$, or just above 2 percent of price. Even this small markup could bring big gains to selling countries if total sales are large, but buying countries would not experience a large percent price increase.

Why Cartels Erode with Time

The theory summarized in the formula above also suggests forces that work increasingly against the cartel over time. When the cartel is first set up, it may well enjoy low elasticities and a high market share. Yet, its very success in raising price is likely to set four anticartel trends in motion: sagging demand, new competing supply, declining market share, and cheating.

Sagging Demand.   First, the higher price will make buying countries look for new ways to avoid importing the cartel's product. If the search for substitutes has any success at all, imports of the buying countries will drop increasingly for any given cartel price, making these countries' long-run demand curve for imports of the product more elastic than their short-run demand curve. The elasticity d will become more negative with time. This happened to OPEC. As theory predicts, and as some OPEC oil ministers had feared, the oil-importing countries slowly came up with ways to conserve on oil use, such as more fuel-efficient cars.

New Competing Supply.   Second, the initial cartel success will accelerate the search for additional supplies in noncartel countries. If the cartel product is an agricultural crop, such as sugar or coffee, the cartel's price hike will cause farmers in other countries to shift increasing amounts of land, labor, and funds from other crops into sugar or coffee. If the cartel product is a depletable mineral resource, such as oil or copper, noncartel countries will respond to the higher price by redoubling their explorations in search of new reserves. If the noncartel countries have any luck at all, their competing supply will become increasingly elastic with time, and s_0 will rise. Again, that happened to OPEC—other countries discovered new oil at a faster rate.

Declining Market Share.   Third, the cartel's world market share (c) will surely fall after the cartel's initial price hike. To raise its price without piling up ever-rising unsold inventories, the cartel must cut its output and sales. Since nonmembers will be straining to raise their output and sales, the cartel's share of the market must drop even if all of its members cooperate solidly. Thus, c will fall while the absolute values of the key elasticities d and s_0 rise, undercutting the cartel's optimal markup and its profits on three fronts at once.

Cheating.   Theory and experience add a fourth reason for a decline in cartel power—the incentive for members, especially members with small individual market shares, to cheat on the cartel agreement.

To see why, suppose that you were a small member of the successful oil export cartel shown back in Figure 13.4 and that when the cartel was set up, your exports were only 1 percent of the cartel total. Yet, let us say, you have enough oil reserves to go on pumping and selling 3 percent of the total cartel exports for as long in the future as you need to plan. Raising your output above the 1 percent share might cost you only, say, $6 a barrel at the margin. Buyers are willing to pay close to $42.50 for each barrel you sell, since the larger cartel members are faithfully holding down their output. Why not attract the extra buyers to you by shaving your price just a little bit below $42.50, say, to $41? Why not do so in grand style, until you are competitively selling the 3 percent of the cartel's market that you can afford to sell without depleting your reserves too fast? You can do so in the hope that you are still so small a share of the cartel that your individual actions will not cause the cartel price to drop much, if at all. Theory says that if a large share of cartel output consists of the outputs of individually small members, their incentive to cheat undermines the whole cartel. The individually large members can keep the cartel effective to some extent by drastically cutting their own outputs to offset the extra sales from the cheaters. Their aggregate size determines how long they can hold out.

OPEC members cheated on the cartel, even openly, just as theory would predict. Up to the mid-1980s, the largest producer, Saudi Arabia, had to hold the cartel together by cutting its production while others cheated. Then the Saudis themselves shifted to a more competitive stance. By the late 1990s, as noted, the real price of oil had fallen back close to its pre-1973 level.

The usual theory of cartels thus correctly explains why cartel profit margins and profits will erode with time—that is, if no new members with large individual shares of the world market join the existing cartel.[7] Yet, the theory does not say that cartels are unprofitable or harmless. On the contrary, it underscores the profitability of cartel formation to cartel members. Even a cartel that eventually erodes can bring vast fortunes to its members. What the theory does do is offer a listing of four key indicators to watch when judging the prospects for an existing or potential cartel: the demand elasticity for the product, the competing-supply elasticity, the members' initial market share, and the share of the cartel held by cheating-prone small members.

---

[7]These same reasons also subtly imply that a cartel would be wise to charge a lower markup, even at the start, than the markup implied by short-run elasticities and the preceding formula. The higher the initial markup, the faster the erosion of the cartel's market share and the lower the optimal markup that the cartel can charge later on. Charging the optimal markup at each point in time is a more delicate art than the simple static formula implies.

Other Primary Products

Do theory and OPEC experience hold out hope for developing countries wanting to make national gains by joining cartels in other primary products besides oil? Not much. There are good reasons for believing that international cartels would collapse faster, with less interim profit, for the non-oil primary products. For agricultural crops in particular, there is the problem of competing supply (leading to a large s_0 and a small c in the preceding formula): Other countries can easily expand the acreage they devote to this crop. Similarly with animal products and forests. History agrees with this verdict. Of 72 commodity cartels set up between the two world wars, only two survived past 1945. Of the few dozen set up in the 1970s, only five lived as late as 1985: cocoa, coffee, rubber, sugar, and tin. All five have been forced into passivity for most of the time since 1985.

Given the limits of international cartel power, a developing nation could still tax its own primary-product exports for the sake of economic development. In principle, the strategy could work well. A tax on exports of Nigerian oil, Ghanaian cocoa, Philippine coconuts, or copper from the Congo (formerly Zaire) could generate revenues for building schools, hospitals, and roads. Or the export-tax revenues could replace some other tax, reinforcing market incentives within the country. It is an excellent idea, as long as there are external benefits to the newly encouraged activities.

Unfortunately, the political economy of many countries seems to divert the export-tax revenues away from the most productive uses (as we hinted in Chapter 9 when discussing the developing government argument for import tariffs). So it has been with the four examples just imagined. Nigeria's oil revenues are lost in a swollen government bureaucracy. For two decades Ghana's cocoa marketing board used its heavy taxation of cocoa farmers to support luxury imports by officials. The Marcos government distributed the Philippine coconut-tax revenues among a handful of Marcos's friends and relatives. And Mobutu kept much of Zaire's revenues from copper and other exports to himself. The potential merits of taxing exports of a primary product are so abused in practice that having no policy would be better.

Exports of Manufactures to Industrial Countries

Since 1980, developing countries turned increasingly toward our fourth trade-policy choice, emphasizing new exports of manufactured goods to the industrialized countries. As Figure 13.5 shows, the switch from primary-product exports to manufactured exports gained momentum in the 1980s and continued into the 1990s. Disillusionment with both primary-product cartels and ISI was probably a factor in the new push.

Is it wise for a developing nation to plan on being able to raise its exports of manufactures to the already industrialized countries? Should Mexico, Ghana, and India follow the example of South Korea, making strategic plans to become major exporters of manufactures? Would the same thing happen without planning, as in the market-directed development of Hong Kong and Taiwan?

	1970	1975	1980	1985	1990	1994
Nonfuel primary products	49.9%	25.8%	18.7%	22.4%	18.7%	17.2%
Fuels	32.4	58.6	61.3	42.2	27.5	17.7
Manufactures	17.4	15.2	18.5	32.4	52.9	64.3

FIGURE 13.5

The Changing Mix of Exports from Developing Countries, 1970–1994

Note: Columns do not add to 100% because of a small amount of unclassified exports in each year.

Source: United Nations Conference on Trade and Development, *Handbook of International Trade and Development Statistics,* 1987 and 1995 (New York: United Nations, 1988 and 1997).

For their part, the industrialized countries have not made the task easy. They have, in fact, discriminated against exports of manufactures from developing countries. Nontariff import barriers apply to a greater percentage of goods from developing countries than to goods from other industrial countries. As for tariffs, the rates are in principle nondiscriminatory. Tariff rates differ, however, by type of product. In general, the highest tariff rates among manufactures are those on textiles, apparel, and footwear—the kind of manufactures in which developing countries have their broadest comparative advantage.

Developing countries are thus justified in charging the industrial nations with hypocrisy. The industrial nations have not practiced the policies of free trade and comparative advantage that they have urged on developing countries. Furthermore, the departures of practice from preaching have been greatest on manufactures exported from developing countries. Tensions will continue over this issue.

Despite some discrimination against their exports, developing countries have been able to break into world markets for their exports of manufactures. One reason is that developing countries have been able to become exporters in standardized manufacturing lines where technological progress has cooled down, such as textiles, tires, and simple electrical appliances. A second reason is that developing countries have become locations for low-cost assembly of more technologically advanced products like computers, with multinational firms from the industrialized countries providing the advanced technology, the components, and the marketing and distribution of the finished products.

A third reason is that barriers against imports of manufactures from developing countries are not all that solid. Consider barriers based on voluntary export restraints, antidumping duties, or countervailing duties. These barriers can limit increases in exports from countries that have already succeeded in establishing their exports to the industrialized countries. But newcomers can gain market access for new manufactured-product exports because they are not hindered by such country-specific barriers. In this way a developing country can gain valuable new export markets, despite the protectionism of the industrialized countries, although there may eventually be limits on how large these export sales can grow.

All in, betting on exports of manufactures is part of the most promising strategy for most developing countries. And as Figure 13.5 has made clear, the developing countries are relying more and more on this strategy.

The Special Challenges of Transition

In 1989, a massive transition from central planning to market economies began in the formerly socialist countries of Central and Eastern Europe. With the breakup of the Soviet Union in 1991, the former Soviet Union (FSU) countries (also called newly independent states, NIS) joined in this transition. This is the most dramatic episode of economic liberalization in history. What role have changing policies toward international trade played in the transition efforts? And what have we learned about trade and transition?

Prior to the transition beginning in 1989–1991, central planning by each national government directed the economies in these countries. National self-sufficiency was a goal of policy. Imports were used to close gaps in the plan, mainly imports of materials and products that were not (yet) available locally, and a state bureaucracy controlled exports and imports. When international trade was necessary, the Soviet Union and its bloc of countries in Central and Eastern Europe favored trade among themselves and strongly discouraged trade with outside countries. But among themselves these countries had a tough problem—what and how to trade in a balanced way. They tended to use bilateral barter trade, with long lists of exports and imports for each pair of countries. In 1949, six countries set up the Council for Mutual Economic Assistance (CMEA) to promote more efficient and multilateral trade.[8] Still, bilateral trade accounts predominated. The trade pattern that emerged had the Soviet Union specializing in exporting oil and gas (at prices well below world prices) and the other countries exporting industrial and farm products.

As the transition began, these countries had a legacy of poor decision making under central planning, including overdevelopment of heavy industries (like steel and defense), outdated technology, environmental problems, and little established trade with market economies. The countries needed to remove state control of transactions and undertake a major reorientation and reorganization of production. They could expect severe negative effects during the transition, including major decreases in national production. Each country faced daunting problems: Before the turnaround, how bad would it be, and for how long?

Transition involves accomplishing five challenging tasks: (1) shifting to markets and market-determined prices, with a new process of resource allocation; (2) reducing subsidies; (3) establishing private ownership, with privatization of state businesses; (4) establishing a legal system, with contract laws and property rights; and (5) opening the economy to international competition and trade. A key question is one of speed. Should the transition be fast (shock therapy), or should it be gradual?

Domestic and international reforms usually advance together in a country. Keeping this in mind, let's focus on the role of trade policy in transition. Figure 13.6 reports a number of indicators of trade, trade policy, and growth in the transition economies. The European Bank for Reconstruction and Development has

---

[8]The six original members of CMEA were Bulgaria, Czechoslovakia, Hungary, Poland, Romania, and the Soviet Union. Late in 1949, Albania and East Germany joined. In 1962, Albania left and Mongolia joined. Cuba joined in 1972. CMEA disbanded in 1991.

	Progress in Trade and Foreign Exchange Reform (4 = Most)		*Exports to Former CMEA Countries as Percentage of Total Exports, 1997*	*Percentage Change in Real GDP, 1996 Compared to 1989*	*Year of Resumption of Real GDP Growth*
Country	*1994*	*1997*			
Central and Eastern Europe Countries					
Albania	4	4	NA	−15%	1993
Bulgaria	4	4	21%	−23	1994
Croatia	4	4	9	−30	1994
Czech Republic	4	4	29	−11	1993
Hungary	4	4	15	−14	1994
Macedonia	4	4	15	−45	1996
Poland	4	4	20	4	1992
Romania	4	4	11	−12	1993
Slovak Republic	4	4	47	−10	1994
Slovenia	4	4	11	−5	1993
Baltic FSU Countries					
Estonia	4	4	28	−29	1995
Latvia	4	4	43	−48	1996
Lithuania	4	4	47	−58	1994
Other FSU Countries					
Armenia	2	4	35	−63	1994
Azerbaijan	1	2	51	−61	1996
Belarus	1	1	86	−36	1996
Georgia	1	4	64	−69	1995
Kazahkstan	2	4	57	−43	1996
Kyrgyzstan	3	4	69	−43	1995
Moldova	2	4	80	−65	post-1996
Russia	3	4	35	−43	post-1996
Tajikistan	1	2	43	−63	post-1996
Turkmenistan	1	1	49	−40	post-1996
Ukraine	1	3	60	−61	post-1996
Uzbekistan	2	2	65	−15	1996

FIGURE 13.6

Trade Reform and Growth in Transition Economies

Note: "Progress in Trade and Foreign Exchange Reform" is a four-category index: (1) widespread conrols remain, (2) some liberalization, (3) removal of almost all restrictions, and (4) removal of all restrictions. For 1997, four countries (Czech Republic, Hungary, Poland, and Slovenia) earned a 4+ rating, indicating standards and norms of advanced industrialized countries. The "Year of Resumption of Real GDP Growth" is the first year in which the country begins at least two consecutive years of positive real GDP growth.

Sources: European Bank for Reconstruction and Development, *Transition Report,* 1994 and 1997; and International Monetary Fund, *Direction of Trade Statistics Yearbook, 1998.*

analyzed each country's progress on trade reform (and other types of reform not reported here). The first two columns of numbers show its estimates of the progress of trade and foreign exchange reforms for 1994 and 1997. Reforms proceeded at different speeds in different sets of countries.

The Central and Eastern European countries and the Baltic countries pursued strong, rapid liberalizations, achieving a rating of 4 (all trade restrictions removed) by 1994. Poland and Hungary led the way. For example, Poland's "big bang" in 1990 eliminated most import barriers (removing quotas and establishing low tariffs), removed export controls, and abolished state trading monopolies, as well as shifting 90 percent of prices in Poland to the market. As another example, in 1992, Estonia, soon after the breakup of the Soviet Union, removed almost all export restrictions, eliminated all import quotas, and kept tariffs low or zero, as well as removing most domestic price controls. Most of these countries strove to meet the standards for membership in the World Trade Organization (WTO). The Czech Republic, Poland, Romania, the Slovak Republic, Slovenia, and Estonia became WTO members in 1995, and Bulgaria in 1996. In addition, all of these countries except Albania, Croatia, and Macedonia established Association Agreements with the European Union (EU) during 1992–1995. They gained free access to the EU market for most manufactures, and are considered to be on a path for full EU membership.

The other FSU countries (the members of the Commonwealth of Independent States) have instead followed the path of slow liberalization. As shown in Figure 13.6, none had removed all trade restrictions by 1994, and half had not begun to liberalize (a rating of 1). As an example of no liberalization, Ukraine maintained state trading and administrative controls to keep domestic prices below world prices. Tight export controls prevented foreign sales, a policy needed to maintain the low domestic prices. Explicit import barriers were low, but little foreign exchange was available to buy imports. As an example of partial liberalization, Russia substantially liberalized domestic prices and import controls in 1992, but maintained extensive export restrictions until 1995. In other countries, the lack of liberalization included new import controls, such as high tariffs and strict product quality standards. By 1997, export restrictions in most of these countries (except Belarus, Turkmenistan, and Uzbekistan) had been removed. Substantial liberalization of imports had been completed in six of the countries (those with ratings of 4). In addition, all except Tajikistan had established Partnership and Cooperation Agreements with the EU, a weaker form of EU relationship, with mutual most-favored-nation tariffs and removal of quotas.

How will the trade pattern evolve as transition occurs? One pressure is clear, toward rapid growth of imports, especially consumer goods, based on pent-up demand. Transition economies must export in order to pay for their rising imports, and Western Europe and other industrialized countries were crucial as major markets for expanding their exports. (In addition, foreign buyers of the country's exports are a source of additional demand for the country's production, which can provide employment for the country's labor and other resources. This is especially important, given the collapse of demand from domestic buyers in the early stages of transition.)

Will the transition country be able to export more to Western Europe and other market economies? There are two sets of challenges. One is the set of initial limitations of the country's products and businesses, including poor product quality, lack of marketing capabilities, and lack of trade financing. The other is the set of actual and threatened import barriers. For instance, exports from the transition economies face nontariff barriers in Western Europe that limit imports of "sensitive products," including agriculture and food, textiles and clothing, leather goods, chemicals, and metals. And transition countries risk incurring antidumping duties and countervailing duties if their export success is deemed to be "unfair trade." Some transition countries have succeeded in increasing their exports of light manufactured goods, including textiles, clothing, and footwear. Another base for success is these countries' low-cost skilled labor, leading to exports of products like vehicles and machinery. Multinational corporations from industrialized countries have invested into these countries to employ their labor in production, with the multinationals providing the designs, advanced components, quality control, and marketing that the transition economies lack.

An indicator of success in reorienting trade is a shift to exporting to countries outside the former socialist bloc. In the later 1980s, before transition began, nearly all trade of each republic of the former Soviet Union was with other Soviet republics and other CMEA countries, and 40 percent or more of the trade of the Central and Eastern European members of the CMEA was with other CMEA countries. (Albania and Yugoslavia, not members of the CMEA, did not trade that much with CMEA countries, so the issue of shifting trade patterns is not so important for Albania and countries that had been part of Yugoslavia.)

The reorienting of trade patterns is indicated by the third column of numbers in Figure 13.6. By 1997, the Central and Eastern European countries and Estonia sent more than 70 percent of their exports to countries outside the former CMEA (except for the Slovak Republic, half of whose exports to the former CMEA countries went, unsurprisingly, to the Czech Republic). In contrast, most other FSU countries still sold over half of their exports to former CMEA countries (including other FSU countries). Rapid liberalization, along with the favorable geographic location closer to the markets of Western Europe, has facilitated a faster shift by Central and Eastern European countries to a more desirable export pattern.

More generally, the speed of transition seems to matter. Studies by the World Bank and others have examined broad experiences with the two approaches to trade reform and reached conclusions that favor the rapid approach. Rapid liberalization is a quick shift toward free trade, with substantial gains in economic efficiency. World prices act as signals to guide resource reallocation. Efficiency gains can be large, given the previous policy of aiming for self-sufficiency and the other inefficiencies of central planning. Free trade also places competitive pressure on domestic businesses to raise productivity and product quality. This process is disruptive, but, as we saw starting in Chapter 2, the gains from opening to trade are based largely on disrupting previous patterns of production and consumption activities. A rapid shift has the advantage that it is completed before vested interests can form to oppose liberalization.

Continuation of trade controls, with only gradual liberalization, might be a way to reduce the disruption of transition, but the savings are small and the losses can be large. Other aspects of transition also cause large disruptions, so that an economy in transition will suffer large losses in production in any case. In fact, for an FSU country, inability to trade freely is itself disruptive, because producers in the country often rely on imported materials as inputs into their own production. Without the imported inputs, domestic production declines. In addition, continued trade controls are part of continued wide-ranging government interference in domestic business management. And government controls and interference breed corruption and evasion.

One indicator of the overall success of transition is the growth or decline of domestic production (real GDP). We expect to see large falls in measured production early in transition. In fact, these declines are probably overstated for two reasons. First, the value of output is overstated before transition because many goods are of low quality and little true value. Second, the value of output during transition is understated because growing private production in the "informal" or "underground" economy is not included. Still, the broad patterns in the data are probably meaningful. The final two columns of Figure 13.6 show (1) how real GDP in 1996 compared with real GDP in 1989 for each transition country and (2) when a substantial period of real growth resumed.

For all countries except Poland, real output was apparently lower in 1996 than it had been in 1989. Still, there is a clear difference between the rapid liberalizers in Central and Eastern Europe and the gradual liberalizers in the FSU. For most Central and Eastern European countries, 1996 real GDP is close to its 1989 value, with growth resuming in 1992, 1993, or 1994 after a relatively short but deep GDP decline after 1989. For most of the FSU countries, 1996 real GDP remains much below its 1989 value, and growth resumed in 1996 or later. For them, the deep decline in real output lingers.

Thus, the policy of rapid liberalization seems to be more successful, with a shorter period of deep recession and a faster return to economic growth. Rapid trade liberalization and integration into the global economy provide direct benefits, and they also tend to lock in other reforms. But the Central and Eastern European countries also had more favorable initial situations—they had a geographic location closer to Western European markets, and they had spent less time as centrally planned economies. Perhaps the interesting test cases are the Baltic countries, which liberalized rapidly but did not have such favorable geography. Estonia has fared rather well, but Latvia and Lithuania resemble other FSU countries. Latvia and Lithuania have been less successful in reorienting trade, and their output levels remain well below those of 1989. Geography, or at least the ability to reorient trade, may be as important as rapid liberalization in explaining the comparative success of the Central and Eastern European countries.

Looking to the future, many of the transition countries have a solid foundation for economic success based on a well-educated, healthy labor force, with high levels of literacy and numeracy and strength in engineering skills. But the mixture of politics, policy decisions, and geography seems to be driving toward two sets of countries with very different transition results. Most transition countries in Central and Eastern Europe, and perhaps the Baltic countries as well, are positioned for growth and rising living standards. Most other FSU countries have failed to reverse their declines and have uncertain futures. This high variance in transition experiences mirrors the high variance in the experiences of developing countries more generally.

Summary

The gaps in living standards are widening among developing countries. Developing countries in East Asia have grown quickly, but some were set back by the Asian crisis beginning in 1997. For many poor countries in Africa, average incomes have been declining for several decades. And countries in transition from central planning to market economies experienced large declines in output and income during the early years of transition, with most countries of the former Soviet Union (FSU) experiencing especially large and lingering declines.

Developing countries must decide what trade policies to adopt toward industrial imports, primary-product exports, and industrial exports.

One strategy open to developing countries is that of import-substituting industrialization (ISI). It could raise national skill levels, bring terms-of-trade gains, and allow planners to economize on market information (since they can just take industrial imports themselves as a measure of demand that could be captured with the help of protection). Detailed studies of ISI and related policies, however, have given ammunition to critics of ISI. A study of 41 nations shows that income growth is negatively correlated with antitrade policies like ISI. The available evidence supports the fears about ISI raised by the analysis of Chapters 7 through 9.

A traditional fear about relying on exports of primary products is that the world market price trends are unfavorable to producers, especially those in developing countries. The evidence shows a downward trend in the relative prices of most primary products, as commonly feared, but the decline has been gradual since 1900. Two factors lowering the relative price of primary products are Engel's law and the development of modern synthetic substitutes for primary materials. Two opposing forces, which would tend to raise primary-product prices, are natural resource limits and the fact that productivity growth is often slower in the primary sectors than in the rest of the economy.

Joining an international cartel could bring gains to a developing country that exports the cartelized product. The greatest cartel success by far is OPEC's pair of price victories in 1973–1974 and 1979–1980. With all international cartels, even OPEC, success breeds decline. Four forces dictate the speed at which a cartel erodes: the rise in product demand elasticity, the rise in the elasticity of competing supplies, the decline in the share of the cartel in the world market, and the rise in cheating by smaller members of the cartel. Because of supply conditions, it is unlikely that cartels in other primary products could achieve anything close to OPEC's success.

Another strategy is to concentrate on developing exports of manufactured goods. This has been a slowly prevailing trend since the 1960s, though ISI also remains widely practiced among developing countries. Relying on exports of manufactures has its risks, however. Developing nations have rightly complained about import barriers against their new manufactures erected by the developed countries. Such barriers have indeed been higher than the barriers on manufactures traded between developed countries, and have risen since the late 1960s. Still, evidence shows that an outward-oriented trade policy encouraging exports of manufactures is part of the most promising strategy for most developing countries.

Changes in international trade policy are an important part of the process of transition from central planning to a market economy. A key issue is the speed of liberalization of trade policy (and other reforms like shifting from controlled prices to market prices). Countries in Central and Eastern Europe and the Baltic countries chose strong, rapid liberalizations, and most achieved substantial reorientations of their exports to Western European and other industrialized-country markets. After deep declines in national output in the first several years of transition, they have achieved economic growth and most seem to be positioned for continued growth. Other FSU countries liberalized slowly, and their output declines have been both deep and lingering. As with developing countries generally, we see widening gaps in living standards between these two groups of transition countries, and we see greater success for those countries adopting more open and outward-oriented trade policies.

Suggested Reading

Studies of the ISI and outward-oriented strategies are the World Bank's *World Development Report* (1983, 1986, 1987), Krueger (1993), Choksi et al. (1991), Edwards (1992, 1993), Sachs and Warner (1995), and Bruton (1998).

Overviews of the vast literature on long-run trends in the relative prices of primary products are Scandizzo and Diakosawas (1987) and Grilli and Yang (1988). An excellent narrative of the events leading to the 1973–1974 OPEC victory, and of the roles played by several countries and the major oil companies, is to be found in Vernon (1976).

Institutional details on commodity cartel schemes are helpfully cataloged by Gordon-Ashworth (1984). Suslow (1988) analyzes why some cartels died faster than others before World War II. The World Bank's *World Devel-opment Report 1986,* pp. 133–173, and Gilbert (1996) discuss the failures of cartels in recent decades.

The implications of the pattern of protection in North America and Europe for developing countries seeking to export manufactures are explored at length by Cline (1984). The rationale for, and developing countries' experience with, export-promotion strategies are surveyed in Milner (1990).

The World Bank's *World Development Report 1996* presents a thorough survey of reforms necessary for transition. The European Bank for Reconstruction and Development issues an annual *Transition Report.* Michalopoulos and Tarr (1996) and Gacs (1997) discuss trade policies in transition countries.

Questions and Problems

✦ 1. List the main pros and cons of taking the import-replacing road to industrialization versus concentrating government aid and private energies on developing new comparative advantages in manufacturing exports.

2. (An alternative to question 1) Under what conditions would ISI have the greatest chance of being better than any alternative development strategy? What other policies should accompany it?

✦ 3. "The terms of trade move against primary producers in the long run." What is the evi-dence in support of this proposition? How solid is the evidence?

4. You are an adviser to the government of a country whose exports are mainly a few primary products and whose imports are mainly manufactured products. You are asked to prepare a short report on the forces that are likely to drive the country's terms of trade during the next two decades. What will the main points of your report be?

✦ 5. The United States, China, India, Brazil, and Turkey have formed an international association known as Tobacco's Altruistic Raisers to set the world price of tobacco at the most profitable level. TAR covers 60 percent of world exports. The price elasticity of world demand for tobacco is –0.6, and the price elasticity of competing supply from non-TAR countries is 0.75. For as long as these elasticities persist,

a. What is the price elasticity of demand for TAR's tobacco exports?

b. What is the profit-maximizing rate of cartel markup?

6. Drawing on material from this chapter and earlier chapters, weigh the pros and cons of restricting and taxing exports of primary products. How could it raise national income? What are the drawbacks of such a policy for a developing country?

✦7. What is the optimal cartel markup if the price elasticity of demand for a cartel's exports is less than 1 in absolute value (e.g., if it is –½)? How do we interpret an optimal markup in this situation? Could this elasticity hold at all prices? Why or why not?

8. In Figure 13.2, Argentina is listed as having a strongly inward trade policy. Around 1990, it shifted to an outward-oriented policy. What is your prediction for Argentina's growth rate of income per capita during the 1990s? Does the data reported in Figure 13.1 support your prediction?

✦ 9. One of your friends believes that the challenges of a transition from central planning to a market economy are so large that policies should be changed slowly. If you disagree, what are your major arguments?

10. Ukraine has to decide on a trade-policy strategy to go with other reforms for promoting development. Comment on the merits and drawbacks of the following available choices:

a. Unilaterally taxing its grain exports.

b. Joining a grain cartel with North America, Argentina, and Australia, the other main exporters.

c. Choosing manufactures it could export (e.g., batteries), giving them a profitable home-market base protected by tariffs, and encouraging exports to other countries at competitive world prices.

CHAPTER 14

The Political Economy of Trade and Agriculture

Understanding the causes and consequences of trade policies requires a mixture of political and economic insights. It also requires separate treatment of policies toward agriculture since they are distinctive both in their motivation and in their effects on trade. This chapter rounds out our pursuit of such understanding in Parts I and II. The preceding chapters have handled the main task by judging the economic consequences of trade policies in general. Here we face three remaining questions:

1. Shifting from the consequences to the cause of trade policies, we ask, What forces have created our trade barriers?
2. What forces in particular have made agricultural trade policy so strange?
3. What are the consequences of these strange agricultural trade policies?

What Explains Our Trade Barriers in General?

Several broad facts about real-world trade barriers demand an explanation:

- *The overall level of trade barriers.* Why are they generally higher than the welfare analysis of Chapters 7 through 9 would warrant?
- The *"tariff escalation" pattern.* Why are tariffs and other trade barriers higher for consumer goods than for raw materials and intermediate goods?
- *Allowing more imports as a "concession."* Why, in international trade negotiations, does each nation act as if lowering its own import barriers is a concession to foreigners, when doing so benefits that same nation?
- *The sudden-damage effect.* Why are trade barriers raised more in recessions than in booms and inflations, and why are they raised quickly when imports suddenly rise?

Economists and political scientists tend to agree on at least some answers to these questions, even though they have only begun to think about the longer-run trends. There is a growing literature on the "political economy of trade barriers," which explains the incentives that motivate activities by individuals and pressure groups in the political system and the self-interested behavior of political representatives who seek to maximize their influence and their chances for staying in office.

The Basic Politics of Protection

Let's take a look at the political process that leads to a decision about whether or not to impose a tariff on imports of a good, say, socks. As we have seen in previous chapters, imposing the tariff will have different effects on the well-being of different groups in the country, with both winners and losers. In addition, we presume that the tariff would cause some economic inefficiency—a decrease in national well-being because the losers lose more than the winners gain. When will such a tariff be enacted? Why?

There are a number of key elements in our political-economic analysis:

1. *The size of the gains for the winners from protection, and how many individuals are in the group of winners.* Let's call the total gains B_P, and presume that this is the producer surplus gained from securing government protection—the same thing as area a in diagrams like Figures 7.2 and 7.3 in Chapter 7. N_P is the number of individuals benefiting from the protection.

2. *The size of the losses for the losers from protection, and how many individuals are in the group of losers.* In the political fight, they gain by defeating the tariff. Their total gains are B_C, which we presume to be at least as large as areas $a + b + d$ in Figure 7.3. (Consumers may not view the tariff revenue area c as a loss to them, if the government uses the revenue to reduce other consumer taxes or spends the revenue on projects valued by the consumers). N_C is the number of individuals losing from protection (gaining from defeating protection).

3. *Individuals' reasons for taking positions for or against protection.* We presume that direct gains and losses of well-being (B_P and B_C) are reasons for taking positions. There may be other reasons. One is sympathy for groups who are suffering losses. Another is ideology or other closely held core beliefs about politics and economics.

4. *Types of political activities and their costs.* Individuals (and groups of individuals sharing a common interest) can engage in a range of different political activities. Assuming that the country has elections, individuals can vote. Individuals can themselves engage in lobbying of their government officials, in which the individuals provide information on their position and try to persuade the officials to support their position, or they can hire others to lobby for them. Individuals can provide campaign contributions to politicians running for office. Or individuals can provide

bribes or other side payments to attempt to gain the support of government officials. The costs of these different types of political activities include both money cost and the opportunity cost of any time or other efforts used in the activity.

5. *Political institutions and the political process.* We will closely examine two types of political process: first, direct voting on the tariff by all individuals and, second, elected representatives voting on the tariff. These seem most relevant to a democratic system like that used in most industrialized and many developing countries. (Other possibilities include a single decision maker or decision making by an appointed committee of experts, among others.)

When Are Tariffs Unlikely?

Under some circumstances, inefficient trade barriers would be rejected, and we would have a world closer to free trade than we observe. Let's consider two sets of circumstances.

Our first case is direct democracy. Consider what will happen if we have (1) a direct vote by individuals on each tariff (or other import barrier), with (2) voting (almost) costless so that (almost) everyone votes, and (3) each person voting based on his or her direct interest as a winner or a loser from protection. Nearly always the number of losers N_C (the number of consumers of the product) is larger than the number of winners N_P (the number of people involved in production of the import-competing product). In the example of socks, nearly everyone buys socks, but only a small number of people work in (or provide substantial amounts of other resources like land or capital to) the sock industry. The sock tariff would be defeated by a large margin. Most trade barriers protect only a minority, and this is probably true even if many trade barriers are combined into a single vote. So the trade barriers that we see in most countries depart from what simple majority-rule democracy would give us. Indeed, countries usually do not use direct votes to set protection. Rather, a group of elected representatives (or some other government officials) decides. Winning the political fight is gaining the support of a majority of these representatives or officials.

Are forms of government like representative democracy inherently protectionist? Our second case shows that representative democracy can also lead to little or no protection. Consider what will happen if (1) each group is willing to devote all of its total gain (B_P and B_C) to political activity like lobbying or contributions, and (2) politicians decide which side to support according to the amount of lobbying or contributions they receive. The fact that the tariff causes economic inefficiency means that B_C is larger than B_P. Those opposed to the tariff would be willing to spend up to B_C to prevent the tariff, while the protectionists would not rationally spend more than the smaller stake B_P. The inefficiency of the tariff (equal to $B_C - B_P$) dooms that tariff. Even if the political process does not work exactly like this, it still would tend to reject the more inefficient of protectionist proposals.

When Are Tariffs Likely?

Lobbying and contributions by different groups can lead to political decisions enacting protection, if some groups are more effective than other groups in organizing their political activities. In this case we reach a surprising conclusion: The group with the smaller number of individuals can be more effective. We can see two different reasons for this surprising conclusion. Both are based on the fact that each individual in the smaller group tends to have a larger individual gain.

First, consider what happens when there is some minimal cost per individual to the individual being involved in any political activity. This cost could be a minimum amount of time that must be spent, or it could be the per person cost of organizing a group effort to engage in lobbying. If the benefit to the individual is less than the cost to participate, the individual will probably decide not to participate. The average gain per supporter of protection is B_P/N_P, and the average gain per opponent of protection is B_C/N_C. The individual gain tends to be larger as the number of individuals in the group is smaller. In our sock example, the number of sock producers is small, but the gain to each from protection is large (perhaps hundreds or thousands of dollars per year). The number of sock consumers is large, but the loss to each from protection is small (probably a few tens of dollars or less per year). If consumers' benefits from defeating the protectionist measure are small per person, many (or all) of them may decide that it is not worth the fight against protectionism. (That is, they see that B_C/N_C is less than the minimum per person cost of participating.) The protectionist minority is the only active interest group, and they gain the majority of representatives' votes.

Second, consider what happens when some members of the group can decide to "free-ride" on the contributions of others in the group. This **free-rider problem** usually afflicts the large-group opposition more seriously than it affects the small group. The free-rider problem arises whenever the benefits of a group effort fall on everyone in the group, regardless of how much each individual does (or does not) spend (in time, effort, voting, or money). Each individual knows that his individual contribution to the group is not likely to be crucial. Therefore, each selfishly rational individual tries to get a free ride, letting others advance the common cause. The individual's benefits from the common cause do depend on the group's victory or defeat, but that does not depend much on the individual's own effort. In a large group, the impact of any one individual is very small, so that the incentive to be a free rider is very high. But if all or most try to free-ride, the large group is not organized or has few resources to use for political activity. A group with a smaller number of individual members is more likely to get individual participation for two reasons. Each individual recognizes that his individual contribution is very important to the group and its success, so he is less likely to free-ride. And the contributors can use peer pressure more effectively to cajole other individuals to participate rather than free-ride. Conquering the free-rider problem is what political action groups—special interests—are all about.

The small number of import-competing producers are motivated to participate in the politics of protection and often overcome the free-rider problem to become a well-organized group with substantial resources to use in political activity. The group lobbies vociferously in favor of protection. The group uses campaign contributions to enhance the chances of electing representatives friendly to their position, to gain access to the representatives for lobbying, to influence the representatives' positions on votes, and to reward votes in favor of industry protection. In contrast, each individual in the large, diffuse consumer group has a small incentive to become active and a large incentive to free-ride. In our sock example, a trade association may organize and represent the interests of the sock-producing firms, and, if the industry is unionized, the labor unions represent the interest of workers. The "organization of sock consumers" is unlikely.

The outcome is often that the well-organized protectionist lobby sways a majority of representatives, even though this protection is economically inefficient and hurts a majority of voters. In these cases, the politicians in favor of protection trade a small reduction in the individual well-being of many voters, with some loss of votes possible in the next election, for the votes and largess of those protected, including the ability to use their campaign contributions to gain votes in the next election.

In addition to this recognition of the important general role of lobbying and contributions by special interest groups, other specific features of the country's political institutions affect the political economy of protection. Here are two that are documented for the United States. First, the U.S. Senate gives exactly two senators to each state, regardless of population. States that are mainly rural and agricultural are overrepresented, providing extra support for protection of agricultural industries. Second, for the U.S. House of Representatives, in which there is one representative for each district, it helps to have the production activities of an import-competing industry spread over a large number of states or districts, so that a large number of representatives are likely to become a core of supporters for protection for the industry.

Applications to Other Trade-Policy Patterns

The simple model of political activity in a representative democracy can also explain other patterns besides the overall favoring of producer interests over consumer interests. Some of these patterns are extensions of the same producer-bias pattern; some are not.

Another general symptom of the importance of group size and concentration into effective lobbying units is the **tariff escalation** pattern. Economists have found that effective and nominal tariff rates rise with the stage of production. That is, they are typically higher on final consumer goods than on intermediate goods and raw materials sold to producing firms.[1] The explanation would seem to be that consumers of final products are a peculiarly weak lobby, being many people who are not well organized into dues-collecting lobbying associations. Consumer groups fight only weakly against the producers of final products, whose

---

[1] The tariff escalation pattern does not apply to agricultural products, however. Farmers get at least as much effective protection as the wholesalers and retailers to whom they sell.

cause is championed by influential large firms and trade associations. When it comes to fights over protecting sellers of intermediate goods, the story can be quite different. The buyers of intermediate goods are themselves firms and can organize lobbying efforts as easily as their suppliers can. The outcome of a struggle over tariffs on intermediate goods is thus less likely to favor protection.

The same bias in favor of producer interests over final-consumer interests shows up in international negotiations to liberalize trade, such as the eight postwar rounds of multilateral trade negotiations. There are curious explicit guidelines as to what constitutes a fair balance of concessions by the different nations at the bargaining table. A *concession* is any agreement to cut one's own import duties, thereby letting in more imports. Each country is pressured to allow as much import expansion as the export expansion it gets from other countries' import liberalizations. It is odd to see import liberalization treated as a concession by the importing nation. After all, cutting your own import tariffs should usually bring net national gains, not losses, according to Chapters 7 through 9. The concession-balancing rule can only be interpreted as further evidence of the power of producer groups over consumer groups. The negotiators view their own import tariff cuts as sacrifices simply because they have to answer politically to import-competing producer groups but not to masses of poorly organized consumers. In addition, another producer group in the country—producers of exportable products—is also usually active in lobbying to influence the trade negotiations. The balancing "concessions" by other countries to lower foreign import barriers bring benefits to export producers, so that they politically support the multilateral trade liberalization.

So far we have presumed that each individual takes a position in favor of or against protection according to her own direct self-interest. But, in some cases, it seems that sympathy (or other reasons) determines an individual's position.

Interest groups are often victorious because they gain the sympathy of others, that is, of people who will not directly gain if policy helps the interest group. Political sympathy often surges when a group suffers a big income loss all at once, especially in a general recession. Sympathy creates the **sudden-damage effect.** The sympathy can spring from either of two sources. One is simply compassion for those suffering large income losses. Political sentiments often yield to pleas for protection when a surge of import competition wipes out incomes, just as we provide generous relief for victims of natural disasters. The other source shows up more when a deep recession hits the whole economy. In a recession, an increased number of people are at risk of having their incomes cut. More of them identify with the less fortunate, thinking, That could be me. One policy response is to help those damaged by import competition, whose pleas are heard above the mild complaints of many consumers who would suffer small individual losses from import barriers. Thus, both a surge in import competition and a general recession raise sympathy for protectionism.

Our discussion began with the general question of why the overall level of trade barriers is higher than the welfare analysis of economic efficiency would justify. But now that we have examined the political economy of trade barriers, we might easily ask the opposite question. Given the power of well-organized import-competing producers favoring protection, as well as the appeal of sympathy for local producers struggling against imports produced by foreign firms, why are our import barriers not so very high? One reason is that there are organized producer groups that are opposed to protection. These include firms that use imported products in their own production, including the wholesalers and retailers who distribute imports, as well as export producers who generally favor free trade. A second reason is that we have used mutual "concessions" during multilateral trade negotiations to lower trade barriers. There is probably also a third reason. Economic ideology probably does have some impact. Politicians who espouse the merits of free enterprise, markets, and competition probably do see that protection is inconsistent with these concepts, and this does make them somewhat less likely to support protection.

The Protection and Taxation of Agriculture

Agriculture is another matter. Wherever the farm population is directly involved, government intervention has become a highly developed art form, with major effects on international trade.

In today's high-income countries, government protection and subsidization of agriculture have been carried to such extremes that the laws of nature have been turned upside down. We naturally expect that food grains, for example, will be exported by the countries with the best climates and soils for growing grain. Yet, since the early 1980s, Saudi Arabia has grown more wheat than that country can consume, forcing it to subsidize wheat exports! Why? The government has placed such a high priority on being able to see wheat fields in the desert around Riyadh that it has not only blocked wheat imports but has heaped subsidies (and expensive water) on home-grown wheat, leading to a surplus for export. Wheat is also exported by other countries with unfavorable climates and soils, including Great Britain and France. And crowded industrial Japan has often been a net exporter of rice.

Presumably, with enough government intervention, bananas could be grown in Antarctica and exported to Ecuador.

As extremely as agriculture is protected in some settings, it is taxed and exploited in others, primarily in developing countries. Take the case of cocoa in Ghana around 1980. Ghanaian cocoa farmers had to sell their crops to the government's cocoa marketing board, which gave them only about 40 percent of the world price at which the board sold the same cocoa beans. In addition to pocketing the other 60 percent, the government put up import barriers that made industrial imports (e.g., clothing, fuel) artificially expensive for farmers to buy. Under such policies, Ghanaian agriculture had reached a ruinous state by the early 1980s, although it has had some recovery since then. Similarly, heavy taxation of exportable crops, especially beverages (cocoa, coffee, tea) and cotton, is common among developing countries.

Global Patterns in Agricultural Policy

In fact, economists have found that extremes like these are part of two policy patterns that show up both in history and in today's global comparisons. While there are exceptions, and there are difficulties of getting precise measurements, two general patterns stand out:

- *The developmental pattern.* Low-income countries generally burden farm producers with taxes and poor terms of trade, whereas high-income countries generally subsidize and protect their agriculture.
- *The antitrade bias.* Policies tend to tax producers of exportable agricultural products, especially in developing countries, while protecting producers of importables against import competition.

To discover these patterns, economists needed measurements of the effects of government policy on agricultural incomes. There is a trade-off in measures of policy impact, a trade-off between availability and accuracy. The most available measure is the **nominal protection coefficient (NPC):**

$$\text{NPC} = \frac{P_{\text{prod}}}{P_{\text{world}}} = \frac{\text{ratio of price received by domestic producers to}}{\text{world price of same product at nation's border}}$$

- NPC > 1 means producers are protected by government.
- NPC < 1 means they are effectively taxed.

The main limitation of the NPC is that it cannot take account of government policies that affect farmers' incomes without affecting domestic agricultural prices. For example, if a government paid its farmers generous income subsidies but let free trade dictate domestic prices, NPC would equal 1, wrongly implying no government help at all. Another limitation is that it does not take account of what the government is doing to the prices of things farmers buy. The NPC fails to reflect the fact that government protection of industry raises the prices of farm inputs and the consumer goods farm families buy. Yet because the NPC requires only the measurement of two prices, it is available. And because it is available, we use it.

A better measure, introduced in Chapter 7, is the **effective rate of protection (e.r.p.):**

$$\text{e.r.p.} = \frac{P_{\text{prod}} - P_{\text{world}} - \text{input cost markup due to government policies}}{\text{unit value added at free-trade prices}}$$

or

$$\text{e.r.p.} = \frac{\text{NPC} - 1 - \text{input cost markups as share of } P_{\text{world}}}{\text{unit value added as share of } P_{\text{world}}}$$

Relative to the NPC, the e.r.p. has the virtue of taking account of the effects of government policy on the prices of farm inputs. It can thus capture subsidies to fertilizer use, where they exist, or government protection of industries supplying farm inputs. Its two most serious omissions are (1) government subsidies or taxes that do not affect prices and (2) government effects on farm families' cost of living.

A third, more comprehensive, measure of policy impacts on agricultural incomes has been developed by economists connected with the U.S. Department of Agriculture and the Organization for Economic Cooperation and Development. Subsidies and taxes are expressed as shares of farmers' original incomes and combined with the percent income effects of price-affecting policies. In rough schematic summary, this **producer subsidy equivalent (PSE)** can be described as

$$\text{PSE} = \frac{P_{\text{prod}} - P_{\text{world}} + \text{government subsidies} - \text{input price markups}}{P_{\text{world}}}$$

or

$$\text{PSE} = \text{NPC} - 1 + \frac{\text{government subsidies} - \text{input price markups}}{P_{\text{world}}}$$

The PSE measure has the advantage of its greater comprehensiveness in capturing effects of government policy on agricultural incomes. Even it, though, omits important effects. In practice, it quantifies only some of the government's influences on the prices of farm inputs. Specifically, it quantifies the influences of farm policies, not all policies. Government's protection of industry often raises agricultural costs in ways missed by the PSE's focus on policies aimed directly at agricultural producers. And the PSE, like all the other measures, misses effects of government on farm families' cost of living. No measure has yet reached the goal of quantifying all the effects of government on agricultural incomes. When PSE measures are refined for many countries, they will be the best available measures. For the present, only the cruder NPCs offer broad international coverage.

How agricultural policy evolves over the course of economic development, and how it is biased against trade, can be shown with NPC estimates for several dozen countries around 1980. Figure 14.1 graphs NPCs separately for importable and exportable goods, with trend (regression) lines showing how NPCs for the average importable and average exportable good tend to advance with GDP per capita. Both tend to rise, showing the developmental pattern. In Figure 14.1, the rise is not steady, but occurs mainly as a jump toward protection, or away from taxation, as a country first joins the ranks of the developed industrial countries. History shows the rise, but not necessarily the same jump. Aside from a temporary jump in agricultural protection and subsidies in the Great Depression of the 1930s, the drift toward protected agriculture was more gradual in the modern history of Japan, North America, and Western Europe than in the global snapshot shown for 1980 in Figure 14.1. It is important to remember that in all cases, the drift was more pronounced than such nominal protection coefficients can show. While the NPCs were rising over the course of economic development, the protection of industry was falling. Thus, governments shifted both toward raising

FIGURE 14.1

*The Net
Protection or
Taxation of
Agricultural
Producers, 249
Cases in 39
Countries, Circa
1980*

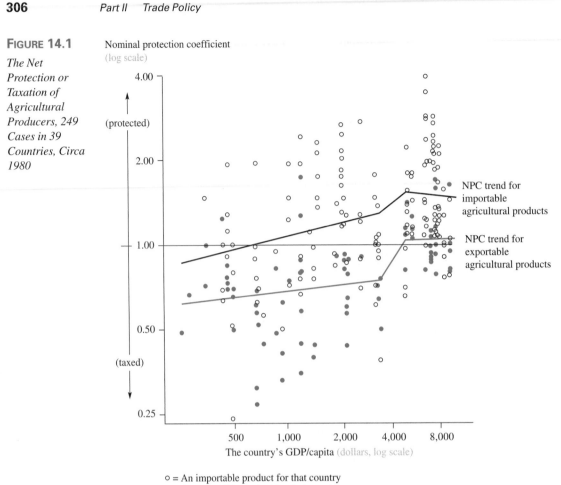

Nominal protection coefficient (log scale)

NPC trend for importable agricultural products

NPC trend for exportable agricultural products

The country's GDP/capita (dollars, log scale)

o = An importable product for that country

● = An exportable product for that country

Source: Binswanger and Scandizzo (1983) and Anderson and Hayami (1986).

agricultural incomes and toward removing policies that raised the farm cost of living and the cost of inputs into farming.

The antitrade bias is evident in the separation of the two trend lines in Figure 14.1. In developing countries, producers of exportables are clearly burdened, mainly through export barriers denying them the world price for their product. Examples of such low NPCs include those between 0.32 and 0.74 for African beverage crops, cotton, and groundnuts, 0.39 for Thai rubber, and 0.64 for Argentine wheat. Producers of importable agricultural products are treated more ambiguously. Some are protected. The NPC is 1.13 for Kenyan wheat, 1.30 for Kenyan rice, and 1.50 for Turkish rice. Others are forced to accept a below-world price (typically as part of a program to subsidize consumers). Among industrial countries, farmers producing for export are given only slight net help from gov-

	Country	1979–1981	1986–1988	1995–1997
FIGURE 14.2				
Agricultural	United States	20	30	15
Subsidies as	Japan	61	73	72
Measured by	European Union	35	48	45
Producer	Canada	25	42	21
Subsidy	Switzerland	63	79	77
Equivalents as	Norway	69	74	71
Percentages of	Australia	9	10	9
Agricultural	New Zealand	16	18	3
Output for				
OECD	Average of 24 OECD countries	37	45	37
Countries,				
1979–1997				

Sources: For 1979–1981, Lipsey and Swedenborg (1996). For 1986–1988 and 1995–1997, Organization for Economic Cooperation and Development, *Agricultural Policies in OECD Countries, 1998* (Paris: OECD, 1998).

ernment. This is one reason why the average NPC is close to one for the naturally agricultural-exporting nations of North America and Australia. By contrast, importable farm products are heavily protected, especially sugar and dairy products, but also beef and grains in the case of the EU and Japan.

The antitrade bias also shows up strongly when we use the more comprehensive producer subsidy equivalent measure instead of the NPCs. Recent PSEs are available for the industrial countries of the OECD. As we see in Figure 14.2, producer subsidies generally increased during the 1980s. These estimates of generally high and rising subsidies were important in the tense multilateral trade negotiations that led to the agreement on agricultural trade as part of the Uruguay Round. The agreement, described in the last section of this chapter, begins to reverse agricultural subsidies and protection. PSEs did decline during the 1990s, though only slightly in some of the countries shown in Figure 14.2.

Figure 14.2 also demonstrates that the heaviest overall subsidies are given to farmers in countries that are destined to be net importers of agricultural products, because they lack the right climate and land endowment: Switzerland, Norway, and Japan. At the other extreme, the governments that least protect farmers' income are the governments of countries that are net exporters of farm products. The least protective are Australia and New Zealand, both heavy net exporters of agricultural products. Not far behind are Canada and the United States. The antitrade pattern seems clear from PSEs as well as from the NPC measures. Farmers in countries that would be large importers with free trade get lots of government assistance; farmers in countries that would be large exporters get modest government assistance.

Tentative Explanations for the Patterns in Agricultural Policy

I don't want to hear about agriculture from anybody but you. . . . Come to think of it, I don't want to hear about it from you either.

President Kennedy to his top agricultural policy adviser

Why do governments intervene in the agricultural sector with policies so different from those applied to other sectors? Why do they drift from taxing agriculture to protecting it, while drifting in the opposite direction for industrial sectors? Why are they harder on farmers producing for export than on those competing against imports? The answers surely depend on history and on political institutions. Yet more can and should be said. The patterns summarized in Figure 14.1 emerge from dozens of countries, some of them democracies and some of them dictatorships. The earlier histories of the leading countries suggest the same patterns. It seems unlikely that a global tendency is just the accidental result of unique events and institutions in separate countries. Broad patterns call for broad explanations. But which ones?

The developmental pattern seems to result from two changes—both illuminated by our simple model of trade policy:

1. The shrinkage of the agricultural sector raises its lobbying efficiency and the sympathy of the nonagricultural population.
2. The agricultural lobby is increasingly mobilized by its rising sensitivity to price movements, movements that government could control.

First, over the course of economic development, agriculture shrinks faster as a share of the labor force and GDP than does any other sector. While no sector would welcome decline for its own sake, a drop in the population earning a living from agriculture has the political advantage of solving some of the problem of organizing a large, diverse group. The more the fortunes of agriculture, good and bad, accrue to fewer farmers and landlords with higher individual stakes, the more effectively they band together to lobby for government support. In addition, the more agriculture declines as a "way of life," the more the nonagricultural population reveres it and feels sympathy for the cause of protecting that way of life. It is odd that people who reject the farm life willingly pay to revere it, but that sentiment is common in industrialized countries, and it seems to have been fed by the sheer magnitude of agriculture's decline.

Second, as the national economy develops, agricultural household incomes become more sensitive to market prices. The clearest reason for this is the fact that the share of their incomes derived from trading with markets goes up. In early settings, say in 17th-century England, farm families consumed up to half their own production. A 10 percent drop in the price of all farm products would lower the farm sector's real income by only 5 percent. In the United States in 1910, the share marketed off the farm had risen to 78 percent. Today it is over 90 percent, so a 10 percent drop in farm product prices would now cut farm real income by more than 9 percent (90 percent of the 10 percent price drop). Although there may be other forces raising farmers' income sensitivity to prices, this one clear force, the rise in farm families' exposure to market prices, suggests that rising sensitivity to price was one source of increasing farmer agitation.

The antitrade bias in the developed countries is explained by these same forces, which often result in high levels of protection against imports. The antitrade bias in developing countries typically includes both taxing exports and taxing imports. The most likely suspect in developing countries is the government's own desire to raise revenues. (Recall the developing government argument for tariffs in Chapter 9.) Taxing agricultural exporters such as Thai rice farmers or Ghanaian cocoa farmers has historically forged a powerful private–public alliance. Private urban interests, say in Bangkok or Accra, approve of using export revenues from agricultural products to pay for investments in modernizing the urban–industrial sector. For government officials the export tax revenues spell budgetary relief.

The Effects of Developed Countries' Agricultural Policies

In developed countries most policies toward agriculture are designed to increase farmers' incomes. In some cases this is accomplished through protection against imports, using tariffs and quotas, with effects that we have presented in Chapters 7 through 9. But in many cases the direct government policy is one of establishing minimum domestic prices for the agricultural products, with the government buying any amounts that farmers cannot sell into the market at the minimum price. When the government establishes a price support for a product, domestic farmers receive at least this minimum price for their product, and domestic consumers must pay at least this minimum price. This sounds like a domestic policy, not a trade policy. But a price support requires that imports be limited (as long as the support price is above the world price for the product, which it almost always is). Otherwise, cheap imports would flood into the country and undermine the price support. And if the country has production available for export, an export subsidy is needed, so that the products can be exported competitively at the lower world price. The Organization for Economic Cooperation and Development estimates that about two-thirds of the government assistance to agriculture in developed countries is through price supports.

The methods of supporting agricultural prices vary across countries and products. A few examples can show the basic features and key effects of price-support policies. The first is straightforward. If the product would be imported with free trade, and the support price is higher than the world price but less than the no-trade price, then the analysis mirrors our previous analysis of import barriers, presented in Chapters 7 and 8. For example, the United States has a policy of supporting sugar prices. In 1997, the sugar price in the United States was about double the world price, forcing U.S. consumers to pay about $1 billion more per year than they would with the world price. Even at this high domestic price, U.S. consumption still exceeds U.S. production. The U.S. government then uses a set of import quotas, one for each foreign country that is permitted to export sugar to the United States, to allow a limited amount of sugar imports into the country while maintaining the high domestic price. Not only does the policy yield the usual effects on consumer surplus, producer surplus, and economic inefficiency, but the allocation of quotas across exporting countries is based more on political considerations (favoring former colonies and current protégés) than on economic efficiency (low-cost production).

The next two examples look at price supports in cases in which the country exports the supported product. First, we examine the effects of a price support for a product that the country would export with free trade and no price support. Then we examine the surprising case in which the price support turns an import-competing product into an export product.

Price Support of an Exportable Product

The basic economics of price supports for an exportable product can be shown with the stylized portrayal of U.S. price supports for wheat in Figure 14.3. Price supports are intended to redistribute income from nonfarmers to farmers. The government mandates a minimum price that exceeds the world price by enough to satisfy society's desire to raise the incomes of farmers. The government buys any excess production that farmers cannot sell at this support price. The government must also enforce import barriers on wheat to keep people from bringing low-world-price wheat into the country.

In Figure 14.3 the support price of $6 a bushel exceeds the world price of $5 a bushel. At the $6 price, domestic consumers buy Q_1 bushels, and domestic farmers grow Q_4 bushels. No wheat can be exported at $6 a bushel (because the world price is only $5 a bushel), so the government must purchase the surplus supply ($Q_4 - Q_1$, equal to EJ). The government's next problem is to decide what to do with the government-held wheat. If it were destroyed, the full amount ($6 \times EJ$) would be lost, and there would be a public outcry about wasting food that somebody needs. To some extent the government tries to give the surplus to needy citizens in a way that keeps it from spilling back onto the market. This is done with partial success through food stamps and other aid-in-kind programs. But there are limits to how much surplus can be disposed of in this way without the recipients' reselling some of it back onto the market, undercutting the intention of keeping prices high.

Government thus turns to the export market and sells the surplus abroad at the lower world price. In Figure 14.3, it is selling EJ of surplus wheat abroad at $5 a bushel. Buying at $6 and selling at $5 means a loss—the government is using an export subsidy to sell its high-priced wheat into foreign markets.[2]

The welfare effects of a price support of an exportable product are predictable. As consumers of expensive wheat and as taxpayers paying to lose a dollar on every bushel of government-purchased wheat, nonfarmers lose twice over while farmers gain, as intended. The nation as a whole loses because (1) consumers are unnecessarily discouraged from buying wheat products (the nation loses triangle AEH) and (2) extra wheat is grown and delivered at a marginal cost of up to $6 when its world-price value is only $5 (the nation loses triangle BCJ).

---

[2]The government could also try to reduce the excess production through acreage and output restriction, perhaps by paying farmers not to plant certain crops on acreage that they had used to grow these crops in previous years. The welfare effects of such a system depend on what else is done with the land. If the acreage is left unused, then this restriction brings a net loss. If less is produced, then there is less to consume. If, instead, the acreage is shifted into growing other crops, then the net effect is less certain, depending on the economic value lost by not growing the supported crop compared to the economic value gained by growing the new crop.

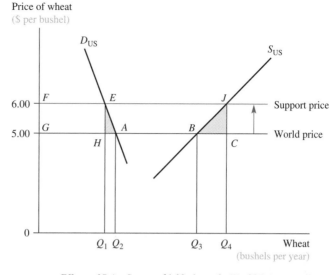

FIGURE 14.3

*Price Support
for an
Exportable
Crop: The Case
of U.S. Wheat*

Effects of Price Support $1.00 above the World Price

On prices and quantities:

Assume no change in world price. Domestic buyers must pay $1 more, and will buy less.

Domestic producers get $1 more, and will produce more. Government pays the high support price for the surplus *EJ* and cuts its losses by exporting the surplus at the world price.

On welfare:

U.S. consumers lose area *AEFG.*

U.S. producers gain area *BJFG.*

U.S. government pays $6 times *EJ,* but resells at $5 times *EJ,* to foreign buyers. It therefore loses $1 times *EJ,* or area *CJEH.*

Total effect: United States as a whole loses the shaded triangles *BCJ* and *AEH.*

As time passes, the social loss *BCJ* will grow because the supply curve will become more elastic. Elastic supply plagues all price-support programs. Farmers respond to the better price with greater and greater supplies, raising the budgetary cost and social loss.

As Figure 14.3 is drawn, the world price is assumed to be fixed, even though more exports are being dumped on the international wheat market. For a small exporter, the diagram's assumption is valid. For a larger exporter, like the United States or Canada, however, dumping more surplus grain into the world market is likely to push down the world price of wheat. Pushing down the world price means a further loss for the United States not shown in Figure 14.3. And other exporters of wheat like Australia suffer a decline in their terms of trade and complain that the U.S. policy is unfairly harming their farmers. On the other side, the lower world price of wheat means a bargain for countries importing wheat. The main beneficiaries of lower world prices are such wheat-importing areas as Russia, Egypt, the OPEC countries, West Africa, and industrial East Asia.

Price Support Creates an Exportable Product

Dramatic effects have occurred in recent experience with what could be called *switch-over goods*—goods that countries convert from importables to exportables by offering very generous price supports to domestic producers. Wheat itself is a switch-over good in the case of the EU. As mentioned at the start of this chapter, its traditional importance as an import has been replaced since the 1970s by EU wheat exports.

An outstanding case of a switch-over good is butter (and other dairy products) in the EU.[3] The effects are similar to those of the U.S. wheat-support program, but with a little more complexity because of the switch from excess domestic demand to excess supply. Figure 14.4 sketches how the EU support for butter prices has worked.

With free trade and no supports, Western European dairy farmers would compete with butter imported from New Zealand and elsewhere at the low world price P_w, as shown in the left panel of Figure 14.4. Imports would equal *AB*. No problem so far.

To give farmers the higher support price P_{EU}, the member governments pool tax funds to buy up the surplus butter represented by *EJ*. The support price has been pushed so far above the world price (sometimes twice it, sometimes four times it) that farmers have raised their butter production enormously, converting the EU into a heavy net exporter of butter, as shown in the right panel of Figure 14.4.

The welfare effects of EU butter supports resemble those of U.S. wheat supports. EU dairy farmers have prospered, gaining extra producer surplus (area *AJFG* in Figure 14.4). EU butter consumers have paid a large part of the bill in lost consumer surplus (area *BEFG*). Taxpayers lose (area *CJEH*) when butter bought at the high EU price is exported at the low world price—an export subsidy.

Again, as with wheat, foreign customers stand to gain from the bargain in butter. Now that the EU has become the world's largest butter exporter, their venting of surpluses is likely to bid down the world price. This brings gains to butter importers, while forcing the EU taxpayers to take an even bigger loss. And other butter exporters like New Zealand complain about their own loss of income because of the lower world price.

Because it is international, the EU's farm-support system has an extra problem beyond those that plague the support programs of the United States or Canada. Which countries will pay the taxes (to cover the lost *CJEH*)? A large part

---

[3]Butter policy is only one part of the EU's Common Agricultural Policy (CAP). The CAP covers a broad range of agricultural products and involves these main policy dimensions:

1. A straightforward customs union for some agricultural products.
2. Price support programs for dairy products, sugar, poultry, other meats, wheat, and wine, like the butter program illustrated in Figure 14.4.
3. A controversial and potentially unstable formula for distributing the net tax burdens of the CAP across member nations.

The CAP represents more than half of total EU fiscal expenditures, and it is estimated to cause inefficiency equal to a loss of about 1 percent of EU GDP.

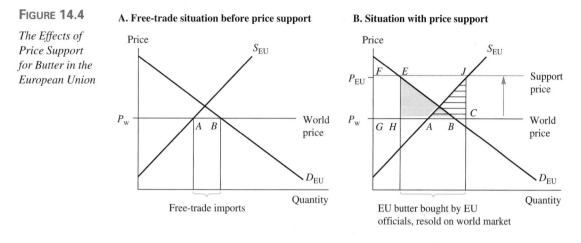

FIGURE 14.4

*The Effects of
Price Support
for Butter in the
European Union*

Official EU price support for butter has been generous enough to move Western Europe beyond self-sufficiency into the net exporting range. Officials buy up surplus butter (*EJ*) at the high support price, and resell it outside the EU so that it cannot be available to EU buyers. The welfare effects are

- EU consumers lose area *BEFG*.
- EU producers gain area *AJFG*.
- EU taxpayers lose *CJEH*.
- EU as a whole loses the overlapping shaded triangles *ACJ* and *BEH*.

of the heavy tax burden is raised through duties on agricultural imports from outside the EU. Part is proportioned to sales of all products through a uniform value-added tax. The tax burden does not end up being nicely proportional to farmers' benefits from country to country. France, with about a quarter of EU output, is the main net gainer from the farm support programs, which give its farmers more than it pays in extra taxes and higher farm-product prices to consumers. Britain has often been the biggest loser since it has only a tiny farm population and must pay the EU duty on its continuing heavy imports of non-EU food. This sort of international redistribution has generated frictions beyond those felt in the usual agricultural policy debates within countries.

The Food Security Issue

Reliable food supplies help to minimize the threat of malnutrition and famine during times of poor harvests. In the name of ensuring reliable supplies, many governments try to encourage domestic food supply with barriers against food imports.

What are the pros and cons of different ways of trying to ensure the best possible food supply? Should countries strive for self-sufficiency, meaning no net food imports? Do they do so in practice? It turns out that raising domestic food supplies up to a self-sufficiency level is not the main farm-policy goal of most governments, even among those paying lip service to that ideal. And it turns out that the goal of food security does not really call for import protection in the first place.

In actual practice, few developing countries protect their domestic food suppliers despite the intellectual popularity of the self-sufficiency goal. Food production, like domestic agriculture in general, tends more often to be taxed and discouraged. As we saw in Figure 14.1, the majority of nominal protection coefficients are less than 1 in developing countries, indicating bias against local production.

Among the industrialized countries, food security also fails to explain the degree and pattern of agricultural protection we observe. Take the case of rice in Japan, supposedly the focus of food security fears exacerbated by World War II. Since 1968, the government of Japan has been disposing of surplus rice beyond what the nation wants to stockpile for emergency reserves. Japan has even been a net exporter of rice for a number of years in the late 1970s and 1980s. In addition, in various years since 1969, the government has been paying farmers to take land out of rice production. Sometimes the intent has been to encourage shifts to other food crops, but sometimes the subsidy allows shifts to nonfood crops and to fallow. Nor is Japanese rice the only case of a glaring departure from food security goals. Canada, the United States, and the EU also subsidize acreage reductions and exports of food crops. EU dairy products, as we have seen, were converted from importables to exportables by generous producer subsidies. While food security rhetoric continues, it is cheap. The types and levels of farm subsidies among the high-income countries reveal that farm income support, not food security, is the driving motive.

There are good economic reasons to doubt that import protection is the right road to food security. Food security does not call for protecting growers. What it calls for is maximizing crisis supply at the lowest cost. The right form of food insurance depends on the type of crisis that is most likely. The four main possibilities are

1. Temporary bad harvests
2. Prolonged bad harvests (e.g., Sahelian drought)
3. Temporary siege or embargo by a hostile power
4. Prolonged siege or embargo by a hostile power

The first two cases are ones in which growing food yields low returns.

Whatever causes the bad harvests is also likely to make subsidies to growers look particularly unpromising relative to the obvious option of stockpiling imported food at noncrisis prices. While the biblical advice of Joseph to the pharaoh is as valuable as ever, protection against imports does little to offset bad harvests. If the concern is hostile interruption of food supplies from other countries, the prescription depends on the likely length of the interruption. If the interruption is not likely to extend beyond the next full crop season or animal-breeding cycle (as in case 3), what the nation must have ready is a stockpile of food, not a stockpile of farmers. Protecting farmers during noncrisis is a

food security policy only for the contingency of a prolonged interruption of import supply (case 4). This case seems least likely for the high-income countries that are doing the protecting. It also requires a strained argument about supply dynamics, claiming that only years of noncrisis subsidy can build up a food-growing capacity to be mobilized in the crisis, and years of stockpile management cannot do the job. While the economics of food supply insurance says that protecting growers against imports could be better than doing nothing in some cases, it is almost never the best food security policy.

The Uruguay Round Agreement on Agriculture

As we noted at the beginning of our discussion, agriculture is another matter. And it has been treated as different in the international trade rules of the WTO and the GATT. In contrast to the international rules for industrial products, governments have been permitted to use quotas and other more esoteric barriers to agricultural imports (like variable tariffs and tariff-quotas in which a low tariff applies to a limited quantity of imports and any more imports incur a higher tariff). And, in contrast to the rules for industrial products, governments have been permitted to use export subsidies.

But things are changing. The agricultural provisions of the Uruguay Round trade agreement signed in 1994 make agriculture less different, especially for the developed countries. Governments are converting all quotas and other nontariff import barriers into tariff rates, a process called "tariffication." Each developed country is reducing its agricultural tariffs (including these new tariffs replacing the NTBs) by an average of 36 percent, with each individual tariff reduced by at least 15 percent. Each developed country is reducing its budget outlays for export subsidies by 36 percent and its volume of subsidized exports by 21 percent. Each developed country must reduce its domestic subsidies to agriculture by 20 percent, with some exceptions. The requirements for developing countries are less stringent.

The effects of these changes are not as large as one might expect. There is little actual liberalization of imports from the tariffication and tariff cuts, except for Japan and other high-income Asian countries. Most developed countries have maintained import protection through artful implementation of the agreement. In many cases the tariff rates that replaced the NTBs were much higher than the tariff equivalent of the NTBs. So even after the tariff cuts, the level of protection is not diminished. In addition, the tariff cuts were not proportional, with lower percentage cuts for products that the government wished to continue protecting. Generally, highly protected products remain highly protected. The reduction of export subsidies is having some impact, particularly in reducing subsidization of exports of wheat, beef, and some dairy products and especially in reducing subsidization of exports by the European Union. The effects of the general reduction in domestic subsidies are moderate, especially because major subsidy programs in the United States and the EU are exempt from the cuts. Of course, other unusual aspects of agricultural trade are not addressed by the Uruguay Round agreement. It has no effect on the bias against agricultural exporters in developing countries, and it has no impact on the use of monopoly governmental export agencies and import buying agencies.

After the Uruguay Round agreement, agriculture is less different. The agreement is forcing some reforms toward more market-oriented and less trade-distorting policies. Even though the actual liberalization is modest, the agreement is important. Tariffication puts import barriers into a form in which they can be compared across countries, and the reduction in subsidies is a step toward less distorted markets. The agreement pulls agriculture toward the mainstream of international trade rules, and it lays the groundwork for future negotiations that may be able to achieve more substantial liberalization.

Summary

Three tasks are undertaken in this chapter: a partial explanation of some economy-wide patterns in trade barriers, a partial explanation of patterns in agricultural policy, and comments on the effects of agricultural policies on trade and welfare.

The political economy of trade barriers explains them (partially) in terms of the gains for the winners from protection, the losses to those hurt by protection, the costs of engaging in political activities like voting, lobbying, and campaign contributions, and the way that the political process works. We can imagine political systems in which protection would be unlikely. If everyone voted directly, the majority would probably vote against a tariff or NTB, because more people are hurt as consumers than are helped as producers of the protected product. Or, if everyone was willing to devote the entire amount that they would gain or lose to political activities like lobbying or campaign contributions, then political representatives would probably oppose protection, because the loss to consumers from protection is larger than the gain to producers. But, in reality, some groups are more effective than others at taking political actions to influence the votes of representatives. Producer groups are often more effective than consumer groups, because the benefits of protection are concentrated in a small group of producers. The benefits are large enough to spur actions by individual producers, and the free-rider problem is more easily solved in a small group. In addition, support for protection often increases when recent reverses for the group hurt by rising imports or declining business generate sympathy among the rest of the population.

Considerations such as these, especially the small-group argument, also help to explain other patterns. The tariff escalation pattern is explained by the group-size effect: A few big firms buying intermediate goods make a stronger lobby against protection of the products they are buying than do masses of final consumers, each of whom has too small an interest to go to battle over consumer-good import policy. The same greater concentration of producer interests into more effective lobbies explains why, in international trade negotiations, each nation treats its own tariff reductions as if they were sacrifices. They are indeed sacrifices for politicians who must answer to small, well-organized import-competing producer groups. And the concessions offered by other countries to reduce their trade barriers mobilize well-organized groups of export producers to support the multilateral agreement.

The long-run trend in agricultural policy, however, is very different. The developmental pattern of agricultural policy is that as a nation becomes more developed, its policy switches from heavily taxing agriculture to heavily subsidizing it. There is also an antitrade pattern: Governments tend to tax exportable-good agriculture and to subsidize (protect) importable-good agriculture. The two patterns together

mean that the greatest departures of agricultural policy from laissez-faire and free trade are the taxing of exportable-good agriculture in developing countries and the protection of importable-good agriculture in industrialized countries.

Two partial explanations for the developmental pattern are that (1) the shrinkage of the agricultural sector raises its lobbying efficiency and the sympathy of the nonagricultural population and (2) the agricultural lobby is increasingly mobilized by its rising sensitivity to price movements, movements that government could control. A partial explanation for the antitrade bias in developing countries is that it serves the government's own demand for extra revenue. Taxing trade can generate revenues, either when imports are taxed (protecting domestic farmers), or when exports are taxed (hurting domestic farmers). In such cases officials can ally, either explicitly or implicitly, with private interests in favor of restricting trade.

In developed countries price supports are a common form of agriculture assistance. The government sets a minimum domestic price that is higher than the world price, limits imports, and may also subsidize exports to sell surplus production into the world market. While farm incomes are raised, the price support harms consumers of agricultural products and creates significant net social costs (inefficiencies).

The goal of providing food security against future harvest failures or hostilities is not well served either by existing policies in developing countries or by the protectionist goal of enforced self-sufficiency. In the spirit of Chapter 9's specificity rule, the key element in ensuring food security is stockpiling for emergencies. For instance, in the face of threats of harvest failure or short-term hostilities, stockpiling of imported food supplies provides food security at reasonable cost. Only in the case of hostilities that would last more years than a nation's storage capacity (but fewer years than it takes to shift people and resources back into a previously unprotected agriculture) would protection against imported food be the preferred policy tool. This is a relatively unlikely case.

As a result of the Uruguay Round trade agreement, agricultural policies are changing, especially in developed countries. Quotas and other nontariff import barriers are being converted to tariffs, and export and domestic subsidies are being reduced. Actual trade liberalization is rather small, but the way is marked for additional multilateral reforms of agricultural policies in the future.

Suggested Reading

Two pioneering theories of political behavior and lobbying biases are Downs (1957) and Olson (1965). Downs deals with tariff examples at some length. Breton (1974) offers similar theories with applications to Canada. Magee, Brock, and Young (1989) take us on an imaginative and sometimes technical tour of political-economic models that might describe the shaping of trade policy.

The vast empirical literature testing many hypotheses about trade-policy pressure groups includes

On Canadian protection: Caves (1976), Helleiner (1977), Saunders (1980), and Cline (1984).

On U.S. protection: Ray (1981), Lavergne (1983), Baldwin and Krueger (1984), Cline (1984), and Ray and Marvel (1984).

On other countries: Baldwin (1984), Cline (1984, Appendix C), and Ray and Marvel (1984).

Comparative international perspective on agricultural policies is offered by the World Bank's *World Development Report* for 1982 and 1986, Anderson and Hayami (1986), Tyers and Anderson (1991), Lindert (1991), and Krueger, Schiff, and Valdes (1992).

Excellent economic analyses of the effects of agricultural policies on international trade appear in McCalla and Josling (1985) and Gardner (1988). Guides to the complexities of the EU's Common Agricultural Policy are found in Bowler (1985) and Moyer and Josling (1990, Chapters 2 to 4 and 9). Hathaway and Ingco (1996) provide a summary and analysis of the agricultural agreement reached during the Uruguay Round.

Questions and Problems

✦ 1. In Chapter 2 we introduced the "one-dollar–one-vote rule." If political decisions in a small country about imposing tariffs were based on this rule, how many tariffs would this country have?

2. What is the free-rider problem, and how does it affect trade policy?

✦ 3. Elected legislative representatives are considering enacting a quota on imports of baseball bats, with the rights to import the quota amount of bats to be given for free to the three companies that currently distribute imported baseball bats. Identify the groups who have a direct interest in whether or not the quota is enacted. How effective do you think each will be in lobbying?

4. What are the major international exports and imports of your home district, province, or state? (Local banks, chambers of commerce, and governments often publish brochures on this subject.) Where do your elected representatives stand on national trade-policy issues?

✦ 5. What is the tariff escalation pattern? Why does it exist in many countries?

6. What is the nominal protection coefficient? What does it measure? What dimension(s) of agricultural policy does it omit?

◆ 7. What is the producer subsidy equivalent (PSE)? What does it measure, and what dimension(s) of agricultural policy does it omit?

8. Describe the general features of agricultural policy that you would expect for each of the following countries. In your answers, refer as appropriate to the developmental pattern and the antitrade bias.

    a. A relatively poor developing country that has a comparative advantage in a small number of agricultural products

    b. A developed country that is poorly endowed with land

◆ 9. Consider the price support for wheat (an exportable agricultural product) shown in Figure 14.3. What are the effects of a decline in the world price of wheat to $4.00 per bushel, assuming that the domestic support price remains at $6.00 per bushel? Show the effects using a graph and explain them.

10. Suppose that Nigeria wants to give wheat and rice farmers higher prices than the world prices, yet wants to make wheat and rice cost domestic millers of flour less than the world price, to keep down the cost of living to consumers.

    a. Describe a policy or set of policies that could do this.

    b. [More difficult.] Try diagramming a grain market subject to such a policy or policies and determining its (their) welfare costs.

PART III

Understanding Foreign Exchange

CHAPTER 15

Payments Among Nations

Throughout Parts I and II we focused on international trade in products. This focus is justified by the need to understand the basis for international trade and the effects of various government policies toward trade. In that discussion countries seemed to exchange exports of goods and services for imports of goods and services. Little attention was given to the monetary and financial aspects of international transactions.

In Parts III and IV we add money and international finance to our discussion. We will recognize (1) that many international transactions are trades in financial assets like bonds, loans, deposits, stocks, and other ownership rights and (2) that nearly all international transactions involve the exchange of money (or some other financial asset) for something else—for a good, service, or a different financial asset.

This chapter examines the framework used to summarize a country's international transactions. The bridge that links all the separate parts of international economics is the **balance of payments,** the set of accounts recording all flows of value between a nation's residents and the residents of the rest of the world during a period of time. Until one is familiar with the balance of payments, it is hard to see what the U.S. government's borrowing abroad has to do with the decision to buy a Sharp hand calculator in a department store, how repaying that foreign debt relates to our sales of aircraft, or how trade events like the purchase of the calculator or the sale of the aircraft could affect the nation's money supply and interest rates. Understanding the balance of payments is also key to understanding how people trade one country's money for that of another country. Even the international flow of humans shows up in the balance of payments, when the migrants make purchases or send money back home. Fortunately, for all the diverse traffic over that bridge, its design is straightforward. We now cross it to widen our view from trade alone to all the exchanges of values between nations, with their many links to macroeconomic concerns like growth, inflation, and unemployment.

Two Sides to Any International Exchange

An exchange between a country and the rest of the world involves two flows of value to be recorded in the balance-of-payments accounts. From that country's point of view each exchange, each transaction, involves two opposite flows of equal value:

A **credit** (+) is a flow for which the country is paid. Exports are an example.

A **debit** (−) is a flow for which the country must pay. Imports are an example.

Any exchange automatically enters the balance-of-payments accounts twice: as a credit (+) and as a debit (−) of the same value. This is just an international application of the fundamental accounting principle of double-entry bookkeeping.

To build a set of accounts showing useful summary information, accountants distinguish between different categories of flows and put the two flows for each transaction into two of the different categories. The main kinds of flows in the balance-of-payments accounts are

Merchandise trade flows (flows of goods)

Service flows

Income flows

Unilateral transfers (gifts)

Private capital (asset) flows

Official asset flows

To show how international transactions affect these six useful categories, let us imagine a set of five illustrative transactions between the United States and the rest of the world in a short time period.

First, suppose that the U.S. government sells $29 million worth of wheat to Russia from its surplus stockpiles, being paid with $29 million in gold by the Russian government. There is an outflow of $29 million worth of wheat, an export of merchandise, for which the United States must be paid. The offsetting inflow is the payment itself, in this case $29 million in gold to the U.S. government. The wheat-for-gold transaction creates these two bookkeeping entries (in millions of dollars):

	Credit (+) ($ million)	Debit (−) ($ million)
Merchandise exports (wheat)	$29	
Increase in official assets (gold)		$29

Note that the payment of gold is a debit item, an inflow of value. It qualifies as a debit because it is something for which the United States must give up something else, namely, wheat.[1] Gold is viewed as an official asset, but wheat is not,

---

[1] In every case, the credit and debit entries have the opposite signs in the accounts of the other country. In Russia's balance of payments, this transaction entails a credit of $29 million for gold exports and a debit of $29 million for wheat imports.

even though the wheat might have been held by government officials. The term *official assets* here refers more strictly to official moneylike assets, an attribute possessed by gold but not by wheat. The moneylike assets such as gold that are generally recognized as official assets are called **official international reserves.**

Consider a second international transaction also involving merchandise trade. Northern Illinois Gas, a U.S. utility company, buys $34 million in natural gas from a Canadian firm. Suppose that it pays for the natural gas by writing a check on its deposits in a New York bank. Two accounting entries are made regarding the U.S. accounts:

	Credit (+) *($ million)*	*Debit (−)* *($ million)*
Merchandise imports (natural gas)		$34
Private capital inflow (bank's deposit liability to a foreign resident)	$34	

The debit entry probably seems easier and more natural than the credit entry in this case. It is clear that importing natural gas is an inflow of something valuable for which the United States must pay. But why should the payment be recorded as a "private capital inflow"? Because the writing of the check placed a bank liability (obligation to pay) into the hands of foreign residents. Before the purchase, the bank owed that bank deposit to Northern Illinois Gas, a resident of the United States. That was a purely domestic matter, not involving the balance of international payments. Once the gas is paid for, however, the New York bank owes an obligation—the right to redeem the checking deposit for cash—to a resident of Canada. This means that the New York bank is borrowing (incurring a new obligation to repay in the future) from Canada, which the bank used to cancel its obligation to somebody in the United States (Northern Illinois Gas). When you borrow, you gain the right to be paid now. In this key respect, borrowing is like an export of goods. It entitles you to be paid now. It is a credit item.

The rules regarding capital flows are:

Capital inflows are credits (+). They take the form of either an increase in a nation's liabilities to foreign residents or a decrease in assets previously obtained from other countries. Each of these is a flow for which the nation must be given payment right now, so each is a credit entry.

Capital outflows are debits (−). They take the form of either an increase in a nation's assets obtained from other countries or a decrease in its liabilities to other countries. Each of these is a flow for which the nation must give up payment right now, so each is a debit entry.[2]

---

[2]*Capital inflow* (or *capital import*) and *capital outflow* (or *capital export*) refer to the directions in which the funds (payments) are flowing (in or out of the country). Capital inflows can also be considered "asset exports" and capital outflows can also be considered "asset imports" if we focus instead on the direction of flows of the financial assets themselves.

A capital outflow arises in the example to which we now turn.

Next, imagine that Brazilian soccer fans spend $6 million as tourists in the United States during a soccer tournament, paying for their hotels, meals, and transportation through New York bank deposits. The two flows are entered in the U.S. accounts as

	Credit (+) ($ million)	Debit (−) ($ million)
Service exports (travel)	$6	
Private capital outflow (reduction in bank's obligations to foreign residents)		$6

Again, one entry fits intuition more easily than the other. It is easy to see that the sales of tourist services to Brazilians are a U.S. export, for which the United States must be paid. And if that is clearly a credit item, it makes sense that the other entry must be a debit item. But why would it be labeled a "private capital outflow"? The answer is because reducing your liability to foreigners is like buying a claim on them, the usual sense of the phrase *capital outflow*. It is a use for which you must pay right now, just like any form of lending. Both repaying your liabilities and lending (buying somebody else's IOUs) are debits.

Our fourth transaction offers a further look at the financial side of the accounts. Suppose that the U.S. Treasury pays $25 million in interest on its past borrowing from Japanese investors, paying with checks on a New York bank. The two accounting entries are

	Credit (+) ($ million)	Debit (−) ($ million)
Income payment (interest paid)		$25
Private capital inflow (increase in bank's obligations to foreign residents)	$25	

The payment of interest to Japanese owners of U.S. government bonds is a payment of income to foreign residents, so this is a debit. The means of payment is a credit. Why is this credit counted as a "private capital inflow"? The private New York bank on which the U.S. government wrote the checks now has a new liability to residents of Japan. It is borrowing anew from foreigners. The bank uses the borrowing from foreigners to cancel an equal checking-account obligation to the U.S. government, which has less claim on the private bank now that it has written checks.

So far, we can see that every transaction has two equal sides. If we add up all the credits as pluses and all the debits as minuses, the net result is zero. That is, the total credits must always equal the total debits. That is correct. To see just how correct it is, though, let us turn to a case that might look like a violation of this accounting balance.

Our fifth hypothetical transaction involves giving something away. Suppose that the U.S. government simply gives $8 million in foreign aid to the government of Egypt in the form of wheat from U.S. government stockpiles. This case differs from our earlier example of the sale of wheat to Russia because Egypt is not paying, with gold or checks or anything else. The correct way to record the credit and debit flows is as follows:

	Credit (+) ($ million)	Debit (–) ($ million)
Merchandise export (wheat)	$8	
Unilateral transfer to Egypt		$8

The $8 million credit is straightforward since this is just another merchandise export, for which the United States must be paid. The accountants get around the fact that the United States was *not* paid by Egypt by inventing a debit item for the unilateral transfer (gift) to Egypt. They invent the fiction that the United States received $8 million in goodwill—or gratitude—from Egypt for its gift of wheat. That goodwill is something received, a debit, for which the United States pays in wheat. In this way, even a one-way flow is transformed by accounting fiction into a two-way flow, preserving the all-in zero balance of double-entry bookkeeping.

Putting the Accounts Together

To arrange the credit and debit flows from separate transactions into a useful summary set of accounts, group them according to the six types of flows. Figure 15.1 does this for our simplified set of five transactions. In this set of transactions, the United States was a slight net exporter of merchandise (exporting $37 million of wheat and importing $34 million of natural gas). It was a net exporter of services (its sales of travel services to the Brazilian soccer fans). For all goods and services together, the United States was a net exporter by $9 million, which is a surplus in the **goods and services balance** of $9 million. It made net payments of income to foreigners (its interest payments to Japan). For all goods, services, and income together, the United States had a deficit in its **goods, services, and income balance** of $16 million. In addition, the nation gave away $8 million in unilateral transfers to Egypt, so there were $24 million that had to be paid for (or financed) somehow.

The net flow of currently used goods, services, income, and gifts is the **current account balance.** If this is positive (a surplus), the nation earns that much in extra assets or reduced liabilities in its dealings with other countries. If it is negative (a deficit), the country must pay by giving up assets or increasing its liabilities. In the

FIGURE 15.1   *A Simple Balance-of-Payments Account for the United States, Resulting from Only Five*
Transactions ($ millions)

Flows and Balances	Credits (+)	Debits (−)	Credits Minus Debits = Net Surplus (+) or Deficit (−)
Merchandise trade flows	$(29 + 8 =) 37	$34	$ 3
Service flows	6		6
Income flows		25	−25
Unilateral transfers (gifts)		8	−8
Private capital flows	(34 + 25 =) 59	6	53
Official asset flows		29	−29
Grand balance of credits minus debits:			0

Six Key Balances

Merchandise trade (goods) balance	3
Goods and services balance	9
Goods, services, and income balance	−16
Current account balance (goods, services, income, gifts)	−24
Net private capital flows	53
Overall balance (current account + private capital flows)	29

simple case of Figure 15.1, the United States has a current account deficit of $24 million. It paid for this by incurring greater debts to foreigners. In this case, its extra debts took the form of extra private-bank deposit liabilities to foreigners, worth $53 million, minus a buildup of $29 million in official gold reserves acquired from Russia, or net new liabilities of $24 million covering the $24 million deficit for goods, services, income, and gifts.

The simple view of Figure 15.1 shows us a skeletal balance of payments with the main categories in clear view: goods flows, service flows, income payments, gifts, private capital flows, and official asset flows. Now that we understand the main categories, let us take a closer look at the varieties of entries that actually go into those categories. Figure 15.2 gives some extra detail, using the actual balance-of-payments accounts of the United States for 1997.

At the top of the accounts, there is little detail to add. Merchandise exports and imports are easy to understand. The only wrinkle is that some of them go unrecorded, due to smuggling, negligence, or national secrecy (such as hiding some military sales and gifts from the U.S. balance of payments).

Services take a miscellany of forms. In the simple example above, we only considered travel services. In addition to travel or tourism services, nations trade transportation, insurance, education, financial, technical, telecommunications, and other business and professional services. Nations also pay each other royalties for use of technologies or brand names. The net balance of trade in goods and services (line 24) is often called the *trade balance,* although this

FIGURE 15.2

*U.S. Balance-
of-Payments
Account, 1997
($ billions)*

		Credit (+)	*Debit (−)*
1.	**Exports of goods and services and income received**	**$1,179**	
2.	Merchandise exports	679	
3.	Service exports (travel, business services, etc.)	258	
4.	Income receipts from foreigners	242	
5.	**Imports of goods and services and income paid**		**−1,295**
6.	Merchandise imports		−877
7.	Services imports (travel, business services, etc.)		−171
8.	Income payments to foreigners		−247
9.	**Unilateral transfers, net**		**−39**
10.	U.S. government transfers to foreigners		−16
11.	Private remittances and other transfers		−23
12.	**Changes in U.S. holdings of foreign assets (excluding official international reserves), net**		**−478**
13.	U.S. direct investments abroad		−122
14.	Other U.S. investments abroad		−356
15.	**Changes in foreign holdings of U.S. assets (excluding official international reserves), net**	**718**	
16.	Foreign direct investments in the U.S.	93	
17.	Other foreign investments in the U.S.	625	
18.	**Changes in holdings of official international reserves, net**	**15**	
19.	Foreign official holdings of U.S. assets	16	
20.	U.S. holdings of official reserve assets		−1
21.	**Statistical discrepancy**		**−100**
22.	Net balance of credits minus debits	0	
	Six Key Balances		
23.	Merchandise trade balance (lines 2 and 6)		−198
24.	Goods and services balance (lines 2, 3, 6, and 7)		−110
25.	Goods, services, and income balance (lines 1 and 5)		−116
26.	Current account balance (lines 1, 5, and 9)		−155
27.	Net private capital flows and statistical discrepancy*	140	
28.	Overall balance (lines 26 and 27, or the negative of line 18)		−15

In the source, lines 12 and 20 are included in the category "U.S. assets abroad, net," and lines 15 and 19 are included in the category "Foreign assets in the United States, net."

*Lines 12, 15, and 21.

Source: U.S. Bureau of Economic Analysis, *Survey of Current Business,* July 1998, p. 69.

somewhat imprecise term also sometimes refers to the merchandise trade balance (line 23).[3]

Income flows are mainly payments to holders of foreign financial assets. In addition to interest, these payments include dividends and other claims on profits by the owners of foreign businesses. Income flows also include payments to foreign

---

[3]Prior to January 1994, the merchandise trade balance received considerable attention in the United States because it was the only information about the U.S. balance of payments reported monthly. The United States now reports the goods and services balance monthly. This provides monthly information that is meaningful for most economic analyses. Nonetheless, there is considerable noise or variation in these data, so be careful when interpreting month-to-month changes.

workers who are only in the country for a short time, such as the honorarium paid to a U.S. professor for giving a talk at a Canadian university.[4]

Unilateral (or unrequited) transfers also take a variety of forms. There are official government grants in aid to foreigners, as in the simple example of a U.S. grant of wheat to Egypt. Private individuals also make unilateral transfers. Historically, the largest kind of private transfer is international migrants' remittances of money and goods back to their families in the home country. Another kind of private aid is charitable giving, such as international famine relief.

The net flows of financial assets and similar claims (excluding official asset flows) is the private **capital account balance.**[5] The values reported in this account are for the principal amounts only of assets traded—any flows of earnings on foreign assets are reported in the current account.[6] Some varieties of private capital flows call for special comment here and in Part V. **Direct investments** are defined as any flow of lending to, or purchases of ownership in, a foreign enterprise that is largely owned by residents of the investing country. Chapter 27 offers a more detailed definition. Foreign investments that are not direct include international flows of securities, loans, and bank deposits. The securities are bonds and stocks. An investment in a bond or a stock that is not a direct investment is sometimes called a *portfolio investment,* indicating that the investor's home country does not own a large share of the enterprise being invested in, but is just investing as part of a diversified portfolio.

The distinction between private capital flows and official capital flows is not quite the same as the distinction between private and government. The term *official* in Lines 18 through 20 refers to official reserve assets held by *monetary*-type officials, not all government. Other ("nonofficial") government assets are included in the private category. The purpose of that distinction is to focus on the monetary task of regulating currency values, to which we return in discussing the overall surplus or deficit.

Early in this century gold was the major official reserve asset. While gold is still held as a reserve asset, it is now little used in official reserve transactions. The majority of countries' official reserve assets are now foreign exchange assets, financial assets denominated in a foreign currency that is readily acceptable in international transactions. For the United States, these foreign exchange assets feature euro (formerly German mark) and Japanese yen assets. For other countries

---

[4]We are following current practice in showing regular service flows and income flows as separate categories in the balance of payments. In some other presentations (including previous editions of this book), these two categories are combined into a single category, service flows, defined broadly. Payments of interest and dividends can be considered payments for the services of using someone else's money (or capital) for a period of time. Similarly, wages and salaries are payments for the services of the workers.

[5]The IMF in its publications now uses the name "financial account" for what we call the "capital account." (But, confusingly, the IMF has a separate item called "capital account" that is mostly capital transfers that are included in our "unilateral transfers.")

[6]Note that each asset or liability category is defined as an increase in that asset or liability. Decreases in one or the other will have the opposite sign. Thus, for example, Mexican repayment of principal on a U.S. bank loan would reduce the bank (asset) claims of the United States against foreigners, bringing a credit entry (a capital inflow) on line 14 in Figure 15.2. Another example: U.S. repayment of principal on a Treasury bond held by investors in Japan would bring a debit entry (a capital outflow) on line 17.

these foreign exchange assets are often U.S. dollar assets. Two other small categories of official reserve assets are certain claims that a country has on the International Monetary Fund (IMF), especially its reserve position in the Fund, and the country's holdings of Special Drawings Rights (SDRs), a reserve asset created by the Fund.

At the bottom of the accounts comes the suspicious item, statistical discrepancy. If the flows on the two sides of every transaction are correctly recorded, there should not be any statistical discrepancy at all. Line 21 in Figure 15.2 should be zero. In fact, it is a debit of $100 billion, meaning that the debit items for the United States are less fully measured than its credit items. The accountants add the statistical discrepancy to make the accounts balance and to warn us that something was missed. In fact, the statistical discrepancy may understate what was missed. It is the net result of errors and omissions on both the credit and debit sides. In truth, more than $100 billion of debits were missed, but some were offset by failure to count all the credits.

How do the measurement errors arise? Which items appear to be most seriously undermeasured? It is hard to know just by looking at one nation's accounts. We get good clues, however, by adding up all the balance-of-payments accounts in the world. These should balance, but they do not. For the world as a whole, there is a tendency to underreport merchandise imports, income receipts (especially investment incomes), and capital exports. (See the following box, "Planet Earth's Balance of Payments.") The main difficulty is probably that many people succeed in hiding their imports, their foreign investment incomes, and their capital flight from their own government officials.

The Macro Meaning of the Current Account Balance

The current account balance has several meanings. To discuss these, let's consider a country that has a current account surplus. The first meaning of a surplus on goods, services, income, and gifts has already been introduced. When all these flows for current uses have been netted out, what is left is the increase in all of the foreign financial assets minus all of the country's foreign financial liabilities. The reason is straightforward. The only (nonhuman) things being exchanged between nations are goods, services, income, gifts, and financial assets. If all credits must equal all debits, then the surplus on goods, services, income, and gifts—that is, the current account surplus—must equal **net foreign investment,** the net accumulation of foreign assets minus foreign liabilities.

The fact that the current account (CA) surplus equals net foreign investment (I_f) links it to national saving, investment, and income. A nation that has net foreign investment ($I_f > 0$) is a nation that is investing part of its national saving (S) abroad instead of in domestic capital formation (I_d). So the value of *national saving equals domestic investment plus foreign investment: $S = I_d + I_f$.*

The net foreign investment, or $I_f = S - I_d$, also equals something else. It is the amount by which all national income or domestic product (Y) exceeds what the nation is spending for all purposes including domestic capital formation. These

Planet Earth's Balance of Payments

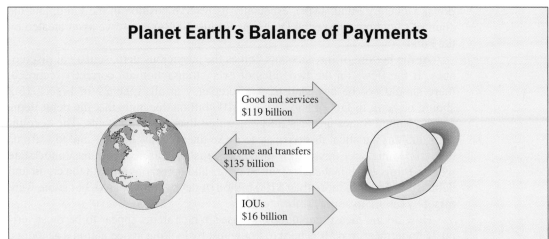

Planet Earth has been trading heavily with the rest of the galaxy for years. Since the early 1980s and perhaps earlier, we have been exporting billions of dollars of goods and services into space, for which we are entitled to payment. But we have been sending even bigger amounts of income payments and transfers to space. To cover our current account deficit, we have been sending out IOUs (promises to repay somebody out there in space). In 1997, for example, we exported $119 billion in goods and services, made income and transfer payments of $135 billion, and sent out $16 billion in promises to repay. How long can this continue?

You may feel that something is wrong with the basic facts here. Yet these flows are consistent with all the world's official balance-of-payments statistics. If you add up the current account flows of every country in 1997, you will find that $116 billion of merchandise imports, $3 billion of services imports, $100 billion of income receipts, and $35 billion of transfers received are unaccounted for. How could that happen? We cannot rule out the possibility that the missing flows went to the rest of the galaxy, as suggested. A more likely explanation, however, is that there are systematic patterns of misreporting international flows right here on Earth. The $116 billion of lost merchandise imports are probably imports

that went unreported because of smuggling or other incentives to underreport. (Drug traffic is probably not the reason, since drug trade is unreported on both the export and the import sides.) The $100 billion in lost income receipts is probably income on foreign investments, hidden to avoid taxes and regulation. A related problem arises in the world's capital account, in which the world appears to be a recipient of capital inflows from the rest of the galaxy. This most probably represents unreported "capital flight," the secret sending of wealth to foreign countries, away from the supervision of one's home government. Separate estimates suggest that unreported capital flight is particularly severe from developing nations, especially Latin America.

How serious are errors of this magnitude? The world's missing net current account surplus has usually been about 2 percent of the value of world exports of goods, services, and income since the early 1980s. By itself, that is an acceptable rate of error. However, it is just a *net* error, the result of offsetting errors in both directions.

Sources: IMF, *Balance of Payments Yearbook, 1998,* Parts 2 and 3, and IMF, *International Financial Statistics Yearbook* 1998.

total expenditures (E) are expenditures for private consumption of home plus foreign goods and services (C), plus government purchases of goods and services (G), plus investment purchases of capital goods (I_d again). You can see the link between this total national expenditure and domestic product by remembering a domestic product identity from introductory courses:

Domestic product = all purchases of our domestic product

$$Y = C + I_d + G + X - M$$

This implies that domestic product (Y) differs from national expenditure ($E = C + I_d + G$) by the amount of the current account balance, or the difference between exports and imports of goods and services,[7] $X - M$:

$$Y - E = X - M$$

So the current account surplus in the balance of payments turns out to equal three other things:

Current account surplus	$CA = X - M$
= Net foreign investment	$= I_f$
= National saving not invested at home	$= S - I_d$
= Difference between domestic product and national expenditure	$= Y - E$

The same identities apply to a country with a deficit in its current account—all expressions are negative in value. The current account deficit ($M > X$) is financed by foreign borrowing (negative net foreign investment I_f). The deficit also represents an excess of domestic capital investment over national saving ($I_d > S$) and an excess of national expenditure over domestic product ($E > Y$).

These identities help us see what must be changed if the current account balance is to be changed. For instance, consider a country that seeks to reduce its current account deficit (that is, increase the value of its current account balance, making it less negative). An improvement in the country's current account balance must be accompanied by an increase in the value of domestic product (Y) relative to the value of national expenditure (E). If domestic production cannot expand much, then national spending must fall in order to decrease imports or to permit more local production to be exported.

The identities also help us to understand what forces might be causing changes in the current account balance. To see some uses for the current account, let's look at how it has behaved since the early 1960s for the four countries in Figure 15.3. Figure 15.3 shows both the country's current account balance and its net exports of goods and services—its goods and services balance—each as a share of the country's gross domestic product. The two measures differ by the country's net income flows and transfers. (It is good to look at these latter two

---

[7]In equating $X - M$, exports minus imports of goods and services, with the current account balance, we are ignoring income flows and unilateral transfers. This is one of several simplifications generally used in macroeconomic analysis. (Another is equating domestic product with national income.)

FIGURE 15.3

*Current Account
Balances and
Goods and
Services
Balances for the
United States,
Canada, Japan,
and Mexico,
1963–1997*

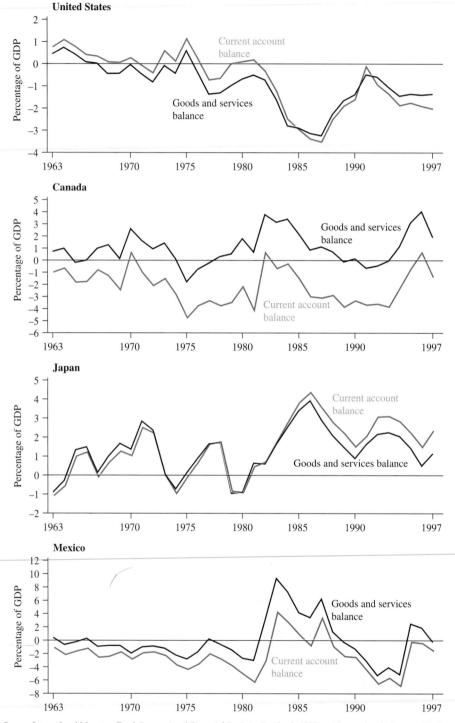

Source: International Monetary Fund, *International Financial Statistics Yearbook, 1998;* and International Monetary Fund,
International Financial Statistics, January 1999.

items here, especially income flows, although we usually ignore them in broad macroeconomic analysis.)

The first panel in Figure 15.3 shows that the United States has evolved from a net exporter and lender after World War II to a borrower. Up through the 1960s, the United States had a positive current account balance and a positive trade balance. The United States was a net exporter and lender largely because Europe and Japan, still recovering from World War II, badly needed American goods and loans (and foreign aid under the Marshall Plan). During the 1970s and up through 1981, a new pattern began to emerge. The United States became a net importer of goods and services, but still kept its current account approximately in balance, thanks largely to interest and profit earnings on previous foreign investments. After 1982, the United States shifted into dramatic trade and current account deficits, becoming the world's largest borrower. The underlying reason: Led by new federal government deficits, the United States cut its rate of national saving (S/Y) much faster than its domestic investment (I_d/Y) and therefore borrowed heavily from Japan and other countries (negative I_f/Y = negative CA/Y). In the late 1980s and early 1990s, the trade and current account deficits then decreased as a percentage of GDP, but deficits continued into the late 1990s. (The current account deficit for 1991 was unusually low because of transfer payments from the allied countries to the United States related to Operation Desert Storm against Iraq.)

Canadian experience fits a classic pattern of a borrowing country with good growth potential. Most of the time Canada has borrowed capital from other countries (especially from the United States), as shown by Canada's current account deficits for most years. Canada has used its goods and services surplus to pay foreign investors some of the earnings on their earlier investments. The payment of interest and profits on past borrowings is much of the gap between the goods and services surplus and the current account deficit in Figure 15.3.

Japan's goods and services balance and current account balance were nearly the same until the mid-1980s. These typically have been in surplus since the early 1960s. The surpluses became large and controversial in the 1980s, as Japanese goods gained major shares of foreign markets. Of course, the other way to look at this is that Japan's net foreign investment (I_f = CA > 0) became large in the mid-1980s. In those years Japanese foreign investment, including heavy lending to the United States, became the dominant force in international finance (although its role then diminished in the 1990s). Behind this shift to net foreign lending in the early and mid-1980s lay a widening gap between Japan's outstanding national savings and its domestic capital formation. (Again, $I_f = S - I_d$.) In addition, the income from Japan's holdings of foreign assets has created a positive gap between the current account balance and the goods and services balance since the mid-1980s.

Until the debt crisis of 1982, Mexico was a consistent borrower. Its current account was in deficit (negative I_f), and net payments of interest and dividends to foreign creditors showed up as a widening gap between the goods and services balance and the current account balance. Figure 15.3 shows part of the tremendous shock Mexico felt when its debt crisis hit in 1982. Its trade balance jumped to a surplus of more than 9 percent of GDP in 1983, not because exports grew (they did not) but because it had to cut out two-thirds of its imports in the belt tightening necessary to meet most of its swollen interest and repay principal to foreign creditors. Between 1983 and 1987, Mexico was actually a net "investor," in that it reduced its net foreign liabilities by running current account surpluses. From 1988 to 1994, Mexico returned to being a net foreign borrower (CA < 0). The peso crisis of late 1994 again forced Mexico into a radical readjustment of its current account, with a shift to a goods and services surplus in 1995 and 1996 and almost no net foreign borrowing (CA about equal to zero) during those years.

The Macro Meaning of the Overall Balance

The overall balance should indicate whether a country's balance of payments has achieved an overall pattern that is sustainable over time. Unfortunately, there is no one indicator that represents overall balance perfectly. The indicator often used is based on the division of net foreign investment (or borrowing), I_f, into two components: the balance on net private (or nonofficial) capital flows (KA) and flows of official reserve assets (OR). The **official settlements balance** (B) measures the sum of the current account balance plus the private capital account balance,[8]

$$B = CA + KA$$

Because all items in the balance of payments must sum to zero, any imbalance in the official settlements balance must be financed (or paid for) through official reserves flows:

$$B + OR = 0$$

If the overall balance B is in surplus, it equals an accumulation of the country's official reserve assets or a decrease in foreign official reserve holdings of the country's assets (that is, a debit in the remaining official reserve items in the account). If the overall balance is in deficit, it equals a decrease in the country's holdings of official reserve assets or an accumulation of foreign official reserve holdings of the country's assets (that is, a credit in the remaining items in the accounts). In some situations such changes in official reserve holdings can be specifically desired by the monetary authorities (for instance, gradually to increase the country's holdings of official reserve assets). In other situations these changes are not specifically desired and indicate an overall imbalance.

The official settlements balance measures the net flows of all private transactions in goods, services, income, transfers, and (nonofficial) financial assets. However, it is the counterbalancing items—the changes in official reserve holdings—that show the macroeconomic meaning of the official settlements balance. Most of the transactions by countries' monetary authorities that result in changes in official reserve holdings are official intervention by these authorities in the foreign exchange markets. The monetary authorities enter the foreign exchange

---

[8]The official settlements balance also includes the statistical discrepancy, because we assume that the discrepancy results from mismeasurement of private transactions.

markets to buy and sell currencies, usually exchanging domestic currency and some foreign currency. For instance, the monetary authority of a country can buy domestic currency and sell foreign currency. The selling reduces the authority's holdings of foreign exchange assets that count as official international reserves. Or the authority can sell domestic currency and buy foreign currency. The buying adds to its official international reserves.

We can see some of these relationships by returning to the U.S. balance of payments for 1997 in Figure 15.2. Foreign monetary authorities increased their official reserve holdings of U.S. dollar assets by $16 billion, mostly by intervening in foreign exchange markets to buy dollars. Their willingness to acquire dollars and dollar assets provided essentially all of the financing for the United States to run its official settlements balance deficit of $15 billion. This can also be viewed as providing part of the financing for the U.S. current account deficit of $155 billion.

As we will see in the chapters that follow in Parts III and IV, changes in official international reserves resulting from foreign exchange intervention can have impacts on many other economic variables. This activity can affect exchange rates, money supplies, interest rates, private international financial capital flows, domestic capital formation, domestic product, and exports and imports of goods and services.

The International Investment Position

Complementing the balance of payments accounts is a balance sheet called the **international investment position,** a statement of the stocks of a nation's international assets and foreign liabilities at a point in time, usually the end of a year. The change in the international investment position is closely related to the current account balance. Any imbalance in the current account contributes to the change in the nation's net foreign assets during a time period.[9] The link between the two kinds of accounts relates to a subtle but common semantic distinction. We say that a nation is a *lender* or a *borrower* depending on whether its current account is in surplus or deficit during a time period. We say that a nation is a *creditor* or *debtor* depending on whether its net stock of foreign assets is positive or negative. The first refers to flows over time, and the second to stocks (or holdings) at a point in time.

Within the 20th century, the United States has come full circle in its international investment position. As shown in Figure 15.4, the nation was a net debtor before World War I. World War I suddenly transformed the United States into the world's leading creditor, a role the country played reluctantly for the next 20 years. Over several decades after 1945, the United States was increasingly a creditor in nominal dollar terms, though not as a share of GDP, reaching a peak nominal creditor position by the end of 1983. However, the large current account deficits that the United States experienced during the 1980s required financing through increased international borrowing. The creditor position built up over 60 years was erased and reversed in the

---

[9]Changes in the market values of assets previously acquired can also change the international investment position.

FIGURE 15.4   *U.S. International Investment Position at the End of Selected Years, 1897–1997 ($ billions)*

	1897	*1914*	*1930*	*1946*	*1960*	*1982*	*1997*
U.S. investments abroad	$1.3	$5.0	$21.5	$39.4	$85.6	$958.8	$5,007.1
Private	0.7	3.5	17.2	13.5	49.3	740.7	4,790.8
Direct investments*	0.6	2.6	8.0	7.2	31.9	226.6	1,793.7
Other	0.1	0.9	9.2	6.3	17.4	514.1	2,997.1
U.S. government (nonofficial)	0.0	—	—	5.2	16.9	74.7	81.5
U.S. official reserve assets†	0.6	1.5	4.3	20.7	19.4	143.4	134.8
Foreign investments in the United States	3.4	7.2	8.4	15.9	40.9	693.8	6,329.6
Direct investments*	—	1.3	1.4	2.5	6.9	130.4	1,620.5
Other	3.4	5.9	7.0	13.4	34.0	563.4	4,709.1
U.S. net international investment position	−2.1	−2.2	13.1	23.5	44.7	265.0	−1,322.5

*Direct investment refers to any international investment in a foreign enterprise owned in large part by the investor's home country. For 1982 and subsequent years, these investments are reported at estimated market values. For previous years, they are reported at historic cost.

†U.S. official reserve assets consist of gold and foreign exchange assets plus the reserve position at the IMF and Special Drawing Rights. For 1982 and subsequent years, reserve gold is reported at market values.

Sources: U.S..Bureau of the Census, *Historical Statistics of the United States: Colonial Times to 1970* (Washington, DC: U.S. Government Printing Office, 1976); and U.S. Bureau of Economic Analysis, *Survey of Current Business,* June 1994 and December 1998.

next 6 years.[10] By early 1989, the United States again became a net debtor, and the indebtedness kept rising into the 1990s. Figure 15.4 dramatizes the change with the stark contrast in the net positions at the end of 1982 and the end of 1997. The United States used to lend on long term and borrow on short term, acting as a world banker and making a large net interest income off the fact that it lent at higher interest (and dividend and profit) rates than it borrowed. That has all changed. Even direct foreign investment, long an American specialty, is now nearly balanced in the U.S. accounts.

---

[10]The data cited here use market or current values for all items. If, instead, some items, especially direct investments, are valued at historic cost and reserve gold is valued at its artificially low "official" price, then the United States appeared to become a net debtor at the beginning of 1985. In the 1980s, the United States shifted to reporting data that use market or current values.

Summary

Basic definitions abound in this chapter. Terms introduced here appear constantly in the news media, and they will reappear throughout this book. Definitely review any of them that are not familiar at first sight.

A country's **balance of payments** is a systematic account of all the exchanges of value between residents of that country and the rest of the world during a given time period. Two flows occur in any exchange, or transaction, according to double-entry bookkeeping:

A **credit** (+) is a flow for which the country is paid.

A **debit** (−) is a flow for which the country must pay.

Flows from international transactions are grouped into six flow categories. Each category contains flows of more detailed types whose definitions also should be learned. The six flow categories, with some important subcategories, are

1. **Merchandise trade** flows (i.e., goods flows).
2. **Service flows,** including such services as travel, transportation, and insurance.
3. **Income flows,** especially earnings of interest, dividends, and profits.
4. **Unilateral transfers,** including government foreign aid grants and private gifts and remittances.
5. **Private capital flows,** including direct foreign investments, portfolio investments in securities, changes in bank deposits, changes in other financial claims, and statistical discrepancy.
6. **Official asset flows,** including changes in official gold and foreign exchange assets, changes in other official reserve assets related to the IMF, and changes in liabilities that foreign countries consider to be their official reserve assets.

To highlight what is happening to wealth and reserves and currency markets, flow categories are summed into six net balances, each defined so that a surplus is positive and a deficit is negative:

1. The **merchandise trade balance** equals the net credits minus debits, or net exports, on merchandise flows. This is one meaning of the term *trade balance.*
2. The **goods and services balance** equals the net exports of both goods and services. It is a more meaningful definition of a trade balance.
3. The **goods, services, and income balance** adds net income flows to the goods and services balance.
4. The **current account balance** equals the net credits minus debits on the flows of goods, services, income, and unilateral transfers. It also equals the change in the nation's foreign assets minus foreign liabilities, also known as **net foreign investment.**
5. The net private **capital account balance** equals net credits minus debits involving changes in private national residents'

foreign financial assets and liabilities. This balance is in surplus if the nation is a net private *borrower,* or *capital importer,* or in deficit if it is a net lender, or *capital exporter,* accumulating more foreign assets than liabilities.

6. The **overall balance** (or **official settlements balance**) equals the sum of the current account balance plus the private capital account balance. If it is in surplus, it is counterbalanced by an accumulation of official net assets (a debit item at the bottom of the accounts). If it is in deficit, it is counterbalanced by an accumulation of official net liabilities (a credit item at the bottom of the accounts).

The current account balance has special macroeconomic meaning. As net foreign investments (I_f) it equals the part of national saving (S) that is not used in domestic capital formation (I_d). That is, it fits into the basic identity that saving equals investment: $S = I_d + I_f$. A nation that is running a current account deficit, like the United States since 1982, is a nation that is saving less than its domestic capital formation, so that the current account deficit represents its net foreign borrowing. The current account deficit also equals the excess of current national expenditures (E, expenditure on consumption, domestic capital formation, and government goods and services) over current domestic production of goods and services (Y). Viewed another way, a net current account deficit represents intertemporal trade, with the nation importing more goods and services (and gratitude for any gifts) for current use and promising to repay with net exports of goods and services (and gratitude for any gifts) in the future. Japan, by contrast, has run large current account surpluses, accumulating claims to future goods and services (and gratitude).

The overall balance is intended to indicate whether the overall pattern of the country's balance of payments has achieved a sustainable equilibrium. The official settlements balance does not quite match this concept, but it is still useful in macroeconomic analysis. It indicates the extent of official intervention in the foreign exchange markets—the buying and selling of currencies by the monetary authorities. As we will see in subsequent chapters, such intervention can have effects on exchange rates, money supplies, and many other macroeconomic variables.

A nation's **international investment position** shows its stocks of international assets and liabilities at a moment of time. These stocks are changed each year by the flows of private and official assets measured in the balance of payments. As a result of large current account deficits since the early 1980s, the United States switched from being the world's largest net creditor to being its largest net debtor.

Suggested Reading

The balance-of-payments accounts of most nations are summarized in the IMF's *International Financial Statistics* and also in its *Balance of Payments Yearbook.* More detailed accounts for the United States appear regularly in the *Survey of Current Business,* and those for Canada are in the *Canada Yearbook.*

Questions and Problems

✦1. What is the current account balance of a nation with a government budget deficit of $128 billion, private saving of $806 billion, and domestic capital formation of $777 billion?

2. "A country is better off running a current account surplus rather than a current account deficit." Do you agree or disagree? Explain.

✦3. "National saving can be used domestically or internationally." Explain the basis for this statement, including the benefits to the nation of each use of its saving.

4. "Consider a country whose assets are not held by other countries as official international reserves. If this country has a surplus in its official settlements balance, then the monetary authority of the country is decreasing its holdings of official reserve assets." Do you agree or disagree? Explain.

✦5. Which of the following transactions would contribute to a U.S. current account surplus on the balance of payments?

a. Boeing barters a $100 million plane to Mexico in exchange for $100 million worth of hotel services on the Mexican coast.

b. The United States borrows $100 million long term from Saudi Arabia to buy $100 million of Saudi oil this year.

c. The United States sells a $100 million jet to Turkey for $100 million in bank deposits.

d. The U.S. government makes a gift of $100 million to the government of Greece, in the form of New York bank deposits, to pay for injuries caused by Turkish jet attacks.

e. The German central bank buys $100 million in U.S.-dollar bank deposits from a New York bank, paying by providing DM (deutsche mark) bank deposits to the New York bank.

6. Which of the transactions in question 5 contribute to a U.S. deficit in the overall (official settlements) balance?

✦ 7. Using the line numbers in Figure 15.2, decide which lines should contain the credit and debit items for each of the following transactions from the point of view of the United States:

  a. Pepsico signs an agreement with Russia bartering Pepsico's managerial services and trademarks in making Pepsi Cola in Russia for an equivalent dollar value of Stolichnaya vodka and Soviet merchant ships.

  b. Citibank of New York lends the government of Brazil $184 million in a new loan so that Brazil simultaneously pays Citibank $184 million in interest on an old loan.

  c. The city of Kyoto, Japan, pays Americans $3 billion in Kyoto city bonds (IOUs) to buy the Dallas Cowboys football franchise (i.e., Kyoto acquires all future paper title to profits from the Cowboys and their name).

  d. U.S. tourists pay $280, with a check written on a Vermont bank, to stay in Toronto's SkyDome Hotel overlooking the Blue Jays baseball stadium.

8. You are given the following information about a country's international transactions during a year:

Merchandise exports	$330
Merchandise imports	198
Service exports	196
Service imports	204
Income flows, net	3
Unilateral transfers, net	−8
Increase in the country's holding of foreign assets, net (excluding official reserve assets)	202
Increase in foreign holdings of the country's assets, net (excluding official reserve assets)	102
Statistical discrepancy, net	4

  a. Calculate the values of the country's merchandise trade balance, goods and services balance, current account balance, and official settlements balance.

  b. What is the value of the change in official reserve assets (net)? Is the country increasing or decreasing its net holdings of official reserve assets?

✦ 9. What are the effects of each of the following on the U.S. international investment position?

  a. Foreign central banks increase their official holdings of U.S. government securities.

  b. U.S. residents increase their holdings of stocks issued by Japanese companies.

  c. A British pension fund sells some of its holdings of the stocks of U.S. companies in order to buy U.S. corporate bonds.

10. On December 31, a country has the following stocks of international assets and liabilities to foreigners.

  • The country's residents own $30 billion of bonds issued by foreign governments.

  • The country's central bank holds $20 billion of gold and $15 billion of foreign-currency assets as official reserve assets.

  • Foreign firms have invested in production facilities in the country, with the value of their investments currently $40 billion.

  • Residents of foreign countries own $25 billion of bonds issued by the country's companies.

  a. What is the value of the country's international investment position? Is the country an international creditor or debtor?

  b. If the country during the next year runs a surplus in its current account, what will the impact be on the value of the country's international investment position?

CHAPTER 16

The Foreign
Exchange Market

In foreign commerce, as in international dialogue, somebody has to translate. People in different countries use different currencies as well as different languages. The translator between different currencies is the exchange rate, the price of one country's money in units of another country's money. You can go only so far using just one currency. If an American wants to buy something from a foreign resident, the foreign resident will typically want to have the payment translated into her home currency. They are less willing to keep dollars than the American, just as they are less willing to speak only English.

What determines the exchange rate, or the pressures on it, is the subject of the rest of Part III. This chapter introduces the real-world institutions of currency trading. It also begins to build a theory of exchange rates, starting with the role of forces that show up in the balance-of-payments entries of Chapter 15.

Much of the study of exchange rates is like a trip to another planet. It is a strange land, far removed from the economics of an ordinary household. It is populated by strange creatures—hedgers, arbitrageurs, the Gnomes of Zurich, the Snake in the Tunnel, the crawling peg, and the dirty float.

Yet the student of exchange rates is helped by the presence of two familiar forces: profit maximization and competition. The familiar assumption that individuals act as though they are out to maximize the real value of their net incomes (profits) appears to be at least as valid in international financial behavior as in other realms of economics. To be sure, people act as though they are maximizing a subtle concept of profit, one that takes account of a wide variety of economic and political risks. Yet, the parties engaged in international finance do seem to react to changing conditions in the way that a profit-maximizer would.

It also happens that competition prevails in most international financial markets despite a folklore full of tales about how groups of wealthy speculators manage to corner those markets. There is competition in the markets for foreign exchange and in the international lending markets. Thus, for these markets, we can use the familiar demand and supply analysis of competitive markets. Here again, it is important to make one disclaimer: It is definitely not the case that all markets in the international arena are competitive. Monopoly and oligopoly are evident in much of the direct investment activity we shall discuss in Part V as well as in the cartels already discussed in Chapter 13. Ordinary demand and supply curves would not do justice to the facts in these areas. Yet, in the financial markets that play a large role in the material of Parts III and IV, competitive conditions do hold, even more so than in most markets usually thought of as competitive.

The Basics of Currency Trading

Foreign exchange is the act of trading different nations' moneys.[1] The moneys take the same forms as money within a country. The greater part of the money assets traded in foreign exchange markets are demand deposits in banks. A very small part consists of coins and currency of the ordinary pocket variety.

An **exchange rate** is the price of one nation's money in terms of another nation's money.[2] There are actually two basic types of exchange rate, depending on the timing of actual exchange of the moneys. The **spot exchange rate** is the price for "immediate" exchange. (For standard large trades in the market, immediate exchange for most currencies actually means exchange or delivery in two working days after the exchange is agreed, while it means one working day after the exchange is agreed for exchanges between U.S. dollars, Canadian dollars, and Mexican pesos.) The **forward exchange rate** is the price for an exchange that will take place sometime in the future. Forward exchange rates are prices that are agreed today for exchanges of moneys that will occur at a specified time in the future, such as 30, 90, or 180 days from now. This chapter focuses on foreign exchange in general and spot exchange rates specifically. Chapter 17 examines forward foreign exchange and its uses.

In today's increasingly international world, many newspapers keep daily track of exchange rates with quotations like those shown in Figure 16.1. Notice that each price is stated in two ways: first as a U.S. dollar price of the other currency and next as the price of the U.S. dollar in units of the other currency. The pairs of prices are just reciprocals of each other. Saying that the British pound sterling costs 1.6355 U.S. dollars is the same as saying the U.S. dollar is worth £0.6114 (1.6355 = 1/0.6114), and so forth. Each exchange rate can thus be read in either of two directions. This is done simply because both sides of the price are money, unlike regular prices of goods and services where only one of the things being traded is money (as in $1.15 per gallon of gasoline). To avoid unnecessary

---

[1] The term *foreign exchange* also refers to holdings of foreign currencies.

[2] Exchange rates are one kind of price that a national money has. Another is its ability to buy goods and services immediately. The second kind of price, the usual "value of the dollar," is just the reciprocal of the money cost of buying a bundle of goods and services. A third kind of price of money is the cost of just renting it, and having access to it, for a given period of time. This is (roughly) the rate of interest that borrowers pay for the use of money, and it is analogous to other rental prices such as the price of renting an apartment or a rental car.

FIGURE 16.1 *Exchange Rate Quotations*

FOREIGN EXCHANGE RATES

Thursday, February 18, 1999
The New York foreign exchange mid-range rates below apply to trading among banks in amounts of $1 million and more, as quoted at 4 p.m. Eastern time by Telerate and other sources. Retail transactions provide fewer units of foreign currency per dollar. Rates for the 11 Euro currency countries are derived from the latest dollar-euro rate using the exchange ratios set 1/1/99.

Country	U.S. $ equiv. Thu	U.S. $ equiv. Wed	Currency per U.S. $ Thu	Currency per U.S. $ Wed	Country	U.S. $ equiv. Thu	U.S. $ equiv. Wed	Currency per U.S. $ Thu	Currency per U.S. $ Wed
Argentina (Peso)	1.0001	1.0002	.9999	.9998	Lebanon (Pound)	.0006631	.0006631	1508.00	1508.00
Australia (Dollar)	.6355	.6353	1.5736	1.5741	Malaysia (Ringgit-b)	.2632	.2632	3.800	3.800
Austria (Schilling)	.08138	.08175	12.288	12.232	Malta (Lira)	2.5674	2.5674	.3895	.3895
Bahrain (Dinar)	2.6525	2.6525	.3770	.3770	Mexico (Peso)	....	....	....	....
Belgium (Franc)	.02776	.02789	36.024	35.861	Floating rate	.1010	.1011	9.9000	9.8920
Brazil (Real)	.5236	.5208	1.9100	1.9200	Netherland (Guilder)	.5081	.5105	1.9679	1.9590
Britain (Pound)	1.6355	1.6350	.6114	.6116	New Zealand (Dollar)	.5399	.5391	1.8522	1.8549
1-month forward	1.6347	1.6342	.6117	.6119	Norway (Krone)	.1280	.1294	7.8103	7.7303
3-months forward	1.6340	1.6337	.6120	.6121	Pakistan (Rupee)	.02001	.02001	49.980	49.980
6-months forward	1.6339	1.6339	.6121	.6120	Peru (new Sol)	.2950	.2955	3.3895	3.3845
Canada (Dollar)	.6726	.6685	1.4867	1.4959	Philippines (Peso)	.02587	.02584	38.660	38.705
1-month forward	.6725	.6684	1.4869	1.4961	Poland (Zloty)	.2634	.2614	3.7965	3.8250
3-months forward	.6725	.6684	1.4870	1.4961	Portugal (Escudo)	.005586	.005611	179.03	178.22
6-months forward	.6726	.6688	1.4867	1.4951	Russia (Ruble) (a)	.04363	.04373	22.920	22.870
Chile (Peso)	.002011	.002010	497.15	497.55	Saudi Arabia (Riyal)	.2666	.2666	3.7506	3.7505
China (Renminbi)	.1208	.1208	8.2785	8.2785	Singapore (Dollar)	.5889	.5888	1.6980	1.6985
Colombia (Peso)	.0006372	.0006404	1569.40	1561.53	Slovak Rep. (Koruna)	.02592	.02617	38.580	38.205
Czech. Rep. (Koruna)	....	....	....	....	South Africa (Rand)	.1615	.1627	6.1930	6.1450
Commercial rate	.02955	.02954	33.840	33.858	South Korea (Won)	.0008461	.0008506	1181.90	1175.70
Denmark (Krone)	.1507	.1513	6.6350	6.6090	Spain (Peseta)	.006730	.006761	148.59	147.91
Ecuador (Sucre)	....	....	....	....	Sweden (Krona)	.1253	.1261	7.9793	7.9288
Floating rate	.0001321	.0001374	7570.00	7280.00	Switzerland (Franc)	.7000	.7040	1.4285	1.4205
Finland (Markka)	.1883	.1892	5.3096	5.2856	1-month forward	.7020	.7060	1.4245	1.4163
France (Franc)	.1707	.1715	5.8578	5.8312	3-months forward	.7066	.7105	1.4152	1.4075
1-month forward	.1710	.1717	5.8496	5.8232	6-months forward	.7131	.7171	1.4024	1.3946
3-months forward	.1715	.1723	5.8302	5.8044	Taiwan (Dollar)	.03098	.03098	32.278	32.278
6-months forward	.1724	.1732	5.7999	5.7743	Thailand (Baht)	.02700	.02703	37.040	36.995
Germany (Mark)	.5725	.5752	1.7466	1.7387	Turkey (Lira)	.00000291	.00000291	344140.00	343392.00
1-month forward	.5733	.5759	1.7441	1.7363	United Arab (Dirham)	.2723	.2723	3.6725	3.6725
3-months forward	.5753	.5778	1.7383	1.7307	Uruguay (New Peso)	....	....	....	....
6-months forward	.5783	.5808	1.7293	1.7217	Financial	.09149	.09158	10.930	10.920
Greece (Drachma)	.003482	.003499	287.20	285.81	Venezuela (Bolivar)	.001733	.001732	576.92	577.25
Hong Kong (Dollar)	.1291	.1291	7.7480	7.7475				– – –	
Hungary (Forint)	.004448	.004478	224.81	223.31	SDR	1.3763	1.3797	.7266	.7248
India (Rupee)	.02356	.02354	42.438	42.472	Euro	1.1198	1.1249	.8930	.8890
Indonesia (Rupiah)	.0001140	.0001151	8775.00	8690.00					
Ireland (Punt)	1.4219	1.4283	.7033	.7001					
Israel (Shekel)	.2458	.2466	4.0688	4.0553	Special Drawing Rights (SDR) are based on exchange rates for the				
Italy (Lira)	.0005783	.0005810	1729.12	1721.28	U.S., German, British, French, and Japanese currencies. Source: International Monetary Fund.				
Japan (Yen)	.008356	.008410	119.67	118.90					
1-month forward	.008388	.008441	119.22	118.47	a-Russian Central Bank rate. Trading band lowered on 8/17/98.				
3-months forward	.008458	.008510	118.23	117.51	b-Government rate.				
6-months forward	.008562	.008615	116.79	116.07	The Wall Street Journal daily foreign exchange data from 1996				
Jordan (Dinar)	1.4104	1.4104	.7090	.7090	forward may be purchased through the Readers' Reference Service				
Kuwait (Dinar)	3.2938	3.2938	.3036	.3036	(413) 592-3600.				

confusion *the rest of the book will refer to the exchange rate as the price of the foreign currency.* When the home currency is the dollar, the exchange rates will be dollar prices of other currencies, like $1.6355 per pound, $0.700 per Swiss franc, and other figures in the left columns of Figure 16.1.[3]

The foreign exchange market is not a single gathering place where traders shout buy and sell orders at each other. Rather, banks and the traders who work at banks are at the center of the foreign exchange market. These banks and their traders—using computers, telephones, and other telecommunications—conduct foreign exchange trades with their customers and also with each other. The trading done with customers is called the *retail part of the market.* Some of this is trading with individuals in small amounts. We see this part of the market, for instance, when we travel to a foreign country, but individuals' exchange is a very small part of overall foreign exchange trading. Most of the retail part of the market involves nonfinancial companies, financial institutions, and other organizations that undertake large trades as the customers of the banks that actively deal in the market. The trading done between the banks active in the market is called the *interbank part of the market.*

The banks active in foreign exchange trading are located in countries around the world, so this is a 24-hour market. On working days, foreign exchange trading is always occurring somewhere in the world. Although banks throughout the world participate, about half of foreign exchange trading involves banks in two locations: London and New York.

The total volumes traded in the foreign exchange market are enormous and have been growing rapidly. Foreign exchange trading in 1998 has been estimated at about $1.5 trillion *per day* versus a daily turnover of only about $200 billion for U.S. government securities and only about $30 billion on the New York Stock Exchange. Yet the number of people employed as traders in banks in this industry is only a few thousand for the world as a whole. (See the box "Foreign Exchange Trading" on page 352.)

Most foreign exchange trading involves the exchange of U.S. dollars for another currency. Indeed, although some trades are made directly between currencies other than the U.S. dollar, many such trades are actually done in two steps. One foreign currency is exchanged for dollars, and these dollars are exchanged for the other foreign currency. Because the dollar is often used in this way to accomplish trading between two other currencies, the dollar is sometimes called a *vehicle currency.*

---

[3]Traders in the market also have conventions for stating exchange rates. In the market, most rates referring to the U.S. dollar are quoted as units of other currency per U.S. dollar, but some (including the euro, British pound, Australian dollar, and Canadian dollar) are quoted as U.S. dollars per unit of this currency. In addition, traders who are willing to buy or sell foreign exchange quote two exchange rates: one for buying and the other for selling. The resulting *bid–ask spread* is a source of profits to these traders. Furthermore, the difference between buying and selling rates (or the bid–ask spread) varies by size (or type) of trade. It is larger for smaller trades, and largest for small transactions in actual currency and coins. The difference between buying and selling rates typically is relatively small for large trades in major currencies. We will ignore differences in buy and sell rates in most subsequent discussion, talking instead about the exchange rate as a single number.

Using the Foreign Exchange Market

In the customer or retail part of the spot foreign exchange market, individuals, businesses, and other organizations can acquire foreign moneys to make payments, or they can sell foreign moneys that they have received in payments. The spot foreign exchange market thus provides clearing services—serving to permit payments to flow between individuals, businesses, and other organizations that prefer to use different moneys. These payments are for all of the types of items included in the balance-of-payments account, including payments for exports and imports of goods and services and payments for purchases or sales of foreign financial assets.

An example can show how this works. The example also demonstrates the role of demand deposits as the major form of money traded in the foreign exchange market. Consider a British firm that has purchased a small airplane (a corporate jet) from the U.S. producer of the plane and now is making the payment for it. If the British firm pays by writing a check in pounds sterling, the U.S. firm receiving the sterling check must be content to hold on to sterling bank deposits or sell the sterling for dollars. Alternatively, if the U.S. firm will accept payment only in dollars, then it is the British buyer who must sell sterling to get the dollars to pay the U.S. exporter.

Let's assume that the latter is the case. The British firm contacts its bank and requests a quotation on the exchange rate for selling pounds and acquiring dollars. If the rate is acceptable, the British firm instructs its bank to take the pounds from its demand deposit (checking) account, convert these pounds into dollars, and transfer the dollars to the U.S. producer. The British bank holds dollar demand deposits in the United States, at its correspondent bank in New York. The British bank instructs its correspondent bank in New York to take dollars from its demand deposit account and transfer the dollars to the U.S. producer, by transferring them to the U.S. producer's bank for deposit into the producer's demand deposit account.[4]

As with most payments that are purely domestic, demand deposits are used in this foreign exchange trade and in completing the international payment for the airplane. The British firm used the pounds in its demand deposit account to purchase the dollars needed. The U.S. producer used its demand deposit account to receive the dollar payment. The British bank used its dollar demand deposits in its correspondent bank in New York for two purposes: (1) as the dollars that it sold to its customer in the foreign transaction and (2) as the (same) dollars that were then transferred to the U.S. producer as payment.

Two systems that utilize modern computer and telecommunication technologies are likely to be used in this and similar foreign exchange and international payments activities. The first is SWIFT (the Society for Worldwide Interbank Financial Telecommunications), which is used to transmit instructions from one member bank to another (in our example, from the British bank to its correspondent bank in New York). Such messages are sent through SWIFT instantly, error-

---

[4]The British bank could also use dollars available at its own U.S. branch to carry out this payment in the United States, if it has a branch there.

Birth of a Currency € Euro Currency Symbol

One of the currencies shown in Figure 16.1 was not there a few months earlier. On January 1, 1999, a major new currency, the *euro,* was born. The European Union (EU) created the euro to replace the various national currencies of the EU members; 11 of the 15 EU countries joined immediately. The fixed conversion rates, set on December 31, 1998, are that 1 euro is equal to each of:

Austrian schilling	13.7603
Belgium franc	40.3399
Finnish markka	5.94573
French franc	6.55957
German mark	1.95583
Irish punt	0.787564
Italian lira	1936.27
Luxembourg franc	40.3399
Netherlands guilder	2.20371
Portuguese escudo	200.482
Spanish peseta	166.386

(To remember which countries are in the euro, try the mnemonic BAFFLING SIP.) The euro replaced the European Currency Unit (ECU), a unit of account (not a true currency) that was a combination of specific amounts of EU national currencies.

As recently as the late 1980s, the idea of merging the EU national currencies seemed like science fiction. But, in 1991, the EU countries drafted the Maastricht Treaty, and it became effective in 1993 after all EU countries approved it, some by close national votes. The Maastricht Treaty set a process for establishing a monetary union and a single union-wide currency, including a timetable and criteria for a country to join. But the system that preceded the euro, the Exchange Rate Mechanism of the European Monetary System, came under severe pressure in 1992–1993 and nearly collapsed. Monetary union still looked far away. By early 1995, only one EU country (Luxembourg!) met the five criteria, covering the country's inflation rate, long-term interest rate, exchange-rate value of its currency, government budget deficit, and government debt.

free, securely, and at low cost. SWIFT has over 1,000 member banks in many countries. The second is CHIPS (the Clearing House International Payments System). CHIPS clears dollars transfers among its member banks, which include all large and internationally active banks. In our example CHIPS would be used if the New York correspondent bank and the bank of the U.S. producer were members. CHIPS handles several hundred thousands of payments totaling over $1 trillion each day, safely and at low cost. Each bank's payments and receipts through CHIPS are totaled at the end of each day, and only the differences are settled up by actual flows of dollar funds among the banks. CHIPS reinforces the role of the U.S. dollar as a vehicle currency by ensuring that dollar transfers between its member banks can be done very efficiently.

Interbank Foreign Exchange Trading

Most foreign exchange trading, perhaps 90 percent or more, is trading between banks in the interbank part of the foreign exchange market. The interbank part of the market serves several functions. Participation in the interbank part of the market provides a bank with a continuous stream of information on conditions in the

The national governments persisted, and people began to believe. In early 1998, 11 EU countries were deemed to meet the criteria (after some fudging on government debt). Three countries—the United Kingdom, Denmark, and Sweden—could have met the criteria but chose not to join the euro at the beginning. Each had serious political concerns about the loss of national power and the loss of the national money as a symbol. The fifteenth EU country, Greece, wanted to join the euro but did not meet the criteria. For the 11 countries joining the euro, the exchange rates between their currencies during 1998 were remarkably steady, a smooth run-up to the euro launching.

In 1998, banks spent months revising and testing their computer systems and communications links to financial exchanges, clearinghouses, and interbank settlement systems. This culminated in "changeover weekend," the days from December 31, 1998, when the actual permanent exchange rates were announced, to January 4, 1999, when financial markets reopened after the New Year's holiday. Financial securities had to be re-denominated in euros, and final tests made on systems. A goodly number of financial folks had no New Year's Eve parties and no holiday. The preparations and work paid off—banks and financial markets performed with no major glitches on January 4.

The transition from national currencies to the euro will take several years. From January 1, 1999, all stocks and bonds are quoted in euros, and all interbank transactions are in euros. People and companies can use euros for bank accounts, including checking accounts (demand deposits), as well as loans and traveler's checks, but national currencies continue in these uses as well. Euro paper money notes and coins are not scheduled to appear until the beginning of 2002, with a transition period then of up to six months during which both euros and national currencies will be used. (This will create quite a challenge for retail stores—there are not enough slots in the cash registers.) By mid-2002, the euro will completely replace the 11 national currencies.

Overnight (or, really, over a weekend) the euro became one of the three major world currencies, along with the U.S. dollar and the Japanese yen. It is part of the growing integration within the EU, a process that includes the "Europe 1992" drive for a single European market (discussed in Chapter 11), as well as the current drive for Economic and Monetary Union (EMU). In Part IV we will examine the implications of the euro for macroeconomic performance of the EU countries.

foreign exchange market through talking with traders at other banks and through observing the prices (exchange rates) being quoted. Interbank trading allows a bank to readjust its own position quickly and at low cost when it separately conducts a large trade with a customer. For instance, if Citibank buys a large amount of yen from Toyota (and sells dollars to Toyota), Citibank may be unwilling to continue holding the yen. Citibank then can sell the yen to another bank (and buy dollars) quickly and at low cost. Interbank trading also permits a bank to take on a position in a foreign currency quickly if the bank and its traders want to speculate on exchange rate movements in the near future. Such speculative positions are usually held only for a short time, typically being closed out by the end of the day.

Some interbank trading is conducted directly between the traders at different banks. In this case the traders know to whom they are quoting exchange rates for possible trades. Other trades between banks are conducted through foreign exchange brokers. The use of brokers provides anonymity to the traders until an exchange rate is agreed on for a trade. The use of brokers can also economize on the costs of searching for the best available exchange rates, as the broker's business is to know the rates at which various banks are willing to trade. Brokers earn commissions for their services.

Skilled traders work at desks in their separate banks dealing with each other (and with brokers) by computer and by phone. Computer terminals show current exchange rate ranges on all major currencies for delivery at various dates. Major banks post the exchange rates at which each is probably willing to trade currencies with other banks. If a bank is shopping for the best rate directly, it consults the ranges quoted on the computer screens. Finding a likely prospect, the buyer bank deals with the other bank directly by phone to get a firmer price bid. Within about a minute, as a rule, any haggling is settled and a transaction is made by verbal agreement. If necessary, documents consummating the trade are mailed later. To repeat, what the banks are trading are demand deposits denominated in different currencies.

Foreign exchange trading in this interbank part of the market is not for the little guy. Notice that the quoted interbank rates in Figure 16.1 are for amounts of $1 million or more. In fact, traders often save time on the phone by referring to each million dollars as a "dollar." With millions being exchanged each minute, extremely fine margins of profit or loss can loom large. For example, a trader who spends a minute shopping and secures 10 million pounds at $1.6354 per pound, instead of accepting a ready offer at $1.6355 has brought his bank an extra $1,000 within that minute. That's equivalent to a wage rate of $60,000 an hour. Correspondingly, anyone who reacts a bit too slowly or too excitedly to a given news release transmitted over the wire services (e.g., announcement of rapid growth in the Canadian money supply, rumors of a coup in Libya, or a wildcat steel strike in Italy) can lose money at an even faster rate. On the average, these professionals make more than they lose, enough to justify their rates of pay. But foreign exchange trading is a lively and tense job. That department of a large bank is usually run as a tight ship with no room for "passengers" who do not make a good rate of return from quick dealings at fine margins.

Demand and Supply for Foreign Exchange

To understand what makes a country's currency rise and fall in its exchange rate value, you should proceed through the same steps used to analyze any competitive market. First, portray the interaction of demand and supply as determinants of the equilibrium price and quantity, and then explore what forces lie behind the demand and supply curves.

Within the foreign exchange market, people want to trade moneys for various reasons. Some are engaged in trading goods and services and are making or receiving payments for these products. Some are engaged in international flows of financial assets. They are investing or borrowing internationally, and need to convert one nation's money to another money in the process of buying and selling financial assets, incurring and paying back debts, and so forth.

A nation's export of goods and services typically causes foreign moneys to be sold in order to buy that nation's money. For instance, the importer in a foreign country desires to pay using his currency, while the U.S. exporter desires to be paid in dollars. Somewhere in the payments process, foreign money is exchanged for dollars. We saw a specific example of this in the previous section on using the foreign exchange market. Thus, U.S. *exports of goods and services will create a supply of foreign currency* and a demand for U.S. dollars to the extent that foreign buyers have their own currencies to offer and U.S. exporters prefer to end up holding U.S. dollars and not some other currency. Only if U.S. exporters are happy to hold on to pounds (or the United Kingdom importers somehow have large holdings of dollars to spend) can U.S. exports to Britain keep from generating a supply of pounds and a demand for dollars.

Importing goods and services correspondingly tends to cause the home currency to be sold in order to buy foreign currency. For instance, if a U.S. importer desires to pay in dollars, and the British exporter desires to be paid in pounds because he wants to end up holding his home currency, then somewhere in the payments process dollars must be exchanged for pounds. Thus, U.S. *imports of goods and services will create a demand for foreign currency* and a supply of U.S. dollars to the extent that U.S. importers have dollars to offer and foreign exporters prefer to end up holding their own currencies. Only if foreign exporters are happy to hold on to dollars (or the U.S. importers somehow have large holdings of foreign currencies to spend) can U.S. imports keep from generating a supply of dollars and a demand for foreign currency.[5]

Similar reasoning applies to transactions in financial assets. Consider a U.S. insurance company that wants to replace some of its current holdings of U.S. dollar–denominated bonds with British-pound–denominated bonds, perhaps because it expects a higher rate of return on the sterling investment. The company will need to sell dollars and buy pounds in the foreign exchange market, and then use these pounds to make payment in the process of buying the pound-denominated bonds. U.S. *capital outflows will create a demand for foreign currency* and a supply of U.S. dollars to the extent that the investors begin with dollars and desire to invest in foreign financial assets that must be paid for in foreign currencies.

In another case, a British resident currently holding sterling demand deposits wishes to buy shares in Microsoft. The person will need to sell pounds and buy dollars in the foreign exchange market, and then use these dollars to make payment in the process of buying the stock. U.S. *capital inflows will create a supply of foreign currency* and a demand for dollars to the extent that investors begin with foreign currency and desire to invest in U.S. financial assets that must be paid for in dollars.

All of these transactions create supply and demand for foreign exchange. The supply and demand determine the exchange rate, within certain constraints imposed by the nature of the foreign exchange system or regime under which the country operates.

---

[5]International payments of income and unilateral transfers can also result in demand or supply of foreign currency. For instance, if a foreign company pays a dividend in its own currency, U.S. holders of its stock supply foreign currency if they want to take payment in dollars. As another example, some people in the United States and Canada demand foreign currency in order to be able to send remittances and cash gifts to relatives in Italy, Mexico, or some other country from which they emigrated.

Foreign Exchange Trading

In 1998, foreign exchange trading reached the astounding pace of $1.5 trillion per day. It is difficult to comprehend how large this number is. One comparison offers some guidance. In just *6 days* the amount of money traded in the foreign exchange market is a little larger than the value of U.S. production of goods and services for an *entire year.*

What exactly is being traded in the huge global foreign exchange market? Where is the trading done? And who are the traders?

First, the what: In addition to spot and forward foreign exchange, there is one other traditional foreign exchange trade, the foreign exchange swap. The foreign exchange swap is a package trade that includes both a spot exchange of two currencies and an agreement to the reverse forward exchange of the two currencies (the future exchange back again). This type of package contract is useful when the parties to the trade have only a temporary need for the currency each is buying spot. In the global market, spot exchange is about 40 percent of trading, forward exchange about 10 percent, and foreign exchange swaps about 50 percent. For all of this foreign exchange trading in 1998, the U.S. dollar was involved in 87 percent of all trades, the German mark in 30 percent, the Japanese yen in 21

percent, the British pound in 11 percent, and the Swiss franc in 7 percent.

Second, the where: The global business was distributed in 1998 as follows:

United Kingdom	32%
United States	18
Japan	8
Singapore	7
Germany	5
France	4
Hong Kong	4
Switzerland	4
Australia	2
Canada	2
Netherlands	2
Other countries	2

Half of global trading is done in the United Kingdom (mostly London) and the United States (mostly New York). This concentration has been rising over the past decade. For instance, in 1992, the United Kingdom had 27 percent of global trading, and the United States 16 percent. Even though the British pound

---

The simplest system is the **floating exchange rate system** without intervention by governments or central bankers. The major countries have been on something close to this system since 1973. The spot price of foreign currency is market-driven, determined by the interaction of private demand and supply for that currency. The market clears itself through the price mechanism.

The two parts of Figure 16.2 (page 354) show how such a system could yield equilibrium exchange rates for the pound sterling and the Swiss franc at the E points. We can indicate the logic behind the slopes of the curves in Figure 16.2 by focusing on the demand curve for foreign currency.

What makes the demand curve slope downward? That is, why should a lower (higher) price of a currency generally mean that more (less) of it is demanded? To see the likelihood of the downward slope, imagine that the exchange rate in Figure 16.2A has just shifted from $1.98 to $1.60. As the pound declines below $1.98, Americans will discover more uses for it. One use would be to buy wool sweaters in Britain. Before the pound sinks, a sweater selling for £50 in London would cost American tourists $99 (= 50 × 1.98). If the pound suddenly sinks to $1.60, the

©David Wells, The Image Works

©David Wells, The Image Works

itself is not that important in foreign exchange contracts, London is clearly the center of global foreign exchange trading.

Now, the who: Most foreign exchange trading is done by and through a network of several hundred banks worldwide, banks that actively "make a market" in foreign exchange by quoting rates and being willing to buy or sell currencies for their own account. Most trading is done by a few thousand traders who are employed at these banks. This is a surprisingly small number of traders, relative to the huge volume of trading conducted.

There are good reasons why there are so few foreign exchange traders. One is the capital intensity of this particular business. It takes a lot of money and substantial investments in computer and telecommunications hardware and software, but only a few decision makers. Another is the nature of the work itself.

Trading millions of dollars of foreign exchange per minute is a harrowing job; it's almost in the same category with being an air traffic controller or a bomb defuser. A trader should be somebody who loves pressures and can take losses. Many who try it soon develop a taste for other work. Once an economics student visiting a foreign exchange trading room in a major bank asked a trader, "How long do people last in this job?" The enthusiastic answer: "Yes, it is an excellent job for young people."

same £50 wool sweater would cost American tourists only $80. They would start buying more. To pay for the extra sweaters, they would want more pounds sterling, to be paid to British merchants. As long as the level of business remains higher, there is more demand for pounds to conduct that business.

The case of British wool sweaters is just one illustration of the forces that might make the demand curve for a currency slope downward. There are usually many such responses of trade to a change in the exchange rate. A sinking pound means more bicycles bought from British companies and fewer bought from Schwinn. There is more reason to buy British and therefore more reason for a demand for pounds as a currency to facilitate such transactions. As long as a lower exchange rate raises the quantity demanded, the demand curve will slope downward.[6]

---

[6]Similar logic can be applied to examine the slope of the supply curve for foreign exchange, but the actual slope of the supply curve is not so clear-cut. We presume for now that the supply curve has the usual upward slope.

FIGURE 16.2

*The Spot
Exchange
Market with and
Without Official
Intervention*

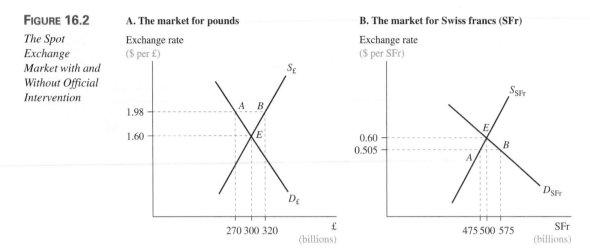

A. The market for pounds

B. The market for Swiss francs (SFr)

The demand and supply curves represent all demand and supply for that currency except for any official intervention by the official government authorities (like the central banks). With no official intervention, the market reaches an equilibrium at point *E* in panels A and B. If the government wishes to fix the exchange rate at a different level, then it must intervene to buy or sell the currency to meet any difference between private (or nonofficial) demand and supply, the gaps *AB* in panels A and B.

To explain what makes the floating exchange rate rise or fall over time, we need to know the forces that shift the supply and demand curves. Again, let's focus on the demand curve. The demand curve is shifted by a variety of changes in the economy. Many of the demand-side forces relate to the balance-of-payments categories of Chapter 15. Shifts in trade demand away from the United States and toward the United Kingdom (caused by forces other than changes in the exchange rate) would result in extra attempts to sell dollars and buy pounds. This can be graphed as an upward (rightward) shift of the demand for foreign exchange. Similarly, a rise in U.S. residents' willingness to lend money to U.K. borrowers or to invest in pound-denominated financial assets usually requires that extra dollars be converted into pounds, thus shifting the demand curve for pounds to the right. In a floating-rate system, if for any reason the demand curve for foreign currency shifts to the right (representing increased demand for foreign money), and the supply curve remains unchanged, then the exchange rate value of the foreign currency rises. Such a shift is shown in Figure 16.3. The rightward shift in demand for pounds to D_2 increases the price of pounds from $1.60 to $1.80 per pound, as the market equilibrium shifts from *E* to E_2.

Figure 16.2 can be used to introduce the other main foreign exchange regime, the **fixed exchange rate system.** Here, officials strive to keep the exchange rate virtually fixed (or pegged) even if the rate they choose differs from the current equilibrium rate. Their usual procedure under such a system is to declare a narrow "band" of exchange rates within which the rate is allowed to vary. If the exchange rate hits the top or bottom of the band, the officials must intervene. In

FIGURE 16.3

A Shift in Demand for Pounds in the Spot Exchange Market

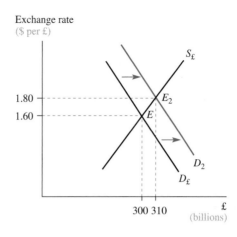

The demand curve for foreign exchange can be shifted to the right (or raised) by either of the following changes related to the balance of payments:

A shift of trade demand away from U.S. goods and services toward those of other countries.

A rise in U.S. willingness to lend money to or invest in other countries.

If the demand curve shifts to the right, then the market equilibrium exchange rate value of the pound rises. (Chapters 18 and 19 discuss in more depth the forces that shift the curves and change the exchange rate.)

Figure 16.2A, consider an officially declared "par value" of $2.00 at which the pound is substantially overvalued relative to its market-clearing rate of $1.60 per pound. British officials have announced that they will support the pound at 1 percent below par (about $1.98), and the dollar at 1 percent above par (about $2.02). In Figure 16.2A, they are forced to make good on this pledge by officially intervening in the foreign exchange market, buying £50 billion (and selling $99 billion, equal to £50 billion times $1.98 per pound). This intervention fills the gap *AB* between nonofficial supply and demand at the $1.98 exchange rate.[7] Only in this way can they bring the total demand for pounds, private plus official, up to the 320 billion of sterling money supplied. If their purchases of pounds with dollars fall short, total demand cannot meet the supply and the price must fall below the official support point of $1.98. British officials wanting to defend the fixed exchange rate may not have sufficient reserves of dollars to keep the price fixed indefinitely, a point to which we will return several times.

Another case of official intervention in defense of a fixed exchange rate is shown in Figure 16.2B. Swiss government officials have declared that the par value of the Swiss franc (SFr) shall be 50 cents in U.S. currency, and that the support points are 50.5 cents and 49.5 cents. As the demand and supply curves are

---

[7]Such official intervention could also be pictured as shifting the demand or supply curves. However, it seems more descriptive, when examining the defense of a fixed rate, to consider official exchange market intervention as filling the gap between quantity demanded and quantity supplied in the absence of the intervention.

drawn, the franc is substantially undervalued relative to the market-clearing rate of $0.60 per franc. To defend the fixed rate, government officials must intervene in the foreign exchange market and sell 100 billion SFr to meet the strong demand at 50.5 cents. If the Swiss government officials cannot tolerate buying enough dollars to plug the gap *AB* and keep the exchange rate down at 50.5 cents, they may give up and let the price rise.

Changes in exchange rates are given various names depending on the kind of exchange rate regime prevailing. Under the floating-rate system a fall in the market price (the exchange rate value) of a currency is called a **depreciation** of that currency; a rise is an **appreciation.** We refer to a discrete official reduction in the otherwise fixed par value of a currency as a **devaluation; revaluation** is the antonym describing a discrete raising of the official par. Devaluations and revaluations are the main ways of changing exchange rates in a nearly fixed-rate system, a system where the rate is usually, but not always, fixed.

Arbitrage Within the Spot Exchange Market

We have pictured foreign exchange as a single market for trading between two currencies. Yet, we have also noted that trading occurs in different locations around the world. For instance, for a period of time each day, trading is occurring in both New York and London as well as in other money centers in Europe. Will the rates in the different locations be essentially the same at a point in time, or can they diverge as local supply and demand conditions differ? Furthermore, exchange rates exist for many different currencies, both rates representing the dollar price of various foreign currencies and the cross-rates between foreign currencies. Are these exchange rates and cross-rates related in some way, or can they have independent levels?

Arbitrage, the process of buying and selling to make a (nearly) riskless pure profit, ensures that rates in different locations are essentially the same, and that rates and cross-rates are related and consistent among themselves. What would happen if pounds were being exchanged at $1.70 per pound in London, and $1.60 per pound at the same time in New York? If foreign exchange trading and money transfers can be done freely, then there is an opportunity to make a riskless profit by arbitraging between the two locations. Buy pounds where they are cheap (in New York) and simultaneously sell them where they are expensive (in London). For each pound bought and sold at the initial exchange rates, the arbitrage profit is 10 cents. Such arbitrage would occur on a large scale, increasing the demand for pounds in New York and increasing the supply of pounds in London. The dollar–pound exchange rate then would increase in New York and/or decrease in London, and the two rates would be driven to be essentially the same (that is, within the small range reflecting transactions costs that prevent any further profitable arbitrage).

What would happen if the exchange rate for the pound in terms of dollars is $1.60, the exchange rate for the Swiss franc in terms of dollars is $0.50, and the cross-rate between the franc and the pound is 3 francs per pound? Although it is more subtle, there is also an opportunity to make a riskless profit by arbitraging through the three rates—a process called **triangular arbitrage.** To see this, start with some number of dollars, say, $150. Your $150 buy 300 francs (100/0.50). Use these francs to buy pounds at the cross-rate, and you have 100 pounds (300/3). Convert these pounds back into dollars and you end up with $160 (100 × 1.60). Your triangular arbitrage has made $10 profit for each $150 that you start with. This profit occurs almost instantly and with essentially no risk if you establish all three spot trades at the same time.

As a large amount of this triangular arbitrage occurs, pressures are placed on the exchange rates to bring them into line with each other. The extra demand for francs tends to increase the dollar–francs exchange rate. The extra demand for pounds (paid for by francs) tends to increase the franc–pound cross-rate. The extra supply of pounds (to acquire dollars) tends to reduce the dollar–pound exchange rate. One or more of the exchange rates will change (due to demand and supply pressures) so that the cross-rate of francs per pound essentially equals the ratio of the dollar–pound exchange rate to the dollar–franc exchange rate. For instance, if only the cross-rate changes, then its value must shift to 3.2 francs per pound (1.60/0.50). At this cross-rate there is no further opportunity for profits from triangular arbitrage.

Just the threat of arbitrage of these types usually keeps the exchange rate between two currencies essentially the same in different locations, and keeps cross-rates in correct alignment with other exchange rates. Opportunities for actual arbitrage of these types are rare.

Summary

A **foreign exchange** transaction is a trade of one national money for another. The **exchange rate** is the price at which the moneys are traded. Spot foreign exchange is for immediate delivery, while forward foreign exchange is for future delivery at a price that is agreed to now. Banks and their traders are at the center of the foreign exchange market. They use telephones, other telecommunications, and computers to conduct foreign exchange trades with customers (the retail part of the market) and with each other (the interbank part of the market).

Spot foreign exchange serves a clearing function, permitting payments to be made between entities who want to hold or use different currencies. The exchange rate is determined by supply and demand, within any constraints imposed by the governmental choice of an exchange rate system or regime. Under a freely flexible or floating exchange rate system, market supply and demand set the equilibrium price (exchange rate) that clears the market. A floating exchange rate changes over time as supply and demand shift over time. Under a fixed-rate or pegged-rate system, officials buy and sell a currency so as to keep its exchange rate within an officially stipulated band. When the currency's value lies at the bottom of its official band, officials must buy it by selling other currencies. When the currency's value presses against the top of its official price range, officials must sell it in exchange for other currencies.

Suggested Reading

Four good alternative textbook views of the foreign exchange market are Levich (1998, Chapter 3), Eun and Resnick (1998, Chapter 4), Giddy (1994, Chapter 2), and Eiteman, Stonehill, and Moffet (1998, Chapter 4).

Questions and Problems

✦ 1. What are the major types of transactions or activities that result in demand for foreign currency in the spot foreign exchange market?

2. What are the major types of transactions or activities that result in supply of foreign currency in the spot foreign exchange market?

✦ 3. What has happened to the exchange rate value of the dollar in each case?

   a. The spot rate goes from $0.50/SFr to $0.51/SFr.

   b. The spot rate goes from SFr 2/$ to SFr 1.96/$0.

   c. The spot rate goes from $0.010/yen to $0.009/yen.

   d. The spot rate goes from 100 yen/$ to 111 yen/$.

4. A U.S. firm must make a payment of 1 million yen to a Japanese firm that has sold the U.S. firm sets of Japanese baseball-player trading cards. The U.S. firm begins with a dollar checking account. Explain in detail how this payment would be made, including the use of the spot foreign exchange market and banks in both countries.

✦ 5. A British bank has acquired a large number of dollars in its dealings with its clients. How could this bank use the interbank foreign exchange market if it was unwilling to continue holding these dollars?

6. A trader at a U.S. bank believes that the euro will strengthen substantially in exchange rate value during the next hour. How would the trader use the interbank market to attempt to profit from her belief?

✦ 7. For each of the following, is it part of demand for yen or supply of yen in the foreign exchange market?

   a. A Japanese firm sells its U.S. government securities to obtain funds to buy real estate in Japan.

   b. A U.S. import company must pay for glassware purchased from a small Japanese producer.

   c. A U.S. farm cooperative receives payment from a Japanese importer of U.S. oranges.

   d. A U.S. pension fund uses some incoming contributions to buy equity shares of several Japanese companies through the Tokyo stock market.

8. You have access to the following three spot exchange rates:

   $0.01/yen

   $0.20/krone

   25 yen/krone

   You start with dollars and want to end up with dollars.

   a. How would you engage in arbitrage to profit from these three rates? What is the profit for each dollar used initially?

   b. As a result of this arbitrage, what is the pressure on the cross-rate between yen and krone? What must the value of the cross-rate be to eliminate the opportunity for triangular arbitrage?

✦ 9. The spot exchange rate between the dollar and the Swiss franc is a floating, or flexible, rate. What are the effects of each of the following on this exchange rate?

a. There is a large increase in Swiss demand for U.S. exports as U.S. culture becomes more popular in Switzerland.

b. There is a large increase in Swiss demand for investments in U.S. dollar–denominated financial assets because of a Swiss belief that the U.S. economy and political situation have improved markedly.

c. Political uncertainties in Europe lead U.S. investors to shift their financial investments out of Switzerland, back to the United States.

d. U.S. demand for products imported from Switzerland falls significantly as bad press reports lead Americans to question the quality of Swiss products.

10. Assume instead that the spot exchange rate between the dollar and Swiss franc is a fixed or pegged rate within a narrow band around a central rate. For each change shown in problem 9, assume that just before the change private (or nonofficial) supply and demand intersected at an equilibrium exchange rate within this narrow band. For each change shown in problem 9, what intervention is necessary by the monetary authorities to defend the fixed rate if the change shifts the intersection of private supply and demand outside of the band?

CHAPTER 17

Forward Exchange

Many international activities lead to money exchanges in the future. This is true of many international trade activities, whose payments are not due until sometime in the (usually near) future. It is also true of international financial activities, which are specifically designed to create future flows of moneys as returns are received, debts are repaid, or financial assets are sold to others. A major challenge in conducting all of these activities is that we do not know for sure the exchange rates that will be available in the future to translate one country's money into another country's money.

This chapter examines future exchanges of moneys and the exposure to the risks of uncertain future exchange rates. It discusses how forward foreign exchange contracts can be used to reduce the risk exposure or to speculate on future exchange rates. The chapter pays special attention to the returns and risks of investments in foreign financial assets.

Exchange Rate Risk Exposure

Exchange rates change over time. In a floating-rate system, spot exchange rates change from minute to minute as supply and demand are constantly in flux. Indeed, as we have seen since the early 1970s, floating rates sometimes change quickly by large amounts as a result of large shifts in supply and demand. In a fixed-rate system, spot exchange rates also can change from minute to minute, but the range of the rate is typically limited to a small band around the par value as long as the fixed rate is defended successfully by the government authorities. Nonetheless, even in a fixed-rate system large changes can and do sometimes occur if the currency is devalued or revalued by the authorities. While some portion of the change in spot exchange rates in either system can be predicted by participants in the foreign exchange market, another part—often a large part—of exchange rate change cannot be predicted.

A person (or an organization like a firm) is exposed to **exchange rate risk** if the value of the person's income, wealth, or net worth changes when exchange rates change unpredictably in the future. This is a broad concept, but it has specific meanings in particular situations. If you take a vacation in Japan and bring U.S. dollars along with you to convert as needed into yen to pay for your expenses and purchases, you are exposed to exchange rate risk. The dollar value of the things that you buy and the number of things that you can afford to do will be affected by the dollar–yen exchange rates during your vacation. While you have some expectation of what those exchange rates will be, the actual rates could be substantially different. From your point of view, the risk is that the yen could appreciate substantially so that it would take more dollars to obtain the same number of yen. The dollar prices of the things that you want to do and to buy will be higher, and you will enjoy your vacation less. Of course, the yen might instead depreciate, in which case you will be pleasantly surprised by the increased buying power of your dollars. Still, as you begin your vacation you are exposed to exchange rate risk because you do not know what will happen to the yen during your vacation.

Another example of exposure to exchange rate risk is your first purchase of a financial asset denominated in a foreign currency—for instance, an investment in Mexican stocks. You may have heard that an investment in emerging markets is "where the action is." This may turn out to be too true. The dollar value of your investment depends not only on changes in the market prices of your Mexican stocks (valued in pesos), but also on changes in the dollar value of the peso. If the peso depreciates, the dollar value of your stock investment falls. Even if you expect some amount of peso depreciation, and incorporate that into the overall dollar return that you expect on your investment, the risk to you is that the peso could depreciate more than you are expecting.

The fact that exchange rates can change over time leads people to two types of responses. These appear contradictory, but actually just represent the responses of different people to different situations. Some people do not want to gamble on what exchange rates will be in the future. They have acquired exposures to exchange rate risk in the course of their regular activities, but they seek to reduce or eliminate their risk exposure by hedging.

Hedging a position exposed to rate risk, here foreign-currency or exchange rate risk, is the act of reducing or eliminating a net asset or net liability position in the foreign currency.

Other people, thinking they have a good idea of what will happen to exchange rates, are quite willing to gamble on what exchange rates will be in the future. They are willing to take on or to hold positions that are exposed to exchange rate risk, betting that the rates are going to move in their favor so that they make a profit.

Speculating is the act of taking a net asset position ("long") or a net liability position ("short") in some asset class, here a foreign currency.

These two attitudes have been personified into the concepts of hedgers and speculators, as though individuals were always either one or the other. Actually, the same person can choose to behave like a hedger in some situations and like a speculator in others.

The Market Basics of Forward Foreign Exchange

There are a number of ways to hedge an exposure to exchange rate risk, or to take on additional exposure in order to speculate. For your vacation in Japan, you could buy yen (or yen-denominated traveler's checks) before you depart, thus having yen money to pay for your yen expenses and purchases.

For larger transactions involving international trade in goods and services, international financial investment, or pure speculation on future exchange rate movements, forward foreign exchange and forward exchange rates are often useful. As we mentioned in the previous chapter, a **forward foreign exchange contract** is an agreement to exchange one currency for another on some date in the future at a price set now (the forward exchange rate).

Banks acting as foreign exchange dealers generally are willing to meet the needs of their customers for the specific size of the forward exchange contract (the amount of foreign exchange) and the specific date in the future for the exchange. Common dates for future exchange are 30, 90, and 180 days forward (one, three, and six months).[1] For instance, to buy £100,000 of 90-day forward sterling at $1.6340/£, you sign an agreement that 90 days from now you will deliver $163,400 in dollar bank deposits and receive £100,000 in pound bank deposits. The exchange of these amounts will take place to carry out the forward contract, regardless of what the actual spot exchange rate turns out to be in 90 days. In the opposite trade, somebody agreeing now to sell 90-day forward sterling must be prepared to deliver it at the agreed price of $1.6340 in 90 days. That person need not own any sterling at all until then, but the rate at which he gives it up in 90 days is already set now. *Do not confuse the forward rate with the future spot rate,* the spot rate that ends up prevailing 90 days from now. The actual spot price of sterling that exists in 90 days could be above, below, or equal to the forward rate. In this respect, a forward exchange rate is like a commodity futures price or an advance hotel reservation.

The forward exchange market is particularly convenient for large customers, typically corporations, that are viewed by their banks as acceptable credit risks. These customers typically do not need to commit anything other than the written agreement until the exchange actually occurs in the future. Other customers typically must pledge a margin that the bank can seize if the customer fails to fulfill the contract in the future, but this margin is only a fraction of the total size of the contract (because the bank only needs to recover any net loss on the other party's position).

Hedging Using Forward Foreign Exchange

Hedging involves acquiring an asset in a foreign currency to offset a net liability position already held in the foreign currency, or acquiring a liability in a foreign currency to offset a net asset position already held. Hedgers in international dealings are persons who have a home currency and insist on having an exact balance

---

[1]In the usual forward exchange contract, the actual exchange of currencies will occur two (or one) days after the stated time period, to match the two-day (or one-day) delay in settling standard spot contracts. The discussion in this chapter ignores the two- or one-day delay in actually exchanging the currencies.

between their liabilities and assets in foreign currencies. In financial jargon, hedging means avoiding both kinds of "open" positions in a foreign currency—both "long" positions (holding net assets in the foreign currency) and "short" positions (owing more of the foreign currency than one holds). An American who has hedged a position in euros has ensured that the future of the exchange rate between dollars and euros will not affect her net worth. Hedging is a perfectly normal kind of behavior, especially for people for whom international financial dealings are a sideline. Simply avoiding any net commitments in a foreign currency saves on the time and trouble of keeping abreast of fast-changing international currency conditions.

There are usually a number of ways to hedge a position that is exposed to exchange rate risk. For many types of exposure, a forward exchange contract is a direct way of hedging.

Consider a U.S. company that has bought some merchandise and will have to pay £100,000 three months from now. Assuming that this represents an overall net liability position in pounds (perhaps because the company has no other assets or liabilities in pounds), the company is exposed to exchange rate risk. It does not know the dollar value of its liability because it does not know the spot exchange rate that will exist 90 days from now. One way to hedge its risk exposure is to enter into a forward contract to acquire (or buy) £100,000 in 90 days. If the current forward rate is $1.6340/£, then the company must deliver (or sell) $163,400 in 90 days. The company has an asset position in pounds through the forward contract (the company is owed pounds in the contract). This exactly matches its pound liability to pay for the merchandise, creating a "perfect hedge." The company now is assured that the merchandise will cost $163,400 regardless of what happens to the spot exchange rate in the next 90 days.[2]

Forward exchange contracts can be used to hedge exposures to exchange rate risk in many other situations. A U.S. company that will receive a payment of £1 million in 60 days is unsure of the dollar value of this receivable, because the spot exchange rate in 60 days is uncertain. It can hedge by selling pounds (and buying dollars) in a 60-day forward exchange contract, using the forward exchange rate to lock in the number of dollars it will receive. A British firm needing to pay $200,000 in 30 days on its dollar-denominated debt can hedge its exchange rate risk exposure by buying dollars (and selling pounds) in a 30-day forward contract. A British individual inheriting $2 million that will be disbursed (in dollars) in 180 days can hedge by selling the dollars (and buying pounds) in a 180-day forward contract.

---

[2]There are several other ways that the U.S. company can acquire an asset in pounds that hedges its pound liability. It could sell merchandise to someone else and bill the buyer in pounds payable in 90 days. Or it could use dollars that it has now to buy pounds now at the current spot rate, and invest those pounds to earn interest for 90 days. The pound proceeds from the investment can then be used to pay the pound debt. Or it could enter into a long position (buying pounds) in a pound futures contract traded on an organized exchange. Or it could buy a currency option call contract that gives the company the right to buy pounds at a price set in the option contract (the exercise or strike price). Each of these establishes an asset in pounds that hedges its pound liability. The company's decision to hedge using a forward contract or one of the other methods depends on the costs of the methods and the extent to which the hedge closely offsets its exposed position. In many cases the forward contract is a low-cost way of establishing the exact hedge desired by the company. Futures and options contracts are discussed further in the box "Futures, Options, and Swaps."

Speculating Using Forward Foreign Exchange

Speculating means committing oneself to an uncertain future value of one's net worth in terms of home currency. A rich imagery surrounds the term *speculator.* Speculators are usually portrayed as a class apart from the rest of humanity. These speculators are viewed as being excessively greedy—unlike us, of course. They are also viewed as exceptionally jittery and as adding an element of subversive chaos to the economic system. They come out in the middle of storms—we hear about them when the markets are veering out of control, and then it is their fault. Although speculation has indeed played such a sinister role in the past, it is an open empirical question whether it does so frequently. More to the present point, we must recognize that the only concrete way of defining speculation is the broad way just offered. Anybody is a speculator who is willing to take a net position in a foreign currency, whatever his motives or expectations about the future of the exchange rate.[3]

There are a number of ways deliberately to establish speculative foreign-currency positions. One direct way of speculating on future spot exchange rate values is a forward foreign exchange contract. Forward foreign exchange provides the same bridge to future currency exchanges for speculators as for hedgers, and there are no credentials checks that can sort out the two groups in the marketplace. If a speculator thinks she has a fairly good idea of what will happen to the spot exchange rate in the future, it is easy to bet on the basis of that idea using the forward market. It is so easy, in fact, that the speculator can even bet with money she does not have in hand.

To illustrate this point, suppose that in February you are convinced that the pound sterling will take a dive from its current spot exchange rate value of about $1.64 and be worth only $1.20 in May. Perhaps you see a coming political and economic crisis in Britain that others do not see. You can make an enormous gain by using the forward market. Contact a foreign exchange trader at your bank and agree to sell £10 million at the current 90-day forward rate of $1.6340. If the bank believes in your ability to honor your forward commitment in May, you do not even need to put up any money now in February. Just sign the forward contract. How will you be able to come up with £10 million in May? Given your knowledge

---

[3]By contrast, most practitioners would use definitions more laden with judgments about speculators' motives, as in the following passage from author Holbrook Working: "In ordinary usage and in much economic discussion the word *speculation* refers to buying and selling (or, more accurately, holding) property purely for the sake of gain from price change, and not merely as an incident to the normal conduct of a producing or merchandising business or of investment" (Chicago Board of Trade. *Selected Writings of Holbrook Working.* Chicago: Board of Trade, 1977, p. 253).

A drawback of this common usage is that there is no way of measuring how much net owning or owing of an asset is done "purely for the sake of gain from price change." Furthermore, knowing that the party in question gains a certain percentage of its income from "producing," "merchandising," and "investment" sheds no light on the motives for holding a particular asset. Our definition, by contrast, is easily measurable.

Semantic confusion about speculation is often deliberately fostered by persons aware of the term's pejorative connotation. Banks and other international investors often claim that *they* invest while *others* speculate, implying that the latter action is more risky and foolhardy. We see the distinction but not the difference, unless the party claiming not to be speculating can show balance sheets revealing no net positions in any of the foreign currencies in question.

Futures, Options, and Swaps

A forward foreign exchange contract is one type of agreement that can be reached now about an exchange of currencies that will occur in the future. This traditional form of future-oriented currency agreement has some relatives that have been introduced since the early 1970s. Someone wishing to hedge or speculate can now choose from among currency futures, currency options, and currency swaps in addition to traditional forward exchange.

Currency futures are contracts that are traded on organized exchanges, such as the Chicago Mercantile Exchange. By entering into a currency futures contract, you can effectively lock in the price at which you buy or sell a foreign currency at a set date in the future. This sounds very much like a forward foreign exchange contract, and it is. There are some differences, though. First, a futures contract is a standard contract (making it tradable on the organized exchange)—for instance, 12.5 million yen to be exchanged for dollars in March of next year. A forward contract can be customized by the bank to meet the needs of the customer. Second, if you enter into a futures contract, the exchange requires that you put up a margin to ensure that you will honor the contract. A margin might be required in a forward contract, but often it is not. Third, the profits and losses on your futures contract accrue to you daily, as the contract is "marked to market" daily. Too many losses and you will receive a call to add to your margin account. The profit or loss on a forward contract usually is not taken until the maturity date. Fourth, and perhaps most important from your perspective, almost anyone able to put up a margin can enter into a futures contract, whereas banks usually are willing to enter into forward contracts only for large amounts (millions of dollars) with suitably creditworthy customers. Futures contracts give ordinary people and small businesses access to a low-cost direct method for currency hedging or speculation.

For some purposes a major drawback to the usual forward and futures contracts is that losses on your open positions can become very large. You must honor your agreements. If the spot rate has moved in a way that is against your position, you will have to buy high and sell low, resulting in what can be a large loss. Some hedgers and speculators may dislike this feature. There is another alternative—an option contract.

A *currency option* gives the buyer (or holder) of the option the right, but not the obligation, to buy (a call option) or to sell (a put option) foreign currency at some time in the future at a price set today. The price set into the contract now for the foreign exchange transaction that the holder may make in the future is called the *exercise* or *strike price*. The option is a valuable right, and the buyer pays a premium (a fee) to the seller (or writer) of the option to acquire the option.

Let's say that you believe that the Swiss franc is going to appreciate substantially during the next month. The current spot price is $0.70 per franc and the current 30-day forward rate (or, for that matter, the current futures price for franc contracts maturing next month) is $0.71 per franc. You expect the spot value of the franc to be $0.74 in 30 days. If you speculate using a forward (or futures) contract, going long in francs, you will make a profit if the actual spot rate in 30 days is above $0.71 per franc. But if the actual spot rate in 30 days is below $0.71 per franc, you will make a loss, and the loss is larger the lower is the spot rate in 30 days. If the actual spot rate in 30 days is $0.67, you must buy francs at the forward price of $0.71 when the francs are worth only $0.67. You have a large actual loss.

You can instead speculate on the franc exchange rate using a currency option contract. The disadvantage of the option is that you must pay a premium to obtain it. (There is no comparable charge to obtain a forward contract.) The advantage of the option is that the size of any loss on the contract is limited to this premium—you cannot lose more. For instance, you can buy a 30-day currency call option that gives you the right to buy Swiss francs at an exercise price of $0.71 per franc. If the actual spot rate in 30 days is above $0.71 per franc, you exercise the option. Your overall profit here is somewhat lower than the comparable forward contract, because you had to pay the premium to buy the option. Still, your profit can be large if the actual spot rate in 30 days has moved well above the $0.71 exercise price. (You buy francs low by exercising the option and sell the francs high at the higher spot rate.) If the actual spot rate in 30 days is below $0.71, you let the option expire unexercised. You have lost the premium, but you are not required to lose any more, even if the actual spot rate is substantially below the exercise price.

Another important future-oriented currency agreement is the *currency swap*. In a currency swap two parties agree to exchange flows of different currencies during a specified period of time. For instance, Microsoft might enter into a swap with its bank in which Microsoft agrees (1) to deliver a large number of dollars in exchange for a comparable number of euros now, (2) every three months to make dollar interest payments and to receive euro interest payments, and (3) at the end of the swap to return the large number of dollars and receive back the comparable number of euros. Because Microsoft has committed to exchanging dollars for euros at various times now and in the future, you might think that this sounds something like spot and forward foreign exchange contracts, and you would be right. A swap is basically a set of spot and forward foreign exchanges packaged into one contract. The advantages of the swap over a package of separate foreign exchange contracts are two: lower transactions costs by using one contract and a subtle but important decrease in risk exposure. In a swap any failure by the other side to honor the contract cancels all future obligations, while in the separate package the other side might try to default on some contracts but force you to honor others.

Why would Microsoft want to enter into such a swap? One reason could be that Microsoft discovers that it has an unusual opportunity to issue euro-denominated bonds at a low interest rate, perhaps because EU investors strongly desire to add some Microsoft bonds to their portfolios. But Microsoft actually needs dollars to finance the expansion of its business and wants to pay dollar interest on its debt. Microsoft can take advantage of the EU opportunity by issuing euro-denominated debt, and then swapping the euros into dollars. Microsoft must pay euro interest to its EU investors, but it is receiving euro interest in the swap. These euro flows approximately equal each other, so Microsoft mostly is left with the obligation to pay dollar interest into the swap. Microsoft accomplishes two things with the combination of euro bonds and swap. First, Microsoft can lower its overall cost of financing by taking advantage of the unusually low interest cost in the EU, even though it really does not want euro-denominated debt. Second, Microsoft effectively does not have euro-denominated debt—the cash flows (on net) are converted through the swap into the dollar cash flows that Microsoft prefers to have.

Currency futures, options, and swaps are relatively recent additions to the set of foreign exchange products. The first foreign-currency futures contract was offered in 1972. The first exchange-traded foreign-currency option was offered in 1982. Foreign-currency options are also offered directly by banks and other financial institutions in customized contracts with their customers. The first major currency swap was contracted in 1981 between the World Bank and IBM (dollars for German marks and Swiss francs).

Exchange-traded currency futures and options are of some importance, with the equivalent of $68 billion and $35 billion in existence at mid-year 1998. Still, most foreign exchange is transacted directly among banks, other financial institutions, and their customers. The size of the "over-the-counter" products (spot exchange, forward exchange, directly written currency options, and currency swaps) is much larger than the size of the exchange-traded foreign-currency futures and options. Currency swaps have become a big product, with nearly $2 trillion of swap contracts in force at mid-year 1998. And about $4.6 trillion of directly written currency options existed at mid-year 1998.

of a coming crisis, there is nothing to worry about. Relax. Take a three-month vacation in Hawaii. From time to time, stroll off the beach long enough to glance at the newspaper and note that the pound is sinking, just as you knew it would. On the contract date in May, instruct your bank to settle the forward contract against the actual spot rate, which has sunk as you expected to $1.20. Effectively, you are buying £10 million in the spot market at $1.20 (total cost of $12 million) and selling the pounds at $1.6340 into the forward contract (total receipt of $16.340 million). You net a profit of $4.340 million for a few minutes' effort, a lot of foresight, and an understanding of "buy low, sell high." If you are smarter than the others in the marketplace, you can get rich using the convenient forward exchange market.

Your speculation may turn out differently, however. Suppose you were wrong. Suppose that Britain's prospects brighten greatly between February and May. Suppose that when May comes around, the spot value of the pound has risen to $2.00. Now you must come up with $20 million to get the £10 million you agreed to sell in exchange for only $16.340 million. It does not take much arithmetic to see what this means for your personal wealth. It is time to reevaluate your lifestyle.

What happens if in February *many* people expect the spot exchange rate value of the pound to depreciate to $1.20 by May, and they are willing to speculate using the forward exchange market? They will sell pounds forward in large amounts. The increased supply of pounds forward will put downward pressure on the forward exchange rate value of the pound, driving it toward $1.20. Generally, all speculators will not have the exact same view as to the expected future spot exchange rate. Nonetheless, *speculators' pressures on supply and demand should drive the forward exchange rate to equal the average expected value of the future spot exchange rate.* For instance, the 90-day forward rate should indicate what informed opinion thinks the pound should be worth spot in 90 days' time. It should be an average expectation of the future spot value, much as the point spread in football betting is the number of points by which the average bettor expects the stronger team to win.

The Difference That Forward Cover Makes

Exposure to exchange rate risk is of major importance to international financial investment, which has grown rapidly in recent decades. Decisions about international investments, including decisions about whether to hedge the exposure to exchange rate risk, are based upon the returns and risks of the available investment alternatives. How do we calculate the overall returns on financial assets denominated in foreign currencies? What are the sources of risk that apply specifically or especially to foreign financial investments? The remainder of this chapter explores these questions about international financial investment. Although our discussion focuses on investing, most of the principles also apply to a borrower deciding whether to take out loans or issue securities denominated in foreign currencies.

Consider an investor who holds dollars now and plans to end up a year from now also holding dollars (or, at least, who calculates her wealth and returns in dollars). If she invests in a dollar-denominated financial asset like a U.S. government security or a dollar time deposit, then she will earn dollar returns and have dollar wealth a year from now. No currency translation is necessary. If she invests in a foreign-currency–denominated financial asset, like a U.K. government security or a pound time deposit, her situation is not so simple. First, she must convert her dollars into pounds at the initial spot exchange rate. Then, she uses the pounds to buy the pound-denominated financial asset. She holds this asset, earning pound returns and having wealth in pounds a year from now. This can be converted back into dollars (either actually or simply to determine the dollar value of wealth) at some dollar–pound exchange rate that applies to foreign exchange transactions a year from now.

What exchange rate can be used to convert pounds back into dollars a year from now? There are two major alternatives, and these correspond to our concepts of hedging and speculation. First, she can contract now for the exchange of pounds back into dollars at the one-year *forward exchange rate* using a forward exchange contract. Her pound liability in the forward contract matches her pound asset position, so she has hedged her exposure to exchange rate risk. She has a hedged or **covered international investment.** Second, she can wait and convert back into dollars at the *future spot exchange rate,* the one that will exist a year from now. She does not now know for sure what this future spot exchange rate will be so her investment is exposed to exchange rate risk. This unhedged investment has a speculative element to it, and it is called an **uncovered international investment.**

Covering an International Financial Investment

We can compare domestic investment and covered international investment using Figure 17.1, which shows ways of investing as paths around a "lake." A movement from one side to the other of the lake represents a currency exchange in the spot or forward exchange market, where the two currencies considered are dollars and pounds.

People moving their assets from left to right are buying sterling and selling dollars, whereas those transferring from right to left are buying dollars with pounds. People moving upward in either country are investing or lending, whereas those moving downward from future to current positions are either selling off interest-earning assets or actually borrowing at interest. The corresponding expressions in terms of exchange rates (the spot rate r_s and the forward rate r_f) and interest rates (i_{US} and i_{UK}) show how the value of one's assets gets multiplied by each move.[4]

---

[4]Note that the interest rates used here are for the actual time period examined and are measured in decimal, not percent, form. They are not annual rates unless the time period is one year. If interest rates are quoted as annualized rates, they must be converted. For instance, the 90-day interest rate is approximately one-quarter the annualized interest rate.

FIGURE 17.1

*Current and
Future Asset
Positions in Two
Currencies: The
"Lake"
Diagram*

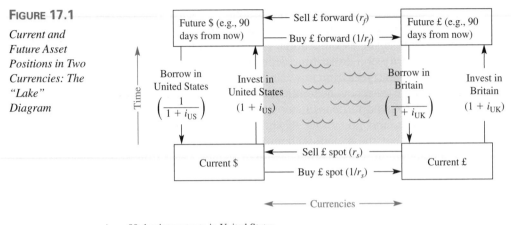

i_{US} = 90-day interest rate in United States
i_{UK} = 90-day interest rate in Britain
r_S = Spot price of the pound ($/£)
r_f = Forward price of the pound ($/£)

Studying how one gets from any corner to any other for any purpose, you will find that the choice of the more profitable of the two possible routes always depends on the comparison of two expressions. Suppose we want to convert present dollars into future dollars. We could route our money through Britain, buying pounds in the spot market, obtaining $1/r_s$ pounds for each dollar. We would then invest these pounds at interest and have $(1 + i_{UK})/r_s$ pounds at maturity for each initial dollar. At the time of the investment we also sell the upcoming pounds in the forward market (at the rate r_f) to get an assured number of dollars in the future. Overall, this yields $(1 + i_{UK}) \times r_f / r_s$ future dollars for every dollar invested now. Or we could simply invest our money at interest in America, getting $(1 + i_{US})$ future dollars for every present dollar. Which road we should take depends on the sign of the difference between the two returns. This difference is sometimes called the **covered interest differential** (CD) "in favor of London" or

$$CD = (1 + i_{UK})r_f/r_s - (1 + i_{US})$$

It is not hard to see why this can be called a differential in favor of London. If it is positive, one would be better off investing in Britain, probably in London. If it is negative (a differential "against London" or "in favor of New York"), one should avoid investments in Britain, investing in America instead. Why is it called *covered?* Because it shows a difference between two ways of getting from one currency to the same currency, with the investor fully hedged or covered against exchange rate risk.

In the literature on the forward exchange market, we sometimes meet a slightly different formula for the covered differential, a handy one that can be derived by using an approximation. First, we need to define the **forward premium** (or discount, if negative) as the proportionate difference between the current forward exchange rate value of the pound and its current spot value.[5]

$$F = (r_f - r_s)/r_s$$

The forward premium (converted into a percentage) shows the rate at which the pound gains value between a current spot transaction and the forward rate that can be obtained now. If the pound is at a forward discount, F is negative. Given this definition, the covered interest differential is approximately equal to the forward premium on the pound plus the regular interest rate differential:[6]

$$CD = F + (i_{UK} - i_{US})$$

The formula shows that the net incentive to go in one particular direction around the lake depends on how the forward premium on the pound compares with the difference between interest rates.

There is another way to interpret the approximation. The overall covered return (in dollars) to a U.S. investor from investing in Britain is approximately equal to the sum of two components: the gain (or loss) from the spot and forward currency exchanges (the forward premium F on the pound) plus the interest return on the pound investment itself (i_{UK}). The covered interest differential is then approximately equal to the difference between the overall covered return to investing in pound-denominated assets ($F + i_{UK}$) and the return to investing in dollar-denominated assets (i_{US}).[7]

---

[5]This is often stated on an annualized percent basis:

$$F = \frac{(r_f - r_s)}{r_s} \times \frac{360}{n} \times 100$$

where n is the number of days forward and a year is taken to be 360 days for convenience.

[6]To see the approximation involved, first rearrange the terms in the previous equation:

$$CD = r_f/r_s + i_{UK}r_f/r_s - 1 - i_{US}$$

Next, add and subtract i_{UK}

$$CD = r_f/r_s + i_{UK}r_f/r_s - i_{UK} - 1 + i_{UK} - i_{US}$$

Now group terms to form the forward premium:

$$CD = F + i_{UK} - i_{US} + i_{UK}F$$

In decimal form, the last term usually is the product of two small fractions and is considered to be zero in the approximation.

[7]The approximation is also useful because all rates can be stated on an annualized basis and in percent terms—the way we usually say them. In this case, F is the annualized percent forward premium (as defined in footnote 5) and the interest rates are annualized percent rates, regardless of the number of days forward being considered.

Covered Interest Arbitrage

The covered differential is such a handy guide to the profitable transfer of money across currencies that banks have developed the art of covered interest arbitrage in order to cash in on any differential. **Covered interest arbitrage** is buying a country's currency spot and selling it forward, while making a net profit off the combination of the higher interest rate in that country and any forward premium on its currency. Covered interest arbitrage is essentially riskless, although it does tie up some assets for a while. One way of engaging in arbitrage is in fact the ultimate in hedging: We can start with dollars today and end up with a guaranteed greater amount of dollars today by going all the way around the lake.

To see how this arbitrage works, let's suppose that British and U.S. interest rates are $i_{UK} = .04$ (4 percent) and $i_{US} = .03$ (3 percent), respectively, for 90 days, and that both the spot and forward exchange rates are \$2.00/£, so that there is neither a premium nor a discount on forward sterling ($F = 0$). Seeing that this means CD = .01 (1 percent), a New York arbitrageur uses the telephone and sets up a counterclockwise journey around the lake. He contracts to sell, say, \$20 million in the spot market, buying £10 million. He informs his London correspondent bank or branch bank of the purchase and instructs that bank to place the proceeds in British Treasury bills that will mature in 90 days. This means that after 90 days he will have £10 million × 1.04 to dispose of. He covers himself against exchange rate risk by contracting to sell the £10.4 million in the forward market, receiving \$20.8 million deliverable after 90 days. He could leave the matter there, knowing that his phone trip in and out of Britain will give \$20.8 million in 90 days' time, instead of the \$20.6 million he would have received by investing his original \$20 million within the United States. Or if he has excellent credit standing, he can celebrate his winnings by borrowing against the \$20.8 million in the United States at 3 percent, giving himself \$20,194,175 = \$20.8 million/(1.03) right now, or about 1 percent more than he had before he used the telephone. So that's \$194,175 in arbitrage gains minus the cost of the telephone calls, any transactions fees, the use of part of a credit line in the United States, and a few minutes' time. Not a bad wage. The operation is also riskless as long as nobody defaults on a contract. [The reader can confirm that if forward sterling instead were at a 2 percent discount ($F = -.02$ because $r_f = \$1.96$), the New York arbitrageur would invest in the United States, buy forward sterling, borrow or sell bills in Britain, and sell pounds spot, making a net profit of about 1 percent.]

Interest arbitrage looks like the perfect money machine. It is especially attractive today, now that telecommunications and computers have reduced transactions costs close to zero. If bankers failed to take advantage of such opportunities, we should wonder about their business acumen.

In fact, though, arbitrage is such a sure thing that it is an endangered species. Banks can program their computers to tell their traders instantly of any discrepancy in rates that would seem to allow profitable arbitrage. Such opportunities can persist only as long as other banks deal at rates that pass up arbitrage profits for themselves, or until market pressures from supply and demand alter the rates.

Soon enough the rates change, removing the chance for instant moneymaking. Traders still make money on pure arbitrage, such as covered interest arbitrage as described here, but they have to be fast. The chance is usually gone within a minute or two.

Covered Interest Parity

John Maynard Keynes, himself an interest arbitrageur, argued that the opportunities to make arbitrage profits would be self-eliminating because the forward exchange rate would adjust so that the covered interest differential returned to zero. Since Keynes we have referred to the condition CD = 0 as **covered interest parity.**

> **Covered interest parity:** A currency is at a forward premium (discount) by as much as its interest rate is lower (higher) than the interest rate in the other country.

In the numerical example on page 372, covered interest parity would exist if the forward rate is \$1.98/£ (rather than \$2.00/£). Then the forward discount on the pound of 1 percent (equal to the proportionate difference between the 1.98 forward rate and the 2.00 spot rate) offsets the amount by which the British interest rate (4 percent) is higher than the U.S. interest rate (3 percent). U.S. investors would earn only 3 percent on their covered investments in pound-denominated assets—the 4 percent interest minus the 1 percent lost in the currency exchanges. This 3 percent is equal to the rate that they receive on investments in dollar-denominated assets, so there is no incentive for arbitrage.

Covered interest parity provides an explanation for differences between current spot and current forward exchange rates. A country with an interest rate that is lower than the corresponding rate in the United States will have a forward premium on its currency, with the percentage point difference in the interest rates equal to the percent forward premium. Referring back to the exchange rate quotations in Figure 16.1, the currencies of Japan and Switzerland, as well as the currencies of France and Germany (both fixed to the euro and to each other), all have 90-day forward rates (dollars per this currency) above their current spot rates. These currencies are at a forward premium, and we could confirm that their 90-day interest rates were less at that time than the interest rates on comparable assets denominated in dollars. The currencies of Britain and Canada have forward rates below their current spot rate—a forward discount that is related to relatively high interest rates in these countries.

Covered interest parity links together four rates: the current forward exchange rate, the current spot exchange rate, and the current interest rates in the two countries. If one of these rates changes, then at least one of the other rates also must change to maintain (reestablish) covered interest parity. For instance, if the spot exchange rate increases and the interest differential is unchanged, then the forward exchange rate also must rise to keep the forward premium steady. In this case, whatever moves the spot rate up (or down) will do the same to the forward rate. In fact, short-term interest differentials have not varied much over the past several decades for the major world currencies, so spot and forward rates between any two of these currencies have tended to go up or down together over time. That is, the current spot and current forward rates are highly positively correlated over time.[8]

International Investment Without Cover

Uncovered international financial investment involves investing in a financial asset denominated in a foreign currency without hedging or covering the future proceeds of the investment back into one's own currency. In the simplest case, the foreign currency proceeds will be translated back into domestic currency using whatever spot exchange rate exists at the future date (either actually, or to calculate wealth and overall returns in one's own currency). The future spot rate is not known for sure at the time of the initial investment, so the investment is exposed to exchange rate risk (assuming that the investor has no other offsetting liability in this currency).

At the time of the initial investment, the investor presumably has some idea of what the future spot rate is likely to be. The investor's expected future spot rate (r_s^e) can be used to determine an expected overall return on the uncovered international investment. (This expected future spot rate is the same type of rate used in deciding whether to speculate using a forward contract.)

A kind of "lake" diagram similar to that used in Figure 17.1 applies here, but the top side of the lake refers to currency exchanges in the future at the future spot exchange rate. At the time of the foreign investment ("ex ante"), we only have a notion or an expectation of what the future spot rate will be. Of course, once we get to the future date (the end or maturity of the foreign investment—"ex post"), we will know what the future spot rate actually is, and then we can determine the actual overall return on the uncovered foreign investment.

To see how this works, again consider that we want to convert present dollars into future dollars. We again could route our money through Britain, but in this case we decide not to cover against exchange rate risk. We first buy pounds in the spot market, obtaining $1/r_s$ pounds for each dollar. We then invest these pounds, and we will have $(1 + i_{UK})/r_s$ pounds at maturity for each initial dollar. We have an expectation that we can convert these pounds back into dollars at the rate r_s^e, to obtain $(1 + i_{UK}) \times r_s^e/r_s$ future dollars expected for each dollar invested now. This can be compared to the future dollars $(1 + i_{US})$ that we could obtain simply by investing each present dollar in a dollar-denominated asset, and we have the **expected uncovered interest differential (EUD)** "in favor of London":

---

[8]Covered interest parity also has implications for our earlier discussion of hedging a future pound liability. Here the goal is to get from current dollars to future pounds (needed to pay for the merchandise). If covered interest parity holds, then the cost of hedging using a forward contract (going up the lake and then across at the top toward the right) will essentially equal the cost of hedging by buying pounds spot now and investing these pounds for 90 days (going across the lake to the right at the bottom and then going up).

$$\text{EUD} = (1 + i_{UK})r_s^e/r_s - (1 + i_{US})$$

If this is positive, then the expected overall return favors uncovered investing in a pound-denominated asset. If it's negative, then the expected overall return favors staying at home.[9]

The expression for the expected uncovered interest differential is almost the same as the expression for the covered interest differential. The only difference is that the expected future spot rate r_s^e replaces the forward rate r_f. This is not surprising—the difference between the two is specifically the decision not to cover or hedge the exposure to exchange rate risk by using a forward contract.

We can also show that the expected uncovered interest differential has a handy approximation. It approximately equals the expected rate of appreciation (depreciation, if negative) of the foreign currency plus the regular interest rate differential:[10]

$$\text{EUD} = \text{expected appreciation} + (i_{UK} - i_{US})$$

For a different view of this, note that the expected overall uncovered return (in dollars) to a U.S. investor from investing in Britain is approximately equal to the sum of the expected gain (or loss) from the currency exchanges (current spot and future spot) as the pound appreciates (or depreciates) during the time of the investment, plus the interest return on the pound investment itself. This expected overall return on the pound investment (currency appreciation + i_{UK}) is compared to the return on investing in dollar-denominated assets (i_{US}) to approximate the expected uncovered interest differential.

Let's consider a numerical example similar to the one used in the section on covered investment. The current spot exchange rate r_s is \$2.00/£, and the current interest rates on 90-day investments are $i_{UK} = 0.04$ (4 percent) and $i_{US} = 0.03$ (3 percent). If a U.S.-based investor expects the spot rate (r_s^e) to remain at \$2.00/£ in 90 days, what is the expected uncovered interest differential? Because he expects no change in the pound's exchange rate value, the expected differential is 1 percent (equal to the interest rate differential, 4 − 3) in favor of the pound investment. The investor expects a higher return to investing uncovered in pound assets, but he is not certain of the extra return. The actual spot exchange rate in 90 days could be quite different from what he is expecting.

---

[9]From the perspective of a U.K. investor, the expected uncovered interest differential is $(1 + i_{US})r_s/r_s^e -$ $(1 + i_{UK})$ if we continue to quote exchange rates as dollars per pound. This expression is mathematically very similar to EUD for the U.S. investor. Specifically, if the two have the same expected future spot rate, the EUD is negative for the U.K. investor when it is positive for the U.S. investor (and positive when negative).

[10]For the actual time period involved, the expected rate of appreciation equals $(r_s^e - r_s)/r_s$. This is often stated instead on a percent annualized basis,

$$\frac{r_s^e - r_s}{r_s} \times \frac{360}{n} \times 100$$

where n is the number of days in the future for the expected future spot rate.

The World's Greatest Investor

George Soros was born Dzjchdzhe Shorask (pronounced "Shorosh") in Budapest in 1930. The son of a lawyer, he became a global investment superstar, with a net worth in 1998 estimated at $3.5 billion.

As a Jewish boy, he and his family struggled to evade the Nazis, and they managed to survive. In 1947 he went to England, expecting to continue his engineering studies. Instead, he enrolled in the London School of Economics and graduated in 1952. He began working at a small London brokerage, but he was frustrated by the lack of responsibilities.

In 1956, Soros moved to New York City, where he worked at two securities firms before joining the firm Arnold & Bleichroeder in 1963. In 1967, he became head of investment research, and he was successful at finding good investment opportunities in undervalued European stocks. In 1969, he founded an offshore hedge fund, using $250,000 of his own money and about $6 million from non-American investors whom he knew. (A hedge fund is an investment partnership that is not restricted by regulations of government agencies like the U.S. Securities and Exchange Commission. Each hedge fund can establish its own investment style and strategy, and these vary. While some hedge funds do use investment strategies that involve different kinds of hedging, others do not. The manager of a fund usually gets fees and a percentage of the profits, as well as having a substantial amount of his or her own money invested in the fund.)

Soon Soros left Arnold & Bleichroeder, taking his Soros Fund with him. While the 1970s were poor years for the U.S. stock market generally, the Soros Fund prospered. As the manager, Soros focused on finding undervalued sectors in the United States and other countries. He bought unpopular low-priced stocks and sold short popular high-priced stocks. He

expected oil demand to outstrip oil supply, so he bought stocks of companies in oil-field services and oil drilling before the first oil shock in 1973. In the mid-1970s, he invested heavily in Japanese stocks. In 1979, he changed the name of the fund to Quantum Fund, in honor of Heisenberg's uncertainty principle in quantum mechanics. In 1980, the fund return was 103 percent. It had grown to $380 million.

In 1981, *Institutional Investor* magazine named him "the world's greatest investor." But 1981 was a difficult year: The fund lost 23 percent, and one-third of his investors withdrew their investments. This was their mistake—spectacular returns were still to come.

In early September 1985, Soros became convinced that the U.S. dollar was overvalued relative to the Japanese yen and the German mark, and that a correction was coming soon. He decided to establish speculative investment positions to try to profit from the changes he expected. For instance, he borrowed dollars, used the dollars to buy yen and marks, and bought Japanese and German government bonds. In total, he established an $800 million position, a position larger than the entire capital of the fund. In late September the major governments announced the Plaza Agreement, in which they vowed to take coordinated actions (like intervention in the foreign exchange markets) to raise the values of other major currencies relative to the dollar. Within a month, as the dollar depreciated,

If an uncovered foreign financial investment is exposed to exchange rate risk, why would anyone want to invest uncovered? The answer has two components: one related to return and one to risk. First, the expected overall return on the uncovered investment may be higher than the return that can be obtained at home (EUD is positive), as in the numerical example just completed. In a sense, an uncovered pound investment is then another way to speculate on the future dollar–pound

Soros had profits of $150 million. The fund's total return for 1985 was 122 percent, as he had also invested in foreign stocks and long-term U.S. treasury bonds. Of course, not all of his positions turned out so well. For instance, in 1987, the Quantum Fund lost up to $840 million when the U.S. and other stock markets crashed in October. But the fund still earned a return of 14 percent for the entire year.

In September 1992, Soros placed his most famous bet. Following German unification in 1989, German interest rates increased, and the mark tended to appreciate. But most EU currencies were pegged to each other in the Exchange Rate Mechanism (ERM) of the European Monetary System. So the other countries had to raise their interest rates to maintain the pegged exchange rates. Soros predicted that the British government could not sustain this policy, because the British economy was already weak and unemployment high. He expected that Britain would either devalue the pound within the ERM or pull out of the ERM. In either case, the exchange rate value of the pound would decline. He established his speculative investment positions short in pounds and long in marks, using pound borrowings and mark investments, as well as futures and options. And the positions were big— $10 billion. As Soros and other speculative investors established their positions, they sold pounds, putting downward pressure on the exchange rate value of the pound. The central banks tried to defend the pegged rate, but soon the British government gave up and pulled out of the ERM. The pound depreciated against the mark. Within a month the Quantum Fund made a profit of about $1 billion on its pound positions, and a profit of up to $1 billion on other European currency positions. The *Economist* magazine called Soros "the man who broke the Bank of England."

After 1992, Soros turned over most trading decisions in the Quantum Fund to his chosen successor, Stanley Druckenmiller. The Quantum Fund remains very active and continues to have some large suc-

cesses and some large losses. In early 1997, Soros and Druckenmiller foresaw weakness in the Thai baht, and Quantum established short baht positions in January and February. The crisis hit in July, the Thai baht depreciated, and Quantum made money. But, when the Thai baht and other Asian currencies continued to depreciate, they thought that the market had taken the rates too far. For instance, when the Indonesian rupiah fell from 2,400 per dollar to 4,000 per dollar, they established long positions in rupiah, and then lost money as the rupiah continued to fall beyond 10,000 per dollar. In 1998, the Quantum Fund lost $2 billion on investments in Russia when Russian financial markets and the ruble collapsed. But the fund still earned more than 12 percent for the entire year. In 1998, the Quantum Fund value was about $20 billion.

As he reduced his role in fund management, Soros turned to writing articles and books and to philanthropy. His writings are curious. He is deeply critical of excessive capitalism and individualism—what he calls "market fundamentalism." He believes that unregulated global financial markets are inherently unstable, and he calls for greater national regulation and the establishment of new global institutions like an international credit-insurance organization to guarantee loans to developing countries.

Although Soros is not active much in investment decisions anymore, he remains the quintessential international speculative investor. His name is synonymous with hedge funds, especially those that take large speculative positions. He is denounced by government officials, like Prime Minister Mahathir Mohamad of Malaysia in 1997, as the source of immense and unjustified speculative pressures on their countries' currencies and financial markets. Soros continues to defend his own investment activities, stating that he merely perceived changes that were going to happen in any case. But, as his writings indicate, at a broader level he has mixed feelings about the current global financial system.

exchange rate. Presumably, the investor would undertake such an uncovered investment if she expects to be adequately compensated for the risks that she is taking on, especially the exchange rate risk that the actual future spot rate could be much lower than she is expecting.

However, the issue of risk exposure is really more subtle. It is not the risk of this individual investment that matters, but rather the contribution of this uncovered investment to the riskiness of the investor's full investment portfolio. While we will not develop this fully, analysis of portfolios indicates that the addition of an uncovered foreign investment can sometimes increase overall riskiness, but in other cases it can instead lower it because of the benefits of diversification of investments. If it lowers overall riskiness, then the investor would look favorably on an uncovered foreign investment even if the expected uncovered interest differential is somewhat negative.

To see the importance of uncovered foreign investments and the expected uncovered interest differential, let's examine what is likely to be true if risk considerations are small. Risk considerations can be small if investors do not care much about risk exposures (they are *risk neutral*) or if the benefits of diversification indicate that additional uncovered investments add little or nothing to the overall riskiness of the investor's portfolio. In this case each investor is willing to undertake uncovered foreign investments if the uncovered interest differential is positive. As investors make shifts in their portfolios, they place supply and demand pressures on the current spot exchange rate, by buying or selling pounds for dollars to shift into or out of pound-denominated investments. (They may also place pressures on the interest rates as they buy and sell the financial assets themselves.)

Generally, the pressures on the rates will subside only when there is no further incentive for large shifts in investments—when the expected uncovered differential equals zero, at least for the average investor. If this is true, then we have a condition in which EUD = 0, called *uncovered interest parity*.

> **Uncovered interest parity:** A currency is expected to appreciate (depreciate) by as much as its interest rate is lower (higher) than the interest rate in the other country.

Consider the rates used in our previous numerical example: a current spot rate of \$2.00/£ and British and U.S. interest rates of 4 and 3 percent. For these rates uncovered interest parity holds if investors generally expect the future spot rate in 90 days to be \$1.98/£. Then the expected depreciation of the pound of 1 percent (from the current spot rate of 2.00 to a future spot rate of 1.98) equals the 1 percent by which British interest rates exceed U.S. interest rates (4 − 3).

If uncovered interest parity holds, then it links together four rates: the current spot exchange rate, the spot exchange rate that is currently expected to exist (on average) in the future, and the current interest rates in the two countries. As with covered interest parity, if one of these four rates changes, then at least one of the other rates must change to maintain or reestablish uncovered interest parity. Consider several possible changes that can lead to quick appreciation of the pound. If the interest rate in the United Kingdom increases, this can increase the current spot exchange-rate value of the pound, thus reducing the expected rate of further pound appreciation (or increasing the expected rate of pound depreciation) into the future (assuming that the value of the expected future spot rate is unchanged). If, instead, the value of the expected future spot rate increases and there is no change in interest rates, then the value of the current spot exchange rate must increase to maintain the same rate of further pound appreciation (or depreciation) expected into the future. We will look at these relationships more deeply in the next two chapters, when we search for the determinants of spot exchange rates.

Does Interest Parity Really Hold? Empirical Evidence

The relationships among exchange rates and interest rates that we have discussed in this chapter are powerful concepts. In this final section we look at the empirical evidence. Do these rate relationships hold for actual exchange rates and interest rates?

Evidence on Covered Interest Parity

Covered interest parity states that the forward premium should be (approximately) equal to the difference in interest rates. All of these rates can be seen in the foreign exchange markets and the short-term financial markets, so a test of covered interest parity is straightforward. The only further requirement is to identify comparable financial assets denominated in different currencies. Generally, we want to use financial assets with little or no risk of default so that any subtle differences in default risk do not muddy the empirical test.

A basic test is to examine financial assets offered by the same institution but differing in their currencies. A good choice is the set of Eurocurrency deposits offered by large banks to their international customers. A bank active in the Eurocurrency market is willing to accept interest-paying time deposits denominated in any of a number of currencies, not just the currency of the country in which the bank is located. [The box "Eurocurrencies—Not (Just) Euros and Not Regulated" says more about this market.] Various tests have shown that covered interest parity applies almost perfectly to Eurocurrency deposits. That is, the difference in interest rates between Eurodollar deposits and Eurosterling deposits, for instance, equals the forward premium on the pound (within the limits of the small amount of transactions costs incurred in making the various exchanges). This is full support for covered interest parity, but it is perhaps not surprising. The same banks are quoting all four rates (forward and spot exchange rates and the Euro-interest rates), and they base their quotes of the forward exchange rates on the interest rate differential.

A more stringent test of covered interest parity involves closely comparable assets issued by different institutions in separate national financial markets. Figure 17.2 on page 382 shows the results from one careful study that examined the covered interest differentials between short-term financial assets in the United States and those in Germany, Japan, and France. For Germany and Japan, the covered interest differential is consistently very close to zero (and thus within the small range created by modest transactions costs) beginning in about 1985. For France this is true beginning in about 1987. Since about the mid-1980s, covered interest parity has held for comparable short-term assets for these four currencies (and for a number of others not shown as well).

The divergences in the earlier period, especially the large divergences for France, appear to reflect actual or threatened government restrictions on the ability to move moneys internationally. Germany, Japan, and France all had various forms of **capital controls** that limited the ability of financial investors to transfer moneys in or out of these countries. Germany and Japan largely eliminated these

Eurocurrencies—Not (Just) Euros and Not Regulated

The Eurocurrency market is a worldwide wholesale money market of enormous scope, one beyond the easy control of any government. In this market any large business or government can borrow or lend at interest any weekday, day or night. This large, complex, and sometimes mysterious market has sprung up since the late 1950s.

The traditional definition of a Eurocurrency deposit is a bank deposit denominated in a currency different from the currency of the country where the bank is located. However, this definition is no longer completely accurate—since 1981, the equivalent of Eurodollar deposits can be booked in New York in the International Banking Facility of a U.S. bank. The better definition of a Eurocurrency deposit is a bank deposit that is not subject to the usual regulations imposed by the country of the currency in which the deposit is denominated. Eurodollar deposits are dollar deposits that are not subject to the same regulations imposed by the U.S. banking authorities on regular dollar deposits. In fact, the prefix *Euro* has now come to be used in international finance to refer not to geographic location but rather to financial instruments or activities that are subject to little or no government regulation. Eurobonds are bonds that are issued outside of the usual regulations imposed by the country in whose currency the bond is denominated.

Eurocurrency deposits are large time deposits. In 1998, banks in various areas of the world, including Europe, North America, Asia, and the Caribbean, had Eurocurrency deposits totaling about $9 billion. A little less than half of these were Eurodollar deposits.

Eurosterling, Euromark, Eurofranc, and Euroyen deposits were important too. With the birth of the euro as a currency in 1999, we now also have euro Eurodeposits! (And we have some confusing terminology—the *euro* as a currency is different from *Euro* as a prefix.)

Eurocurrencies in their modern form seem to have begun in Europe in the late 1950s. Several reasons explain the development and rapid growth of Eurocurrencies. First, European firms active in international trade began to hold dollars temporarily, because the dollar had become the currency used for many trade transactions. These firms found it convenient to deal with their local banks that were willing to accept dollar deposits. Second, the Soviet Union was acquiring dollars in its foreign transactions. With the Cold War in full force, the Soviets feared that the United States might block any deposits that they made in U.S. banks so they began to deposit dollars in European banks. In the 1970s, Arab countries earning dollars on oil exports also feared possible restrictions if they placed their dollars on deposit in the United States, and turned to Eurodollar deposits. Third, and most important to the long-run development of the market, banks involved in taking these deposits (and making loans with the funds) found that they could avoid various regulations otherwise imposed on their banking activities.

One type of regulation that can be avoided is any restriction of international flows of moneys. Thus, in the late 1950s, the British government restricted the ability of British banks to lend pounds to foreigners,

capital controls in the early 1980s. With freer flows of moneys, covered interest arbitrage became possible, and covered interest parity has held between the United States and these two countries since the mid-1980s.

With the election of Mitterrand, a socialist, as president of France in 1981, foreign investors began to fear the imposition of more severe capital controls. This added a risk to covered investments into France, the political risk that investors will not be able to remove their moneys from France when they want. Because of this additional risk, major deviations from covered interest parity arose in 1981, at times reaching an annualized covered interest differ-but permitted them to lend dollars to foreigners. In the 1960s, the U.S. government attempted to restrict capital outflows. Borrowers turned to the Eurodollar market to obtain dollars that they could no longer borrow from the United States.

Other regulations that can be avoided in the Eurocurrency market are the standard regulations imposed on domestic banking activities. For instance, in the 1960s in the United States, government-imposed ceilings (Regulation Q) were limiting the interest rates that U.S. banks could pay on their deposits. Depositors turned to Eurodollar deposits to earn interest rates above the ceilings. Other examples of regulations that can be avoided in the Eurocurrency market are the reserves that banks are normally required to hold against their deposits and the insurance premiums that banks are normally required to pay for deposit insurance. Countries that wish to attract Eurocurrency deposit activity generally do not impose such reserve requirements or deposit premiums, and they lighten or eliminate other regulations as well. The lack of the burdens and extra costs of various regulations permits banks to offer somewhat higher interest rates on Eurocurrency deposits than are available on regular domestic bank deposits (even with no interest rate ceilings domestically) and perhaps also to charge somewhat lower interest rates on loans funded by these deposits. The lack of regulation implies that Eurocurrency deposit claims are somewhat riskier for depositors—they face somewhat more uncertainty about whether their claims will be honored if the bank should fail.

Some effects of Eurocurrency markets are straightforward, while others are controversial. Eurocurrency deposits and loans are generally credited with enhancing the efficiency of international financial markets. Eurocurrencies offer large corporations, financial institutions, and governments another alternative as to where they can invest their funds to earn interest or where they can borrow to obtain low-cost financing. Some of the efficiencies here come from the lack of burdens and costs imposed by government regulations, while others come from additional and fierce competition among banks from many countries for the same business.

The possible effects of Eurocurrencies on money supplies and inflation pressures are more controversial. Eurocurrency deposits are time deposits. They are not part of the narrowly defined money supply (currency, coin, and demand deposits—M1 in the United States). But they would be part of the more broadly defined money supply that includes "near moneys" such as time deposits (M2 or M3 in the United States).

Various studies have concluded that (1) the rise of Eurocurrencies generally has not reduced the ability of monetary authorities to control national money supplies and influence national inflation rates and (2) there is little impact on the growth rate of world money or on average world inflation. Nonetheless, the large amount of near-money existing in Eurocurrency deposits, and the ability of the market to grow quickly, could still influence inflation pressures in the future. In subsequent chapters we will examine the relationships between money and inflation in different countries, and how these in turn influence exchange rates and the international performance of different countries.

ential of 10 percentage points. Foreign investors were correct to fear capital controls. France tightened its controls in 1981 and did not substantially liberalize these controls until 1986. Once the controls were removed, and the risk that they might be reimposed subsided, covered interest parity began to hold in 1987.

Thus, covered interest parity is an important and empirically useful concept. It applies almost perfectly in the Eurocurrency market, and it applies to a growing number of countries that have liberalized or eliminated their capital controls on international movements of moneys.

FIGURE 17.2

Covered Interest Differentials: The United States Against Germany, Japan, and France, 1978–93

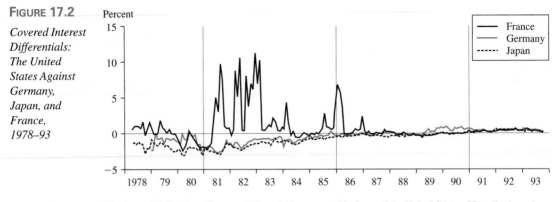

The (annualized) covered interest differential is measured in favor of the United States, $CD = F + i_{US} - i_F$, where F is the forward premium on the dollar, and i_F is the interest rate for the other country (Germany, Japan, or France). The forward rate and the interest rates are 90-day rates. The interest rates are for commercial paper in the United States and for interbank borrowing in the other three countries.

Source: Pigott (1993–1994).

Evidence on Uncovered Interest Parity

Uncovered interest parity states that the expected rate of appreciation of the spot exchange rate value of a currency should (approximately) equal the difference in interest rates. Testing uncovered interest parity is much more difficult than testing covered interest parity. We have no direct information on people's actual expectations of exchange rate changes.

One approach is to survey knowledgeable market participants about their exchange rate expectations (and hope that they answer truthfully.) The average expected future spot rate can then be used to calculate the expected appreciation and the expected uncovered interest differential. Figure 17.3 shows the results of one study using this approach. The two panels show the uncovered interest differential in favor of the United States relative to Germany and to Japan. In both panels it appears that market participants often expected large uncovered interest differentials. This suggests that uncovered interest parity does not hold nearly as closely as does covered interest parity.

A second approach is to examine actual returns on uncovered international investments to draw out inferences about expected returns and exchange rate expectations. Looking at the *actual* overall return (including both the foreign interest return and the actual gain or loss on the currency exchanges) on any *one* uncovered foreign investment does not tell us much. The actual uncovered return may not equal the return on a comparable domestic investment simply because the actual future spot exchange rate turned out to be somewhat different from the future spot exchange rate that was expected at the time of the investment. Nonetheless, if expected uncovered returns are typically at parity, then over a *large number* of investments the actual uncovered differentials should be random and on average approximately equal to zero. Various studies have shown that the actual uncovered differentials are not completely random and for some time peri-

FIGURE 17.3

Uncovered Interest Differentials: The United States Against Germany and Japan, 1991–1993

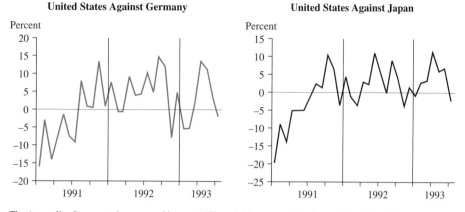

The (annualized) expected uncovered interest differential is measured in favor of the United States, EUD = expected appreciation of the dollar + $i_{US} - i_F$. The expected 90-day appreciation of the dollar is based on forecasts of currency movements from *Consensus Forecasts*. Interest rates are those on 90-day Eurocurrency deposits.

Source: Pigott (1993–1994).

ods are not on average equal to zero. Uncovered interest parity applies roughly, but there also appear to be deviations of some importance.

Why does uncovered interest parity not hold perfectly? One possible explanation is simple—exchange rate risk matters. Investors will not enter into risky uncovered foreign investments unless they expect to be compensated adequately for the risk that this adds to their portfolios. Divergences from uncovered interest parity then reflect the risk premium necessary to compensate for exchange rate risk. However, some studies conclude that the uncovered interest differential is often larger than the risk premium necessary to compensate for this risk.

To the extent that the differential is larger than that necessary to compensate for risk, it appears that the expectations of market participants about future spot exchange rates are biased. For some periods of time the market participants are consistently expecting an exchange rate change that is different from what will actually occur. Current research is attempting to determine the nature of the biases that appear to exist in market expectations of future spot exchange rates. One possible explanation is troubling. If the biases are simply consistent errors, the foreign exchange market is an inefficient market. Other possible explanations are more subtle and probably less troubling. One is that market participants learn slowly about exchange rate behavior, but their forecasts are biased while they are learning. Another is that market participants (correctly) expect a large, rather sudden shift in the exchange rate at some point in the future. During the time before the large shift occurs, forecasts appear to be biased because they give some probability to the much different exchange rate that has not yet arrived. For instance, if the market expects a large devaluation of a now fixed-rate currency, the expected value of the spot exchange rate 90 days from now is an average of the current spot rate (if the devaluation does not occur within the next 90 days) and a much lower rate (if the devaluation does occur within the next 90 days). During the time before the devaluation actually occurs, the expected exchange rate appears to be biased—it is consistently lower than the actual (fixed) rate that continues to hold.

The conclusions that we reach are cautious. Uncovered interest parity is useful at least as a rough approximation empirically, but it also appears to apply imperfectly to actual rates.

Evidence on Forward Exchange Rates and Expected Future Spot Exchange Rates

If there is substantial speculation using the forward exchange market, then the forward rate should equal the average market expectation of the future spot exchange rate. Although this seems quite different from the interest parity relationships, it is actually closely related to them. If covered interest parity applies to actual rates, then testing whether the forward rate is a predictor of the future spot exchange rate is the same as testing uncovered interest parity. The only difference between covered and uncovered interest parity is the replacement of the current forward exchange rate with the currently expected future spot exchange rate.

For currencies for which covered interest parity holds, conclusions about the forward rate are then the same as those about uncovered interest parity. The forward exchange rate is roughly useful as an indicator of the market's expected future spot rate or as a predictor of this future spot rate, but there are also indications of biases in the predictions. Some part of the biases probably reflect risk premiums, but another part appears to reflect biases in the forecasts themselves. In addition, the forward rate is not a particularly accurate predictor of the future spot exchange rate—the errors in forecasting are often large. Indeed, as we will see in the next two chapters, no method of forecasting exchange rates into the near future is particularly accurate!

Summary

A person holding a net asset position (a *long* position) or a net liability position (a *short* position) in a foreign currency is exposed to **exchange rate risk.** The value of the person's income or net worth will change if the exchange rate changes in a way that the person does not expect. **Hedging** is the act of equating your assets and liabilities in a foreign currency so as to become immune to risk resulting from the future changes in the value of foreign currency. **Speculating** means taking a long or a short position in a foreign currency, thereby gambling on its future exchange value. There are a number of ways to hedge or speculate in foreign currency.

A forward foreign exchange contract is an agreement to buy or sell a foreign currency for future delivery at a price (the forward exchange rate) set now. Forward exchange contracts are useful because they provide a straightforward way to hedge an exposure to exchange rate risk or to speculate in an attempt to profit from future spot exchange rate values. An interesting condition that emerges from the use of the forward market for speculation is that the forward exchange rate should equal the average expected value of the future spot rate.

International financial investment has grown rapidly in recent years. It is more complicated than domestic investment because of the need for currency exchanges, both to acquire foreign currency now and to translate the foreign currency back in the future. If the rate at which the future sale of foreign currency will occur is locked in now through a forward exchange contract, we have a hedged or **covered international investment.** If the future sale of foreign currency will occur at the future spot rate, we have an **uncovered international investment,** one that is exposed to exchange rate risk and therefore is speculative.

As a result of **covered interest arbitrage** to exploit any covered differential between the returns on domestic and covered international investments, we expect that **covered interest parity** will exist (as long as there are no actual or threatened government restrictions on international money flows). Covered interest parity states that the percentage by which the forward exchange value of a currency exceeds its spot value equals the percentage point amount by which its interest rate is lower than the other country's interest rate. For countries with no capital controls and for comparable short-term financial assets, covered interest parity holds almost perfectly when actual rates are examined empirically.

At the time of the investment, the expected overall return on an uncovered international investment can be calculated using the investor's expected future spot exchange rate. The overall expected return on the uncovered international investment can be compared to the return available at home. The differential in these returns is one factor in deciding whether to make the uncovered international investment. Exposure to exchange rate risk must also be considered in the decision. If this risk is of little or no importance, then we expect that **uncovered interest parity** would exist—the expected rate of appreciation of a currency equals the percentage point amount by which its interest rate is lower than the other country's interest rate. Uncovered interest parity is not easy to test or examine empirically using actual rates, because we do not directly know the expected future spot rate or the expected rate of appreciation. It appears that uncovered interest parity is useful as a rough approximation, but it does not apply almost perfectly. Rather, exchange rate risk appears to be of some importance, and investors' expectations or forecasts of future spot exchange rates appear to be somewhat biased. (A similar conclusion is that, empirically, the forward exchange rate is a rough but somewhat biased predictor of the future spot exchange rate.)

Suggested Reading

Good presentations of theory and evidence on the parity relationships among forward exchange rates, spot exchange rates, and interest rates include Pigott (1993–94), Koedijk and Ott (1987), Taylor (1989), and Marston (1995). Froot and Thaler (1990) and Levich (1989) discuss evidence about the efficiency or inefficiency of the foreign exchange market. A good textbook view of foreign exchange futures, options, and swaps is found in Levich (1998, Chapters 11, 12, and 13). Stern and Chew (1988) offer further discussion of these and other innovations in foreign exchange and other aspects of international finance.

On Eurocurrencies, a readable guide is Goodfriend (1986). For more depth, see Dufey and Giddy (1994).

Questions and Problems

✦1. "For an investment in a foreign currency–denominated financial asset, part of the return comes from the asset itself and part from the foreign currency." Do you agree or disagree? Explain.

2. You have been asked to determine whether covered interest parity holds for one-year government bonds issued by the U.S. and British governments. What data will you need? How will you test?

✦3. Explain the nature of the exchange rate risk for each of the following, from the perspective of the U.S. firm or person. In your answer, include whether each is a long or short position in foreign currency.

   a. A small U.S. firm sold experimental computer components to a Japanese firm, and it will receive payment of 1 million yen in 60 days.

   b. An American college student receives as a birthday gift Japanese government bonds worth 10 million yen, and the bonds mature in 60 days.

   c. A U.S. firm must repay a yen loan, principal plus interest totaling 100 million yen, coming due in 60 days.

4. The current spot exchange rate is $0.010/yen. The current 60-day forward exchange rate is $0.009/yen. How would each U.S. firm or person shown in question 3 use a forward foreign exchange contract to hedge their risk exposure? What are the amounts in each forward contract?

✦5. The current spot exchange rate is $0.50/SFr. The current 180-day forward exchange rate is $0.52/SFr. You expect the spot rate to be $0.51/SFr in 180 days. How would you speculate using a forward contract?

6. The current spot exchange rate is $1.20/euro. The current 90-day forward exchange rate is $1.18/euro. You expect the spot rate to be $1.22/euro in 90 days. How would you speculate using a forward contract? If many people speculate in this way, what pressure is placed on the value of the current forward exchange rate?

✦7. You have access to the following rates:

   Current spot exchange rate: $0.0100/yen
   Current 180-day forward exchange rate: $0.0105/yen
   180-day U.S. interest rate (on dollar-denominated assets): 6.05%
   180-day Japanese interest rate (on yen-denominated assets): 1.00%

   The interest rates are true 180-day rates (not annualized). You can borrow or invest at these rates. Calculate the actual amounts involved for the two ways around the lake (Figure 17.1) to get between each of the following.

   a. Start with $1 now and end with dollars in 180 days.

   b. Start with $1 now and end with yen in 180 days.

   c. Start with 100 yen now and end with yen in 180 days.

8. The following rates are available in the markets:

   Current spot exchange rate: $0.500/SFr
   Current 30-day forward exchange rate: $0.505/SFr

   Annualized interest rate on 30-day dollar-denominated bonds: 12% (1.0% for 30 days)

   Annualized interest rate on 30-day Swiss franc–denominated bonds: 6% (0.5% for 30 days)

   a. Is the Swiss franc at a forward premium or discount?

   b. Should a U.S.-based investor make a covered investment in Swiss franc–denominated 30-day bonds, rather than investing in a 30-day dollar-denominated bond? Explain.

c. Because of covered interest arbitrage, what pressures are placed on the various rates? If the only rate that actually changes is the forward exchange rate, to what will its value be driven?

✦9. The following rates exist:

Current spot exchange rate: $1.80/£

Annualized interest rate on 90-day dollar-denominated bonds: 8% (2% for 90 days)

Annualized interest rate on 90-day pound-denominated bonds: 12% (3% for 90 days)

Financial investors expect the spot exchange rate to be $1.77/£ in 90 days

a. If he bases his decision solely on the difference in the expected rate of return, should a U.S.-based investor make an uncovered investment in pound-denominated bonds rather than investing in dollar-denominated bonds?

b. If she bases her decision solely on the difference in the expected rate of return, should a U.K.-based investor make an uncovered investment in dollar-denominated bonds rather than investing in pound-denominated bonds?

c. If there is substantial uncovered investment seeking higher expected returns, what pressure is placed on the current spot exchange rate?

10. Why is testing whether uncovered interest parity holds for actual rates more difficult than testing whether covered interest parity holds?

CHAPTER 18

What Determines Exchange Rates in the Long Run?

Thinking in terms of supply and demand is a necessary first step toward understanding exchange rates. The next step is the one that has to be taken in any market analysis: finding out what underlying forces cause supply and demand to change.

We need to know what forces have caused the changes in exchange rates observed since the start of widespread "floating" back in the early 1970s. Figure 18.1 reminds us just how variable exchange rates have been. Between 1971 and the end of 1973, most currencies of other industrialized countries rose in value relative to the dollar, the average rise being about 20 percent. After 1973, when the modern era of floating exchange rates clearly took hold, we can see three types of variability for these exchange rates.

First, there are long trends. As shown in Figure 18.1A, over the entire period the Japanese yen, Swiss franc, and German mark (DM) have tended to appreciate, with the yen and the Swiss franc about tripling in value, and the DM more than doubling. As shown in Figure 18.1B, over the entire period the Italian lira, British pound, and Canadian dollar have tended to depreciate. The lira has lost about half its exchange rate value against the dollar, the pound has lost about a third, and the Canadian dollar has lost about a third. Still other currencies, such as the Israeli shekel or Argentine peso, dropped so far in value that the vertical axis would need to be extended down (close) to zero if we wanted to add them to Figure 18.1B.

Second, there are medium-term trends (over periods of several years), and these medium-term trends are sometimes counter to the longer trends. For instance, the Swiss franc, DM, and to a lesser extent the yen depreciated during the period 1980–1985. Another trend is the appreciation of the pound and the lira from 1985 to 1988. Furthermore, the French franc has experienced a series of medium-term swings, but its value in 1998 was not much different from its value back in the early 1970s.

Third, there is substantial variability in these exchange rates from month to month (and indeed, from day to day, hour to hour, and even minute to minute).

FIGURE 18.1   *Selected Exchange Rates, 1970–1998 (Monthly)*

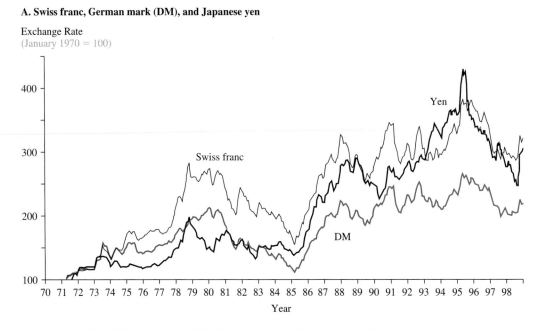

A. Swiss franc, German mark (DM), and Japanese yen

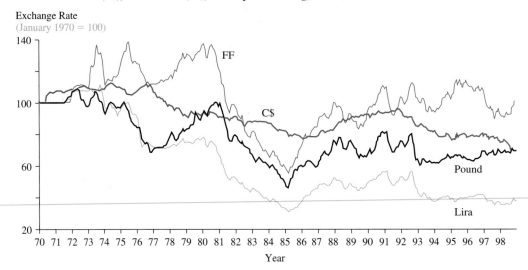

B. Canadian dollar (C$), French franc (FF), British pound sterling, and Italian lira

For each currency, the dollar price of that currency (e.g., $/£) is shown, with units adjusted so that its January 1970 value is 100. For any currency, an increase in the value shown from one time to another indicates that the currency has increased in exchange rate value (appreciated) relative to the U.S. dollar during that time period; a decrease in the value shown indicates that the currency has depreciated relative to the U.S. dollar. For the currencies shown, over the entire 28-year period, the Japanese yen, Swiss franc, and German mark have appreciated, while the Italian lira, British pound sterling, and Canadian dollar have depreciated. The French franc has fluctuated, and its 1998 value is similar to its 1970 value. At the beginning of 1999, the DM, French franc, and Italian lira were fixed to the euro and will eventually be replaced by this new currency.

Source: International Monetary Fund, *International Financial Statistics.*

We can look at the movements in the exchange rate value of the dollar as the reverse of those for each foreign currency, or we can calculate the average movement against a set of other currencies. On average against the currencies of other industrialized countries, after losing about 20 percent in exchange rate value during 1971–73, the dollar gained back almost 10 percent, but then lost about 13 percent from 1977 to 1979. After it changed little during the next two years, nearly all observers were stunned as the dollar rallied. By the time the dollar peaked in early 1985, it had gained over 50 percent in value since 1980 and was about 20 percent above its value in 1970. From early 1985 to early 1988, the dollar then fell (even more quickly) by a little more than it had risen in the previous five years. From early 1988 to 1998, the dollar fluctuated somewhat in average value against the currencies of the other industrialized countries, but it did not show any pronounced overall trend.

Why do we see large changes in the values of floating exchange rates? We need to know because exchange rate movements set off many macroeconomic effects, some of them negative. This chapter and the next one present what economists believe, what they think they know, and what they admit they do not know about this challenging puzzle.

This chapter focuses on what we know about the determinants of the *long trends* in exchange rates. Why do some currencies tend to appreciate over the long run, while others tend to depreciate? A key economic "fundamental" that appears to explain these long trends is the difference in national rates of inflation of the prices of goods and services. The first part of this chapter explores the concept of **purchasing power parity** as the basis for the relationship between product prices and exchange rates in the long run.

The second part of the chapter examines the role of money as the determinant of national product price levels and inflation rates. Through the link of money to price levels and inflation rates, the **monetary approach to exchange rates** emphasizes the importance of money supplies and demands as key to understanding the determinants of exchange rates. A major conclusion of the monetary approach is that the spot exchange rate r_s, the price of foreign currency in units of our currency, is raised *in the long run* by the following changes in fundamentals:

- A rise in our money supply relative to the foreign money supply (M^s/M_f^s).
- A rise in foreign real domestic product relative to our real domestic product (Y_f/Y).

Purchasing Power Parity (PPP)

Our understanding of exchange rates in the long run is based on the proposition that there is a predictable relationship between product price levels and exchange rates. The relationship relies on the fact that people can buy goods and services from one country or another, depending on the prices that they must pay.

Products that are substitutes for each other in international trade should have similar prices in all countries when measured in the same currency. This should hold, at least, after a run long enough for market equilibrium to be restored after major shocks. The belief that international trade irons out differences in the prices of traded goods has led to the **purchasing power parity hypothesis** linking national currency prices to exchange rates:

$$P = r_s \times P_f$$

or

$$r_s = P/P_f$$

Here the exchange rate r_s is again the spot price of the foreign currency (say, the pound) in dollars, and the price levels P and P_f are product price levels in the home country (say, the United States) and the rest of the world (say, Britain), respectively, each denominated in its own currency.

Something like the purchasing power parity theory has existed throughout the modern history of international economics. The theory keeps resurfacing whenever exchange rates have become more variable as a result of wars or other events. Sometimes the hypothesis is used as a way of describing how a nation's general price level must change to reestablish some desired exchange rate, given the level and trend in foreign prices. At other times it is used to guess at what the equilibrium exchange rate will be, given recent trends in prices within and outside the country. Both of these interpretations crept into the British "bullionist–antibullionist" debate during and after the Napoleonic Wars, when the issue was why Britain had been driven by the wars to dislodge the pound sterling from its fixed exchange rates and gold backing, and what could be done about it. The purchasing power parity hypothesis came into its own in the 1920s, when Gustav Cassel and others directed it at the issue of how much European countries would have to change either their official exchange rates or their domestic price levels, given that World War I had driven the exchange rates off their prewar par values and had brought varying percentages of price inflation to different countries. For instance, PPP was a rough guide to the mistake made by Britain in returning to the prewar gold parity for the pound sterling in 1925 despite greater price inflation in Britain than in Britain's trading partners. With the restoration of fixed exchange rates following World War II, the purchasing power parity hypothesis again faded from prominence, ostensibly because its defects had been demonstrated, but mainly because the issue it raised seemed less compelling as long as exchange rates were expected to stay fixed. After the resumption of widespread floating of exchange rates in the early 1970s, the hypothesis was revived once again.

General Evidence on PPP

The purchasing power parity hypothesis has received mixed empirical support. Using levels or movements in P/P_f to predict the level or movements of the exchange rate r_s leads to small errors in some settings and large errors in others.

PPP predicts well at the level of one heavily traded commodity, either at a point in time or for changes over time, as long as governments permit free trade in the commodity. Such heavily traded commodities include gold, other metals, crude oil, and various agricultural commodities. Consider, for example, No. 2 soft red Chicago wheat, and suppose that it costs $4.80 a bushel in Chicago. Its dollar price in London should not be much greater, given the cheapness of transporting wheat from Chicago to London. To simplify the example, let us say that it costs nothing to transport the wheat. It seems reasonable, then, that the dollar price of the same wheat in London should be $4.80 a bushel. If it is not, it would pay someone to trade wheat between Chicago and London to profit from the price gap. Now if some major disruption temporarily forces the price of wheat in London up to $6.00, yet free trade is still possible, we would certainly expect that the two prices would soon be bid back into equality, presumably somewhere between $4.80 and $6.00 for both countries. In the case of wheat (a standardized commodity with a well established market), we would expect the two prices to be brought into line within a week. For a highly traded good like wheat, something called the **law of one price** is a fair approximation. It says that a single commodity will have the same price everywhere, once the prices at different places are expressed in the same currency. Thus, in the wheat example, if the exchange rate is $1.60 per pound and wheat costs $4.80 a bushel in Chicago, the law of one price predicts that the London price of wheat will be £3.00, so that wheat costs $4.80 a bushel (= 3.00×1.60) in London as well as in Chicago.

PPP predicts only moderately well at the level of all traded goods, either at a point in time or for changes over time. If P_T is a domestic price index for the whole bundle of products that our nation exports and imports, and P_{Tf} is a foreign-currency price index for the similar bundle in other countries, it will turn out that P_T/P_{Tf} is only a fair predictor of the exchange rate r_s. Once we get up to the level of several goods, we get into technical difficulties of comparing index numbers. We also confront a wide range of products, some of which have significant transport costs and official trade barriers, so that their prices differ between countries. In addition, some firms with market power attempt to separate or segment different national markets so that they can increase profits by charging different prices in different markets.

PPP predicts least well at the level of all products in the economy. The broadest kind of price level and the one that relates most closely to overall inflation in a country, is the GDP (or GNP) price deflator, the price index for the whole bundle of all goods and services that make up gross domestic (or national) product. Unfortunately, this broad price concept includes many prices that fail to equalize between countries. As the box "Price Gaps and International Income Comparisons" on page 398 makes clear, price levels that the PPP theory assumes equal can be in a 5:1 ratio to each other. In fact, there is a clear pattern to the international failure of PPP to hold for GNP price deflators. The "worst" behaved prices are those for nontraded products, such as housing, haircuts, and other local services. The prices of nontraded products differ radically between lower-income and higher-income countries, as the box explains.

At any level of aggregation, *PPP predicts better over the long run than in the short run.* It takes time for market equilibrium to return after any given shock. The longer the number of years over which we examine prices and exchange rates, the closer we come to the PPP condition $r_s = P/P_f$.

For all its limitations, the purchasing power parity theory has its uses. It implies that countries with relatively low inflation rates have currencies whose values tend to appreciate in the foreign exchange market. Looked at the other way, countries with relatively high inflation rates have currencies whose values tend to depreciate in the foreign exchange market. In fact, a strict application of PPP implies that each percentage point more of domestic inflation per year tends to be related to a 1 percent faster rate of currency depreciation (or slower rate of currency appreciation) per year. PPP thus has an important message to offer countries such as Switzerland, which are seeking to keep domestic prices stable when the rest of the world is inflating. If prices elsewhere are rising 10 percent a year, in the long run, a country can keep its domestic prices stable only by accepting a rise of about 10 percent a year in the exchange value of its currency in terms of inflating-country currencies.

PPP: Recent Experience

We just suggested that PPP holds reasonably well in the long run, but poorly in the short run. We can examine specific evidence about PPP for recent years. Figure 18.2 provides evidence on the long run during the current period of floating exchange rates. For each country included in samples of industrialized and developing countries, the average annual rate of change of its currency's exchange rate against the U.S. dollar is compared to the difference between the average U.S. inflation rate and the country's inflation rate.[1] PPP predicts that when the inflation differential is positive (the U.S. has a higher inflation rate, or the country has a lower one), the country's currency should appreciate. When the inflation differential is negative, the country's currency should depreciate. Looking across the countries in each sample, this relationship is clear. In fact, the relationship is very close to the one-to-one relationship implied by a strict version of PPP.[2]

---

[1] The time period is 1975–1998. The beginning year 1975 is somewhat arbitrary; it was chosen to be close to the beginning of the current floating-rate period, but also to allow several years of adjustment following the end of the previous fixed-rate period. Inflation rates are measured using the consumer price index, a broad price index.

[2] A standard statistical test of the relationship is to fit the best straight line to the data points using a simple regression. For the industrialized countries, the slope of the line is not significantly different from 1 (and the intercept is not significantly different from zero), strongly supporting the one-to-one relationship. For the developing countries, the slope coefficient is 0.93, statistically significantly different from 1, and the intercept is –2.88, statistically significantly different from zero. These results indicate a mild divergence from the one-to-one relationship predicted by PPP. The currencies of developing countries tend to depreciate by about 3 percent per year, in addition to changing by somewhat less than the difference in inflation rates. In both cases the straight lines fit the data very well—over 95 percent of the variation in the rates of exchange rate changes across the countries is "explained" by the inflation rate differences.

FIGURE 18.2   *Purchasing Power Parity: Inflation Rate Differences and Exchange Rate Changes, 1975–1998*

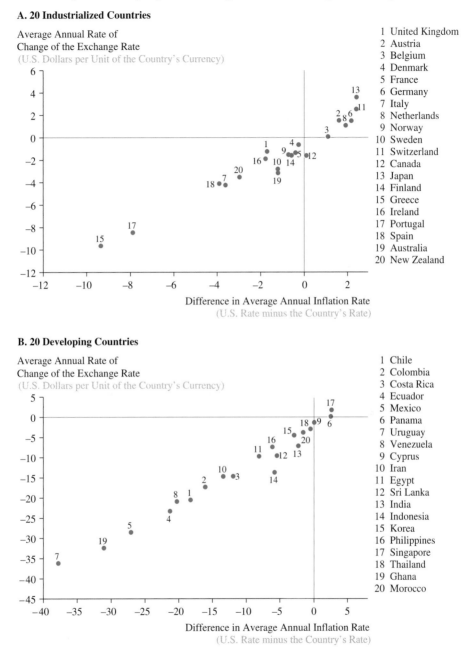

On average from 1975 to 1998, strong support is found for PPP. If the U.S. inflation rate is higher than the other country's inflation rate, the country's currency tends to appreciate; if the U.S. inflation rate is lower, the currency tends to depreciate.

Inflation rates are measured using consumer price indexes. Annual rates of change are calculated using differences in natural logarithms.

Source: International Monetary Fund, *International Financial Statistics.*

We can also examine recent performance of PPP for both short and long periods of time using data on the exchange rates of individual countries over time. Figure 18.3 shows the actual exchange rates against the U.S. dollar and the exchange rates that would be consistent with PPP, month-by-month, for the German mark (DM) and Japanese yen. The exchange rate consistent with PPP is the rate that equals the ratio of the national price levels P/P_f (where Germany and Japan are the foreign countries).[3] If PPP always held, the actual exchange rate would equal the exchange rate implied by PPP. As we can see easily in the figure, the deviations of the actual exchange rate from its PPP value can be large and can persist for a number of years. The DM was substantially undervalued relative to the implied PPP value from 1981 through 1986, and then was somewhat overvalued for much of the first half of the 1990s. The yen tracked its PPP value reasonably well from 1976 through 1986, but then became overvalued. In the long run there is also a tendency for the actual exchange rates to move in a manner consistent with PPP. According to PPP, both the DM and the yen should have appreciated over this entire period, and they did.

If we examine evidence for other countries, we would generally reach similar conclusions: noticeable deviations from PPP in the short run, but a tendency for PPP to hold in the long run. In a survey of recent studies, Froot and Rogoff (1995) conclude that, for the exchange rates of major industrialized countries, it takes about four years on average for a deviation from PPP to be reduced by half.

Money, Price Levels, and Inflation

Purchasing power parity indicates that, at least in the long run, exchange rates are closely related to the levels of prices for products in different countries. But this also suggests the next question: What determines the average national price level (or the rate at which it changes, the inflation rate)? Economists believe that the money supply (or its growth rate) determines the price level (or the inflation rate), in the long run. This suggests that money supplies in different countries, through their links to national price levels and inflation rates, are closely linked to exchange rates in the long run. Indeed, this is not surprising—an exchange rate is the price of one money in terms of another. Trying to analyze exchange rates or international payments without looking at national money supplies and demands is like presenting *Hamlet* without the Prince of Denmark.

Relative money supplies affect exchange rates. On the international front as on the domestic front, a currency is less valuable the more of it there is to circulate. Extreme cases of hyperinflation dramatize this fundamental point. The trillionfold increase in the German money supply in 1922–1923 was the key

---

[3]The price index used here is the wholesale or producer price index. Use of this price index, somewhat narrower than the price index for all GDP, should be favorable to finding that PPP holds, because nearly all of the items in the index are traded goods. The deviations from PPP shown in Figure 18.3 are not due to divergences in the prices of nontraded products.

FIGURE 18.3   *Actual Exchange Rates and Exchange Rates Consistent with PPP, Monthly, 1975–1998*

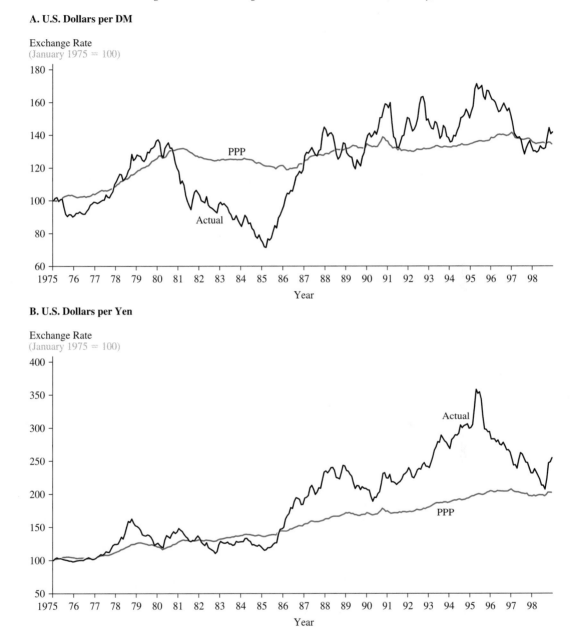

A. U.S. Dollars per DM

B. U.S. Dollars per Yen

The exchange rate implied by PPP equals the ratio of national price levels P/P_f. The actual exchange rate can differ substantially from this PPP rate, and the divergences can persist for several years. Nonetheless, there is a tendency for the actual exchange rate to follow the PPP rate in the long run.

National price levels are measured by wholesale (or producer) price indexes.

Source: International Monetary Fund, *International Financial Statistics.*

Price Gaps and International Income Comparisons

There is tremendous social importance to international comparisons of average production or income levels. To judge whether Japan has overtaken the United States, we compare Japanese and U.S. gross production per capita. To judge which nations are most in need of United Nations aid, World Bank loans, and other help, officials compare their incomes per capita. All such comparisons are dangerous as well as unavoidable. The comparisons are likely to contain a host of large errors.

One of the worst pitfalls comes in converting from one national currency to another. It turns out that the market exchange rate is a poor way to convert, precisely because the purchasing power parity theory is not reliable when applied to all the goods and services that make up GDP (or GNP). To see how exchange rates can mislead, consider what happened to the comparison of Japan and the United States between 1984 and late 1986. As of 1984, according to the World Bank, Japan's GNP per person was only 69 percent of that of the United States, despite the press coverage of Japan's superior efficiency in many industries. In October 1986, a cover story in the *Economist* trumpeted the news that Japan now had an average production that was 12 percent *higher* than that of the United States. Yet data on the real growth rates of the two countries differed very little between 1984 and 1986. How could Japan jump from being so far behind to being ahead in just two years without growing much faster?

The exchange rate did it. By October 1986, the dollar had fallen so much that it took about 33 percent fewer yen to buy a dollar than in 1984. The *Economist* was calculating Japan's 1986 GNP in dollars per capita at a very different exchange rate from that used by the World Bank for 1984. The result was a mirage. No great change in the ratio of Japanese to American production or incomes had really occurred in those two years. The market exchange rate sometimes oscillates wildly.

If the market exchange rate is unreliable, what should we use for comparing values of GDP or GNP per capita between countries? The principle is clear: We want to take the national products per capita measured using whatever prices exist in each country and convert these into values of national products per capita using a set of common international prices like those that would exist if PPP applied. That way, we are comparing how many units of a consistently priced bundle of goods and services the average resident of each nation produced (or could buy). But it is difficult to get data on the prices of a wide-ranging bundle of goods and services for every country.

That is where the United Nations International Comparisons Project (ICP) came in. A team of economists at the University of Pennsylvania, led by Alan Heston, Irving Kravis, and Robert Summers, did the hard work of measuring the prices of items in separate countries, with financial backing by the United Nations, the World Bank, and the U.S. National Science Foundation. The ICP group has assembled useful annual data on the price structures and income levels of over 130 countries since the 1950s. What they have found, in effect, are the true levels of P and P_f for deflating the current-price national product figures. They confirm what was widely feared: The exchange rate r_s is often far from the ratio P/P_f that PPP says it should equal.

The accompanying table shows the typical pattern in departures from PPP and the importance of replacing exchange rate conversions of GNP per capita with the better comparisons based on common price levels. The data are for the year 1997:

proximate cause of the trillionfold increase in the price of foreign exchange and of everything else in Germany at that time. Hyperinflation of the money supplies is also the key to understanding why the currencies of Israel and several Latin American countries lost almost all their value in recent times.

The relationship between money and the national price level (or inflation rate) follows from the relationship between money supply and money demand.

Country	GNP per Capita, 1997, Relative to the U.S. = 100		Domestic Price Level (This Country/U.S.) as a Percentage of the Level Predicted by PPP
	Using the Exchange Rate	Using Common Prices	
United States	100	100	100%
Singapore	115	101	114
Switzerland	154	92	168
Norway	126	83	151
Japan	132	81	162
Denmark	113	79	143
Canada	67	76	88
France	91	76	119
Netherlands	90	74	121
Germany	98	74	133
United Kingdom	72	71	101
Australia	71	70	102
Italy	70	70	100
Sweden	91	66	138
Israel	55	59	93
Korea	37	47	78
Chile	17	42	42
Czech Republic	18	40	46
Mexico	13	28	45
South Africa	12	26	45
Thailand	10	23	42
Turkey	11	22	49
Poland	12	22	56
Brazil	16	22	76
Russia	10	15	65
Philippines	4	13	33
China	3	12	24
Indonesia	4	12	32
Egypt	4	10	40
Ghana	1	6	21
India	1	6	24
Nigeria	1	3	30

Source: World Bank, *World Development Report 1998/99.*

If purchasing power parity really held, then every number in the right column would be 100. The departures from that PPP norm are great enough to reshuffle some of the international rankings, making the better (PPP-based) measurements of the center column differ from the exchange-rate–based measures on the left. Two patterns are apparent in the figures. One is that the price-difference ratio in the right column is above unity for Japan and most West European nations, so that their PPP-measured real average income is not as high relative to that of the United States as the exchange rate figures imply.

Another pattern is that the usual comparisons— the ones using exchange rates—overstate the real income gaps between rich and poor nations, because the price-difference ratio is below unity for the lower-income countries in the bottom half of the list.

Why should lower-income countries have prices so much lower than U.S. prices? Almost all of the departures come from the wide international gaps in the prices of nontraded goods like housing and other services. The gaps in the prices of these services seem to be widened by two forces. One is the tendency of the price of land to be highly sensitive to the income of the country's residents. So, a country with twice as high an income would have more than twice as high a cost for space, making space-intensive nontraded goods cost much more. A second explanation is that as a country develops, its productivity in making traded goods rises much faster than its productivity in making nontraded goods and services. The higher productivity in making traded goods tends to increase wage rates in more developed countries. Firms making nontraded goods and services must also pay these higher wage rates. With less productivity advantage, this results in costs and prices of nontraded products that are higher in more developed countries.

Turning to the demand for holding money, we recall that money is used as a medium of exchange. A certain stock should be on hand to cover an uncertain value of transactions that may arise requiring the exchange of money for other items. This transaction demand varies with the annual turnover of transactions requiring money, a turnover that is fairly well proxied by the level of domestic product (GDP).

The link between domestic product and the demand for a nation's money is central to the quantity theory of demand for money. The **quantity theory equation** says that in any country the money supply is equated with the demand for money, which is directly proportional to the value of gross domestic product. In separate equations for the home country and the rest of the world, the quantity theory equation becomes a pair:

$$M^s = k \times P \times Y$$

and

$$M_f^s = k_f \times P_f \times Y_f$$

where M^s and M_f^s are the home and foreign money supplies (measured in dollars and foreign currency, respectively), the P and P_f are the home and foreign price levels, and the Y and Y_f are the real (constant-price) domestic products. The k and k_f indicate the proportional relationships between money holdings and the value of GDP. They represent people's behavior. If the value of GDP and thus the value of transactions increase, k indicates the amount of extra money that people want to hold to facilitate this higher level of economic activity. Sometimes quantity theorists assume the ks are constant numbers, sometimes not. (The facts say that any k varies.) For the present long-run analysis, we follow the common presumption that the money supplies (the M^ss) are dictated by monetary policy alone and the Ys are governed by such supply-side forces as factor growth, productivity improvement, or harvest failure.

By taking the ratio of these two equations and rearranging the terms, we can use the quantity theory equations to determine the ratio of prices between countries:

$$(P/P_f) = (M^s/M_f^s) \, (k_f/k) \, (Y_f/Y)$$

Money and PPP Combined

Combining the purchasing power parity equation with the quantity theory equations for the home country and the rest of the world yields a prediction of exchange rates based on money supplies and national products:

$$r_s = P/P_f = (M^s/M_f^s) \, (k_f/k) \, (Y_f/Y)$$

The exchange rate r_s between one foreign currency (say, the British pound) and other currencies (here represented by the dollar, the home currency in our examples) can now be related to just the M^ss, the ks, and the Ys. The price ratio (P/P_f) can be set aside as an intermediate variable determined, in the long run, by the M^ss, ks, and Ys.

The equation predicts that a foreign nation (Britain) will have an appreciating currency (r_s up) if it has some combination of slower money supply growth

(M^s/M^s_f up), faster growth in real output (Y_f/Y up), or a rise in the ratio k_f/k. Conversely, a nation with fast money growth and a stagnant real economy is likely to have a depreciating currency.

Going one step further, we can use the same equation to quantify the percent effects of changes in money supplies or domestic products on the exchange rate. The equation implies that some key elasticities are equal to 1. That is, if the ratio (k_f/k) stays the same, then

> r_s rises by 1 percent for each 1 percent rise in the dollar money supply (M^s), or each 1 percent drop in the pound money supply (M^s_f), or each 1 percent drop in dollar-area real GDP (Y), or each 1 percent rise in British GDP (Y_f).

The exchange rate elasticities imply something else that seems reasonable too: An exchange rate will be unaffected by balanced growth. If money supplies grow at the same rate in all countries, leaving M^s/M^s_f unchanged, and if domestic products grow at the same rate, leaving Y_f/Y unchanged, there should be no change in the exchange rate.

Changes in the ks would have comparable effects on the exchange rate in the long run, but we choose not to examine these here. Instead, let's look a little more closely at the effects of money supply and real income.

The Impact of Money Supplies on an Exchange Rate

If, for instance, the supply of pounds is cut by 10 percent, each pound would become more scarce and more valuable. The cut might be achieved by much tighter British monetary policy. This contractionary policy would restrict the reserves of the British banking system, forcing British banks to tighten credit and the outstanding stock of sterling bank deposits, which represent most of the British money supply. The tighter credit would make it harder to borrow and spend, cutting back on aggregate demand, output, jobs, and prices in Britain. With the passage of time, the fall in output and jobs should reverse, and the reduction in prices should reach 10 percent. Over time, the pound should rise in value. The 10 percent cut in Britain's money supply should eventually lead to a 10 percent higher exchange rate value of the pound. This 10 percent rise is what the preceding quantity theory equations would predict.

The same shift should result from a 10 percent rise in the dollar money supply. If central bankers in the United States and other countries pegged to the dollar let their money supplies rise 10 percent, the extra dollar money available should end up inflating dollar prices by 10 percent. For a time, the higher dollar prices might cause international demands for goods and services to shift in favor of buying the sterling-priced goods, which are temporarily cheaper. Eventually, purchasing power parity should be restored by a 10 percent rise in the exchange rate, r_s. One other result predicted above follows as a corollary: If the preceding equations are correct, a balanced 10 percent rise in all money supplies, both pounds and dollars, should have no effect on the exchange rate.

Tracking the Exchange Rate Value of a Currency

We are often interested in "the" exchange rate value of a currency like the U.S. dollar, but this question is not as simple as it sounds. For each currency there are several hundred exchange rates with other currencies. These "regular" exchange rates are the ones quoted in the foreign exchange markets and are technically termed **nominal bilateral exchange rates.** For many purposes we are only interested in one or a few of these regular market exchange rates with specific other currencies.

For other purposes, including those related to macroeconomic analysis, we are interested in knowing how the exchange rate value of a country's currency is doing overall or on average. Furthermore, we probably do not want a simple average because some countries are more important than others. Rather, we want a weighted average exchange rate value, with the weights showing the importance of the other countries. For instance, an analysis of the effect of exchange rates on the country's exports and imports suggests using weights based on the country's amounts of international trade with the other countries. The weighted-average exchange rate value of a country's currency is called the **nominal effective exchange rate.** We have already used this idea in the introduction to this chapter, when we discussed the average value of the U.S. dollar against the currencies of other industrialized countries. Because an effective exchange rate is a weighted average of a number of distinct bilateral exchange rates, it has no natural units of measurement. It is usually measured as an index with some base year equal to 100.

Another issue in exchange rate analysis is the extent to which the actual exchange rate deviates from PPP. We showed this in Figure 18.3 by comparing the actual nominal bilateral exchange rates (for the DM and yen) to the values that the nominal exchange rates would be if they followed PPP (as P/P_f changed over time). The deviation from PPP can also be measured using the real exchange rate (RER):

$$\text{RER} = \frac{(P_f/P_{f,0}) \times (r_s/r_{s,0})}{P/P_0} \times 100$$

The subscript 0 indicates the values for P_f, P, and r_s in the base year. If PPP holds continuously, then the value of the real exchange rate will always be 100. If PPP holds in the long run, then RER will tend to return to (or fluctuate around) the 100 value (assuming that the base year is chosen judiciously). If the nominal exchange rate value of the currency being priced (the "foreign currency" according to our notation) is above its implied PPP value, then RER is above 100. If the nominal exchange rate value is below its implied PPP value, then the RER is below 100. In addition, increases in RER are called *real appreciations;* decreases are called *real depreciations.* We can calculate a **real bilateral exchange rate** (relative to one other specific country), and we can calculate a **real effective exchange rate** (as a weighted average relative to a number of other countries).

In summary, we have four ways to track the exchange rate value of a country's currency: nominal bilateral, nominal effective, real bilateral, and real effective. Each has its uses. For instance, in Part IV we

The Effect of Real Incomes on an Exchange Rate

The same kind of reasoning can be used to explore how long-run changes in real income should affect an exchange rate. Let us first follow this reasoning on its own terms and then add a word of caution.

Suppose that Britain's real income shifts up to a growth path 10 percent above the path Britain would otherwise have followed. This might happen, for instance, as the result of a spurt in British productivity. The extra transactions associated

will link the real effective exchange rate to the international price competitiveness of a country's products.

The accompanying figure shows the nominal effective exchange rate value of the U.S. dollar and its real effective exchange rate value, monthly from 1976 through 1999, for a broad sample including 44 other countries (21 industrialized and 23 developing countries). We can see that the dollar has tended to appreciate on average on a nominal basis (especially because the dollar has tended to appreciate nominally against the currencies of many developing countries

like Mexico). The real effective exchange rate also fluctuates over time, but it stays closer to the 100 value. The tendency to return to the 100 value indicates the role of PPP in the long run. The divergences suggest a kind of exchange rate "overshooting," which we discuss more in the next chapter. In particular, the dollar went through a large real appreciation (of nearly 50 percent) during 1981–1985. It then experienced a large real depreciation during the next three years that left the real exchange rate for the dollar back close to its 100 value.

Nominal and Real Effective Exchange Rate Values for the U.S. Dollar, Jan. 1976–Jan. 1999 (Monthly)

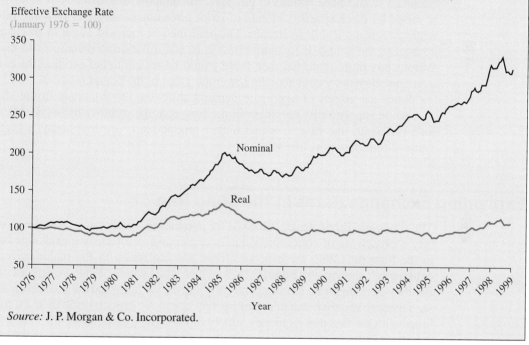

Effective Exchange Rate
(January 1976 = 100)

Source: J. P. Morgan & Co. Incorporated.

with the higher British production and income would call forth a new demand for holding pounds. If the extra productivity results in a 10 percent rise in real British national income, the quantity theory predicts a 10 percent higher transactions demand for the pound. But this extra demand cannot be met, assuming that Britain's money stock has not increased. Instead, the price level must decline in Britain by 10 percent so that the overall money value of British national income is unchanged. Essentially, in this case the increase in productivity is passed forward to buyers in the form of lower product prices. Then, according to PPP, the decline in British prices leads to a rise in the value of the pound. The rise again equals 10 percent. Again, we have two corollaries that can be seen from the equations: A 10 percent decline in U.S. real income should also raise r_s by 10 percent, and a balanced 10 percent rise in incomes in both Britain and the United States should leave the exchange rate the same.

A caution must be added to this tidy result, however. You can be misled by memorizing a single "effect of income" on the exchange rate. Income is not an independent force that can simply move by itself. What causes it to change has a great effect on an exchange rate. In the British productivity example above, real income was being raised for a *supply-side* reason—Britain's ability to produce more with its limited resources. It is easy to believe that this would strengthen the pound, by using the quantity theory equation (or by thinking about the extra British exports, made possible by its rising productivity, as something other countries would need pounds to pay for). But suppose that Britain's real income is raised by the Keynesian effects of extra government spending or some other aggregate-*demand* shift in Britain. This real-income increase might or might not strengthen the pound. If its main effect is to add inflation in Britain (or to make Britons buy more imports), then there would be reason to believe that the extra aggregate demand would actually lower the value of the pound.

Since the effects of aggregate demand shifts tend to dominate in the short run, while supply shifts dominate in the long run, the quantity theory yields the long-run result, the case in which higher production or income means a higher value of the country's currency.

Explaining Exchange Rates in the Long Run

The economic fundamentals stressed by purchasing power parity and the monetary approach are of noticeable value in explaining or forecasting exchange rates in the long run. With these perspectives, we can return to the major-currency experience shown in Figure 18.1. Over the whole long sweep of the flexible–exchange-rate era since the early 1970s, we know part of the reason why the Japanese yen rose: Japan's stronger real economic growth (growth in Y), combined with the fact that its money supply did not grow much faster than the average, kept inflation down in Japan and raised the international value of the yen. The Swiss franc rose because Switzerland kept tight control over its money supply. The lira sank because Italy's money supply rose faster than average.

PPP and the monetary approach are useful in explaining long-run changes in exchange rates, showing us the fundamentals that govern the long run. Whether we can go further and use them to *forecast* or predict exchange rate changes into the future is a greater challenge. To forecast exchange rates, we need forecasts of the fundamentals themselves into the future. If we can develop good predictors of money supplies and real incomes, or of just product prices or inflation rates, we then could have fair predictors of long-run movements in exchange rates.

Summary

This chapter has surveyed what we know about the determinants of exchange rates in the long run. Our understanding begins with **purchasing power parity (PPP)**. PPP states that international competition tends to equalize the home and foreign prices of traded goods and services so that $P = r_s P_f$ overall, where the Ps are price levels in the countries and r_s is the exchange rate price of foreign currency. PPP works tolerably well for longer periods of time, say, a decade or more. Over the long run, a country with a relatively high inflation rate tends to have a depreciating currency, and a country with a relatively low inflation rate tends to have an appreciating currency.

The monetary approach seeks to explain exchange rates by focusing on demands and supplies for national moneys since the foreign exchange market is where one money is traded for another. The transactions demand for a national money can be expressed as kPY, a behavioral coefficient (k) times the price level (P) times the level of real domestic product (Y). The equilibrium $M^s = kPY$ matches this demand against the national money supply (M^s), which is regulated by the central bank's monetary pol-icy. A similar equilibrium holds in any foreign country: $M^s_f = k_f P_f Y_f$.

Combining the basic monetary equilibriums with PPP yields an equation for predicting the exchange rate (r_s), or the value of the currency of a foreign country: $r_s = (M^s/M^s_f) \times (Y_f/Y) \times (k_f/k)$. Ignoring changes in the ks, we can use this equation to explain the exchange rate given data on money supplies and real incomes.

The price of foreign currency (r_s) is raised by:

An increase in (M^s/M^s_f).
An increase in (Y_f/Y).

Furthermore, the elasticities of the impact of (M^s/M^s_f) and (Y_f/Y) on r_s should approximately equal 1.

The monetary approach has success in explaining exchange rate movements in the long run, but it leaves many short-run exchange rate changes unexplained. Over long periods of time, exchange rates tend to move toward values consistent with such economic fundamentals as relative money supplies and real incomes (the monetary approach) or, similarly, relative price levels (PPP).

Suggested Reading

Purchasing power parity (PPP) has been subjected to a wide range of tests. Froot and Rogoff (1995) survey many of these studies. Hakkio (1992) provides an accessible summary of the theory of PPP and its empirical validity.

Surveys of research on the determinants of exchange rates, including work based on the monetary approach, are found in Frankel and Rose (1995) and MacDonald and Taylor (1992).

Questions and Problems

✦ 1. Will the law of one price apply better to gold or to Big Macs? Why?

2. According to PPP and the monetary approach, why did the exchange rate value of the DM (relative to the dollar) rise between the early 1970s and the late 1990s? Why did the exchange rate value of the pound decline?

✦ 3. For your next foreign vacation, would it be better to go to a country whose currency is overvalued relative to PPP or one whose currency is undervalued relative to PPP (other attractions being equal)?

4. "If the growth rate of the money supply in one country is the same as the growth rate of the money supply in another country, then over the long run the exchange rate between their two currencies should be unchanged." Do you agree or disagree? Why?

◆ 5. Mexico currently has an annual domestic inflation rate of about 20 percent. Suppose that Mexico wants to stabilize the exchange rate value of its currency (pesos/dollar) in a world in which dollar prices are generally rising at 3 percent per year. What must the rate of inflation of domestic peso prices come down to? If the quantity theory of money holds with a constant k, and if Mexican real output is growing 6 percent per year, what rate of money growth should the Mexican government try to achieve?

6. New Zealand recently changed the mandate of its central bank in a way that ensures that New Zealand's inflation rate is very likely to remain close to zero in the future. If you believe that this change will be fully effective, what is your prediction for the long-run trend for the exchange rate value of New Zealand's currency? Why?

◆ 7. "A natural disaster wipes out a large part of a country's production capability. According to the monetary approach, this will tend to result in a depreciation of the country's currency." Do you agree or disagree? Why?

8. To aid in its efforts to get reelected, the current government of a country decides to increase the growth rate of the domestic money supply by two percentage points. The increased growth rate becomes "permanent" because once started it is difficult to reverse.

   a. According to the monetary approach, how will this affect the long-run trend for the exchange rate value of the country's currency?

   b. Explain why the exchange rate trend is affected, referring especially to PPP.

◆ 9. In 1975, the price level for the United States was 100, the price level for Pugelovia was also 100, and in the foreign exchange market one Pugelovian pnut was equal to $1. In 2000, the U.S. price level had risen to 260, and the Pugelovian price level had risen to 390.

   a. According to PPP, what should the dollar–pnut exchange rate be in 2000?

   b. If the *actual* dollar–pnut exchange rate is $1/pnut in 2000, is the pnut overvalued or undervalued relative to PPP?

10. Here is further information on the U.S. and Pugelovian economies:

	1975			2000		
	M^s	Y	P	M^s	Y	P
United States	20,000	800	100	65,000	1,000	260
Pugelovia	10,000	200	100	58,500	300	390

   a. What is the value of k for the United States in 1975? For Pugelovia?

   b. Show that the change in price level from 1975 to 2000 for each country is consistent with the quantity theory of money with a constant k.

CHAPTER 19

What Determines Exchange Rates in the Short Run?

Exchange rates change a lot over time, as we saw in the figure at the beginning of the previous chapter. Rates can vary quite a bit even in the short run—periods of time covering minutes, days, or months. In addition, exchange rates sometimes move in medium-term trends that are counter to their long-term trends.

This chapter focuses on short-run movements in exchange rates. Economists believe that exchange rates can best be understood in terms of the demands and supplies of assets denominated in different currencies—the **asset market approach to exchange rates.** The monetary approach presented in the previous chapter is one variant of this. While the monetary approach, which emphasizes the subset of assets that are considered to be money, is useful for understanding long-run movements in exchange rates, it has not proven capable of explaining short-run movements in the exchange rates among the currencies of the major industrialized countries.

A broader asset market approach that incorporates all financial assets is necessary to gain some understanding of short-run movements. This broader approach emphasizes the role of portfolio repositioning by international financial investors. Much of it can be understood as an application of Chapter 17's analysis of uncovered international investments. Major conclusions are that the exchange rate value of a foreign currency (r_s) is raised *in the short run* by the following changes:

- A rise in the foreign interest rate relative to our interest rate ($i_f - i$).
- A rise in the expected future spot exchange rate (r_s^e).

This broad asset market approach helps us to understand short-run movements in exchange rates, including the tendency for exchange rates to "overshoot"—to change more than seems necessary in reaction to changes in government policies or to other important economic or political news.

Although the broad approach gives us insights, we must also admit that there is much that we do not know. Economists and professional traders do agree on

407

some of the fundamentals and other forces that drive exchange rates in the short and medium run,[1] but they all readily admit that their understanding and their ability to forecast are limited.

Asset Markets and International Financial Investment

To understand exchange rates in the short run, we must focus on the perceptions and actions of international financial investors. We believe that rather little of the more than $1 trillion of foreign exchange trading that occurs each day is related to international trade in goods and services. Instead, most of it is related to positioning or repositioning of the currency composition of the portfolios of international financial investors. As demand for and supply of financial assets denominated in different currencies shift around, these shifts place pressures on the exchange rates among the currencies.

This version of an asset market approach to exchange rates incorporates all financial assets. Nonetheless, we can grasp its key elements by focusing on investments in debt securities, such as government bonds, denominated in different currencies. In the analysis we build on the discussion of uncovered international financial investment and uncovered interest parity from Chapter 17. Recall that investors determine the expected overall return on an uncovered investment in a bond denominated in a foreign currency by using (1) the basic return on the bond itself (the interest rate or yield) and (2) the expected gain or loss on currency exchanges (the expected appreciation or depreciation of the foreign currency). While we may not believe that uncovered interest parity holds exactly, we still expect that there will be a noticeable relationship between the return on home-currency bonds and the expected overall return on foreign-currency bonds. These two returns will tend to be equal (or at least not too different). Emerging differences in these two returns will cause international financial investors to reposition their portfolios, and this repositioning creates the pressures that move the two returns toward equality.[2]

Uncovered interest parity (whether exact or approximate) links together four variables: the domestic interest rate, the foreign interest rate, the current spot

---

[1]The forces examined here (and in the previous chapter) are central not only to understanding what causes floating rates to change, but also to understanding the pressures on a system of fixed rates. Whatever would make a floating currency sink or rise would also make a fixed exchange rate harder to defend. The material thus has more uses than simply the search for determinants of floating exchange rates. It also applies to the analysis of the balance of payments under a fixed-rate system or a managed floating rate.

[2]This broad asset market approach built on uncovered interest parity is a kind of portfolio balance approach because it emphasizes the role of portfolio repositioning in the determination of exchange rates. However, the portfolio balance approach can go further than this. One further conclusion of the portfolio balance approach is that a change in the supplies of assets denominated in different currencies affects the deviation from uncovered interest parity (in the form of a risk premium) that is necessary to induce investors to hold (demand) all of these assets. This conclusion results because assets denominated in different currencies actually are not perfect substitutes for each other in investors' portfolios.

FIGURE 19.1

Determinants of the Exchange Rate in the Short Run

Change in Variable	Direction of International Financial Repositioning	Implication for the Current Spot Exchange Rate
Domestic Interest Rate (i)		
Increases	Toward domestic-currency assets	r_s decreases. (Domestic currency appreciates.)
Decreases	Toward foreign-currency assets	r_s increases. (Domestic currency depreciates.)
Foreign Interest Rate (i_f)		
Increases	Toward foreign-currency assets	r_s increases. (Domestic currency depreciates.)
Decreases	Toward domestic-currency assets	r_s decreases. (Domestic currency appreciates.)
Expected Future Spot Exchange Rate (r_s^e)		
Increases	Toward foreign-currency assets	r_s increases. (Domestic currency depreciates.)
Decreases	Toward domestic-currency assets	r_s decreases. (Domestic currency appreciates.)

The analysis for each change in one of the variables assumes that the other two variables are unchanged.

exchange rate, and the expected future spot exchange rate. (The two exchange rates together imply the expected appreciation or depreciation.) Change in any one of these four variables implies that adjustments will occur in one or more of the other three. We will here focus on implications for the current spot exchange rate of changes in each of the other three variables. Figure 19.1 provides a road map by summarizing the effects.

The Role of Interest Rates

Foreign exchange markets do seem sensitive to movements in interest rates. Jumps of exchange rates often follow changes in interest rates. The response often looks prompt—so much so that press coverage of day-to-day rises or drops in an exchange rate typically point first to interest rates as a cause.

If our interest rate (i) increases, while the foreign interest rate (i_f) and the spot exchange rate expected at some appropriate time in the future (r_s^e) remain constant, the return comparison shifts in favor of investments in bonds denominated in our currency. If international financial investors want to shift toward domestic-currency assets, they first need to buy domestic currency before they can buy the domestic-currency bonds. This increase in demand for domestic currency increases the current spot exchange rate value of domestic currency (so r_s decreases). Given the speed with which financial investors can initiate shifts in their portfolios, the effect on the spot exchange rate can happen very quickly (instantaneously or within a few minutes).

Let's consider an example involving the United States, Switzerland, and 90-day bonds. Initially, the U.S. interest rate is 9 percent per year, the Swiss interest rate is 5 percent per year, the current spot rate is $.50 per Swiss franc (SFr), and the spot rate expected in 90 days is about $.505 per SFr, implying that the franc is expected to appreciate at an annual rate of about 4 percent. (Uncovered interest parity holds at these rates, as the expected annualized overall return on the SFr-denominated bonds is about 9 percent—equal to 5 percent interest plus about 4 percent expected currency appreciation.) What happens if the U.S. interest rate increases to 11 percent? Given the other initial rates, the return differential shifts in favor of U.S.-dollar–denominated bonds. International financial investors have an incentive to shift toward dollar-denominated bonds, and this increases the demand for dollars in the foreign exchange market. The dollar tends to appreciate immediately. Furthermore, we can determine that the dollar should appreciate to about $.4975 per SFr, assuming that the interest rates and the expected future exchange rate do not change. Once this new current spot exchange rate is posted in the market, the SFr then is expected to appreciate during the next 90 days at a faster rate, equal to about 6 percent. This reestablishes uncovered interest parity (5 percent interest plus about 6 percent expected appreciation matches the 11 percent U.S. interest) and eliminates any further desire by international investors to reposition their portfolios.

If our interest rate instead decreases, with foreign interest rates and the expected future spot rate unchanged, the spot exchange rate value of our currency is predicted to decrease (r_s increases).

If the foreign interest rate (i_f) increases, the story is similar. Assuming that the domestic interest rate and the expected future spot exchange rate are constant, the return comparison shifts in favor of investments in bonds denominated in foreign currency. A shift by international financial investors toward foreign-currency bonds would require them first to buy foreign currency in the foreign exchange market. This increase in demand for the foreign currency increases the current spot exchange rate r_s (the domestic currency depreciates).

Consider a variation on our previous example. If the U.S. interest rate is 9 percent, the spot exchange rate is $.50 per SFr, and the expected future spot rate is about $.505 per SFr, what is the effect of an increase in the Swiss interest rate from 5 to 7 percent? The return differential shifts in favor of Swiss bonds. The increased demand for francs in the foreign exchange market results in a quick appreciation of the franc (and depreciation of the dollar). The current spot exchange rate must jump immediately to about $.5025 per SFr to reestablish uncovered interest parity.

If instead the foreign interest rate decreases, the spot rate r_s decreases. (The domestic currency appreciates.)

What happens if both interest rates change at the same time? The answer is straightforward. What matters is the interest rate differential $i - i_f$. If the interest rate differential increases, the return differential shifts in favor of domestic-currency bonds, and r_s tends to decrease. (The domestic currency appreciates.) If it decreases, r_s tends to increase.

The Role of the Expected Future Spot Exchange Rate

Expectations of future exchange rates can also have a powerful impact on international financial positioning, and through this on the value of the current exchange rate. Consider what happens when financial investors decide that they expect the future spot exchange rate to be higher than they previously expected. Relative to the current spot rate, this means that they expect the foreign currency to appreciate more, or to depreciate less, or to appreciate rather than depreciate. Assuming that the interest rate differential is unchanged, the increase in the expected future spot rate alters the return differential in favor of foreign-currency–denominated bonds. The story from here is familiar. If international financial investors want to shift toward foreign-currency assets, they first need to buy foreign currency in the foreign exchange market before they can buy the foreign-currency bonds. This increase in demand for foreign currency increases the current spot exchange rate r_s. (The foreign currency appreciates; the domestic currency depreciates.) If instead the expected future spot exchange rate decreases, with the interest rate differential unchanged, the return differential changes in favor of domestic-currency investments, and the current spot exchange rate value of our currency increases (r_s decreases).

Consider another variation on our previous example. With the U.S. interest rate at 9 percent, the Swiss interest rate at 5 percent, and the current spot exchange rate at \$.50 per SFr, what happens if the spot exchange rate expected in 90 days increases from about \$.505 to about \$.515 per SFr, perhaps because international investors believe that the political situation in Switzerland will improve rapidly? Relative to the initial current spot rate, investors now expect the franc to appreciate more in the next 90 days, at about a 12 percent annual rate (rather than the previously expected 4 percent). This shifts the return differential in favor of Swiss-currency bonds. Because investors desire to reposition their portfolios toward Swiss assets, demand for the franc increases in the foreign exchange market. The current spot exchange rate increases—the franc appreciates and the dollar depreciates. In fact, the spot exchange rate moves to about \$.51 per SFr. At this new spot rate, the franc then is expected to appreciate further by only about 4 percent (annual rate). Uncovered interest parity is reestablished, and there is no further incentive for international investors to reposition their portfolios.

As with a change in interest rates, the effect of a change in the expected future spot rate on the current spot exchange rate can happen very quickly (instantaneously or within a few minutes). This can be like a rapid-fire self-confirming expectation. In the Swiss franc example, the expectation that the franc would appreciate more than was previously expected resulted in a rapid and large appreciation of the franc. For another example, consider what happens if international financial investors shift from expecting no change in spot exchange rates (r_s^e equals the initial r_s) to expecting a depreciation of the foreign currency (r_s^e decreases so that it then is below the initial current spot rate r_s). The willingness of international investors to reposition their international portfolios away from foreign-currency bonds results in a depreciation of the foreign currency (r_s decreases)—exactly what they were expecting.

Given the powerful effects that exchange-rate expectations can have on actual exchange rates, we would like to know what determines these expectations. Many different things can influence the value of the expected future exchange rate.

Some investors, especially for expectations regarding the near-term future (the next minutes, hours, days, or weeks), may expect that the recent trend in the exchange rate will continue—extrapolating the recent trend into the future. This is a **bandwagon.** For instance, currencies that have been appreciating are expected to continue to do so. The recent actual increase in the exchange rate value of a country's currency leads some investors to expect further increases in the near future. If they act on this belief, the currency will tend to appreciate further. This bandwagon effect is the basis for fears that "speculation" can sometimes be destabilizing in that the actions of international investors can move the exchange rate away from a long-run equilibrium value consistent with fundamental economic influences. Expectations can be destabilizing if they are formed without regard to these economic fundamentals—which is quite possible if recent exchange rate trends are simply extrapolated into the future.

Expectations can also be based on the belief that exchange rates eventually return to values consistent with purchasing power parity. If the current exchange rate value of a currency is above its estimated PPP value (the currency is overvalued relative to its PPP value), then investors may expect that the currency will depreciate back toward its PPP value. If the exchange rate value is below its PPP value, then investors may expect it to appreciate toward this value. Expectations of this sort are considered stabilizing in the sense that they lead to stabilizing speculation, which tends to move the exchange rate toward a value consistent with some economic "fundamentals" such as those in PPP (relative national price levels).

Changes in expectations can be based on various kinds of "news"—new information that can have an impact on international financial flows. News includes unexpected information about government policies, about national and international economic data or performance, and about political leaders and situations (both domestic politics and international political issues and tensions). An example is that foreign exchange markets often react to news of official figures about a country's trade or current account balances, measures that largely reflect the balance or imbalance between a country's exports and imports of goods and services. There is logic to the market's reactions to such news. For instance, an unexpected increase in a country's trade deficit or (especially) its current account deficit indicates that the country requires an increasing amount of foreign financing of the deficit. If the increased foreign financing is not assured to be forthcoming, then the country's currency will tend to fall in the foreign exchange market. The increasing demand for foreign currency as part of the process of paying for the excess of imports over exports tends to appreciate the foreign currency and depreciate the domestic currency. If this logic is built into the changed expectations of international investors, then the exchange rate change can occur quickly, rather than gradually over time as the trade imbalance would slowly add to market pressures.

What happens when both interest rates and the expected future spot exchange rate change at the same time? Let's examine an increase in nominal domestic interest rates. The nominal interest rate i can change for two reasons. First, a country's nominal interest rate can increase because the ongoing expected rate of product price inflation π^e has increased. The higher nominal interest rate increases only to maintain a steady value of the expected real interest rate $i - \pi^e$. If financial investors base their expectations of future exchange rates on an eventual movement of the exchange rate toward its PPP value, then they will expect the currency to depreciate more (or appreciate less) than they previously expected (because of the higher domestic inflation expected), assuming that the foreign inflation rate is unchanged. The higher (nominal) interest rate then need not result in a shift toward this country's financial assets because the higher interest rate is countered by the expected additional depreciation of the currency.

An extreme case may help drive home the point. Nominal interest rates are sky-high in hyperinflating economies (as in recent times in Israel and some Latin American countries), but foreign investors know better than to be attracted to these high nominal rates. They know that inflation is also high in those countries, and their currencies are rapidly depreciating on the foreign exchange markets.

Second, the nominal interest rate may increase without any increase in the ongoing expected inflation rate. The real interest rate has increased, for instance, because monetary policy has been tightened in the country. With no increase in expected inflation, the expected future exchange rate value of the country's currency can remain the same (or rise)—there is certainly no reason for it to fall. This is essentially the case examined in the previous section—the higher interest rate causes the return differential to shift in favor of the country, and the country's currency appreciates quickly.

Exchange Rate Overshooting

Our view of exchange rates as being determined in the short run by investors' portfolio decisions seems quite removed from the long-run world of purchasing power parity and the monetary approach discussed in the previous chapter. Yet, the two must be related, as the short run eventually flows into the long run. We have already mentioned one basis for this flow, when international investors form their expectations of future exchange rates partly on the belief that exchange rates will move toward their PPP values.

It is useful to consider this relationship in more depth. In doing so we will see that international investors can react rationally to news by driving the exchange rate *past* what they know to be its ultimate long-run equilibrium rate and then slowly back to that rate later on. That is, in the short run the exchange rate actually overshoots its long-run value and then reverts back toward it.

Figure 19.2 shows how exchange rates could overshoot their new equilibrium, even if all investors correctly judge the future equilibrium rate. Suppose that the domestic money supply unexpectedly jumps 10 percent at time t_0 and then resumes the rate of growth investors had already been expecting. Investors understand that this permanent increase of 10 percent more money stock should eventually raise the price of foreign exchange by 10 percent, if they believe that

FIGURE 19.2

*A Case of
Exchange Rate
Overshooting*

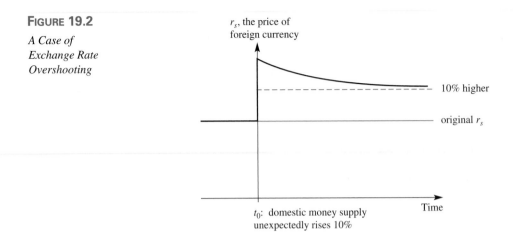

purchasing power parity and the monetary approach hold eventually. In the long run, both the domestic price level (P) and the price of foreign exchange (the exchange rate r_s) should be 10 percent higher.

But two realistic side effects of the increase in the domestic money supply intervene and make the exchange rate take a strange path to its ultimate 10 percent increase:

1. Product prices are somewhat sticky in the short run so that considerable time must pass for domestic inflation to raise domestic prices P by 10 percent relative to foreign prices P_f.
2. Because prices are sticky at first, the increase in the money supply drives down the domestic interest rate, both real and nominal.

With the domestic interest rate (i) lower, the return differential shifts to favor foreign-currency assets. But some other adjustments are also in order. The expected future spot exchange rate should increase, with investors expecting that eventually the future spot rate will be 10 percent higher (as PPP is established in the long run). Relative to the initial spot exchange rate, this implies that the foreign currency is expected to appreciate. At the initial spot exchange rate, the overall return differential actually favors foreign-currency assets for two reasons: The domestic interest rate has decreased, and the foreign currency is expected to appreciate. The desire by investors to reposition their portfolios toward foreign-currency assets increases the demand for foreign currency and results in a quick appreciation of the foreign currency.

By how much will the foreign currency appreciate immediately? If the domestic interest rate i has just dropped and the foreign interest rate i_f remains unchanged, then the current spot exchange rate must rise immediately by *more than* 10 percent. After this rapid adjustment, the much higher spot rate will then slowly decline back toward its expected value. That is, the new current spot rate r_s immediately rises above the new r_s^e so that the foreign currency is then expected to depreciate slowly back toward the new expected rate. This is necessary to reestablish uncovered interest parity once the current spot rate adjusts. The domestic return is lower because of the lower domestic interest rate i. After the current spot rate overshoots, then the overall return on foreign investments also becomes lower, even though the foreign interest rate i_f is unchanged, because the foreign currency is expected to depreciate from its high value. Investors must have the prospect of seeing the foreign currency depreciate later in order to stem their outflow in search of higher foreign interest rates.

So, once the news of the extra 10 percent money supply is out, investors will quickly bid up the spot price of foreign exchange by more than 10 percent (Dornbusch, 1976). One test by Jeffrey Frankel (1979) suggested that perhaps the announcement of a surprise 10 percent increase in the domestic money supply would trigger a jump of the spot rate by 12.3 percent, before it begins retreating back to just a 10 percent increase. In addition, the exchange rate overshoots by even more in the short run if we compare it to the path implied by PPP for each time period. Because the domestic price level rises only slowly toward its ultimate 10 percent increase, PPP alone implies that the exchange rate should rise only gradually toward its 10 percent increase. Thus, in the year or so after the money supply increase, little of the large increase in the actual spot exchange rate appears to be consistent with the limited amount of additional domestic inflation that occurs during that first year.

This case shows how exchange rates can be highly variable in the short run (driven by the reactions of international financial investors to policy surprises and other news), while at the same time exchange rates eventually change in the long run in ways consistent with PPP. The case also shows that it can be difficult to identify clearly cases of destabilizing "speculation." Exchange rate movements that appear to be extreme and inconsistent with the economic fundamentals in the short run can be part of a process that is understandable, reasonable, and stabilizing in the long run.

How Well Can We Predict Exchange Rates in the Short Run?

We would like to be able to forecast exchange rates. One purpose of having theories is to predict tendencies in the real world. International experience since the switch to floating exchange rates in the early 1970s provides a rich data set against which to test the value of our theories.

If they are to be valuable, how accurate would we want our theories to be in predicting changes in exchange rates? Clearly we should not expect perfect forecasts. But presumably we would expect a useful economic model at least to be able to outpredict a naive model that says the future exchange rate is predicted simply to be equal to the current spot exchange rate. This is a minimal standard—the naive model is equivalent to saying that the spot exchange rate follows a random walk, with no ability to predict whether it will go up or down. The predictions of any useful economic structural model presumably ought to be able to do better than this naive model.

Somewhat to our consternation, there is now general agreement that economic structural models are of little use in predicting exchange rates in the short run (for

Forecasting Using a Modified Monetary Model

A simple application of the monetary approach (or any other approach) fails to predict exchange rate changes in the short run. Yet purchasing power parity and the monetary approach do provide insights into movements in exchange rates in the long run. How quickly does the predictive power of the monetary approach assert itself?

To examine this predictive power, we need to develop a modified version of the monetary approach. The modified version admits that the actual exchange rate is often different from the exchange rate predicted by the basic monetary approach. Still, the exchange rate predicted by the basic monetary approach does represent a long-run equilibrium value. Thus, when the actual exchange rate is different from this long-run equilibrium value, the actual rate will then tend to move toward it. If the actual rate is below the long-run value, the actual rate is predicted to increase in the future, and, if above, to decrease. This modified version attempts to use the long-run validity of the monetary approach to make predictions for shorter periods of time. Its basic propositions are essentially those of the overshooting model (although it does not attempt to explain why the overshooting occurs in the first place).

Mark (1995) sets up a test of this modified version of the monetary approach in three stages, following an approach used by Meese and Rogoff (1983) and other similar studies. First, Mark formulates a "structural" model that captures the essence of the modified monetary approach in two equations. The first equation is drawn from the basic monetary approach. The long-run equilibrium exchange rate r_s^* is determined by economic fundamentals—relative money supplies and relative real incomes:

$$r_s^* = (M^s/M_f^s) \times (Y_f/Y)$$

The long-run equilibrium exchange rate value of foreign currency is raised by a rise in the home country's money supply (M^s), a drop in the foreign country's money supply (M_f^s), a rise in foreign real income (Y_f), and drop in home country real income (Y). The second equation shows that the exchange rate predicted for a time in the future (r_s^p) is based on both the current exchange rate r_s and how the long-run

equilibrium value of the exchange rate r_s^* compares to the current rate:

$$r_s^p = r_s \times (r_s^*/r_s)^b$$

The coefficient b shows adjustment—how much of the deviation between the long-run equilibrium and the actual exchange rate is predicted to be eliminated over the time period of the prediction. A larger b indicates that more of the deviation will disappear. Consider, for instance, benchmark values for b. If b is zero, then none of the deviation is predicted to disappear, because r_s^* is irrelevant. (Anything raised to the zero power is simply 1.) If b is 1, then all of the deviation is predicted to disappear, and the actual future exchange rate is predicted to equal its long-run equilibrium value.

The second step toward a direct test is to fit this model statistically to some data. Mark substitutes the first equation into the second, and then uses a logarithmic form of the combined equation. He fits this equation to quarterly data beginning with the second quarter of 1973, for exchange rates between the U.S. dollar and, separately, the Canadian dollar, German mark (DM), yen, and Swiss franc. The initial statistical effort is to estimate, using regression, the values for the adjustment coefficients b, using actual future spot exchange values in place of the predicted values (r_s^p). Mark's estimates of b are shown in the accompanying table. The estimates of b for the different exchange rates and time horizons into the future are all positive and of reasonable value, although the estimates for the Canadian dollar exchange rate are somewhat smaller than those for the other three exchange rates. The estimates of b that are nearly 1 for the three-year horizon for the other three exchange rates indicate that close to all of the deviation of the current spot rate from its long-run equilibrium value tends to be eliminated over the next three years.

Now comes the tough part. The third step taken by Mark is one that any predictive model should have to pass: How well does it predict beyond the time for which is has been fitted statistically? Does it predict better than some crude and simpler forecasting device? Mark lets the model show its stuff by forecasting exchange rates for the period 1981–1991. The results (the second column of numbers in the table) show a statistical measure of the average percent error in the forecasts.

The structural model based on the modified monetary approach has the virtue of making explicit what forces economists think the exchange rate depends on. Yet its predictive power is certainly far from perfect, given the substantial size of the percent forecast errors indicated by the values in this middle column of numbers.

Are these errors large or small? It depends on what you might compare them to. They are large errors relative to perfect foresight. If you made the Faustian bargain to sell your soul for a lifetime of perfect foreign exchange foresight, and managed to keep your information secret from others, you could make huge profits at the expense of other speculators who lacked perfect foresight. Clearly, there is financial value in information that the market does not now have. But perfect foresight is an unrealistic norm.

Another possible norm is a naive model predicting that the future spot exchange rate will simply equal the current spot exchange rate—the random walk. The percent errors that result from using this naive model (the current spot rate) to forecast the future spot rate are shown in the final column of the table.

When we compare the forecast errors from the modified monetary model with the forecast errors from the naive random walk model, we see several patterns. First, the errors in forecasting the Canadian dollar exchange rate using the modified monetary approach are equal to or larger than the errors using the naive model, for all forecast horizons. The structural model provides no ability to forecast this exchange rate. Second, for the other three exchange rates, the errors in forecasting spot exchange rates one quarter ahead using the modified monetary approach are about as large as those using the naive model. The structural model also provides no ability to forecast these exchange rates at short forecast horizons like one quarter into the future. Third, the structural model performs better for longer forecast horizons. The errors using the modified monetary approach are a little smaller than those using the naive model for forecasts of the Japanese yen and Swiss franc exchange rates one year into the future, and the errors are substantially smaller for forecasts of the mark, yen, and Swiss franc exchange rates three years into the future.

Perhaps there is some hope for exchange rate forecasting using economic models, at least for forecasts a year or more into the future, if not yet for shorter forecast horizons.

Forecast Errors, Modified Monetary Approach, and a "Naive" Approach, 1981–1991

Predicted Exchange Rate	Predicted How Far Ahead?	Estimate of the b Coefficient	Forecast Errors Made By	
			Modified Monetary Approach	Just the Current Spot Rate
U.S.$/Canadian $	1 quarter	0.040	2.1%	2.1%
	1 year	0.155	5.0	4.5
	3 years	0.438	15.7	10.9
U.S.$/DM	1 quarter	0.035	6.7	6.6
	1 year	0.205	15.3	14.8
	3 years	0.966	23.4	29.4
U.S.$/yen	1 quarter	0.047	6.8	6.8
	1 year	0.263	13.9	15.0
	3 years	0.945	24.0	33.8
U.S.$/Swiss franc	1 quarter	0.074	7.0	7.0
	1 year	0.285	15.7	16.0
	3 years	0.837	21.6	29.3

The forecast errors are approximate percent root-mean-square errors.

Source: Mark (1995).

future periods up to about one year). Frankel and Rose (1995) survey many studies that use various models based on many different economic fundamentals, including money supplies and real incomes, interest rates, expected inflation rates, and the trade and current account balances. They conclude that structural economic models cannot reliably outpredict the naive alternative of a random walk for short forecast horizons.[3] The box "Forecasting Using a Modified Monetary Model" presented an example of one recent study examining our ability to predict exchange rates.

Why is it so difficult to predict exchange rates in the short run using economic models? There appear to be two parts to the answer. First, and probably more important, the exchange rate reacts strongly and immediately to new information. Exactly because news is unexpected, it cannot be incorporated into any predictions. The reaction to such news often involves large movements in the exchange rate. Actual exchange rate movements appear to overshoot movements in smoothly adjusting long-run equilibrium rates like those from PPP or the monetary approach. Studies have documented the immediate effects of a variety of different types of news on exchange rates, although some of these types seem to have power during some time periods but not others. For instance, the U.S. dollar tends to appreciate when there are unexpected contractions in the U.S. money supply, unexpected increases in U.S. interest rates (relative to foreign interest rates), unexpected growth in U.S. real GDP, unexpected decreases in the U.S. inflation rate, unexpected improvements in the U.S. trade or current account balance, and unexpected increases in the U.S. government budget deficit. In addition, casual observation indicates that the exchange rate reacts to new information concerning both actual events and changes in probabilities about what will happen, not only for economic variables such as those just mentioned, but also for political variables such as elections, appointments, international tensions, and wars.

The second reason is that exchange rate expectations can be formed without much reference to economic fundamentals. Surveys indicate that many foreign exchange market participants just extrapolate the latest trends up to one month ahead. Because the actions taken by investors can make their expectations self-confirming, recent trends in exchange rates can be reinforced and persist for a while. If the resulting movement in the exchange rate appears to be simply inconsistent with any form of economic fundamentals, it is called a **bubble** (or *speculative bubble*). While it is difficult to identify such bubbles with complete certainty, the final stage of the appreciation of the dollar against many other currencies in 1984 and early 1985 appears to have been such a bubble. The strong possibility that bubbles occur in the foreign exchange market from time to time suggests that there is some economic inefficiency in foreign exchange markets. You may recall that we reached a similar conclusion at the end of Chapter 17, when we discussed why estimated deviations from uncovered interest parity appear to be too large to be explained completely by risk premiums.

---

[3] A few studies (e.g., MacDonald and Marsh, 1997; Woo, 1995; MacDonald and Taylor, 1993, 1994) do beat the random walk with a structural model for specific time periods and currencies, but these results have not been replicated for other currencies or time periods.

Summary

This chapter surveyed what we know (and don't know) about the determinants of exchange rates in the short run. The **asset market approach** explains exchange rates as being part of the equilibrium for the markets for financial assets denominated in different currencies. We gain insights into short-run movements in exchange rates by using a variant of the asset market approach that focuses on portfolio repositioning by international investors, especially decisions regarding investments in bonds denominated in different currencies. If uncovered interest parity tends to hold (at least approximately), then any changes in domestic or foreign interest rates (i and i_f) or the expected future spot exchange rate (r_s^e) create an uncovered interest differential and also create pressures for a return toward uncovered interest parity. Focusing on the pressures on the current spot exchange rate r_s, the price of foreign currency, it tends to be raised by

An increase in the interest rate differential ($i_f - i$).
An increase in the expected future spot exchange rate (r_s^e).

Changes in the expected future spot exchange rate tend to be self-confirming expectations in that the current spot rate tends to change quickly in the direction expected. Furthermore, there appear to be several types of influences on the expected future spot exchange rate, including recent trends in the actual spot rate, beliefs that the exchange rate eventually moves toward its PPP value, and unexpected new information ("news") about economic performance or about political situations. The rapid large reaction of the current exchange rate to such news as a change in monetary policy is called **overshooting**—the current exchange rate changes by much more than would be consistent with a long-run standard like purchasing power parity.

We would like to be able to use economic models to predict exchange rates in the future, but our ability to do so is limited. Economic models provide almost no ability to predict exchange rates for short periods into the future, say, about a year or less. This inability is based largely on the importance of unpredictable news as an influence on short-term exchange rate movements, but it may also reflect the role of expectations that extrapolate recent trends in the exchange rate, leading to bandwagon effects and (speculative) bubbles.

Suggested Reading

Surveys of research on the determinants of exchange rates, including work based on the asset market approach, are found in Frankel and Rose (1995) and MacDonald and Taylor (1992). Meese (1990) provides a discussion (not too technical) of the ability of different economic structural models to forecast exchange rates, with comparisons to the forward foreign exchange rate and the random walk. Bosworth (1993, Chapter 4) provides a broader set of empirical tests of economic models' ability to explain exchange rate movements.

Questions and Problems

✦ 1. "Short-run pressures on exchange rates result mainly from gradual changes in flows of international trade in goods and services." Do you agree or disagree? Why?

2. "While flows of foreign financial investment into a country tend to appreciate the country's currency, outflows as foreign investors pull their investments out of a country have little impact on the exchange rate value of the country's currency." Do you agree or disagree? Why?

✦ 3. The United States has been running a trade deficit of about $10 billion per month. Last month this increased slightly to $11 billion. What is likely to be the effect on the dollar's exchange rate value if the announcement for this month is that the trade deficit was $6 billion? Why?

4. A country's government is attempting to steady the exchange rate value of the country's currency, while international financial investors increasingly expect that the county's currency will depreciate. What change in the country's interest rates should the country's government implement? Why?

✦ 5. As a foreign exchange trader, how would you react to each of the following news items as it flashes on your computer screen?

   a. Mexico's oil reserves prove to be much smaller than touted earlier.

   b. The Social Credit Party wins the national elections in Canada and promises generous expansion of the supply of money and credit.

   c. In a surprise vote the Swiss government passes a law that will result in a large increase in the taxation of interest payments from Switzerland to foreigners.

6. The following rates currently exist:

   Spot exchange rate: $1.200/euro.

   Annual interest rate on 180-day euro-denominated bonds: 5%.

   Annual interest rate on 180-day U.S.-dollar–denominated bonds: 6%.

   Investors currently expect the spot exchange rate to be about $1.206/euro in 180 days.

   a. Show that uncovered interest parity holds (approximately) at these rates.

   b. What is likely to be the effect on the spot exchange rate if the interest rate on 180-day dollar-denominated bonds declines to 5 percent? If the euro interest rate and the expected future spot rate are unchanged, and if uncovered interest parity is reestablished, what will the new current spot exchange rate be? Has the dollar appreciated or depreciated?

✦ 7. The current rates are

   Spot exchange rate: $2.00/£.

   Annual interest rate on 60-day U.S.-dollar–denominated bonds: 5%.

   Annual interest rate on 60-day pound-denominated bonds: 11%.

   Investors currently expect the spot exchange rate to be $1.98/pound in 60 days.

   a. Show that uncovered interest parity holds (approximately) at these rates.

   b. What is likely to be the effect on the spot exchange rate if the interest rate on 60-day pound-denominated bonds declines to 8 percent? If the dollar interest rate and the expected future spot rate are unchanged, and if uncovered interest parity is reestablished, what will the new current spot exchange rate be? Has the pound appreciated or depreciated?

8. You observe the following current rates:

   Spot exchange rate: $0.01/yen.

   Annual interest rate on 90-day U.S.-dollar–denominated bonds: 4%.

Annual interest rate on 90-day yen-denominated bonds: 4%.

a. If uncovered interest parity holds, what spot exchange rate do investors expect to exist in 90 days?

b. A close U.S. presidential election has just been decided. The candidate whom international investors view as the stronger and more probusiness person won. Because of this, investors expect the exchange rate to be $0.0095/yen in 90 days. What will happen in the foreign exchange market?

◆ 9. Consider our example of overshooting shown in Figure 19.2, in which the domestic money supply increased by 10 percent. Assume that the path of slow adjustment of prices is that the price level rises by about 2 percent per year for five years. What would the path of the exchange rate be if PPP held for each year? Given the actual path for the exchange rate shown in Figure 19.2, does PPP hold in the short run? Does it hold in the long run?

10. A country has had a steady value for its exchange rate (stated inversely as the domestic currency price of foreign currency) for a number of years. The country now tightens up on (reduces) its money supply dramatically. The country's product price level is not immediately affected, but the price level gradually becomes lower (relative to what it otherwise would have been) during the next several years.

a. Why might the exchange rate change a lot as this monetary tightening is announced and implemented?

b. What is the path of the exchange rate likely to be over the next several years? Why?

CHAPTER 20

Government Policies Toward the Foreign Exchange Market

Chapters 15 through 19 presented the basic analysis of how currencies are exchanged and what seems to determine the exchange rate if the determination is left mainly to market forces. For better or worse, many governments do not usually just let the private market set the exchange rate. Rather, governments have policies toward the foreign exchange market in the form of policies toward exchange rates themselves, policies toward who is allowed to use the market, or both.

Our previous discussion suggests one reason why governments adopt such policies. Exchange rates, if left to private market forces, sometimes fluctuate a lot. They are prone to overshoot, and may occasionally also be influenced by bandwagons among investors or speculators. Exchange rates are very important prices—they can affect the entire range of a country's international transactions. One objective for government policy then can be to reduce variability in exchange rates.

Governments often have other reasons for adopting policies toward the foreign exchange market. A government may want to keep the exchange rate value of its currency low, preventing appreciation or promoting depreciation. This benefits certain activities or groups in the country, including the country's exporters and import-competing businesses. Or, in a different setting, a government may want to do the opposite: keep the exchange rate value of its currency high, preventing depreciation or promoting appreciation. This can benefit other activities or groups—for instance, buyers of imports. It can also be used as part of an effort to reduce domestic inflation by using the competitive pressure of low import prices. In addition, the government policy may reflect other, relatively noneconomic goals. The government may believe that it is defending national honor or encouraging national pride by maintaining a steady exchange rate or a strong currency internationally. Devaluation or depreciation may be feared as a confirmation of the ineptitude of the government in selecting policies.

This chapter has three objectives. First, it provides a framework for understanding the range of possible government policies toward the foreign exchange market. Second, it begins the analysis of these policies, focusing on the economics of official buying and selling of currencies in the market and the economics of restrictions on who can use the market. Third, it explores some lessons of history by surveying exchange rate systems that have existed during the past 130 years, concluding with a description of the current system. Part IV of this book then continues this discussion by examining in depth the broader macroeconomic implications of the foreign exchange policies chosen by governments.

Two Aspects: Rate Flexibility and Restrictions on Use

Government policies toward the foreign exchange market can be divided into those policies that are directly applied to the exchange rate itself and those that directly state who may use the foreign exchange market and for what purposes. Some policies act directly on price (the exchange rate), while others act directly on quantity (by limiting some people's ability to use the foreign exchange market). We saw this distinction before when we examined tariffs and quotas as two forms of government policies toward imports. As in the case of imports, we expect that any one policy has impacts on both price and quantity in the market, even though the policy directly acts on only one of these. A policy toward the exchange rate affects the quantity of foreign exchange traded in the market (the turnover), and a policy restricting use has an impact on the exchange rate.

Government policies toward the exchange rate itself are usually categorized according to the flexibility of the exchange rate—the amount of movement in the exchange rate that the policy permits. In the simplest terms, governments choose between floating and fixed exchange rates, although, as we will see, the reality is often richer than this.

Government policies can also restrict access to the foreign exchange market. One type of policy is no restriction—everyone is free to use the foreign exchange market. The country's currency is fully convertible into foreign currency for all uses, for both trade in goods and services (current account transactions) and international financial activities (capital account transactions). The other type of policy is **exchange control**—the country's government places some restrictions on use of the foreign exchange market. In the most extreme form of exchange control, all foreign exchange proceeds (for instance, proceeds resulting from foreign payments for the country's exports) must be turned over to the country's monetary authority. Anyone wanting to obtain foreign exchange must request it from the authority, which then determines whether to approve the request. Less extreme forms of control limit access for some types of transactions, while permitting free access for other types of transactions. For instance, the government may permit use of the foreign exchange market for all payments for exports and imports of goods and services, but place limits or require approvals for payments related to some (or all) international financial activities. In this case, the country's currency is convertible for current transactions, but the country imposes some form of **capital controls.** Another example of a less extreme form of restriction is limits on the use of the foreign exchange market for transactions related to broad types of imports, such as consumer luxury goods.

Floating Exchange Rate

If government policy lets the market determine the exchange rate, the rate is free to go wherever the market equilibrium is at that time. This policy choice results in a pure or **clean float.** Market supply and demand are solely private (nonofficial) activities. As private market supply and demand shift around, the value of the floating exchange rate changes. A clean float is the polar case of complete flexibility.

Even when the country's exchange rate policy is to permit flexibility by floating the rate, the government often is not willing to simply let the rate go wherever private supply and demand drive it. Rather, the government often tries to have a direct impact on the rate through official intervention. That is, the monetary authority enters the foreign exchange market to buy or sell foreign currency (in exchange for domestic currency). Through this intervention, the government hopes to alter the configuration of supply and demand, and thus influence the equilibrium value of the exchange rate—the rate that clears the market. This policy approach—an exchange rate that is generally floating (or flexible) but with the government willing to intervene to attempt to influence the market rate—is called a **managed float** (if you are an optimist about the capabilities of the government) or a **dirty float** (if you are a pessimist). Often the government is attempting to "lean against the wind" to moderate movements in the floating rate. For instance, if the exchange rate value of the country's currency is rising (and that of foreign currency falling), then the authorities intervene to buy foreign currency (and sell domestic currency). They hope that the intervention and the extra supply of domestic currency can slow or stop their own currency's rise in value (or, correspondingly, that the extra demand for foreign currency can slow or stop its decline). The actual effectiveness of intervention is controversial, and we will examine this issue further in Chapter 23. Nonetheless, most governments that choose a floating exchange rate policy also do manage, or "dirty," the float to some extent.

Fixed Exchange Rate

If the government chooses the policy of a fixed exchange rate, then the government sets the exchange rate that it wants. Often, some flexibility is permitted within a range, called a *band,* around this chosen fixed rate, called the *par value* or *central value.* Nonetheless, the flexibility is generally more limited than would occur if the government instead permitted a floating rate.

In implementing its choice of a fixed exchange rate, the government actually faces three specific major questions: To what does the government fix the value of its currency? When or how often does the country change the value of its fixed rate? How does the government defend the fixed value against any market pressures pushing toward some other exchange rate value?

What to Fix To?

A fixed rate means that the value of the country's currency is fixed to something else, but what is this something else? As we will see later in this chapter, the answer about a century ago was to fix to gold. If several countries all fix the values of their currencies to specific amounts of gold, then arbitrage ensures that the exchange rates among the currencies will also be fixed at the rates implied by their gold values. That is, currencies tied to the same thing (such as gold) are all tied to each other. In principle, any other commodity or group of commodities could serve the same purpose—the gold standard is one example of the broader idea of a commodity standard.

The country could choose to fix the value of its currency to some other currency, rather than to a commodity. Since the end of World War II many countries have often fixed the value of their currency to the U.S. dollar. Any other single currency can serve the same purpose.

Or, the country could choose to fix the value of its currency not to one other currency but to the average value of a number of other currencies. Why would a country choose to fix to such a "basket" of other currencies? The logic is the same as that of diversifying a portfolio (or not putting all your eggs in one basket). If the country fixes to one single other currency, then it will ride along with this other currency if the other currency's value experiences extreme changes against any third-country currencies. Fixing to a basket of currencies moderates this effect, in that the average value is kept steady.

What basket of currencies might the country fix to? There is one ready-made basket—the **special drawing right (SDR),** a basket of the four major currencies in the world.[1] Or a country can create its own basket. For instance, the country might be interested in maintaining a steady exchange rate value to facilitate its international trade activities. In this case the basket would include the currencies of its major trading partners, and the importance of these other countries in the basket would be based on their importance in the country's trade. In designing its

---

[1]As we mentioned in Chapter 15, the SDR is a reserve asset created by the International Monetary Fund. The IMF periodically adjusts the specific composition of the SDR. As of 1999, one SDR equaled the collection of U.S. \$0.572 plus 0.3519 euros plus 31.8 Japanese yen plus British £0.0812. Market exchange rates can then be used to compute the SDR's value in terms of any specific single currency.

basket in this way, the country is using the same logic as that used to calculate an effective exchange rate.

No country today fixes its currency to gold or any other commodity. Although we examine the gold standard later in this chapter, the rest of our fixed-rate discussion presumes that a country fixes the exchange rate value of its currency to one or more other currencies.

When to Change the Fixed Rate?

Once the country has chosen what to fix to, it establishes a specific value for its currency in terms of the item chosen. As the government attempts to maintain this fixed value over time, it faces the question of when to change the fixed rate.

The government may insist that it will never change the fixed rate. A permanently fixed exchange rate is useful as a polar case—the opposite of a clean float. However, it is not clear that the government's commitment is credible. The commitment is not truly binding—the government has the capability to alter its policy. Most probably, nothing is fixed forever. On this basis, we often use the term **pegged exchange rate** in place of *fixed exchange rate,* in recognition that the government has some ability to move the peg.

Although the fixed rate may not be fixed forever, the government may try to keep the value fixed for long periods of time. Nonetheless, in the face of a substantial or "fundamental" disequilibrium in the country's international position, the government may change the pegged rate. This approach is called an **adjustable peg.**

In other situations, the government may recognize that a specific pegged-rate value cannot be maintained for long. For instance, if the country has a relatively high inflation rate, then an attempt to maintain a pegged rate against the currency of a low-inflation country will quickly lead to large violations of purchasing power parity and declining international price competitiveness. Nonetheless, the country may prefer to maintain some form of pegged exchange rate, perhaps because it believes that a floating exchange rate would be too volatile. The solution chosen by some countries in this position is a **crawling peg.** With a crawling peg the pegged exchange rate is changed often (for instance, monthly) according to a set of indicators or according to the judgment of the government monetary authority. If indicators are used, the discussion of Chapter 18 suggests one reasonable choice—the difference between the country's inflation rate and the inflation rate of the country whose currency it pegs to. If the inflation difference is used, the nominal pegged rate will track purchasing power parity over time, and this bilateral real exchange rate will be stabilized. Other indicators that might be used include the country's holdings of official international reserve assets (indicating pressure from the country's balance of payments), the growth of the country's money supply (indicating underlying inflation pressure), or the current actual market exchange rate relative to the central par value of the pegged rate (indicating, within the allowable band, the foreign exchange market pressure away from the par value).

In fact, the choice of the width of the allowable band is closely related to the issue of when to change the pegged rate. If the band is larger, then the actual exchange rate has more room to move around the par value. Market pressures can result in wider variations in the actual exchange rate, without necessarily forcing the government to face the decision of whether to change the pegged-rate value.

At this point, it is useful to summarize the main points of our survey. For government policies toward the exchange rate itself, we often frame the decision facing the government as choosing between a floating or a fixed exchange rate. A floating exchange rate seems to permit substantial flexibility or variability in the actual rate, while a fixed rate seems to impose strict limits on this variability or flexibility. While this proposition is true to a large extent, the reality is also more complicated. In a clean float, the rate is purely market-driven, but in a managed float the government takes actions such as exchange market intervention to influence the floating rate. In a heavily managed float, the exchange rate may show little flexibility—it is almost pegged, even though this is not the way that the government describes its choice. Even with a fixed rate, much variability or flexibility may still exist for several reasons. The band around the central pegged rate can be wide, permitting substantial variability within the band. The exchange rate value of the country's currency can also vary substantially with respect to other currencies that are not involved in the same type of peg. Furthermore, the government can change the pegged rate, sometimes frequently, as in a crawling peg. The polar cases of a clean float and a permanently fixed exchange rate are useful in order to contrast the implications of a country's choice of exchange rate policy. At the same time we must remember that in reality there is more of a continuum in which the country permits more or less flexibility in the movements of the exchange rate value of the country's currency. A full analysis of a specific country requires examination of the true nature of government policy toward the exchange rate.

Defending a Fixed Exchange Rate

The third major question confronting a country that has chosen a fixed exchange rate is how to defend its fixed rate. The pressures of private (or nonofficial) supply and demand in the foreign exchange market may sometimes drive the exchange rate toward values that are not within the permissible band around the par value. The government then must use some means to defend the pegged rate—to keep the actual exchange rate within the band.

How does the government defend the fixed rate that it has announced? There are four basic ways:

1. The government can intervene in the foreign exchange market, buying or selling foreign currency in exchange for domestic currency, to maintain or influence the actual exchange rate in the market.
2. The government can impose some form of exchange control to maintain or influence the exchange rate by constricting demand or supply in the

market. (A closely related approach would use trade controls such as tariffs or quotas to attempt to accomplish this result.)

3. The government can alter domestic interest rates to influence short-term capital flows, thus maintaining or influencing the exchange rate by shifting the supply–demand position in the market.

4. The government can adjust the country's whole macroeconomic position to make it "fit" the chosen fixed exchange rate value. Macroeconomic adjustments, such as changes in fiscal or monetary policy, can alter the supply–demand position in the foreign exchange market, for instance, by adjusting export capabilities, the demand for imports, or international capital flows.

We should also remember that there is a fifth option for the country—to surrender rather than defend:

5. The country can alter its fixed rate (devaluing or revaluing its currency) or switch to a floating exchange rate (in which case the currency will immediately depreciate or appreciate).

The four ways of defending a fixed rate are not mutually exclusive—a country can use several methods at the same time. Indeed, they are often closely interrelated. For instance, changing interest rates to influence short-term capital flows relates to overall macroeconomic management. In the next two sections of this chapter, we turn to a closer examination of the first two options: intervention and exchange control. Part IV is devoted to examining the broader implications of the country's foreign exchange policies for the whole national economy.

Defense Through Official Intervention

In defending a fixed exchange rate, the country's first line of defense is usually official intervention in the foreign exchange market. This is the defense that we introduced in Chapter 16, and we can now examine it in more depth. For much of our discussion in the first parts of this section, we will examine a country that has chosen to peg its currency to the U.S. dollar so that the spot exchange rate r_s is in units of this country's currency per dollar (because the dollar is now the "foreign" currency).

Defending Against Depreciation

Consider first the case in which the pressure from private (or nonofficial) supply and demand in the foreign exchange market is attempting to drive the exchange rate above the top of its allowable band—the country's currency is tending toward depreciation. For instance, say that this is a Latin American country that is attempting to maintain a fixed rate of 25 pesos per dollar, with a band of plus or minus 4 percent (plus or minus one peso). As shown in Figure 20.1, nonofficial

FIGURE 20.1

Intervention to Defend a Fixed Rate: Preventing Depreciation of the Country's Currency

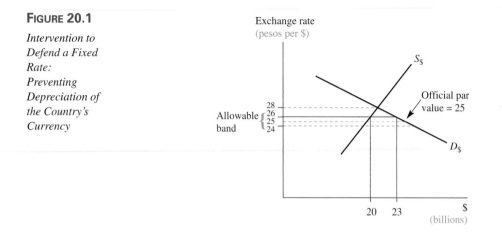

supply and demand are attempting to push the exchange rate to 28 pesos per dollar, the intersection where the market would clear on its own. If the country's monetary authority is committed to defending the fixed rate within its band using intervention, then the authority must enter into the foreign exchange market in its official role. It must sell dollars and buy domestic currency. To keep the currency in the allowable band, it must sell 3 billion dollars into the foreign exchange market at the rate of 26 pesos per dollar (the top of the band), so it is buying 78 billion pesos from the foreign exchange market. The relatively strong demand for dollars is generally related to strong demand by the country for purchases of foreign goods, services, and (nonofficial) financial assets (relative to the demand by foreigners for this country's goods, services, and nonofficial financial assets). This results in an official settlements balance deficit if the country's monetary authority intervenes to defend the fixed rate. The intervention provides the foreign exchange for the country to buy more (in total value) from foreigners than it is selling to them (for goods, services, and nonofficial financial assets). Through intervention the monetary authority is financing the country's deficit in its official settlement balance.

Where does the country's monetary authority get the dollars to sell into the foreign exchange market? This Latin American country cannot just create U.S. dollars. Rather, the authority either uses its own official international reserve assets (or some other similar government assets) to obtain dollars from some foreign source, most likely the U.S. monetary authority (the Federal Reserve), or it borrows the dollars. Let's examine each of these.

As we noted in Chapter 15, there are four major components to a country's official reserve assets: the country's holdings of foreign exchange assets denominated in the major currencies of the world, the country's reserve position with the International Monetary Fund, the country's holdings of special drawing rights, and the country's holdings of gold. To indicate the magnitudes, Figure 20.2 provides information on world holdings of official reserve assets.

FIGURE 20.2		*1970*	*1980*	*1990*	*1997*
Official Holdings of Reserve Assets, End of Year, 1970–1997 (billions of U.S. dollars)	Foreign exchange assets	45	381	806	1,537
	U.S. dollar	34	261	463	942
	German mark	1	57	150	201
	Japanese yen	0	17	71	77
	British pound	6	11	27	54
	Other and unspecified currencies	4	35	95	263
	Special drawing rights	3	15	28	28
	Reserve position in the IMF	8	22	32	65
	Gold	40	573	345	263
	(millions of ounces)	(1,057)	(953)	(940)	(890)
	Total reserve assets	96	991	1,211	1,893

Most official reserves are held as foreign exchange assets. Most of these are in dollar-denominated assets. The two reserve assets provided by the IMF are relatively minor. The value of official holdings of gold has fluctuated as the dollar price of gold has varied, while the amount (ounces) of gold held as official reserves has been declining slowly.

The dollar value of gold reserves is shown at the market price. For 1980, 1990, and 1997, the European Currency Unit is not treated as a separate reserve asset. At the beginning of 1999, as the euro came into existence, all official reserves previously denominated in German marks and the other member currencies became euro-denominated official reserve assets.

Source: International Monetary Fund, *Annual Report,* various years.

Most official reserve assets are in the form of foreign exchange assets, typically invested in safe, highly liquid interest-earning debt securities such as government bonds. Our Latin American country can use this type of asset to obtain dollars by selling it. If the asset is denominated in dollars (as most are, according to Figure 20.2), it obtains dollars that can then be used in its intervention. If the asset is denominated in some other major currency (such as yen or pounds), the currency must be exchanged for dollars, but this can easily be accomplished if the other currency is readily traded.

If our country has a reserve position in the IMF, then it can obtain dollars from the IMF on request. If the country is holding SDRs, then it can use these SDRs to obtain dollars from the U.S. monetary authority or from the IMF. The SDRs actually act as a line of credit permitting the country to borrow dollars, but SDRs are counted as reserves because the country can automatically draw on this line. If the country has gold, then it can sell gold to obtain dollars, but officials today almost never use gold sales to obtain foreign currency.

In addition to using its reserve assets to obtain dollars, the country's monetary authority can borrow dollars. It may be able to borrow dollars (or other major currencies) from the monetary authorities of other countries. Some countries maintain arrangements called *swap lines* with each other to facilitate this type of official borrowing. The monetary authority also may be able to borrow dollars from private—that is, nonofficial—sources. Sometimes these borrowings are disguised to keep them secret from private participants in the foreign exchange market.

These borrowings usually are considered to be different from normal transactions in official international reserves, because the country may not have "automatic" access to dollars through borrowings—the lender must be willing to make the loan. There is, however, a special case, the case of a country (like the United States) whose currency is readily held by the monetary authorities of other countries. If the country's currency is a **reserve currency,** then the country can effectively borrow through official channels by issuing assets that will be held as reserves by the central banks of other countries. Specifically, this has allowed the United States to run what French economist Jacques Rueff called *deficits without tears.* The United States, especially in the 1950s and 1960s, was given extraordinary leeway to finance its deficits. Needless to say, this option is probably not available to the Latin American country that was the focus of our previous example.

What is the implication of the other part of the intervention, that the country's monetary authority is buying domestic currency from the foreign exchange market? In buying domestic currency, the country's monetary authority is removing domestic currency from the economy. This will tend to reduce the domestic money supply unless the authority separately takes another action (called **sterilization**) to restore the domestic money back into the economy. If the authority does take action to prevent the domestic money supply from changing, then the authority is relying only on intervention to defend the fixed rate. This is called **sterilized intervention.** If the monetary authority instead allows the intervention to reduce the money supply, then we have a clear interrelationship with two of the other defense methods. The change in the domestic money supply is likely to alter domestic interest rates, and these changes are likely to influence the entire macroeconomy of the country (including the country's price level).[2] We will examine these broader issues in depth in Part IV.

Defending Against Appreciation

Consider now the case in which the pressure from private (or nonofficial) supply and demand in the foreign exchange market is attempting to drive the exchange rate, the price of foreign currency, below the bottom of its allowable band—the country's currency is tending toward appreciation. For instance, say that this is an Asian country attempting to maintain a fixed rate of 100 "locals" per dollar, with a band of plus or minus 5 percent (plus or minus five locals). As shown in Figure 20.3, nonofficial supply and demand are attempting to push the exchange rate to 85 locals per dollar, the intersection where the market would clear on its own. If the country's monetary authority is committed to defending the fixed rate within its band using intervention, then the authority must enter into the foreign exchange market in its official role. It must buy dollars and sell domestic currency. To keep the currency in the band, it must buy 2 billion dollars from the foreign exchange market at the rate of 95 locals per dollar (the bottom of the band), so it is selling 190 billion locals into the foreign exchange market. The relatively strong demand for locals is generally related to relatively strong

---

[2]The intervention may also change the foreign country's money supply as the monetary authority sells foreign currency, but we usually do not focus much on this effect.

FIGURE 20.3

Intervention to Defend a Fixed Rate: Preventing Appreciation of the Country's Currency

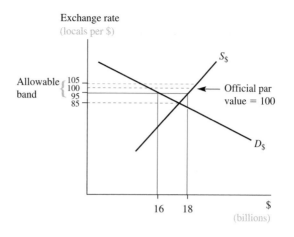

demand by foreigners for the country's goods, services, and (nonofficial) financial assets. This results in an official settlements balance surplus if the country's monetary authority intervenes to defend the fixed rate. The intervention provides the local currency for the foreigners to buy more from the country than they are selling to the country (for goods, services, and nonofficial financial assets).

What does the country's monetary authority do with the dollars that it obtains from the foreign exchange market? It adds these dollars to its official international reserve holdings (or, if appropriate, repays prior official borrowings of dollars). Most likely, the authority will use the dollars to obtain U.S.-dollar–denominated foreign exchange assets, probably U.S. government bonds. The country's holdings of official reserve assets increase. Note that this case is closely related to the idea of a U.S. "deficit without tears." A U.S. deficit is a surplus for some other countries. If the other countries want to prevent an appreciation of their currencies, they may intervene to buy dollars. In the process, the United States finances its own official settlements deficit by issuing financial assets that other countries hold as their reserves.

What is the implication of the other part of the intervention, that the country's monetary authority is selling domestic currency into the foreign exchange market? This will expand the domestic money supply unless the authority separately takes another action to remove the additional domestic money from the economy. If the domestic money supply does increase, then domestic interest rates and the entire macroeconomy of the country are likely to be affected.

Temporary Disequilibrium

A major issue for the use of intervention to defend a fixed exchange rate is the length of time for which the intervention must continue. How long will the gap between nonofficial supply and demand at the edge of the band persist? That is, how long will the imbalance in the official settlements balance persist at this exchange rate?

If imbalances are clearly temporary, then defending the fixed exchange rate purely through intervention can work and makes sense. In this case the monetary authorities can finance a succession of deficits and surpluses indefinitely. In fact, we can make a case that financing temporary deficits and surpluses is better than letting the exchange rate float around.

Consider, for example, a situation in which Canada maintains a fixed exchange rate with its major trading partner, Britain. (The exchange rate r_s is in Canadian dollars per pound, the price of foreign currency if our home country is Canada.) Figure 20.4 gives an example of a successful and socially desirable financing of temporary surpluses and deficits with a fixed exchange rate. We have imagined that the temporary fluctuations in the balance of payments and the foreign exchange market arise from something predictable, such as a seasonal pattern in foreign exchange receipts, with Canada exporting more and earning more foreign exchange (£) during the autumn-winter harvest season than during the nonharvest spring-summer season. To help the example along, let us assume that it is costly for producers of the export crop to refrain from selling it during the harvest season and that something also prevents private investors or speculators from stepping in and performing the equilibrating function being assigned to government officials here. If the officials did not finance the temporary imbalances, the exchange rate would drop to $1.40 at point B in the harvest season, when the nation had a lot of exports to sell, and it would rise to $1.80 in the off-season. In this instance there is some economic loss since it would be better if the people who wanted foreign exchange to keep up imports during the off-season did not have to pay $1.80 for foreign exchange that is readily available for only $1.40 during the harvest season. The officials can recapture this economic gain by stabilizing the price at $1.60. Their stabilization is made possible because they have somehow picked the correct price, $1.60, the one at which they can sell exactly as much foreign exchange during one season as they buy during the other, exactly breaking even while stabilizing the price.

The official financing of spring-summer deficits with autumn-winter foreign exchange reserves brings a net social gain to the world. This gain arises from the fact that the officials gave a net supply of foreign exchange at $1.60 to people who would have been willing to pay up to $1.80 a pound during the spring-summer season, while also buying at $1.60 the same amount of foreign exchange from people who would have been willing to sell it for as little as $1.40. The net social gain is measured as the sum of areas ACD and BDE (or about $1 billion a year). In this case, financing was successful and superior to letting the exchange rate find its own equilibrium in each season.

For intervention to finance temporary disequilibriums to be the correct policy option, some stringent conditions must be met. First, it must be the case that private speculators do not see, or cannot take advantage of, the opportunity to buy foreign exchange in the fall and winter, invest it for a few months, and then sell it in the spring and summer. If private parties could do this, their own actions would bring the exchange rate close to $1.60 throughout the year, and there would be no need for official intervention.

FIGURE 20.4

*A Successful
Financing of
Temporary
Deficits and
Surpluses at a
Stable
Exchange Rate*

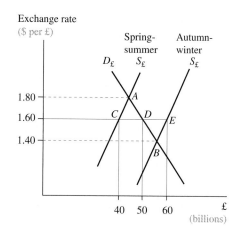

Autumn and winter: officials buy $DE = £10$ billion in foreign exchange.
Spring and summer: officials sell $CD = £10$ billion in foreign exchange.

It is also crucial that the officials correctly predict the future demand and supply for foreign exchange and that they predict what would be an equilibrium path for the exchange rate in the absence of their intervention. If they do not forecast correctly, their attempt to finance a deficit or a surplus at a fixed exchange rate can be costly because their accumulation of official reserves at some times will not balance against their loss of reserves at other times.

Disequilibrium That Is Not Temporary

What happens if the disequilibrium that results in an imbalance in the country's official settlements balance is not temporary? Rather, what if the disequilibrium is ongoing or *fundamental?* If the country defends its fixed rate using intervention, then the country's monetary authority is continually losing reserves (or borrowing foreign exchange) if the imbalance is a deficit, or it is accumulating reserves if the imbalance is a surplus.

If the domestic currency is facing pressure toward depreciation because of an ongoing deficit, the authority must continually intervene to sell foreign currency. Eventually its official reserves will run low, as will its ability to borrow foreign currencies. Furthermore, its problems can become worse if private investors and speculators observe its reserve losses and begin to bet heavily that the currency must be devalued. A one-way speculative gamble exists. As investors and speculators sell domestic currency and buy foreign currency, the gap that must be filled by official intervention widens, hastening the loss of reserves. As the country loses reserves, it also loses the ability to defend the fixed rate by intervention alone. It must shift to one of the other three defenses or surrender (devalue).

To see some of the economic costs of intervening to finance a "temporary" disequilibrium that turns out to be a fundamental disequilibrium, consider a stunning recent example of a failed defense of a currency—the depreciation of the Mexican peso in late 1994. The Mexican monetary authority was using a heavily managed "float" to effectively peg the Mexican currency at about 3.5 pesos per dollar. They were intervening to defend this value, and their holdings of official reserves declined from nearly $30 billion to about $6 billion during 1994. With their reserves so low, on December 20, 1994, they were forced to surrender, and the peso declined by about one-third to about 5 pesos per dollar by year-end. They lost billions of dollars of taxpayers' money. Having bought pesos at about $0.29 per peso, they subsequently had to sell pesos at a much lower dollar value to buy dollars in order to rebuild their official reserves. Buying dear and selling cheap is a formula for large losses.

If, in the opposite case, the domestic currency is facing pressure toward appreciation because of an ongoing surplus, the authority must continually intervene to buy foreign currency. The country eventually accumulates large international reserves. These may be viewed as too large by the country itself for several reasons. First, the basic rate of return on this particular form of national wealth tends to be low, given the types of low-interest investments that are usually chosen for international reserve assets. Second, the value of foreign-exchange assets will decline if the country eventually must "retreat" by revaluing its own currency (which devalues foreign currency). Furthermore, these reserves may be viewed as too large by other countries, because some other countries are running deficits if this country is running a surplus and building its reserve holdings.

An example of this surplus case is Japan in the early 1970s. The Japanese government did not want the dollar value of the yen to rise in August 1971, even though President Nixon had openly invited speculation in favor of the yen by calling for its revaluation (rise in dollar value). Hoping to ride out a temporary surplus situation in order to keep Japan's export and import-competing goods competitive (to the advantage of powerful trading groups but to the disadvantage of Japanese consuming groups), Japanese officials bought up billions of dollars during a few months as a way of financing the "temporary" surplus. Dollars threatened to become the sole asset of the Bank of Japan if the trend continued. Japanese officials soon gave up and let the dollar value of the yen jump. This involved the Japanese officials in the same kind of currency losses as the Mexican officials sustained in 1994. The difference was that the Japanese officials were stuck holding *foreign* currency that was worth less than they had paid for it (the depreciating dollars), whereas the Mexican officials ended up holding less-valuable domestic currency.

These experiences do not prove that it is futile to try to keep exchange rates fixed. They do prove that when the existing official exchange rate is becoming a disequilibrium exchange rate for the long run, trying to ride out the storm with intervention alone is costly. Something more must be added. Fundamental disequilibrium calls for adjustment, not merely financing. However, it is not easy for officials to judge what constitutes fundamental disequilibrium. We are left with the knowledge that a fundamental disequilibrium is one that is too great and/or too enduring to be financed, but we have no clear way of identifying one until after it has happened.

Exchange Control

Among the options for defending a fixed exchange rate, one—exchange control—can be indicated as socially inferior to the others. Oddly enough, exchange control is widely used. According to the International Monetary Fund, in the late 1990s about 100 countries, all developing countries, had fairly comprehensive exchange control policies in place, controls that included requirements related to export proceeds and restrictions on payments for both current and capital transactions. A large number of other countries had some more limited form of exchange control in place. For instance, about 50 other countries, including some industrialized countries, had substantial controls on capital transactions. A number of these countries are responding to persistent deficits in their external payments by defending a fixed exchange rate with elaborate government controls restricting the ability of their residents to buy foreign goods or services, to travel abroad, or to invest abroad.

Exchange controls are closely analogous to quantitative restrictions (quotas) on imports, already analyzed in Chapter 8. In fact, the analogy with import quotas fits very well, so well that the basic economics of exchange controls is simply the economics of import quotas expanded to cover imports of IOUs (investing abroad) and tourist services as well as imports of ordinary products. In Chapter 8 and Appendix E, we demonstrate that an import quota is at least as bad as an import tariff using a one-dollar–one-vote analysis of changes in well-being. So it is with exchange controls as well: They are at least as damaging as a uniform tax on all foreign transactions, and probably they are worse.

To show the economic case against exchange controls, it is useful to start with an oversimplified view of exchange controls that is almost certain to underestimate the social losses coming from real-world controls. Figure 20.5 sketches the effects of a system of binding comprehensive exchange control that is about as well managed and benign as we can imagine. Figure 20.5 imagines that the U.S. government has become committed to maintaining a fixed exchange rate that officially values foreign currencies less, and the dollar more, than would a free-market equilibrium rate. This official rate is $1.00 for the pound sterling, with similar subequilibrium rates for other foreign currencies. The exchange control laws require exporters to turn over all their claims on foreigners (which we shall equate with claims in foreign currencies) to the U.S. government. The U.S. government, in turn, gives them $1.00 in domestic bank deposits for each pound sterling they have earned by selling abroad. At this exchange rate, exporters are earning, and releasing to authorities, only £30 billion. This figure is well below the £63.3 billion that residents of the United States want to buy at this exchange rate to purchase foreign goods, services, and assets. If the U.S. government feels committed to the $1.00 rate, yet is not willing to intervene or to contract the whole U.S. economy enough, to make the demand and supply for foreign exchange match at $1.00, then it must ration the right to buy foreign exchange.

Let us imagine that the U.S. officials ration foreign exchange in a sound but seldom-tried way. Every two months they announce that it is time for another

FIGURE 20.5

The Best of the Worst: Welfare Losses from Well-Managed Exchange Controls

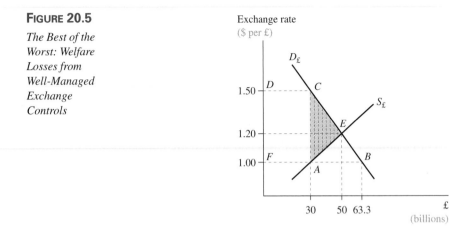

public auction-by-mail. On January 21, they announce that anyone wanting sterling (or any other foreign currency) for the March–April period must send in bids by February 15. A family that plans to be in England in April might send in a form pledging its willingness to pay up to $3 per pound for 700 pounds to spend in England and its willingness to pay $2.50 per pound for 1,000 pounds. An importer of automobiles would also submit a schedule of amounts of foreign currencies he wished to buy at each exchange rate in order to buy cars abroad. Receiving all these bids, the government's computers would rank them by the prices willingly pledged, and the totals pledged would be added up at each price, thus revealing the demand curve $D_{£}$ in Figure 20.5. Estimating that it could allocate £30 billion over a year, or £5 billion for March–April, the government would announce on February 20 that the price of $1.50 per pound was the price that made demand match the available £30 billion per year. The family who wanted to be in England for April would thus be able to get £1,000 by taking a check for $1,500 = £1,000 × $1.50 to the local post office, along with the officially signed pledge form it had submitted before February 15. Thus, all who were willing to pay $1.50 or more for each pound would receive the pounds they applied for, at the price of only $1.50 a pound, even if they had agreed to pay more. Anyone who did not submit bids with prices as high as $1.50 would be denied the right to buy abroad during March or April.

This system would give the government a large amount of revenues earned from the exchange control auctions. Collecting $1.50/£ × £30 billion = $45 billion while paying exporters only $1.00/£ × £30 billion = $30 billion, the government would make a net profit of $15 billion, minus its administrative costs. This government profit could be returned to the general public either as a cut in other kinds of taxes or as extra government spending. Area *DCAF* in Figure 20.5 represents these auction profits taken from importers but returned to the rest of society, and it does not constitute a net gain or loss for society as a whole.

The exchange control just described does impose a welfare loss on society as a whole, however. This loss is measured by the area *CEA*. To see why, remember the interpretation of demand and supply curves as marginal benefit and cost curves. When the exchange controls are in effect and only £30 billion is available, some mutually profitable trades are being prohibited. At point *C*, the demand curve is telling us that some American is willing to pay up to $1.50 for an extra pound. At point *A*, the supply curve is telling us that somebody else, either a U.S. exporter or her customers, would be willing to provide an extra pound per year for as little as $1.00. Yet, the exchange controls prevent these two groups from getting together to split the $0.50 of net gain in a marketplace for pounds. Thus the vertical distance *AC* = $0.50 shows the social loss from not being able to trade freely another pound. Similarly, each extra vertical gap between the demand curve and the supply curve out to point *E* also adds to the measure of something lost because the exchange controls hamper private transactions. All these net losses add up to area *CEA* (£5 billion).

Actual exchange control regimes are likely to have several other effects and costs. First, in practice, governments usually do not hold public foreign currency auctions. Instead, they allocate the right to buy foreign currency at the low official rate according to more complicated rules. To get the right to buy foreign currency, we must go through involved application procedures to show that the purpose of the foreign purchase qualifies it for a favored-treatment category. Importing inputs for factories that would otherwise have to remain idle and underutilized is one purpose that often qualifies for priority access to foreign exchange, over less crucial inputs, or imports of luxury consumer goods, or acquisition of private foreign bank deposits. One difference between actual exchange controls and our hypothetical one is that the actual controls often incur greater administrative costs to enforce the controls, as well as greater private resource costs in dealing with them. Another difference is that some lower-valued uses may be approved in place of higher-valued uses. The government is not necessarily serving the demanders toward the top of the demand curve. For both of these reasons the net loss is larger than area *CEA*.

Second, another effect of exchange controls—efforts to evade them—is predictable. People are frustrated when they are not allowed to buy foreign exchange, even though they are willing to pay more than the recipients of foreign exchange will get from the government when these holders sell their foreign currency. The frustrated demanders will then look for other ways to obtain foreign exchange. One way is to bribe the government functionaries in charge of determining the official approvals. Another is to offer more to the recipients of foreign exchange than the government is offering, thus making it worthwhile for the recipients to "sell direct," in violation of the exchange controls. In this way a second foreign exchange market—a parallel market or black market—develops. Parallel markets exist in most countries that have exchange controls. The degree to which users of these illegal markets are punished varies widely. Some countries ignore violations of the exchange control, while others impose death penalties. If you visit a country that has exchange controls, be sure that you know the penalties before you use the parallel market. Your effort to take advantage of free-market economics might make you decidedly unfree.[3]

The costs of actual exchange controls are generally great enough to raise the question of what good purpose they are intended to serve. Because controls can be used to defend a fixed rate, we might imagine that they reduce economic uncertainty by holding fixed the external value of the national currency. Yet, they are unlikely to help reduce uncertainty if they leave individual firms and households in doubt as to whether they will be allowed to obtain foreign exchange at the official price. Controls are likely to appeal mainly to government officials as a device for increasing their discretionary power over the allocation of resources. Controls undeniably have this effect. A charitable interpretation is that the extra power makes it easier for government officials to achieve social goals through comprehensive planning. A less charitable interpretation, consistent with the facts, is that officials see in exchange controls an opportunity for personal power and its lucrative exercise. In addition, the emergence of parallel markets or other methods to evade the controls calls into question their true effectiveness. Although exchange controls in various forms are used in many countries, especially developing countries, they have sufficiently large costs and questions regarding long-run effectiveness that we focus further discussion here and in Part IV on the other methods for defending a fixed rate.

International Currency Experience

The first part of this chapter has laid out a framework for describing government policies toward the foreign exchange market, and has examined some of the economics of official intervention and exchange control. The rest of the chapter surveys the historical experience of actual government policies since the establishment of a nearly worldwide gold standard over a century ago. It reports some lessons learned from that experience. The history leads into a description of the current system (or perhaps "nonsystem") in the final section of the chapter.

The Gold Standard Era, 1870–1914 (One Version of Fixed Rates)

Ever since 1914, the prewar gold standard has been the object of considerable nostalgia. Both the interwar period and the postwar period saw concerted interna-

---

[3]In a number of countries the government itself creates two or more foreign exchange markets and rates—a dual– or multiple–exchange-rate system. Each rate applies to transactions of a specific type. For instance, a dual-rate system might have one rate for current transactions and another rate for capital transactions. In the late 1990s, about 25 countries had some form of dual– or multiple–exchange-rate system. As part of this type of policy, some form of exchange control is needed to direct each transaction to its appropriate rate. Again, the system creates incentives for evasion. For instance, transactions may be disguised to qualify for a more favorable rate.

High Finance, or the International Beer-Drinking Puzzle

At several points in Part III we have touched briefly on the issue of the welfare aspects of disequilibrium exchange rates. Here are a puzzle and a real-life counterpart to ponder on that subject.

In a certain town lying on the border between Mexico and the United States, a peculiar currency situation exists. In Mexico, a U.S. dollar is worth only 90 centavos of Mexican money, whereas in the United States the value of a Mexican peso (= 100 centavos) is only 90 cents of U.S. money.

One day, a cowhand strolls into a Mexican cantina and orders a 10-centavo beer. He pays for it with a Mexican peso, receiving in exchange a U.S. dollar worth 90 centavos in Mexico. After drinking his beer, he strolls over the border to a saloon in the United States and orders a 10-cent beer. He pays for this with the just-received dollar, receiving a Mexican peso (worth 90 U.S. cents in the United States) in exchange. He keeps on repeating the process, drinking beer happily all day. He ends up just as rich as he started—with a peso.

The question: Who really paid for the beer?

(In addition to explaining who really paid for the beer, discuss the foreign exchange aspects of this situation. What conditions are necessary for such a situation to persist for a long time, and what might bring it to a stop? What are the effects of this situation on the domestic economies of the United States and Mexico?)*

The beer-drinking puzzle may strike you as unrealistic. Not so. The puzzle is but one illustration of the real-world phenomenon of arbitrage profit, the gains accruing to persons taking riskless advantage of price inconsistencies. A part of the high incomes earned by professional traders comes from their ability to engage in arbitrage. (The rest comes as a reward for their risk taking.)

For a real-life example of the same street-level arbitrage between currencies, consider the case of Wendy and Jim of Portland, Oregon, in 1982. They noticed different prices in Portland for the Canadian quarter. Most merchants were willing to accept Canadian quarters as worth 25 U.S. cents. You could also mix Canadian quarters into rolls of U.S. quarters and, again, get 25 U.S. cents for each. But Wendy and Jim were able to get Canadian quarters for much less than 25 U.S. cents. For one thing, the Canadian dollar had fallen from the old parity with the U.S. dollar to being worth only 80 U.S. cents, making the Canadian quarter available at 20 U.S. cents. Some banks would even sell Wendy and Jim Canadian quarters in bulk for as little as 16 cents each just to save the expense of shipping them back to Canada.

So Wendy and Jim engaged in arbitrage. They would get large amounts of Canadian quarters from Portland banks at 16 to 20 U.S. cents each and spend them on whatever they wanted in Portland stores (or mix them into rolls of U.S. quarters at 25 cents each). They made up to $25 an hour that way, though usually somewhat less.

How long could their arbitrage last? For quite a long time if the Canadian dollar stays well below the U.S. dollar in value and if nobody else horns in on their business. Wendy and Jim find the pay better than their alternatives. Wendy was fired from her university job for teaching in the nude, and they have made little profit on their unpublished novels and musical compositions or their trade in rare records.

Who really pays for their profit on Canadian quarters? "That's what we were trying to figure out," says Wendy. "Nobody is, but somebody must be."†

---

*The source of this puzzle is E. Krasner and J. Newman, *Mathematics and the Imagination* (1940), p. 162. Sorry, they didn't include the answer—we leave that to you.

---

†The source in this case is Lisa E. Vickery, "Free Money! Some Folks Snatching $25 an Hour Right Out of Thin Air," *The Wall Street Journal,* August 18, 1982, p. 24.

tional efforts to reestablish fixed–exchange-rate systems whose desirability was viewed as proven by the experience of the gold standard. Among scholars too, the "success" of the gold standard has been widely accepted and research has focused on *why*, not whether, it worked so well.

The international gold standard emerged by 1870 with the help of historical accidents centering on Britain. Britain tied the pound sterling ever more closely to gold than to silver from the late 17th century on, in part because Britain's official gold–silver value ratio was more favorable to gold than were the ratios of other countries, causing arbitrageurs to ship gold *to* Britain and silver *from* Britain. The link between the pound sterling and gold proved crucial. Britain's rise to primacy in industrialization and world trade in the 19th century enhanced the prestige of the metal tied to the currency of this leading country. Also, Britain had the advantage of not being invaded in wars, which further strengthened its image as the model of financial security and prudence. The prestige of gold was raised further by another lucky accident. The waves of gold discoveries both in the middle of the 19th century (California, Australia) and at the end of this century (South Africa, the Klondike) were small enough not to make gold suddenly too abundant to be a standard for international value. The silver mining expansion of the 1870s and 1880s, by contrast, yielded too much silver, causing its value to plummet. Through such accidents, the gold standard, in which each national currency was fixed in gold content, remained intact from about 1870 until World War I.

Under the gold standard each country's government fixed its currency to a specified quantity of gold. The government also freely permitted individuals to exchange domestic money or currency for gold and to export and import gold. Through gold arbitrage the exchange rates between currencies then remained within a band (whose width reflected the transactions costs of gold movements between countries). Furthermore, changes in the government's gold holdings were linked to changes in the country's money supply—and thus to the country's average price level, its inflation rate, and other aspects of its macroeconomic performance.

The actual functioning of the gold standard was not this simple. Indeed, the process of actual payments adjustment under the prevailing fixed exchange rates puzzled Frank Taussig and his Harvard students after World War I. They found that international gold flows seemed to eliminate themselves very quickly, too quickly for their possible effects on national money supplies to change incomes, prices, and the balance of payments. The puzzle was heightened by the postwar finding of Arthur I. Bloomfield that central banks had done little to adjust their national economies to their exchange rates before 1914. Far from speeding up the economy's adjustment to payment surpluses or deficits, prewar central banks, similar to their successors in the interwar period, offset (sterilized) external reserve flows in the majority of cases, so that their national money supplies did not change much. What, then, actually kept the prewar balance of payments in line?

First, it must be noted that most countries were able to run payments surpluses before 1914, raising their holdings of gold and foreign exchange. This removed the cost of adjustment to fixed exchange rates because surplus countries were under little pressure to adjust. Widespread surpluses were made possible by, aside from the slow accumulation of newly mined gold in official vaults, the willingness and ability of Britain—and Germany to a lesser extent—to let the rest of the world hold growing amounts of its monetary liabilities. Between 1900 and 1913, for example, Britain ran payments deficits that were at least as large in relation to official (Bank of England) gold reserves as the deficits that caused so much hand-wringing in the United States in the 1960s. In fact, it would have been impossible for Britain to honor even one-third of its liquid liabilities to foreigners in 1913 by paying out official gold reserves. The gold standard was thus helped along considerably by the ability of the key-currency country to give the rest of the world liquid IOUs whose buildup nobody minded—or even measured.

There were times, of course, when Britain was called on to halt outflows of gold reserves which were more conspicuous than the unknown rise in its liquid liabilities. The Bank of England showed an impressive ability to halt gold outflows within a few months, faster than it could have if it had needed to contract the whole British economy to improve the balance of payments. It appears that higher British interest rates, resulting from monetary tightening by the Bank of England, were capable of calling in large volumes of short-term capital from abroad, even when central banks in other countries raised their interest rates by the same percentage. This command over short-term capital seems to have been linked to London's being the financial center for the world's money markets. As the main short-term international lender (as well as borrower), London could contract the whole world's money supply in the short run if and when the Bank of England ordered private banks in London to do so. In this way, the prewar gold standard combined overall surplus for most countries with short-run defensive strength on the part of the main deficit country.

In retrospect, it is clear that the success of the gold standard is explained partly by the tranquillity of the prewar era. The world economy was not subjected to shocks as severe as World Wars I and II, the Great Depression of the 1930s, and the OPEC oil price shocks of 1973–1974 and 1979–1980. *The gold standard looked successful, in part, because it was not put to a severe worldwide test.*

The prewar gold standard seemed to succeed for one other reason: *"success" was leniently defined* in those days. Central banks were responsible only for fixing the gold or exchange rate value of the currency. Public opinion did not hold central bankers (or government officials) responsible for fighting unemployment or stabilizing prices as much as after World War I. This easy assignment shielded officials from the demand-policy dilemma discussed in Part IV.

The pre-1914 tranquillity also allowed some countries to have favorable experiences with flexible exchange rates. Several countries abandoned fixed exchange rates and gold convertibility in short-run crises. Britain itself did so during the Napoleonic Wars. Faced with heavy wartime financial needs, Britain suspended convertibility of the pound sterling into gold and let the pound drop by as much as 30 percent in value by 1813, restoring official gold convertibility after the wars. Other countries repeated the experience, as shown for selected countries in Figure 20.6. During the American Civil War, the North found itself unable to maintain the gold value of the paper dollar, given the tremendous need to print

FIGURE 20.6   *Selected Exchange Rates, 1860–1913*

Value of this currency in
gold $ (U.S. or Canadian)
(ratio scale)

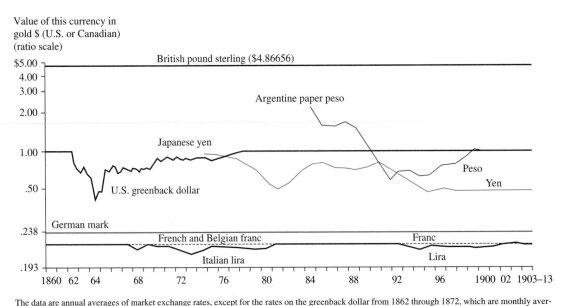

The data are annual averages of market exchange rates, except for the rates on the greenback dollar from 1862 through 1872, which are monthly averages for every third month. The Argentine paper peso rates are the John H. Williams gold premiums cited in Alec G. Ford, *The Gold Standard, 1880–1914: Great Britain and Argentina* (Oxford: Clarendon, 1962), p. 139. The Italian series is from Istituto Centrale di Statistica, *Sommario di Statistiche Storiche Italiane, 1861–1955* (Rome, 1958), p. 166. The gold value of the paper Japanese yen was calculated using the midrange New York dollar value of the metal-backed yen (Bank of Japan, Statistics Department, *Hundred Year Statistics of the Japanese Economy* [Tokyo, 1966], p. 318) and the average price of silver in paper yen for the period 1877–1886 (Henry Rosovsky, "Japan's Transition to Modern Economic Growth, 1868–1885," in *Industrialization in Two Systems*, ed. Henry Rosovsky [New York: Wiley, 1966], pp. 129 and 136). The U.S. greenback dollar series is the W. C. Mitchell series cited in Don C. Barrett, *The Greenback and Resumption of Specie Payments, 1862–1879* (Cambridge, Mass.: Harvard University Press, 1931, pp. 96–98). The virtually fixed rates are available in the *Economist* for prewar years.

dollars to finance the war effort. The newly issued greenback dollars had dropped in value by more than 60 percent as of 1864, before beginning a long, slow climb back to gold parity in 1879. Heavy short-run financial needs also drove other countries off gold parity. War was the proximate culprit in the cases of Russia, Austria–Hungary, and Italy.

This experience with fixed and flexible exchange rates reveals some patterns. Most countries that abandoned fixed exchange rates did so in a context of growing payments deficits and reserve outflows. Note that in Figure 20.6 the end of fixed exchange rates was accompanied by a drop in the value of the national currency. This drop shows indirectly that the fixed-rate gold standard imposed strain mostly on countries that were in payments deficit situations, not on countries in surplus. Indeed, countries in surplus found it easy to continue accumulating reserves with a fixed exchange rate.

In general, the pre-1914 experiences with flexible exchange rates did not reveal any tendency toward destabilizing speculation. For the most part, the exchange rate fluctuations did not represent wide departures from the exchange rate we would have predicted, given the movements in price indexes. Two possible exceptions related to the U.S. greenback dollar and the Russian ruble. In

1864, the greenback dollar fell in value 49 percent between April and July, even though the wholesale price index rose less than 15 percent, suggesting that speculation greatly accelerated the drop in the greenback, which then promptly rebounded. Similarly, in 1888, political rumors caused a dive in the thinly marketed Russian ruble. With the exception of these two possible cases of destabilizing speculation, it appears that flexible rates were quite stable in the prewar setting, given the political events that forced governments to try them out.

Interwar Instability

If the gold standard era before 1914 has been viewed as the classic example of international monetary soundness, the interwar period has played the part of a nightmare that officials have been determined to avoid repeating. Payments balances and exchange rates gyrated chaotically in response to two great shocks: World War I and the Great Depression. Figure 20.7 plots the exchange rate history of the interwar period. The chaos was concentrated into two periods: the first few years after World War I (1919–1923) and the currency crisis in the depths of the Great Depression (1931–1934).

After World War I the European countries had to struggle with a legacy of inflation and political instability. Their currencies had become inconvertible during the war because their rates of inflation were much higher than that experienced in the United States, the new financial leader. In this setting, Britain made the fateful decision to return to its prewar gold parity, achieving this rate by April 1925. Although the decision has been defended as a moral obligation and as a sound attempt to restore international confidence as well as Britain's role at the center of a reviving world economy, the hindsight consensus is that bringing the pound back up to $4.86656 was a serious mistake. It appears to have caused considerable unemployment and stagnation in traded-goods industries, as theory would predict, because the high real exchange rate value of the pound corresponded to a loss of international price competitiveness.

France, Italy, and some other European countries chose a more inflationary route for complicated political reasons. A succession of French revolving-door governments was unable to cut government spending or raise taxes to shut off large budgetary deficits that had to be financed largely by printing new money. Something similar happened in Italy, both before and immediately after the 1922 coup d'état that brought Mussolini to power. The ultimate in inflation, however, was experienced by Germany, where the money supply, prices, and cost of foreign exchange all rose more than a trillionfold in 1922–1923. Money became totally worthless, and by late 1923, not even a wheelbarrowful of paper money could buy a week's groceries. The mark had to be reissued in a new series equal to the prewar dollar value, with old marks forever unredeemable.

The early 1930s brought another breakdown of international currency relations. The financial community, already stunned by the early postwar chaos and the Wall Street collapse, became justifiably jittery about bank deposits and currencies as the depression spread. The failure of the reputable Creditanstalt bank in Austria caused a run on German banks and on the mark because Germany had

FIGURE 20.7

*Selected
Exchange Rates,
1913,
1919–1938*

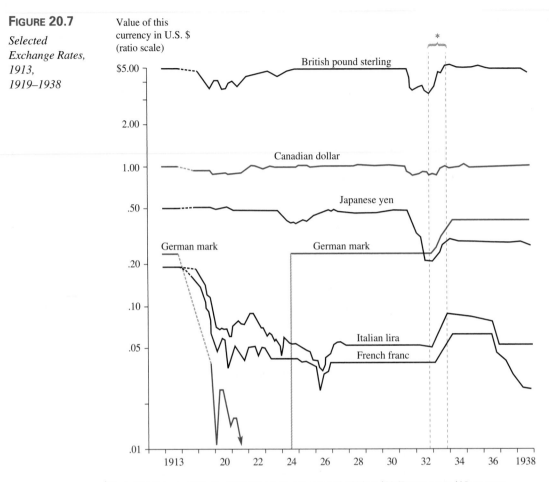

*March 1933–February 1934: The United States raises the price of gold from $20.67 per ounce to $35 per ounce.

Source: Monthly averages from U.S. Federal Reserve Board, Board of Governors, *Banking and Monetary Statistics* (Washington, D.C., 1943).

lent heavily to Austria. The panic soon led to an attack on the pound sterling, which had been perennially weak and was now compromised by Britain's making heavy loans to the collapsing Germans. On September 19, 1931, Britain abandoned the gold standard it had championed, letting the pound sink to its equilibrium market value. Between early 1933 and early 1934, the United States followed suit and let the dollar drop in gold value as President Roosevelt and his advisors manipulated the price of gold in an attempt to create jobs. Other countries also used devaluations, tariffs, and other trade restrictions to boost domestic employment. Such "beggar-thy-neighbor" policies (intended to benefit a country's economy at the expense of other countries) were widespread and probably added to worldwide depression ("beggared almost everyone") as international trade shrank rapidly in the early 1930s.

What lessons does the interwar experience hold for policymakers? During World War II, expert opinion seemed to be that the interwar experience called for a compromise between fixed and flexible exchange rates, with emphasis on the former. The Bretton Woods agreement of 1944 set up the International Monetary Fund and laid down a set of rules calling for countries to change their exchange rates only when fundamental disequilibrium made this unavoidable. This decision was paralleled by Ragnar Nurkse's book *International Currency Experience,* written for the League of Nations in 1944. Nurkse argued, with some qualifying disclaimers, that the interwar experience showed the instability of flexible exchange rates. Figure 20.7 adds some evidence to his premise: Exchange rates did indeed move more sharply during the interwar era than at any other time before the 1970s.

Yet subsequent studies have shown that a closer look at the interwar experience reveals the opposite lesson: *The interwar experience shows the futility of trying to keep exchange rates fixed in the face of severe shocks and the necessity of turning to flexible rates to cushion some of the international shocks.* Studies also have shown that it became more difficult for central banks to maintain defense of fixed rates as central banks came under more political pressure to pursue other goals such as reducing domestic unemployment.

At the same time, these studies have shown that even during the unstable interwar era, speculation tended to be stabilizing—it was domestic monetary and fiscal policy that was destabilizing. This revisionist conclusion began to emerge from studies of Britain's fluctuating rates between 1919 and 1925. Both Leland Yeager and S. C. Tsiang found that the pound sterling fluctuated in ways that are easily explained by the effects of differential inflation on the trade balance. Relative to the exchange rate movements that would be predicted by the purchasing power parity theory of the equilibrium exchange rate (see Chapter 18), the actual movements stayed close to the long-run trend. The cases in which Figure 20.7 shows rapid drops in currency values were cases in which the runaway expansion of the national money supply made this inevitable under any exchange rate regime. This was true of France up until 1926; it was even more true, of course, of the German hyperinflation.

Closer looks at the currency instability of the early 1930s suggest the same conclusion. The pound sterling, the yen, and other currencies dropped rapidly in 1931–1932 due to the gaping disequilibrium built into the fixed–exchange-rate system by the depression (and, for Japan, by the invasion of Manchuria). Once fixed rates were abandoned, flexible rates merely reflected, rather than worsened, the varying health of national economies.

The Bretton Woods Era, 1944–1971 (Adjustable Pegged Rates)

The Great Compromise of 1944

Meeting at the Bretton Woods resort in New Hampshire, the monetary leaders of the Allied powers had an opportunity to design a better system. Everyone agreed that the system needed reform. The United States dominated the Bretton Woods conference, just as it dominated the world economy and the world's gold reserves in 1944. America wanted something like fixed exchange rates. Indeed, all leaders sought to get close to the virtuous fixed–exchange-rate case sketched in Figure 20.4. If only there were enough reserves to tide countries over temporary disequilibria, and if only countries followed policies that made all disequilibria temporary, then we could capture those welfare gains from successful stabilization.

Two expert economists, John Maynard Keynes of Britain and Harry Dexter White of the United States, came up with workable plans to give the world a new central bank that would allow deficit countries enough reserves to ride out their temporary deficits. White's plan also called for international pressure on national governments to change their macroeconomic policies to serve the goal of balanced international payments. The grand design, in other words, was fully fixed exchange rates defended by government intervention, with international reserves sufficient to permit defense by deficit countries.

In the end, however, the United States, Britain, and other governments had difficulty accepting the grand design. The Americans balked at putting billions of dollars at the disposal of other governments and at having to inflate the American economy just because it had a balance-of-payments surplus (as was then expected). Seeing the limits to what the Americans were prepared to give raised the fears of Britain and others about how they could adjust to their likely balance-of-payments deficits. In exchange, they insisted on the right to resort to devaluations and exchange controls when deficits threatened to persist.

The resulting compromise was what we have come to call the **Bretton Woods system.** Its central feature was the **adjustable peg,** which called for a fixed exchange rate and temporary financing out of international reserves until a country's balance of payments was seen to be in "fundamental disequilibrium." A country in that condition might then change its "fixed" exchange rate to a new official par value that looked sustainable. The international reserves were augmented by the International Monetary Fund (IMF). The IMF was set up with contributions of gold and foreign exchange from member governments. It grants all member countries the right to borrow reserves to finance temporary deficits. The IMF, in other words, is something like the global central bank that Keynes and White tried to design in their two different ways. Its resources and prerogatives, however, were more limited than Keynes and White envisioned. Also limited was the international community's ability to bend nations' macroeconomic policies to keep their international payments in line.

After the immediate postwar exchange rate adjustments, which were completed by about 1950, the Bretton Woods system looked remarkably successful for almost two decades. Countries grew rapidly and unemployment stayed low. Most exchange rates stayed fixed for long time periods, as shown in Figure 20.8.

The strong economic growth probably contributed more to the look of success for monetary institutions than they contributed to the strong growth. The good growth climate was consistent with flexible exchange rates, too, to judge from the Canadian experience of floating during 1950–1962. As shown in Figure 20.8, the annual average exchange rates between Canada and the United States showed little movement. By itself this does not prove that the Canadian experi-

FIGURE 20.8   *Selected Exchange Rates, 1950–1981*

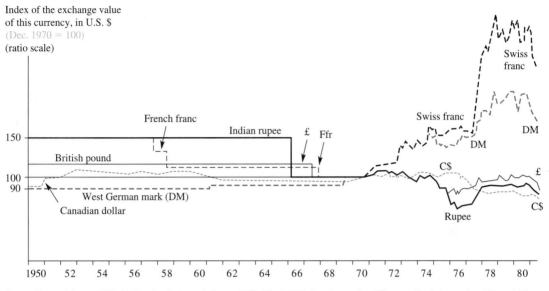

Source: Year-end figures, 1950–1969, and end-of-month figures, 1970–March 1981, from International Monetary Fund, *International Financial Statistics,* various issues.

ence was one in which flexible rates worked well. However, detailed studies of Canada's floating rate have borne out this inference. Statistical regressions have suggested that if the exchange rate on the Canadian dollar had any effect on capital movements, this effect was in the stabilizing direction; that is, a lower value of the Canadian dollar tended to cause greater net capital inflows into Canada, as though investors expected the Canadian dollar to rise more when it was at low levels. Other studies have confirmed that fluctuations in the exchange value of the Canadian dollar were no greater than we would have predicted by following movements in the relative U.S. and Canadian prices of traded goods. In this stable economic environment, the floating rate of the Canadian dollar was well behaved and almost as stable as the fixed rates of other currencies.

The One-Way Speculative Gamble
The postwar experience with adjustable pegged rates recorded only rare changes in exchange rates among major currencies up to 1971, as Figure 20.8 suggests. Yet the adjustable-peg system revealed a new pattern in private speculation, one that caused a great deal of official consternation. As the world economy grew, so did the volume of internationally mobile private funds. The new system of pegged but adjustable exchange rates spurred private speculators to attack currencies that were "in trouble." The adjustable-peg system gave private speculators an excellent one-way gamble. It was always clear from the context whether a

currency was in danger of being devalued or revalued. In the case of a devaluation-suspect currency, such as the pound sterling in the mid-1960s, the astute private speculator knew that the currency could not rise significantly in value. She thus had little to lose by selling the currency in the spot (or forward) market. If the currency did not drop in value, she had lost nothing but a slight gap between the domestic interest rate and the foreign interest rate (or between the forward rate and the spot rate), but if she was right and the currency was devalued, it might be devalued by a large percentage over a single weekend, bringing her a handsome return. In this situation, private speculators would gang up on a currency that was moving into a crisis phase. As one foreign exchange specialist in a leading U.S. bank put it, "In those days we could make money just by following the crowd."

This pattern of speculation under the adjustable-peg system meant serious difficulties for any government or central bank that was trying to cure a payments disequilibrium without adjusting the peg. A classic illustration of these difficulties was the attempt of Harold Wilson's Labor government to keep the pound worth $2.80 between 1964 and November 1967. When Wilson took office, he found that Britain's trade and payments balances were even worse than previous official figures had admitted. His government used numerous devices to make the pound worth $2.80: tighter exchange controls; soaring interest rates; selective tax hikes; promises to cut government spending; and massive loans from the IMF, the United States, and other governments. Speculators who, in increasing number, doubted Britain's ability to shore up the pound were castigated by the chancellor of the Exchequer as "gnomes of Zurich." Yet, in the end, all of the belt-tightening and all of the support loans worked no better than had the attempt to make the pound worth $4.86656 from 1925 to 1931. On November 18, 1967, Britain devalued the pound by 14.3 percent, to $2.40. The gnomes had won handsomely. Those who had, for instance, been selling sterling forward at prices like $2.67 just before the devaluation were able to buy the same sterling at about $2.40, pocketing the 27 cents difference. The British government and its taxpayers lost a similar difference, by paying close to $2.80 to buy sterling that they had to concede was worth only $2.40 after November 18.

The existence of the one-way speculative gamble seems to make the adjustable peg of the Bretton Woods system look less sustainable than either purely fixed rates or purely flexible rates. If speculators believe that the government is willing to turn the entire economy inside out to defend the exchange rate, then they will not attack the exchange rate. Britain could have made speculators believe in $2.80 in the mid-1960s if it had shown its determination to slash the money supply and contract British incomes and jobs until $2.80 was truly an equilibrium rate. But as the speculators realized, few postwar governments are prepared to pay such national costs in the name of truly fixed exchange rates. Alternatively, the speculators might have been more cautious in betting against sterling if the exchange rate had been a floating equilibrium rate. With the float, speculators face a two-way gamble. Because the current spot exchange rate is an equilibrium rate and not an artificial official disequilibrium rate, the actual exchange rate in the future could turn out to be higher or lower than the current spot rate or the rate that speculators expect in the future.

Although the speculative attacks on an adjustable-pegged rate are certainly unsettling to officials, it is not clear that they should be called *destabilizing*. If the official defense of a currency is primarily just a way to postpone an inevitable devaluation and not a way to raise the equilibrium value of the currency, then it could be said that the speculative attack is stabilizing in the sense that it hastens the transition to a new equilibrium rate. Whether it performs this stabilizing function is uncertain, however. Officials may be induced to overreact to the speculative attack and to overdevalue the pegged rate.

The Dollar Crisis

The postwar growth of the international economy led to a crisis involving the key currency of the system, the U.S. dollar. Under the Bretton Woods system, other countries effectively pegged their currencies to the U.S. dollar. The dollar became the major reserve currency, and the U.S. government was committed to exchanging the dollars held as reserves by other countries' monetary authorities for gold at an official price of $35 per ounce. (The system is sometimes described as a *gold-exchange standard*.)

As the European and Japanese economies recovered from the war, and as their firms gained in competitive ability relative to that of U.S. firms, the U.S. payments position shifted into large official settlements balance deficits. In part, those deficits represented the fact that the monetary authorities of other countries wanted to run surpluses to increase their international reserves as international transactions generally grew rapidly. After a time, however, the deficits became a source of official concern in Europe and Japan. More and more dollars ended up in official hands. Something like this had happened in 1914, when other countries accumulated growing official reserves of sterling. In the postwar setting, however, few governments felt that they could be as relaxed about the gold backing of the U.S. dollar as the rest of the world had felt about the link between gold and Britain's sterling before 1914. U.S. gold reserves dwindled as France led the march to Fort Knox (actually, the basement of the New York Federal Reserve Bank), demanding gold for dollar claims. It became questionable whether the U.S. dollar was worth as much gold as the official gold price implied.

In this situation, the United States clearly had the option of shrinking the U.S. economy until foreign central banks were constrained to supply gold to the United States to pay for U.S. exports. Other alternatives were tight exchange controls and devaluing the dollar in terms of gold. Exchange controls were tried to a limited extent (in the form of the Interest Equalization Tax on lending abroad, the "Voluntary" Foreign Credit Restraint Program, and the like), but these controls ran counter to the official U.S. stance of encouraging free mobility of capital between countries. Devaluation of the dollar in terms of gold would have marked up the dollar value of U.S. gold reserves but would have brought politically distasteful windfall gains to the Soviet Union and South Africa (the two major gold producers).

Faced with these choices under the existing international rules, the United States opted for changing the rules. On March 17, 1968, a seven-country meeting hastily called by the United States announced the "two-tier" gold price system. The private price of gold in London, Zurich, and other markets was now free to fluctuate in response to supply and demand. The official price for transactions among the seven agreeing governments would still be $35 an ounce. Nonetheless, the U.S. overall payments deficits continued and had to be financed by increasing sales of U.S. foreign exchange reserves. Eventually, the United States would have to adjust, either by restraining its economy or by imposing exchange controls or by changing the international monetary rules. Again, the United States chose to change the rules.

In August 1971, President Nixon suspended convertibility of dollars into gold, effectively severing the official gold–dollar price link. He also imposed a 10 percent temporary additional tariff on all imports coming into the United States, to remain in place until other countries agreed to revalue their currencies against the dollar (so that the dollar was similarly devalued). Most major currencies then floated against the dollar until December 1971, when the Smithsonian Agreement attempted to patch the system back together. Under this agreement the DM was revalued by about 17 percent, the yen by about 13 percent, and other currencies by smaller percentages, overall creating an effective devaluation of the dollar of close to 10 percent, and the United States removed its import surcharge. The official dollar price of gold also was raised to $38 per ounce, but this was symbolic because the suspension continued. The agreement failed to save the system. By March 1973, most major currencies shifted to floating against the dollar. After effectively ending in 1971, the pegged exchange rate regime known as the Bretton Woods system was officially abandoned in 1973.

The Current System: Limited Anarchy

The current system is sometimes described as a *managed floating regime.* Since the early 1970s, a growing number of countries, including many major industrialized countries, have floating or relatively flexible exchange rates, but government authorities often attempt to have an impact through intervention or some other form of management of the floating or flexible exchange rates.

A noteworthy feature of the experience since 1973 is the extent of official resistance to floating. Some of this resistance is seen in the management of the float. For instance, at various times in the 1970s, 1980s, and 1990s, the government of Japan has tried to hold down the dollar value of the yen, apparently to prevent a loss in the international price competitiveness of Japanese products. In the process, the Japanese central bank has bought huge numbers of dollars (that subsequently declined in yen value anyway, as the yen did appreciate against the dollar). Another part of the resistance is seen in the substantial number of countries that continue to peg their currencies to the dollar or to other currencies.

The European Union has been a center of resistance to floating exchange rates, at least for the cross-rates among the EU currencies. The governments of the

European Economic Community (the forerunner of the European Union) strove to prevent movements in exchange rates among their currencies, first setting up the "snake" within the "tunnel" in December 1971. They agreed on maximum ranges of movement of the most appreciated versus the most depreciated member currency (the tunnel) and on maximum bands within which pairwise exchange rates could oscillate (the snake). This scheme was short-lived. Britain, Italy, and France soon allowed their currencies to drop well below the tunnel, leaving only a fixed set of exchange rates between the West German mark and the currencies of the Benelux countries. The governments of the European Community then developed a successor scheme, the Exchange Rate Mechanism (ERM) of the European Monetary System, in 1979. In the early 1990s, the governments of the European Union established a process for moving toward permanently fixed exchange rates and a single currency. As we discussed in Chapter 16, at the beginning of 1999, the new common currency, the euro, came into existence, with fixed rates of conversion for the currencies of 11 of the 15 EU countries.

The official desire for fixed or managed exchange rates has remained strong, but fixed or steady rates have been hard to maintain. Once the Bretton Woods system broke down, the U.S. governments switched to advocacy of floating rates. It often (e.g., in the early 1970s, 1980–1984, and 1995–1998) has followed a policy of "benign neglect" toward the exchange rate value of the dollar, with almost no official exchange-market intervention by U.S. monetary authorities during these long periods of time. At other times, especially in the late 1980s, the U.S. government has been active in managing the dollar float. After the dollar soared in value during 1981–1985, the U.S. government participated in two major international accords to manage exchange rates through coordinated intervention. The first accord, the Plaza Agreement of September 1985, was intended to promote a decline in the exchange rate value of the dollar, and the dollar did fall. The second accord, the Louvre Agreement of February 1987, was intended to stabilize the exchange rate value of the dollar against other major currencies. Formal coordination faded by the early 1990s, and as we have seen, exchange rates between the dollar and other major currencies still oscillate widely at times.

The series of exchange rate crises in the 1990s show how difficult it is to defend pegged rates or heavily managed floating rates in the face of large flows of private funds. When speculators believe they have spotted attempts by officials to maintain unrealistic exchange rates, they have a one-way speculative gamble that can overwhelm the defenses of the monetary authorities.

The first major crisis of the 1990s centered on the European Union. In the early 1990s, all EU countries but Greece had joined the ERM system of pegged rates among these currencies. (In addition, several European countries, including Sweden and Finland, also pegged to this system, although they were not formally part of it.) Following the shock of German reunification and the subsequent tight monetary policy followed by Germany, a major speculative attack hit the ERM in 1992 and 1993. Governments mounted defenses that included massive intervention, high short-term interest rates, and tightening of capital controls. Nonetheless, Britain and Italy surrendered and dropped out of the ERM in 1992, and Sweden and Finland also ceased their peg to it. Several other currencies that remained in the system were devalued in 1992 and 1993. In addition, in 1993, the bands for most currencies that remained in the system were widened to 15 percent on each side of the central rate (from 2.25 percent) to deter speculation by permitting more room for the pegged rate to fluctuate.

Since 1994, a series of exchange crises have hit developing countries, resulting in dramatic devaluations of pegged exchange rates or depreciations following abandonment of pegged or heavily managed rates. As discussed earlier in this chapter, after using a large part of its official reserve holdings to defend the peso exchange rate, the Mexican government had to abandon its heavily managed rate in late 1994. The CFA franc, a currency used by 13 African countries, was devalued by 50 percent in 1994, after it had been pegged at the same rate to the French franc for 45 years. In 1996, the Venezuelan government abandoned its pegged rate, and the bolivar declined by 42 percent in one day. In May 1997, the Czech government, after spending about 30 percent of its international reserves to defend the pegged rate it had maintained for 6 years, shifted to a floating exchange rate, and the koruna declined by about 10 percent during the first few days of the float.

Then, in July 1997, the Asian crisis began. The Thai baht had been pegged within a narrow band to a currency basket that gave most weight to the U.S. dollar but also included the Japanese yen and the German mark. After mounting a defense in which the Thai central bank used perhaps half of its official reserves, the Thai government shifted to a floating rate. By the end of 1997, the baht had fallen by 45 percent against the dollar. Also in July, Malaysia floated its currency, and by the end of the year the ringgit had fallen by 35 percent. In July, Indonesia widened the trading band for the rupiah exchange rate. This worked for a while, but speculative pressure built in August, and Indonesia switched to a float. By year-end, the rupiah had fallen by 47 percent. Speculative pressure hit the Korean won in November, and the Korean government stopped defending its value. By year-end, the won had fallen by 48 percent. Speculative pressure also drove down the values of other Asian currencies. For instance, the Philippine peso fell by 34 percent during the second half of 1997.

In 1998, the Russian government, after using a substantial part of its official reserves to defend the ruble exchange rate, shifted to a floating rate and the ruble declined by 60 percent in value against the dollar in about a month and a half. Since 1995, the Brazilian government had maintained a crawling peg for its real, in which the pegged value of the real relative to the dollar declined by about 7 percent per year. From April 1998 to January 1999, Brazil used about half of its official reserves defending the pegged value of the real. Capital outflows and other speculative pressures increased, and Brazil shifted to a floating rate in January 1999. In two and a half weeks the real declined by 39 percent.

After all of these schemes and crises, what is the current international monetary system? Perhaps it is best to describe it as a nonsystem—countries can choose almost any exchange rate policies that they want and change them whenever they want. The policies of various countries at the beginning of 1999 (as their governments describe them) are shown in Figure 20.9.

Column 1 in Figure 20.9 shows that 37 countries peg their currencies to the U.S. dollar. Malaysia is one of these countries; it reestablished its currency peg in late 1998, along with extensive exchange controls to help maintain the peg. Columns 2 to 5 show the 34 countries whose currencies are pegged to the euro. The 11 euro-zone countries (column 2) are in the process of replacing their individual currencies with the euro. Two of the other EU members (column 3) peg to the euro through the Exchange Rate Mechanism—Denmark using a rather tight band of 2.25 percent around the central rate, and Greece with the wider 15 percent band. Column 4 shows the 13 countries that use the CFA franc, plus the Comoros, which has similar arrangement. These countries previously pegged to the French franc. Seven other countries (column 5) peg to the euro; most of these countries previously pegged to the German mark.

Column 6 shows that 7 countries peg to some other single currency, usually the currency of a larger neighboring country. Column 7 shows the 17 countries that peg to a basket of currencies.

Moving to the other end of the spectrum, column 10 shows the 45 countries that say their exchange rate is floating and mainly determined by market supply and demand, although the float is managed to a greater or lesser extent by each of these countries. Included here are a number of industrialized countries. The number of countries with floating exchange rates has grown during the past decade. In 1988, only 17 countries indicated that they had a market-determined floating exchange rate.

Columns 8 and 9 show countries in which the government essentially sets the exchange rate but also changes it frequently. Under a heavily managed float (column 9), the monetary authority of the country influences the exchange rate through active intervention without committing to an announced exchange rate target value. Under a crawling peg (column 8), the monetary authority changes the pegged exchange rate value frequently according to specific indicators. In practice, these two approaches may be quite similar.

In summary, under the current system each country chooses its own exchange rate policy. Two major blocs of currencies exist: currencies pegged to the U.S. dollar and currencies pegged to the euro. The exchange rates among the U.S. dollar, the euro, and such other major currencies as the Japanese yen, British pound, Swiss franc, and Canadian dollar are floating rates, with some (usually small) amount of official management. Economists are still debating the merits and demerits of this "nonsystem," as well as the strengths and weaknesses of the policy choices made by individual countries. Critics of floating rates start at the obvious point: Floating exchange rates have fluctuated "a lot," "more than anyone expected." But pegged exchange rates have sometimes been difficult to maintain, so they are prone to currency crises. We will return to these issues in Chapter 24.

FIGURE 20.9 *Exchange Rate Arrangements, January 1, 1999*

| | Currency Pegged To | | | | | | | | |
| (1) | (2) Euro Zone | (3) Exchange Rate Mechanism | (4) CFA Franc Zone | (5) Other | (6) Other Currency | (7) Currency Basket | (8) Crawling Peg | (9) Heavily Managed Float | (10) Market-Driven Float |
U.S. Dollar	Euro	Euro							
Antigua & Barbuda	Austria	Denmark	Benin	Bosnia & Herzegovina	Bhutan (Indian rupee)	Bangladesh	Angola	Algeria	Albania
Aruba	Belgium	Greece	Burkina Faso	Bulgaria	Brunei Darussalam (Singapore dollar)	Botswana	Bolivia	Azerbaijan	Armenia
Argentina	Finland		Cameroon	Cape Verde	Kiribati (Australian dollar)	Burundi	Chile	Belarus	Australia
Bahamas	France		Central African Republic	Croatia	Lesotho (South African rand)	Cyprus	Colombia	Cambodia	Brazil
Bahrain	Germany		Chad	Estonia	Namibia (South African rand)	Fiji	Costa Rica	Czech Republic	Canada
Barbados	Ireland		Comoros	Macedonia	Nepal (Indian rupee)	Iceland	Ecuador	Dominican Republic	Congo, Democratic Republic of
Belize	Italy		Congo, Republic of	San Marino	Swaziland (South African rand)	Kuwait	Honduras	Ethiopia	Eritrea
China	Luxembourg		Cote d'Ivoire			Latvia	Hungary	Jamaica	Gambia
Djibouti	Netherlands		Equatorial Guinea			Libya	Israel	Kazakhstan	Georgia
Dominica	Portugal		Gabon			Malta	Nicaragua	Kenya	Ghana
Egypt	Spain		Guinea-Bissau			Morocco	Poland	Kyrgyz Republic	Guatemala
El Salvador			Mali			Myanmar	Sri Lanka	Lao PDR	Guinea
Grenada			Niger			Samoa	Tunisia	Malawi	Guyana
Hong Kong			Senegal			Seychelles	Turkey	Mauritania	Haiti
Iraq			Togo			Solomon Islands	Uruguay	Nigeria	India
Iran						Tonga	Venezuela	Norway	Indonesia
Jordan						Vanuatu		Pakistan	Japan
Lebanon								Paraguay	Korea
Lithuania								Romania	Liberia
Malaysia								Russia	Madagascar
Maldives								Singapore	Mauritius
Marshall Islands								Slovak Republic	Mexico
Micronesia								Slovenia	Moldova
Netherlands Antilles								Suriname	Mongolia
Oman								Tajikistan	Mozambique
Palau								Uzbekistan	New Zealand
Panama									Papua New Guinea
Qatar									Peru
St. Kitts & Nevis									Philippines
St. Lucia									Rwanda
St. Vincent & the Grenadines									Sao Tome & Principe
Saudi Arabia									Sierra Leone
Syrian Arab Republic									South Africa
Turkmenistan									Sudan
Ukraine									Sweden
United Arab Emirates									Switzerland
Vietnam									Tanzania
									Thailand
									Trinidad & Tobago
									Uganda
									United Kingdom
									United States
									Yemen
									Zambia
									Zimbabwe

Notes: The countries shown as having currencies pegged to the U.S. dollar include nine that state an official policy of a floating exchange rate but informally maintain a peg to the dollar, and five that have an official peg to the SDR but informally maintain a peg to the dollar. In addition, two countries shown as having currencies pegged to the euro have an official policy of floating but informally maintain a peg to the euro.

Source: International Monetary Fund, *International Financial Statistics*, March 1999 and April 1999.

Summary

The two major aspects of government policy toward the foreign exchange market are the degree of exchange rate flexibility and restrictions (if any) on use of the market. Foreign exchange restrictions are called **exchange control.**

Policies toward the exchange rate itself cover a spectrum. The polar case of complete flexibility is a **clean float,** with the exchange rate determined solely by nonofficial (or private) supply and demand. Governments often do not allow a clean float, but rather take actions (such as **official intervention**) to **manage** (or **dirty**) the float.

The other polar case is a permanently fixed exchange rate. The government must decide what to fix to. The alternatives include a commodity like gold, a single other currency, or a basket of other currencies. The government also must decide the width of a band around the central fixed rate. The exchange rate has some flexibility around this par value, but the flexibility is limited by the size of the band. Although a permanently fixed rate is a polar case, it is nearly impossible for a government to commit never to change the fixed rate. If the exchange rate is not permanently fixed, then the government must also decide when to change the fixed rate. If the answer is seldom, the approach is called an **adjustable peg;** if often, it is called a **crawling peg.**

If the government chooses a fixed exchange rate, it must also decide how to defend the rate if private supply and demand pressures tend to push the actual rate outside of the allowable band. One or more of four ways can be used to defend the fixed rate:

1. Use official intervention in the foreign exchange market, in which the monetary authority buys and sells currencies to alter the supply and demand situation.
2. Impose exchange control to restrict or control some or all aspects of supply and demand.
3. Alter domestic interest rates to influence short-term capital flows.
4. Adjust the macroeconomy to alter nonofficial supply and demand.

The government may also exercise a fifth option—to surrender by changing the fixed rate (revaluation or devaluation) or by shifting to a floating exchange rate.

Government intervention in the foreign exchange market is closely related to official reserves transactions and the official settlements balance of the country's balance of payments. If the government attempts to prevent the value of its currency from declining through intervention, it must buy domestic currency and sell foreign currency in the foreign exchange market. As for sources of foreign currency to sell in the intervention, the government can use its official reserve holdings or it can borrow. This provides the financing for the country to run an official settlements balance deficit. If instead the government attempts to prevent the value of its currency from rising, it must sell domestic currency and buy foreign currency. The government can use the foreign currency that it buys to increase its official reserve holdings or to repay past borrowings. The country's official settlements balance is in surplus.

Defense of the fixed rate using only intervention can work and make economic sense if the imbalances in the official settlements balance are temporary and self-reversing. This approach assumes that private speculators cannot perform the same stabilizing function and that officials correctly foresee the sustainable long-run value for the exchange rate. If these assumptions do not hold, the case for financing deficits and surpluses with a fixed exchange rate breaks down.

Defense using exchange control creates deadweight loss similar to that of an import quota, and also probably has high administrative costs. Efforts to evade exchange controls, including bribery of government officials and the development of an illegal "parallel" market, reduce the actual effectiveness of the controls.

The success or failure of different exchange rate regimes has depended historically on the severity of the shocks with which those systems have had to cope. The fixed-rate gold standard seemed successful before 1914, largely because the world economy itself was more stable than in the period that followed. Many countries were able to keep their exchange rates fixed because they were lucky enough to be running surpluses at established exchange rates without having to generate those surpluses with any contractionary macroeconomic policies. The main deficit-running country, Britain, could control international reserve flows in the short run by controlling credit in London, but it was never called upon to defend sterling against sustained attack. During the stable prewar era, even floating–exchange-rate regimes showed stability (with two brief possible exceptions).

The interwar economy was chaotic enough to put any currency regime to a severe test. Fixed rates broke down, and governments that believed in fixed rates were forced into flexible exchange rates. Studies of the interwar period showed that in cases of relative macroeconomic stability, flexible rates showed signs of stabilizing speculation. Those signs were less evident in economies whose money supplies had "run away" or whose previous fixed exchange rates were far from equilibrium.

Postwar experience showed some difficulties with the adjustable-peg system set up in Bretton Woods in 1944. Under this system, private speculators were given a strong incentive to attack reserve-losing currencies and force large devaluations. The role of the dollar as a reserve currency also became increasingly strained in the Bretton Woods era. Under Bretton Woods, foreign central banks acquired large holdings of dollars through official intervention, when the United States shifted to running official settlements balance deficits. At first, these were welcomed as additions to highly liquid official reserve holdings in these foreign countries, but the dollars became unwanted as the reserves grew too large. Foreign central banks' conversions of dollars into gold decreased U.S. official gold holdings, further reducing foreign officials' confidence in the dollar. The United States had to adjust its balance-of-payments position or change the rules. The United States opted for new rules, divorcing the private gold market from the official gold price in 1968, suspending gold convertibility and forcing a devaluation of the dollar in 1971, and shifting to general floating in 1973.

The current exchange rate system permits each country to choose its own exchange rate policy. Two major blocs exist, one of currencies pegged to the U.S. dollar and the other of the euro and currencies pegged to it. The euro is the new common currency that is replacing the currencies of the 11 EU countries that are members of the euro zone. The euro is the successor to previous schemes, including the Exchange Rate Mechanism of the European Monetary System, as the countries that are members of the EU seek a zone of exchange rate stability for transactions within the union.

The dollar bloc and the euro bloc float against each other, and the currencies of a number of industrialized countries—Australia, Canada, Japan, New Zealand, Sweden, Switzerland, and the United Kingdom—float independently. For countries with flexible exchange rates, governments generally are skeptical of purely market-driven exchange rates, and they practice some degree of management of the floating rate.

Most developing countries have a pegged exchange rate of some sort, but the trend is toward greater flexibility and floating. A series of exchange rate crises in the 1990s, including the Mexican peso in 1994, the Asian crisis (Thai baht, Malaysian ringgit, Indonesian rupiah, and South Korea won) in 1997, the Russian ruble in 1998, and the Brazilian real in 1999, show the difficulty of defending a pegged rate against speculative flows of short-term capital when the speculators have a one-way gamble against a currency that they believe is misvalued.

Suggested Reading

Information on each country's policies toward the foreign exchange market can be found in the IMF's *Annual Report on Exchange Arrangements and Exchange Restrictions.* On exchange control, see Bhagwati (1978), Collins (1988), and Dooley (1996). On the issue of stabilizing and destabilizing speculation, see Friedman's classic argument (1953) and Stern (1973, Chapter 3).

For broad surveys of international currency experience during the past century, see McKinnon (1993 and 1996) and Giovannini (1989). The prewar gold standard is analyzed in more depth in Bloomfield (1959), Lindert (1969), Bordo and Schwartz (1984), and Gallarotti (1989).

A masterly survey of the interwar experience is Eichengreen (1992). Two pioneering studies of the stability of fluctuating exchange rates in the interwar period are Tsiang (1959) and Aliber (1962).

For more detail on the Bretton Woods era, see Solomon (1977), Bordo and Eichengreen (1992), and Pauls (1990). The dollar crisis under the Bretton Woods system was predicted and diagnosed in Robert Triffin's classic work (1960) and by Jacques Rueff (translation, 1972).

Organization for Economic Cooperation and Development (1999), Pitchford and Cox (1998), Eichengreen (1997), and Obstfeld (1997) analyze the European Monetary System, monetary union in Europe, and the euro. Higgins (1993) and Whitt (1994) discuss the EMS problems of 1992 and 1993.

Questions and Problems

✦ 1. What is the difference between a clean float and a managed float?

2. What is the difference between an adjustable peg and a crawling peg?

✦ 3. For a country that is attempting to maintain a fixed exchange rate, what is the difference between a temporary disequilibrium and a fundamental disequilibrium? Contrast the implications of each type of disequilibrium for official intervention in the foreign exchange market to defend the fixed exchange rate.

4. "The emergence of expectations that a country in the near future will impose exchange controls will probably result in upward pressure on the exchange rate value of the country's currency." Do you agree or disagree? Why?

✦ 5. A government has just imposed a total set of exchange controls to prevent the exchange rate value of its currency from declining. What effects and further developments do you predict?

6. The Pugelovian government is attempting to peg the exchange rate value of its currency (the pnut, pronounced "p'noot") at a rate of three pnuts per U.S. dollar (plus or minus 2 percent). Unfortunately, private market supply and demand is putting downward pressure on the pnut's exchange rate value. In fact, it appears that under current market conditions, the exchange rate would be about 3.5 pnuts per dollar if the government did not defend the pegged rate.

a. How could the Pugelovian government use official intervention in the foreign exchange market to defend the pegged exchange rate?

b. How could the Pugelovian government use exchange controls to defend the pegged exchange rate?

c. How could the Pugelovian government use domestic interest rates to defend the pegged exchange rate?

✦ 7. Under the gold standard the fixed price of gold was $20.67 per ounce in the United States. The fixed price of gold was £4.2474 per ounce in Britain.

a. What is the "fixed" exchange rate (dollars per pound) implied by these fixed gold prices?

b. How would you arbitrage if the exchange rate quoted in the foreign exchange market was $4.00 per pound? (Under the gold standard, you could buy or sell gold with each central bank at the fixed price of gold in each country.)

c. What pressure is placed on the exchange rate by this arbitrage?

8. Consider the international currency experience for the period of the gold standard before 1914.

a. What type of exchange rate system was the gold standard and how did it operate?

b. What country was central to the system? What was the role of this country in the success of the currency system?

c. What was the nature of economic shocks during this period?

d. What is the evidence on speculation and speculative pressures on exchange rates during this period?

✦ 9. What are the key features of the international currency experience in the period between the two world wars? What lessons did policymakers learn from this experience? Why are these lessons now questioned and debated?

10. Consider the international currency experience for the Bretton Woods era from 1944 to the early 1970s.

a. What type of exchange rate system was the Bretton Woods system? How did it operate?

b. What country was central to the system? What was the role of this country in the success of the currency system?

c. What is the evidence on speculation and speculative pressures on exchange rates during this period?

✦ 11. Why did the Bretton Woods system of fixed exchange rates collapse?

12. The current exchange rate regime is sometimes described as a system of managed floating exchange rates, but with some blocs of currencies that are tied together.

a. What are the two major blocs of currencies that are tied together?

b. What are the major currencies that float against each other?

c. Given the discussion in this chapter and the previous chapters of Part III, how would you characterize the movements of exchange rates between the U.S. dollar and the other major currencies since the shift to managed floating in the early 1970s?

CHAPTER 21

How Does the Open Macroeconomy Work?

The analysis of Part III brought us part of the way toward a judgment of what kinds of policies toward foreign exchange would best serve a nation's needs. Chapters 18, 19, and 20 in particular spelled out some of the implications of different policies for the performance of the foreign exchange market, in terms of the efficiency—or inefficiency—of the market itself.

In Part IV, our focus shifts to the other kind of performance issue previewed when the basic policy choices were laid out at the start of Chapter 20. This and the next two chapters address the problem of *macroeconomic* performance—the behavior of a country's output, jobs, and prices in the face of changing world conditions. There are many ways in which the national economy and the world economy interact. Yet some valuable conclusions about policy can be established. Once these conclusions have been laid out in Chapters 21 through 23, Chapter 24 can provide a series of lessons about where the international macroeconomic system is headed and how well different exchange rate institutions work.

This chapter develops a general framework for analyzing the performance of a national economy that is open to international transactions. It provides a picture of how the open macroeconomy works. This framework will then be used in Chapters 22 and 23 to examine macroeconomic performance in settings of fixed exchange rates and floating exchange rates.

The Performance of a National Economy

Each of us is comfortable judging our own performance in various activities. Did I perform in a sport up to the level that I am capable? How did I perform on an examination relative to my own capabilities in the subject and relative to how others in the class performed? Judgments about performance also drive most macroeconomic analysis. How well is a country's economy performing? Is it performing up to its potential—for instance, its capabilities for producing goods and services? How close is it to achieving broad objectives that most people would agree are desirable, such as stability in average product prices (no inflation), low unemployment, or the maintenance of a reasonable balance of payments with the rest of the world?

We judge a country's macroeconomic performance against a number of broad objectives or goals. We can usefully divide these broad goals into two categories. The first category involves two objectives oriented to the domestic economy. One objective is keeping actual domestic production up to the economy's capabilities so that (1) the country achieves *full employment* of its labor and other resources and (2) the economy's production grows over time. Another domestic objective is achieving *price stability* (or, at least, a low or acceptable rate of product price inflation). These two domestically oriented goals taken together define the goal of achieving **internal balance.**

The other category involves objectives related to the country's international economic activities. This is the problem of **external balance,** which is usually defined as the achievement of a reasonable and sustainable balance of payments with the rest of the world. Specifying a precise goal here is not so simple. Most broadly, the goal may be to achieve balance in the country's overall balance of payments. For instance, the goal may be to achieve a balance of approximately zero in the country's official settlements balance, at least over a number of years, so that the country is not losing official reserves or building up unwanted official reserves. This implies that the sum of the current account and the capital account (excluding official reserves transactions) should be approximately zero. If it is substantially different from zero for a long enough time, then we have the disequilibrium in the country's balance of payments (and exchange rate) that we discussed in Chapter 20.

For some purposes we focus on a somewhat narrower reading of external balance, one that focuses on the country's current account (or balance on goods and services trade). The goal here need not be a zero balance. Rather, it is a position that is sustainable in that the value for the current account balance can readily be financed by international capital flows (or official reserves transactions). Some rich industrialized countries probably achieve external balance by running a current account surplus because this allows the country to use some of its national saving to act as a net investor in the rest of the world (capital outflows or capital account deficit). Other countries that are in the process of developing their economies can achieve external balance while running a current account deficit. The deficit may include imports of machinery that directly are part of the development effort. The deficit can be financed by borrowing from the rest of the world (capital inflows or capital account surplus). As long as the surpluses and deficits on current account are not too large, then the positions are sustainable over time. Each can become too large, however, and can become an external imbalance.

A Framework for Macroeconomic Analysis

To analyze the performance of an economy, we need a picture of how the economy functions. Such a picture is not without controversy—macroeconomists do not fully agree on the correct way to analyze the macroeconomy. One of the main difficulties has been to form a satisfactory framework for predicting both changes in domestic production and changes in the price level. We will use a synthesis that attempts to use the strongest features from several different schools of thought. Our analysis of the behavior of the economy in the short run (say, a time period of one year or less) is relatively Keynesian in that the price level is not immediately responsive to aggregate demand and supply conditions in the economy. The price level is sticky or sluggish in the short run. Our view of the economy in the longer run is more monetarist or classical. As we move beyond the short run, the price level does respond to demand and supply conditions. Furthermore, the amount of price inflation that the economy experiences eventually depends mainly on the growth rate of the country's money supply. In addition, the economy tends toward full employment in the long run. We have already developed some of the key features and implications of this long-run analysis in the discussion of the monetary approach in Chapter 18. Here and in the next two chapters we focus more on the economy in the shorter run. We want to develop a picture of how the economy works in the short run that is pragmatic and useful, even if it is not perfect.

The next three major sections of this chapter focus on the determinants of real GDP (representing both domestic product and national income) and the relationships between international trade and national income. Then the next major section adds the market for money and the country's overall balance of payments, resulting in a broad and flexible model of the open economy in the short run. The final two sections of the chapter take up issues related to product prices in order to enhance the framework. These final sections explore the determinants of changes in the country's product price level (or its inflation rate) over time and the effects of international price competitiveness on a country's international trade.

Domestic Production Depends on Aggregate Demand

A major performance goal of an economy is to achieve production of goods and services that is close to the economy's potential. The economy's potential for producing is determined by the supply-side capabilities of the economy. Supply-side capabilities include both the factor resources (labor, capital, land, and natural resources) that the economy has available—the factor endowments from Parts I and II—and intangible influences such as technology, resource quality, climate, and motivation. The intangibles determine the productivity of the resources.

The value of production of goods and services is the economy's real GDP (Y). Because production activity creates income (in the form of wages, profits and other returns to capital, and rents to landowners), real GDP is nearly the same thing as real national income.

In the short run (and within the economy's supply-side capabilities), domestic production is determined by aggregate demand (AD) for the country's products. Essentially, if someone demands a product, some business (or other organization) will try to produce it. Aggregate demand can be split into four components that represent different sources of demand: household consumption of goods and services (*C*); domestic investment (*I$_d$*) in new real assets like machinery, buildings, housing, and inventories; government spending on goods and services (*G*); and net exports of goods and services (*X − M*). Net exports add foreign demand for our exports (*X*) as a source of demand for our products, but subtract our demand for imports (*M*) because these imports are already included in the other kinds of spending but actually represent demand for the products of other countries.

Equilibrium occurs when domestic production (*Y*, our GDP) equals desired demand for domestically produced goods and services:

$$Y = \text{AD} = C + I_d + G + (X - M) \tag{21.1}$$

The level of actual domestic production (relative to the economy's potential for producing) tends to be closely related to the economy's labor unemployment rate. Increases of actual GDP (relative to potential) tend to decrease the unemployment rate, while decreases tend to increase the unemployment rate.

In order to focus on international trade issues, we can add up the national spending components into national expenditures (*E*) on goods and services:

$$E = C + I_d + G \tag{21.2}$$

From basic macroeconomic analysis, we know something about the determinants of each of these components.

Household consumption expenditures are positively related to disposable income, and disposable income is (approximately) the difference between total income (*Y*) and taxes (*T*) paid to the government. Many taxes are based directly on income or are related indirectly to income because they are based on spending (for instance, sales or value added taxes). Rather than carry around all of this detail, we will summarize the major determinant of consumption as income:

$$C = C(Y) \tag{21.3}$$

remembering that the relationship incorporates taxes that have to paid out of income before consumer spending is done. There are other influences on consumption, including interest rates that set the cost of borrowing to finance the purchase of items like automobiles, as well as household wealth and consumer sentiment about the future. We do not formally build these other influences into the framework to keep the formal analysis simple. Instead, we can treat major changes in these other influences as shocks that occasionally disturb the economy.

Real domestic investment spending is negatively related to the level of interest rates (*i*) in the economy:

$$I_d = I_d(i) \tag{21.4}$$

Higher interest rates increase the cost of financing the capital assets, thus reducing the amount of real investment undertaken. There are a number of other influences on real investment spending, including business sentiment about the future, current capacity utilization, and the emergence of new technologies that require capital investments in order to bring the technologies into use. Again, we can picture these other influences as a source of shocks to the economy.

We treat government spending on goods and services as a political decision. Decisions about government spending are a major part of a country's **fiscal policy**; the other part of fiscal policy is decisions about taxation.

Trade Depends on Income

According to a host of empirical estimates for many countries, the volume of a nation's imports depends positively on the level of real national income or production:

$$M = M(Y) \tag{21.5}$$

This positive relationship seems to have two explanations. One is that imports are often used as inputs into the production of the goods and services that constitute domestic product. The other explanation is that imports respond to the total real spending or "absorption" (E) in our economy. The more we spend on all goods and services, the more we tend to spend on the part of them that we buy from abroad. Although a nation's expenditures on goods and services are not the same thing as its national income from producing goods and services, the close statistical correlation between income and expenditure allows us to gloss over this distinction. We can estimate the amount by which our imports increase when our income goes up by one dollar. This amount is called the **marginal propensity to import** (m).

It is also possible that the volume of our *exports* depends on *our* national income. If domestic national income is raised by a surge in domestic aggregate demand, there is a good chance that the increase in national income will be accompanied by a drop in export volumes, as domestic buyers bid away resources that otherwise would have been used to produce exports. Although such a negative dependence of export volumes on national-income-as-determined-by-domestic-demand is plausible, the evidence for it is somewhat sparse. We will assume that export volumes are independent of this country's national income.[1]

Exports nonetheless do depend on income—the income of foreign countries. If foreign income is higher, then foreigners tend to buy more of all kinds of things, including more of our exports. The amount by which their imports (our exports) increase if foreign income increases is the foreign marginal propensity to import.

Equilibrium GDP and Spending Multipliers

With these pieces of the framework we can gain some major insights into macroeconomic performance in an open economy. To gain these insights we make a few assumptions that are useful now (but will be relaxed in later analysis). We assume that all price and pricelike variables are constant. In relation to our discussion so far, this means that the interest rate (in addition to the average product price level) is constant.

---

[1]Another way that export volumes can vary with our national income is through the supply side. A supply-side expansion of the economy permits production to increase, and some of this extra production may be available to increase exports.

Equilibrium GDP

The condition for equilibrium real GDP is that it must equal desired aggregate demand, which in turn equals desired national expenditure plus net exports. Holding interest rates constant, our desired national expenditure depends on national income, as does our volume of imports. These relationships indicate that the value of aggregate demand itself depends on national income. The equilibrium condition is

$$Y = \mathrm{AD}(Y) = E(Y) + X - M(Y) \qquad (21.6)$$

Although our exports depend on foreign income, we initially ignore this (or assume that foreign income is constant).

Figure 21.1A illustrates the equilibrium level of domestic production and income, showing the matching between domestic product and aggregate demand at point A. At levels of domestic production below 100, the aggregate demand would exceed the level of production, as shown by the fact that the AD curve is above the 45-degree line to the left of A. At any such lower levels of production, the combination of home and foreign demand for what this nation is producing would be so great as to deplete the inventories of goods held by firms, and the firms would respond by raising production and creating more jobs and incomes, moving the economy up toward A. Similarly, levels of production above 100 would yield insufficient demand, accumulating inventories, and cutbacks in production and jobs until the economy returned to equilibrium at point A.

Figure 21.1A does not demonstrate how the nation's foreign trade and investment relate to the process of achieving the equilibrium domestic production. To underline the role of the foreign sector, it is convenient to convert the equilibrium condition into a different form. This can be done with an algebraic step like the one taken in Chapter 15, when we were discussing the current account of the balance of payments. National saving (S) equals the difference between national income (Y) and national expenditures on noninvestment items (C and G). Subtracting ($C + G$) from both sides of Equation 21.6, the condition becomes an equilibrium between saving and investment:

$$Y = E + X - M$$
$$(Y - C - G) = (E - C - G) + (X - M)$$

or

$$S = I_d + I_f \qquad (21.7)$$

In other words, desired saving, which is the nation's net accumulation of assets, must match its desired domestic investment in new real assets (buildings, equipment, and inventories) plus its desired net foreign investment, or its net buildup of claims on the rest of the world.

Figure 21.1B expresses this saving–investment equilibrium in a way highlighting the current account balance ($X - M$, or I_f). As drawn here, Figure 21.1B shows a country having a current account deficit with more imports than exports

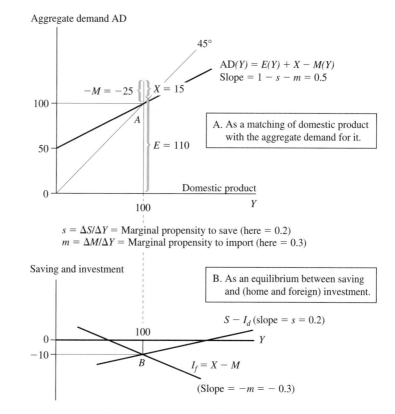

FIGURE 21.1

Equilibrium Domestic Production in an Open Economy Shown in Two Equivalent Ways

of goods and services. For the equilibrium at point *B,* the country's domestic saving is less than its domestic investment, so the extra domestic investment must be financed by borrowing from foreigners (or selling off previously acquired foreign assets, including the country's official reserve assets). This could serve as a schematic view of Canada's usual past situation since Canada typically has a deficit in its current account balance, financed by net capital inflows. This is also the situation of the United States since 1982. In contrast, Japan has usually had its version of point *B* lying above the horizontal axis, representing a net export surplus and positive net foreign investment.

The Spending Multiplier in a Small, Open Economy

When national spending rises in an economy in which actual production initially is below the economy's supply-side potential, this extra spending sets off a multiplier process of expansion of domestic production and income, whether or not the country is involved in international trade. Yet, the way in which the country is involved in trade does affect the size of the spending multiplier. Suppose that the government raises its purchases of goods and services by 10 units and holds them at this higher level. The extra 10 means an extra 10 income for whoever sells the extra goods and services to the government. The extent to which this initial income gain gets transmitted into further income gains depends on how the first gainers allocate their extra income. Let us assume, as we already have in Figure 21.1, that out of each extra dollar of income, people within this nation save 20 cents (part of which is "saved" by the government as taxes on their extra income) and spend the remaining 80 cents (30 cents of it on imports of foreign goods and services). In other words, the marginal propensity to save (s, including the marginal tax rate) is 0.2; the marginal propensity to consume domestic product ($1 - s - m$) is 0.5; and the marginal propensity to import (m) is 0.3.

The first round of generating extra income produces an extra 2 units in saving, an extra 3 in imports, and an extra 5 in spending on domestic goods and services. Of these, only the 5 in domestic spending will be returned to the national economy as a further demand stimulus. Both the 2 saved and the 3 spent on imports represent "leakages" from the domestic expenditure stream. Whatever their indirect effects, they do not directly create new demand or income in the national economy. (Extra imports could feed demand back into our own economy by raising foreign incomes and stimulating their demand for our exports. But we do not consider this possibility until the next section, and we will assume for the present that this is a small country that has no impact on production or income in the rest of the world.) In the second round of income and expenditures, only 5 will be passed on and divided up into further domestic spending (2.5), saving (1), and imports (1.5). And for each succeeding round of expenditures, as for these first two, the share of extra income that becomes further expenditures is ($1 - s - m$), or ($1 - 0.2 - 0.3$) = 0.5.

The overall effects of this process are summarized in the spending multiplier. Its formula is easily derived from the fact that the final change in production and income equals the initial rise in government spending plus the extra demand for this nation's product that was stimulated by the rise in income itself:

$$\Delta Y = \Delta G + (1 - s - m)\, \Delta Y \qquad (21.8)$$

so that

$$\Delta Y(1 - 1 + s + m) = \Delta G \qquad (21.9)$$

and

$$\textbf{Spending multiplier in a small, open economy} = \frac{\Delta Y}{\Delta G} = \frac{1}{(s + m)} \qquad (21.10)$$

In our example, the rise in government spending by 10 billion ultimately leads to twice as great an expansion of domestic production since the multiplier equals $1/(0.2 + 0.3) = 2$. The value of this multiplier is the same, of course, whether the initial extra spending is made by the government or results from a surge in consumption, a rise in private investment spending, or a rise in exports. Note also that the value of the multiplier is smaller in a small open economy than the multiplier in a closed economy. Had m been zero, the multiplier would have been $1/s = 5$.

FIGURE 21.2

The Effect of a Rise in Government Spending on Foreign Trade and Domestic Production

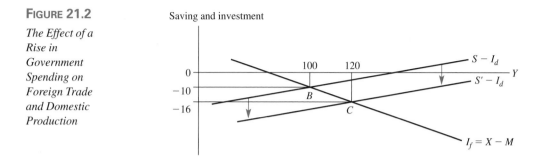

The results of the multiplier expansion in response to a rise in domestic spending can be reexpressed in a diagram like Figure 21.2. Here the initial rise in government spending is portrayed by a downward shift of the $S - I_d$ curve. It can be portrayed this way because a rise in government spending by 10 is a change in government saving by –10 since government saving is the difference between government tax revenue and government spending. The rise in government spending by 10 produces the same final rise in domestic production by 20 here as in the discussion above. Note further that the multiplier of 2 works its effects not only on the final rise in production but also on the final rise in imports. Imports rose by 3, thanks to the first round of new expenditures, but rose by twice as much, or $[m/(s + m)] \times \Delta G = 6$ over all rounds of new expenditures, the amount of trade balance worsening shown in Figure 21.2.

Foreign-Income Repercussions

In describing the marginal propensity to import as a leakage, we have argued as though whatever is spent on imports is permanently lost as a component of aggregate demand for our domestic product. This assumption works well enough for a small country whose trade is negligible as an average or marginal share of world income. However, when a nation looms larger in the economies of its trading partners, this assumption underestimates the multiplier. When a large nation's extra spending leads to extra imports, these imports noticeably raise foreign incomes and create foreign jobs. The expansion of foreign incomes encourages foreign purchases of the first country's exports in amounts dictated by the foreign marginal propensities to import from that country. The extra demand for exports raises the country's income further, thus raising the value of the multiplier response to the initial domestic spending. Thus, *the more our country's imports affect foreign incomes, the more the true spending multiplier exceeds the simple formula* $1/(s + m)$.

Figure 21.3 illustrates the process of foreign repercussions. An initial rise in our government purchases of goods and services, on the left, creates extra income in our national economy. Some fraction (s) of the extra income will be saved, some will be spent on domestic product, and some will be spent on imports. The fraction (m) spent on imports will create an equal amount of demand for foreign production,

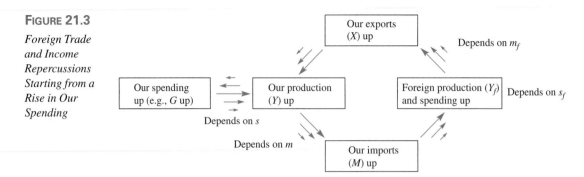

FIGURE 21.3

*Foreign Trade
and Income
Repercussions
Starting from a
Rise in Our
Spending*

as well as income for foreign sellers. They, in turn, will save a fraction of this additional income (s_f), spend some in their own countries, and import a fraction (m_f) from us. We then divide that extra export income into saving, domestic purchases, and imports, and the cycle continues. Each round passes along a smaller stimulus until the multiplier process comes to rest with a finite overall expansion.

The existence of such foreign-income repercussions helps account for the parallelism in business cycles that has been observed among the major industrial economies. Throughout much of the 20th century, when America has sneezed, Europe and Japan have caught cold. Such a tendency was already evident in the business cycles in Europe and the United States in the mid-19th century, though the correlation between the European cycles and the U.S. cycles was far from perfect. The Great Depression of the 1930s also reverberated back and forth among countries, as each country's slump caused a cut in imports (helped by beggar-thy-neighbor import barriers that were partly a response to the slump itself) and thereby cut foreign exports and incomes. Correspondingly, the outbreak of the Korean War brought economic boom to West Germany, Italy, and Japan, as surging U.S. war spending raised their exports and incomes, leading to a further partial increase in their purchases from the United States.

The same interdependence of incomes persists today. The "locomotive theory" represents a recent application of repercussions analysis. The theory is based on the fact that the three largest economies in the world are the United States, Japan, and Germany. During times when world real growth is sluggish, such as the late 1970s, early 1990s, and late 1990s, increasing growth in two or three of these countries may be sufficient to raise world growth overall. Growth in the largest economies raises their imports, tending to pull the rest of the world along, with repercussions reinforcing the higher growth of all countries.

Economists have estimated the spending multipliers in major industrial countries that are subject to foreign-income repercussions. They came up with plausible patterns like those in Figure 21.4. The multipliers tell the tales we would expect of such international multipliers even though they are expressed in elasticity form (*percent* change/*percent* change), instead of the usual multiplier form (absolute change/absolute change). To follow the numbers across the top row, Figure 21.4 says that U.S. production and income would be raised 1.3 percent if aggregate demand rose by 1 percent in the United States alone, or by 0.1 percent if demand rose 1 percent in Japan alone, 0.1 percent if demand rose by 1 percent

FIGURE 21.4

Spending Multipliers with Foreign-Income Repercussions for Five Industrial Countries

The Effects of a 1 Percent Rise of Spending in

On Real Domestic Product in	United States	Japan	Germany	United Kingdom	Canada
United States	1.3	0.1	0.1	<0.05	0.1
Japan	1.0	2.1	0.1	0.1	0.1
Germany	0.9	0.2	1.7	0.3	0.1
United Kingdom	0.5	0.1	0.2	1.1	<0.05
Canada	0.8	0.1	<0.05	<0.05	1.0

Each number gives the *percent* rise in the domestic product of the country whose row is named on the left that is caused by a 1 percent rise in the spending of the country whose column is named along the top of the table. In the analysis short-term interest rates and exchange rates are held constant. The multipliers shown here are the results for the third year after the initial increase in spending.

Source: Richardson (1988), Annex Table 2.

in Germany alone, and so forth. Or following the numbers down the Japan column, the estimates say that a 1 percent rise in Japanese spending would raise U.S. production and income by 0.1 percent, Japanese production and income by 2.1 percent, German production and income by 0.2 percent, and so forth.

A basic pattern emerging from the estimates in Figure 21.4 is the role of *national size.* The bigger the country, the more its spending affects other countries. The effect of U.S. spending in any other country is greater than the effect of any other foreign country's spending. For example, Germany is more affected by spending shifts in the United States (0.9 percent) than it is by those in Japan or Canada (0.2 or 0.1).

How Aggregate Demand and Supply Can Affect the Trade Balance

We have seen that a rise in domestic aggregate demand can, by raising our production and income, raise our imports. To the extent that this worsens the trade balance, it is a force that will contribute (in the chapters that follow) to either a bigger balance-of-payments deficit or to a drop in the exchange value of our home currency. But we cannot simply say that whatever raises our production and income worsens our balance of trade. We must take a more careful look at three realistic cases:

1. *If our production and income are raised by increases in domestic spending,* then the trade balance will *probably*[2] *"worsen"* (shift toward net imports). This is just a corollary of the multiplier process sketched in connection with Figure 21.3. We make use of this in the next two chapters, when analyzing the performance of both the fixed exchange rates implied here and various floating-rate regimes.

---

[2]A rise in domestic spending could actually improve the trade balance. Suppose that the foreign marginal propensity to import from us is larger than our marginal propensity to import from them. Each round of increase in imports by us could trigger not only immediate foreign purchases of our exports, but further export increases as well, in response to the foreign multiplier process. Under some possible parameter values, this could yield the perverse result: Our spending increase would actually raise our trade balance.

2. *If our production and income are raised by an international demand shift* from foreign to home-country goods and services (e.g., due to a change in tastes or a lowering of foreign import barriers), the home country's trade balance will *clearly improve.*

3. *If our production and income are raised by improvements in our supply capabilities,* our trade balance will *probably improve.* The analysis of this case is not easily handled within the framework that dominates this chapter since that framework lets changes in income be dictated by aggregate demand. Yet the importance of supply capabilities is easy to see. Suppose that our aggregate supply is raised by technological improvements (or peaceful settlements of labor strikes) that are evenly distributed across the exportable, import-competing, and nontraded sectors. Our extra ability to supply and compete will win more export markets as well as home markets away from foreign suppliers. This will increase export volumes and may decrease import volumes. The value of the trade balance usually improves, unless the price of exports declines severely as a result of the export expansion.[3]

A More Complete Framework: Three Markets

The discussion of spending multipliers provides insights into macroeconomic performance, but it is too limited to be useful as a full framework for our analysis. We need to be able to picture three major components of the macroeconomy at the same time, adding the supply and demand for money and the country's overall balance of payments. In the process of developing this more complete framework, we can also drop the assumption that interest rates are constant. In fact, we will focus on the level of interest rates in the country as a second variable of major interest in addition to the country's real GDP.

Figure 21.5 sketches the basic approach. The three markets that give us a broader picture of the country's economy are shown in the center. The first two, the goods and services market and the market for money, directly determine two key variables of interest (Y and i). At the same time, these two variables have a major impact on the country's balance of payments and thus on the foreign exchange market. All three of the markets can be affected by different kinds of outside (exogenous) forces, shown on the left side of the figure. These outside forces represent shocks or disturbances that create pressures for macroeconomic changes.

The Domestic Product Market

The aggregate demand for what our country produces depends not only on income (Y). It also depends on the interest rate (i) since a higher real interest rate discourages spending. We can picture these relationships in a graph as an IS

---

[3]Yes, it is necessary to add this last qualifying clause. Improved domestic supply can do more to the trade balance than simply raise the physical volume of exports and cut the physical volume of imports. It can also change prices. In an extreme case of very inelastic demand for our exports, it is conceivable that their price would drop far enough to make the innovation worsen the trade balance. This is closely related to our discussion of immiserizing growth in Chapter 5.

FIGURE 21.5

*An Overview of
the Macromodel
of an Open
Economy*

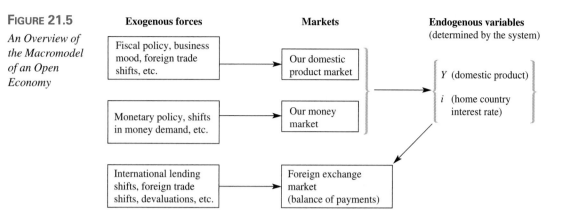

In addition to the linkages shown here, pressure in the foreign exchange market (or imbalance in the country's balance of payments) can feed back into and affect the country through the domestic product market or the money market. The ways in which this occurs depend on whether the country has a fixed or a floating exchange rate. These issues are taken up in the next two chapters.

curve. (IS stands for investment–saving.) The **IS curve** shows all combinations of domestic product levels and interest rates for which the domestic product market is in equilibrium. As in the previous section of this chapter, we can think of this equilibrium as following from the condition $Y = C + I_d + G + (X - M)$, or we can think of it as following from the condition that national saving S equals the sum of domestic and foreign investment ($I_d + I_f$). If we use the latter (following literally the name of the curve), the domestic product market is in equilibrium when

$$S(\overset{+}{Y}) = I_d(\bar{i}) + I_f(\bar{Y}) \tag{21.11}$$

Here the signs above the equation indicate the direction of each influence in parentheses on the values of the variables.[4] The negative influence of domestic product on foreign investment follows because foreign investment is equal to net exports. Net exports themselves are negatively related to domestic product because imports are positively related.

To see why the IS curve slopes downward, let's start with one equilibrium point on it and then ask where other equilibria could lie. Let us start at point A in Figure 21.6, where domestic product equals 100 and the interest rate is 0.07 (7 percent a year). We somehow know that this combination brings an equilibrium in the domestic product market. That is, given other basic economic conditions, having $Y = 100$ and $i = 0.07$ makes investment $I_d + I_f$ match savings S. How could equilibrium in the product market be maintained if the interest rate were lower,

---

[4]Additional influences of Y and i are possible. S may be a positive function of i, for instance, if higher interest rates reduce borrowing (that is, reduce negative saving) by households. I_d may be a positive function of Y, for instance, if high current production levels make the need for new investment to expand capacity more urgent. These additions would somewhat change the slope of the IS curve, but the picture would not be different in its essentials.

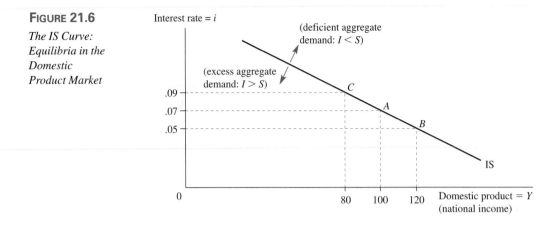

FIGURE 21.6

The IS Curve: Equilibria in the Domestic Product Market

say, only 0.05? The lower interest rate would make the nation invest in more real capital. The higher level of aggregate demand (because I_d is larger) results in a higher level of domestic product. (In fact, because of the spending multiplier, the increase in domestic product is larger than the increase in real domestic investment resulting directly from the lower interest rate.) According to the IS curve, the higher level of domestic product matching aggregate demand for that low interest rate is $Y = 120$, as represented at point B. Similarly, if point A is one equilibrium, then others with higher interest rates must lie at lower production levels, as at point C. So the IS curve must slope downward. The higher the interest rate, the lower the level of domestic product that is consistent with it. Points that are not on the IS curve find the domestic product market out of equilibrium.

Changes in any influence other than interest rates that can directly affect aggregate demand cause a shift in the IS curve. These are the exogenous forces or shocks discussed previously. For instance, an increase in government spending, or an improvement in consumer sentiment that leads people to increase their consumption spending, increases aggregate demand and shifts the IS curve to the right.

The Money Market

The next market in which macroeconomic forces interact is that for the money of each nation. As usual, there is a balancing of supply and demand.

The supply side of the market for owning units of a nation's money is, roughly, the conventional "money supply." **Monetary policy,** the set of central-bank policies, institutions, and bank behavioral patterns governing the availability of bank checking deposits and currency in circulation, is the top influence on money supply.

Our view of the demand for money is an extension of the money demand discussed in Chapter 18. There we posited that the (nominal) demand for money depends on the value of (nominal) GDP, which equals the price level P times Y

(real GDP). Money is held to carry out transactions, and the value of transactions should be correlated with the value of income or production. The larger domestic product is during a time period such as a year, the greater the amount of money balances that firms and households will want to keep on hand to cover uncertain amounts of spending needs. In addition to the benefits of money in facilitating transactions, there is an opportunity cost to holding money. The opportunity cost is the interest that the holder of money could earn if her wealth were instead invested in other financial assets such as bonds. Some forms of money (currency and coin, traveler's checks, zero-interest checking accounts) earn no interest. Others (interest-paying checking accounts) earn some interest, but the interest rate earned is generally relatively low. Interest forgone is an opportunity cost of holding money. This cost leads us to attempt to economize on our money holdings, and we attempt to economize more as the interest rate available on other financial assets rises. A higher interest rate tempts people to hold interest-earning bonds rather than money. That is, it lowers the demand for money.

The demand for (nominal) money L is positively related to nominal GDP and negatively related to the level of interest rates available on other financial assets:

$$L = L(\overset{+}{P}\overset{-}{Y}, i) \tag{21.12}$$

The equilibrium between money supply and money demand is then

$$M^s = L(\overset{+}{P}\overset{-}{Y}, i) \tag{21.13}$$

where the plus and minus signs again serve to remind us of the direction of influence of PY and i.

The money market equilibrium can be pictured as the "LM curve" of Figure 21.7. The **LM curve** shows all combinations of production levels and interest rates for which the money market is in equilibrium, given the money supply (set by policy), the price level P, and the money demand function (representing how people decide their money holdings). LM stands for liquidity–money, where money demand is viewed as demand for the most highly liquid financial assets in the economy.

To see why the LM curve slopes upward, begin with the equilibrium at point A and think of where the other equilibria could lie. If the interest rate were higher, say, at 0.09, people would hold less money in order to earn the higher interest rate by holding bonds instead. To have the money market in equilibrium at that higher interest rate, people would have to have some other reason to hold the same amount of money supply as at point A. They would be willing to hold the extra money only if the level of domestic product and income were higher, raising their transactions demand for holding money. That happens to just the right extent at point F, another equilibrium. In contrast, going in the other direction, we can ask how people would be content to hold the same money supply as at point A if the interest they gave up by holding money were suddenly lower than at point A. By itself, the lower interest rate on bonds would mean a greater demand for cash because cash is convenient. People would be willing to refrain from holding extra

FIGURE 21.7

The LM Curve:
Equilibria in the
Money Market

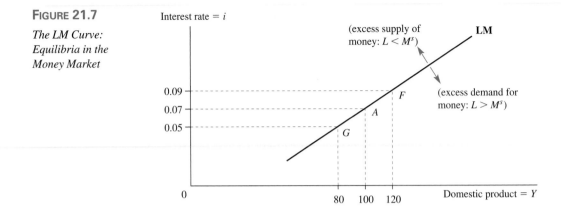

cash only if some other change reduced the demand. One such change is lower domestic product, meaning lower transactions demand for cash. Point *G* is a point at which the lower interest rate and lower production leave the demand for money the same as at point *A*.

Changes in any of the given factors listed above represent exogenous forces that shift the entire LM curve. Consider an increase in the nominal money supply M^s by the central bank. If the price level *P* is sticky in the short run (so there is no immediate effect on the country's price level or inflation rate), then the increase in the money supply tends to reduce interest rates (or, equivalently, the increased money supply can support a higher level of domestic product and transactions). The LM curve shifts down (or to the right).

So far, we have two markets whose equilibria depend on how domestic product (*Y*) and interest rates (*i*) interact in each market. For any given set of basic economic conditions (fiscal policy, the business mood, consumer sentiment, foreign demand for the country's exports, monetary policy, and so forth), these two markets simultaneously determine the level of domestic product and the level of the interest rate in the economy. The intersection of the IS and LM curves shows the levels of *Y* and *i* that represent equilibrium in both the market for goods and services and the market for money. For instance, if the IS curve from Figure 21.6 is added to Figure 21.7, the intersection is at point *A*. The short-run equilibrium level of real GDP (*Y*) is 100, and the equilibrium interest rate is 0.07 (7 percent).

The Foreign Exchange Market (or Balance of Payments)

The third market is the one where the availability of foreign currency is balanced against the demand for it. This market can be called either the "foreign exchange market," if we want to keep the exchange rate in mind, or "the balance of payments," if we are using the country's official settlements balance (*B*) to reflect the net private or nonofficial trading between our currency and foreign currency. In order to picture this third market, it is easier to think through the balance-of-payments approach.

The country's official settlements balance is the sum of the country's current account balance (CA) and its capital account balance (KA, which does not include official reserves transactions). The influences on *B* can be divided into trade flow effects and financial flow effects. How do our key variables—real product or income (*Y*) and the country's interest rate (*i*)—affect the country's balance of payments? Previous discussion has shown two major effects. First, the balance on goods and services trade (or the current account) depends negatively on our domestic product, through the demand for imports. Second, international capital flows depend on interest rates (both at home and abroad). A higher interest rate in our country will attract a capital inflow, provided that the higher domestic interest rate is not immediately offset by higher foreign interest rates.

The easy intuition that a higher interest rate in our economy will attract investment from abroad and give us a capital inflow is valid but only in the short run (say, for a year or less after the interest rate rises). Over the longer run, this effect stops and is even reversed for at least two reasons:

1. A higher interest rate attracts a lot of capital inflow from abroad at first, as investors adjust the shares of their stock of wealth held in assets from our country. Soon, though, the inflow will dwindle because portfolios have already been adjusted.

2. If a higher interest rate in our country succeeds in attracting funds from abroad and raising *B* in the short run, it may have the opposite effect later on for the simple reason that bonds mature and loans must be repaid. If a higher interest rate gives us borrowed funds now, we must repay with interest later. We cannot talk of using higher interest rates to attract capital (lending) to this country without reflecting on the fact that those higher interest rates will have to be paid out in the future, along with the borrowed principal.[5]

For these reasons, the notion that a higher interest rate in our country can "improve" the balance of payments is valid only in the short run. We can use the short-run reasoning if the issue before us is the effect on *B* now. We will often use this short-run focus, but only with the warning that in the long run a higher interest rate has an ambiguous effect on the overall balance of payments.

---

[5]The balance-of-payments cost of attracting the extra capital from abroad could be even greater than the interest rate alone might suggest. To see how, let us suppose that the home country (a) is a net debtor country and (b) is large enough to be able to raise its own interest rate even though it is part of a larger world capital market. Let us imagine Canada is in this position.

Suppose that a rise in Canada's interest rate from 9 percent to 12 percent succeeds in raising foreign investments into Canada from $500 billion to $600 billion. What interest will Canada pay out each year on the extra $100 billion of borrowing (a temporarily higher *B*)? The annual interest bill on the new $100 billion itself comes to $12 billion a year. But, in addition, to continue to hold the original investments of $500 billion within the country—that is, to "roll over" these bonds and loans as they come up for renewal or repayment—Canadian borrowers have to pay an extra $15 billion [= $500 billion × (.12 − .09)]. The total extra interest outflow each year is thus the $12 billion plus the extra $15 billion, or payments of $27 billion just to hold on to an extra $100 billion in borrowings. That's an effective interest rate of 27 percent, not just 12 percent. This is an expensive way to attract international "hot money."

FIGURE 21.8

The FE Curve: Balance-of-Payment Equilibria

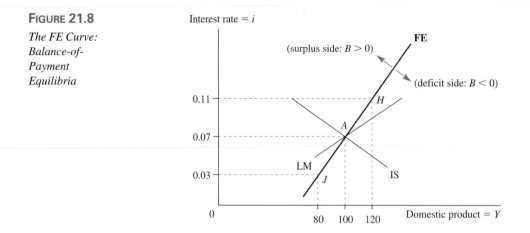

We can reexpress the dependence of the balance of payments (or the foreign exchange market) on production and interest rates in two other ways. One is with an equation. The official settlements balance B equals the current account balance CA (which is approximately equal to net exports, $X - M$) plus the capital account balance KA:

$$B = CA(\overset{-}{Y}) + KA(\overset{+}{i}) \qquad (21.14)$$

Raising our domestic product lowers the current account surplus (or raises the deficit) because it gives us more demand for imports of foreign goods and services. Raising our interest rate, on the other hand, attracts an inflow of capital from abroad, raising our capital account surplus (or reducing the deficit).

To link the balance of payments with i and Y, we can also use the FE curve of Figure 21.8. For a given set of other basic economic conditions that can influence the country's balance of payments, the **FE curve** shows the set of all interest-and-production combinations in our country that result in a zero value for the country's official settlements balance.

The FE curve, like the LM curve, slopes upward. To see why, begin again with an equilibrium at point A. Let's say that this is the same point A as in the previous two figures, although it need not be. If point A finds our international payments in overall balance, how could they still be in balance if the interest rate is higher, say, at 11 percent? That higher interest rate attracts a greater inflow of capital, bringing an official-settlements-balance surplus unless something else also changes. With the higher interest rate, B could still be zero (no surplus, no deficit) if domestic product and income are higher. Higher product and income induce us to spend more on everything, including imports. The extra imports shift the balance of payments toward a deficit. In just the right amounts, extra production and a higher interest rate could cancel each other's effect on the balance of payments, leaving $B = 0$. That happens at point H. Correspondingly, some combinations of lower interest rates and lower production levels could also keep our payments in overall balance, as at point J.

How does the slope of the FE curve compare to the slope of the LM curve? As drawn in Figure 21.8, the FE curve is steeper. This is not the only possibility, though. It depends on how responsive money demand and the balance of payments are to changes in the interest rate and domestic product. If, for instance, capital flows are very sensitive to interest rates, then the FE curve is relatively flat, flatter than the LM curve. The FE curve is relatively flat because only a small increase in the interest rate is needed to draw in capital and offset the decline in the current account if domestic product is higher. (Point H would be lower, with an interest rate that is not much above 0.07.) If capital flows are extremely sensitive to interest rates, then we have the case of **perfect capital mobility,** and the FE curve is essentially completely flat (a horizontal line).

What happens when some other condition or variable that affects the country's balance of payments changes? These are the exogenous forces of Figure 21.5. When one of these changes occurs, it shifts the FE curve (just as a change in an exogenous condition relevant to the IS curve or the LM curve causes a shift in that curve). For instance, an increase in foreign income increases demand for our exports, improving our balance of payments and shifting the FE curve to the right. Or, an increase in foreign interest rates causes a capital outflow from our country, deteriorating our balance of payments, and shifting the FE curve to the left.

Three Markets Together

Bringing the three markets together, we get a determination of the level of domestic product (Y), the interest rate (i), and the overall balance of payments (B). The economy will gravitate toward a simultaneous equilibrium in the domestic product market (on the IS curve) and the money market (on the LM curve). With Y and i thus determined, we also know the state of the balance of payments (B). The official settlements balance is in surplus if the IS–LM equilibrium is to the left of the FE curve; the balance is zero if it is on the FE curve (for example, point A in Figure 21.8), and it is in deficit if the IS–LM intersection is to the right of the FE curve. This section has given the same reasoning about three markets in three alternative forms: the causal-arrow sketch of Figure 21.5, the listing of Equations 21.11, 21.13, and 21.14, and the use of IS–LM–FE diagrams (Figures 21.6 through 21.8).

The way that we use this framework—especially the way that we use the FE curve—depends on the type of exchange rate policy that the country has adopted. As we will examine in the next chapter, if a country adopts a fixed exchange rate, then any divergence between the IS–LM intersection and the FE curve shows that official intervention is needed to defend the fixed rate. The official settlements balance is not zero—official intervention to defend the fixed rate results in official reserves transactions. As we will examine in Chapter 23, if the country adopts a clean float, then the official settlements balance must be zero, and somehow a triple intersection between the IS, LM, and FE curves must occur. In different ways, to be explored in each chapter, these situations create pressures for adjustments that affect the country's macroeconomic performance.

The Price Level Does Change

In developing the framework so far, we have generally ignored the product price level (P). We assumed that the price level is a constant for the short run, given by previous history. While this may be reasonable for most short-run analysis, it is clearly not appropriate generally. The price level does change over time for three basic reasons.

First, most countries have some amount of ongoing inflation. This amount can be anticipated and built into inflation expectations. Generally, ongoing positive inflation requires sufficient ongoing growth of the country's nominal money supply. The role of ongoing inflation was prominent in Chapter 18, especially in discussing the monetary approach.

Second, strong or weak aggregate demand can put pressure on the country's price level. If the price level is somewhat sluggish, then this effect will not be felt in the immediate short run, but it will have an impact as the economy moves beyond the initial short run. The strength of aggregate demand must be evaluated against the economy's supply-side capabilities for producing goods and services. If aggregate demand is very strong, then actual production strains against the economy's supply capabilities. The economy will "overheat" and there will be upward pressure on the price level. (In a setting in which there is ongoing inflation, this really means that the price level will rise more than it otherwise would have anyway. The inflation rate will increase.) If aggregate demand is weak, then product markets will be weak, creating downward pressure on the price level because of the "discipline" effect of weak demand. (Again, in a setting of ongoing inflation, this really means that the inflation rate will be lower than it otherwise would have been—the price level may still be rising, but it will rise more slowly.)

Third, shocks occasionally can cause large changes in the price level even in the short run. One dramatic example was the pair of oil price shocks in the 1970s. Another source of a price shock is a large abrupt change in the exchange rate value of a country's currency. As we will discuss in the next chapter, a large devaluation or depreciation is likely to cause a large increase in the domestic-currency price of imported products. The general price level tends to increase quickly because of both the direct effects of higher import prices and the indirect effects on costs and other prices in the country.

For subsequent analysis using our framework, the effect of strong or weak aggregate demand on the price level is of major interest. As we move beyond the initial short run, we do expect adjustment in the country's product price level. This can have an impact on the country's international price competitiveness, as discussed in the next section. If international price competitiveness is affected, then the country's current account balance changes. In addition, although we will not focus on this effect in subsequent analysis, a change in the price level changes money demand (through the PY term). If the nation's money supply is not changing in line with the change in money demand, then the LM curve will shift over time.[6]

---

[6]If the aggregate demand pressure continues for a sufficient period of time, it can also affect the ongoing rate of inflation. For instance, the United States went into the 1990–1991 recession with an ongoing inflation rate of about 4.5 percent. The weak aggregate demand that caused the recession (and slowed the subsequent

Trade Also Depends on Price Competitiveness

As previously discussed, a country's exports, imports, and net exports depend on production and incomes in both this country and the rest of the world. Standard microeconomics indicates that demand for exports and imports each should also be affected by the prices of these products. Quantity demanded depends on both income and relative prices.

Our demand for imports depends not only on our income, but also on the price of imports relative to the price (P) of domestic products that are substitutes for these imports. What is this relative price? Consider that an imported product (say, a bottle of French wine) is initially priced in foreign currency (say, 10 euros). Once imported into the United States, its price is converted into dollars using the going exchange rate (say, $1.10 per euro). The domestic-currency price of the import is then equal to $P_f r$ ($11.10 for the bottle).[7] Our decision about whether to buy this import depends partly on its dollar price relative to the price of a comparable domestic product (say, a bottle of California wine). The price ratio is $(P_f r)/P$. This ratio may look familiar—it is essentially the real exchange rate introduced in Chapter 18.

Thus, by expanding our previous Equation 21.5, we see that the demand for imports has two major determinants:

$$M = M(\overset{+}{Y}, \overset{-}{P_f r/P}) \qquad (21.15)$$

The volume of imports tends to be higher if our production and income are higher, but lower if imports are relatively expensive (meaning $P_f r/P$ is high).

Foreign demand for our exports depends not only on foreign income, but also on the price of our products exported into the foreign market relative to the prices of their comparable local products (P_f). Our export product (say, a personal computer) is initially priced in our currency (say, $1,500). This can be converted into a foreign currency (say, yen) at the going exchange rate (say, $0.01 per yen). The foreign-currency price of our export is then equal to P/r. (Here $1,500/.01 = 150,000$ yen.) The foreign decision about whether to buy their domestic product (say, an NEC computer) or our exported product is based partly on the relative price, which equals $P_f/(P/r)$ or $(P_f r)/P$. The higher is this ratio, the less attractive is their domestic product, and the more attractive is our exported product.

Thus, the demand for our exports has two major determinants:

$$X = X(\overset{+}{Y_f}, \overset{+}{P_f r/P}) \qquad (21.16)$$

The volume of our exports tends to be higher if foreign production and income are higher or if foreign substitute products are relatively expensive.

---

recovery) reduced the actual inflation rate to less than 3 percent. In addition, the ongoing inflation rate expected to continue into the future (even when the economy had fully recovered from the recession) was reduced to about 3 percent, according to most estimates. (The expected ongoing inflation rate fell to 2–2.5 percent by the late 1990s, largely because technical changes lowered the measured inflation rate.)

[7]To simplify the notation a little, in Part IV we use the symbol r to represent the spot exchange rate. We drop the subscript s.

Thus, in addition to the income effects, net exports $(X - M)$ tend to be higher if the price competitiveness of our products is higher, both because the volume of exports tends to be larger and because the volume of imports tends to be smaller. Our general indicator of international price competitiveness is the ratio $(P_f r)/P$ (the real exchange rate).[8] Our international price competitiveness improves if the foreign-currency price of foreign substitute products (P_f) is higher, if the domestic-currency price of our products (P) is lower, or if the nominal exchange rate value of our currency is lower (r is higher). Over time, our price competitiveness improves if the foreign inflation rate is higher, our inflation rate is lower, or our currency appreciates less (or depreciates more).

Changes in international price competitiveness can be incorporated into our IS–LM–FE framework. They are one of the other economic conditions (or exogenous forces) that can cause shifts in the curves. A change in international price competitiveness shifts two curves: the FE curve and the IS curve. To see this, consider an improvement in a country's international price competitiveness, perhaps because the country has had low product price inflation or because the country's currency has depreciated or devalued. The improved price competitiveness increases exports and decreases imports. If the current account improves, the FE curve shifts to the right. In addition, the increase in net exports increases aggregate demand, so the IS curve shifts to the right.

---

[8]While the real exchange rate provides a useful broad indicator of a country's international price competitiveness, it is not perfect. For any particular product, the relative price is affected by several influences not usually captured in the ratio. First, transport costs and government barriers to imports can alter the price ratio by increasing the price of the imported product. Second, exporters may use strategic pricing so that the local-currency price of the imported product is not just the domestic-currency price in the home market converted at the going exchange rate. This reflects international price discrimination. It is particularly interesting here because exporters may resist passing through the full effect of any exchange rate change into foreign-currency prices for their products. This is called *incomplete pass-through* or *pricing to market*. When the yen appreciated sharply from 1985 to 1987, Japanese firms did raise the dollar prices of the products that they exported to the United States, but by far less than the amount of the exchange rate change. They did this, presumably, to minimize their loss of export sales. From the point of view of the U.S. economy, this means that the volume of imports did not fall as much as might have been expected following the large dollar depreciation.

Summary

The performance of a country's macroeconomy has both internal and external dimensions. We evaluate the country's internal balance against goals oriented toward the domestic economy. **Internal balance** focuses on achieving domestic production that matches the country's supply capabilities so that resources are fully employed, while also achieving price-level stability or an acceptably low rate of inflation. We evaluate external balance against goals related to the country's international transactions. **External balance** focuses on achieving an overall balance of payments that is sustainable over time.

A key aspect of how an open macroeconomy works is the relationship between domestic production and international trade in goods and services. International trade in goods and services is one component of total aggregate demand, which determines domestic product and income in the short run. In addition, domestic production and income have an impact on international trade, especially through the demand for imports.

These relationships influence how shifts in aggregate demand affect our domestic production. Holding interest rates (as well as the product price level and exchange rates) constant, we generally expect that an increase in some component of aggregate demand (like government spending) has a larger effect on domestic production—a phenomenon summarized in the **spending multiplier.** In a closed economy, the size of the multiplier is $1/s$, where s is the marginal propensity to save (including any government saving "forced" through the marginal tax rate). For the open macroeconomy, a rise in domestic product and income increases imports. The size of the spending multiplier for the small open macroeconomy is $1/(s + m)$, where m is the **marginal propensity to import.** The larger is the country's propensity to import, the smaller is the spending multiplier. The leakage into imports, like the leakage into saving, dampens the effects of the initial extra spending on the ultimate change in domestic product and income.

If the country is not small, then changes in its demand for imports have noticeable effects on other countries, with several specific implications. First, any boom or slump in one country's aggregate demand can spread to other countries. Second, the changes in production and income in the other countries can then feed back into the first country—**foreign-income repercussions.** These foreign-income repercussions make the true spending multiplier larger than the simple formula $1/(s + m)$. Swings in the business cycle (recession or expansion) are not only internationally contagious but also self-reinforcing, a conjecture easily supported by the experience of the 1930s. More recently, the "locomotive theory" posits that growth in the United States, Japan, and Germany (the three largest economies in the world) can spur growth in the entire world.

The forces that change domestic product and income might or might not "worsen" our balance of trade (i.e., shift it toward deficit). The result depends on which of three kinds of forces are at work: (1) A rise in domestic spending will probably worsen the balance of trade. (2) An international shift in demand toward our product (e.g., due to a shift in tastes) will definitely improve our trade balance. (3) A rise in our aggregate supply, that is, in our ability to cut costs and to compete, will probably improve our balance of trade.

A more complete framework for analyzing a country's macroeconomy in the short run requires that we are able to picture not only domestic product, income, and aggregate demand but also supply and demand for money and the country's overall balance of payments. The IS–LM–FE approach provides this framework.

The **IS curve** shows all combinations of interest rate and domestic product that are equilibriums in the national market for goods and services. Because lower interest rates encourage borrowing and spending, the IS curve slopes downward. The **LM curve** shows all combinations of interest rate and domestic product that are equilibria between money supply and money demand. For money demand to remain equal to a given, unchanged money supply, the increase in money demand that accompanies a higher domestic product must be offset by a higher interest rate that reduces money demand, so that the LM curve slopes upward.

The **FE curve** shows all combinations of interest rate and domestic product that result in a zero balance in the country's overall international payments (its official settlements balance). The FE curve also generally slopes upward. An increase in domestic product and income increases demand for imports so that the country's current account and overall payments balance deteriorate. This can be offset (at least in the short run) by a higher interest rate that draws in foreign financial capital (or reduces capital outflows) so that the capital account (excluding official reserves transactions) improves.

The intersection of the IS and LM curves indicates the short-run equilibrium values for domestic product Y and the interest rate i for the country. The position of the FE curve relative to this IS–LM intersection indicates whether the official settlements balance is positive, zero, or negative.

Although we often assume that the country's product price level is constant in the short run, over time the price level changes. Most countries have some amount of ongoing inflation that is expected to continue. The monetary approach presented in Chapter 18 emphasizes that ongoing inflation is related to continuing growth of the money supply. In addition, the strength of aggregate demand relative to the economy's supply capabilities can affect the price level or inflation rate. If aggregate demand is too strong, the economy overheats and the price level or inflation rate rises. If aggregate demand is weak, the discipline effect of weak market demand tends to lower the price level or inflation rate. Furthermore, price shocks can cause large changes in the price level or inflation rate even in the short run.

International price competitiveness is another key determinant of a country's international trade in goods and services, in addition to the effects of national income on the country's imports and foreign income on the country's exports. If the price of foreign products relative to the price of our country's products is higher, our demand for imports tends to be lower, and foreign demand for our exports tends to be higher. The real exchange rate (introduced in Chapter 18) is a useful general indicator of this relative price and thus of the country's international price competitiveness. A change in international price competitiveness shifts both the FE curve and the IS curve because the current account balance changes. For instance, if competitiveness improves, then exports increase and imports decline. The improvement in the country's payments position shifts the FE curve to the right, and the increase in aggregate demand shifts the IS curve to the right.

Suggested Reading

Algebraic treatments of foreign-trade repercussions are given in Vanek (1962, Chapters 6–9) and Stern (1973, Chapter 7). Bosworth (1993, Chapter 2) discusses the concepts of internal and external balance and develops the IS–LM–FE model. Richardson (1988) and Bryant et al. (1988) present empirical estimates of the domestic and foreign effects of policy changes using dynamic macroeconomic models that incorporate trade and other linkages among countries. Helliwell and Padmore (1984) summarize earlier empirical work using dynamic linkage models.

Questions and Problems

✦ 1. According to Figure 21.4, which two countries (excluding the United States) have the largest multiplier impacts on each other? Why do you think that this is so?

2. "A recession in the United States is likely to raise the growth of real GDP in Europe." Do you agree or disagree? Why?

✦ 3. An economy has a marginal propensity to save of 0.2 and a marginal propensity to import of 0.1. An increase of $1 billion in government spending now occurs.
(Assume that the economy is initially producing at a level that is below its supply-side capabilities.)

a. According to the spending multiplier for a small open economy, by how much will domestic product and income increase?

b. If instead this is a closed economy with a marginal propensity to save of 0.2, by how much would domestic product and income increase if government spending increases by $1 billion? Explain the economics of why this answer is different from the answer to part *a*.

4. An economy has a marginal propensity to save of 0.15 and a marginal propensity to import of 0.4. Real domestic spending now decreases by $2 billion.

a. According to the spending multiplier (for a small open economy), by how much will domestic product and income change?

b. What is the change in the country's imports?

c. If this country is large, what effect will this have on foreign product and income? Explain.

d. Will the change in foreign product and income tend to counteract or reinforce the change in the first country's domestic product and income? Explain.

✦5. How does the intersection of the IS and LM curves relate to the concept of internal balance?

6. How does the FE curve relate to the concept of external balance?

✦7. Explain the effect of each of the following on the LM curve:

a. The country's central bank decreases the money supply.

b. The country's interest rate increases.

8. Explain the effect of each of the following on the IS curve:

a. Government spending decreases.

b. Foreign demand for the country's exports increases.

c. The country's interest rate increases.

✦9. Explain the effect of each of the following on the FE curve:

a. Foreign demand for the country's exports increases.

b. The foreign interest rate increases.

c. The country's interest rate increases.

10. Explain the impact of each of the following on our country's exports and imports:

a. Our domestic product and income increase.

b. Foreign domestic product and income decrease.

c. Our price level increases by 5 percent, with no change in the (nominal) exchange rate value of our currency and no change in the foreign price level.

d. Our price level increases by 5 percent, the foreign price level increases by 10 percent, but there is no change in the (nominal) exchange rate value of our currency.

CHAPTER 22

Internal and External Balance with Fixed Exchange Rates

Fixed exchange rates can reduce the variability of currency values if governments are willing and able to defend the rates. This chapter examines the macroeconomics of a country whose government has chosen a fixed exchange rate.

Many major countries of the world have instead chosen floating rates (albeit with modest amounts of government management). Why study fixed rates? There are three major reasons. First, within the current system a substantial number of countries do fix their exchange rates. As shown in Chapter 20, there are two major blocs of currencies with fixed exchange rates. A large number of developing countries that fix their currencies to the U.S. dollar form the dollar bloc. The euro bloc includes the 11 European Union countries that plan to replace their national currencies with the euro in 2002, 2 other EU countries that fix their currencies to the euro through the Exchange Rate Mechanism, and a number of countries outside the EU that fix their currencies to the euro. In addition, a number of other countries fix their moneys to currencies other than the dollar or the euro. Second, in the current system a number of countries have floating rates in name, but the rates are so heavily managed by the governments that they are closer to being fixed rates in many respects. Third, there are continuing discussions about returning to a system of fixed rates among the world's major currencies. Proposals range from target zones that would be a kind of crawling peg with wide bands, to a return to the gold standard. Before we can assess the desirability or feasibility of such proposals, we need to understand how a fixed exchange rate affects both the behavior of a country's economy and the use of government policies to affect the economy's performance.

The analysis of the chapter shows that defense of a fixed exchange rate through official intervention in the foreign exchange market dramatically affects the country's monetary policy. The intervention can change the country's money supply, setting off effects that tend to reduce the payments imbalance. But this process also limits the country's ability to pursue an independent monetary policy. Defending the fixed rate also has an impact on fiscal policy, which actually becomes more powerful if international capital is highly mobile. In addition, intervention to defend the fixed rate affects how the country's economy responds to shocks, both shocks that come from within the country and shocks that are international in origin.

Fixed rates challenge government policymakers who are attempting to guide the country to both external balance (balance in the country's overall international payments) and internal balance (actual production equal to the economy's supply potential, or a high level of employment—"full employment"—without upward pressure on the country's inflation rate). Internal and external balance are often hard to reconcile in the short and medium runs. A government that pursues external balance alone, tidying up its balance of payments while letting inflation or unemployment get out of hand at home, may be thrown out of office. On the other hand, controlling domestic production alone, with fiscal or monetary policies, may widen a deficit or surplus in the balance of payments, jeopardizing the promise to keep the exchange rate fixed.

One possible solution is a subtle mixture of policies, with monetary policy assigned to reducing international payments imbalances, and fiscal policy assigned to stabilizing domestic production (GDP). Another possible "solution" is surrender—to change the fixed rate by devaluing, revaluing, or shifting to a floating rate. The chapter looks at both ideas, and concludes by considering the conditions that influence whether a change in the fixed rate will be successful in improving the country's internal and external macroeconomic performance.

From the Balance of Payments to the Money Supply

Once a country's government has decided to have a fixed exchange rate, the government must defend that rate. As discussed in Chapter 20, the first line of defense is official intervention—the monetary authority (central bank) buys or sells foreign currency in the foreign exchange market as necessary to steady the rate within the allowable band around the central value chosen for the fixed rate. Chapter 20 showed that several implications follow from official intervention. First, the holdings of official reserves change as the authority buys or sells foreign currency. Second, the country's money supply may change as the authority sells or buys domestic currency as the other half of its official intervention.

Our goal in this and the next three sections of the chapter is to show how these effects occur and what implications they have for the country's macroeconomy. To begin, let's consider the balance sheet of the country's central bank. For our story, the assets held by the central bank can be divided into two major types: official international reserve assets (R) and domestic assets (D). The domestic assets are not international reserves because they are denominated in domestic currency. Two major types of domestic assets held by the central bank are (1) bonds and similar debt securities issued by the country's government and (2) loans that the central bank has made to (regular) domestic banks or other domestic financial institutions.

On the other side of the balance sheet, the two liabilities of interest to our story are (1) the domestic currency (paper money and coins) issued by the central bank and (2) the deposits that the country's (regular) domestic banks (or other domestic financial institutions) have placed with the central bank. The deposits from regular banks may be required by regulations of the central bank. In addition, the central bank often uses the deposits from banks in the process of settling payments between domestic banks (for instance, in the process of clearing checks drawn on one bank but payable to another).

The country's money supply consists (mainly) of currency held by the public and various types of deposits (like checking accounts) that the public has at regular banks. The country's central bank has the ability to influence the total amount of these bank deposits from the public because banks are required to hold, or wish to hold, certain assets as bank reserves to "back up" these deposit liabilities. We presume that the types of assets that count as bank reserves are a bank's holdings of currency "in its vault" and the bank's holdings of deposits at the central bank. The amount of reserves that a bank is required to hold is typically some fraction of the deposits that the bank owes to its customers—a system called **fractional reserve banking.**[1]

In this setting the central bank controls the country's money supply by controlling its own balance sheet and by setting the reserve requirements that (regular) banks must meet. To see this, consider what happens if the central bank allows its liabilities to increase. This will expand the money supply. If the increase is in the form of an increase in currency that is held by the public, then the money supply increases directly. If the increase is in the form of central bank liabilities that count as bank reserves (either currency in bank vaults or deposits from banks), then banks can increase the value of their deposit liabilities, and they can increase deposits by a multiple amount of the value of the increase in bank reserves. With fractional reserve banking, each dollar of extra bank reserves can back up several dollars of deposits (where *several* is the reciprocal of the reserve requirement fraction). The multiple expansion of the money supply with fractional reserve banking is called the **money multiplier process.**[2]

---

[1]As you can see, the standard terminology seems intended to confuse us. *Bank* shows up in two ways. The country's *central bank* is the official monetary authority that controls monetary policy and also (usually) is the authority that undertakes official intervention in the foreign exchange market. Regular banks, often just called *banks,* conduct regular banking business (making loans, taking deposits, transacting in foreign exchange) with regular customers (for instance, individuals, businesses, and government units) and among themselves (for instance, interbank loans and interbank foreign exchange trading). *Reserves* is an even more dangerous term. A central bank (or the country's relevant monetary authority if it is not exactly a central bank) holds *official reserve* assets. Regular banks hold *bank reserves* as assets, usually in proportion to their deposit liabilities. Part of these bank reserves is usually in the form of deposits that these regular banks have at the central bank. (Just to add to the soup, there is another type of reserve in bank accounting—liability items such as reserves for bad loans—but these are not part of our main story.)

[2]This description of the central bank and the way in which it controls the country's money supply is appropriate for the United States (the Federal Reserve or "Fed") and for many other countries. A number of central banks (including the Bank of Japan) that previously had different procedures have been shifting toward this approach. Still, some countries use different procedures (for instance, implementing monetary policy through limits on the expansion of loans by banks to their customers). Analysis of such countries would need to be modified somewhat to match their procedures, but the major conclusions to be reached in the sections below generally still apply.

With this background on the country's central bank and its control of the country's money supply, let's return to the effects of official intervention used to defend the fixed exchange rate. If the country has an official settlements surplus, so that the country's currency is experiencing upward pressure (a tendency for the exchange rate r to decrease), the central bank must intervene to buy foreign currency and sell domestic currency. On its balance sheet this is an increase in official international reserve holdings (R) and an increase in its liabilities (as the domestic currency is added to the economy). This increase in liabilities could be in the form of an increase in actual currency outstanding (if the central bank delivers the domestic currency as currency itself). More likely, and more efficiently in terms of the process, the central bank probably delivers the domestic "currency" to a regular bank (the bank with whom it is transacting in the foreign exchange market) by increasing the deposits that the bank has at the central bank. In either case, the country's money supply will increase. If, as is likely, the reserves held by banks increase (because their deposits at the central bank increase or their holdings of vault cash increase), then the money supply can increase by a multiple of the size of the central bank intervention in the foreign exchange market.

If instead the country's official settlements balance is in deficit and the country's currency is under downward pressure (a tendency for r to increase), the central bank must intervene to sell foreign currency and buy domestic currency. On its balance sheet this is a decrease in official international reserve holdings (R) and a decrease in its liabilities (as the domestic currency is removed from the economy). The central bank probably collects the domestic "currency" by decreasing the deposits that the regular bank involved in the foreign exchange transaction has at the central bank. Then the reserves held by banks decline (because their deposits at the central bank decrease), and the money supply must decrease by a multiple of the size of the central bank intervention in the foreign exchange market (the money multiplier in reverse).

The conclusion here is that official intervention alters the central bank's assets and liabilities in ways that change not only the country's holdings of official international reserve assets but also the country's money supply, unless the central bank does something else to attempt to resist the change in the money supply. Indeed, under fractional reserve banking, the change in the money supply will be a multiple of the size of the intervention.

From the Money Supply Back to the Balance of Payments

If official intervention changes the country's money supply, what are the implications for the country's balance of payments and for the country's macroeconomic performance in general? The change in the money supply sets off several effects that tend to reduce the payments imbalance.

Consider first the case in which the country begins with a surplus in its balance of payments. The surplus requires official intervention in which the central bank buys foreign currency and sells domestic currency. The domestic money supply increases "automatically" as the central bank increases its liabilities when

FIGURE 22.1   *Expanding the Money Supply Worsens the Balance of Payments with Fixed Rates*

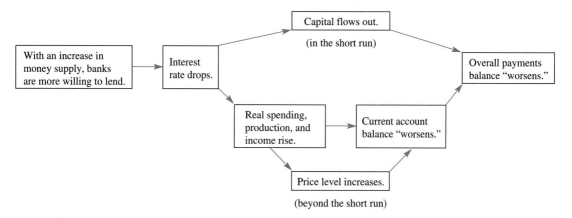

For a decrease in the money supply, reverse the direction of all changes.

it sells domestic currency. The effects of the increase in the money supply on the balance of payments are clear-cut, as Figure 22.1 shows. As the central bank increases bank reserves, banks are more liquid and want to expand their business. They seek to make more loans. In the process, their competition to lend more is likely to bid down interest rates. The lowering of interest rates in the economy, at least in the short run, has several effects on the balance of payments. One is through the country's capital account. The decline in interest rates causes some holders of financial assets denominated in the domestic currency to seek higher returns abroad. The international capital outflow causes the capital account to "deteriorate" (become less positive or more negative).[3] This effect on the capital account can occur quickly, but it may not last long. Once portfolios are adjusted, any ongoing capital flows are likely to be smaller. In fact, the outflows could reverse when bonds mature or loans come due. (In addition, the extra foreign investment is likely to set up a stream of income payments that the country receives in the future.)

Another effect is on the current account because of changes in real income, in the price level, or in both. The decrease in domestic interest rates encourages interest-sensitive spending—for instance, through more borrowing to support additional new real investment projects. The expansion in spending results in an increase in real domestic product and income (assuming that there is some availability of resources to expand production in the economy). The rise in income increases imports of goods and services and "worsens" the current account balance. (A smaller surplus or a larger deficit results.) In addition, the extra spending can put upward pressure on the price level in the economy, especially if the expansion of

---

[3]We are assuming that the change in the domestic interest rate lowers the interest differential because foreign interest rates have not changed or have not changed as much. In addition, we are assuming that expectations of future spot exchange rates have not changed. For instance, international investors believe that the fixed rate will be maintained, so the expected future spot rate remains about equal to the current spot rate.

aggregate demand pushes against the supply capabilities of the economy. If prices and costs in the economy rise, then the country's international price competitiveness deteriorates, and the country's current account worsens. Which of these two effects actually occurs depends on the starting point for the economy and the time frame involved. If the economy begins with unemployed resources, then the effect through real income is likely to be larger. If the economy starts close to full employment, then the effect through the price level is likely to be more important, at least beyond the short-run period when prices are sticky.

Thus, official intervention by a country that initially has a balance-of-payments surplus can increase the money supply, and this increase in the money supply sets off adjustments in the economy that tend to reduce the size of the surplus. Key features of the adjustment can be pictured using an IS–LM–FE diagram. Suppose that the economy is initially at point A in Figure 22.2, the intersection of the initial IS and LM_0 curves. This point is to the left of the FE curve, showing that the country has a surplus in its official settlements balance. Official intervention to defend the fixed rate increases the money supply, shifting the LM curve down or to the right. As the LM curve shifts down, the equilibrium interest rate decreases and domestic product and income increase. The intersection of the IS curve and the new LM curve is moving closer to the FE curve. If the price level does not change, then full adjustment has occurred (probably over several years) when the LM curve has shifted down to the triple intersection at point E. The equilibrium interest rate has fallen from 7 percent to 6 percent, domestic product has risen from 100 to 110, and the official settlements balance is zero (because the economy is on the FE curve).[4]

If the country instead begins with a deficit in its official settlements balance and downward pressure on the exchange rate value of its currency, then all of these effects work in the reverse direction. The domestic money supply decreases, and domestic interest rates increase, at least in the short run. The rise in interest rates draws a capital inflow, improving the capital account. The rise in interest rates also lowers aggregate demand and real domestic product, reducing imports and improving the current account. The weak aggregate demand also puts downward pressure on the economy's price level, at least beyond the short-run period in which prices are sticky. This increases the country's international price competitiveness and improves its current account. The overall balance of payments improves—the deficit declines toward zero. The country's IS–LM intersection is initially to the right of the FE curve. The LM curve then shifts up or to the left, and eventually a triple intersection is achieved.

The thrust of the analysis is clear. If an external imbalance exists, intervention to defend the fixed rate changes the domestic money supply. The money supply change causes adjustments that move the country back toward external balance. So what is the problem? Possible problems are of two types. First, the process is based on changes in the country's holdings of international reserve

---

[4]If the price level also increases, then both the FE and IS curves will shift to the left as the country loses international price competitiveness. The LM curve will shift by less, and the triple intersection will occur with a somewhat lower real domestic product.

FIGURE 22.2

*Payments
Adjustments
for a Surplus
Country with
Fixed Rates*

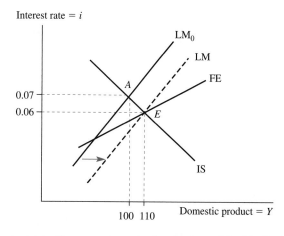

If the country begins at point *A* with a payments surplus, intervention to defend the fixed exchange rate
results in an increase in the money supply. The LM curve shifts down or to the right, and the surplus falls
toward zero as the IS–LM intersection shifts toward point *E*.

assets. For a country that begins with a payments surplus, the monetary authority
will acquire official international reserve assets. For a deficit, the authority will
lose official reserves. Officials may view either change as undesirable. However,
this may not really be a problem if the authority *accepts* that the money supply
must change (and the LM curve must shift). The central bank can simply use its
domestic operations to speed up the adjustment. For instance, the country can use
open market operations in which it buys or sells government securities. In the
surplus situation, the country could expand the money supply more quickly, and
lower interest rates more quickly, by buying domestic government securities.
This open market operation adds to both the domestic assets and the liabilities of
the central bank. In paying for the securities, the central bank increases bank
reserves. By changing monetary conditions more quickly, external balance is
achieved more quickly. Official reserve assets (R) increase by less because some
of the increase in the domestic money supply is the result of the increase in
domestic assets (D) held by the central bank. In the deficit situation, the country
could contract the money supply by selling domestic government bonds in an
open market operation. Bank reserves decrease, the money supply contracts, and
interest rates rise more quickly. The payments deficit shrinks more quickly, and
external balance is achieved more quickly. Official international reserves do not
decrease as much; instead, part of the money supply decrease is the result of a
decrease in domestic assets held by the central bank.

A second possible problem with the adjustment toward external balance is
that it may not be consistent with internal balance. In the surplus situation, the
increase in the money supply can put upward pressure on the country's price
level, and this pressure toward a positive (or higher) rate of inflation may be
viewed as undesirable—a shift toward internal imbalance. In the deficit situation,
the decrease in the money supply can result in a recession (declining real production), with rising unemployment.

Short of Reserves? Call 1-800-IMF-LOAN

The International Monetary Fund (IMF) is considered by some to be the friend of countries in need during their times of large payments deficits. But others think it's a big bully and the front man for the rich countries, as the IMF imposes economic constraints on the world's poorer countries. What view is right?

The IMF was designed as part of the 1944 Bretton Woods agreement that also set up the postwar fixed-rate system. The IMF began operation in 1946 and by 1999 had 182 member countries. On joining the IMF, each member contributes a quota—one-quarter in the form of assets generally recognized as official international reserves and the other three-quarters in its own currency. The size of the quota is roughly related to the country's economic size, and the size determines the country's voting rights on the Board of Directors. For instance, the United States has about 18 percent of the voting rights. Periodically, the sizes of the countries' quotas are increased to expand the IMF's financial resources. The IMF also borrows from some of its members and receives voluntary contributions from some.

The IMF has several major purposes. It promotes the expansion of international trade and international monetary cooperation among countries. It seeks to maintain orderly foreign exchange arrangements through surveillance of the exchange rate policies of its member countries. Especially, countries should not manipulate their exchange rate to gain unfair competitive advantages. The IMF seeks to establish unrestricted convertibility of currencies for current account payments. It created the special drawing right (SDR) as a new official reserve asset and occa-sionally makes new allocations to its members (the most recent during 1979–1981). The IMF collects and publishes national economic and financial data. And, most important to our purpose here, the IMF lends to its members when appropriate to give them time to correct payment imbalances. In the early years, most such loans were to industrialized countries recovering from wartime destruction and disruptions. In recent decades nearly all IMF loans have been to developing countries.

Most IMF lending is to countries with large payments deficits, countries whose official reserves are declining to low levels. The loans provide additional official reserve assets to the country. The country can use these additional reserves to buy time for the country to make orderly macroeconomic adjustments to reduce the deficit, without resorting to exchange controls or trade restrictions. Ideally, the adjustment can occur without excessive costs or disruptions to the country or to other countries. Loans from the IMF are extended under a number of different programs. The standard loans, made from the country's "credit tranches" linked to the country's quota contributions to the Fund, are general-purpose. Other programs target specific purposes or types of countries, including loans to cover temporary shortfalls in export earnings due to declines in world commodity prices, loans to countries making the transition from central planning to freer markets, and loans with very low interest rates to very poor countries. Most IMF loans are to be repaid in 5 years; some are to be repaid in 10 years. Maximum amounts of loans from various programs are in proportion to a country's quota.

Sterilization

Rather than allowing automatic adjustments to proceed (or speeding them up), the monetary authority instead may want to *resist* the change in the country's money supply. One reason for resistance is that the money supply change would tend to create an internal imbalance, as just described. Another is that the authority may believe that the international imbalance is temporary and will soon reverse. This was the case of temporary disequilibrium discussed in Chapter 20.

The IMF only makes loans that it expects to be repaid. The IMF requires a borrowing country to agree to how it intends to correct its payments imbalance. That is, the IMF imposes **conditionality**—the IMF makes a loan only if the borrowing country commits to and enacts changes in its policies, with quantified performance criteria. The policies should promise to achieve external balance within a reasonable time. The IMF disburses some loans in pieces over time. It withholds pieces if the performance criteria are not met, as it did for Russia in 1998. The policy changes that are usually included in an IMF adjustment program are not surprising. They include fiscal and monetary restraint, liberalization of restrictions on domestic markets and on international trade, and deregulation.

What is the record for these IMF loans? Do they work? One answer is repayment. Prior to the mid-1980s, nearly all loans had been repaid on time. However, from 1985 to 1992, rising amounts, reaching over 10 percent of IMF loans outstanding, had not been repaid on time. These overdue payments then declined to less than 5 percent of loans outstanding by the late 1990s.

Do the loans assist payments adjustment? Evaluation of the effects of the loans and the conditions attached to them is difficult—what would have happened without them? Nonetheless, the programs accompanying IMF loans typically appear to result in increases in a country's exports, decreases in imports, and reduction in the payments deficits, but these changes are often temporary. Many countries appear to be chronically dependent on IMF loans. Sixty countries have borrowed in almost every year since their first borrowing from the IMF.

The IMF also sometimes makes mistakes. Its programs to address the Asian crisis have been particularly controversial. As the Asian crisis hit in 1997, Thailand, Indonesia, and South Korea had rather large current account deficits and rather large amounts of short-term foreign debt. But they did not have large government budget deficits and they had little inflation. For Thailand, Indonesia, and South Korea to receive IMF loans, the IMF required the contractionary monetary and fiscal policies that are typically conditions for its loans. But these conditions were too severe—the policy changes led to deep recessions that were much larger than necessary to reduce the countries' external imbalances. The IMF also demanded changes in basic economic structures and institutions, including changes in labor rules and business governance. Critics viewed these structural conditions as unnecessary to address the external imbalances, and perhaps even counterproductive in that the IMF's criticisms of the country's government practices and business systems undermined the willingness of foreign investors to renew lending to the countries.

Our conclusions about IMF loans and the adjustment programs that accompany them are cautious. The IMF is neither the great friend nor the outside bully, but perhaps more like a stern but fallible teacher. In many cases the IMF adjustment programs seem appropriate and necessary if the borrowing countries are to reduce their payments deficits. But the programs often seem to be ineffective. This does not mean that the programs are wrong (though perhaps they were for the Asian countries in 1997). Instead, the ineffectiveness often has more to do with local politics—many countries fail to comply with the conditions set in the loan agreements.

The central bank can keep the external surplus or deficit from having an impact on the domestic money supply by taking an *offsetting* domestic action. **Sterilization** is the practice of taking an action to reverse the effect of official intervention on the domestic money supply. If the central bank is intervening to defend the fixed rate in a situation of payments surplus by selling its national currency in exchange for foreign currency, the money supply would tend to increase. This can be sterilized if the central bank, for instance, undertakes an open market operation in which the central bank sells domestic government bonds. While the intervention in currency markets tends to expand the money supply, the open market operation tends to reduce it by reducing both the domestic assets held by the central bank and the central bank liabilities that serve as the base for the domestic money supply. In the case of a deficit, the central bank can sterilize the official intervention (buying the nation's currency) by buying domestic government bonds with that same currency in an open market operation.

Sterilized intervention does not change the money supply. Instead, in the case of a surplus, the central bank increases its holdings of official reserve assets and decreases its holdings of domestic assets like government bonds. (*D* decreases as *R* increases.) The changes are on the asset side of the central bank's balance sheet, and thus sum to zero. If the central bank's liabilities do not change after the combination of the two activities, then the money supply should not change either.

Because a sterilized intervention does not change the money supply, the LM curve does not change. In Figure 22.2 the economy's equilibrium remains at point *A*. There is no adjustment toward external balance. Often this is a wait-and-see or a wait-and-hope strategy. Perhaps something else will shift the FE curve toward point *A*, or some other source of change will shift the IS–LM intersection toward the FE curve. If nothing else moves the economy toward external balance, there are limits to the ability of the monetary authority to use sterilized intervention to continue to run a payments imbalance. In the case of the payments surplus, the limit may be (1) the unwillingness of the central bank to continue to increase its holdings of official reserve assets or (2) the complaints by other countries about the country's ongoing surplus. Taiwan found itself in this situation in the 1980s, when its intervention resulted in official reserve holdings that grew rapidly to a value equal to about three-quarters of the value of its annual national income. Pressure by the U.S. government then induced Taiwan to allow its currency to appreciate quickly during 1986–1987. Or, more concretely, the limit may come when the central bank has decreased its holdings of domestic assets to zero and thus has no domestic assets left to sell in open market operations.

In the case of a payments deficit, the limit is the inability of the central bank to obtain foreign currency to sell in the official intervention. The country's official reserve assets may dwindle toward zero (and it also cannot borrow more foreign currencies because of its precarious international position).[5] This limit can be dramatic—if international investors and speculators believe that the central bank is low in its holdings of official reserves, a currency crisis based on the one-way speculative gamble discussed in Chapter 20 can develop.

Monetary Policy with Fixed Exchange Rates

The discussion of the preceding two sections has a major implication—*fixed exchange rates greatly constrain a country's ability to pursue an independent monetary policy.* To a large degree the country's monetary policy must be consistent with maintaining the value of the fixed rate. Payments imbalances place pressure for changes in the money supply driven by the intervention to defend the fixed rate.

---

[5]In situations like this, the country's government may turn to the International Monetary Fund, as the box on page 498 discussed.

Sterilization can be used to resist these money supply changes, but there are limits to how long the country's central bank can use sterilization, especially if the central bank's holdings of official reserves are declining because of a payments deficit.

Even if the country begins with a payments balance, its ability to pursue an independent monetary policy is greatly constrained. To see this, consider a country that initially has an official settlements balance of zero. While the country has achieved external balance, the country may believe that it has not achieved internal balance. Specifically, it has a high unemployment rate and wants to expand its domestic product. To pursue this goal with monetary policy, it attempts to implement an expansionary monetary policy. For a time this policy may increase real product. But the country's official settlements balance will go into deficit through the process shown in Figure 22.1. Both the current account and capital account will deteriorate. The country then must intervene to defend its fixed rate, selling foreign currency and buying domestic currency. This reduces the domestic money supply, effectively forcing the country to abandon its expansionary policy. Even if the central bank resists this for a while using sterilization, it cannot continue to sterilize indefinitely. Eventually, the country must allow its money supply to shrink (or pursue some other adjustment like an exchange rate change).

This process can be seen in Figure 22.3, where the country is initially at point *E*, a triple intersection. The increase in the money supply shifts the LM curve down or to the right. The IS–LM intersection at point *H* indicates that real domestic product has increased, but the new intersection is to the right of the FE curve, indicating a payments deficit. As the country intervenes, the money supply shrinks and the LM curve shifts back. If nothing else changes, the LM curve shifts back to the original triple intersection. In this example, in contrast to the analysis in the earlier sections, we are starting from payments balance and conducting the analysis as "from the money supply to the balance of payments" and then "from the balance of payments back to the money supply." In the process we conclude that the

FIGURE 22.3

Expansionary Monetary Policy with Fixed Rates

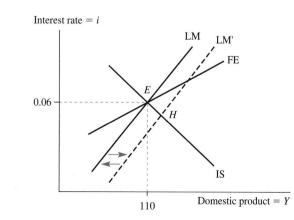

Starting from point *E* with an overall payments balance of zero, the country attempts to implement an expansionary policy. The LM curve shifts down or to the right, but at point *H* the payments balance is in deficit. Intervention to defend the fixed exchange rate decreases the money supply, and the LM curve shifts back up, eventually returning the country to point *E*.

ability to change the money supply is limited, and eventually stops, because of the feedback from the balance of payments and the need to defend the fixed rate.

Fiscal Policy with Fixed Exchange Rates

Fiscal policy is implemented by changing government spending and taxes. A change in fiscal policy affects the balance of payments through both the current account and the capital account. Let's examine the case of an expansionary fiscal policy, say a rise in government purchases of goods and services. This case is summarized in Figure 22.4. (Contractionary fiscal policy is analyzed in the same way, with all of the changes occurring in the opposite direction.)

The extra government spending means a bigger government budget deficit (or a reduced budget surplus). We'll tell the story using a budget deficit. To finance the larger budget deficit, the government is borrowing more and driving up interest rates. The higher interest rates should attract a capital inflow, "improving" the country's capital account.

The extra government spending also increases aggregate demand and increases real domestic product (assuming that some resources are available to expand production).[6] The extra spending spills over into extra import demand, "worsening" our current account balance. In addition, the extra aggregate demand may put upward pressure on the price level once we pass beyond the short-run period in which the price level is sticky. If the price level increases, then the country loses international price competitiveness, another reason that the current account deteriorates.

The effect on the country's overall balance of payments depends on the magnitudes of these changes. Given the worsening of the current account, we can examine the effect on overall balance as a question of how responsive international capital flows are to interest rate changes. If international capital flows are very responsive to interest rate changes, then the capital inflows will be large, and the official settlements balance will go into surplus. If the capital flows are unresponsive, then the capital account will improve only a little, and the overall balance will go into deficit. The effect on the overall balance is probably also affected by timing—the capital inflows may be large at first, but they probably will dwindle as international portfolios are adjusted to the new economic conditions.

Figure 22.5 shows the effects of a fiscal expansion with fixed exchange rates in the short run assuming that the price level is steady. For both cases we begin with a triple intersection at point E. The shift to an expansionary fiscal policy shifts the IS curve to the right, to IS'. The new intersection with the LM curve is at point K, with a higher interest rate and a higher level of real domestic product.[7]

---

[6]In the short run real GDP increases even if there is partial crowding out, as interest-sensitive domestic spending decreases somewhat when interest rates increase.

[7]Another way to see the pressure for a higher interest rate is to use the direct logic of the IS–LM analysis. The increase in real income and spending increases the transaction demand for money, but there is no increase in the money supply (assuming, at least initially, that the central bank does not permit any increase because of an unwillingness to shift its monetary policy). The extra money demand must be choked off by an increase in interest rates. (All of this represents a movement along the LM curve from E to K.)

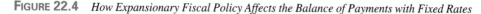

FIGURE 22.4   *How Expansionary Fiscal Policy Affects the Balance of Payments with Fixed Rates*

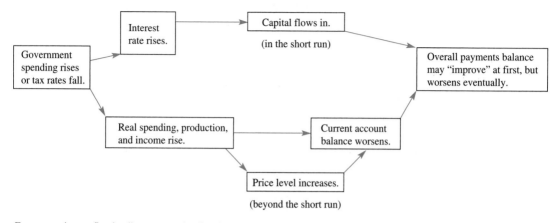

For contractionary fiscal policy, reverse the direction of all changes.

The two cases shown in Figure 22.5 differ in how responsive international capital flows are to changes in the interest rate. The left graph shows the case of relatively responsive capital flows so that the FE curve is relatively flat. The right graph shows the case of unresponsive capital flows so that the FE curve is relatively steep. If capital flows are responsive, as in Figure 22.5A, then the new intersection point *K* lies to the left of the FE curve, and the overall payments

FIGURE 22.5

Expansionary Fiscal Policy with Fixed Exchange Rates

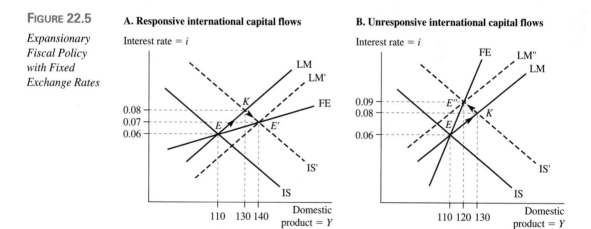

Expansionary fiscal policy shifts the IS curve to the right and the IS–LM intersection shifts from *E* to *K*. The effects of fiscal policy depend on how strongly international capital flows respond to the interest rate increase. In panel A, the overall payments balance goes into surplus. (*K* is to the left of FE.) In panel B, the overall payments balance goes into deficit. (*K* is to the right of FE.) In either case the payments imbalance leads to a change in the money supply (assuming that the central bank does not or cannot "sterilize" it). In panel A, intervention to defend the fixed rate increases the money supply, shifting the LM curve down, and the economy shifts toward a new full equilibrium at point *E'*. In panel B, intervention to defend the fixed rate decreases the money supply, shifting the LM curve up, and the economy shifts toward a new full equilibrium at point *E''*.

balance goes into surplus. If they are unresponsive (Figure 22.5B), then point K lies to the right of FE, and the overall balance goes into deficit.[8]

The discussion so far has offered conclusions about the effects of a fiscal policy change on the domestic economy and on external balance. It might seem that we can stop here, but we should not. If the official settlements balance shifts into surplus or deficit, then official intervention is needed to defend the fixed exchange rate, and the country's money supply will change (although this effect might be postponed if the intervention is sterilized). If the intervention is not sterilized, then interest rates and domestic product will be affected further as the money supply changes. The direction of this effect depends on whether the overall balance shifts into surplus or deficit.

If capital flows are very responsive to interest rates, then overall payments go into surplus, and the central bank must intervene by selling domestic currency and buying foreign currency. With no sterilization, the domestic money supply expands, reducing interest rates and supporting a further expansion in domestic product. In Figure 22.5A, the increase in the money supply shifts the LM curve down or to the right. It will eventually shift to the dashed LM′, where a new triple intersection is achieved at point E'. In this case, fiscal policy becomes more powerful in increasing real GDP because the monetary authority expands the money supply as it intervenes to defend the fixed exchange rate.[9]

If capital flows instead are not that responsive, then the overall payments deficit requires official intervention in which domestic currency is purchased and foreign currency is sold. If the intervention is not sterilized, then the domestic money supply decreases, raising interest rates and reversing some of the increase in real domestic product. In Figure 22.5B the decrease in the money supply shifts the LM curve up or to the left, eventually to the dashed LM″. In this case, expansionary fiscal policy loses some of its power to increase real GDP.

Perfect Capital Mobility

The case of perfect capital mobility is an extreme case of how international movements can alter the effectiveness of monetary and fiscal policies under fixed rates.

> **Perfect capital mobility** means that a practically unlimited amount of international capital flows in response to the slightest change in one country's interest rates.

Perfect capital mobility may be a good basis to analyze countries whose capital markets are open to international activity and whose political and economic situation is considered stable (so that no perceptions of political and economic

---

[8]The slope of the FE curve does not matter much in analyzing monetary policy, because there is no ambiguity in the direction of effects on the overall balance for an attempted shift in monetary policy such as that analyzed in Figure 22.3.

[9]If the price level also increases, the FE curve shifts to the left, and the IS curve shifts back somewhat to the left. Real domestic product does not increase by as much in this case and in the one discussed in the next paragraph.

risks limit capital inflows). Indeed, the success of a system of fixed exchange rates makes perfect capital mobility more likely. If investors are convinced that exchange rates will remain fixed, they will be more willing to move back and forth between currencies in response to small differences in interest rates.

For a small country (one that is too small to influence global financial markets by itself), perfect capital mobility implies that the country's interest rate must be equal to the interest rate in the larger global capital market. When exchange rates were fixed, this gave substance to the Canadian complaint that "Canadian interest rates are made in Washington." There is evidence that interest rate correlations between countries grew stronger during prolonged periods of fixed rates (the gold standard and Bretton Woods periods).

If international capital flows are highly sensitive to slight temporary interest rate changes, then they practically dictate the country's money supply, even in the short run. Why? Consider what happens if an incipient reduction of the money supply begins to increase the country's interest rates. The slightly higher interest rates draw a large capital inflow. Intervention to defend the fixed exchange rate requires selling domestic currency, thus expanding the money supply. Furthermore, sterilization is nearly impossible under such circumstances because of how large the capital inflows could be. Conversely, a nearly unlimited outflow of capital could occur if the country expanded its money supply and lowered interest rates slightly. The capital outflow forces the money supply back down to its original level to eliminate the slight drop in interest rates. The balance of payments rules the money supply. Perfect capital mobility with fixed exchange rates robs monetary policy of its ability to influence interest rates or the domestic economy.

For fiscal policy, perfect capital mobility actually means enhanced control over the domestic economy in the short run. Expansionary fiscal policies do not raise interest rates because the extra government borrowing is met by a large influx of lending from abroad. Thus, the government borrowing does not crowd out private domestic borrowers with higher interest rates, allowing fiscal policy its full spending multiplier effects on the economy. In other words, with perfect capital mobility and interest rates set outside the country, fiscal expansion cannot be guilty of crowding out private real investment from lending markets. This extra potency of fiscal policy under fixed exchange rates and perfect capital mobility may be a poor substitute for the loss of monetary control since government handling of spending and taxes is often crude and subject to the vagaries of politics. Yet this is apparently a fact of life for small countries under truly fixed exchange rates.[10]

Figure 22.6 shows the effect of perfect capital mobility on the IS–LM–FE picture. The FE curve is flat because the tiniest change in interest rates would trigger a potentially infinite international flow of capital. If the global interest rate is 6 percent, then any point above the flat FE, corresponding to a domestic interest rate greater than 6 percent, results in a massive capital inflow and payments

---

[10]With perfect capital mobility, as with the other cases discussed in this chapter, we must remember that any attracted capital must be paid for later with reflows of interest and principal back to the foreign creditors.

FIGURE 22.6

*With Perfect
Capital
Mobility,
Monetary
Policy Is
Impotent but
Fiscal Policy Is
Strong*

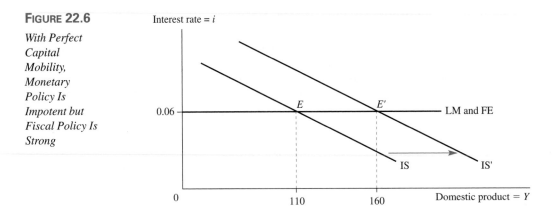

surplus. Any point below results in a massive capital outflow and payments deficit.

With perfect capital mobility the LM curve is also effectively flat and the same as FE. Any flood of international capital swamps any other influence on the nation's money supply. The money supply must be whatever is necessary to keep the domestic interest rate at 6 percent. Only the interest rate of 6 percent, dictated by financial conditions in the world as a whole, is consistent with equilibrium in the country's market for money. Under the conditions shown in Figure 22.6, the country has no independent monetary policy. The monetary authorities cannot change the domestic interest rate or control the money supply.

By contrast, fiscal policy takes on its greatest power under these conditions. Raising government spending or cutting tax rates causes the usual rightward shift of the IS curve to IS'. As soon as the extra government deficit raises the home country's interest rate even slightly, there is a rush of capital inflow, as international investors seek the slightly higher interest rate in this country. The inflow raises the money supply until the interest rate is bid back down to 6 percent. So a rightward shift of the IS curve has a large effect on domestic product and no effect on the interest rate.[11]

The case of perfect capital mobility shows clearly that monetary policy is subordinated to the defense of the fixed exchange rate, and that fiscal policy can be powerful with fixed exchange rates. For the rest of this chapter we now return to the case of moderate capital mobility and an upward-sloping FE curve. Perfect capital mobility can be considered the limiting case (flat) of the general case (upward-sloping) that we examine.

---

[11]In fact, fiscal policy's impact on domestic product fits the spending multiplier formula of Chapter 21. For example, suppose that the country in Figure 22.6 had a marginal propensity to save of 0.2 and a marginal propensity to import of 0.3. This would make the multiplier equal to 2, according to Chapter 21. In this case, the rightward shift of $\Delta Y = 50$ from point E to point E' in Figure 22.6 could be achieved by $\Delta G = 25$.

Shocks to the Economy

From time to time a country's economy is hit by major shocks—both shocks that represent changes in basic conditions in the domestic economy and those that arise externally in the international economy. What are the effects of these exogenous forces on an economy that has a fixed exchange rate? To provide a simple base for our analysis, we will usually examine cases in which the country has achieved external balance (a triple intersection in the IS–LM–FE graph) just before the shock hits the economy.

Internal Shocks

One type of internal shock arises in the market for money. A **domestic monetary shock** alters the equilibrium relationship between money supply and money demand because (1) the money supply changes or (2) the way in which people decide on their money holdings changes. The latter can arise, for instance, from financial innovations like money market mutual funds, the spread of credit cards, or automated teller machines (ATMs). A domestic monetary shock causes a shift in the LM curve. Its effect on domestic interest rates and domestic product is quite limited with fixed rates. As we saw in our analysis of the attempt to run an independent monetary policy, a shift in the LM curve tends to reverse itself as the central bank must intervene to defend the fixed rate. A major effect of a monetary shock instead can be on the country's holdings of official reserve assets, if intervention is the basis for the money supply change that shifts the LM curve back toward its initial position.

Another type of domestic shock arises from exogenous changes in domestic spending on goods and services. A **domestic spending shock** alters domestic real expenditure (E) through an exogenous force that alters one of its components (consumption, real domestic investment, or government spending). A change in fiscal policy is one such shock. Another would be a change in the business mood or consumer sentiment, resulting in a change in real investment or consumption spending. The discussion of fiscal policy provides an example of the analysis of this type of shock. In addition, it is important to remember that effects on foreign countries will be transmitted through changes in our imports, and that this can have repercussions back to our economy if the induced changes in the foreign economies alter their imports from us (as discussed in Chapter 21).

International Capital-Flow Shocks

One type of external shock arises from unexpected changes in the country's capital account. An **international capital-flow shock** is the unpredictable shifting of internationally mobile funds in response to such events as rumors about political changes or new restrictions (capital controls) on international asset holdings. Let's examine an international capital-flow shock in the form of a shift by international investors and speculators to a belief that the country's government is likely to devalue its currency (raise r) in the near future. Although this is not necessary to the analysis, we begin with a country that has an external balance. (In this case the shift in belief is not related to a payments imbalance today—rather, it may be related to doubts about the political leadership of the country, or to a belief that the country may try to use devaluation to boost international price competitiveness in order to increase net exports and lower domestic unemployment.)

The shift in belief leads to a capital outflow as international investors attempt to reposition their portfolios away from assets denominated in this country's currency *before* the devaluation occurs. This type of capital outflow is a form of "capital flight," in which investors flee a country because of doubts about government policies. If the country begins with an external balance, then the overall balance shifts into deficit as the capital account deteriorates. There is downward pressure on the exchange rate value of the country's currency, and the central bank must intervene to defend the fixed rate. The central bank buys domestic currency and sells foreign currency. If the intervention is not sterilized, then the domestic money supply shrinks. Interest rates increase, and real domestic product decreases. The increase in interest rates here becomes part of the defense of the fixed exchange rate. If the interest differential shifts in favor of this country, then international investors are more willing to keep investments in this country's financial assets (or are less interested in fleeing) even if there is some risk of devaluation. (Recall our discussions of uncovered financial investments in Part III.) In fact, countries faced with this form of capital outflow often immediately shift policy to raise short-term interest rates dramatically, for instance, from annual rates of less than 10 percent to annual rates of over 100 percent. This is an example of using monetary policy *actively* to reestablish external balance, rather than waiting for the slower effects of intervention on the domestic money supply to move the country toward external balance.

The effects of this shock are pictured in Figure 22.7. The economy begins at point E. The international capital-flow shock causes the FE curve to shift up or to the left. Once the FE curve has shifted, the official settlements balance is in deficit at point E. The central bank must intervene to defend the fixed rate. The central bank may attempt to keep the economy at point E by sterilizing the intervention. The central bank may hope that the disequilibrium in the overall balance is temporary, perhaps because the fears of the international investors will subside and the FE curve will shift back to the right in the near future. If the monetary authority cannot or does not sterilize the intervention, then the LM curve will begin to shift up or to the left. If the new FE curve remains where it is, the LM curve must shift to LM', with a new triple intersection at point T. External balance has been reestablished at point T. However, real domestic product has declined. The country now has an internal imbalance, in the form of low aggregate demand and higher unemployment, assuming that the country did not begin with the opposite imbalance of excessively strong aggregate demand. Under fixed exchange rates, external capital flow shocks can have powerful impacts on internal balance through the changes in the money supply driven by official intervention to defend the fixed rate.

Figure 22.7

*An Adverse
International
Capital-Flow
Shock*

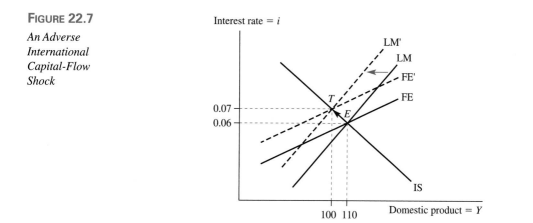

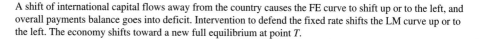

A shift of international capital flows away from the country causes the FE curve to shift up or to the left, and overall payments balance goes into deficit. Intervention to defend the fixed rate shifts the LM curve up or to the left. The economy shifts toward a new full equilibrium at point T.

International Trade Shocks

A second type of external shock arises from exogenous changes in the country's current account. An **international trade shock** is a shift in a country's exports or imports that arises from causes other than changes in the real income of the country. For instance, demand for a country's exports can change for many reasons. This variability seems to be largest for countries specializing in exporting a narrow range of products, especially primary commodities for which demand is sensitive to the business cycle in importing countries. Instability has strongly affected exporters of metals, such as Chile (copper), Malaysia (tin), and, to a lesser extent, Canada. Import shocks can occur if our consumers unexpectedly alter their purchases between import products and domestically produced substitutes, for instance, because of changing perceptions of the relative quality of the products. Trade shocks can also occur because of shifts in the prices or availability of domestic and foreign products. An important example of this type of shock is a shock to the supply of a major import, such as oil for most industrialized countries.[12]

An international trade shock alters the country's current account. Thus, it directly affects both the country's overall balance of payments and aggregate

---

[12]The analysis of a decline in the supply of a major import is a bit complicated. Examples of such supply shocks for crucial imports are the oil shocks of 1973–1974 and 1978–1979, and the smaller one of 1990. The shock is likely to lower the quantity of imports of this product while raising its price. The analysis is similar to that about to be discussed in the text if the cutback in foreign supply initially raises the total value of imports and lowers national purchasing power (with the higher price acting like a "tax" on the economy imposed by the exporters). These conditions hold if imports of the product take a large share of our national spending and our demand for the product is very price-inelastic (at least in the short run). An additional twist is that the oil price shocks quickly increased the price level P so that the LM curve also shifted up or to the left as a result of the shock.

FIGURE 22.8

*An Adverse
International
Trade Shock*

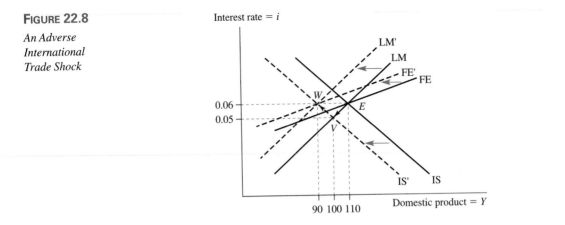

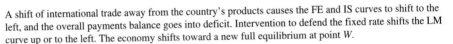

A shift of international trade away from the country's products causes the FE and IS curves to shift to the left, and the overall payments balance goes into deficit. Intervention to defend the fixed rate shifts the LM curve up or to the left. The economy shifts toward a new full equilibrium at point W.

demand for the country's domestic production. For instance, a shift of foreign demand away from our exports, or a shift of our demand toward imports (and away from our own products), leads to a worsening of the current account and the overall balance (assuming that there is little effect on international capital flows). It also reduces aggregate demand, lowering real domestic product.[13] In addition, the country's central bank must intervene to defend the fixed rate by buying domestic currency and selling foreign currency. If the intervention is not sterilized, then the domestic money supply contracts, leading to a further decline in aggregate demand. External balance can be reestablished through these changes, but the internal imbalance of low aggregate demand and high unemployment will be increased.

Figure 22.8 shows the effects of this shock. Beginning at point E, the adverse international trade shock shifts the FE curve to the left and the IS curve to the left as well. At the new IS–LM intersection (point V), real domestic product declines (as does the domestic interest rate). With point V to the right of the new FE' curve, the country's overall payments are in deficit. Intervention to defend the fixed rate reduces the domestic money supply (assuming that it is not sterilized). The LM curve begins to shift up or to the left. External balance is reestablished at point W when the LM curve shifts to the dashed LM'. However, real domestic product has declined even more.[14]

---

[13]We are assuming that the current account actually does deteriorate even though the reduction in our real income will offset some of the initial decline by lowering the country's demand for imports through the domestic-income effect on imports. In Figure 22.8 this ensures that point V is to the right of the new FE curve even if the FE curve is steeper than the LM curve.

[14]As shown, the interest rate returns to 0.06. This is not the only possibility—the interest rate could be higher or lower, depending on the magnitudes of the curve shifts and the slopes of the curves.

Thus, as with international capital-flow shocks, international trade shocks can have a powerful effect on the country's internal balance. The intervention needed to defend the fixed rate tends to magnify the effect of the shock on domestic production.

Imbalances and Policy Responses

A country wants to achieve both internal balance and external balance. Yet, its actual performance is often short of these goals. In many situations it has imbalances in both its internal and external situations as a result of shocks that hit the economy, or previous government policies that resulted in poor economic performance.

Internal and External Imbalances

Figure 22.9 catalogs the four possible cases in which the country has both internal and external imbalances. With fixed exchange rates a country's policymakers could get lucky and face the straightforward problems represented by the upper-left and lower-right cells. The government of a country experiencing high unemployment and a payments surplus can use expansionary policies to address both problems. Most obviously, an expansion of the domestic money supply can increase aggregate demand and lower unemployment, while also reducing the payments surplus (as summarized previously in Figure 22.1). This shift occurs automatically if the country intervenes to defend the fixed exchange rate and does not sterilize, but the country can also speed it up by using active monetary policy to expand the money supply more quickly. The government of a country experiencing an inflation rate that is viewed as being too high and a payments deficit can use contractionary policies to address both. Again, an obvious choice is a contraction of the money supply (or perhaps more realistically, a reduction of the growth rate of the money supply). Even in these cases the exact policy solution may be tricky because balance in one dimension may be achieved while part of the other imbalance remains. Nonetheless, the initial direction of the desirable policy change that reduces (if not eliminates) both imbalances is clear.

What about the other two cells in Figure 22.9? In broad terms the correct policy response is not clear. The dilemma of having to choose which goal to pursue has been felt most acutely by countries in the lower-left cell, where low aggregate demand has resulted in high unemployment, but the balance of payments is in deficit. This was the near tragedy of Britain after it rejoined the gold standard in 1925 at its prewar gold parity, with the high value for the pound making British products uncompetitive in international trade. This was the problem facing the United States in the early 1960s. France faced a similar problem in the early 1990s, as discussed in "A Tale of Three Countries," pages 516 to 518. In these cases, reducing unemployment called for raising aggregate demand with expansionary policies. However, this would worsen the trade balance and tend to worsen the overall balance. The dilemma was not well solved in any of the cases.

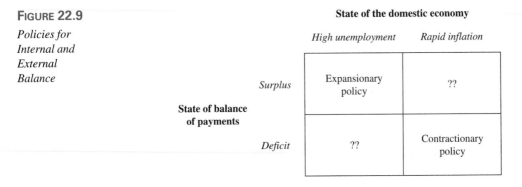

FIGURE 22.9

Policies for Internal and External Balance

In some situations a policy to change aggregate demand can serve both internal and external goals, but in some cases (marked "??" here) it cannot. To deal with high unemployment and a payments surplus, policy-makers should expand aggregate demand (upper-left case). To deal with inflation and a payment deficit, they should cut aggregate demand (lower-right case). But with the other two combinations of imbalances, there is no clear prescription for aggregate-demand policy.

Britain was driven off the gold standard in 1931. The United States reduced its unemployment rate with a series of fiscal policy changes (the tax cut of 1964, domestic "Great Society" spending programs, and Vietnam War spending) but the payments imbalance led toward the breakup of the Bretton Woods fixed-rate system. Through mid-1990s, France continued to suffer from high unemployment.

The opposite dilemma faces governments worried about a rising or high inflation rate while the country is running a payments surplus (the upper-right cell of Figure 22.9). This was the sort of position frequently faced by Germany and Switzerland during the Bretton Woods fixed-rate years. The unacceptably high inflation rate calls for restraint on aggregate demand, but the surpluses are likely to be increased as the demand restraint improves the current account balance.

The government of a country in one of the two dilemma cells has three basic choices:

1. It can abandon the goal of external balance, which eventually means that the country will abandon its fixed exchange rate.

2. It can abandon the goal of internal balance, at least in the short run, and set its policies (especially its monetary policy and money supply) to achieve external balance. This is sometimes called the "rules of the game" in a fixed-rate system such as the gold standard. Defending the fixed rate is the highest goal.

3. The government can try to find more policy tools or more creative ways to use the tools that it already has.

Giving up is unpopular, and the natural tendency is to search for more tools and creative solutions.

A candidate for addressing the dilemma of high unemployment and payments deficit is enhancement of the economy's supply capabilities. Why not come up with policies that create more national income by improving our productivity? Productivity improvements would enhance our ability to compete in international trade, thereby shifting demand to our products, expanding production and employment, and improving our current account balance. It sounds too good to be true. And it probably is. Policymakers usually have no fast, low-cost way of improving the economy's supply capabilities. That comes through sources of growth, such as the advance of human skills and technology, that respond sluggishly, if at all, to government manipulation.

A Short-Run Solution: Monetary–Fiscal Mix

There is a way to buy time and serve both internal and external goals using conventional demand-side policies while staying on fixed exchange rates. Looking more closely at the basic policy dilemma, Robert Mundell and J. Marcus Fleming noticed that monetary and fiscal policies have different relative impacts on internal and external balance. This difference can be the basis for a creative solution.

The key difference between the impacts of fiscal and monetary policies is that easier monetary policy tends to lower interest rates and easier fiscal policy tends to raise them, as noted in Figures 22.1 and 22.4. An expansion of aggregate demand and domestic product can be achieved with different mixes of fiscal policy and monetary policy, and the mix matters for the resulting level of the interest rate, at least in the short run. Expansion of domestic product can result in a low interest rate if it is driven mainly by expansionary monetary policy. Expansion can result in a high interest rate if it is driven mainly by expansionary fiscal policy. Because interest rates affect the country's payments balance, the interest rate is important. If the interest rate is lower, the payments balance deteriorates, but if the interest rate is pushed high enough (for instance, by using very expansionary fiscal policy coupled with somewhat contractionary monetary policy), the payments balance improves.

More generally, *monetary and fiscal policies can be mixed so as to achieve any combination of domestic product and overall payments balance in the short run.* Figure 22.10 illustrates the opportunities for solving one of the four policy challenges posed in Figure 22.9, namely, the case of excessive unemployment and payments deficits, starting at point Z. The goal is to raise the economy to full employment, which can be achieved at the level of domestic product Y_{full}. Shifting only one policy would not work, as we have seen, but shifting both can work. In this case, it is best to shift to tighter (contractionary) monetary policy to attract foreign capital with higher interest rates, and to easier (expansionary) fiscal policy in pursuit of full employment. In the right amounts, the monetary tightening and fiscal easing can bring us exactly to full employment and payments balance. In Figure 22.10, this is achieved by shifting IS to IS' and LM to LM'.[15]

---

[15]The prospect of mixing tight money with fiscal ease starting from point Z raises interest rates, as increased government borrowing and the tightening of the money supply combine to squeeze out private borrowers. It is reasonable to fear that such a jump in interest rates would hold back productive private investment. Something of the sort happened in the early 1980s, when the combination of the Federal Reserve's restraint on money growth and the Reagan administration's tax cuts and deficits seems to have held back U.S. capital formation.

FIGURE 22.10

*How Monetary
and Fiscal
Policy Could
Combine to
Cure Both
Unemployment
and a Balance-
of-Payments
Deficit*

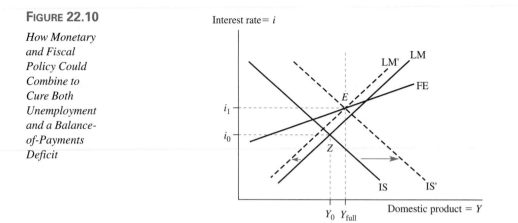

At the starting point Z, domestic product Y_0 is below the full employment level Y_{full} and the balance of payments is in deficit. To reach full employment and payments balance at point E, combine the right amounts of tight monetary policy and easy fiscal policy.

A similar recipe can be used to get from any starting point to internal balance and payments balance. The principle is clear: As long as there are as many different policies as target variables, as in the present case of two policies and two targets, there is a solution.

Furthermore, the pattern of policy prescriptions reveals a useful guideline for assigning policy tasks to fiscal and monetary policy. This is Robert Mundell's **assignment rule:** Assign to fiscal policy the task of stabilizing the domestic economy only, and assign to monetary policy the task of stabilizing the balance of payments only. We can see from Figure 22.11 that such marching orders would guide the two arms of policy toward internal balance and payments balance. Studying the different cases in Figure 22.11, you will find that the assignment rule generally steers each policy in the right direction. There are exceptions, as Figure 22.11 notes, but even in these cases it is likely that following the assignment rule does nothing worse than make the economy follow a less direct route to the goal of internal and external balance.

The assignment rule is handy. It allows each arm of policy to concentrate on a single task, relieving the need for perfect coordination between fiscal and monetary officials. It also directs each arm to work on the target it tends to care about more, since the balance of payments (and exchange rate stability) have traditionally been of more concern to central bankers than to politicians who make fiscal decisions.

The rule might or might not work in practice. We have already mentioned problems with the interest rate effect on capital flows that is supposed to guarantee the existence of a solution. Furthermore, if either branch of policy lags in getting signals from the economy and responding to them, the result could be unstable oscillations that are even worse than having no policy at all. Or, monetary policy may be run largely to accommodate the country's fiscal policy (and the need of the government to fund its deficit spending), so that independent policies are not really possible. In addition, the mix influences both the composition of domestic spending and the level of foreign debt. A policy of high interest rates,

FIGURE 22.11

Monetary–Fiscal Recipes for Internal and External Balance

		High unemployment	Rapid inflation
	Surplus	Easier monetary policy, easier fiscal policy	Easier monetary policy, tighter fiscal policy
	Deficit	Tighter monetary policy, easier fiscal policy	Tighter monetary policy, tighter fiscal policy

State of the domestic economy

State of the balance of payments

These recipes conform to the **assignment rule:** Assign monetary policy the task of balancing the country's international payments, and assign fiscal policy the task of bringing the domestic economy to full employment without excessive inflation. There are exceptional cases, however, when the assignment rule fails to follow the most direct route to the goal. In the diagram below, the assignment rule is wrong for monetary policy at points like *B* and *G*, and it is wrong for fiscal policy at points like *D* and *I*.

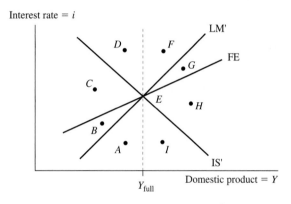

such as that used in Figure 22.10, reduces domestic real investment. This can harm the growth of the economy's supply capabilities by reducing the growth of the capital stock. It also builds up foreign debt, which must be serviced in the future, reducing the amount of national income that the country keeps for itself.[16]

Surrender: Changing the Exchange Rate

If an imbalance in a country's overall balance of payments is large enough or lasts for long enough (a "fundamental disequilibrium"), the country's government may be unwilling to change domestic policies by enough to eliminate the imbalance. The country's government instead may conclude that surrendering the fixed rate is the best choice available. If the payments balance is in deficit, a devaluation may be used; if it's in surplus, revaluation may occur.

---

[16]Another possible problem might seem to be the case of perfect capital mobility because the country has no control of its money supply. This is not a problem. In fact, the case of perfect capital mobility effectively forces the government to follow the assignment rule. Monetary policy must allow the money supply to be whatever is necessary to achieve external balance on the FE curve. Fiscal policy can then be directed toward achieving internal balance, addressing any problems of domestic unemployment or inflation pressures.

A Tale of Three Countries

In 1992, unemployment in France was high and rising. Inflation was almost nothing. The French government seemed to respond by tightening up on money and raising interest rates.

Madness? Not really, but an example of the policy dilemma that can arise with fixed exchange rates. France was a member of the Exchange Rate Mechanism (ERM) of the European Monetary System (EMS). Membership committed the French government to keep the exchange rates between the French franc and the currencies of the other member countries within small bands around the central rates chosen for the fix.

To understand France we actually need to start with Germany, the largest member of the ERM. The Berlin Wall fell in 1989, and German unification proceeded rapidly over the next year, politically, financially, and economically. German government policy toward unification included support for the eastern part in the form of transfers, subsidies, and other government expenditures on such things as public infrastructure investments. This expansionary fiscal policy increased aggregate demand. Domestic production expanded rapidly in 1990 and 1991, and unemployment fell, but the economy began to overheat as demand exceeded production capabilities, so that the inflation rate increased. German policymakers, especially those at the Bundesbank (Germany's central bank), loathe inflation. History matters—the hyperinflation of the 1920s in Germany is considered to be the economic disaster of the century for Germany.

In response to the rise in inflation, the German monetary authorities tightened up on monetary policy, after a spurt in money growth in 1990–1991 resulting from monetary unification. Interest rates rose. This monetary tightening slowed the economy during 1992–1993.

We can capture the main elements of the German story in an IS–LM picture. Germany began at point A. The fiscal expansion shifted IS_1 to IS_2, and the increased growth rate of the money supply shifted LM_1 to LM_2. At the new equilibrium point B, real domestic product was higher, but the economy was trying to push past its supply capabilities. In response

to the internal imbalance of rising inflation, the Bundesbank reduced money growth, shifting LM_2 to LM_3. Interest rates rose (on a nominal basis, although less so on a real basis), and domestic product declined as the economy moved toward point C.

In this way the German government adopted policies that focused almost completely on internal political and economic problems. (In fact, although we could add the FE curve to Germany's picture, we have instead omitted it to emphasize this internal focus of German policy.) Meanwhile, back in France . . .

In 1990, the French economy was already weak and weakening. The unemployment rate was 9 percent and rising. For internal reasons the French government probably wanted to shift to an expansionary policy. But it had an external problem. Rising interest rates in Germany could set off a capital outflow that would threaten the fixed exchange rate between the franc and the DM. France had to respond to this incipient external imbalance by tightening up on money and raising French interest rates. (Given France's low inflation rate, the higher nominal interest rates also were higher real interest rates.) Unfortunately, for political reasons, fiscal policy could not turn expansionary. The assignment rule could not be used. Instead, the higher interest rates made the French economy worse. The growth rate of real French GDP declined from 1989 through 1993, and real GDP actually declined in 1993. The French unemployment rate rose from 1990 through 1994.

In France's picture, France began at point F, with aggregate demand already weak and unemployment high. The rise in Germany's interest rate shifted France's FE curve up or to the left (FE_1 to FE_2). To avoid capital outflows and a payments deficit, the French monetary authorities responded by tightening money, shifting LM_1 to LM_2. As the economy moved toward point H, demand and production weakened and the unemployment rate rose.

However, this was not always enough. International investors and speculators doubted the resolve of the French (and most other non-German members of the ERM) to stick to fixed exchange rates. Major speculative attacks occurred in September 1992, November 1992, and July 1993. In these the FE curve for France shifted sharply up or to the left. The French government responded with massive official intervention, buying francs and selling DM, and with high short-term interest rates to discourage the speculative outflows. Total intervention by all ERM members in September 1992 was over $100 billion, with capital losses of about $5 billion to the central banks that bought currencies of the countries (Britain, Italy, Spain, and Portugal) that then devalued or depreciated anyway. Total intervention in July 1993 was also more than $100 billion, with the French central bank alone selling more than $50 billion of DM in defense of the franc. Official reserve holdings of the French central bank declined close to zero, but the French government was "successful." The franc was not devalued.

The third largest economy in the European Union is Britain. Britain's journey through these years was different. Britain was not a member of the ERM until joining in 1990, when it committed to a pound–DM rate of about 0.35. The next two years were not good for Britain. To defend the fixed rate, the growth rate of the British money supply had to be kept low (although at the same time British interest rates could decline, starting from a high level). A severe recession with two years of decline in real GDP hit, and the unemployment rate rose to about 10 percent. Broadly, this picture is similar to that of France, but the recession was worse.

In 1992, Britain's story diverges. As a result of the speculative attack on non-DM currencies in September 1992, Britain left the ERM. The British government spent close to half of its official reserves defending the pound before surrendering. Britain shifted to a floating exchange rate, and the pound depreciated by over 10 percent against the DM. This improved British price competitiveness. In addition, the British government could allow its money supply to grow more quickly. Interest rates fell sharply in 1993, and real GDP began to grow. Britain's unemployment rate plateaued in 1993 and declined in 1994 (while the unemployment rate was still rising in both France and Germany). After declining in 1993, the inflation rate increased a little in Britain in 1994, but not even close to enough to reverse the gain in price

competitiveness from the currency depreciation. Britain's depreciation of 1992 seems to have been successful.

Let's pick up Britain's picture as Britain left the ERM in 1992. (Its picture for 1990–1992 is similar to that of France.) The initial situation, just before the departure, was at point J. With the depreciation of the pound, the improvement in price competitiveness shifts FE_1 right to FE_2 and moves IS_1 right to IS_2. The money expansion shifts LM_1 right as well to LM_2. The British economy shifts toward point K, with higher real domestic production and a lower interest rate.

Tales have lessons. The lesson of this tale is that countries must choose between fixed exchange rates and control over their internal balance. When large countries choose internal balance, the choice gets tougher for smaller countries. Germany, the largest economy in the EU, ran its policies mainly to satisfy internal objectives (like the United States in the 1960s). This created problems for other ERM members—conflicts for them between internal and external balance. Both France and Britain faced a dilemma: high unemployment and a tendency toward payments deficits. For a while, both responded with tight money that tried to achieve external balance but made the internal imbalance (high unemployment) worse. All of this did not completely convince international investors and speculators. With the speculative attack of September 1992, the paths diverged. France defended the fixed rate, at further cost to internal balance. Britain surrendered, withdrawing from the ERM. This allowed Britain to address its internal imbalance. Expansionary policy and the competitiveness gained from the pound's depreciation rekindled economic growth. The unemployment rate declined. The speculative attack in July 1993 led to a semisurrender even by France and other ERM members. They widened the allowable bands around the central rates from plus or minus 2.25 percent to plus or minus 15 percent. This widening of the band forestalled any further speculative attacks. But, during the next years, the franc–DM rate seldom was more than 3 percent from its central value. France continued to direct its policies to keeping the franc exchange rate steady against the DM, and France's unemployment rate remained high.

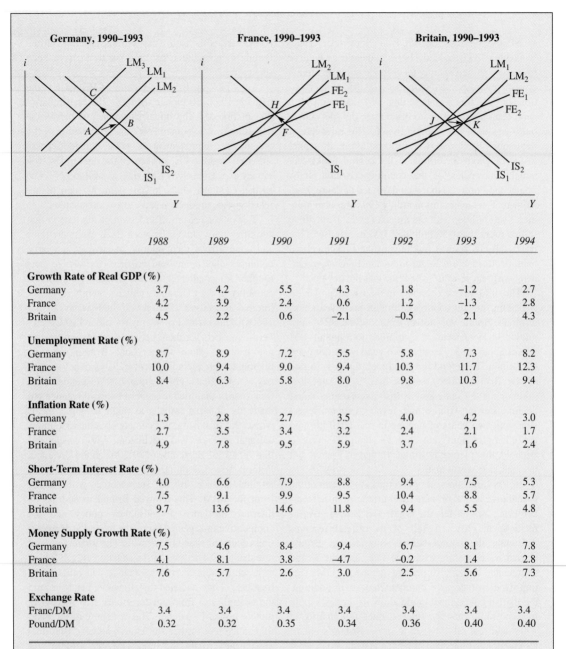

Germany, 1990–1993   France, 1990–1993   Britain, 1990–1993

	1988	1989	1990	1991	1992	1993	1994
Growth Rate of Real GDP (%)							
Germany	3.7	4.2	5.5	4.3	1.8	−1.2	2.7
France	4.2	3.9	2.4	0.6	1.2	−1.3	2.8
Britain	4.5	2.2	0.6	−2.1	−0.5	2.1	4.3
Unemployment Rate (%)							
Germany	8.7	8.9	7.2	5.5	5.8	7.3	8.2
France	10.0	9.4	9.0	9.4	10.3	11.7	12.3
Britain	8.4	6.3	5.8	8.0	9.8	10.3	9.4
Inflation Rate (%)							
Germany	1.3	2.8	2.7	3.5	4.0	4.2	3.0
France	2.7	3.5	3.4	3.2	2.4	2.1	1.7
Britain	4.9	7.8	9.5	5.9	3.7	1.6	2.4
Short-Term Interest Rate (%)							
Germany	4.0	6.6	7.9	8.8	9.4	7.5	5.3
France	7.5	9.1	9.9	9.5	10.4	8.8	5.7
Britain	9.7	13.6	14.6	11.8	9.4	5.5	4.8
Money Supply Growth Rate (%)							
Germany	7.5	4.6	8.4	9.4	6.7	8.1	7.8
France	4.1	8.1	3.8	−4.7	−0.2	1.4	2.8
Britain	7.6	5.7	2.6	3.0	2.5	5.6	7.3
Exchange Rate							
Franc/DM	3.4	3.4	3.4	3.4	3.4	3.4	3.4
Pound/DM	0.32	0.32	0.35	0.34	0.36	0.40	0.40

Source: Growth rate of real GDP, unemployment rate, (CPI) inflation rate, and money supply growth rate (M1 for France, M3 for Germany, and M0 for Britain) from Economic Intelligence Unit, *Country Report,* various issues for these three countries. Short-term (money market) interest rates and exchange rates from International Monetary Fund, *International Financial Statistics Yearbook,* 1998.

The government may hope that the exchange rate change can adjust the external imbalance without excessive disruption to the domestic economy. Nonetheless, the exchange rate change will affect aggregate demand, domestic production, unemployment, and inflation. In some situations these domestic changes represent a departure from internal balance. The internal effects of the exchange rate change may then need to be offset by other policy changes, creating a rationale for a policy mix that includes the exchange rate change and one or both of a fiscal policy change and a monetary policy change.

In other situations the internal effects of an exchange rate change can themselves be desirable. Interestingly, these are precisely the dilemma cases of Figure 22.9. Consider a country that has a fixed exchange rate, a payments deficit, and also a rather high unemployment rate (the lower-left cell in Figure 22.9). This country's government is not willing to allow an "automatic" adjustment through a decline in the money supply, because this would raise interest rates, lower demand and production, and increase unemployment further. Instead, the government has been sterilizing its intervention. It is also not capable of following the assignment rule, perhaps because domestic politics precludes adopting the right policy mix.

What happens if this country devalues (or shifts to a floating exchange rate and allows its currency to depreciate)? What effects does this exchange rate surrender (an increase in r) have on external and internal balance?

The devaluation should improve international price competitiveness (as long as any changes in the domestic price level or the foreign price level do not offset the exchange rate change). Exports tend to increase as firms from this country can lower the foreign-currency prices of their products (and as higher profits draw resources into producing for export). Imports tend to decrease as the domestic-currency price of imported products rises (and as higher profits in producing domestic products that can now compete more successfully with imports draws resources into producing these import substitutes). Thus, the current account tends to improve. The effects on the capital account are less clear-cut. The capital account may also improve. If some capital was fleeing the country in fear of the impending devaluation, then this flight could stop or even reverse once the devaluation is done. Overall, we expect an improvement in the payments balance (a decrease in the deficit).

If exports increase and imports decrease, then these changes increase aggregate demand and domestic production, reducing domestic unemployment. However, import prices in local currency increase, and this increase puts some upward pressure on the average price level or inflation rate in the country. The extra demand could also put upward pressure on the price level, but this effect may be small if the economy begins with high unemployment.

Figure 22.12 shows these effects in the IS–LM–FE diagram, assuming that the domestic price level is steady. The country begins at point B with a payments deficit, and the (low) level of domestic production at B results in rather high unemployment. The devaluation improves the current account (and may also improve the capital account), shifting the FE curve down or to the right. The increase in net

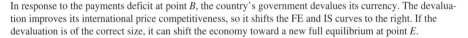

FIGURE 22.12

*Devaluation of
the Country's
Currency*

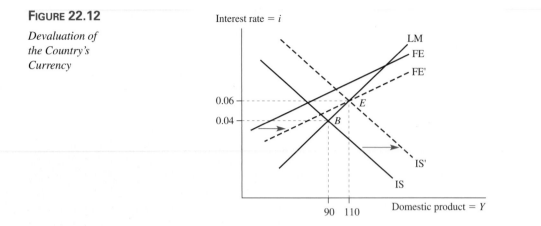

In response to the payments deficit at point *B*, the country's government devalues its currency. The devaluation improves its international price competitiveness, so it shifts the FE and IS curves to the right. If the devaluation is of the correct size, it can shift the economy toward a new full equilibrium at point *E*.

exports as a result of the change in price competitiveness shifts the IS curve to the right. The figure shows that a devaluation (of the correct size) can shift the economy to a triple intersection (external balance) with a higher domestic product (and lower unemployment). The new equilibrium at point *E* may not exactly be internal balance (full employment), but it is a move in the correct direction.[17]

This sounds good—another possible answer to the dilemma of deficit and unemployment. In some cases it seems to work well. (See the discussion of Britain in the box "A Tale of Three Countries.") The comparable analysis, with all the signs reversed, indicates that a revaluation (or appreciation after the government allows the country's currency to float) can be an appropriate policy response to surplus and inflation (the upper-right cell in Figure 22.9) because it can lower a surplus while reducing inflation pressure in the economy by decreasing demand and lowering the local-currency price of imports.

However, there are also times that a devaluation fails to reduce the external imbalance. One possible reason for failure is taken up in the next section—the value of the current account may not actually increase because of low responsiveness of export and import volumes to the exchange rate change. Another possible reason for failure is that the government pursues fiscal or monetary policies that themselves are driving to expand the deficit, and these are so strong that they overwhelm the benefits of the devaluation. For instance, expansionary monetary policy can expand income and import demand, and also increase the price level

---

[17]If the price level also rises as a result of the devaluation, the FE and IS curves do not shift as much, and the LM curve shifts up or to the left. This reduces the effect on the payments balance and on domestic product. In fact, if the price level rises by enough, there is no gain in competitiveness, and the benefits of devaluation on external and internal balance are lost.

through extra inflation so that the improved price competitiveness is lost. A third possible reason is that capital flows react in the "wrong" direction. For instance, a devaluation could lead to fears among international investors that the devaluation will not be successful in reducing the deficit (perhaps for one of the first two reasons). They then expect that another devaluation will be needed soon. Rising capital outflows (capital flight) could deteriorate the capital account and make the payments deficit bigger.

A key to much of this is how other government policies are used with the devaluation. If other government policies (especially monetary policy) can limit any increase in the country's price level or inflation rate, then the devaluation probably will improve the current account balance. International investors, seeing this, are less likely to fear that another devaluation will be needed. If the current account improves and the capital account does not deteriorate, then the devaluation will be successful in reducing the payments deficit.

How Well Does the Trade Balance Respond to Changes in the Exchange Rate?

According to the discussion in the preceding section, a change in the nominal exchange rate r should alter net exports, at least as long as it alters international price competitiveness. The conclusion is straightforward for effects on the *volumes* (or quantities) of exports and imports, although we can still wonder about the speed or magnitude of the changes. However, the effect on the *value* of the trade balance is not so obvious because both prices and volumes are changing. Yet, the effect on the value of net exports or current account is what matters for the country's balance of payments and for its FE curve.

Following a devaluation, consider the likely directions of change in a nation's trade quantities and trade prices (measured in foreign currency, here pounds), when its currency (here the dollar) drops in value:

CA (our current account balance, measured in £/year)	=	$P_x^£$	·	X	−	$P_m^£$	·	M

		£ Price of Exports	*Quantity of Exports*	*£ Price of Imports*	*Quantity of Imports*
Effects of a devaluation of the dollar	=	↓ No change or *down*	↑ · No change or *up*	↓ − No change or *down*	↓ · No change or *down*

As indicated in shorthand here, a dollar devaluation is likely to lower the pound price of exports (if it has any net effect on this price). This is because U.S. exporters are to some extent willing to lower pound prices while still receiving the same (or even higher) dollar prices because pounds are now worth more. If there is any effect of this price change on export quantities, the change is upward, as foreign buyers take advantage of any lower pound prices of U.S. exports to buy more from the United States. It is already clear that the net effect of devaluation on export value is of uncertain sign since pound prices probably drop and quantities exported probably rise. On the import side, any changes in either pound price or quantity are likely to be downward. The devaluation is likely to make *dollar* prices of imports look higher, causing a drop in import quantities as buyers shift toward U.S. substitutes for imports. If this drop in demand has any effect on the *pound* price of imports, that effect is likely to be negative. The sterling value of imports thus clearly drops, but if this value is to be subtracted from an export value that could rise or fall, it is still not clear whether the value of the net trade balance rises or falls. We need to know more about the underlying price elasticities of demand and supply in both the export and import markets.

How the Response Could Be Unstable

A drop in the value of the dollar (i.e., a rise in r, the price of foreign exchange) actually could worsen the trade balance. It would clearly do so in the case of *perfectly inelastic demand* curves for exports and imports. Suppose that buyers' habits are rigidly fixed so that they will not change the quantities they buy from any nation's suppliers despite changes in price. Examples might be the dependence of a non-tobacco-producing country on tobacco imports, or a similar addiction to tea or coffee, or to petroleum for fuels. In such cases of perfectly inelastic demand, devaluation of the country's currency backfires completely. Given the perfect inelasticity of import demand, no signals are sent to foreign suppliers by devaluing the dollar. Buyers go on buying the same amount of imports at the same pound price, paying a higher dollar price without cutting back their imports. No change in the foreign exchange value of imports results. On the export side, the devaluation leads suppliers to end up with the same competitive dollar price as before, but this price equals fewer pounds. U.S. exporters get fewer pounds for each bushel of wheat they export, yet foreigners do not respond to the lower price by buying any more wheat than they would otherwise.

In the case of perfectly inelastic demand curves for exports and imports, the changes in the current account are as follows:

$$CA^£ = P_x^£ \cdot X - P_m^£ \cdot M$$
$$down = (down \cdot no\ change) - (no\ change \cdot no\ change)$$

A numerical illustration of this case is given in Figure 22.13A. There, devaluing the dollar merely lowers the value of foreign exchange the United States earns on exports, from 80 (= 1.00×80) to 60 (= 0.75×80), worsening the trade balance.

It might seem that this perverse, or unstable, result hinges on something special about the export market. This is not the case, however. It only looks as

FIGURE 22.13

Devaluation Affects the Trade Balance

A. How Devaluation Could Worsen the Trade Balance

Exchange Rate	$P_x^£$	•	X	–	$P_m^£$	•	M	=	$CA^£$
Before dollar devaluation: $1.60/£	1.00	•	80	–	1.00	•	120	=	–40
After dollar devaluation: $2.00/£	0.75	•	80	–	1.00	•	120	=	–60

The key to this case: Demand curves are inelastic, so the volumes of exports and imports do not change. Devaluing our currency just lowers the value of foreign exchange we earn on exports, worsening the trade deficit.

B. The Small-Country Case

Exchange Rate	$P_x^£$	•	X	–	$P_m^£$	•	M	=	$CA^£$
Before dollar devaluation: $1.60/£	1.00	•	80	–	1.00	•	120	=	–40
After dollar devaluation: $2.00/£	1.00	•	105	–	1.00	•	100	=	+ 5

The small-country case illustrates the ability of high demand elasticities to guarantee that devaluation improves the trade balance. The essence of the small-country case is that foreign curves are infinitely elastic so the world (£) prices are not affected by our country's actions. On the export side, the infinite elasticity of foreign demand means that our own supply elasticity dictates what happens to the volume of exports (X). We probably export more, raising our earnings of foreign exchange. On the import side, the infinite elasticity of foreign supply means that our demand elasticity dictates what happens to volume (M). We probably import less, cutting our demand for foreign exchange.

Appendix G generalizes from such special cases, showing how larger demand elasticities raise the ability of devaluation to improve the trade balance.

though the change is confined to the export side because we are looking at the equation expressed in sterling. If we had looked at the CA equation in dollar prices, the deterioration would still appear:

$$CA^\$ = P_x^\$ \cdot X - P_m^\$ \cdot M$$
$$Down = (no\ change \cdot no\ change) - (up \cdot no\ change)$$

Why the Response Is Probably Stable

In all likelihood, however, a drop in the value of the home currency improves the current account balance, especially in the long run. The reason, basically, is that export and import demand elasticities end up being sufficiently high, and, as Appendix G proves, this is enough to ensure the stable response.

One quick way to see why the case of perfectly inelastic demand does not prevail is to note its strange implications. It implies, first, that we make it harder for ourselves to buy foreign goods with each unit of exports (i.e., $P_x^£/P_m^£$ drops), yet this impoverishing effect fails to get us to cut our spending on imports. The result looks even stranger upside down. It implies that a country could succeed in cutting its trade deficit and at the same time buy imports more cheaply (in terms of the export good) by cleverly *revaluing* its currency (for example, raising the value of the dollar from $1.60/£ to $1.00/£). If that were a common occurrence, governments would have discovered it long ago, and they would have solved their trade deficits by happily raising the values of their currencies.

Over the long run, price elasticities tend to be higher, and each nation tends to face elastic curves from the outside world, both the foreign demand curve for its exports and the foreign supply curve for its imports. In the extreme *small-country case,* the home country faces infinitely elastic foreign curves. Foreign-currency (£) prices are fixed, and the current account balance is affected by a drop in our currency as follows:

$$CA^£ = (P^£_x \cdot X) - (P^£_m \cdot M)$$
$$Up = (no\ change \cdot up) - (no\ change \cdot down)$$

We know that if the real volume of exports (X) changes, it will rise, because the same pound price of exports means more dollars per unit for sellers. They will respond to the new incentive with extra production and export sales. Similarly, we know that any change in the real volume of imports (M) will be a drop because the same pound price for imports leaves the dollar-country consumers with a higher dollar price. In the small-country case, both sides of the current account move in the right direction: Export revenues rise and import payments decline. Figure 22.13B provides a numerical illustration that underlines the contrast with the pessimistic case of Figure 22.13A. The crucial role of elasticities, illustrated in the two halves of Figure 22.13, also emerges from the technical formulas of Appendix G.

The fact that the elasticities of response to a given change (here, the devaluation or depreciation of the dollar) usually rise over time brings a second key result: *Devaluation is more likely to improve the trade balance, the longer the span of elapsed time.* The current account balance may dip for several months after a devaluation or depreciation of the home currency. The changes in prices are likely to occur faster than any changes in trade quantities. The changes in trade quantities at first are small because it takes time for buyers to respond to the price changes by altering their behavior. Contracts previously concluded must expire or be renegotiated, and alternative sources of products must be identified and evaluated. Eventually the quantity responses become larger, as buyers do switch to lower-priced products. As quantity effects become larger, the current account balance improves.

Figure 22.14 gives a schematic diagram of what economists think is a typical response of the current account balance to a drop in the home currency. The typical pattern is called a **J curve** because of its shape over the first couple of years of response to devaluation. The value of the current account at first deteriorates, but then begins to improve. After a moderate time period, perhaps about 18 months, the value of the current account returns to where it started, and thereafter it moves above its initial value. This analysis indicates that it may take some time for a large decrease in the exchange rate value of the country's currency to have a positive impact on the current account. The shift in the FE curve is more complicated than

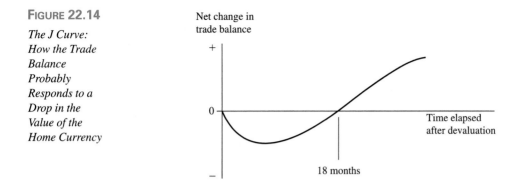

FIGURE 22.14

*The J Curve:
How the Trade
Balance
Probably
Responds to a
Drop in the
Value of the
Home Currency*

in the previous section. In the short run the FE curve could (perversely) shift to the left unless a capital inflow (perhaps based on the anticipation of the eventual beneficial effects of the devaluation) stabilizes the curve. Eventually the FE curve should shift to the right, but perhaps not until a year or more after the devaluation.

Summary

If a country has a fixed exchange rate, it must defend the fixed rate chosen. The first part of this chapter examined four major implications of having a fixed exchange rate and defending it using official intervention.

The first implication is that intervention to defend the fixed rate alters monetary conditions in the country. Faced with an external imbalance in the country's overall international payments, the central bank defends the fixed rate by buying or selling domestic currency in the foreign exchange market. The intervention changes the central bank's liabilities that serve as the base for the domestic money supply. The change in the domestic money supply then results in macroeconomic adjustments that tend to reduce the external imbalance. The domestic interest rate changes, altering international capital flows, at least in the short run. The change in real domestic product and income alters demand for imports. In addition, a change in the domestic price level can alter both exports and imports by changing the country's international price competitiveness.

The central bank can attempt to resist this monetary process through **sterilization**, which prevents the domestic money supply from changing. But there are limits to how long the central bank can use sterilized intervention to defend the fixed exchange rate. If the external imbalance continues, then the country's holdings of official reserves continue to change because the central bank is also selling or buying foreign currency as the other half of the intervention. Eventually the change in official reserve holdings forces the central bank to make some adjustment. For instance, if the central bank is selling foreign currency in its intervention, then eventually the central bank runs low on its holdings of official reserves.

The second implication is that a fixed exchange rate and its defense constrain a country's ability to pursue an independent monetary policy. If the country begins with an external deficit, the defense of the fixed rate eventually forces the country to contract its money supply. If the country begins with an external surplus, the defense of the fixed rate eventually forces the country to expand its money supply. If the country begins with an external balance, then any change in monetary policy and the money supply would create an external imbalance, and the intervention to defend the fixed rate would tend to reverse the monetary change.

The third implication is that the effects of fiscal policy are also altered by a fixed exchange rate. A change in fiscal policy causes the country's current and capital accounts to change in opposite directions in the short run, so the effect on the overall payments balance depends on how large the two changes are. If international financial capital flows are not that responsive to interest rate changes, then the resulting external imbalance following a fiscal policy change leads to intervention that changes monetary conditions in the other direction, reducing the effect of the fiscal policy change on domestic product. If international capital flows are sufficiently responsive, the resulting external imbalance leads to intervention that changes monetary conditions in the same direction, enhancing the effect of fiscal policy on real product. In the extreme case of **perfect capital mobility,** the fiscal change can have the full spending multiplier effect because the domestic interest rate remains unchanged and equal to the foreign interest rate. (However, with perfect capital mobility the country has *no* independent monetary policy.)

The fourth implication is that defending a fixed exchange rate without sterilization alters how different exogenous shocks affect the country's macroeconomy in the short run. The effects of **domestic monetary shocks** are greatly reduced without sterilization. The effects of **domestic spending shocks** on domestic product depend on how responsive international financial capital flows are to changes in the interest rate. If international capital is more responsive, a domestic spending shock has more effect.

International capital-flow shocks can have major effects on the domestic economy because they require intervention to defend the fixed rate as the shock hits. For instance, a shift to capital outflow leads to intervention that results in a lower domestic money supply.

Domestic interest rates tend to increase, and domestic product and income tend to decline.

International trade shocks affect the economy directly by changing aggregate demand. In addition, the resulting intervention to defend the fixed exchange rate causes a monetary change that generally reinforces the change in demand, resulting in a larger change in domestic product and income.

The second part of the chapter examined broad policy issues for countries that have fixed exchange rates. A country wants to achieve both internal and external balance. Yet, stabilizing an open macroeconomy with a fixed exchange rate is not easy. If a country has only one policy for influencing aggregate demand (for instance, monetary policy that changes the money supply), it would have to be very lucky for the level of aggregate demand that is best for the domestic economy to turn out to be the one that keeps external payments in balance. One way out of the dilemma was proposed by Robert Mundell and J. Marcus Fleming. They noted that expansionary monetary and fiscal policies have opposite effects on domestic interest rates. The difference can be used to influence international capital flows in the short run.

This means that monetary policy has a comparative advantage in affecting the external balance, whereas fiscal policy has a comparative advantage in affecting the domestic economy. We can thus devise a monetary–fiscal mix to deal with any pairing of imbalances in the external accounts and the domestic economy, as shown in Figure 22.11.

When policymakers cannot confidently estimate the positions of the curves, they can still follow a simpler **assignment rule** with fair chances of at least approaching the desired combination of internal and external balance. When policies are adjusted smoothly and take quick effect, internal and external balance can be reached by assigning the internal task to fiscal policy and the external task to monetary policy.

Faced with a large or continuing external imbalance, a country's government may decide to react by surrendering—by changing the exchange rate: devaluing, revaluing, or shifting to a floating exchange rate that immediately depreciates or appreciates. A change in the exchange rate can reduce the external imbalance by altering the country's international price competitiveness. Changes in exports and imports alter the current account balance. The exchange rate change also has an impact on internal balance. The export and import changes alter aggregate demand, and the change in the domestic prices of imported goods can alter the country's general price level or inflation rate.

However, it is not certain that the exchange rate change actually does reduce the external imbalance. The effect on the value of the current account balance depends on changes in both the volumes (quantities) and prices of exports and imports. Consider a devaluation. Measured in foreign currency, the price of exportable prod-

ucts tends to decrease, the quantity of exports tends to increase, and the price and quantity of imports tend to decrease. The value of exports could increase or decrease. If the value of exports decreases, the current account balance only improves if the decline in the value of imports is larger. A general condition that ensures that the current account balance improves is that the price elasticities of demand for exports and imports be sufficiently high so that the changes in the volumes of exports and imports are large enough. In practice, the price effects, especially the decrease in the foreign-currency price of exports, often occurs quickly, while the volume effects occur more slowly but eventually become sufficiently large. The current account balance thus deteriorates at first, but after a period of months it tends to improve, tracing out a pattern called the **J curve.**

Suggested Reading

A technical treatment of the economics of fixed exchange rates is presented in Rivera-Batiz and Rivera-Batiz (1994, Chapter 14). Some of Robert Mundell's pioneering articles on internal and external balance and the implications of international capital mobility are reprinted in Mundell (1968, Chapters 16 and 18). The same path-breaking analysis was simultaneously developed by Fleming (1962).

Fieleke (1994) discusses the purposes and activities of the International Monetary Fund. Feldstein (1998) provides a critique of IMF programs for the Asian-crisis countries. Aylward and Thorne (1998) present statistical analysis of countries that are overdue in repaying loans from the IMF. Kamin (1988) reviews the effects of nearly 100 instances of currency devaluations since the early 1950s.

Questions and Problems

✦1. "A country with a deficit in its overall international payments runs the risk of increasing inflation if it defends its fixed exchange rate by (unsterilized) official intervention in the foreign exchange market." Do you agree or disagree? Why?

2. A country with a fixed exchange rate has achieved external balance. Government spending then increases in an effort to reduce unemployment. What is the effect of this policy change on the country's official settlements balance? If the central bank uses

unsterilized intervention to defend the fixed rate, will intervention tend to reduce the expansionary effect of the fiscal policy?

✦3. What does perfect capital mobility mean for the effectiveness of monetary and fiscal policies under fixed exchange rates?

4. What is the assignment rule? What are its possible advantages and drawbacks?

✦5. "According to the logic of the J-curve analysis, a country that revalues its currency should have an improvement in the value of its current account in the months immediately after the revaluation." Do you agree or disagree? Why?

6. The Pugelovian central bank intervenes in the foreign exchange market by selling U.S. $10 billion to prevent the Pugelovian currency (the pnut) from depreciating.

   a. What impact does this have on the Pugelovian holdings of official international reserves?

   b. What effect will this have on the Pugelovian money supply if the central bank does not sterilize? Explain.

   c. What effect will this have on the Pugelovian money supply if the central bank does sterilize (using an open market operation in Pugelovian government bonds)? Explain.

✦7. A country initially has achieved both external balance and internal balance. International financial capital is reasonably mobile, so the country's FE curve is upward sloping (and flatter than the LM curve). The country has a fixed exchange rate and defends it using official intervention. The country does not sterilize. As a result of the election of a new government, foreign investors become bullish on the country. International financial capital inflows increase dramatically and remain higher for a number of years.

   a. What shift occurs in the FE curve because of the increased capital inflows?

   b. What intervention is necessary to defend the fixed exchange rate?

   c. As a result of the intervention, how does the country adjust back to external balance? Illustrate this using an IS–LM–FE graph. What is the effect of all of this on the country's internal balance?

8. A country initially has achieved both external balance and internal balance. The country prohibits international financial capital inflows and outflows, so its capital account

(excluding official reserves transactions) is always zero because of these capital controls. The country has a fixed exchange rate and defends it using official intervention. The country does not sterilize. An exogenous shock now occurs—foreign demand for the country's exports increases.

   a. What is the slope of the country's FE curve?

   b. What shifts occur in the IS, LM, or FE curves because of the increase in foreign demand for the country's exports?

   c. What intervention is necessary to defend the fixed exchange rate?

   d. As a result of the intervention, how does the country adjust back to external balance? Illustrate this using an IS–LM–FE graph. What is the effect of all of this on the country's internal balance?

✦9. What is the mixture of monetary and fiscal policies that can cure each of the following imbalances?

   a. Rising inflation and overall payments deficit (e.g., point *H* in Figure 22.11).

   b. Rising inflation and overall payments surplus (e.g., point *F* in Figure 22.11).

   c. Insufficient aggregate demand and overall payments surplus (e.g., point *C* in Figure 22.11).

10. The Pugelovian government has just devalued the Pugelovian currency by 10 percent. For each of the following, will this devaluation improve the Pugelovian current account deficit? Explain each.

   a. People are very fixed in their habits. Both Pugelovian importers and foreign buyers of Pugelovian exports buy the same physical volumes no matter what.

   b. Pugelovian firms keep the Pugelovian pnut prices of Pugelovian exports constant, and foreign firms keep the foreign-currency prices of exports to Pugelovia constant.

CHAPTER 23

Floating Exchange Rates and Internal Balance

One way to reconcile the goals of external balance and internal balance is to let the exchange rate take care of external balance and to direct macroeconomic policy toward the problem of internal balance. If the exchange rate is allowed to float cleanly, without government intervention, then the exchange rate changes to achieve external balance. If there are no transactions in official reserves, then the official settlements balance must be zero, and the exchange rate must change to whatever value is needed to achieve this external balance. Changes in the exchange rate are the "automatic" mechanism for adjusting to achieve external balance.

Even if a floating exchange rate is used to achieve external balance, this still leaves the problem of achieving internal balance. How does use of floating exchange rates affect the behavior of the economy and the effectiveness of monetary and fiscal policies that might be directed to achieving internal balance? The purpose of this chapter is to examine the macroeconomics of floating exchange rates. It first examines how monetary policy and fiscal policy work in an economy that has a floating exchange rate. Then it explores the impacts of various shocks on such an economy. The shocks are the same types that we examined in Chapter 22, so we can see how the choice of fixed or flexible exchange rates alters how the economy responds to different shocks.

In our analysis of floating exchange rates, we use the same basic model of the open macroeconomy that we developed in Chapter 21 and applied to fixed rates in Chapter 22. The key difference from the previous chapter is that the exchange rate r is now a variable determined endogenously by the macroeconomic system rather than a rate set (and defended) by the government. With a floating rate, the exchange rate brings the foreign exchange market (or the overall balance of payments) into equilibrium, as was the case in most of Part III, by affecting peoples' choices about whether to buy goods and services abroad or at home and whether to invest in this country's financial assets or another country's financial assets.

The impact on demand for goods and services then has a feedback effect on the country's domestic product.

The analysis of how a country with a floating exchange rate responds to a policy change or another type of economic shock can usefully proceed through three steps:

1. At the initial value of the exchange rate, what are the effects of the shock on the country's economy? In particular, does the shock push the official settlements balance away from a zero value?

2. If there is a tendency away from zero for the official settlements balance, what change in the exchange rate value of the country's currency (appreciation or depreciation) is needed to move back to a zero balance?

3. What are the additional effects on the country's macroeconomy of this change in the exchange rate?

The additional effects indicate the "special" ways in which floating rates alter the behavior of the economy (just as the additional effects resulting from intervention to defend the fixed rate indicated the "special" ways in which fixed rates alter the behavior of the economy). The additional effects show how floating rates alter the effectiveness of government policies. They also suggest how floating rates alter the country's ability to keep internal balance in a changing world.

Monetary Policy with Floating Exchange Rates

With floating or flexible exchange rates, monetary policy exerts a strong influence over domestic product and income. To see how, let us consider the case of a deliberate expansion of the domestic money supply. Such a change is implemented by using a domestic tool of monetary policy. For instance, the country's monetary authority might use open market operations to buy domestic securities. As the monetary authority pays for its securities purchase, it issues new liabilities that expand money in the economy.

An expansion of the money supply increases banks' willingness to lend, and interest rates decrease. Borrowing and spending rise. As we saw in Chapter 22, the drop in interest rates tends to worsen the overall balance of payments in the short run. The capital account tends to worsen as capital flows out of the country, and the current account worsens as imports rise. The demand for foreign currency is now greater than the supply. In the fixed-rate analysis of Chapter 22, the government had to intervene to defend the fixed rate against the pressure resulting from this payments deficit. With floating exchange rates, the pressure results in a depreciation of the exchange rate value of the country's currency (foreign currencies rise in value), as summarized in Figure 23.1.

Depreciation of our currency increases the international price competitiveness of the products produced by our country's firms (assuming that the nominal depreciation is larger than any increase in domestic prices and costs in the short run—a form of overshooting like that discussed in Chapter 19). The improve-

FIGURE 23.1   *Effects of Expanding the Money Supply with Floating Exchange Rates*

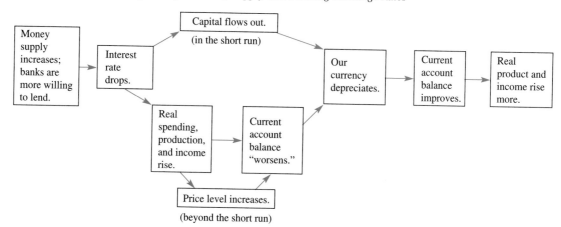

For a decrease in the money supply, reverse the direction of all changes.

ment in our firms' ability to compete with foreign firms is likely to improve our current account balance, as export volumes increase and import volumes decline. (Improvement in the current account balance occurs only after the initial stage of the J-curve has played itself out. This assumes that the stability conditions of Chapter 22 and Appendix G eventually hold. In this chapter we focus on situations in which the response is stable.)

The improvement in the current account balance lowers the overall payments deficit, reducing and eventually eliminating pressure for further depreciation of the exchange rate value of our currency. External balance is restored through the exchange rate change.

The new competitive edge for the country's firms raises aggregate demand for what the country produces. Such extra demand due to the depreciation augments the direct domestic effects of the increase in the money supply. Due to the extra demand, real domestic product and income may rise even more. However, the depreciation may also enhance the effects of monetary policy on the price level and inflation rate as well. The depreciation results in higher domestic prices for imported products, and the extra demand can create general upward pressure on prices.

Thus, under floating exchange rates, monetary policy is powerful in its effects on internal balance. The induced change in the exchange rate reinforces the standard domestic effects of monetary policy. Monetary policy gains power under floating exchange rates, whereas, as we saw in the previous chapter, it loses power under fixed exchange rates.

This general conclusion holds whatever the degree of capital mobility. Whatever the degree, expanding the money supply causes a depreciation, and this further expands aggregate demand. Consider, for instance, perfect capital mobility. Capital flows respond to both interest rates and the expected change in the

FIGURE 23.2

*Expansionary
Monetary
Policy with
Floating
Exchange Rates*

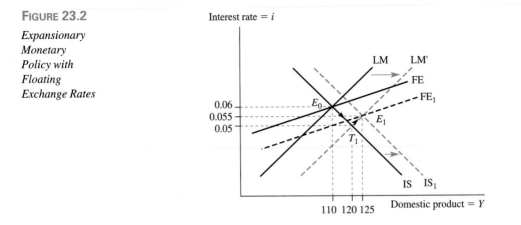

Starting from point E_0 with an overall payments balance of zero, the country implements an expansionary policy. The LM curve shifts down or to the right, but at point T_1 the payments balance tends toward deficit. The country's currency depreciates, and the FE and IS curves shift to the right, reestablishing external balance at E_1.

exchange rate into the future. Perfect capital mobility implies that uncovered interest parity always holds, because nearly unlimited flows of international financial capital occur if there is any deviation from this parity.[1] The overshooting discussed in Chapter 19 is a form of perfect capital mobility. There we saw that if a monetary expansion reduced the domestic interest rate, the exchange rate value of the country's currency would depreciate immediately by a large amount. The overshooting results in a large improvement in the country's international price competitiveness in the short and medium runs.

We can see the effects of monetary policy in the IS–LM–FE picture used in the previous two chapters. Consider a country that begins with external balance— a triple intersection shown as point E_0 in Figure 23.2. The country's central bank now uses a domestic change (such as an open market purchase of domestic securities) to expand the domestic money supply, and the LM curve shifts down to LM'. Even if the exchange rate value of the domestic currency were unchanged, the direct domestic effects of this policy change reduce the domestic interest rate from 6 percent to 5 percent and increase real domestic product from 110 to 120. In addition, the country's balance of payments tends to go into deficit. (The intersection of LM' and the original IS curve at point T_1 is to the right of the initial FE curve.) The country's currency depreciates in the foreign exchange market. As the country's price competitiveness improves, exports increase and imports decrease. The current account balance improves, so the FE curve shifts to the right and the IS

---

[1]For the fixed-rate analysis of Chapter 22, perfect capital mobility also implied uncovered interest parity, but the expected change in the exchange rate was assumed to be approximately zero if investors expected the fixed rate to hold into the future. With no change expected in the fixed rate, uncovered interest parity means that the domestic interest rate is equal to the foreign interest rate.

FIGURE 23.3   *Effects of Expansionary Fiscal Policy with Floating Exchange Rates*

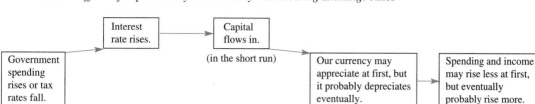

For contractionary fiscal policy, reverse the direction of all changes.

curve shifts to the right. If the floating exchange rate adjusts to maintain external balance (a zero balance in the country's official settlements balance), then the economy will be at a triple intersection of all three curves after the exchange rate has adjusted. The new triple intersection is point E_1. Because of the depreciation, real GDP increases even more, to 125. Monetary policy is powerful in affecting real GDP in the short run under floating exchange rates.[2]

Fiscal Policy with Floating Exchange Rates

How fiscal policy works with floating exchange rates is a little more complicated. Fiscal policy can affect exchange rates in either direction, as shown in Figure 23.3. The left side of the figure shows the same effects of expansionary policy as we saw in Chapter 22. The fiscal expansion bids up domestic interest rates as the government borrows more. Higher domestic interest rates tend to attract capital from abroad, at least temporarily. Meanwhile, aggregate spending, product, and income are raised by higher government spending and/or lower tax rates. This raises imports and worsens the current account balance. So there are two opposing tendencies for the country's overall balance of payments and thus for the exchange rate value of the country's currency. The interest rate rise tends to draw a capital inflow that strengthens the

---

[2]The monetary expansion and the induced depreciation are also likely to increase the domestic price level through inflation, especially beyond the short run. If the domestic price level increases, then the LM curve shifts back up (or does not shift down by as much in the first place). The higher domestic price level reverses some of the gain in international price competitiveness, so the FE and IS curves also shift back (or do not shift by as much in the first place). The increase in real GDP is not as large. Indeed, in the long run, the currency depreciation will be exactly offset by the higher price level if money is neutral in the long run and purchasing power parity holds.

FIGURE 23.4

*Expansionary
Fiscal Policy
with Floating
Exchange Rates*

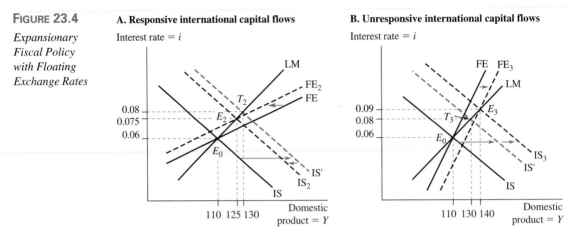

Expansionary fiscal policy shifts the IS curve to the right, and the IS–LM intersection shifts from E_0 to T_2 or T_3 initially. The effects of fiscal policy depend on how strongly international capital flows respond to the interest rate increase. In panel A, the overall payments balance tends toward surplus. (T_2 is to the left of FE.) In panel B, the overall payments balance tends toward deficit. (T_3 is to the right of FE.) In either case the payments imbalance leads to a change in the exchange rate. In panel A, the country's currency appreciates, and the FE and IS curves shift to the left, reestablishing external balance at E_2. In panel B, the country's currency depreciates, and the FE and IS curves shift to the right, reestablishing external balance at E_3. Here we assume that the LM curve does not move, because the central bank can keep the money supply steady if it doesn't need to defend a fixed exchange rate.

country's currency, but the rise in aggregate demand and imports weakens it. Which tendency will prevail? There is no firm answer. If capital is mobile internationally, then the capital inflow effect at first is probably large enough to appreciate the country's currency. Eventually the aggregate-demand effect is probably stronger and longer lasting, so eventually the currency depreciates.[3]

The "feedback" effects on the domestic economy depend on which way the exchange rate changes. If the country's currency at first appreciates, then the country loses price competitiveness. The country's exports decline and its imports increase. The decline in the country's current account reduces the expansionary effects of the fiscal change on the country's domestic product. That is, the expansionary effect is reduced by "international crowding out"—the appreciation of the country's currency and the resulting decline in the current account. If the country's currency instead (or eventually) depreciates, the enhanced price competitiveness and resulting increase in the current account give a further trade-based stimulus to domestic production.

The effects of fiscal expansion can be pictured using an IS–LM–FE graph. Figure 23.4 shows the two cases possible. In both cases the economy begins at the triple intersection E_0. The fiscal expansion directly shifts the IS curve to IS',

---

[3]The extreme case of perfect capital mobility is also consistent with this pattern. The initial interest rate increase leads to an immediate appreciation of the domestic currency. The exchange rate overshoots so that the currency is expected subsequently to depreciate slowly. Uncovered interest rate parity is reestablished because the interest differential in favor of the country is offset by the expected depreciation.

increasing the domestic interest rate from 6 percent to 8 percent and boosting domestic product from 110 to 130.

The two cases differ by whether the country's overall payments balance tends to go into surplus or deficit. The left graph in Figure 23.4 shows the case of a tendency to surplus because the capital inflow effect is larger. In this graph the incipient payments surplus is shown by the IS'–LM intersection to the left of the initial FE curve. The country's currency appreciates, the current account balance worsens, and the FE and IS curves shift to the left. The new triple intersection is at point E_2. Because of the currency appreciation, domestic product declines somewhat from 130 to 125 (or does not rise as much from its initial value of 110). International crowding out reduces the expansionary thrust of the fiscal change.[4]

The right graph in Figure 23.4 shows the case of a tendency to deficit, because the aggregate-demand effect is larger—the IS'–LM intersection is to the right of the initial FE curve. The country's currency depreciates, the current account balance improves, and the FE and IS curves shift to the right. The new triple intersection is at point E_3. Because of the currency depreciation, domestic product rises to 140 rather than 130.

The large U.S. fiscal expansion implemented in the early 1980s illustrates the nature and timing of the effects of a change in fiscal policy under floating exchange rates. The box "U.S. Deficits: Twins or Cousins?" discusses the U.S. experience.

Shocks to the Economy

Major shocks occasionally strike a country's economy. What are the effects of these exogenous changes on a country that has a floating exchange rate? We will look at the same shocks that we examined in Chapter 22 for a country with a fixed exchange rate so that we can contrast the results.

Internal Shocks

Domestic monetary shocks affect the equilibrium relationship between money supply and money demand, causing a shift in the LM curve. A change in the country's monetary policy is an example of such a shock. As we saw in the analysis of expansionary monetary policy, domestic monetary shocks have powerful effects on an economy with a floating exchange rate. If the monetary shock tends to expand the economy, then the exchange rate value of the country's currency tends to depreciate, further increasing domestic product (or putting additional upward pressure on the country's price level or inflation rate). If the

---

[4]If the fiscal expansion causes the price level to increase, then the LM curve also shifts up, and both the FE and IS curves shift to the left somewhat (or do not shift as much to the right) as a result of some loss of international price competitiveness due to the higher domestic prices. For either of the two cases discussed here in the text, these additional shifts reduce the amount by which real domestic product increases from its initial value of 110.

U.S. Deficits: Twins or Cousins?

The performance of the U.S. economy since 1980 dramatically shows the effects of government policies for a country that has a floating exchange rate. In the early 1980s, a major shift in U.S. fiscal policy resulted in a large increase in the government budget deficit. This seemed to be closely related to a large appreciation of the U.S. dollar and a large deterioration in the U.S. trade balance. The experience is usually summarized as the "twin deficits." But are they really twins?

The accompanying figure shows the U.S. government budget deficit (as a percentage of U.S. GDP, to make the sizes more comparable over time), the U.S. deficit in goods and services trade (also as a percentage of U.S. GDP), and the real effective exchange rate value of the dollar (to indicate the exchange rate value of the dollar in a way that shows changes over time in the international price competitiveness of U.S. products).

Let's begin our story in the late 1970s. The United States had relatively small government budget deficits (actually small surpluses in 1978 and 1979) and small deficits in goods and services trade. Major changes began about 1981. The first change was a tightening of U.S. monetary policy, and the dollar began to appreciate. This tightening was relaxed in 1982 as the U.S. inflation rate declined to about 4 percent.

The second change was the important one for our story. In 1981, the Reagan administration sought and obtained a major change in U.S. fiscal policy, reducing U.S. taxes, while government expenditures continued to grow. The government budget deficit increased to over 4 percent of GDP, remaining high through 1986. The trade deficit also rose, reaching over 3 percent of GDP and remaining high through 1987. In the second half of the 1980s, both deficits fell. Thus, during the 1980s, the deficits appeared to be twins—or at least very closely related.

Our model provides insight into these relationships. Expansionary fiscal policy shifts the IS curve to the right, increasing both U.S. interest rates and U.S. national income. The rise in income alone tends to increase the trade deficit, but not by nearly as much as we actually saw (given that the U.S. marginal propensity to import is not that high). The additional effect comes from the relatively high U.S. interest rates, which draw capital inflows. The real value of the dollar increases. This large increase in the real value of the dollar greatly reduces U.S. price competitiveness. With a lag of about a year and a half (recall the J-curve), the trade balance begins to deteriorate.

In 1985, the U.S. trade deficit became so large, and the real value of the dollar climbed so high, that international investors became worried. Capital inflows slowed down, so the trade deficit became an important driver of the exchange rate value of the dollar. The dollar began to depreciate in early 1985. (In September, the governments of the major countries announced an agreement to reinforce this depreciation by intervening if necessary to ensure the decline.) The real value of the dollar fell from 1985 through 1988, returning to about its value in 1980. With a somewhat longer lag of about two years, the trade balance responded to this improvement in U.S. price competitiveness.

Were the government budget deficit and the trade deficit really twins? Even in the early 1980s, they were not exactly twins—they did not correlate precisely. The government budget deficit increased before the trade deficit increased. U.S. experience since 1988 suggests that the deficits were not twins, but rather cousins, and perhaps distant cousins at that.

monetary shock tends to contract the economy, then the country's currency tends to appreciate, decreasing domestic product.

Domestic spending shocks alter domestic expenditure, causing a shift in the IS curve. A change in fiscal policy is an example. As we saw for fiscal policy, the effect of this kind of shock on the exchange rate depends on which changes more: international capital flows or the country's current account.

Between 1988 and 1992, the government budget deficit increased while the trade deficit decreased. Since 1992, the government budget deficit declined steadily, becoming a surplus toward the end of the 1990s. The trade deficit has been relatively steady at a little less than 1 percent of GDP, and the real exchange rate value of the dollar was also relatively steady from 1988 to 1996. (The real appreciation of the dollar in the late 1990s had not yet had much impact on the trade balance, as of mid-1998.)

Why are the deficits only cousins? We benefit by returning to the accounting for balance of payments and national income from Chapter 15. Recall that national saving can be used for either domestic real investment or foreign investment. National saving itself is comprised of private saving and government saving. (A deficit is government dissaving.) If the relationship between private domestic saving and domestic real investment is steady, then the govern-

ment budget deficit will closely track the trade deficit (which roughly equals borrowing from foreigners, negative foreign investment). For much of the 1980s, the relationship between domestic private saving and domestic real investment was rather steady so the deficits appeared to be twins. But since 1988, the paths of private domestic saving and domestic real investment have diverged. During the 1990–1991 recession, domestic real investment declined by a large amount, more than private domestic saving declined. Since 1992, domestic real investment has grown strongly, while growth of private domestic saving has been weak. As a result, the close relationship between the government budget deficit and the trade deficit has been severed. The two deficits appeared to be twins during the 1980s, when changes in fiscal policy were the driving force behind them. But they were barely related during the 1990s, when private domestic saving and domestic real investment diverged.

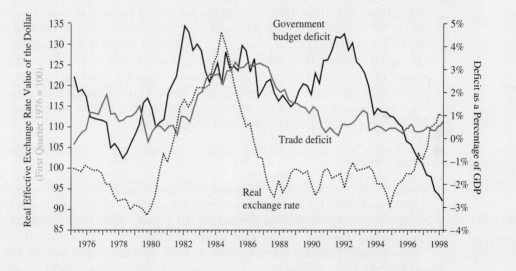

Source: J. P. Morgan & Co., Incorporated; IMF, *International Financial Statistics; Economic Report of the President 1995 and 1999; Survey of Current Business,* July 1990 and July 1991; and *National Income and Product Accounts, 1959–88.*

International Capital-Flow Shocks

Shocks to international capital flows occur because of changes in investors' perceptions of economic and political conditions in various countries. For instance, an adverse international capital-flow shock, leading to a capital outflow from our country, can occur because foreign interest rates increase, because investors shift to expecting more depreciation of our currency in the future, or because investors fear negative changes in our country's politics or policies.

The shift leads to a capital outflow. The outflow puts downward pressure on the exchange rate value of the country's currency, and the currency depreciates. The depreciation improves the international price competitiveness of the country's products. Our exports increase, and our imports decrease, improving the country's current account. The extra demand tends to increase our domestic product.

The effects of this shock are pictured in Figure 23.5. The economy begins at point E_0, a triple intersection. The adverse international capital-flow shock causes the FE curve to shift to the left to FE'. The country's overall payments balance tends to go into deficit, as the intersection of the (initially unchanged) IS–LM curves at E_0 is below FE'. The country's currency depreciates, shifting the FE and IS curves to the right. A new triple intersection occurs at point E_4, with domestic product and the interest rate higher.

Thus, under floating exchange rates external capital-flow shocks can have effects on internal balance, by altering the exchange rate and the country's international price competitiveness. Interestingly, an adverse shock tends to expand the domestic economy by depreciating the country's currency. We probably should add several cautions about this result. First, the reason for the capital-flow shift is important. If capital is flowing out because of political or economic problems in the country, then these problems may cause the economy to contract even though the exchange rate depreciation is pushing in the other direction. Second, the capital outflow may disrupt domestic financial markets in ways that go beyond our basic analysis. Any disruptions in domestic financial markets may harm the broader domestic economy, also tending to contract it. It is probably risky to conclude, on the basis of the simpler analysis, that an adverse capital-flow shock is simply good for the country's economy.

International Trade Shocks

Shocks to international trade flows cause the value of the country's current account balance to change. For instance, an adverse international trade shock might occur because of a decline in foreign demand for our exports, an increase in our taste for imported products, or a decline in the supply of an important import such as oil.

An adverse international trade shock reduces both the current account and the country's domestic product and income.[5] As the current account worsens, the overall payments balance tends to go into deficit, and the country's currency depreciates. The improvement in price competitiveness leads to an increase in the country's exports and a decline in imports. The current account improves and domestic product and income rise. If all of this happens with no change in international capital flows, then the currency must depreciate enough to completely reverse the deterioration in the current account, putting the overall payments balance back to zero.

---

[5]We presume that the current account does actually decline. The shock itself worsens the current account. The decline in national income lowers demand for imports, but we assume that this is not enough to reverse the deterioration of the current account. In Figure 23.6, page 540, this assumption ensures that the new IS'–LM intersection at T_5 is to the left of the new FE', even if the FE curve is steeper than the LM curve.

FIGURE 23.5

*An Adverse
International
Capital-Flow
Shock*

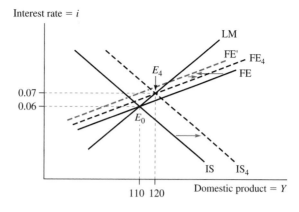

A shift of international capital flows away from the country causes the FE curve to shift up or to the left, and the overall payments balance tends toward deficit. The country's currency depreciates, and the FE and IS curves shift to the right, reestablishing external balance at E_4. Here again we assume that the LM curve does not shift, because the central bank can keep the money supply steady.

Figure 23.6 shows the effects of this adverse international trade shock. The shock causes the FE and IS curves to shift to the left. The intersection of IS' with LM at T_5 is below the new FE'. The country's currency depreciates, resulting in shifts back to the right in the FE and IS curves. If nothing else changes (such as international capital flows or the domestic price level), then the curves shift back to their original positions, and the new triple intersection is back to E_0.[6]

With floating exchange rates, the effects of international trade shocks on internal balance are mitigated by the effects of the resulting change in the exchange rate. An adverse trade shock tends to depreciate the country's currency, and this reverses some of the effects of the shock. By reversing all of the directions of change, we would also conclude that a positive trade shock appreciates the country's currency, reversing both the improvement in the country's current account balance and the increase in demand for the country's domestic product.

Internal Imbalance and Policy Responses

Shocks to the economy alter both the international performance of the country's economy and its domestic performance. With floating exchange rates a change in the exchange rate takes care of achieving external balance following a shock. If the country's overall payments tend to go into deficit, then the country's currency depreciates, reversing the tendency toward deficit. If the country's overall payments tend to surplus, then appreciation reverses the tendency to surplus.

---

[6]The depreciation of the currency may put some upward pressure on the country's price level by increasing the domestic-currency price of imported products. If the overall domestic price level increases, then the LM curve shifts up somewhat, and the new triple intersection will still result in some decline in domestic product. Nonetheless, the decline is less than what would occur without the currency depreciation.

FIGURE 23.6

*An Adverse
International
Trade Shock*

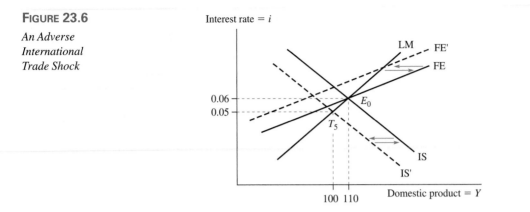

A shift of international trade away from the country's products causes the FE and IS curves to shift to the left, and the overall payments balance tends toward deficit. The country's currency depreciates, and the FE and IS curves shift back to the right. Here, to simplify the diagram, we imagine the case in which external balance is reestablished at E_0.

A floating exchange rate does not ensure that the country achieves internal balance, but changes in the floating rate do affect the country's internal balance. A depreciation tends to expand the country's economy. If the country begins with excessive unemployment before the exchange rate change, then the expansionary thrust of the depreciation is welcome, as it reduces the internal imbalance. If the country instead begins with internal balance or with an inflation rate that is rising or too high, then the expansionary thrust of the depreciation will create or add to the internal inflationary imbalance.

An appreciation tends to contract the country's economy. If the economy begins with inflationary pressure, then this may be welcome. But if the economy is already in or tending toward a recession with excessive unemployment, then the exchange rate change adds to the internal imbalance.

Government monetary or fiscal policy can be used to address any internal imbalances that do arise. If excessive unemployment is the internal imbalance, then expansionary monetary or fiscal policy can be used. The size of the change in policy needed to address the imbalance depends on the change in the exchange rate that will occur. Monetary policy is powerful with floating exchange rates, so a relatively small change may be enough to reestablish internal balance. The power of fiscal policy is more variable and may be difficult to predict if it is difficult to predict the appreciation or depreciation of the exchange rate following the fiscal change.

International Macroeconomic Policy Coordination

The policies adopted by one country have effects on other countries. With floating exchange rates these spillover effects happen in several ways, including foreign income repercussions as changes in incomes alter demands for imports, and changes in international price competitiveness as floating exchange rates change.

Financial Times, April 21, 1995. Picture: Reuters.

One danger is that a policy change that benefits the country making it can harm other countries. For instance, a shift to expansionary monetary policy causes the currencies of other countries to appreciate. This can appear to be a beggar-thy-neighbor policy in that the first country benefits from increased growth, but the exchange rate appreciation can harm the price competitiveness and trade of other countries.

Another danger is that each country acting individually may fail to make a policy change whose benefits mostly go to other countries. If a number of countries could coordinate so that they all make this policy change, all would reap substantial benefits. For example, following the nearly global stock market crash of October 1987, the global financial system needed additional liquidity to counteract the decline in banking and financial activity. If any one central bank added liquidity, the rest of the global system would benefit, probably more than the individual country would. Each individual central bank might be slow to act, or reluctant to add liquidity aggressively, on its own. Fortunately, several central banks coordinated their actions to inject liquidity, and the financial markets stabilized.

Given these spillover effects and interdependencies, it seems that it should be possible to improve global macroeconomic performance through international cooperation and international coordination. International policy cooperation refers to such activities as sharing of information about each country's performance, problems, and policies. Sharing of information occurs in many places, including high-level meetings of national finance ministers and heads of state as well as international organizations such as the International Monetary Fund and the Bank for International Settlements. International cooperation of this sort is not controversial.

International macroeconomic policy coordination is more than this. It is the joint determination of several countries' macroeconomic policies to improve joint performance. It implies the ability of one country to influence the policies of other countries and the willingness of a country to alter its policies to benefit

Can Governments Manage the Float?

Floating exchange rates allow a country to achieve external balance while maintaining control over its money supply and monetary policy. But floating exchange rates are also highly variable, more variable than we expected when many countries shifted to floating rates in 1973.

Governments that have chosen floating exchange rates worry about the large amount of variability, and nearly all manage the float to some extent. Some governments manage their floating rates closely. If the floating exchange rate is heavily managed, then it behaves more like a fixed exchange rate, and the analysis of the previous chapter is relevant. Other governments, including the governments of most major countries that have chosen floating rates, use management selectively. Occasionally the government intervenes in the foreign exchange market.

Is selective or occasional intervention effective in influencing exchange rates? Fifteen years ago the conventional wisdom was clear. If the intervention is not sterilized, then it can be effective. However, it is effective not because it is intervention but rather because it changes the money supply. Unsterilized intervention is simply another way to implement a change in the domestic money supply and monetary policy. By changing the money supply, it can have a substantial effect on the exchange rate. If the intervention is sterilized, the conventional wisdom was that it would not be effective in changing the exchange rate, at least not much or for long. Yet, interventions by the U.S. monetary authorities are fully sterilized. The Japanese and European authorities claim that they routinely sterilize their interventions—and they do to a large extent but probably not fully.

The conventional wisdom was based on a number of studies that showed little effect of sterilized intervention. Perhaps most dramatically, Taylor (1982) studied the profitability of foreign exchange intervention in the 1970s and concluded that central banks generally incurred losses. These losses suggested that intervention was ineffective. The central banks were buying currencies in an effort to enhance the exchange rate values of these currencies, but the

losses indicate that the values subsequently fell. Other studies completed in the early 1980s also concluded that the effects of sterilized interventions were at most small and transitory.

The conventional wisdom was also based on the relatively small sizes of interventions. In the late 1980s the average daily size of U.S. interventions was about $200 million, and the average daily size of German interventions was about $100 million. Occasionally central banks would engage in more than $1 billion of intervention in a day, but such instances were unusual. In a market where total daily trading is hundreds of billions of dollars, the size of such interventions seems too small to have much impact.

More recent studies have challenged this conventional wisdom. How might sterilized intervention be effective, even though it does not change the domestic money supply and is relatively small? The most likely way is by changing the exchange rate expectations of international financial investors and speculators. Intervention can act as a signal from the monetary authorities that they are not happy with the current level or trend of the exchange rate. The authorities show that they are willing to do something (intervention) now and they signal that they may be willing to do something more in the future. For instance, the authorities may be willing to change monetary policy and interest rates in the future if the path for the exchange rate remains unacceptable. Sterilized interventions then can be a type of news that influences expectations. If international investors take the signal seriously, they adjust their exchange rate expectations. Changed expectations alter international capital flows, changing the exchange rate in the direction desired by the authorities. For instance, in 1985 the major governments announced in the Plaza Agreement that they were committed to reducing the exchange rate value of the dollar. They intervened to sell dollars. International investors shifted to expecting the dollar to depreciate by more than they had previously thought, and the exchange rate value of the dollar declined rapidly.

Recent studies indicate that sterilized intervention can be effective. One study concluded that during the

1980s the U.S. monetary authority made a profit of over $12 billion on its dollar–DM intervention activities, with large profits earned during 1980, 1985–1986, and 1988–1989. It made a profit of over $4 billion on its dollar–yen interventions during this period, with especially large profits earned during 1985–1988. Another study concluded that interventions during the mid- and late 1980s significantly affected exchange rate expectations in the direction intended.

Dominguez and Frankel (1993) studied major episodes of intense intervention, usually by more than one central bank. As the accompanying table shows, they concluded that in 10 of the 11 episodes of intervention to affect the dollar–DM exchange rate during 1985–1991, the change in the exchange rate during the month following the intervention was in the direction intended by the monetary authorities, and in 6 of these 10 interventions, the direction that the exchange rate was moving was reversed from what it had been in the month before the intervention.

Our belief about the effectiveness of sterilized intervention is now cautious. There are times when it appears to work, as documented by studies of intervention during the late 1980s. There are other times when it has little or no impact. The ineffectiveness of intervention seemed to be the rule in the 1970s. More recently, during 1994–1995, central banks repeatedly intervened to buy U.S. dollars, but the dollar continued to fall against the Japanese yen and the German mark. For other cases of intervention, it is simply difficult to decide whether intervention was successful or not. Intervention to affect the dollar–yen exchange rate during 1998 provides a good example. The exchange rate value of the yen had been declining during the early part of the year, and billions of dollars of intervention by the Japanese central bank failed to reverse this trend. On June 17, the Japanese and U.S. central banks used a coordinated intervention to sell about $4 billion for yen. (This was the first intervention by the U.S. Federal Reserve in the foreign exchange market since August 1995.) The intervention was clearly successful during the day of the intervention, as the yen rose by about 4 percent (from 143 yen per dollar to 137). A month later the exchange rate was 139 yen per dollar. But by the end of July, the yen had declined in value to 144 yen per dollar, and it was only from August that the yen strengthened noticeably, ending 1998 at 116 yen per dollar.

Was the June 17 coordinated intervention successful? During the day of the intervention it was, and the intervention succeeded in stopping the trend of depreciation of the yen. But the yen did not strengthen further in the weeks after the intervention, and it then weakened substantially beginning about a month and a half after the intervention. The picture of the success or failure of this specific intervention is mixed—a conclusion that also summarizes our view of the effectiveness of sterilized intervention generally.

Intervention Episode	Percentage Change in $/DM Rate, Month Before	Intervention Dollars Bought (Sold) ($ billions)	Percentage Change in $/DM Rate, Month After
Jan. 11–Mar. 4, 1985	−2.3	−4.1	8.3
Sep. 23–Nov. 12, 1985	−4.5	−4.4	3.5
Mar. 11–June 3, 1987	−1.3	5.6	−0.8
Oct. 19, 1987–Jan. 21, 1988	0.5	7.7	−2.0
May 31–Oct. 7, 1988	−2.5	−12.9	3.7
Oct. 31–Dec. 2, 1988	5.8	3.0	−3.0
Dec. 8, 1988–Feb. 6, 1989	1.3	−2.4	0.9
Mar. 3–Oct. 12, 1989	0.9	−19.7	1.5
Feb. 23–Apr. 9, 1990	1.1	−1.8	2.0
May 29–July 17, 1990	0.2	1.0	5.1
Feb. 4–Feb. 12, 1991	2.6	1.3	−8.0

Intervention dollars bought (or sold, if negative) show intervention by the U.S. and German central banks combined, except for the last four episodes, which show only intervention by the U.S. central bank (because data for the German central bank were not available).
Source: Dominguez and Frankel (1993, p. 96).

other countries. In some situations coordination could be easy. For instance, in a deep global recession with no inflation, the advantages of mutual expansionary policies are clear. All countries can benefit if each country finds an alternative to beggar-thy-neighbor policies that harm other countries. In other situations coordination is more controversial.

We have several examples of major coordination efforts in the past quarter-century. At the Bonn Summit of 1978, the United States agreed to implement policies to reduce U.S. inflation while also agreeing to reduce oil imports by decontrolling domestic oil prices. Germany agreed to increase its government spending to stimulate its economy. Japan also agreed to continue its expansionary policies, while taking steps to slow its growth of exports. In the Plaza Agreement of 1985, the major countries agreed to intervene in the foreign exchange markets to lower the exchange rate value of the U.S. dollar (but there was no other coordination of policies). In the Louvre Accord of 1987, the United States committed to reduce its fiscal deficit, while Germany and Japan committed to expansionary policies. All committed to stabilize the exchange rate value of the dollar, if necessary through higher U.S. interest rates and lower interest rates in Germany and Japan, as well as through official intervention.[7]

We can see possible benefits of coordination by examining the Louvre Accord. Tightening of U.S. policies (both fiscal and monetary) would tend to slow down the U.S. economy, and slow down the economies of other countries by reducing U.S. demand for imports. Expansionary policies in Germany and Japan could offset the contractionary effects of the U.S. policy shift, not only in these two countries, but also in other countries (including the United States) by expanding German and Japanese demands for imports. If this is done on a coordinated basis, the result can be a reduction of the U.S. current account deficit, reductions in the German and Japanese current account surpluses, and a stabilization of the exchange rate value of the dollar, without a global recession caused by the tightening of U.S. policies.

If the benefits of international policy coordination seem clear, why do we actually see rather little of it? There seem to be several reasons. First, the goals of different countries may not be compatible. For instance, the United States may want to maintain growth while stabilizing the exchange rate value of the dollar. Policymakers at the European Central Bank are mandated to focus solely on preventing inflation, so they may be unwilling to expand the money supply, lower interest rates, and expand the EU economy. It is simply difficult for a government to adopt policies that do not suit the economic and political conditions of the country, even if these policies would benefit other countries. Indeed, governments may disagree about how the domestic and global macroeconomy works. For instance, they may disagree about how much expansion is possible before inflation begins to increase noticeably.

Second, the benefits of international policy coordination may actually be small in many situations. Often the appropriate "coordinated" policies actually

---

[7]The preceding box "Can Governments Manage the Float?" discussed the use of intervention to influence floating exchange rates.

appear to be close to the appropriate policies that would be chosen by the countries individually (as long as blatant beggar-thy-neighbor policies such as new trade barriers are avoided). For instance, in 1987, the United States on its own probably should have shifted to somewhat contractionary policies and reduced its government budget deficit. In turn, both Germany and Japan, for their own benefit, probably should have shifted to more expansionary policies. Even in this situation, a coordination agreement could have some benefit, not because governments do something different from what each wants to do, but rather because each government can use the commitment to international coordination to firm up domestic support for the policy changes that are in the best interests of the individual countries.

Major instances of international macroeconomic policy coordination are rare. Coordination is more likely when countries clearly see and agree to goals and the means to achieve these goals. In practice this means that the countries commit to doing what they largely should have done on their own. Even in these cases, governments often have difficulty delivering on their commitments. For instance, during the 1980s, international commitments by the U.S. government to reduce its government budget deficit seem to have had little impact.

Summary

With a cleanly floating exchange rate, the exchange rate changes to maintain external balance. If a country is tending toward a surplus in its overall international payments, the exchange rate value of the country's currency will appreciate enough to reverse the tendency. If the country is tending toward a deficit, the currency will depreciate. The contrast with fixed exchange rates is clear. With a clean float external balance is not an issue, but the exchange rate can be quite variable or volatile.

Monetary policy is more powerful with floating exchange rates. After a shift in monetary policy, the exchange rate is likely to change in the direction that reinforces or magnifies the effect of the policy shift on aggregate demand, domestic product, national income, and the price level. In contrast, as we saw in Chapter 22, with fixed exchange rates monetary policy loses power because the need to defend the fixed rate tends to reverse the policy thrust (assuming that the intervention is not or cannot be sterilized).

The effects of floating exchange rates on fiscal policy are not clear. Consider a fiscal expansion. If the resulting inflow of international financial capital is the dominant effect on external balance, then the country's currency appreciates. The loss of international price competitiveness leads to international crowding out, as the current account balance deteriorates. This reduces the effectiveness of fiscal policy in altering domestic product and income. If, instead, the initial deterioration in the current account balance is the dominant effect on external balance, then the country's currency depreciates. The gain in international price competitiveness improves the current account, and this enhances the effectiveness of fiscal policy. We also saw an ambiguity in how fixed exchange rates affect fiscal policy. But the conclusions are the opposite. With fixed exchange rates, fiscal policy is more effective in altering domestic product and income if capital is highly mobile internationally; it is less effective if capital is less mobile.

The ways in which different kinds of shocks affect the country's economy also differ according to whether the country has a fixed or floating exchange rate. Figure 23.7 summarizes

FIGURE 23.7   *Ranking of Exchange Rate Systems by Unit Impacts of Various Exogenous Shocks on Domestic Product and Income*

	More Disruptive– Less Stable	Less Disruptive– More Stable
Internal Shocks		
Domestic monetary shock	Floating	Fixed
Domestic spending shock	Floating*	Fixed*
External Shocks		
International trade shock	Fixed	Floating
International capital-flow shock	Fixed†	Floating†

Comparison is between (1) a fixed exchange rate defended by intervention with no sterilization, so adjustment is through money supply changes, and (2) a floating exchange rate with adjustment through exchange rate changes. If sterilized intervention is used to defend the fixed exchange rate, this raises the disruptiveness of internal shocks, and it lowers the disruptiveness of external shocks, each relative to fixed rates with unsterilized intervention.

---

*This is the result if international capital flows are unresponsive to interest rate differences, or if the current account change eventually is the dominant pressure on the exchange rate. The opposite result applies if the capital account change is the dominant pressure.

†The effect of the shock on national income is in the opposite direction for the two cases. The sense in which the shock is less disruptive under a floating exchange rate is that the induced exchange rate change with floating exchange rates shifts the FE curve back toward its original position.

the conclusions of the analysis of this chapter and Chapter 22. This figure indicates whether a particular shock would change domestic product and income more (be more disruptive or less stable) with fixed or with floating exchange rates. We can reach several general conclusions. First, internal shocks, especially domestic monetary shocks, are more disruptive to an economy with a floating exchange rate, and are less disruptive with a fixed exchange rate. Second, external shocks, especially international trade shocks, are more disruptive to an economy with a fixed exchange rate, and are less disruptive with a floating exchange rate. Floating exchange rates provide some insulation from foreign trade shocks.

While cleanly floating exchange rates can ensure that the country achieves external balance, they do not ensure internal balance. In several situations the exchange rate change that reestablishes external balance can make an internal imbalance worse. If a country has rising inflation and a tendency toward external deficit, the depreciation of the currency can exacerbate the inflation pressures in the country. If the country has excessive unemployment and a tendency toward surplus, the appreciation of the currency can make the unemployment problem worse. To achieve internal balance, the country's government may need to implement domestic policy changes (contractionary to fight inflation, expansionary to fight unemployment).

In theory, **international macroeconomic policy coordination** can improve global macroeconomic performance. International policy coordination means that countries set their policies jointly. The benefits of coordination include the opportunity to consider spillover effects on other countries that arise from interdependence and the opportunity to avoid beggar-thy-neighbor policies that benefit one country at the expense of others. In practice, major instances of international policy coordination are infrequent.

Suggested Reading

See Bergsten (1991) for a discussion of the experience with external adjustment under floating exchange rates during the late 1980s and early 1990s. Genberg and Swoboda (1989) present a technical analysis of the effects of government policies on current account balances under floating exchange rates. Fieleke (1996) provides estimates of how often external shocks hit industrialized countries. International macroeconomic policy coordination is discussed in Feldstein (1988, Parts One and Two), Espinosa and Yip (1993), Bryant (1995), and Bergsten and Henning (1996).

Edison (1993) and Dominguez and Frankel (1993) survey what we know about the effectiveness of official intervention used to manage the float. Taylor (1995) discusses official intervention as well as other recent research on the determinants of floating exchange rates. Leahy (1995) and Taylor (1982) examine the profitability of official intervention. Humpage (1994) explains how the United States undertakes official intervention.

Questions and Problems

✦1. "Overshooting is the basis for the enhanced effectiveness of monetary policy under floating exchange rates." Do you agree or disagree? Why?

2. A country has a floating exchange rate. Government spending now increases in an effort to reduce unemployment. What is the effect of this policy change on the exchange rate value of the country's currency? Under what circumstances does the exchange rate change reduce the expansionary effect of the fiscal change?

✦3. "A drop in the foreign demand for our exports has a larger effect on our domestic product and income under floating exchange rates than it would under fixed exchange rates." Do you agree or disagree? Why?

4. Describe the effects of a sudden decrease in the domestic demand for holding money (a shift from wanting to hold domestic money to wanting to hold domestic bonds) on our domestic product and income under floating exchange rates. Is the change in domestic product and income greater or less than it would be under fixed exchange rates? (*Hint:* A decrease in the demand for money is like an increase in the supply of money.)

✦5. A country has a rising inflation rate and a tendency for its overall payments to go into deficit. Will the resulting exchange rate change move the country closer to or further from internal balance?

6. Britain has instituted a contractionary monetary policy to fight inflation. The pound is floating.

   a. If the exchange rate value of the pound remained steady, what are the effects of tighter money on British domestic product and income? What is the effect on the British inflation rate? Explain.

   b. Following the shift to tighter money, what is the pressure on the exchange rate value of the pound? Explain.

   c. What are the implications of the change in the exchange rate value of the pound for domestic product and inflation in Britain? Does the exchange rate change tend to reinforce or counteract the contractionary thrust of British monetary policy? Explain.

✦7. In the late 1980s, the United States had a large government budget deficit and a large current account deficit. The dollar was floating. One approach suggested to reduce both of these deficits was a large increase in taxes.

a. If the exchange rate value of the dollar remained steady, how would this change affect U.S. domestic product and income? How would it affect the U.S. current account balance and the U.S. capital account balance? Explain.

b. What are the possible pressures on the exchange rate value of the dollar as a result of this change in fiscal policy? Explain.

c. If the dollar actually depreciates, what are the implications for further changes in U.S. domestic product and the U.S. current account balance? Explain.

8. What are the effects of a sudden surge in foreign money supplies on our domestic product and income under floating exchange rates? (*Hint:* The increase in the foreign money supplies will have an impact both on demand for our exports and on international capital flows as well as on exchange rates.)

◆ 9. A country initially has achieved both external balance and internal balance. International financial capital is reasonably mobile, so the country's FE curve is upward sloping (and flatter than the LM curve). The country has a floating exchange rate. As a result of the election of a new government, foreign investors become bullish on the country. International financial capital inflows increase dramatically and remain higher for a number of years.

a. What shift occurs in the FE curve because of the increased capital inflows?

b. What change in the exchange rate occurs to reestablish external balance?

c. As a result of the exchange rate change, how does the country adjust back to external balance? Illustrate this using an IS–LM–FE graph. What is the effect of all of this on the country's internal balance?

10. A country initially has achieved both external balance and internal balance. The country prohibits international financial capital inflows and outflows, so its capital account (excluding official reserves transactions) is always zero because of these capital controls. The country has a floating exchange rate. An exogenous shock now occurs—foreign demand for the country's exports increases.

a. What shifts would occur in the IS, LM, and FE curves because of the increase in foreign demand for the country's exports if the exchange rate value of the country's currency were to remain unchanged?

b. What change in the exchange rate value of the country's currency actually occurs? Why?

c. As a result of the exchange rate change, how does the country adjust back to external balance? Illustrate this using an IS–LM–FE graph. How does all of this affect the country's internal balance?

CHAPTER 24

National and Global Choices

FLOATING RATES AND THE ALTERNATIVES

Parts III and IV examined many aspects of international economic and financial performance. This chapter provides a capstone for the construct by exploring the issues that surround countries' choices of policies toward the exchange rate.

What exchange rate policy should a country use? Should it use a clean float in which private supply and demand determine the exchange rate? Should it commit to a fixed rate that it defends and attempts never to change? Should it generally use a floating, market-driven exchange rate but manage that rate to try to modify the market outcome some of the time? Should it use a fixed rate but be willing from time to time, or perhaps even quite frequently, to change the pegged-rate value?

Each country must choose its policy. The analysis of Parts III and IV provides a broad range of insights into the economics of this choice. This chapter pulls these insights together by exploring the key issues to consider. We will see that the issues suggest that each policy has both strengths and weaknesses, so different countries might wisely choose different policies.

The composite of all countries' choices results in the global exchange rate system. As we noted in Chapter 20, at times in the past century countries have created a coherent global regime around a single policy—fixing to gold during the gold standard, and the adjustable pegged system based on the U.S. dollar that we call the Bretton Woods system. At other times countries have made more varied choices, so characterizing the system during those times is not so easy. For instance, the period between the two world wars did not have a dominant policy, especially after the attempt to return to the gold standard broke down in the early 1930s.

In the current period different countries use different exchange rate policies. Our analysis provides insights into their choices and into the general trend toward floating exchange rates. After discussing this trend, the chapter takes a look at three paths in the opposite direction, toward fixed exchange rates that are (nearly) permanent. The members of the European Union are on the most far-reaching of these paths, to a monetary union with a single European currency.

Key Issues in the Choice of Exchange Rate Policy

A country must choose its exchange rate policy from a menu of many alternatives. The aspect of the policy that we examine is the extent of flexibility that is permitted by the policy. On the one side is a policy that permits substantial flexibility, with a rate that is floating and largely (if not completely) market-driven. The polar case here is a cleanly floating exchange rate, but a lightly managed floating rate also fits the type. On the other side is a policy that fixes or pegs the exchange rate value of the country's currency to a major foreign currency or a basket of foreign currencies.[1] A permanently fixed exchange rate is the polar case, but an adjustable peg is more common, given that it is impossible for a country to commit never to change its policy.

Our previous analysis suggests that five major issues can influence the country's choice: the effects of macroeconomic shocks; the effectiveness of government policies; differences in macroeconomic goals, priorities, and policies; controlling inflation; and the real effects of exchange rate variability. Let's look at each major issue and what it says about the advantages and disadvantages of floating or fixing.

Effects of Macroeconomic Shocks

The analysis of Chapters 22 and 23 has shown that the effects of various macroeconomic shocks depend on the exchange rate policy adopted by the country.[2] A country would look favorably on an exchange rate policy that reduced the domestic effects of macroeconomic shocks. The performance of the country's economy is better if shocks are less disruptive because the economy is more stable. Our analysis indicates that the effects of various macroeconomic shocks depend not only on the exchange rate policy but also on the type of shock.

Internal shocks generally cause less trouble with a fixed rate than with a float.

A *domestic monetary shock* is less disruptive with a fixed exchange rate because the intervention to defend the fixed rate tends to reverse the shock and its effects. With a floating exchange rate the resulting change in the exchange rate would actually magnify the domestic effects of the monetary shock. For example,

---

[1]The country could also choose to fix the value of its currency to a commodity like gold. The box "What Role for Gold?", page 560, explores this possibility.

[2]Most of our discussion here continues to make the assumptions that product prices are rather sticky in the short run, but that they do adjust to spending and monetary pressures in the long run. The discussion of the effects of shocks focuses on the short and medium runs, when shocks can cause cyclical movements in spending, production, and unemployment. In addition, our discussion of macroeconomic effects under fixed exchange rates focuses on the case in which the government does not or cannot sterilize, so the intervention does affect the domestic money supply.

consider what happens if the demand for holding money increases unexpectedly, perhaps because people become wary of using credit cards and begin to pay more often with cash. The extra money demand increases domestic interest rates and reduces domestic product by discouraging interest-sensitive spending. The country's overall balance of payments tends toward surplus, as the capital account improves because of increased capital inflows and the current account improves because of lower domestic spending and demand for imports.

1. With a fixed exchange rate, the country's central bank must intervene to prevent the country's currency from appreciating. As the central bank sells domestic currency, the intervention increases the domestic money supply. (Recall the analysis of Chapter 22.) The extra money demand is now met by an increased money supply, and interest rates can fall back toward their original level. The fall in interest rates spurs a recovery of interest-sensitive spending and domestic product.

2. With a floating exchange rate, the tendency toward surplus causes the domestic currency to appreciate, reducing the country's international price competitiveness. (Recall the analysis of Chapter 23.) As exports decline and imports rise in response to the shift in price competitiveness, the effect of the shock on the domestic economy is magnified. Domestic product tends to decline more.

The effects of a *domestic spending shock,* such as an unexpected change in real domestic investment spending or in consumption spending, or a sudden shift in fiscal policy, depend on how responsive international flows of financial capital are to interest rate changes. If capital is not responsive, then domestic spending shocks are also less disruptive with fixed rates than with floating rates. For instance, a decline in domestic spending tends to improve the country's current account balance as the demand for imports declines. If this is the dominant effect, the country's overall international payments also tend toward surplus. As in the monetary example, the payments surplus results in intervention that expands the domestic money supply if the country has a fixed exchange rate, and this tends to expand domestic spending, stabilizing the economy to some extent. With a floating exchange rate, the appreciation of the currency tends to lower demand and production further. Of course, if capital is highly responsive, then the reverse is true—domestic spending shocks are more disruptive with fixed rates.

For *external shocks,* we reach opposite conclusions about stability and disruption. We can see this most clearly for *foreign trade shocks.* Suppose that foreign demand for our exports declines (or, for that matter, that our country's demand shifts toward imported foreign products and away from the comparable domestic products). The decrease in demand for our products tends to put the economy into a recession. In addition, the country's current account balance tends to deteriorate, and this tends to worsen the country's overall payments balance. With a fixed exchange rate, the central bank must intervene to defend the fixed rate by buying domestic currency. The resulting contraction of the domestic money supply reinforces the initial contraction of demand for our products, adding to the recession. With a floating exchange rate, the tendency to deficit depreciates the value of our currency. The improvement in price competitiveness boosts demand for our products, countering the recession tendency.

The effects of foreign trade shocks are important because changes in foreign trade are a major way in which business cycles are transmitted from one country to another. With fixed exchange rates business cycles are transmitted through foreign trade and foreign repercussions, and the intervention to defend the fixed rate can magnify the transmission. With floating exchange rates the transmission is muted because exchange rate changes tend to insulate the economy from foreign trade shocks.

International capital-flow shocks have domestic effects under both fixed and floating exchange rates, but there is a sense in which they are less disruptive under floating exchange rates. With a fixed exchange rate, an adverse capital-flow shift, which results in a capital outflow, requires intervention to defend the fixed rate by buying domestic currency. The reduction in the domestic money supply (if the intervention is not sterilized) has an adverse effect on the economy by raising interest rates and reducing spending. Under floating exchange rates, the currency depreciates. Any adverse effect that the capital outflow itself might have on the economy's production is countered by the improvement in trade that results from better international price competitiveness.

The differences in the effects of shocks on the economy can have an impact on a country's choice of exchange rate policy. If the country believes that it is buffeted mainly by internal shocks, the country would favor a fixed exchange rate. If it believes that most shocks are external, then it would favor a floating exchange rate.

However, we also must add a caution to this conclusion. While its conceptual basis is clear, its practical importance is actually debatable for several reasons. The most important reason is that the effects of shocks under fixed exchange rates depend on whether interventions are sterilized. The previous discussion has assumed that intervention is not sterilized. If, instead, the intervention is sterilized, the domestic money supply does not change. This reduces the stabilizing properties of fixed rates when internal shocks hit the economy, and it also reduces the disruptive effects when external shocks hit. (Of course, continued sterilization may not be feasible if the payments imbalance persists, but the short-run behavior is still altered.)

The Effectiveness of Government Policies

Chapters 22 and 23 showed that government policies' influence on aggregate demand and domestic product is altered by the type of exchange rate policy chosen by the country. Monetary policy loses its control over the money supply if the country has a fixed exchange rate because monetary policy is constrained by the need to defend the fixed exchange rate. If the country tries to implement an expansionary monetary policy, the payments balance tends to go into deficit, and intervention to defend the fixed rate reduces the domestic money supply and reverses the monetary expansion. Indeed, if the country has a payments deficit for any reason, the intervention reduces the domestic money supply. If instead the country tries to implement a contractionary monetary policy, the payments balance tends to go into surplus, and the intervention to defend the fixed rate increases the domestic money supply and reverses the monetary contraction. In fact, a payments surplus for any reason expands the domestic money supply. The country's monetary authority can attempt to regain some control over domestic monetary policy by sterilizing to reverse the effect of the intervention on the money supply, but there is a limit to how long it can continue to sterilize.

Monetary policy gains effectiveness under floating exchange rates. The resulting change in the exchange rate reinforces the thrust of the policy change. A shift to expansionary monetary policy results in a depreciation of the country's currency. The improvement in price competitiveness further expands demand for the country's products. A shift to contractionary policy appreciates the country's currency, resulting in a further reduction in demand for the country's products.

The effectiveness of fiscal policy depends on how responsive international capital flows are to interest rates. If capital is highly mobile, then fiscal policy gains effectiveness under fixed rates. The intervention to defend the fixed rate reduces the change in domestic interest rates, so that there is less domestic crowding out. With floating exchange rates and highly mobile capital, fiscal policy loses effectiveness. The resulting exchange rate change leads to international crowding out. If capital is not that mobile, or if capital flows decline beyond a short-run period, the reverse is true. Fiscal policy then loses effectiveness with a fixed exchange rate and gains effectiveness with a floating rate.

The country's choice of exchange rate policy can be influenced by its impact on the effectiveness of fiscal policy. A country whose capital markets are closely linked to the rest of the world, so that capital is highly mobile, will view a fixed exchange rate more favorably if it wants fiscal policy to be highly effective in the short run. A country whose capital flows are less responsive, or one that is worried about the effectiveness of fiscal policy beyond the short-run period when capital flows are responding, will look more favorably on floating rates.

While the impact of fiscal policy effectiveness on the choice of exchange rate policy is conditional, the impact of monetary policy effectiveness is straightforward. *If a country desires to use monetary policy to address domestic objectives, then the country will favor a floating exchange rate.* A floating rate frees monetary policy from the need to defend the exchange rate.

Differences in Macroeconomic Goals, Priorities, and Policies

Government policymakers in each country must decide on the goals and objectives of macroeconomic policy. Even if countries generally pursue the same set of macroeconomic performance goals—including real economic growth, low unemployment, low inflation, and external balance—the priorities that governments place on the goals can differ, as can the specific policies adopted to achieve the goals.

For fixed exchange rates between the currencies of two or more countries to be successful, a kind of consistency or coordination between the countries involved is necessary. A country choosing a fixed exchange rate must follow policies that permit successful defense of the rate, given the policies and performance of the other countries linked by the fixed rates. If the policies diverge noticeably, large payments imbalances are likely to develop, making the defense of the fixed rates difficult or impossible.

One example is that countries should be willing to refrain from policy changes that lead to large international capital flows, or coordinate such changes in policies across countries. For instance, a big reduction in the taxes that one country imposes on financial investments can lead to large international capital flows into the country. If the other countries must intervene to defend the fixed rates as capital flows out of their countries, their international reserve holdings decline, threatening their ability to continue to defend the fixed rates. To maintain fixed rates, the first country may need to temper policy changes such as this. Or the other countries may need to adopt their own policy changes to mute the incentives for capital flows. For instance, the other countries could also lower their taxes on financial investments, or they could raise their interest rates. These changes would create a kind of consistency or coordination that reduces the threat to the viability of the fixed-rate system.

Another example is the priority that each country places on controlling inflation, or the trade-off that each country is willing to make between inflation and unemployment. For instance, Germany and Switzerland have placed the highest priority on maintaining a very low inflation rate. The United States has been somewhat less concerned with inflation and more concerned with stabilizing employment. Even if there is no long-run trade-off between inflation and unemployment, such differences in priorities can still influence policy in the short run. The United States would be willing to risk somewhat higher inflation to reduce unemployment in the short run, while Germany and Switzerland would not. If the United States ends up with a higher inflation rate than Germany or Switzerland, and neither side is willing to compromise to achieve consistency, fixed rates probably cannot be maintained. We examine the relationship of inflation rates and exchange rate policy in more depth in the next subsection.

Floating exchange rates are tolerant of diversity in countries' goals, priorities, and policies. As long as the country is willing to permit the exchange rate to change according to market pressures, external balance in the country's overall payments is maintained whatever the country's policies. International policy coordination is still possible across countries, as we discussed in the previous chapter, but it is not necessary. There is no doubt that floating exchange rates permit a country to be more independent in its choices of policies, but we should also be a little cautious with this proposition. Policymakers in a country often are concerned about movements in the exchange rate value of the country's currency, so their policy choices are somewhat constrained even with floating rates. For instance, in the early 1980s unemployment rates were high in a number of the major European countries. However, they did not shift to expansionary policies because their currencies were already weak against the dollar. In fact, they tightened up and raised their interest rates to prevent their currencies from weakening further.

Controlling Inflation

The relationship between the choice of exchange rate policy and a country's inflation rate is an important issue for the country. In addition, this issue has broad meaning for global macroeconomic performance, especially for the average rate of global inflation.

Countries that choose to fix the exchange rates among their currencies are committing to have similar inflation rates over the long run. This is the prediction of purchasing power parity—a nominal exchange rate can be steady only if the difference in inflation rates between the countries is about zero. The logic is based on the need to maintain reasonable price competitiveness for the products of each country. If inflation rates were consistently different over a substantial period of time, and exchange rates were fixed, a low-inflation country would steadily gain international price competitiveness, leading to current account surpluses. A high-inflation country would steadily lose price competitiveness, leading to deficits. These continuing and growing surpluses and deficits are not sustainable, and something would need to adjust. The inflation rate in the low-inflation country could increase, the inflation rate in the high-inflation country could decrease, or the exchange rate could change. If inflation rates change, then the fixed rate can be maintained, but the inflation difference instead could result in surrender of the fixed rate.

A number of implications follow from the conclusion that countries that fix their exchange rates should have similar inflation rates. First, proponents of fixed rates argue that fixed rates create a discipline effect on national tendencies to run high inflation rates. For the fixed rate to be sustained, a country cannot have an inflation rate that is much above the inflation rate(s) of its partner(s).[3] In fact, a country embarking on a serious effort to reduce its high inflation rate may deliberately choose to fix its currency to the currency of another country that has a lower inflation rate. The high-inflation country is using the discipline effect as part of its anti-inflation program. The high-inflation country hopes that the peg to the other country's currency can establish the credibility of its anti-inflation program. If it can gain credibility, it has a greater chance of success because people will lower their estimate of how much inflation will occur in the future. If inflation expectations are lowered, then it is easier to lower actual inflation and keep it low. Argentina used this strategy successfully in the early 1990s. In 1989, prices in Argentina rose by about 3,000 percent; in 1990, they climbed by about 2,300 percent. Argentina began an anti-inflation program and, in 1991, fixed the value of peso to the U.S. dollar. The discipline of this peg helped to reduce the growth rate of the money supply and the inflation rate in Argentina. By 1994, Argentinean inflation was about 4 percent, nearly the same as that in the United States, and it remained close to zero through the rest of the 1990s.

---

[3]There is a limit to this discipline effect. Rather than reducing its inflation rate, the country instead can change its exchange rate, devaluing or switching to a floating exchange rate.

Second, a fixed-rate system in which most countries participate may also impose discipline to lower the average global rate of price inflation. This **price discipline** argument runs as follows: The fixed-rate system puts more pressure on governments whose countries have international deficits than on governments that have surpluses. Deficit countries face an obvious limit on their ability to sustain deficits; they soon run out of reserves and creditworthiness. Even if they attempt to sterilize their interventions, they must tighten up on their money supplies fairly quickly if they are to maintain the fixed rate. This forces them to contract, which lowers their money growth and inflation rate. Surplus countries, in contrast, face only more distant and manageable inconveniences from perennial surpluses. As long as they are willing to accumulate additional official reserves, they should be able to use sterilized intervention for an extended period. Thus, the deficit countries tend to lower their money growth, while the surplus countries tend not to raise theirs. Overall there is less money growth in the world and a lower average inflation rate.

With the price discipline of fixed exchange rates, there is a greater chance that countries have similar inflation and that the average inflation rate may be somewhat lower than the average that each country would choose on its own. If the system has a leading country, such as the United States in Bretton Woods, then countries tend to have to match the inflation rate of this lead country. For countries that would have had a higher inflation rate, the system is imposing a discipline effect. But other countries might prefer an even lower inflation rate.

This observation leads to the third implication. With fixed exchange rates, a country that prefers to have a lower inflation rate than that of other countries, especially the lead country in the system, will have difficulty maintaining this low inflation rate. With a low inflation rate the country will tend to have payments surpluses. Intervention to defend the fixed rate tends to expand their money supply. Sterilization can prevent the money growth. But sterilization may not be perfect, and in any case the country will come under political pressure to reduce its surplus. It may be forced to expand and inflate against its will. It will tend to "import inflation" from the other countries. Germany complained of this pressure in the 1960s as the inflation rate in the United States rose.

In contrast to all of this, floating exchange rates simply permit countries to have different inflation rates. According to purchasing power parity, high-inflation countries tend to have depreciating currencies, and low-inflation countries tend to have appreciating currencies. The exchange rate changes maintain reasonable price competitiveness for both types of countries in the long run. Proponents of floating rates generally view this as a virtue. Different countries' policymakers may have different beliefs as to what an acceptable inflation rate is. These beliefs may be the result of historic events, such as the hyperinflation of the 1920s in Germany that has resulted in a strong German preference for very low inflation. Or they may be the result of a series of decisions about acceptable trade-offs of a little more inflation in order to reduce unemployment. This was the situation of the United States in the 1970s, and it resulted in rather high inflation. Or the government may choose to "finance" its large budget deficit by printing money (rather than by borrowing through the issue of government bonds). The rapid money growth leads to high rates of inflation. This has been the case in some developing countries.

Opponents of floating exchange rates suggest that the ability of each country to choose its own policies toward inflation results in more inflation worldwide. The exchange rate does not impose any discipline on money growth and inflation. Instead, with floating exchange rates a country can be caught in a vicious circle in which (1) high inflation leads to currency depreciation and (2) the depreciation increases the domestic currency prices of imports so the high inflation rate is reinforced. Continuing high inflation requires further depreciation and so forth. Domestic money growth simply accommodates this dynamic.

The world experience in the first decade after the shift to general floating in 1973 seemed to be consistent with the concerns of these opponents of floating rates. Average world inflation in the 1970s was substantially higher than it had been in the 1950s or 1960s. The seeds for some of this higher inflation had been sown, especially in the United States, beginning in the fixed-rate 1960s. In addition, the two oil shocks of the 1970s presumably would have resulted in higher average inflation even if exchange rates had remained fixed. Nonetheless, some of the higher inflation was probably the result of the removal of the discipline of fixed rates.

The world experience since the early 1980s indicates that the tendency toward higher inflation with floating rates actually may not be a serious problem. The inflation rates in many of the major countries whose currencies have generally been floating—including Japan, the United States, and Britain—fell noticeably and remain low. The experience since the early 1980s indicates that what really matters in controlling national inflation rates is the discipline and resolve of the national monetary authorities.

Real Effects of Exchange Rate Variability

A major concern about floating exchange rates is that they are highly variable. Some variability presumably is not controversial, including exchange rate movements that offset inflation rate differentials and exchange rate movements that promote an orderly adjustment to shocks. However, the substantial variability of exchange rates within fairly short time periods like months or a few years is more controversial. What are the possible effects of exchange rate variability that might concern us?

If the variability simply creates unexpected gains and losses for short-term financial investors who deliberately take positions exposed to exchange rate risk, we probably would not be much concerned. However, we would be concerned if heightened exchange rate risk discourages such international activities as trade in goods and services or foreign direct investment. Exchange rate variability then would have real effects, by altering activities in the part of the economy that produces goods and services.

Consider international trade in goods and services. Does exchange rate variability create risk that leads to lower volumes of trade? First, simple short-run variability may have little direct impact on trade activities. Anyone engaged in international trade has a range of foreign exchange contracts, including forward foreign exchange, currency futures, and currency options, that can be used to hedge exposures to exchange rate risk in the short run, at least for the major currencies in the world. These contracts can be obtained with low transactions costs. Second, exchange rate variability beyond the short run can affect the real investments that must be made to support export-oriented production. If exchange rate variability raises the riskiness of these real investments, they tend to be lower if firms are risk-averse. This form of exchange rate risk is more difficult to hedge because (1) longer maturities of many contracts do not exist or are rather expensive to buy and (2) the specific amounts of payments that might need to be hedged several years in the future are themselves often highly uncertain. Economists have studied the overall effect of increased exchange rate risk on the volumes of international trade activities. Early studies typically found almost no effect of exchange rate variability on trade volumes. Some more recent studies have found negative effects, although the effects generally are estimated to be rather small.

Overshooting raises another concern about the real effects of the variability of floating exchange rates. When exchange rates overshoot (as discussed in Chapters 19 and 23), they send signals about changes in international price competitiveness that seem to some observers to be far too strong. Big swings in price competitiveness create incentives for large shifts in real resources. For example, if overshooting leads to a large appreciation of the country's currency (for instance, the U.S. dollar in the early 1980s), this creates the incentive for labor to move out of export-oriented and import-competing industries, as the country loses a large amount of price competitiveness. New capital investment in these industries is strongly discouraged, and some existing facilities are shut down. However, as the overshooting then reverses itself, these resource movements appear to have been excessive. Resources then must move back into these industries. Relative price adjustments are an important and necessary part of the market system. They signal the need for resource reallocations. The concern here is not with relative price changes in general. The concern is with the possibility that the dynamics of floating exchange rates sometimes send false price signals or signals that are too strong, resulting in excessive resource reallocations.

This discussion of exchange rate variability and the real effects of this variability leads into a broader debate. Proponents and defenders of floating exchange rates agree that variability has been high, and that some real effects occur. But they believe that this is what markets should do. Exchange rates as prices send signals about the relative values of currencies. These signals represent the summary of information about the currencies that is available at that time. As economic and political conditions change, the prices and signals should change. The variability of exchange rates represents the ongoing market-based quest for economic efficiency. The proponents of floating rates believe that the supporters of fixed rates delude themselves by claiming that the lack of variability of fixed rates is a virtue. A fixed exchange rate is simply a form of price control. Price controls are generally inefficient because the price is often too high or too low. That is, with a fixed rate the country's currency is often overvalued or undervalued by government fiat. In addition, a fixed rate is sometimes changed, often suddenly and by a large amount, when the peg is adjusted through a devaluation or a revaluation. This sudden change can be highly disruptive, and it often occurs in a crisis atmosphere brought on by large capital flows as speculators believe that they have a one-way speculative gamble on the direction of the exchange rate change.

Detractors and opponents of floating exchange rates believe that floating exchange rates are excessively variable, and that this variability has real effects that are inefficient. Some of these detractors view the variability of floating rates as excessive because the exchange rates themselves are sometimes inefficient, as they are affected by speculative bandwagons and bubbles that do not reflect the underlying economic fundamentals. Other detractors, while conceding that floating exchange rates are reasonably efficient prices from the point of view of their function within the international financial system, believe that exchange rates set in this way do not serve the broader economy well. Variability and overshooting may have a logic in international finance, but they nonetheless cause undesirable real effects like discouragement of international trade and excessive resource shifts. To these opponents, with floating exchange rates the market often undervalues or overvalues a country's currency, at least in relation to the signals that should be sent to the goods-and-services part of the economy. Exchange rates should make transactions between countries as smooth and easy as possible. To the opponents of floating rates, exchange rates, like money, serve their transactions functions best when their values are stable.

National Choices

We have just examined five major issues that can affect a country's choice of its exchange rate policy. Each country must make its own decision, and that decision depends on the balancing of a number of factors, including the economic issues explored here as well as political concerns. While each country will have its own important issues because of its own economic and political situation, we can nonetheless discern in our set of five issues several factors that are likely to be of major importance for most countries.

There are several strong arguments in favor of a country adopting a floating exchange rate. First, a floating exchange rate provides more effective use of two important tools for adjusting toward internal and external balances. Exchange rate changes can promote adjustment to external balance, and monetary policy can be directed toward achieving internal balance because it does not need to be directed toward defending the exchange rate. Second, a floating exchange rate permits a country to pursue goals, priorities, and policies that meet its own domestic preferences and needs, with less concern about how these will put pressure on the exchange rate. Third, the country does not need to defend a fixed rate

What Role for Gold?

Gold was at the center of the international monetary system during the gold standard. As we discussed in Chapter 20, individuals had the right to obtain or sell gold (in exchange for national money) with the country's central bank at the fixed official gold price. Gold was also an important part of the Bretton Woods system of fixed exchange rates. The U.S. government was expected to sell gold to foreign central banks (but not to individuals) at the official U.S. dollar price of gold.

What is the role for gold now? Gold remains an official reserve asset, but currently central banks make almost no official use of gold. Gold is also held by private individuals as part of their investments. Let's look at both the official role and private role for gold more closely.

Official Role: The Once and Future King?

Most observers of the current system are comfortable with the lack of a role for gold in official international activity. Indeed, some believe that central banks and the International Monetary Fund should sell off their current official holdings of gold. One reason to sell is that gold plays no active role and earns no interest. The part of national wealth (or IMF assets) held in gold could be invested more productively. Another reason is that the proceeds of gold sales could be used for assistance to the poorer countries of the world. Central banks and the IMF have made some gold sales into the private market in recent decades (a process called *demonetization of gold*), and they plan to continue gold sales. IMF sales have been used to add funds to programs of lending to developing countries.

A small group of people are strong advocates of a return to a real gold standard in which countries tie their currencies to gold. These proponents believe that a return to a gold standard would greatly reduce national and average global rates of inflation by creating a strong discipline effect on countries' abilities to expand their money supplies. They also believe that a return to a gold standard would eliminate the variability of exchange rates by establishing full confidence in the system and by enforcing monetary adjustments to achieve external balance. By creating

stability and confidence in national moneys and exchange rates, they believe that the return to a gold standard would stabilize and lower both nominal and real interest rates.

Most international economists oppose a return to the gold standard. To most, a gold standard is not nearly as stabilizing as its proponents claim, except perhaps in the very long run. The supply of new gold to the world is governed not by some master regulator, but rather by mining activities. A major discovery of new minable gold deposits leads to a rapid expansion of the world gold supply. As central banks buy gold to defend the fixed gold prices, national money supplies would expand rapidly and inflation rates would increase. On the other hand, if there are no new discoveries, and if current mines slow output as mines are exhausted (or if major strikes or similar disruptions slow output), national central banks would have to sell gold to defend its price (assuming that private demand continues to grow). National money supplies would shrink, and countries would enter into painful deflations (with weak economic conditions forcing price levels lower). Looking at the other side of the market for gold, decreases in private demand for gold would require central banks to buy gold to defend its price, expanding money supplies. Increases in private demand would force central banks to sell gold, shrinking national money supplies.

Such swings were evident even during the classical gold standard. Between 1873 and 1896, the British price level fell by about one-third, and it then inflated back up from 1896 to 1913. These shifts were closely related to changes in the growth rates of world stocks of monetary gold, and these were closely related to cycles in mining driven by gold discoveries. Between 1850 and 1873, the world gold stock grew by 2.9 percent per year, with discoveries leading to mining booms in California and Australia. This permitted money supplies to keep up with the growing real demand for money, so that price levels remained about steady. Between 1873 and 1896, the world gold stock grew by only 1.7 percent per year. This was not enough to keep up with continued growth in real money demand, and the price level was forced down. Then from 1896 to 1913, new discoveries of gold led to mining booms in the Klondike (Canada) and the Transvaal (South Africa). The world gold stock rose 3.2 percent per year, faster than real money demand was growing, so the price level increased. With such fluctuations in the growth of monetary gold, it is difficult to claim that the gold standard ensured steady expansion of the world money base (although the gold standard did limit money growth and inflation in the long run).

Because a gold standard probably would not be nearly as stable as its proponents claim, most international economists oppose a return to a gold standard. Bolstering their belief are the more typical arguments about the advantages of flexible or floating exchange rates, including independence in choosing priorities and using policies. In addition, the resource costs of expanding official gold reserves is itself high. New gold must be mined. This seems to be an inefficient use of resources, to produce something that will largely sit in the vaults of central banks.

Private Role: A Sound Investment?

The official link between gold and currencies effectively ended in 1968, and it seems unlikely to be revived. Even though its official role has largely ended, should gold play a role in the investments of private individuals? Holding gold pays no interest, so any return to gold comes from increases in its price. (The return earned is actually lower than the price increase suggests, because of the costs of buying and selling as well as the costs of storing and safekeeping.) The accompanying graph shows the monthly dollar price of gold since 1970. There are three lessons from this graph. First, anyone who bought gold in the early 1970s earned a high rate of return through 1980, as the dollar price increased from under $100 per ounce to over $600 per ounce. This increase far exceeded general price inflation or the rates of return available on most financial assets. Second, anyone who bought gold since 1980 would generally be disappointed. The typical price of gold stayed slightly below $400 between 1982 and 1997, and it fell below $300 in 1998. The gold price has not kept up with broad price inflation, and it has underperformed compared to the returns available on many financial assets like stocks and bonds. Third, far from being stable, or tracking general price inflation as an "inflation hedge," the gold price has fluctuated a lot, soaring during 1979–1980, falling back during 1980–1982, rising strongly during 1982, and so forth.

Why has the price of gold jumped around so much during the past several decades? Shifts in supply have

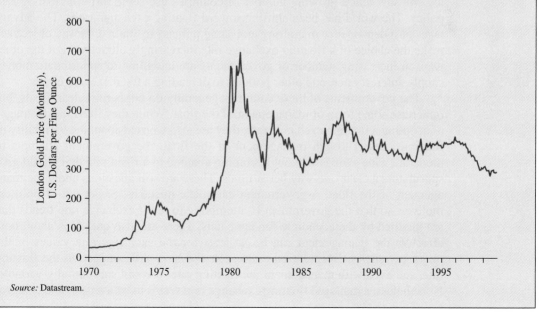

Source: Datastream.

some impact, and the depressed gold price since early 1998 seems to reflect the expectation that central banks and the IMF will accelerate their sales of gold into the private market. Still, pressure often comes from shifts in demand. To a large extent gold is what frightened people invest in. Suppose you are wealthy and live in an unstable region of the world. Clandestine gold ownership can protect you from having your assets seized or heavily taxed. Or suppose you fear an explosion of inflation. Holding real assets like gold provides at least some protection against the loss of purchasing power that will afflict most paper assets. These demands increase and decrease as fears and tensions rise and subside.

Thus, private investments in gold are bets about the future course of gold prices. Over the long term the price of gold has roughly kept up with the rise of general prices (though past performance is no indicator of future performance). But for any short- or medium-term period of time, gold's value is anybody's guess. For a commodity that symbolizes stability, unpredictable shifts in demand and supply can and do cause large swings in gold's real price.

against speculative attacks, a task that is increasingly difficult as large amounts of internationally mobile capital can be shifted quickly from country to country.

The strongest argument against a country adopting a floating exchange rate is that floating rates have been disturbingly variable since 1973. This variability increases exchange rate risk, and this risk does seem to have some effect in discouraging international activities such as trade in goods and services. In addition, overshooting of floating exchange rates may have promoted too much adjustment into or out of trade-oriented production from time to time. A major advantage of fixed rates is the substantial reduction in variability and exchange rate risk if the fixed rate can be defended and the peg is not adjusted too often.

In Chapter 20 we presented countries' current choices of exchange rate policy. We saw that a growing number of countries use some form of floating-rate policy. The world has been shifting toward floating exchange rates. The advantages of independence in crafting and using policies to attain domestic objectives make the choice of a floating exchange rate increasingly attractive. Put the other way, an increasing number of governments are unwilling to subordinate money supply, interest rates, and other policies to defending a fixed exchange rate.

The governments of these countries generally do not permit clean floats, but rather use some form of management of the float. While they like the advantages of adopting a floating exchange rate, they are also worried about the variability of floating rates. Through management of the float, the government attempts to moderate wide swings without becoming chained to a fixed rate that would give speculators a clear one-way bet at times. There are still questions about the management of the float. A government can make mistakes, or act out of political motives, so that the government is attempting to resist exchange rate trends that are justified by the economic fundamentals. There are also questions about how effective the management can be, at least for the exchange rate values of the major currencies. Intervention often seems to have little impact on the floating rate, and even with management the floating rates are still substantially variable. Nonetheless, a managed floating exchange rate seems to be a reasonable compromise choice. It gains much of the policy independence while offering governments some ability to reduce exchange rate variability. It is not surprising that managed floating is increasingly the policy adopted by countries.

While the global trend is toward floating, a number of countries continue to maintain fixed exchange rates. For most of these countries, the compelling argument is that floating exchange rates are too variable. A number of these countries are smaller countries that fix to the currency of a major trading partner (or to a basket of currencies of major trading partners). For these countries reducing exchange rate risk to promote smooth trade and avoiding overshooting that would disrupt their trade-oriented industries seem to be the major objectives in choosing an exchange rate policy. These countries are willing to sacrifice some economic policy autonomy to obtain exchange rate stability.

However, a fixed exchange rate that is adjustable—that leaves room for the country's monetary authority to change or abandon the fixed value—sometimes invites attack through a one-way speculative gamble. Such a speculative attack can all but force the monetary authority to surrender, as in Mexico in late 1994, in Thailand, Indonesia, and South Korea in 1997, and in Brazil in early 1999. In response, some countries have adopted or are considering arrangements that create more permanent fixes.

Extreme Fixes

The general trend in national exchange rate policies is toward greater flexibility. But some countries have moved in the opposite direction—to exchange rates that are not only fixed but also rather difficult or nearly impossible to change. In this section we examine currency boards and "dollarization," two "extreme" forms of fixed rates that can be adopted by a single country. In the final section of the chapter we examine what may be the ultimate form of fixed rates—a monetary union among several countries that agree to a single unionwide currency.

Currency Board

A currency board attempts to establish a fixed exchange rate that is long-lived by mandating that the board, acting as the country's monetary authority, should focus almost exclusively on maintaining the fixed rate. A currency board holds only foreign-currency assets (official reserve assets). The board issues domestic currency liabilities only in exchange for foreign currency assets that it acquires. Because the board owns no domestic-currency assets, it has no ability to sterilize. This arrangement increases the credibility of a country's commitment to maintaining the fixed exchange rate by automatically linking the domestic money supply to the defense of the fixed rate. For instance, if increased private selling is putting downward pressure on the exchange-rate value of the country's currency, the currency board defends the fixed rate by buying domestic currency and selling foreign currency. As the board buys domestic currency, the domestic money supply decreases. This money supply decrease sets in motion the adjustments discussed at length in Chapter 22, and the currency board has no power to resist. With no domestic assets, the currency board cannot sterilize the intervention—the domestic money supply must decrease.

Several very small countries have had currency boards since before 1970. Argentina set up its currency board in 1991. During the 1990s, four transition countries—Estonia, Lithuania, Bulgaria, and Bosnia and Herzegovina—established currency boards.

The experience of Argentina shows the advantages and disadvantages of a currency board. Argentina's government established a currency board to signal its commitment to stop the country's hyperinflation, by imposing strict discipline to limit the growth of Argentina's money supply. As we saw earlier in the chapter, this effort was completely successful. With inflation quickly reduced, interest rates decreased, and economic growth increased. After almost no growth of its real GDP during the 1980s, Argentina's real growth averaged nearly 4 percent during 1992–1998. But the Argentinean economy has also been vulnerable to adverse external shocks. The fallout from the Mexican peso crisis caused a recession during 1995, and the Asian crisis, the Russian crisis, and the devaluation of Brazil's currency led to a recession during 1998–1999. In these periods of foreign financial turmoil, international investors pulled back from investments in Argentina, its money supply shrank, and its interest rates increased. In addition, especially in 1995, concerns about whether Argentina would maintain its fixed rate led to speculative outflows that further decreased Argentina's money supply. Argentina did stick with its currency board and the fixed dollar–peso exchange rate, but probably at the cost of deeper recessions both times.

"Dollarization"

A currency board establishes a strongly fixed exchange rate, but it is still at risk of a speculative attack, because the country's government could decide to shift to some other exchange-rate policy for its currency. A more extreme form of fixed exchange rate is for the country's government to abolish its own currency and use the currency of some other country. Because the other currency is often the U.S. dollar, this arrangement is called "dollarization." Panama, Micronesia, and the Marshall Islands use the U.S. dollar as their official local currency, and several other very small countries use the currency of a large neighboring country as their own currency.

The late 1990s saw serious discussions of whether some larger countries, especially Latin American countries, should replace their national currencies with dollars. Polls in Mexico showed that a majority of Mexicans favored dollarization, but it seemed unlikely that the Mexican government would do so. The discussion was most advanced in Argentina, with expression of support for dollarization by the Argentinean president.

In comparison with Argentina's currency board, which already maintains a tight fixed rate between the peso and the dollar, what would be the advantages and disadvantages of full dollarization? The major advantage for Argentina would be ending speculative attacks on the peso, such as those that occurred in 1995. Such speculative attacks are disruptive because the peso money supply shrinks and peso interest rates rise. In addition, if Argentina were to abandon its currency board, it would face the risk of rising inflation, as the discipline of the currency board would be lost. The major disadvantage of full dollarization is the loss of interest income on Argentina's holdings of official international reserve assets. The Argentinean government would have to replace all pesos with dollars. To do this, the government would use about $15 billion of its holdings of U.S. government bonds to obtain dollars. Argentina's government would lose about $700 million per year in interest income, equal to about 0.2 percent of Argentinean national income. That is, with dollarization the seigniorage profits from issuing currency circulating in Argentina would go to the U.S. government (the issuer of dollar bills) rather than to the Argentinean government (the issuer of peso currency).[4]

One effect of dollarization in Argentina would be surprisingly small. The peso and the dollar already circulate freely together, and about 60 percent of Argentina's bank deposits are dollar-denominated. Informally, Argentina is already partly dollarized, so the Argentinean people would find it easy to adjust to full dollarization.

With full dollarization, Argentina completely cedes its monetary policy to the United States. The U.S. Fed will make its monetary policy decision based on economic conditions in the United States, with almost no concern for economic conditions in Argentina. This sounds like a major drawback, but if Argentina is fully committed to the currency board, then it has already almost completely given up its own monetary policy anyway.

The International Fix—Monetary Union

Since the breakup of the Bretton Woods fixed-rate system, the countries of the European Union have attempted to establish and maintain fixed exchange rates among their currencies. In 1979, they established the European Monetary System, and a subset of the countries established fixed exchange rates among their currencies through the **Exchange Rate Mechanism (ERM).** The Maastricht Treaty, approved in 1993, committed the countries to a monetary union and a single currency, the euro. In a **monetary union**, exchange rates are permanently fixed and a single monetary authority conducts a single unionwide monetary policy. Eleven EU countries established the monetary union on January 1, 1999. This final section of the chapter examines the economics of monetary union as the ultimate fixed exchange rate arrangement, by looking at the experience of the EU during the past several decades.

---

[4]The Argentinean government could attempt to negotiate an agreement with the U.S. government to gain a share of the forgone interest, but the U.S. government has not appeared to be receptive to encouraging dollarization by sharing seigniorage profits with other countries.

Exchange Rate Mechanism

In 1979, Germany, France, Italy, the Netherlands, Belgium, Denmark, Ireland, and Luxembourg began to fix the exchange rates among their currencies as participants in the Exchange Rate Mechanism. Until 1993, most countries in the ERM committed to maintaining their actual exchange rates within a band of plus or minus 2.25 percent around the central rate. Until 1990, Italy had a larger band of plus or minus 6 percent for the lira exchange rates. Spain joined the ERM in 1989, Britain in 1990, and Portugal in 1992—all with bands of 6 percent.

The ERM was an adjustable-peg system. When a realignment of some or all central rates seemed necessary, it was a collective decision of the members, not a unilateral action by one country. There were 11 realignments during the first nine years, 1979–1987. Then from 1987 through 1992, there were no realignments. In fact, the discipline effect on national inflation rates seemed to work quite well. Germany was generally regarded as the lead country in the system due to its economic size and the prestige of its central bank. Germany maintained a low inflation rate, and the other ERM countries were disciplined by the fixed exchange rates to lower their inflation rates toward the German level. In 1979, the range of inflation rates was about 10 percentage points. In the early 1990s, the average inflation rate was lower and the range was halved.

Figure 24.1 shows the exchange rates of EU countries' currencies relative to the German mark (pictured as the DM value of the other currency). Of the original ERM members shown in the top half, the DM value of the Netherlands guilder is the steadiest—it changed little from 1979 to 1998. The general tendency for the Belgian franc, Danish kroner, French franc, and Italian lira to devalue in the realignments is seen clearly from 1979 into 1987. From 1987 to 1992, the curves flatten, and the exchange rate values steady in the absence of realignments. The figure also shows that the exchange rate values (relative to the DM) of all of these ERM members were less variable than that of the British pound up to 1990. Britain was the EU country that deliberately did not join the ERM in 1979.

By mid-1992, the ERM seemed to be working very well. At that time all EU countries but Greece were in the ERM. No realignments had occurred since 1987. As part of "Europe 1992," the general effort to dismantle barriers to permit free movements of goods, services, and capital within the EU, most countries had removed capital controls by 1990. The EU countries had completed the drafting of the Maastricht Treaty, which contained the plans for monetary union, and they were in the process of approving it.

As we discussed in Chapters 20 and 22, the ERM exchange rates came under serious pressure beginning in September 1992. Several things contributed to the severity of the pressure. International investors became worried that the exchange rate values of several currencies in the ERM were not appropriate. For instance, the lira appeared to be overvalued, given that the Italian inflation rate had remained above that of the other ERM members. In addition, international investors became worried by policy tensions among the ERM members. German policymakers were placing full emphasis on reducing and controlling German inflation, while policymakers in several other countries, including France and

FIGURE 24.1 *Exchange Rates for the Currencies of the European Union Countries, 1979–1998 (Monthly)*

A. EU members in 1979

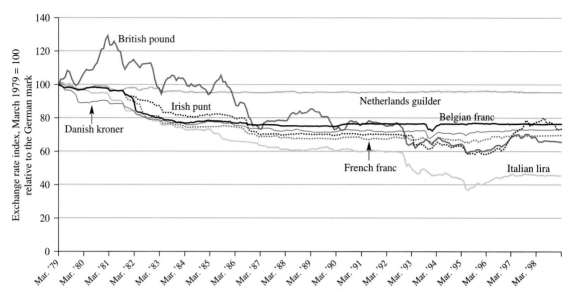

B. Countries that joined the EU after 1979

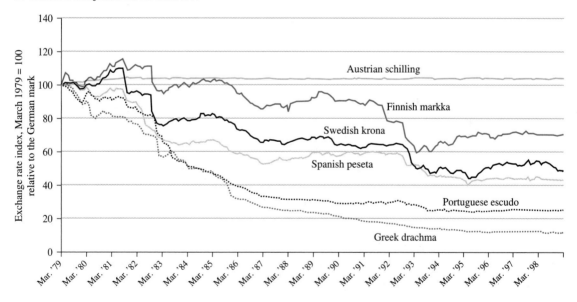

The figure shows the nominal exchange rate values of EU currencies as German marks per other currency, shown as an index with a value of 100 in March 1979, the date that the Exchange Rate Mechanism began. The original members of the ERM were Germany, the Netherlands, Belgium, Ireland, France, Italy, and Luxembourg. (The Luxembourg franc is the same as the Belgian franc, so it is not shown separately.) The Belgian franc, Danish kroner, French franc, Italian lira, and Irish punt were devalued during realignments from 1979 to 1987. Spain joined the ERM in 1989, Britain in 1990, and Portugal in 1992. Britain and Italy withdrew from the ERM in 1992, and their currencies quickly depreciated. Austria, whose currency had been effectively pegged to the German mark for many years, joined the ERM in 1994, Finland in 1996, and Greece in 1998. Italy rejoined in 1996. With the exception of the Irish punt, the DM values of other ERM member currencies were generally steady from late 1993 to the end of 1998.

Source: International Monetary Fund, *International Financial Statistics.*

Britain, probably preferred to shift the emphasis to reducing unemployment. Furthermore, in a general vote in 1992, Denmark rejected the Maastricht Treaty, and the upcoming French vote was expected to be close. These votes raised doubts about eventual monetary union, and they also raised doubts about the countries' current commitments to fixed exchange rates. Finally, the removal of capital controls meant that international investors and speculators could move large amounts of financial capital quickly from one country and currency to another. Official defense of the fixed rates was difficult in the face of these large speculative flows.

As international investors and speculators shifted to expecting devaluations against the DM by a number of ERM countries, large amounts of capital flowed, and the central banks mounted massive defenses. Italy and Britain surrendered and left the system. Figure 24.1 shows the quick depreciation of the pound and lira as they switched to floating. Over the next year speculative attacks continued. The Spanish peseta was devalued three times, the Portuguese escudo twice, and the Irish punt once.

Another large speculative attack occurred during July 1993. As a result, on August 1, 1993, the ERM changed the allowable band to plus or minus 15 percent (though the DM–guilder rate remained fixed within a 2.25 percent band). Though the bands were widened, there was no realignment. Exchange rates among the ERM currencies then were generally calm during the next years, mostly staying within or close to the old 2.25 percent bands. However, in March 1995, the peseta and escudo were devalued again. Also, at the end of 1994, Austria joined the ERM as it joined the EU. The entry of the Austrian schilling was easy. It had been effectively pegged closely to the DM for many years, as the bottom half of Figure 24.1 shows. Finland joined the ERM in 1996, Italy rejoined in 1996, and Greece joined in 1998.

As this brief history indicates, the ERM illustrates many of the points made in the first half of the chapter about the strengths and weaknesses of fixed exchange rates. The ERM exchange rates were generally steadier than floating rates were during this period, although occasional realignments disturbed the stability. The fixed rates applied pressure on other ERM countries to reduce their inflation rates toward the German level. Differences in goals between Germany and several other ERM countries in the early 1990s led to strains in the system, and these other countries could not use monetary policy to address their internal imbalances. The removal of capital controls made the defense of the fixed rates through official intervention more difficult in 1992 and 1993. In fact, several countries temporarily reimposed or tightened their capital controls as part of their defense efforts. These controls helped in the defense of the fixed exchange rates, but they ran counter to the broad efforts to create a single EU market.

European Monetary Union

In 1991, the EU countries completed the draft of the Maastricht Treaty (named for the Dutch town where it was negotiated). The **Maastricht Treaty** amended the Treaty of Rome, the founding charter of the European Union, to set a process for establishing a monetary union and a single unionwide currency. After several close national votes, including a defeat in Denmark that was later reversed, all EU countries approved the treaty, and it became effective in November 1993.

The Maastricht Treaty set a specific process for the establishment of the **European Monetary Union.** To participate in the monetary union, a country had to meet five criteria. The country's inflation rate must be no higher than 1.5 percentage points above the average inflation rate of the three EU countries with the lowest inflation rates, its exchange rates must be maintained within the ERM bands with no realignments during the preceding two years, and its long-term interest rate on government bonds must be no higher than 2 percentage points above the average of the comparable interest rates in the three lowest-inflation countries. In addition, the country's government budget deficit must be no larger than 3 percent of the value of its GDP, and the gross government debt must be no larger than 60 percent of its GDP (or the country must show satisfactory progress to achieving these two criteria in the near future). These criteria were intended to measure whether the country's performance had converged toward that of the best-performing EU countries so that the country was ready to enter the monetary union.

In May 1998, a summit of EU leaders decided which countries met the five criteria and would be members of the new euro-zone. With some liberal use of the "satisfactory progress" exception for the government debt criterion, 11 of the countries were deemed to meet the criteria and chose to join the monetary union. Greece did not qualify. Britain, Denmark, and Sweden could have qualified but chose not to join the union at its inception. EU countries not joining at the beginning can join later if they meet the criteria.

As discussed in Chapter 16, the monetary union began on January 1, 1999, with each national currency fixed in value to the new unionwide currency, the euro. In 2002, euro coins and paper currency will begin to circulate and will completely replace the national currencies. The **European Central Bank (ECB)** was established in 1998 as the center of the European System of Central Banks, a federal structure that also includes the national central banks as operating arms. On January 1, 1999, the ECB assumed responsibility for unionwide monetary policy in the euro-zone.

What can the EU countries achieve with monetary union and what are they giving up or risking? European Monetary Union provides examples of almost all of the issues that we discussed in the first half of the chapter.[5]

The gains from monetary union are based on the elimination of all exchange rate concerns. The shift to a common currency is a permanent fix and more. It will end exchange rate variability and risk. It will end one-way speculation about changes in pegged exchange rates. It will end all foreign exchange transactions costs.

Eliminating transactions costs will free up resources to be devoted to other productive activities. The costs of currency transactions within the euro-zone were about 0.4 percent of GDP. This is not a large resource cost saving, but it is not absolutely small either. Furthermore, by reducing costs and risks, larger volumes of trade will occur. In this sense monetary union is part of the broad drive to European integration and single European markets. In addition, it may benefit

---

[5]This discussion is also largely an application of the analysis of an *optimum currency area*—the size of the geographic area that shows the best economic performance with fixed exchange rates (or one currency) within the area and floating exchange rates with currencies outside the area.

macroeconomic performance in individual EU countries. Because the smaller EU countries are very open to international flows, some observers believe that exchange rate changes often harm the countries' performance. For these countries depreciation or devaluation quickly adds to domestic inflation pressures, while appreciation or revaluation quickly harms price competitiveness and has a large adverse effect on aggregate demand.

There are two major sources of risks and possible losses from European Monetary Union. The first risk is about how effective the new European Central Bank (ECB) will be in its conduct of unionwide monetary policy. The second risk is about how each member country's economy will perform when economic shocks affect different countries in different ways.

Uncertainties about the ECB arise from the different reasons that different countries supported full monetary union and from the ECB's unusual structure. Before monetary union, monetary policy within the ERM was effectively set by the German central bank. This arrangement was very successful in reducing EU inflation to almost nothing, but the Bundesbank set its policy mainly to achieve good German economic performance. Other EU countries, especially France, supported monetary union as a way of gaining more say over unionwide monetary policy, by establishing the ECB as a unionwide institution. However, the Germans would only support monetary union if the ECB was modeled closely after the Bundesbank. The ECB is designed to be independent from direct political influence and mandated to conduct unionwide monetary policy to achieve price stability. Tensions arose immediately, during the first months of 1999, as economic growth weakened and unemployment rose in many countries of the euro-zone. National politicians publicly called for loosening of euro monetary policy and pressured the ECB to focus more on growth and employment, and certainly not only on price stability. (In April 1999, the ECB did shift to an expansionary monetary policy, by lowering its interest rate targets.) The ECB's monetary policy decisions are made by a majority vote of the governing council, composed of the 11 heads of the national central banks and the 6 members of the executive committee. While not overtly political, there is room for national economic concerns to sway unionwide policy decisions. It is uncertain whether or not this structure will be successful in setting unionwide monetary policy that achieves a high level of macroeconomic performance for the euro-zone.

The second risk is to the national economic performance of each member country. The economies of the member countries are different. It is likely that shocks will affect the countries differently, so that economic conditions sometimes will vary across the countries. Especially, weak demand will cause recessions in some countries, while demand in other countries is growing and their economies are strong. With monetary union, each country has given up both the ability to run an independent monetary policy that could respond to domestic imbalances and the ability to use exchange rate changes as an adjustment tool.

Each country, then, must rely on other mechanisms to reduce national imbalances. Fiscal policy remains available, but there are two concerns about how effective it can be. First, there is little fiscal policy that includes the entire euro-zone. With almost no unionwide fiscal policy, there are almost no "automatic stabilizers" across countries. That is, higher tax revenues from the growing countries are not "automatically" shifted to the recession countries through lower taxes and larger expenditures in the recession countries. And there is no active unionwide fiscal policy to help the recession countries.

This leads to the second concern, whether each country will be able to use its national fiscal policy effectively to improve its domestic performance. A major constraint on the effective use of national fiscal policy is political. Fiscal policy can be changed only with lags created by the political process of enacting changes and the bureaucratic process of implementing them. In addition, as part of the process of moving toward monetary union, the German government insisted on the "Stability and Growth Pact," which establishes the ongoing rule that national government budget deficits should be no more than 3 percent of GDP, with temporary exceptions for unusual external shocks or severe national recessions. Countries that have a budget deficit above 3 percent of GDP are subject to monetary penalties, unless an exception is granted. If this agreement is taken seriously, it will limit the use of national fiscal policy, and it could at times turn national fiscal policy into a destabilizer. For instance, if the government budget deficit begins close to 3 percent, and a mild national recession hits, the government may be compelled to raise taxes or cut government expenditures to prevent the deficit from rising above 3 percent. These fiscal changes would make the recession worse.

Another method of adjustment to national imbalances is for resources to move from areas of weak demand to areas of strong demand. If labor mobility is high, adjustments to internal imbalances can be speeded by people moving from places where unemployment is high to places where demand for labor is strong. However, most studies conclude that labor mobility across EU countries (and even within these countries) is relatively low and is likely to remain low. In contrast, capital mobility is high within the EU. Adjustment could occur with capital moving to seek out and employ underutilized resources like unemployed labor. But, given rigidities in labor markets and labor practices, capital may not move in this way—in fact, capital may instead flee from problem areas to those that are booming.

Our discussion indicates that a major risk facing each member nation of the euro-zone is the inability to address national recession (or some other internal imbalance) quickly, especially if the thrust of unionwide monetary policy is not helping. There is essentially no unionwide fiscal policy, and national fiscal policy may be limited and clumsy. Labor mobility is generally low, and capital movements may not be enough.

In conclusion, the European Monetary Union is an unprecedented effort by a group of countries that had separate monetary policies and separate central banks to establish a common central bank, a common monetary policy, and a common currency. While there are risks, there are also major benefits, as well as strong political commitments in the member countries to deepen the economic and political union. If the European Monetary Union and the euro work well, other countries that favor fixed exchange rates are likely to consider forming monetary unions (or replacing their national currencies with the dollar or the euro). One global trend is toward floating exchange rates, but another trend may be developing as well—toward more permanent regional fixes and fewer currencies.

Summary

A major decision for a country's government is its choice of exchange rate policy. This chapter has examined the extent of rate flexibility that a country's policy allows. We discussed what five major issues say about the advantages and disadvantages of choosing a floating rate or a fixed rate.

Figure 24.2 summarizes the major points of the discussion. For each issue there are usually ways in which the issue favors a floating rate and other ways in which the issue favors a fixed rate. Because countries differ in their economic situations, policymaking institutions, economic histories, and political interests, different countries can view the balance of advantages and disadvantages differently, leading to different policy choices. Indeed, as economic and political conditions change over time, the policy chosen by a country can change.

In a country's choice between a more flexible rate and a more fixed-rate policy, several points shown in Figure 24.2 are typically prominent. Strong arguments in favor of a floating exchange rate include the country's ability to use independent monetary policy and exchange rate changes to adjust internal and external imbalances; the country's ability, more generally, to pursue goals and policies that meet its own domestic needs; and the difficulty of defending fixed rates against speculative attacks, given the large and growing amounts of financial capital that can move quickly between countries. The strongest argument in favor of a fixed exchange rate is that floating rates have been too variable, which disrupts and discourages international trade and other international transactions.

In recent decades, countries have shifted toward choosing more flexible exchange rates. Countries generally attempt to manage the float in order to moderate the variability of the floating rate, although the effectiveness of this management, at least for the major currencies, is questionable.

Still, a number of countries continue to have fixed exchange rates. However, fixed rates that are adjustable seem at times to encourage speculative attacks. Some countries use forms of fixed rates that are more nearly permanent. A **currency board** is a monetary authority that holds only international reserve assets, so sterilization is not possible. With a currency board, the country's money supply is automatically linked to the intervention to defend the fixed exchange rate. **"Dollarization"** involves completely replacing the local currency with a foreign currency (for instance, the U.S. dollar). Monetary conditions in the country are almost completely controlled by the foreign central bank (for instance, the U.S. Federal Reserve).

The most ambitious fixed-rate effort is occurring in the European Union, where 11 EU countries joined the **European Monetary Union** at the beginning of 1999. In a **monetary union,** exchange rates are permanently fixed, and a single monetary authority conducts a unionwide monetary policy. The European Monetary Union is the successor to the fixed exchange rates of the **Exchange Rate Mechanism (ERM)** of the European Monetary System, established in 1979. Under the ERM, the fixed exchange rates were generally less variable than comparable floating exchange rates, although the fixed ERM rates were occasionally adjusted in realignments. Inflation rates in other ERM countries declined toward the low German inflation rate. However, following the removal of capital controls by some ERM countries, differences in macroeconomic goals between Germany and some other ERM countries led to speculative attacks in 1992 and 1993. Britain and Italy left the ERM, and the allowable bands were widened for all rates but the mark–guilder rate. After 1993, the ERM exchange rates were generally steady.

The **Maastricht Treaty** took effect in 1993 and set the criteria for EU countries to enter into a monetary union. In 1998, 11 EU countries were

FIGURE 24.2   *Advantages of Floating Exchange Rates and Fixed Exchange Rates in Terms of Various Issues*

Issue	Advantage of Floating Exchange Rates	Advantage of Fixed Exchange Rates
Effects of macroeconomic shocks	With floating rates external shocks, especially foreign trade shocks, are less disruptive.	With fixed rates internal shocks, especially domestic monetary shocks, are less disruptive.
Effectiveness of government policies	With floating rates monetary policy is more effective in influencing aggregate demand.	—
	With floating rates fiscal policy is more effective if capital flows are not very responsive to interest rates.	With fixed rates fiscal policy is more effective if capital flows are sufficiently responsive to interest rates.
Differences in macroeconomic goals and policies	Floating rates allow goals and policies to differ across countries.	Fixed rates require coordination or consistency of goals and policies across countries.
Controlling inflation	Floating rates allow each country to choose its own acceptable inflation rate.	With fixed rates countries should have about the same inflation rates. This creates a discipline effect on high-inflation countries (but low-inflation countries may "import" higher inflation).
Real effects of exchange rate variability	Variability of floating rates is desirable. It shows that the market is working well as supply and demand shift. The rates reflect unstable economic and political environments. Real effects on international trade are not that large because much exchange rate risk can be hedged.	Variability of floating rates, especially between the major currencies, is excessive. The rates may be driven at times by bandwagons and speculative bubbles. The variability causes undesirable real effects. Exchange rate risk lowers trade volumes. Overshooting causes excessive resource shifts into and out of trade-oriented industries.
	A fixed rate is simply a form of price control. The fixed rate is often inefficiently low or high, causing inefficient resource allocations.	The relative stability of fixed rates may promote higher levels of international transactions, especially trade.

deemed to meet the criteria and agreed to join the union. The **European Central Bank (ECB)** was established to conduct unionwide monetary policy. On January 1, 1999, the national currencies of these 11 countries were fixed to the euro, the new union currency, and the euro will completely replace the national currencies in 2002.

The European Monetary Union can be used to indicate the major advantages and disadvantages of a monetary union. First, the union brings greater gains, the larger are the trade and other transactions among its members. The gains flow largely from reduced transactions costs and reduced exchange rate risk. For the European Monetary Union, with its shift to a single currency, these gains are probably substantial. Second, the establishment of the unionwide monetary authority can bring uncertainty, at least at first, about what its priorities and decision-making procedures will be. The ECB was established to be largely free from direct political influence, but it came under substantial political pressures to loosen monetary policy in the first months of the monetary union.

Third, if the structures of the members' economies are different, economic shocks affect them differently, with some countries in recession and others growing quickly. When this occurs, the countries will need ways to adjust their internal imbalances, but each nation no longer has national monetary policy or national exchange rate policy. Fiscal policy at the union level could be useful, by providing automatic stabilizers as well as active fiscal policy changes. If unionwide fiscal policy is not sufficient, each nation may need to use national fiscal policy actively. In addition, labor mobility can assist in adjusting imbalances, as people move from areas of high unemployment to areas of low unemployment. European Monetary Union faces its major challenges in this third broad area of shocks, national imbalances, and policy and adjustment responses. The member countries are different and experience different internal imbalances, there is almost no fiscal policy at the union level, national fiscal policies are limited, and labor mobility is low.

Suggested Reading

The classic article favoring floating exchange rates is Friedman (1953). Shortcomings of current floating are discussed in Whitt (1990). Obstfeld and Rogoff (1995) discuss why fixed rates have been so hard to defend. Edison and Melvin (1990) survey our knowledge of the influence of exchange rate variability on international trade. McKinnon (1988) and Williamson (1985) propose reforms to the current system that incorporate shifts back toward relatively fixed (or less flexible) exchange rates. Enoch and Gulde (1998) look at currency boards. Mundell (1961), McKinnon (1963), and Tower and Willett (1976) examine fixed rates within optimum currency areas. Wyplosz (1997), Feldstein (1997), and Eichengreen (1993) review and critique European Monetary Union. Wynne (1999) examines the European Central Bank.

Questions and Problems

✦1. "Countries whose currencies are linked to each other through fixed exchange rates usually should pursue very different monetary and fiscal policies." Do you agree or disagree? Why?

2. "If most countries adhered to a system of fixed exchange rates, global inflation would be lower." Do you agree or disagree? Why?

✦3. A country is worried that business cycles in other countries tend to disrupt its own economy. It would like some "insulation" from foreign business cycles. Why would this country favor having a floating exchange rate?

4. "If a country's government decides to have a flexible exchange rate, then it should have a clean float." Do you agree or disagree? Why?

✦5. A country now has a floating exchange rate. Its government would like to fix the exchange rate value of its currency to another currency. You have been hired as an advisor to the country's government. Suggest three major criteria for deciding what other country's currency to fix to. Why is each important?

6. The variability of floating exchange rates since 1973 has been higher than most economists expected.

a. Why are some economists not concerned about this?

b. Why are other economists quite worried about this?

◆7. A new government has been elected in a country that now has a high inflation rate and a floating exchange rate. The new government is committed to reducing the country's inflation rate.

a. If the government continues to use a floating exchange rate, what will the government need to do to reduce the high inflation rate?

b. As part of its effort to reduce the country's inflation rate, why might the country's government consider a change to using a currency board and a fixed exchange rate with one of the major currencies of the world?

8. According to the Maastricht Treaty, what are the five convergence criteria for an EU country to be allowed to join the European Monetary Union? What logic do you see for having each as a requirement? Which of the five criteria seem to be more or less important as a basis for excluding a country from the monetary union?

◆9. The time is 2003. The European Monetary Union and the euro have worked reasonably well, and the euro is now the sole currency in the euro-zone. Britain has remained outside. You are attempting to convince a British friend that Britain should join the monetary union as soon as possible. What are your two strongest arguments?

10. Consider the same scenario in question 9. Your British friend is trying to convince you that Britain should stay out of the monetary union. What are her two strongest arguments?

PART V

Factor Movements

CHAPTER 25

The International Movement of Labor

Of all the flows that take place between nations, none is more sensitive than the flow of humans. As we saw in Chapter 1, several events of the 1990s showed that the sensitivity of this issue is once again on the rise. In response to the growing numbers of refugees from Eastern Europe, Germany put up new immigration barriers. Anti-immigrant campaigns became vocal in some other European countries. In response to rising legal and illegal immigration from Mexico and Central America, a majority of Californians voted to deny all non-emergency public services to any non-natives who could not show they had entered the country legally. And the U.S. government enacted a federal law to deny legal immigrants access to many social programs, though subsequent laws restored some of the benefits.

For political reasons, the migration issue does not lend itself to clean, simple solutions. At the one extreme, simply stopping immigration or emigration may not be feasible. Stopping all immigration offends foreign countries and domestic ethnic groups, and harms businesses and individuals who wish to employ the immigrants. It has the further drawback of being almost impossible to enforce. Stopping all immigration, like stopping all emigration, practically requires a Berlin Wall and a complete police state. Even Switzerland—the best example of a highly prosperous country threatened by a massive influx of foreigners—has to allow some to stay.

The other extreme also often does not work for a key political reason: Simply allowing free migration is politically unpopular because *the group that benefits most from international migration has almost no political voice.* Even without an economic model, we know who that group is: the migrants themselves.

For those who migrate, the dangers are great but the average gain is high. A migrant risks disease or victimization by others, and may fail to find a better income in the country of destination. Many migrants return home unsuccessful and disillusioned. Still, they experience great gains on the average, as we might expect from so risky an activity. In some cases political and physical freedom itself is a large gain, as in the case of refugees from repressive regimes. In other cases, the economic gains stand out. Doctors, engineers, and other highly trained personnel from low-income countries such as India and Pakistan have multiplied their incomes severalfold by migrating to North America, Australia, Britain, and the Persian Gulf. Mexican craftspeople and campesinos earn enough in Texas or California to retire early (if they wish) in comfortable Mexican homes and to support their children generously. Turkish "guestworkers" in Germany have also ensured themselves a comfortable living and a quantum jump up the income ranks.

Yet allowing complete freedom for migrants brings objective costs to some vocal nonmigrants. In the sending countries, having people emigrate can wound national pride and bring economic losses to some who remain behind. Thus promoting emigration is not politically popular, even in countries like Mexico where the overall economic gains are unmistakable. In the receiving countries, ethnic prejudice, general xenophobia, and the direct economic stake of groups who fear competition from immigrants keep the issue especially sensitive. Wherever the concentration of immigrants swells suddenly, violent backlash threatens. Light-footed politicians know better than to campaign on a slogan of free migration.

Behind these pressures lies the migrants' basic political weakness: In any political arena, the migrating minority is "them," not "us." To migrate or to request help in migrating is to lose voting rights. In a sending country, potential emigrants who speak up on behalf of their right to leave are signaling that they do not plan to be a part of that country's political future. The majority may demand compensation or make emigration inconvenient, especially if the issue of national pride surfaces. In the receiving country, the interests of possible future immigrants do not command enough votes to make immigration easy. Only lobbying by employers and church groups represents their cause. The gains they would make by migrating, as opposed to their future employers' gains, have almost no vote.

If we want to understand just the economic pros and cons, and set aside the political bias against free migration, how do all these opposing forces balance out? What are the net economic gains to nations and the world, and how do they stack up against the less economic side effects of migration?

This chapter comes to grips with these issues. We begin by noting the dramatic swings in immigration in the main receiving countries. We then turn to the controversial effects of migration on labor markets and national incomes in the sending and receiving countries. These effects are both positive and negative, and we will show how the net balance might work out. Thereafter, we turn to the sensitive issue of whether immigrants contribute more in taxes than they claim from other taxpayers. Finally, we examine the policy choices facing host countries today.

Waves of Migration in the Past

International migration has played an enormous role in the past expansion of receiving counties. Indeed, almost the entire population of the Western Hemisphere and of Australia and New Zealand consists of descendants of those who immigrated in the past 200 years. One of the most striking features of this immigrant flow is its instability over the decades.

FIGURE 25.1

Gross Immigration Rates into the United States, 1820–1996 and Canada, 1851–1997

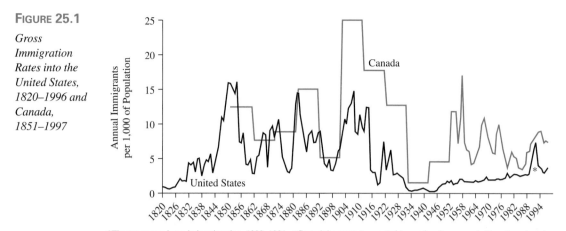

*The temporary jump in immigration, 1989–1991, reflected the amnesty granted to previously unrecorded immigrants and their families under the Immigration Reform and Control Act of 1986.

Source: U.S. annual rates, 1820–1970, from U.S. Bureau of the Census, *Historical Statistics of the United States, Colonial Times to 1970* (1976); and 1971–1996, from U.S. Bureau of the Census, *Statistical Abstract of the United States, 1987, 1994, and 1998;* Canadian decennial averages, 1851–1951, and the 1951–1954 average from Statistics Canada, *Canada Yearbook 1994;* Canadian annual rates 1955–1993 from the *Canadian Economic Observer 1993/94,* and 1994–1997 from SOPEMI, *Trends in International Migration, Annual Report, 1998* (OECD, 1998).

The basic modern history of immigration flows into North America and Europe is sketched in Figures 25.1 and 25.2. Figure 25.1 shows that the rising tide of immigration into North America since World War II has still not reached its levels before World War I, when both Canada and the United States opened their doors to immigrants and even advertised in Europe to attract them. After World War I, the door was partly shut by immigration restrictions in both the United States and Canada. The United States severely restricted immigration in 1924, using a system of quotas by national origin, in response to unprecedented public fear of strange cultures, revolutionary radicalism, and job competition. Canada also switched from actively recruiting immigrants to limiting them, especially when hard times hit in the 1930s.

After the war, both countries relied on partial controls that favored immigrants arriving with training and experience. In 1965, the United States replaced the national-origin quotas with a system that gave preference to applicants with family relatives already in the United States, and subsequent changes opened the door to more refugees. In 1974, Canada also shifted to a liberal policy toward relatives. Family members and refugees began to arrive at a quickening rate in the 1980s. In the Immigration Reform and Control Act (IRCA) of 1986, the United States tried to solve two immigration policy problems at once: cutting the further inflow of "illegal" (undocumented) immigrants and giving amnesty (permanent residence rights) to those who came earlier. One result of IRCA was the temporary jump in legal immigration for 1989–1991, a jump that helped reawaken natives' concern about being burdened with a new wave of immigrants. Even without the post-IRCA bulge, more immigrants were moving to North America in the 1990s,

FIGURE 25.2

*Net Immigration
Rates into the
European
Union,
1960–1996*

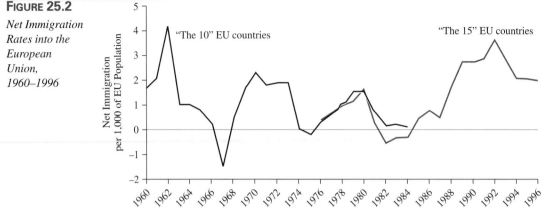

Net immigration = (Gross) immigration minus emigration, per 1,000 of population.
"The 10" EU countries = The original six (Belgium, France, Germany, Italy, Luxembourg, and the
                                    Netherlands) plus the UK, Ireland, Denmark, and Greece.
"The 15" EU countries = "The 10" plus Portugal, Spain, Austria, Finland, and Sweden.

Source: European Communities, Statistical Offices (Eurostat), Bevölkerungsstatistik (Demographic Statistics), Brussels,
1986; and Eurostat, *Eurostat Yearbook '97*, Brussels, 1997.

especially people from Mexico and the former Soviet Union into the United
States, and Asians into Canada.

The doors in the European Union (EU) have also swung open, then shut, and
then temporarily more open again, in this case within the shorter period since it
was formed in 1957. In the 1950s and 1960s, the EU countries welcomed and
even recruited workers from Turkey and other nonmember countries to help with
the postwar reconstruction boom. In the early 1970s, however, the mood
changed, as suggested by Figure 25.2. One EU country after another tightened up
its immigration policy, partly out of rising cultural frictions and partly to protect
jobs after the first oil crisis began to raise unemployment in 1974. Fewer immigrants were granted entry into the EU from 1974 to 1988. Then, however, the
inflow began to rise again. The reason is not that EU immigration policy liberalized after 1988, but rather that a change in conditions outside the EU forced more
immigrants through the same half-open doors. In particular, the rise of asylum
seekers from East Europe made greater demands on those countries whose laws
allowed for compassion toward refugees. The strain was particularly great on
Germany because of its prosperity, the reunification of West and East Germany,
Germany's proximity to the transition countries of East Europe, and the German
constitution's provision that refugees must be given safe haven. Finally, in 1993,
Germany repealed the constitutional safe-haven guarantees and began clamping
down on immigration.

How Migration Affects Labor Markets

To see the impact of allowing immigration, let's explore the economic effects of migration in two stages. First, we squeeze as much as we can out of a thrice-squeezed orange, the familiar static welfare analysis already used extensively in Parts I and II. In this stage, repetition is a positive advantage, showing that our familiar demand–supply framework is useful once again. The second stage introduces social and economic dimensions of migration that do not lend themselves well to the usual analysis. Exploring the public-finance effects and social externalities of migration calls for more complicated analysis.

We begin with the standard effects of migration on labor markets in the two countries. To simplify the analysis, we shall aggregate the whole world into two stylized countries: a low-income "South" and a high-income "North." Let's start with a situation in which no migration is allowed, as at the points *A* in the two sides of Figure 25.3. In this initial situation northern workers earn $6.00 an hour and southern workers of comparable skill earn $2.00 an hour. (Realistically, we presume that factor-price equalization, as discussed in Chapter 4, does not hold, perhaps because of governmental barriers to free trade or differences in technologies.)

If all official barriers to migration are removed, southern workers can go north and compete for northern jobs. If moving were costless and painless, they would do so in large numbers until they had bid the northern wage rate down and the southern wage rate up enough to equate the two.

Yet moving also brings costs to the migrants. Economic costs include the transportation and other money expenses of migration, as well as lost wages while relocating. In addition, migrants usually feel uprooted from friends and relatives. They feel uncertain about many dimensions of life in a strange country. They may have to learn new customs and a new language. They may have to endure hostility in their new country. All these things matter, so much so that we should imagine that wide wage gaps would persist even with complete legal freedom to move. Thus only a lesser number of persons, 20 million of them in Figure 25.3, find the wage gains from moving high enough to compensate them for the migration costs (*c*), here valued at $1.80 per hour of work in the North. The inflow of migrant labor thus bids the northern wage rate down only to $5.00 at point *B,* and the outflow of the same workers only raises southern wages up to $3.20. The new equilibrium, at point *B,* finds the number who have chosen to migrate just equal to the demand for extra labor in the North at $5.00 an hour.

Those who decide to migrate earn $5.00 an hour in the North, but it is worth only as much as $3.20 in the South because of the costs and drawbacks of working in the North. To measure their net gain, we take the area above the migrants' labor supply curve between the old and new wage rates ($2.00 and $3.20), or areas *e* and *f*.[1]

---

[1] The migrants' labor supply curve S_{mig} can be derived by subtracting the curve S_r from the combined curve $S_r + S_{mig}$. Note that their welfare gain does not equal the full product of ($3.20 – $2.00) times the 20 million unless their labor supply curve (S_{mig}) is perfectly vertical, in which case the amount of time they devote to work is independent of the wage rate. (Remember that their supply curve can be interpreted as a curve showing the marginal cost of their time.)

FIGURE 25.3

*Labor-Market
Effects of
Migration*

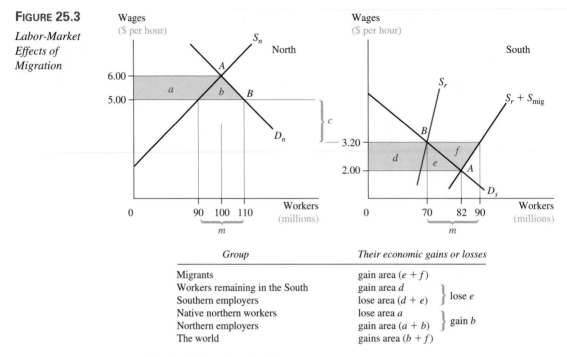

Group	Their economic gains or losses	
Migrants	gain area (*e* + *f*)	
Workers remaining in the South	gain area *d*	
Southern employers	lose area (*d* + *e*)	} lose *e*
Native northern workers	lose area *a*	
Northern employers	gain area (*a* + *b*)	} gain *b*
The world	gains area (*b* + *f*)	

m = Number of migrants = 20 million
c = Annuitized cost of migrating, both economic and psychic
    (being uprooted, etc.), which offsets $1.80 per hour of extra pay

(By holding the labor demand curves fixed, we gloss over the slight shifts in them that would result from the
migrants' own spending.)

It is not hard to identify the other groups of net gainers and losers in the two
regions. Workers remaining in the South, whose labor supply curve is S_r, gain
because the reduction in competition for jobs raises their wage rates from $2.00
to $3.20. We can quantify their gains with a standard producer surplus measure,
area *d*, in the same way used to quantify the gains to producers in Parts I and II of
this book. Their employers lose profits by having to offer higher wage rates. The
southern employers' loss is area (*d* + *e*). Employers in the North gain, of course,
from the extra supply of labor. Having the northern wage rate bid down from
$6.00 to $5.00 brings them area (*a* + *b*) in extra surplus. Workers already in the
North lose area *a* by having their wage rate bid down. So here, as in the analysis
of product trade in Part I, some groups absolutely gain and others absolutely lose
from the new international freedom.

The analysis in Figure 25.3 shows some clear and perhaps unexpected effects
on the welfare of entire nations of nonmigrants. Let's turn first to the effects on
the North, here defined so as to exclude the migrants even after they have arrived.

As a nation these northern "natives" gain in standard economic terms—the gain to employers (and the general public buying their products) clearly outweighs the loss to workers; area b is the net gain. The case for restricting immigration cannot lie in any net national economic loss unless we can introduce large negative effects not yet shown in Figure 25.3. The sending country, defined as those who remain in the South after the migrants' departure, clearly loses. Employers' losses of $(d + e)$ exceed workers' gain of d alone. So far it looks as though receiving countries and the migrants gain, while sending countries lose. The world as a whole gains, of course, because freedom to migrate sends people toward countries where they will make a greater net contribution to world production.

Does migration really work that way? Does it make wage rates more equal in different countries? Are competing workers harmed in receiving countries? Do immigrants catch up with them in pay? Does the world as a whole gain? Several studies have shown that the predictions of Figure 25.3 are borne out by the history of migration, both in the great integration of the world economy before 1914 and again in experience since the mid-1970s. Here are some of the main findings of the empirical studies:[2]

- Freer migration makes wage rates in the migrant-related occupations more equal between countries.
- Directly competing workers in the receiving countries do have their pay lowered, relative to less immigrant-threatened occupations and relative to such nonlabor incomes as land rents. However, these directly competing workers are fewer in number than most people think because immigrants often take jobs that are increasingly unpopular with natives of the prosperous receiving countries (taxi driving, long hours in small convenience stores, etc.). In the United States the major group of workers hurt by rising immigration since 1980 is the least-skilled American workers (e.g., high school dropouts).
- Immigrants catch up partly, but not completely, within their own lifetimes. Numerous studies have traced their convergence toward the better pay enjoyed by native-born workers, but the deficit is not erased in the first generation after migration. The pay deficit has grown more pronounced in Canada and the United States since the 1970s.
- World output is raised by allowing more migration.

Average-Income Paradoxes of Migration

The gains for receiving countries and the losses for sending countries pose what might be called average-income paradoxes. That is, they clash with some intuitions we might have about the effects of migration on that crude standard

---

[2]For a recent sampling from this vast literature, see Borjas, Freeman, and Katz (1997, on the United States); Abowd and Freeman (1991, on North America and Australia); Pope and Withers (1993, on Australia); Bloom, Grenier, and Gunderson (1994, on Canada); O'Rourke, Taylor, and Williamson (1993 and 1994, on pre-1914); Friedberg and Hunt (1995); and Zimmerman (1995).

measure of welfare, national income per capita or "average income." Intuition might lead us to ask two questions:

1. If the immigrants have a lower income than others in the new country, won't their arrival lower average income in this country? How can this be reconciled with the receiving-country gains shown in Figure 25.3?
2. If the same migrants had lower-than-average income in the sending country, won't their departure raise average income in that country? How can this be reconciled with the sending-country losses shown in Figure 25.3?

What is here imagined about average incomes is likely to be true—yet there is no contradiction. The logical consistency of the usual results is shown with a numerical example in Figure 25.4, an example based on recent population and income levels of the United States and Mexico. Each country is divided into the same three groups featured in our discussion of the welfare effects in Figure 25.3: the migrants themselves, competing permanent-resident workers whose job markets the migrants affect, and a group consisting of employers and others benefiting from extra labor supply and population.

The example in Figure 25.4 starts from a realistic premise about the position of typical migrants: Their income would be closer to the average in the sending country than in the receiving country. Numerous studies have found that international migrants are typically average or almost average in their earning power in the home country before they emigrate. They are usually not from the ranks of the poorest. The lowest-income groups in the low-income countries lack the hope, the money, and the information to migrate internationally in large numbers. The international migrants tend to be venturesome individuals from more middling backgrounds. To underline our paradoxes, however, let's assume the Mexican migrants in this example have initially below-average incomes in Mexico.

If 2 million adults of working age were to migrate from Mexico to the United States, the movement of their labor supply would probably have effects like those shown in Figure 25.4. The "net change" row at the bottom shows two average-income paradoxes: The United States loses average income yet gains total income, whereas Mexico gains average income yet loses total income. There's more: Within the United States, there is a net gain for the 140 million permanent residents as well as for the migrants, but the U.S. average income declines; within Mexico, there is a net income loss for all permanent residents, but Mexico's average income rises!

The key to all the paradoxes is that the migrants and their incomes are counted in the calculation of Mexico's average income before they migrate, but they are counted in the calculation of U.S. average income afterwards. Let's look first at the receiving country, the United States. Migration had all the effects on separate northern groups that we discussed in connection with Figure 25.3. Competing permanent-resident workers, especially unskilled workers, tend to lose income because of extra competition from immigrants. Employers, landowners, and others tend to gain income from the arrival of the immigrants—from their

FIGURE 25.4   *A Realistic Example of an Average-Income Paradox from Migration*

Group	United States			Mexico		
	No. of Persons of Working Age (million)	Average Income	Total Income ($ million)	No. of Persons of Working Age (million)	Average Income	Total Income ($ million)
Before Migration						
Competing permanent-resident workers	20 ×	$12,000 =	$ 240,000	19 ×	$3,750 =	$ 71,250
Potential emigrants	—	—	—	2 ×	3,750 =	7,500
Employers and others	120 ×	55,582 =	6,669,840	19 ×	13,940 =	264,860
Nation as a whole	140 ×	49,356 =	6,909,840	40 ×	8,590 =	343,610
After Migration						
Competing permanent-resident workers	19 ×	11,000 =	209,000	20 ×	3,950 =	79,000
Immigrants*	2 ×	11,000 =	22,000	—	—	—
Employers and others	121 ×	55,942 =	6,769,000	18 ×	13,833 =	249,000
Nation as a whole	142 ×	49,296 =	7,000,000	38 ×	8,632 =	328,000
Net change	+2	−60	+90,160	−2	+42	−15,610

*The costs of migration (psychological and other) have *not* been subtracted here, as they should be for judgments of overall well-being. This example also leaves the migrants' incomes in their pockets, not remitted to relatives and friends back in Mexico. Any remittances are here viewed as income for the donor and not the recipient, taking account of the donor's satisfaction from being able to send the remittances but not of the value of remittances to the recipients.

Note the Paradox: Average income drops by $60 in the United States and rises by $38 in Mexico—yet total income rises for the United States and the world as a whole, while declining for Mexico! Here is the key: The migrants are counted as Mexicans before they move but as residents of the United States after they move.

labor and from their demand for housing and other products. If they did not gain, we would have a hard time explaining why so many employers in California, Texas, and Florida spend a lot of dollars on lobbying against laws to cut immigration. Furthermore, both Figure 25.3 and Figure 25.4 realistically imagine that the gain to native employers and others outweighs the loss to competing workers, so that U.S. natives as a whole receive a small gain from the immigrants' arrival. The migrants receive greater percent gains. The seeming drop in U.S. average income is a mirage caused by inconsistently redefining the working-age population of the United States as excluding the migrants before they arrive but including them afterwards. If we carefully define the United States either with the migrants both before and after or without them both before and after, then we come to the correct conclusion: Average income rises for either definition of the United States, the receiving country.

The paradox for the sending country can be unraveled in the same way. If we carefully define Mexico as excluding the migrants both before and after they leave, Mexico loses average income. If we take the broader consistent definition of Mexico—one including the migrants both before and after they leave—then Mexico, as thus defined, gains.[3]

Public-Finance Effects of Migration

Thus far our analysis has ignored the effects of migrants on taxes and public spending. Figure 25.3 implicitly assumed that everybody breaks even on the public-finance side effects of migration, both on the average and at all the relevant margins. Yet this dimension of the migration issue is rightly controversial and deserves a fuller treatment.

There are many possible effects. Migrants stop paying taxes in their countries of origin, but they face new taxes at their destination. These include income taxes, sales taxes, property taxes (either directly or through rents), and social security contributions. They are also liable to military draft. Migrants also switch from one set of public goods to another. They benefit from the new nation's national defense, police protection, natural scenery, and public schools, while giving up the same services in the old country. They also switch from old to new rights to such transfer payments as unemployment insurance, social security, and ordinary welfare. How are all these possible effects likely to net out?

For the migrants themselves, it is not clear whether the net gain on public goods minus taxes rises or falls with the move. By changing countries they may forfeit some accumulated entitlements, such as public pensions and social insurance, without being entitled to the same in the new country. On the other hand, migrants generally drift toward higher-income countries, and public goods and services as a whole may be a better bargain there. The net public-finance effect for the migrants themselves is not clear. (Its unknown positive or negative value is buried within *c,* the perceived nonmarket cost of moving to the new country.)

Effects in the Sending Country

For the sending country, the loss of future tax contributions (and military service) from the emigrants is likely to outweigh the relief from having to share public goods and services with them. Many public-expenditure items are true "public goods" in the economics sense of being equally enjoyable to each party regardless of how many enjoy them. Having some leave does not greatly raise the oth-

---

[3]For another interesting average-income paradox, suppose that the migrants have above-average incomes in the sending countries but move to higher incomes that are nonetheless below average in the receiving county. In this case, the usual careless way of defining income per capita (including the migrants wherever they show up) yields this sort of paradox: The migration lowers income per capita in both countries yet raises it for the world as a whole! Demographers will recognize the average-income paradoxes as the sort of compositional-shift paradox that abounds in demography. Readers of Part I of this book can discover a similar paradox there. In Chapter 4, when we analyzed the effects of opening trade on factor use in a two-sector economy, we found that opening trade lowered the land/labor ratio in both sectors, yet kept the overall land/labor ratio unchanged (by shifting resources toward the land-intensive industry). See the box "A Factor-Ratio Paradox" in Chapter 4.

ers' enjoyment of such public goods as national defense or flood-control levees. The likelihood of a net fiscal drain from emigration is raised by the life-cycle patterns of public goods and migration. People tend to migrate in early adulthood. This means that emigrants tend to be concentrated in the age group that has just received some public schooling at taxpayer expense, yet the migrants will not be around to pay taxes from their adult earnings.

The sending country, then, may very well suffer a net public-finance loss from having people migrate.[4] The loss is likely to be the largest for highly skilled emigrants—the "brain drain." They have received substantial education at public expense, and they would pay substantial taxes on their above-average earnings if they stayed.

To reduce the net public-finance loss of emigration in general and the brain drain in particular, the sending country's government could try to reduce emigration. It could simply block departures. A more defensible policy response would be a tax on outward-bound persons that is roughly equal to the net contribution society has made to the emigrants through public schooling and the like. An alternative policy approach is to encourage return after the emigrant has been gone for a while by appealing to national pride, ensuring good employment, and so forth. Taiwan and South Korea have encouraged the return of their scientists and engineers to work in their rapidly developing high-tech industries.

In judging the sending country's stake in the emigration issue, we must also note the flows of voluntary remittances sent back to relatives and friends in the home country. These are often large, as Italian and Mexican experiences have shown. In fact, a country (defined as including the back-home family and friends) might reap a handsome rate of return from letting people leave.[5]

Effects in the Receiving Country

It is widely suspected that immigrants are a fiscal burden, swelling welfare rolls, using public schools, and raising police costs more than they pay back in taxes. This suspicion, applied to the "illegal" immigrants, was the basis for California's voting that public services should be denied to those immigrants whose papers are not in order. It was also the basis for the U.S. law that made legal immigrants ineligible for some forms of public assistance.

---

[4]We can think up hypothetical counterexamples in which the sending country gets all of its chronically unemployed, its welfare recipients, and its felons to leave, relieving itself of a net fiscal burden through emigration. But actual migrations almost never take such a form. As mentioned earlier, emigrants tend to be from the more energetic and productive ranks that probably would be net taxpayers.

[5]Do migrants' remittances back to their home country represent a loss to the country they have moved to? The first instinct might be to say yes, it's a drain on the new country's balance of payments. But reflect further on the meaning of the remittances. Migrants' remittances are a voluntary gift on their part and do not represent a loss to the migrants themselves, any more than voluntarily giving to a charity makes a person worse off. We could say the migrants are buying psychic satisfaction with their remittances to family and friends in the home country. And if importing this psychic satisfaction from the old country is not a clear welfare loss to them, it is not a welfare loss to their new country because the payment is being made only by the migrants from money they earned.

FIGURE 25.5   *Immigrant Households as U.S. Welfare Recipients and as Taxpayers, 1970–1990*

	1970	1980	1990
Immigrants as a percentage of all household heads	6.8%	7.6%	8.4%
Immigrants as a percentage of household heads receiving public assistance	6.7	8.3	10.1
Percentage of public assistance received by immigrants	6.7	9.1	13.1
Immigrant households' share of the tax base (share of nonwelfare income)	6.3	7.0	8.3

Source: See Figure 25.7, page 592.

The true fiscal effects of immigrants are hard to measure. A good set of clues and deductions on the recent fiscal effects of immigration comes from George Borjas's study of the incomes and welfare entitlements of U.S. immigrants between 1970 and 1990. Figures 25.5 through 25.7 present the key points. In the top two rows of Figure 25.5, we see that immigrant households have been rising faster as a share of the welfare population (those receiving public assistance aimed at the poor) than as a share of the whole population. To say it another way, the tendency to be on welfare was rising faster among immigrants than among others. The third row accentuates this trend. The share of welfare dollars going to immigrants has been rising even faster than their share of all welfare cases, meaning that their average claims per welfare case are rising faster than the claims of native welfare recipients.

So far, the first three rows of Figure 25.5 seem to confirm the anti-immigrant suspicion, at least the suspicion about changes over time. Yes, immigrants are becoming a rising welfare burden. But they are also paying a higher and higher share of the taxes, as shown by the fourth row.

Which trend is greater: their rising welfare receipts or their rising tax payments? Figure 25.5 cannot answer this question by itself. You might think that it shows a rising net burden on native taxpayers, just because the share of public assistance taken by immigrants jumped more (from 6.7 percent up to 13.1 percent) than their share of taxes (from 6.3 percent to 8.3 percent). Yet this comparison of shares can deceive. The total amount of taxes is a much greater dollar figure than the total amount of welfare spending. By paying a "mere" 8.3 percent of the tax base in 1990, for example, immigrants are paying more than they receive in the form of 13.1 percent of public assistance payments.

To reach a conclusion about the net burden or benefit on native taxpayers, we must even go beyond the taxes immigrants pay and the welfare payments they receive.

What nonwelfare public services do they get for the part of their taxes that does not go into welfare payments? And are these services actually taken away from natives, or is it costless to share them? No clear answer has yet emerged. Figures 25.6 and 25.7 show the two extremes between which the truth must lie for 1990. First, we have the optimistic extreme, based on the assumption that the arrival of extra immigrants does not detract at all from native taxpayers' enjoyment of government expenditure programs other than welfare. We can imagine,

FIGURE 25.6   *An Optimistic Range of Possible Dollar Flows to Native Taxpayers, 1990 (in $ billions)*

	Immigrants' Average Tax Rate		
	20%	*30%*	*40%*
Taxes paid by immigrants on their $284.7 billion of nonwelfare income	$56.9	$85.4	$113.9
Benefits to immigrant households on welfare programs	23.8	23.8	23.8
Net payment from immigrants to native taxpayers	$33.1	$61.6	$ 90.1

If all government spending other than welfare payments is a free "public good" that immigrants can enjoy without taking any of its value away from natives, then in 1990 immigrants clearly paid more in taxes than they took in public assistance payments. The positive net balance depends on the tax rate immigrants pay.

Source: See Figure 25.7, page 592.

for example, that receiving the extra immigrants does not compromise the effectiveness of our national defense budget at all. (Indeed, the extra immigration might add effective soldiers.) In this optimistic case, immigrants contributed far more taxes—from $57 billion to $114 billion, depending on the average tax rate they paid—than they took back in welfare payments, only $24 billion.

Yet immigrants' sharing in some public services (hospitals, schools, etc.) probably does detract from the natives' consumption of the same public services. In the pessimistic extreme shown in Figure 25.7, every dollar of taxes paid by immigrants goes back to them, either as welfare payments or as nonwelfare public services. In this case, native taxpayers do not gain any taxes from the immigrants, but they lose the part of the welfare expenditures on immigrant families that was not covered by immigrants' tax contributions. So, depending on the tax rate, the natives might have lost nearly $14 billion to $19 billion to immigrants through government budgets in 1990.

So, as of 1990, the fiscal balance between immigrants and natives might have tipped in either direction. For earlier years, though, most studies found that immigrants were major net taxpayers, not a net fiscal drain.

This kind of analysis provides a snapshot of the fiscal effects of immigrants during a year. Another way to look at the issue is to examine the fiscal effects of immigrants over their entire lifetimes, and even to examine the fiscal effects of their descendants. Is a wave of immigrants a net burden on native taxpayers over the life span of the immigrants and their descendants? For government programs that have costs for recipients of some ages but generate tax revenues from these same recipients at other ages, the lifetime approach is clearly the most sensible way to answer the question of fiscal effects. One example is public schooling. Immigrants' children substantially increase the cost of providing public schooling. But the schooling increases the children's future earning, so the government collects more taxes. Another example is social security. While working, immigrants pay social security taxes. But in the future they will collect social security payments.

Analysis of the fiscal effects of immigrants over lifetimes is complicated and requires many assumptions, including assumptions about how much immigrants

FIGURE 25.7 *A Pessimistic Range of Possible Dollar Flows to Native Taxpayers, 1990 (in $ billions)*

	Immigrants' Average Tax Rate		
	20%	*30%*	*40%*
Taxes paid by immigrants on their $284.7 billion of nonwelfare income	$56.9	$85.4	$113.9
Nonwelfare benefits taken away from native taxpayers	51.8	77.8	103.8
Benefits to immigrant households on welfare programs	23.8	23.8	23.8
Net payment from native taxpayers to immigrants	$18.7	$16.2	$ 13.7

If immigrants receive their proportional share of all nonwelfare government spending, and take the same value away from native taxpayers in addition to their welfare-program receipts, then they are a net fiscal burden on native taxpayers.

The "nonwelfare benefits taken away from native taxpayers" data are based on a balanced-budget assumption: They are the 90.1 percent share of the immigrants' own tax payments that is estimated not to be spent on welfare payments, and therefore spent on other public programs.

Source: George Borjas (1995a, Tables 9 and 10).

add incremental costs as they consume various public services. Smith and Edmonston (1997, Chapter 7) examined all fiscal effects of immigrants in the United States in 1996. Over the lifetime of the average immigrant (not including descendants), the net fiscal effect is slightly negative, about a $3,000 net cost to native taxpayers. However, the effects depend strongly on how educated the immigrant is. (Education is used as an indicator of earnings potential based on labor skill or human capital.) The average immigrant who has not completed high school imposes a lifetime net cost of $89,000, and the average immigrant who is a high school graduate imposes a net cost of $31,000, but the average immigrant who has at least a year of college provides a lifetime net fiscal *benefit* of $105,000.

In addition, the study concludes that the descendants of the typical immigrant provide a net fiscal benefit of $83,000. Thus, the typical immigrant and his descendants provide a net fiscal benefit of $80,000 (= –$3,000 + $83,000). Interestingly, this net fiscal benefit is not spread evenly over government units. State and local governments bear a net fiscal cost of $25,000, while the U.S. federal government receives a net benefit of $105,000.[6] We can see a clear basis for tension between states and the federal government over immigration policies. Especially, we can see the basis for California's efforts to limit its outlays for immigrants, because California has by far the largest proportion of immigrants of any state.

Taken together, these findings indicate that the fiscal effects of immigration depend very much on the levels of labor skills of the immigrants. More educated, more skilled immigrants have higher earnings, resulting in larger payments of taxes. Immigrants with greater skills and higher earnings are less likely to use public assistance. For the United States since 1970, the fiscal balance is shifting toward immigrants being a fiscal burden, because the average skill level of immigrants is declining relative to that of natives.

---

[6]This differential is not unique to immigrants. The average native-born child also imposes a net fiscal cost on state and local governments. They largely bear the costs of education, health care, and other transfers early in the child's life, while the federal government collects much of the taxes paid after the child grows up.

FIGURE 25.8

Education and Wages, Immigrant and Native Men Aged 25–64, United States, 1970–1990

	Average Years of Education	Percent Less Than High School Graduate	Percent College Graduate	Wage Rate (native = 100 for each year)
1970				
Natives	11.5	40	15	100
Immigrants				
All	10.7	48	19	101
Recently arrived*	11.1	45	28	83
1980				
Natives	12.7	23	23	100
Immigrants				
All	11.7	37	25	91
Recently arrived*	11.8	36	30	72
1990				
Natives	13.2	15	27	100
Immigrants				
All	11.6	37	27	85
Recently arrived*	11.9	35	32	68

*Recently arrived immigrants are those entering the United States during the previous 5 years.
Source: Borjas (1995b, Table 1) and Borjas (1994, Tables 3 and 4).

The relative decline in immigrant skill levels can be seen in changes in immigrant education and earnings. Figure 25.8 shows these changes from 1970 to 1990 for immigrant men in the United States. (For immigrant women, the trends are very similar, except that the decline in relative wages is not so large.) As we noted earlier, years of education is one indicator of labor skills. Especially since 1980, immigrants have less education on average than do natives, and a far larger percentage of immigrants have not completed high school. While a larger percentage of immigrants were college graduates in 1970, this difference disappeared by 1990. The relative decline in the wages of immigrants is also an indicator of the declining relative skills of immigrants. In 1970, the immigrants' average wage rate was about equal to that of natives. Although recent immigrants earned about 17 percent less than natives in 1970, immigrants who had been in the country for more than 5 years had sufficient labor market advantages to earn somewhat more than natives earned. By 1990, immigrants' relative position had deteriorated markedly. On average, immigrants earned 15 percent less than natives, and recent immigrants earned 32 percent less.

External Costs and Benefits

Other possible effects of migration elude both labor-market analysis and our fiscal accounting. Migration may generate external costs and benefits outside private and public-fiscal marketplaces. Three kinds of possible externalities merit mention:

1. *Knowledge benefits.* People carry knowledge with them, and much of that knowledge has economic value, be it tricks of the trade, food recipes, artistic talent, farming practices, or advanced technology. American examples include migrants Andrew Carnegie, Albert Einstein, and many virtuosi of classical music. Often only part of the economic benefits of this knowledge accrues to the migrant and those he sells his services to. Part often spills over to others, especially others in the same country. Migration may thus transfer external benefits of knowledge from the sending to the receiving country.

2. *Congestion costs.* Immigration, like any other source of population growth, may bring external costs associated with crowding: extra noise, conflict, and crime. If so, then this is a partial offset to the gains of the receiving country and the losses of the sending country. This effect is probably small, however, if the migration flow is gradual.

3. *Social friction.* Immigrants are often greeted with bigotry and harassment—even from native groups that would benefit from the immigration. Long-lasting restrictions on the freedom to migrate, such as American discrimination against Asian immigrants at the turn of the century, the sweeping restrictions during the "red scare" of the early 1920s in the United States, and Britain's revocation of many Commonwealth passport privileges since the 1960s, have been motivated largely by simple dislike for the immigrating nationalities. Although the most appropriate form of social response to this kind of prejudice is to work on changing the prevailing attitudes themselves, policymakers must also weigh the frictions in the balance when judging how much immigration and what kind of immigration to allow.

There is at least indirect support for the idea that admitting immigrants only gradually would go far to removing social frictions. The United States experienced its worst surge of anti-immigrant feeling in the early 1920s, when the immigration rate was increasing toward the peak rate it had reached just before World War I. The immigration rate was higher then, just before and after World War I, than it is today, even if we add reasonable estimates of the number of unrecorded illegal aliens. Even though some of the historic reasons for the anti-immigrant sentiment of that time (e.g., the Bolshevik Revolution) transcend economics, the high rate of immigration itself must have contributed to the fears and resentments of those Americans whose families migrated earlier.

What Policies to Select Immigrants?

The major industrialized countries have policies to limit the rate of immigration. If a country is going to limit immigration, on what basis should it select its immigrants? Our economic analysis offers some insights. Two features of the analysis are prominent. First, the types of immigrant workers admitted will affect which groups within the native population win and which groups lose, as a result of the immigration. For instance, if relatively less educated and less skilled immigrants are admitted, these immigrant workers will compete for jobs against less skilled native workers, further reducing their already low earnings. Second, the types of immigrants admitted will affect the net fiscal benefit or burden of immigration. To gain greater fiscal benefits, the country should admit young adults who have some college education. In addition, admitting highly educated and skilled immigrants is likely to enhance the external knowledge benefits we just examined.

Australian policies toward immigration seem to draw from these economic lessons. Australia has used a point system to screen applicants, focusing on those whose age and skills are likely to be beneficial to the Australian economy. Canada also uses a point system to screen some of its applicants, but about four-fifths of immigrants into Canada enter based on family links or refugee status. Immigration into the United States is even more heavily skewed toward family and refugees, with less than one-tenth entering based on their worker skills. For both the United States and Canada, the results of these policies are that the average skill levels of their immigrants have been declining.

Economic analysis can make a strong case for a country like the United States or Canada to tilt its immigration policies toward encouraging and selecting more skilled immigrants while reducing the number of less skilled immigrants that it admits. Of course, economic objectives are not the only national goals. A shift toward pursuing these would come at a cost of achieving less toward other worthy goals, including promoting family reunification and providing humanitarian assistance to refugees. And the shift toward pursuing economic objectives by reducing immigration of the less skilled would leave more people in the rest of the world with very low income levels.

Summary

Free international migration, like free trade, is the policy most likely to maximize world income. Yet perfect freedom to migrate is politically unlikely. The main beneficiaries of such a liberal policy, the migrants themselves, have little political voice in any country. More vocal are groups that resent the departure of emigrants or, more often, the arrival of immigrants.

The labor-market analysis of migration flows shows who wins and who loses from extra migration, and by how much. The main winners and losers from migration are the ones intuition would suggest: the migrants, their new employers, and workers who stay in the sending country all gain; competing workers in the new country and employers in the old country lose. Yet, the net effects on nations, defined as excluding the migrants themselves, may clash with intuition. The receiving country is a net gainer according to the labor-market analysis. The sending country as a whole loses, both in the labor markets and on the public-finance front. A case can be made for a brain-drain tax that compensates the sending country for its public investments in the emigrants.

It has often been true that immigrants pay more to their new country in taxes than they receive in public services. In the United States in the 1980s and 1990s, however, the trend has been in the other direction. Immigrants' use of welfare entitlements has risen at a faster percent rate than the taxes they pay. Whether this means that they are a net fiscal burden depends on what one assumes about the degree to which nonwelfare public services can be shared. If there is perfect sharing, so that having more immigrants benefit from public services does not detract at all from natives' benefits from the same services, then immigrants clearly pay more in taxes than they take away from other taxpayers. If there is no sharing, then by 1990 the immigrants have become a net fiscal burden to other taxpayers. The truth is probably somewhere in between.

Analysis of fiscal effects over the lifetimes of immigrants and their descendants indicates that current U.S. immigrants themselves impose small net fiscal costs on native taxpayers, while the immigrants' descendants provide substantial fiscal benefits. For the immigrants themselves, the largest net fiscal costs are for immigrants with less education and lower skills, because they pay less taxes on their lower earnings and because they are more likely to use public assistance and similar welfare programs. More educated, more skilled immigrants provide net fiscal benefits.

Immigrants also cause externalities, both positive (new knowledge) and negative (congestion, social friction).

The reason for the U.S. drift toward having immigrants be a net fiscal burden is that the relative education and skill levels of immigrants has declined, as U.S. admission policy has given preference to family relatives and refugees since the mid-1960s. A country can improve the net fiscal effects of immigration by skewing its admissions toward selecting young, educated, and skilled adults and away from less skilled persons. While this policy would improve the fiscal side of the immigration accounts, it may clash with other objectives such as reuniting families and providing humanitarian aid to refugees.

Suggested Reading

Smith and Edmonston (1997), Borjas, Freeman, and Katz (1997), Borjas and Hilton (1996), Borjas (1990, 1991, 1994, 1995a, 1995b), and Chiswick (1988) analyze U.S. immigration and immigration policy. Simon (1989) gives an optimistic view of the benefits of allowing immigration. See also the studies cited in footnote 2 of this chapter.

Questions and Problems

◆ 1. For each of the following observed changes in wage rates and migration flows from the low-wage South to the high-wage North, describe one shift in conditions that, by itself, could have caused all those changes:

  a. A rise in wage rates in both South and North, and a fresh migration from South to North.

  b. A drop in wage rates in both South and North, and a fresh migration from South to North.

  c. A drop in northern wage rates, a rise in southern wage rates, and a fresh migration from South to North.

2. What are two reasons that immigration into the United States was so low in the 1930s?

◆ 3. Review the areas of gain and loss to different groups in Figure 25.3. Why do the migrants gain only areas *e* and *f*? Why don't they each gain the full southern wage markup ($3.20 – $2.00)? Why don't they each gain ($5.00 – $2.00)?

4. Consider the labor effects of migration shown in Figure 25.3. What is the effect of a decrease in the annualized cost of migration (a decrease in c) on each group?

✦5. Describe how a single international migrant can raise her own income by moving from country A to country B, yet still lower the average income per capita both in A and in B.

6. Using the numbers shown in Figure 25.4, explain how counting immigrants as part of the United States both before and after immigration resolves the "average income paradox" for the United States.

✦7. Which of the following kinds of immigrants probably contributed the greatest net taxes, after deducting welfare payments, to the U.S. government? Which probably contributed the least?

   a. Political refugees arriving around 1990.

   b. Electrical engineers arriving around 1970.

   c. Earlier immigrants' grandparents, arriving around 1990.

8. "Sending countries should cheer for emigration because the migrants improve their economic well-being." Do you think this statement is true or false? Why?

✦9. Japan currently has a very low rate of immigration, because of a very restrictive Japanese government policy. You are trying to convince your Japanese friend that Japan should change its laws to permit and encourage substantially more immigration. What are your three strongest arguments?

10. Continuing from question 9, your Japanese friend is skeptical. What are his three strongest arguments that Japan should continue its policy of permitting little immigration?

CHAPTER 26

International Lending and Financial Crises

Capital, like labor, moves between countries. As we saw in the discussion of balance-of-payments accounting in Chapter 15, the term *international capital movement* refers to the flow of financial claims between lenders and borrowers.[1] The lenders give the borrowers money to be used now in exchange for IOUs or ownership shares entitling them to interest and dividends later. International capital flows are conventionally divided into different categories by type of lender or investor (private versus official), by maturity (long term versus short term), by existence of management control (direct versus portfolio), and by type of borrower (private or government). For the first three distinctions, here are the key categories:

A. Private lending and investing
  1. Long term
     a. Direct investment (lending to, or purchasing shares in, a foreign enterprise largely owned and controlled by the investor)
     b. Loans (to a foreign borrower, maturity more than one year, mostly by banks)
     c. Portfolio investment (purchasing stock or bonds with maturity of more than one year, issued by a government or a foreign enterprise not controlled by the investor)
  2. Short term (lending to a foreign borrower, or purchasing bonds issued by a government or a foreign enterprise not controlled by the investor, maturing in a year or less)

B. Official lending and investing (by a government or a multilateral institution like the International Monetary Fund or the World Bank, mostly lending, both long term and short term)

---

[1]Physical capital goods also flow between countries, but this is typically viewed as an ordinary trade flow, not a "capital" flow.

The subtleties of control that go with direct investments are explored in Chapter 27. Here we concentrate on bank lending and portfolio investments.

International lending and investing have been revolutionized. From before World War II to the early 1980s, the main lender was the United States, joined in the 1970s by the newly rich oil exporters. Since the early 1980s, the United States has been the world's largest net borrower, and the oil exporters have also become borrowers. The dominant lender since then has been Japan. The major type of lending has been private loans and portfolio investments, a shift from the official loans from governments and direct foreign investment that were dominant from the late 1940s to the early 1970s.

International lending can bring major benefits of two types. First, it represents intertemporal trade, in which the lender gives up resources today in order to get more in the future, and the borrower gets resources today but must be willing to pay back more in the future. Second, it allows lenders and investors to diversify their investments more broadly. The ability to add foreign financial assets to investment portfolios can lower the riskiness of the entire portfolio of investments through greater diversification. The chapter begins with an analysis of some of the benefits of international lending and borrowing.

International lending is not always well-behaved. International lending to developing countries swings between surges of lending and crises of confidence. During the financial crises, lending shrinks and lenders scramble to get repaid. The rest of the chapter discusses why these financial crises occur, how we try to resolve them, and what we might be able to do to make them less frequent.

Gains and Losses from Well-Behaved International Lending

If the world is stable and predictable, and if borrowers fully honor their commitments to repay, then international lending can be efficient from a world point of view, bringing gains to some that outweigh losses to others. In such a world, the welfare effects of international lending are exactly parallel to the welfare effects of opening trade (Chapter 2) or those of allowing free labor migration (Chapter 25).

Figure 26.1 shows the normal effects of allowing free international lending and borrowing. We divide the world into two large countries: "Japan," having abundant financial wealth and less attractive domestic investment opportunities; and an "America" in the image of Argentina, Brazil, Canada, and the United States, having less wealth relative to its abundant opportunities for profitable investment (for instance, in its new technologies or its open areas rich in natural resources). The length of the horizontal axis in Figure 26.1 shows total world wealth, equal to Japan's wealth W_J plus America's wealth W_A. This wealth is used to finance capital investments. The vertical axes indicate percentage rates of return (say, rates of interest) earned on capital investments. Capital investment opportunities in Japan are shown as the marginal-product-of-capital curve MPK_{Japan}, which begins at the left vertical axis, and ranks possible investments in Japan according to the real returns the investments produce. Investment opportunities in America are shown as the marginal-product-of-capital curve $MPK_{America}$, which

FIGURE 26.1

Gains and Losses from Well-Behaved International Lending

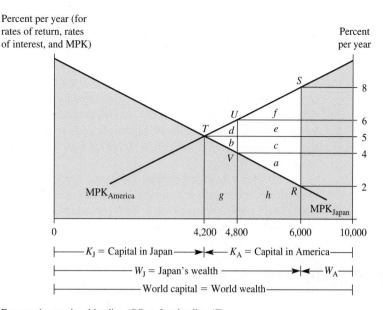

Percent per year (for rates of return, rates of interest, and MPK)

Percent per year

From no international lending (RS) to free lending (T):

Japan	gains ($a + b + c$)	= 27
America	gains ($d + e + f$)	= 27
World	gains (a through f)	= 54

If Japan imposes a 2 percent per year tax on lending abroad (from T to UV):

Japan	gains ($e - b$)	= 9
America	loses ($d + e$)	= 15
World	loses ($b + d$)	= 6

If America imposes a 2 percent per year tax on borrowing abroad (from T to UV):

Japan	loses ($b + c$)	= 15
America	gains ($c - d$)	= 9
World	loses ($b + d$)	= 6

begins at the right vertical axis and ranks investments in the opposite direction, from right to left.

We begin with a situation in which international financial transactions are prohibited. In this situation each country must use its financial wealth to finance its own stock of real capital. If all Japanese wealth W_J is used domestically, Japan's lenders must accept a low rate of return, because the return on domestic capital investments follows the declining MPK_{Japan} curve. Competition thus forces lenders in Japan to accept the low real rate of return of 2 percent per year at point R. Meanwhile, in America, the scarcity of funds prevents any real capital formation to the left of point S since W_A is all the wealth that America has. Competition for borrowing the W_A of national wealth bids the American real rate of interest on lending up to 8 percent at point S. The world's product equals the areas under the marginal-product-of-capital curves, the shaded area in Figure 26.1.

Now imagine that there are no barriers to international finance. Wealthholders in Japan and borrowers in America have a strong incentive to get together.

Why should one group lend at only 2 percent and the other borrow at 8 percent, if, as we assume here, the riskiness or creditworthiness of the different borrowings is the same? Lenders in Japan should do part of their lending in America. Over time, their lending to America will allow more capital formation in America, with less capital formation in Japan. The international lending leads to a different equilibrium, one in which the worldwide rate of return is somewhere between 2 percent and 8 percent. Let's say that it ends up at 5 percent, at point T. In this situation the wealth of Japan exceeds its stock of domestic real assets by the same amount $(W_J - K_J)$ that America has to borrow to finance its extra real assets $(K_A - W_A)$.

With international financial freedom, world product is maximized. It equals everything under either marginal product curve or all the shaded area plus area RST. This is clear gain of area RST (or areas a through f) over the situation in which international lending was prohibited. The reason for this gain is that freedom allows individual wealthholders the chance to seek the highest return anywhere in the world.

The world's gains from international lending are split between the two countries. Japan's national income is the whole area under its MPK_{Japan} curve down to point R *plus* the area $(a + b + c)$, which is gained by the chance to lend wealth abroad at 5 percent instead of accepting the less productive domestic investments from point T down to point R. Similarly, America gains area $(d + e + f)$ because it has expanded its productive real capital from point S out to point T, paying foreign lenders the rectangle $(a + b + c + g + h)$ for the funds borrowed at 5 percent.

Within each country there are gainers and losers from the new freedom. Japanese lenders gain from lending at 5 percent instead of at 2 percent. That harms Japanese borrowers, though, because competition from foreign borrowers forces them to pay the same higher rate on their borrowings. In America borrowers have gained from being able to borrow at 5 percent instead of 8 percent. Yet American lenders will be nostalgic for the old days of financial isolation, when borrowers still had to pay them 8 percent. In addition, the smaller capital stock in Japan lowers the productivity and earnings of other resources (like labor and land) in Japan, whereas the larger capital stock in America raises the productivity and earnings of other resources in America. Note that the pattern of gains and losses is identical to the one established in the analysis of trade and migration: International freedom benefits the world as a whole and the groups for whom the freedom means opportunity, whereas it harms the groups for whom the freedom means tougher competition or fewer resources to work with.

Taxes on International Lending

We have compared free international lending with no international lending and have found the orthodox result: Freedom raises world product and national incomes. Another standard result also carries over from trade analysis: the **nationally optimal tax.** *If* a country looms large enough to have power over the world market rate of return, it can exploit this market power to its own advantage, at the expense of other countries and the world as a whole.

In Figure 26.1, Japan can be said to have market power. By restricting its foreign lending, it could force America's borrowers to pay higher interest rates (moving northeast from point *T* toward point *S*). Let us say that Japan exploits this power by imposing a tax of 2 percent per year on the value of assets held abroad by residents of Japan. This will bid up the rate that America's borrowers have to pay and bid down the rate that domestic lenders can get after taxes. Equilibrium will be restored when the gap between the foreign and domestic rates is just the 2 percent tax. This is shown by the gap *UV* in Figure 26.1. Japan's government collects total tax revenues (areas *e* and *c*) equal to the tax rate times the international assets that Japan continues to have after the adjustment to the tax. Japan has made a net gain on its taxation of foreign lending. It has forced America to pay 6 percent instead of 5 percent on all continuing debt. This markup, area *e*, is large enough to outweigh Japan's loss of some previously profitable lending abroad (triangle *b*). Setting such a tax at just the right level (which might or might not be the one shown here) gives Japan a nationally optimal tax on foreign lending.

Two can play at that game, of course. Figure 26.1 shows that America also has market power, since by restricting its borrowing it could force Japan's lenders to accept lower rates of return (moving southeast from point *T* toward point *R*). What if it is America (instead of Japan) that imposes the 2 percent tax on the same international assets? Then all the results would work out the same as for the tax by Japan—except that the American government pockets the tax revenue (areas *c* and *e*). America, in this case, gains income (area *c* minus area *d*) at the expense of Japan and the world as a whole. (If both countries impose taxes on the same international lending, the amount of international lending shrinks. At most, one country can gain compared to its position with free lending, and it is rather likely that both countries lose.)

International Lending to Developing Countries

International lending and borrowing between industrialized countries generally is well-behaved and provides the sort of mutual benefits that we have discussed. Financial capital flows from industrialized countries like Japan and Germany, where it is relatively abundant, to countries like the United States that offer rich investment opportunities. Both lender and borrower benefit from the gains from intertemporal trade, as countries with net savings get higher returns and countries that are net borrowers pay lower costs. Additional gains arise as international financial investments are used to lower risk through portfolio diversification. Conflicts sometimes arise over tax policies, but these are manageable.

International lending by industrialized countries to developing countries is another story. It should create these same gains from intertemporal trade and risk diversification, and to large extent it does. But there are also periodic international crises—lending from industrialized countries to developing countries is sometimes not well-behaved. In a financial crisis the borrowing country experiences difficulties in servicing its debts, and it often *defaults*—that is, fails to make payments as specified in the debt agreements. Lenders cut back or stop new lending, as the borrower is viewed as too risky. This section presents a brief history of capital flows to developing countries and the nature of the financial crises. Subsequent sections look at why crises occur, how they are resolved, and suggestions for ways to reduce the frequency of crises.

The Surge in International Lending, 1974–1982

Before World War I there was a large amount of international lending, with Britain as the main creditor and the growing newly settled countries (the United States, Canada, Argentina, Australia) as the main borrowers. To a large extent this international lending fit the well-behaved model of Figure 26.1, as lending sought out high returns (although defaults were also common). During the 1920s, a large number of foreign governments issued foreign bonds, especially in New York, as the United States became a major creditor country. But in the 1930s, the depression led to massive defaults by developing countries, which frightened away lenders through the 1960s. Lending to developing countries remained very low for four decades.

The oil shocks of the 1970s led to a surge in private international lending to developing countries. Between 1970 and 1980, developing country debt outstanding increased over sevenfold, with long-term debt rising from 5.4 percent of the countries' national product in 1970 to 15.5 percent in 1980.

The oil shocks quadrupled and then tripled the world price of oil, and these shocks caused recessions and high inflation in the industrialized countries. How did the shocks also revive the lending? Four forces combined to create the surge. First, the rich oil-exporting nations had a high short-run propensity to save out of their extra income. While their savings were piling up, they tended to invest them in liquid form, especially in bonds and bank deposits in the United States and other established financial centers. The major international private banks thereby gained large amounts of new funds to be lent to other borrowers. The banks had the problem of "recycling" or reinvesting the "petrodollars." But where to lend?

Second, there was widespread pessimism about the profitability of capital formation in industrialized countries. Real interest rates in many countries were unusually low. One promising area was investment in energy-saving equipment, but the development of these projects took time. For a time the banks' expanded ability to lend was not absorbed by borrowers in the industrial countries, which encouraged banks to look elsewhere. Attention began to shift to developing countries, which had long been forced to offer higher rates of interest and dividends to attract even small amounts of private capital.

Third, in developing countries, the 1970s was an era of peak resistance to direct foreign investment (DFI), in which the foreign investor, usually a multinational firm based in an industrialized country, keeps controlling ownership of foreign affiliated enterprises. Banks might have lent to multinational firms for additional DFI, but developing countries were generally hostile to DFI. Populist ideological currents and valid fears about political intrigues by multinational firms brought DFI down from 25 percent of net financial flows to developing countries in 1960 to less than 10 percent by 1980. To gain access to the higher returns offered in developing countries, banks had to lend outright to governments and companies in these countries.

Fourth, "herding" behavior meant that the lending to developing countries acquired a momentum of its own once it began to increase. Major banks aggressively sought lending opportunities, each showing eagerness to lend before competing banks did. Much of the lending went to poorly planned projects in mismanaged economies. But everyone was doing it.

The Debt Crisis of 1982

In August 1982, Mexico declared that it was unable to service its large foreign debt. Dozens of other developing countries followed with announcements that they also could not repay their previous loans. Several factors explain why the crunch came in 1982. Interest rates increased sharply in the United States, as the U.S. Federal Reserve shifted to a much tighter monetary policy to reduce U.S. inflation. The United States and other industrialized countries sank into a severe recession. Developing countries' exports declined and commodity prices plummeted, while real interest rates remained high. The debtors' ability to repay fell dramatically.

At first the responses of the bank creditors depended on how much each bank had lent. Smaller banks (those holding small shares of all loans) headed for the exits and eliminated their exposure by selling off their loans or getting repaid. The larger banks could not extricate themselves without triggering a larger crisis, and they hoped that the problems were temporary. They rescheduled loan payments to establish repayment obligations in the future, and they loaned smaller amounts of new money to assist the debtors to grow so that repayment would be possible. Figure 26.2 provides information on long-term financial flows to developing countries. Bank loans, which were most of the private lending to developing countries in the early 1980s, declined somewhat in 1983 and 1984. As shown in Figure 26.3, the long-term debt of developing countries doubled between 1980 and 1985, the ratio of debt to national product rose from 21 percent in 1980 to over 35 percent in 1985, and the share of export revenues that was committed to service the debt nearly doubled, to almost 25 percent. As large banks reassessed the prospects for developing country debtors, they concluded that it was imprudent to lend more. The net flows of bank loans to developing countries became small in 1985 and remained low until 1995.

As the debt crisis wore on through the 1980s, it became clear that the debtor countries were suffering low economic growth and lack of access to international finance, but that this cost was not leading to repayments that would end the crisis. In response, U.S. Treasury officials crafted the Brady Plan (named after U.S. Treasury Secretary Nicholas Brady). Beginning in 1989, each debtor country

FIGURE 26.2 *Net Long-Term Financial Flows to Developing Countries, 1980–1998 (billions of U.S. dollars)*

Source and Type	1980	1981	1982	1983	1984	1985	1986	1987	1988	1989
Official	35	34	35	35	34	41	45	45	42	42
Loans	22	22	24	24	21	25	28	27	23	23
Grants	13	11	11	10	13	16	17	18	19	20
Private debt	44	53	45	31	27	22	10	10	15	14
Bank loans	30	44	33	23	23	9	2	2	9	6
Bonds	1	1	4	2	0	6	2	1	4	5
Other loans	12	8	8	6	5	8	6	7	3	4
Portfolio equity (stock)	0	0	0	0	0	0	0	0	0	4
Direct foreign investment	4	13	11	9	9	11	10	14	20	23
Total	83	100	91	74	72	73	65	68	76	83

Source and Type	1990	1991	1992	1993	1994	1995	1996	1997	1998
Official	57	63	54	53	46	53	32	39	48
Loans	28	28	23	25	14	21	3	13	25
Grants	29	35	31	28	32	32	29	26	23
Private debt	16	19	38	49	54	60	100	105	58
Bank loans	3	5	16	3	14	32	44	60	25
Bonds	1	11	11	37	37	27	54	43	30
Other loans	11	3	11	9	4	1	3	3	3
Portfolio equity (stock)	4	8	14	51	35	36	49	30	14
Direct foreign investment	25	34	46	67	89	105	126	163	155
Total	101	123	152	220	224	255	308	338	275

Note: Net inflows of short-term finance have been variable: $20 billion in 1990, rising to $61 billion in 1995, then declining to $5 billion in 1998.

Source: 1980 and 1990–1998: World Bank, *Global Development Finance, 1999;* 1985–1989: World Bank, *World Debt Tables, 1992–93;* 1981–1984: Rachel McCulloch and Peter A. Petri, "Equity Financing of East Asian Development," in Kahler (1998).

could reach a deal in which its bank debt would be partially reduced, with most of the remaining loans repackaged as "Brady bonds." By 1994, most of the bank debt had been reduced and converted into bonds. The debt crisis that began in 1982 was effectively over.

The Resurgence of Capital Flows in the 1990s

Beginning in about 1990, lending to and investing in developing countries began to increase again. Four forces converged to drive this new lending. First, the size and scope of the Brady Plan led investors to believe that the previous crisis was being resolved. As each debtor country agreed to a Brady deal, it was usually able to receive new private lending almost immediately. Second, low U.S. interest rates again led lenders to seek out higher returns through foreign investments. Third, the developing countries were becoming more attractive places to lend as governments reformed their policies. Governments were opening up opportunities for financing profitable new investments as they deregulated industries, privatized state-owned firms, and encouraged production for export with

FIGURE 26.3   *Developing Countries' Debt Outstanding, 1970–1998 (billions of U.S. dollars, unless otherwise indicated)*

Type of Debt	1970	1980	1985	1990	1995	1998
Long-term debt	61	452	899	1,181	1,674	1,957
Public and publicly guaranteed	46	381	797	1,116	1,454	1,637
Private nonguaranteed	15	71	102	66	220	320
Loans from the IMF	1	12	41	35	61	95
Short-term debt	NA[a]	146	184	257	427	412
Total debt	NA	610	1,123	1,473	2,163	2,465
Debt–GNP ratio (percentage)	NA[b]	21.0	35.4	33.5	38.2	37.3
Debt service–exports of goods and services ratio (percentage)	NA	13.1	24.7	17.4	16.0	17.6

[a]NA: Not available.

[b]Long-term debt–GNP ratio was 5.4% in 1970, and this rose to 15.4% in 1980.

Source: World Bank, *Global Development Finance, 1999;* and World Bank, *World Debt Tables, 1992–93.*

outward-oriented trade policies (as discussed in Chapter 13). Fourth, individual investors, as well as the rapidly growing mutual funds and pension funds, were looking for new forms of portfolio investments that could raise returns and add risk diversification. Developing countries became the emerging markets for this portfolio investment.

Figure 26.2 shows the rapidly growing flows of long-term investments into developing countries in the 1990s, as total net financial inflows increased every year from 1989 to 1997. The majority of this money went to a small number of developing countries viewed as the major emerging markets—Mexico, Brazil, and Argentina in Latin America and China, Indonesia, Malaysia, South Korea, and Thailand in Asia. The types of investments were different from those that drove the lending surge in the late 1970s. Foreign portfolio investors' net purchases of stocks and bonds rose from almost nothing in 1990 to one-third of total net financial flows in 1996. Bank lending was less important, but even bank lending increased substantially from 1993 to 1997. Figure 26.3 shows that developing country debt outstanding rose as a percentage of national product from 33.5 percent in 1990 to 38.2 percent in 1995, but that lower interest rates actually lowered the share of exports of goods and services that had to be devoted to debt service.

The Mexican Crisis, 1994–1995

Three periods of crisis punctured the generally strong flows of international lending to developing countries during the 1990s. The first of these struck Mexico in late 1994.

Mexico received large capital inflows in the early 1990s, as investors sought high returns and were impressed with Mexico's economic reforms and its entry into the North American Free Trade Area. But strains also arose. The real exchange rate value of the peso increased, because the government permitted only a slow nominal peso depreciation, while the Mexican inflation rate was higher than that of the United States, its main trading partner. The current account deficit increased to 8 percent of Mexico's GDP in 1994, although this was readily financed by the capital inflows. Mexico's banking system was rather weak, with inadequate bank supervision and regulation by the government. With the capital inflows adding funds to the Mexican banking system, bank lending grew rapidly, as did defaults on these loans. The year 1994 was an election year with some turmoil, including an uprising in the Chiapas region and two political assassinations. The peso came under some downward pressure. The government used sterilized intervention to defend its exchange rate value, so its holdings of official international reserves fell.

Mexico's fiscal policy was reasonable, with a modest government budget deficit. Still, the fiscal authorities made the change that became the center of the crisis, by altering the form of the government debt. Beginning in early 1994, the government replaced peso-denominated government debt with short-term dollar-indexed government debt called *tesobonos*. By the end of 1994, there were about $28 billion of *tesobonos* outstanding, most maturing in the first half of 1995.

The crisis was touched off by a large flight of capital, mostly by Mexican residents who feared a currency devaluation and converted out of pesos. In December the currency was allowed to depreciate, but Mexican holdings of official reserves had declined to about $6 billion. The financial crisis arose as investors refused to purchase new *tesobonos* to pay off those coming due, because it appeared that the government did not have the ability to make good on its dollar obligations. Each investor wanted to be paid off in dollars—a rush to the exit—but what was rational for each investor individually was not necessarily rational for all of them collectively. The Mexican government might not be able to repay all of them within a short time period. As investors reassessed their investments in emerging markets, they pulled back on investments not only in Mexico but also in many other developing countries (the "tequila effect").

The U.S. government became worried about the political and economic effects of financial crisis in Mexico, and it arranged a large rescue package that permitted the Mexican government to borrow up to $50 billion, mostly from the U.S. government and the International Monetary Fund (IMF). The Mexican government did borrow about $25 billion, using the money to pay off the *tesobonos* as they matured and to replenish its official reserve holdings. The currency depreciation and the financial turmoil caused rapid and painful adjustments in Mexico. The Mexican economy went into a severe recession, and the current account deficit disappeared as imports decreased and exports increased.

As the rescue took hold, the pure contagion that led investors to retreat from nearly all lending to developing countries calmed after the first quarter of 1995. The adverse tequila effect lingered for a smaller number of countries, as investors continued to pull out of Argentina, Brazil, and to lesser extents, Venezuela and the Philippines. Still, much of the Mexican financial crisis of 1994–1995 was resolved quickly. As shown in Figure 26.2, overall capital flows to developing countries continued to increase in 1995 and 1996.

The Asian Crisis, 1997

In the early and mid-1990s, foreign investors looked favorably on the rapidly growing developing countries of Southeast and East Asia. In these countries macroeconomic policies were solid. The governments had fiscal budgets with surpluses or small deficits; steady monetary policies kept inflation low, and trade policies were outward-oriented. Most of the foreign debt was owed by private firms, not by the governments.

A closer look showed a few problems. In Thailand and South Korea, much of the foreign borrowing was by banks and other financial institutions. Government regulation and supervision were weak. The banks took on significant exchange rate risk by borrowing dollars and yen and lending in local currencies. And the lending boom led to loans to riskier local borrowers and rising defaults on loans. In Indonesia, much of the foreign borrowing was by private nonfinancial firms, which took on the exchange rate risk directly.

The external balance of the countries also showed some problems. The real exchange rate values of these countries' currencies seemed to be somewhat overvalued, and the growth of exports slowed beginning in 1996. With the exception of Thailand, the current account deficits were not large. Thailand's current account deficit rose to 8 percent of GDP in 1996. Still, the strong capital inflows provided financing for the deficits.

Crisis struck first in Thailand. Beginning in 1996, the expectation of declining exports led to large declines in Thai stock prices and real estate prices. The exchange rate value of the Thai baht came under downward pressure. By mid-1997, the pressures had become intense. Banks and other local firms that had borrowed dollars and yen without hedging rushed to sell off baht to acquire foreign currency assets. The Thai government could not maintain its defense, and the baht was allowed to depreciate beginning in July 1997.

Throughout the rest of 1997 the crisis spread to a number of other Asian countries, especially to Indonesia and South Korea, but also to Malaysia and the Philippines, as foreign investors lost confidence in local bank borrowers and the local stock markets, and as local borrowers scrambled to sell local currency to establish hedges against exchange rate risk.

In response, the IMF organized large rescue packages, with commitments to lend up to $17 billion to Thailand ($13 billion actually borrowed), up to $42 billion to Indonesia ($9 billion borrowed), and up to $58 billion to South Korea ($27 billion borrowed). As in Mexico, these large rescue packages and policy changes did contain the crises, though not without costs. Currency values continued to fall throughout 1997, and these countries went into severe multiyear recessions. The currency depreciations and the recessions did lead to improvements in the current account balance, largely through decreases in imports.

The Russian Crisis, 1998

Russia weathered the Asian crisis in 1997 very well, but its underlying fundamental position was remarkably weak. It had a large fiscal budget deficit, and government borrowing led to rapid increases in government debt to both domestic and foreign lenders. In mid-1998, lenders balked at buying still more Russian government debt. In July 1998, the IMF organized a lending package under which the Russian government could borrow up to $23 billion, and the IMF made the first loan of $5 billion. However, the Russian government failed to enact policy changes included as conditions for the loan. The exchange rate value of the ruble came under severe pressure as capital flight by wealthy Russians led to large sales of rubles for foreign currencies. With substantial debt service due on government debt during the second half of 1998, investor confidence declined, with selling pressure driving down Russian stock and bond prices.

In August 1998, the Russian government announced drastic measures. The government unilaterally "restructured" its ruble-denominated debt, effectively wiping out most of the creditors' value. It placed a 90-day moratorium on payments of many foreign currency obligations of banks and other private firms, a move designed to protect Russian banks. And it allowed the ruble to depreciate by shifting to a floating exchange rate. Russia requested the next installment of its loan from the IMF, but the IMF refused, because the government had not met the conditions for fiscal reforms.

Foreign lenders were in shock. They had expected that Russia was too important to fail and that the IMF rescue package would provide Russia with the funds to repay them. They reassessed the risk of investments in all emerging markets and rapidly sought to reduce their investments. The selloff caused stock and bond prices to plummet, with a general flight to high-quality investments like U.S. government bonds. The reversal of international bank lending and stock and bond investing in 1998 led to the first decline in net long-term financial flows to developing countries since the mid-1980s (see Figure 26.2).

Brazil was among the countries hit hard by the fallout from the Russian crisis. In November 1998, the IMF organized a package that allowed the Brazilian government to borrow up to $41 billion, in an effort to allow Brazil to fight pressures toward a crisis. Brazil had a large current account deficit, and the government was defending its crawling exchange rate with intervention and high domestic interest rates. However, the government failed to enact the fiscal reforms called for in the IMF loan, and capital outflows increased. In January 1999, the Brazilian government ended its fixed exchange rate, and the real depreciated. However, this situation did not escalate into a full crisis. By April 1999, Brazil and other developing countries were able to issue new bonds to foreign investors. More generally, the market prices of emerging market financial assets began to increase, although the net capital flows to developing countries remained lower than they had been in 1997.

Financial Crises: What Can and Does Go Wrong

International lending to developing countries brings benefits, but, as we just saw in the history of the past several decades, it also brings recurrent financial crises. How can we understand the frequency and scope of these crises? We gain major insights by focusing on five major forces that can, and do, lead to financial crises:

1. Waves of overlending and overborrowing
2. Exogenous international shocks
3. Exchange rate risk
4. Fickle international short-term lending
5. Global contagion

Waves of Overlending and Overborrowing

Our model of well-behaved lending, shown in Figure 26.1, assumes that lenders only lend (and that borrowers only borrow) for investment projects that generate the returns in the future that can be used to service the debt. This is not always true. In the late 1970s and again in the mid-1990s, lenders seemed to lend excessive amounts to some countries.

The classic explanation of overlending and overborrowing is that it results from excessively expansionary government policies in the borrowing country. These policies lead to government borrowing to finance growing budget deficits, and the government may also guarantee loans to private borrowers in order to finance the growing current account deficits. Lending to national governments seems to be low risk, but it's not. When the government realizes that it has borrowed too much, it has an incentive to default, and a financial crisis arises. (The box "The Special Case of Sovereign Debt," page 614, examines these defaults in more depth.)

The Asian crisis (and to a lesser extent the Mexican crisis of 1994–1995) presented a new form of overlending and overborrowing: too much lending to private borrowers rather than to national governments. In the 1990s, lending to banks in Asian countries seemed to be low risk, because the countries' governments provided a guarantee that creditors would be repaid. Large capital inflows lead to easy domestic credit. In a domestic lending boom, some of the lending is for current consumption, so that it is not invested to generate future returns.[2] Other lending goes to investments that are of low quality—projects that offer low returns or are too risky (too likely to fail to produce returns). More generally, the capital inflows and lending boom tend to inflate stock and real estate prices. For a while the capital inflows appear to be earning high returns, until the price bubble bursts.

Once foreign lenders realize that too much has been lent and borrowed, each has the incentive to stop lending and to try to get repaid as quickly as possible (before available money runs out). All cannot be repaid quickly, and a financial crisis erupts. The excessive lending and borrowing that can lead to a financial crisis is sometimes called a **debt overhang**—the amount by which the debt obligations exceed the present value of the resource transfers that will be made to service the debt.

---

[2]Borrowing for current consumption can be sensible, if it is part of a strategy to smooth the country's consumption over time. It makes sense if the country's income will be higher in the future, so that part of the higher future income can be used to repay the loan. But borrowing for current consumption also is risky, because it is not adding to future income potential.

Exogenous International Shocks

When exogenous international shocks hit a country's economy, international lenders and the borrower must reassess the borrower's ability to meet its obligations to service its debt. For instance, a decline in export earnings, perhaps due to a decline in the world price of the country's key export commodity, makes it more difficult for the country to service its debt and thus more likely to default.

The experiences of the early 1980s and mid-1990s indicate that a change in U.S. real interest rates is a major exogenous shock. New funding flows to developing countries decrease, as fewer projects meet this higher required return. In addition, projects previously funded may not be profitable enough, leading to difficulties in servicing bank loans and to decreases in the market prices of stocks and bonds in the developing countries. Foreign investors can sour on their investments and try to sell them off before values decline further. The abrupt shift in flows can result in a crisis if the borrowers cannot adjust quickly enough.

Exchange Rate Risk

Sometimes the form of the debts can help us understand financial crises. In the Mexican and Asian crises, private borrowers took on large liabilities denominated in foreign currency while acquiring assets valued in local currency. The borrowers took on these positions exposed to exchange rate risk because they expected (hoped?) that the government would continue to defend the fixed or heavily managed exchange rate value of the foreign currency. A major part of this uncovered foreign borrowing was the "carry trade," in which financial institutions borrow dollars or yen at a low interest rate, exchange the money to local currency, and lend in the borrowing country at a higher interest rate. This is very profitable as long as the exchange value of the local currency is steady (so that local currency can be exchanged back to dollars or yen at the same rate in the future, to repay the foreign borrowing).

When the likelihood of devaluation or depreciation becomes noticeable, the borrowers attempt to hedge their exposed positions by selling local currency, but this puts additional pressure on the government defense of the fixed exchange rate. If the government gives up the fixed rate, borrowers suffer losses to the extent that their positions are still unhedged. The losses make it more difficult for them to service their foreign debts. Foreign lenders then may reduce new lending and try to be repaid more quickly, leading to a financial crisis.

Fickle International Short-Term Lending

Another form of debt can help us understand financial crises. Short-term debt—debt that is due to be paid off soon—can cause a major problem because foreign lenders can refuse to refinance it. The inability of the Mexican government to refinance the large amount of short-term *tesobonos* that were coming due was a major contributor to the Mexican crisis of 1994–1995. In the Asian crisis, the large amount of short-term borrowing by banks that was coming due created a policy dilemma for the countries' governments. The governments could raise interest rates to attract continued foreign financing, but this would weaken local borrowers and hurt the banks' loan returns. Instead, the governments could guarantee or take over the banks' foreign borrowings, based on the need to prevent the local banks from failing. But the governments themselves did not have sufficient foreign exchange to pay off the debts, so they risked setting off a financial crisis on their own if foreign lenders demanded repayment.

Short-term debt is risky to the borrowing country because international lenders can readily shift from one equilibrium to another, based on their opinion of the country's prospects. In one equilibrium, the lenders refinance or roll over the short-term debt, and this can continue into the future. But a rapid shift to another equilibrium in which lenders demand repayment is also possible. If the borrowing country cannot come up with the payoff quickly, a financial crisis occurs.

Global Contagion

The four forces already discussed—overlending and overborrowing, exogenous shocks, exchange rate risk, and short-term borrowing—provide major insights into why a financial crisis could hit a country. But the financial crises of the 1980s and 1990s were more than this. When a crisis hits one country, it usually spreads and affects many other countries. It appears that some kind of **global contagion** is at work (an issue we first discussed in Chapter 1).

This contagion could be an overreaction by foreign lenders as they engage in a scramble for the exits. Herding behavior can occur. Borrowers often do not provide full information to lenders. Asymmetric information can lead some lenders to imitate other lenders who may have better information about the borrowers, or to fear that other borrowing countries are likely to have similar problems to those of the crisis country, even if there is no evidence that this is true.

But contagion can also be based on new recognition of real problems in other countries that are similar to those in the country with the initial crisis. The financial crisis in one country can serve as a "wake-up call" that other countries really do have similar problems. The crisis in Mexico led to a more severe tequila effect in countries that had problems similar to those of Mexico—currencies that had experienced real appreciations, weak banking systems and domestic lending booms, and relatively low holdings of official international reserves. In Asia the crisis in Thailand led to a recognition that Indonesia and South Korea had similar problems, including a weak banking sector, declining quality of domestic capital formation, a slowdown in export growth, and fixed exchange rates that may not be defensible for very long.

Analysis suggests that both forms of contagion are probably important and occur together in many crises. The initial reaction to a crisis in one country is often pure contagion, as international lenders pull back from nearly all investments in developing countries. Lenders then examine the other countries more closely. International lenders resume lending to those countries that do not seem to have problems. But the financial crisis spreads to those countries that seem to have similar problems. Although the spread of the crisis has a basis in the recognition of actual problems, it is still a kind of contagion effect. Without the crisis in the first country, the other countries probably would have avoided their own crises.

The Special Case of Sovereign Debt

Most debt of developing countries is *sovereign debt*—debt of the government of the country or debt of private borrowers that is guaranteed by the country's government. According to the information in Figure 26.3, sovereign debt was 94 percent of total long-term debt in 1990, and this was still 84 percent in 1998, notwithstanding the rising importance of investments in the securities of private companies.

Sovereign borrowers are different. They cannot be legally forced to repay if they do not wish to do so. Creditors cannot sue them in court or seize their assets. Granted, there have been times in the past when creditors could force repayments: Britain and France were able to take over Egyptian tax collections in the latter half of the nineteenth century after Egypt failed to repay English and French creditors, and creditors were backed by gunboats when they demanded repayment from Venezuela at the beginning of the twentieth century. But the gunboat days are over. If Malaysia defaults on its debts, the United States and other lending countries cannot send gunboats to Malaysia. Nor can they send thugs to beat up the Malaysian finance minister.

If sovereign debtors cannot be forced to repay, why should they ever repay? The usual answer—that the debtor will repay on time to protect its own future creditworthiness—surprisingly turns out to be false, at least by itself. If fresh loans keep growing fast enough, the debtor country can afford to repay an ever-growing debt service. But this is no solution, if the debtor never actually repays the full amount. If lenders tire of "repaying themselves" and cut their new lending, the debtor then defaults.

The correct answer to why sovereign debtors repay requires that they have something more to lose than just access to future loans. In domestic lending, collateral works well as the something more to lose. National laws allow the creditor to take over assets of the nonrepaying debtor, but only in amounts tied to the value defaulted.

Aside from creditworthiness, what might the sovereign debtor lose when it defaults? There are ways to create seizable international collateral, even though they are not perfect counterparts to the collateral

recognized by domestic law. Often debtor countries have assets in the creditor country that make them fear retaliation by that country. If a debtor country has actual gross investments in the banks and enterprises of the creditor country, it should worry that these could be seized in retaliation, as when the United States froze Iranian assets in response to the Teheran hostage crisis in 1979–1981 and several countries froze Iraqi assets after Iraq invaded Kuwait in 1990. In practice, however, the international collateral mechanism is not finely tuned. The value of such assets is not necessarily close to the size of the possible default by the debtor country, and it may be legally difficult for the creditors to seize them.

There are two other sources of loss to the debtor country from default. First, the country can experience macroeconomic costs. We have seen that defaults linked to financial crises disrupt the domestic financial system and the domestic economy. The economy goes into a severe recession, exacting a large cost on the country. In addition, the debtor country may lose some ability to export and import if it loses access to trade financing or if new barriers are erected to its trade by the creditor countries. Second, the country can experience a general loss of reputation that results in a loss of other benefits. For instance, multinational firms may see the default as a sign of increased country risk. If multinationals fail to invest or they pull out of the country, it loses the spillover benefits from the technology, management practices, worker training, and marketing skills that the multinational firms bring to the country.

These extra losses create a true benefit–cost problem for the sovereign debtor considering default. And the answer to this benefit–cost problem indicates the limits to prudent lending to the sovereign borrower. The key forces are summarized in the accompanying graph. To simplify, let's examine the case in which the sovereign borrower owes full payment of all debt and interest at the end of the period, equal to the stock of debt (D) plus the interest due on this debt (iD). The debtor is considering full default, so that the straight line $(1 + i)D$ shows the benefits of not repaying. The debtor's cost (C) of not repaying also depends on the stock of debt, but only to some extent. There is a fixed cost (C_0) to any nonrepayment, regardless of the amount of debt. The fixed cost could be in the form of reduced creditworthiness, macroeconomic costs, or some loss of general reputation. Beyond C_0, the cost of not repaying probably rises with the amount of debt not honored, but not as fast as the stock of debt itself. Loss of access to future loans, asset seizures, macroeconomic costs, and more serious loss of general reputation are probably larger if the default is larger, but these losses are limited. A bigger default does not bring a much bigger penalty.

The fact that the cost of not repaying rises more slowly with extra debt than does the benefit of default means that the sovereign debtor repays debt faithfully as long as the debt is not too large. However, beyond some threshold amount of debt (D_{limit}), the willingness to repay disappears. Well-behaved lending occurs to the left of the limit, because the cost of nonrepayment exceeds the amount of debt service that could be avoided.

Default can occur for any of several reasons. First, the borrower may amass debt larger than D_{limit}. This

is the overlending and overborrowing discussed in the text for the special case of sovereign borrowing. We gain a subtle insight from the analysis here. Sovereign debtors may decide that it is not wise to repay even if they are *able* to repay. Second, a rise in the real rate of interest raises the benefit of not repaying. This is an upward rotation of the benefit line $(1 + i)D$ in the graph. If the sovereign debt just equaled D_{limit} before the increase in the interest rate, then it is now above the new D_{limit} for the higher interest rate. The country has the incentive to default. This is an example of how exogenous shocks discussed in the text apply to the special case of sovereign debt.

Should lenders make new loans if the sovereign debtor announces that it "cannot" repay without new loans to cover its current debt service? The graph suggests a negative answer. The debtor's announcement suggests that the stock of debt is already over the safe limit ($D > D_{limit}$). Extending more loans to cover current interest payments moves us farther to the right (D rises). The gap between the debtor's benefits and the costs of not repaying grows wider. Unless something else changes, default will occur.

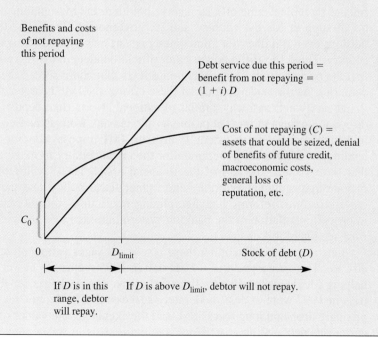

Resolving Financial Crises

A financial crisis has serious negative consequences for the borrowing country and its economy. As new lending to the country dries up, the economy goes into recession. Also, a financial crisis in one country can threaten the economies of other countries and the broader global financial system, through contagion effects that reduce capital flows to other borrowers and can send some into their own crises. In the crises of the past several decades, the two major types of international efforts to resolve financial crises are rescue packages and debt restructuring. Let's look at each of these, how they work, and the questions that arise about their efforts.

Rescue Packages

When a financial crisis hits a country, that country's government usually seeks a rescue package of loan commitments to assist it in getting through the crisis. As indicated in the discussion of the history of lending to developing countries, the sizes of these rescue packages were large in the 1990s, ranging from $17 billion for Thailand to $58 billion for South Korea. The lenders generally included the IMF, the World Bank, and some national governments.

A rescue package can have several purposes. First, the loans in the rescue package compensate for the lack of private lending during the crisis. The money allows the country to meet its needs for foreign exchange, to provide some financing for new domestic investments, and to cushion the decline in aggregate demand and domestic production. Second, the package can restore investor confidence by replenishing official reserve holdings and by signaling official international support for the country and its government. This can stem the capital outflow, even if it does not immediately restart new private foreign lending to the country. Third, the IMF and the other official lenders in the rescue package hope that the package will limit contagion effects that could spread the crisis to other countries. As the leader in most of these efforts, the IMF is organizing an international safety net, in a way similar to national efforts (like deposit insurance and discount lending) to prevent problems at one bank from spreading to other banks in the national financial system. Fourth, the IMF imposes conditions as part of its lending, to require the government of the crisis country to make policy changes that should speed the end of the financial crisis. These policy reforms usually include tighter monetary policy and tighter fiscal policy, and they may include other structural reforms like liberalizing restrictions on international trade or improving regulation of the banking system (an issue that we will take up in the final section of this chapter).

One major question about these rescue packages is how effective they actually are. The rescue package for Mexico in 1995 seemed to be very successful in helping Mexico to resolve its financial crisis. The packages for the Asian countries in 1997 were at best moderately successful. The economies went into surprisingly deep and long recessions, and the exchange rate values of the countries' currencies declined greatly before stabilizing. Russia was a nontest—Russia did not abide by the IMF conditions, so the package never took hold. The package for Brazil did not prevent a currency fall, probably largely because the Brazilian government did not enact the fiscal reforms that it promised. But the package appeared to be helpful in heading off a full financial crisis.

The other major question about the rescue packages is whether they actually increase the likelihood of financial crises because they encourage overlending and overborrowing. A rescue package provides a bailout for lenders and borrowers when a crisis hits. But if lenders and borrowers expect to be bailed out, then they should worry less about the risk of a financial crisis. This leads them to lend and borrow more than is prudent—an example of **moral hazard,** in which insurance leads the insured to be less careful because the insurance offers compensation if bad things happen. Given the costs that the borrowers incur when a crisis hits, it seems that the moral hazard for them is probably not too large. Borrowers still lose a lot even with a rescue package.

The rescue package can create moral hazard for lenders. In the Mexican crisis of 1994–1995, the rescue package was used to pay off foreign investors, including full payment to the holders of the *tesobonos*. The lack of large losses to rescued creditors in the Mexican crisis probably encouraged too much international lending during 1996–1997 because the lenders worried too little about the risks of the lending.

In the Asian crisis, lenders to banks in the crisis countries were generally repaid in full, using money from the rescue packages. Still, the scope for moral hazard had its limits. Foreign investors in private bonds and stocks suffered large losses as the market price of these securities declined, and foreign banks suffered large losses on loans to private nonfinancial borrowers.

The failure of the rescue package for Russia led to large losses for all foreign creditors. Many of these lenders were specifically relying on a rescue to limit their downside risk (moral hazard in action), so they received quite a surprise. Some of the caution in lending to developing countries after the Russian crisis is probably the result of a reappraisal of the risks of this lending. Moral hazard has declined because lenders realize that rescue packages may not provide a bailout.

Debt Restructuring

Debt restructuring refers to two types of changes in the terms of debt: *Debt rescheduling* changes when payments are due, by pushing the repayments schedule further into the future. The amount of debt is effectively the same, but the borrower has a longer time to pay it off. *Debt reduction* lowers the amount of debt.

When a financial crisis hits a country because the country has more debt than it is willing or able to service, resolution of the crisis often requires debt restructuring. By stretching out payments or reducing debt, the borrowing country has a better chance of meeting a more manageable stream of current and future payments for debt service. A key issue is the process of reaching a restructuring agreement among creditors and borrowers. There is a free-rider problem here. Each individual creditor has the incentive to hold out, hoping that others restructure their lending agreements, but not altering its own. Then the free rider can be repaid faster or fully, while other creditors that agreed to restructuring must wait longer or get less. But if free riding prevents a restructuring deal, then all creditors will probably lose, as the crisis is not resolved.

The debt crisis of 1982 dragged on through the 1980s partly because there was no framework for overcoming the coordination problem among the hundreds of banks that had lent to the crisis countries. In addition to the free-rider problem, legal clauses in many syndicated loan agreements limited debt restructuring. As we saw earlier, the Brady Plan of 1989 finally established a process for debt restructuring. It offered a menu of choices to the creditor banks, as well as coercion when necessary, to overcome the free-rider problem. In a typical Brady deal, each creditor bank was offered a choice between partial debt reduction and continuance of its loan agreements along with required new lending to the crisis country. The debt reduction occurred when the bank exchanged its bank loans for a smaller amount of new bonds that were backed by collateral (usually U.S. government bonds). The borrowing country was able to establish the collateral by borrowing part of the value from the IMF and World Bank. (As usual, the IMF also imposed conditions for policy changes by the country along with its loan). Brady deals succeeded in reducing the debt of 18 crisis countries by $65 billion, about one-third of their total debt. As the Brady deals resolved the lingering crisis, international lending to these countries resumed.

During the crises of the 1990s, restructuring of bank debt went smoother. The limited number of debtors and creditors eased the negotiations. The key issue that arose in the 1990s was the great difficulty of restructuring bonds. There are often hundreds or thousands of bondholders. The legal terms of the typical international bond require that all bondholders agree to the terms of a restructuring. And a small number of bondholders can sue to force immediate full repayment if the issuer defaults on any payment. Given the growing importance of bonds in financial flows to developing countries, there are a number of suggestions to revise the terms of the bonds, to mandate majority voting on restructuring, to share equally any partial payments, and to limit the ability of small numbers of bondholders to force immediate full repayment or take other legal actions concerning the bond. But these suggestions have not yet been adopted, so bond restructuring remains nearly impossible.

Reducing the Frequency of Financial Crises

Financial crises create large losses for international lenders though defaults, debt rescheduling, debt reduction, and declines in the market prices of bonds, stocks, and loans that are traded on secondary markets. Financial crises also impose large costs on borrowing countries through sudden declines in access to lending and the macroeconomic costs of recessions and slow economic growth that usually accompany the crises. While we have ways for trying to resolve crises once they occur, it would also be great to find ways to prevent financial crises from occurring, or at least to reduce their frequency. The goal of reducing how often financial crises occur has taken on new urgency as the series of major crises hit the developing countries beginning in 1994.

There is no scarcity of proposals for improving the "international financial architecture." Four proposed reforms enjoy widespread support. First, developing countries should pursue sound macroeconomic policies, to avoid creating conditions in which overborrowing or a loss of confidence in the government's capability could lead to a crisis. Second, countries should improve the data that they report publicly, to provide sufficient details on total debt and its components, as well as on holdings of international reserves, and they should report these data promptly. The belief is that with better data lenders would make more informed decisions on lending and investing, making overlending less likely and also reducing the risk of pure contagion against emerging markets debt. In addition, the commitment to release data should encourage developing countries to follow better policies, under threat of having to report poor performance resulting from poor policies. While the call for more information is not controversial, it also has its limits. Developing country governments have the incentive to provide misleading or incomplete data at exactly the times when lenders most need accurate information. Third, developing country governments should avoid short-term borrowing denominated in foreign currencies, to avoid crises that begin when foreign lenders abruptly demand repayment. In the next part of this section we look more closely at a fourth proposal that enjoys widespread support—better regulation and supervision of banks in developing countries.

Several proposed reforms are radical and have no chance of being adopted. These include proposals for a global organization to insure international debt, a global superregulator of financial institutions and markets, a global central bank, and a single global currency.

Other proposals for reform are more controversial, and in some cases serious competing proposals suggest moving in opposite directions. One proposal is that developing countries should end efforts to fix or heavily manage the exchange rate values of their currencies. Among other possible benefits, the shift to more flexible exchange rates makes the existence of exchange rate risk palpable, so that private borrowers are less likely to build up large unhedged liabilities in foreign currencies. But a competing proposal is that developing countries should move to nearly permanently fixed exchange rates, with greater use of currency boards and similar arrangements. Such arrangements discipline government macroeconomic policies to be more sound. In another set of competing proposals, one is that the IMF should receive more resources so that it can establish large lines of credit to developing countries with sound economic policies. These countries then can use this backing to fight off any financial attacks. The other is that the IMF should be abolished, or at least that its rescue activities be severely limited, because it creates substantial moral hazard with its lending. By encouraging overlending, it makes crises more likely.

After we discuss proposals for better bank regulation, which is *not* controversial, we conclude the chapter with a look at a proposal that is controversial: expanding the use capital controls to limit borrowing.

Bank Regulation and Supervision

Banks are considered to have a special role in an economy. They are at the center of the payments system that facilitates transactions in the economy. They acquire deposits from customers based on trust that the banks can pay back the deposits in the future, but if this trust is broken, depositors create a run on the bank as they all try to get their money out quickly. And this run can spread to other banks, creating the risk that the banking system ceases to function. Governments believe they must back up banks by assuring that depositors can get their money out, to prevent a problem at one bank from spreading to the whole system. But bank managers then have an incentive to take too many risks, because government insurance provides a rescue if the risks go bad (another case of moral hazard). Strong government regulation and supervision of banks is then needed to limit how much risk banks take on.

In developing countries banks are often especially important, because bank lending is also the major source of financing for local businesses. Stock and bond markets are often underdeveloped. But government regulation and supervision of banks in developing countries is often weak. With weak regulation, banks engage in more risky activities. Banks make loans based on relationships—"crony capitalism" loans to bank directors, managers, friends of directors and managers, politically important people, and their businesses. Banks take on large exposures to exchange rate risk by borrowing foreign currencies to fund local-currency loans (the carry trade). Banks operate with little equity capital, so they are more likely to take risks and require government rescues. In addition, the government often exerts direct influence on lending decisions, to favor some borrowers based on the government's strategy for economic development.

Thus, with weak supervision and an explicit or implicit guarantee that the government will rescue banks in trouble, banks have incentives to borrow too much internationally (and lenders are comfortable lending so much), and banks are more willing to take the risk of unhedged foreign-currency liabilities. A financial crisis becomes more likely. There is a clear need for better government regulation and supervision of local banks in the borrowing countries. Regulators should require banks to use better accounting and disclose more information publicly, to use risk assessment and risk management to reduce risk exposures, to recognize bad loans and make provision for them, and to have more equity capital. The regulators should be willing to identify weak banks, to insist on changes in practices and management at these banks, and to close them if they are insolvent. In addition, the government probably should permit more foreign banks to operate locally because these foreign banks bring better management and better techniques for controlling risks.

In the abstract, the proposal for better bank regulation and supervision in developing countries is not controversial. The challenge is in the implementation. There is likely to be political resistance—from the banks, from the borrowers favored by crony capitalism, and from the government officials who lose some power to direct bank lending. Even if such political resistance can be overcome, there is also a lack of people with the expertise to regulate banks effectively.

Bank regulation and supervision has improved in some countries like Mexico, and it will continue to improve in developing countries more generally, but the improvement is likely to be a slow process.

Capital Controls

A controversial proposal for reducing the frequency of financial crises is to increase developing countries' use of controls or impediments to capital inflows.[3] Such controls could take any of several forms, including an outright limit or prohibition, a tax that must be paid to the government equal to some portion of the borrowing, or a requirement that some portion of the borrowing be placed in a deposit with the country's central bank. (If this deposit does not earn interest, then it is effectively a tax on the borrowing.) There are three ways in which such controls can reduce the risk of financial crisis. First, the controls can prevent large inflows that could result in overlending and overborrowing. Second, the controls can be used to discourage short-term borrowing. Third, the controls can reduce the country's exposure to contagion by limiting the amount that foreign lenders could pull out of the country.

Chile is usually offered as the example of a country that seems to have used controls on capital inflows successfully during the 1990s. The Chilean government has required that a percentage of the value of new lending and investments into the country be placed in an interest-free deposit with the central bank for one year. And the government has required that foreign investors keep their investments in Chile for at least one year. These requirements seem to have had their major effect by altering the mix of borrowing—less short-term debt. The Chilean government has also changed the percentage that must be deposited to tune it to changing market conditions over time. It began at 20 percent, was raised to 30 percent, then lowered to 10 percent and to zero in 1998, as capital inflows fell off following the Russian crisis.

What are the overall benefits and costs of controls on capital inflows? A major cost of the controls is the loss of the gains from international borrowing, to the extent that they discourage capital inflows. While they can provide benefits by reducing the risk of a financial crisis, they are a second-best policy. It would be better if the government of the borrowing country could identify the specific problems that might lead to a crisis and address these directly (recall the specificity rule from Chapter 9). For instance, if overborrowing or too much

---

[3]Another possible use of capital controls is to limit capital outflows during a financial crisis. Malaysia adopted such controls as a temporary measure in 1998. The goal is to prevent continued capital flight and remove the pressures that it places on local financial institutions, local capital markets, and the exchange rate value of the country's currency. Government fiscal and monetary policy can then be directed to addressing the internal imbalance of recession, with less fear that the shift to expansionary policies will worsen the financial crisis. Such controls are probably only effective for a short time, as pressures build and investors find ways around the controls. The major cost of such controls is that they are likely to scare off new capital inflows in the future, even after the controls are removed, so that the country loses the gains from international borrowing.

short-term foreign-currency borrowing occurs because of the excessive risks taken by local banks, the direct policy response is to improve bank regulation and supervision. If bank regulation cannot be improved immediately, then capital controls can be a second-best policy response. However, the capital controls are likely to lose their effectiveness over time, as investors and borrowers find ways to circumvent them. They probably only buy time for the government to adopt the direct policy improvement like better bank regulation. Furthermore, governments can also make mistakes with controls on capital inflows. For instance, South Korea removed controls on short-term bank borrowing while continuing to restrict longer term capital inflows like foreign purchases of stocks and direct foreign investments. Korean banks then borrowed on a massive scale, and this became a key part of the Korean crisis of late 1997.

In conclusion, we have a variety of proposals for reducing the frequency of financial crises, ranging from the unrealistic to the controversial to the useful and feasible, and some reforms are being implemented. International lending brings major benefits to both the lending and the borrowing countries. But international lending is prone to financial crises from time to time. We can hope to reduce the frequency of crises while resolving those crises that do occur and trying to minimize contagion.

Summary

Well-behaved international lending (or international capital flows) yields the same kinds of welfare results as international trade in products. International lending increases total world product and brings net gains to both the lending and borrowing countries, although there are some groups who lose well-being in each country. The lending-country government or the borrowing-country government can impose taxes on international lending. If either country has market power (that is, if it is able to affect the world interest rate), it can try to improve its well-being by imposing a nationally optimal tax on international lending. But if the other country retaliates with its own tax, both countries can end up worse off.

The history of international lending to developing countries shows surges of lending and recurrent financial crises. The dramatic increase of lending in the 1970s as banks recycled petrodollars led to the debt crisis beginning in 1982. This crisis stretched throughout the 1980s, with low capital flows to developing countries. The Brady Plan of 1989 led to the resolution of the crisis through debt reductions and the conversion of much bank debt to Brady bonds. Capital flows to developing countries increased dramatically during the 1990s, with more in the form of portfolio investments in bonds and stocks. However, the 1990s also saw a series of financial crises: Mexico in 1994–1995, several Asian countries in 1997, and Russia in 1998.

We can identify five major forces that can lead to or deepen financial crises. First, overlending and overborrowing can occur, as a result of government borrowing to finance expansionary government policies, excessive borrowing by banks, or the herding behavior of lenders seeking what seem to be high returns. For sovereign debt owed by borrowing governments, lending can turn out to be excessive even if the government has the ability to repay, because the benefits of default exceed the costs. Second, exogenous shocks like increases in foreign (especially U.S.) interest rates can shift flows away from developing country borrowers and make repaying their debts more difficult. Third, borrowers, especially banks, can take on too many unhedged foreign currency liabilities, which then become very expensive to pay off if the local currency depreciates unexpectedly. Fourth, the borrowing country can borrow too much using short-term loans and bonds. The borrower can experience difficulties if foreign investors refuse to refinance or roll over the debt. And finally, contagion can spread the crisis from the initial crisis country to other countries. These other countries may be vulnerable because of problems with their policies or economic performance, but it is the contagion from the initial crisis country that leads foreign lenders to fear a crisis and pull back from lending to these other countries. Financial crises have elements of self-fulfilling panics, in which investors fear defaults, so they stop lending and demand quick repayment. If many lenders try to do this at once, the borrower cannot repay, and default and crisis occur.

The two major types of international efforts to resolve financial crises are rescue packages and debt restructuring. A rescue package provides temporary financial assistance, can help to restore foreign investor confidence, and can try to limit contagion. In the 1990s, these packages were large. A key question is whether these packages create substantial moral hazard, in which lenders believe that they can lend with little risk because a rescue will bail them out. Debt restructuring attempts to make debt service more manageable for the borrowing country. Debt rescheduling stretches out the repayments further into the future, and debt reduction lowers the amount of debt. Restructuring can be difficult because each individual creditor has the incentive to free-ride, hoping others will restructure while the free rider receives full repayment on time. The Brady Plan set up a process of successful restructuring of bank debt from the 1980s' crisis. Because of legal clauses in international bonds, they are very difficult to restructure.

There are a range of proposals for reforms of the "international financial architecture" to reduce the frequency of financial crises. Some are radical and unlikely, and others are controversial. Several are widely supported: Developing country governments should have sound macroeconomic policies, they should provide better data for lenders and investors to use in their decision making, they should minimize short-term debt, and they should improve their regulation and supervision of their banks. One controversial proposal is that developing country governments should make greater use of controls on capital inflows. While this could limit overborrowing, short-term borrowing, and exposure to contagion, it would also reduce the benefits to be gained from international borrowing.

Suggested Reading

Obstfeld (1998) and Mahler (1998) provide broad discussions of international capital movements. Eichengreen (1999) and Goldstein (1998) discuss recent financial crises and proposals for reform. Cline (1995), Edwards (1995), and Eichengreen and Lindert (1989) examine the debt crisis of the 1980s. *Global Development Finance* (previously called *World Debt Tables*), published annually by the World Bank, is a good source for current information and data.

Questions and Problems

✦1. "It is best for a country never to borrow from foreign lenders." Do you agree or disagree? Why?

2. "Because a national government cannot go bankrupt, it is safe to lend to a foreign government." Do you agree or disagree? Why?

✦3. Why was there so much private lending to developing countries from 1974 to 1982, although there had been so little from 1930 to 1974?

4. What triggered the debt crisis in 1982?

✦5. Consider Figure 26.1. What is the size of each of the following? (Each answer should be a number.)

   a. World product without international lending

   b. World product with free international lending

   c. World product with Japan's tax of 2 percent on its foreign lending

   What does the difference between your answers to parts *a* and *b* tell us? What does the difference between your answers to parts *b* and *c* tell us?

6. Consider Figure 26.1. In comparison with free international lending, what happens if each country imposes a 2 percent tax on the international lending (so that there is a total of 4 percent of tax)? What is the net gain, or loss, for each country?

✦7. How could each of the following cause or contribute to a financial crisis in a developing country?

   a. A large amount of short-term debt denominated in dollars

   b. A financial crisis in another developing country in the region

8. Consider the graph in the box "The Special Case of Sovereign Debt."

   a. Show graphically the effect of an increase in the interest rate *i*. If the country's government would not default before this change, could this change lead to default?

   b. Show graphically the effect of an increase in the cost of defaulting. If the country's government would not default before this change, could this change lead to default?

✦9. How could each of the following reforms reduce the frequency of financial crises?

   a. Quick release of detailed, accurate information on the debt and official reserves of most developing countries

   b. Use by more developing countries of controls to limit capital inflows

10. The "Optimal Deadbeat" Problem: The World Bank is considering a stream of loans to the Puglian government to help it develop its nationalized oil fields and refineries. This is the only set of loans that the World Bank would ever give Puglia. Whether the Puglian government repays the loan or defaults has no impact on Puglia. If the World Bank's stream of loans would have the effects shown in the accompanying table, would it ever be in Puglia's interest to default on the loans? If not, why not? If so, why and when?

Loan Effects ($ millions)

Year	Inflow of Funds from World Bank	Stock of Accumulated Borrowings at End of Year	Interest Paid on Borrowings (at 8 percent)	Profits on Extra Oil Export Sales
1	$200	$200	0	0
2	100	300	16	30
3	50	350	24	30
4	0	350	28	30
5	−50 (repayment)	300	28	30
6	−50 (repayment)	250	24	30
7	−50 (repayment)	200	20	30
8	−50 (repayment)	150	16	30
9	−50 (repayment)	100	12	30
10	−50 (repayment)	50	8	30
11	−50 (repayment)	0	4	30

CHAPTER 27

Direct Foreign Investment and the Multinationals

One of the most sensitive areas in international economics today is direct foreign investment (DFI). Developing countries worry both that foreigners will invest in them and that they won't. They fear exploitation on the one hand and inadequate access to foreign capital, technology, marketing, and management skills on the other. Industrialized countries worry about being both the sources and the recipients of direct investments. As direct investments flow out, don't these reduce employment opportunities at home? As direct investments flow in, won't foreigners establish undue influence and control over the local economy? In some cases, won't foreigners gain control over facilities that compromise national security and national defense?

These issues are important because governments must decide their policies toward direct foreign investments. All governments prohibit or restrict direct investment into the country in certain lines of activity. Which lines are prohibited vary from one country to another, but the prohibitions are directed toward those activities that are regarded as particularly vulnerable to foreign influence—including natural resources, banking, newspapers and other communications media, and defense industries. Governments also can regulate the operations of foreign firms in a number of ways. They can require local participation in the ownership or management of the local operations, or they can require training, locally purchased components and parts, local research, or exports. Governments can also use tax policy to influence both the flows of direct investments and the division of the investment returns between the firms and the governments. On the other hand, many governments actively court multinational firms by offering various forms of subsidies to attract them to locate in their countries.

This chapter provides a broad survey of what we know about DFI. It explores why direct investments occur. It also examines whether either the source country or the host country has good reasons to try to restrict (or encourage) it.

A Definition

Balance-of-payments accountants define **direct foreign investment** as any flow of lending to, or purchases of ownership in, a foreign enterprise that is largely owned by residents (usually firms) of the investing country. The proportions of ownership that define *largely* vary from country to country. For the United States 10 percent ownership by the investing firm suffices as an official definition of direct investment. Here are some examples of investments that do and do not fit the U.S. definition of direct foreign investment:

U.S. Direct Foreign Investments	*U.S. Portfolio Investments Abroad**
Alcoa's purchase of stock in a new Jamaican bauxite firm that is 50 percent owned by Alcoa	Alcoa's purchase of stock in a new Jamaican bauxite firm that is 5 percent owned by Alcoa
A loan from Ford U.S.A. to a Canadian parts-making subsidiary in which Ford holds 55 percent of shares	A loan from Ford U.S.A. to a Canadian parts-making firm in which Ford U.S.A. holds 8 percent of shares

*As discussed in Chapter 26.

Note that direct investment consists of any investment, whether new ownership or simple lending, as long as the investing firm owns over 10 percent of the foreign firm being invested in.[1] The distinction between direct and portfolio (nondirect) investment is thus meant to focus on the issue of control.

A firm that owns and controls enterprises in more than one country is a **multinational firm.** In a multinational firm the parent company is based in the home country (the source country for the DFI). The parent has one or more foreign affiliates (subsidiaries or branches) in one or more host countries. The parent company uses DFI to establish a new foreign affiliate or to expand or finance an existing one.

Direct Investment Is Not Just a Capital Movement

The fact that the investor has substantial control over the foreign subsidiary enterprise makes direct investment more complex in nature than portfolio investment. A controlled subsidiary often receives direct inputs of managerial skills, trade secrets, technology, rights to use brand names, and instructions about which markets to pursue and which to avoid.

In fact, direct investment is so much more than just a capital movement that in many cases it begins with little or no net flow of financial capital at all. Sometimes the parent company borrows the initial financial capital exclusively in the

---

[1]Balance-of-payments accountants also define direct investment as any lending in, or purchase of stock in, firms controlled by parties in the investor's home country (e.g., the United States) even if each *individual* investor does not own 10 percent of the firm being invested in.

host country, adding only its brand name, managerial formulas, and other assets of the less tangible variety. Once the subsidiary becomes profitable, it grows from reinvested internal profits and newly borrowed funds, while sending a part of profits back to the parent whose financial investments were so hard to see.

Why should it often be the case that little or no financial capital initially flows? One reason is that the purpose of DFI is not so much to move capital internationally, as it is to move the firm's intangible assets: technology, managerial capabilities, and marketing skills and assets. Another reason is that the parent company wants to reduce the risks that its foreign activities are exposed to. One risk is exchange rate risk. A good hedging strategy for a parent company that has foreign-currency assets in its affiliates is to take on foreign-currency liabilities as well, by borrowing in foreign currencies that are used to finance the affiliate.

Another risk is political risk, the risk that the government of the country will alter its policies in ways that harm the multinational company. A major political risk is the possibility of expropriation or nationalization by the host government. Since World War I and the Russian revolution, host countries have shown willingness to seize the assets of multinationals, sometimes without compensating the investors. Realizing the danger of expropriation, many multinationals have hedged their direct foreign investments in a way analogous to hedging in the foreign exchange market. They have matched much of their tangible assets in a host country with borrowings in that country (for which the tangible assets serve as collateral). If political change brings expropriation, the parents also can tell the host-country creditors to try to collect their repayments from their own (expropriating) government. With freedom from liabilities offsetting part or all of its asset losses in that country, the parent could not be held hostage. Its technology, market secrets, and managerial skills could typically elude expropriation.

When and Where DFI Occurs

Direct foreign investment has been rising and falling, mainly rising, throughout the 20th century. It had its fastest growth, and took its largest share of all international investment, in the postwar generation dating roughly from the Korean War (1950–53) to the first oil shock (1973–74). During that period, international investments were dominated by investment outflows from the United States. The Americans have historically shown a greater preference for DFI and direct control than have other investing countries, particularly Britain, France, and the oil-rich nations, all of which have channeled a greater proportion of their foreign investments into portfolio lending.[2] Thus the early postwar rise of American capital exports propelled DFI and American-based multinationals into international prominence. In the 1970s and early 1980s, DFI grew more slowly, being eclipsed by two waves of portfolio lending: the ill-fated surge of lending to developing

---

[2]Japan has occupied an intermediate position. Much of its outward investment in the 1970s took the form of DFI, but in the 1980s, it shifted relatively toward portfolio lending, especially lending to the U.S. government, although it also became a large direct investor.

countries in 1974–82 (discussed in Chapter 26) and the surge of lending to the United States in the 1980s. Since the mid-1980s, DFI has again grown quickly, driven by increasing DFI by Japanese firms in the second half of the 1980s and by increasing DFI by U.S. firms, European firms, and firms based in South and East Asia in the 1990s.

Direct foreign investment has also changed direction. First, in the 1970s and 1980s, it moved away from the developing countries, where it had met with resistance and expropriations climaxing in the 1970s. This trend reversed itself beginning in 1992 as DFI flows into developing countries increased dramatically. Growing domestic markets, low production costs, and reforms of economic policies attracted direct investment, especially into a small number of developing countries in South and East Asia and Latin America. Included in these is the People's Republic of China, following its opening to foreign trade and investment in the late 1970s. Second, the United States attracted more DFI inflows than any other nation in the 1980s. The share of the United States then declined somewhat, but it continued to receive about one-fifth of new DFI flows in the mid- and late 1990s. Third, the deepening of integration in the European Union has encouraged DFI into and within the EU, and the formation of NAFTA (along with Mexico's own policy reforms) has encouraged DFI into Mexico.

Figure 27.1 shows the geographic pattern of direct investments by the eight largest source countries at the end of 1996. While the previous paragraphs' descriptions focused on changes in the flows of new direct investments, Figure 27.1 shows the stocks of direct investments, the cumulations of past flows into established positions. These eight countries are the source of about 76 percent of all existing direct investments, which totaled about $3.1 trillion in 1996. In fact, industrialized countries as a group are overwhelmingly the home countries of direct investments, accounting for about 90 percent of the world total.

The six columns toward the right in Figure 27.1 indicate different regions that host the direct investments. Reading across a row shows where the eight source countries invest. Close to half of U.S. direct investment is in Europe. The United States is also a major investor in Canada. (Most of the $111 billion of U.S. direct investment in the other two countries of NAFTA is in Canada.) Canada has placed a little over half of its investment in the United States. Japan is the dominant investor in South and East Asia, and it also built a large position in the United States in the 1980s. Britain, Germany, France, the Netherlands, and Switzerland have close to half of their direct investments in other European countries.

Two-thirds of the stock of direct investment is in industrialized countries, and over nine-tenths of that is in West European countries, Canada, and the United States. To a large extent, DFI involves firms from industrialized countries investing in other industrialized countries. With one exception, the major home countries are also major host countries. The exception is Japan. The way that Japan is truly different from other major industrialized countries is that it is host to little direct investment. In 1996, the stock of direct investment in Japan was only $30 billion, about one-quarter of what even the Netherlands had received.

FIGURE 27.1   *Major Home Countries' Direct Investments, End of 1996 (billions of U.S. dollars)*

Host Region

Home Country	Total Outward DFI	NAFTA[a]	European Union	Other Industrialized	Latin America	South and East Asia[b]	Other Developing[c]
United States	777	111	337	106	128	68	27
Canada[d]	130	71	27	7	14	7	5
Japan	276	104	45	13	6	85	23
United Kingdom	327	96	141	30	20	26	13
Germany	280	67	152	31	14	10	6
France	198	41	97	13	17	5	24
Netherlands[d]	191	51	93	18	13	10	6
Switzerland	156	44	74	10	19	6	3

These eight largest home (or source) countries accounted for about three-quarters of the world's stock of existing DFI. DFI shows noticeable regional patterns, with substantial direct investments between the United States and Canada, from Japan into the developing countries of South and East Asia, and between European countries.

[a]North American Free Trade Area: Canada, Mexico, and the United States.

[b]Includes South Korea, even though it is a member of the Organization for Economic Cooperation and Development.

[c]Includes DFI not allocated to specific host countries. The amount not allocated is rather large for Japan and France, so their large numbers for "Other Developing" should be interpreted cautiously.

[d]The total outward stock of DFI by Canada and the Netherlands at the end of 1996 is distributed to the host regions according to each country's actual regional pattern of DFI at the end of 1995.

Source: Organization for Economic Cooperation and Development, *International Direct Investment Statistics Yearbook, 1998.*

In which industries does DFI occur? That has changed over time. In 1970, about one-quarter of the world's direct investment was in the primary sector, mainly mining and extraction activities. About half was in the manufacturing sector, and about a quarter was in the services sector. The share of mining and extraction has since declined, especially in the 1970s as developing countries nationalized many firms and exerted greater control over the extraction of their natural resources. The share of manufacturing has declined somewhat, and the importance of direct investment in services has risen. In manufacturing, firms that produce pharmaceuticals and other chemicals, electrical and electronic equipment, automobiles, machinery, and food tend to be active in direct investment, while firms in industries like textiles, clothing, and paper products tend to do rather little direct investment. Within the services sector substantial direct investment occurs in banking and other financial services, in business services such as consulting, accounting, and advertising, and in wholesaling and retailing.

What Explains DFI?

Before we can sense what policies the source countries and host countries should adopt toward direct foreign investment, we need to survey the competing explanations for its private profitability.

Not Just Financial Flows or Simple Competition

One possible explanation of DFI is that it is simply another form of international flow of financial capital based on differences in returns and risks between countries. Although return and risk must play a role in the decisions by firms about whether to make direct investments, this financial theory of direct investment is not adequate. It does not explain why these international investments would be large enough to establish managerial control over the foreign companies. If the challenge is to transfer capital from one country to another, international portfolio investment can accomplish this task better than direct investment by firms whose major preoccupation lies in production and marketing.

Another possible explanation of DFI is that it is merely the outcome of perfect competition in which some firms almost accidentally happen to operate in more than one country. This approach also does not seem to be generally adequate. DFI is usually not easy or accidental, because establishing and managing successful operations in a foreign country are difficult. Local firms have inherent advantages in operating in their own environment. A foreign firm is at a disadvantage because it does not initially have the native understanding of local laws, customs, procedures, practices, and relationships. In addition, the foreign firm has the extra costs of maintaining management control. It is expensive to operate at a distance, expensive in travel, and communication, and especially expensive in misunderstanding.

What makes it possible for a foreign firm to overcome the inherent disadvantages of being foreign? To be successful, the firm entering from abroad must have some firm-specific advantage(s) not held by its local competitors in the host country. The firm-specific advantage sometimes lies in technology or patents. It may inhere in special access to very large amounts of capital, amounts far larger than the ordinary national firm can command. Or, as in the case of petroleum refining or metal processing, the firm may coordinate operations and invested capital requirements at various stages in a vertical production process and, because of heavy inventory costs and its knowledge of the requirements at each stage, it may be able to economize through synchronizing operations. Or the firm may have marketing advantages based on skilled use of advertising and other promotional methods that establish product differentiation—for instance, through highly regarded brand names. Or it may have truly superior management. But some special advantage is necessary for the firm to overcome the disadvantage of operating at a distance.

DFI as Imperfect Competition: Two Views

The key role played by firm-specific advantages has led scholars to move away from models of simple competition toward perspectives associating DFI with one or another kind of market power. Two variants, with differing policy implications, stand out: the Hymer view and the appropriability theory.

The Hymer View.

A provocative thesis and book by Stephen Hymer saw the role of firm-specific advantages as a way of marrying the study of direct foreign investment with classic models of imperfect competition in product markets. To Hymer, a direct foreign investor is a monopolist or, more often, an oligopolist in product markets. It invests in foreign enterprises to stifle competition and protect its market power. It insists on having a controlling interest in those same enterprises, and it refuses to share ownership to keep them from competing with its other branches—and also to keep its company secrets secure.

Hymer's approach does help explain the frequent pattern of "defensive investment." Major companies often seem to set up enterprises abroad that look only marginally profitable, yet do so with the stated purpose of beating their main competitors to the same national markets. Kodak may set up a foreign affiliate mainly because it fears that if it doesn't Fuji will. Ford and GM seem to have set up automaking firms in developing countries to shut each other out. Although such defensive investment may seem like good-old competition, Hymer plausibly viewed it as oligopolistic behavior, characteristic of "nonprice competition among the few" in pursuit of market power.

If direct foreign investment really betrays power in product markets, as Hymer implied, then host-country governments should be ready to impose controls on it. An oligopolist or monopolist that seeks to protect market power may well act against the national interest. For example, a U.S.-based subsidiary in Singapore may be told by its parent company not to sell in Thailand or India, whose markets bring high markups to its subsidiaries there. The prospective host government, here Singapore, may wish to constrain such a foreign parent to either allow more competition or stay out of Singapore, in favor of another investor who will export more aggressively from Singapore. The defensive investment pattern should also cause some concern because it implies that the company is likely to lobby the host government for special market protection, such as import barriers, which benefit the company but not the host nation as a whole.

The Appropriability Theory.[3]
Looked at in a different mirror, the key firm-specific advantages that seem to make DFI happen do not imply such major threats to competition in product markets. The firm must make costly investments to develop excellent management, superior information about buyers, new technologies, and better products. The firm's challenge is then to earn an adequate return on these investments, and to continue to invest to continually upgrade its firm-specific advantages. The returns that it can earn are limited by competition from other firms in the product market. These other firms are attempting to build and exploit their own firm-specific advantages.

Firm-specific advantages make the firm engage in direct investment abroad for the same reasons that make it build its own facilities, instead of buying from others, at home. The economics of whether to engage in DFI is an international extension of the decision about the boundaries of the firm (whether to make or

---

[3]The appropriability theory as described here is, in fact, a hybrid. As a theory of DFI and the scope of multinationals, it is associated with Stephen P. Magee. We have also mixed in traces of Ronald Coase's discussion of the nature of the firm.

buy, whether to own or rent, etc.). In order to *appropriate* the potential gains from its advantage, the firm often finds that it is better to keep control and ownership to itself. If it did not keep tight control, and if it offered to share its foreign enterprise with other owners, its firm-specific productive advantages might be lost. For example, where production workers must be organized and supervised as only the firm knows how, efficiency and product quality might suffer if the firm were to share control with others. (Japanese automakers feared as much about their American subsidiary branches, though Toyota then turned out to be successful in its joint production venture with General Motors.) If a firm made some of its secrets freely available to partners in the host country, that knowledge might be used to compete against the firm itself, either by defecting partners or by others.

The appropriability theory has different predictive powers from the Hymer view. Its relative strength is that it predicts both the prevalence of, and problems with, high technology industries among direct foreign investments. DFI tends to be far heavier in high tech industries because their dependence on complex skills and valuable knowledge makes firms in this sector especially aware of the advantages of keeping direct control of all affiliate enterprises. Problems arise, however, when it is difficult to guarantee that the fruits of a firm's technological advantages will be appropriated by the firm itself when it operates in some other country. If it fears it cannot keep effective control over its foreign subsidiaries, it will refrain from some productive investments, with losses to all parties (the firm itself, the host country, and the world as a whole).

The appropriability theory also has different policy implications from the Hymer view. Its emphasis on the productive nature of most of the firm-specific advantages motivating DFI favors host-country policies that either leave DFI alone or positively encourage it with favorable government treatment. Whether DFI should be left alone or actually favored again depends on how well the firm is able to appropriate the fruits of its own productive investment. If it can do so, then the government can presumably leave it alone. If it cannot, and there are "external benefits" of its productivity that would spill over to competitors and others, the government should positively subsidize the incoming direct investment.

Taxation of Multinational Firms' Profits

The profits of multinational firms come from the operations of the parent firm and of their foreign affiliates. Governments impose taxes on business profits, and the taxation of the profits of multinational firms can become complicated and contentious. Let's look first at how the profits of these global firms are taxed, and then at two important issues that arise from this taxation.

Part of how multinational firms' profits are taxed is conceptually straightforward (although the details can be vexing). The host-country government taxes the profits of the local affiliates of foreign multinationals, and the home-country government taxes the parent companies' "local" profits earned on their own activities. A key question is, then, whether the home-country government also imposes any taxes on the profits earned by the foreign affiliates of the parent companies.

Because the profits of these foreign affiliates have been taxed already by the host government, the home government usually tries to avoid double taxation of the foreign affiliate profits. While the exact rules vary by country and can be very complicated, the outcome is that the home-country government collects little or no extra taxes on the profits of foreign affiliates. Thus, the tax rate on the profits of a foreign affiliate is largely that imposed by the host government. Two important issues arise because tax rates vary across host countries, and because a global multinational firm tries to minimize the total taxes that it pays (as long as lower tax payments increase global after-tax profits).

First, multinational firms can shop around among governments and locate affiliates in the jurisdictions of governments offering lower tax rates.[4] DFI allows a multinational firm to settle in countries with lower taxes. Whether this is good or bad from a world point of view depends on the uses to which tax revenues are put and whether the productivity of the investing firm is lower in the lower-tax country.

Second, multinational firms can engage in *transfer pricing* and other devices for reporting most of their profits in low-tax countries, even though the profits were earned in high-tax countries. Transfer pricing is an art form that can be practiced by accountants of any firm dealing with itself across national borders. To lower its corporate income taxes, the firm can have its unit in the high-tax country be overcharged (or underpaid) for goods and services that the unit buys from (sells to) the less taxed affiliate. That way, the unit in the high-tax country doesn't show its tax officials much profit, while the unit in the low-tax country shows high profits. Profits are "transferred" from the unit in the high-tax country to the unit in the low-tax country. The result: net tax reduction for the multinational firm in question.

Governments know that multinational firms can use transfer prices to shift their profits and lower their taxes. Many governments attempt to police transfer pricing to ensure that the transfer prices used between units within a multinational firm are similar to the market prices that independent firms would pay to each other for similar transactions. However, determining whether transfer prices differ from market prices is complex and costly, so multinational firms usually have some scope to use transfer pricing to alter the taxes the firms pay (and which countries they pay taxes to).

DFI and International Trade

It is natural to think of direct foreign investment into a host country as a substitute for exports by the parent firm (or other home-country firms) to the host, just as we concluded in Chapter 4 that trade and international movements of production factors are substitutes. But it turns out that multinational firms are actually heavily involved in international trade. About one-third of the world's international trade

---

[4]Here and in what follows, we assume that higher tax rates in one nation are *not* matched by higher values of public programs in the eyes of the firm. If they were, then higher taxes might not be something to avoid. In practice, though, firms often feel that the public programs redistribute tax money toward others, and they view taxes as losses to the firms.

occurs as **intra-firm trade** between units of the multinational firms located in different countries (that is, trade between a parent and one its foreign affiliates or trade between foreign affiliates of a multinational). Another third of the world's international trade involves a multinational firm as the seller (exporter) or buyer (importer), trading with some other firm.

Why are multinational firms so involved in world trade? Especially, why is intra-firm trade so important? When are trade and DFI substitutes? Can DFI complement trade? We will answer these questions, first for the easier case in which a parent and its affiliates are engaged in different stages of overall production, and then for the harder case in which the affiliate is largely doing the same types of production activities as the parent (or other affiliates).

As long as transport costs and trade barriers are low enough, DFI can be used to reduce total costs by locating different stages of overall production in different countries. With DFI, the firm can maintain full control over these international production activities just as it could if it undertook all stages in its home country. For instance, for electronics products like televisions or communications equipment, the development and design of new products and improved production methods can be done in one country, the manufacture of components can be done in several other countries, the assembly of finished products can be done in yet other countries, and the design and implementation of marketing and distribution can be managed from another set of countries. When we buy a product like this today, we are buying an international value added sandwich: values added in different countries that add up to the final value that we pay.

Compared with the situation in which the firm would perform most of these activities in a single country, DFI leads to more trade as the firm's overall production is spread across units in different countries. Each stage of production can be located according to the country's comparative costs advantage (or, in the case of marketing and distribution, according to the need to locate close to the customers for the final products). For instance, design and development is located in countries (often the home country) abundant in engineers and other skilled labor, and assembly is located in countries abundant in less skilled labor. In this case, DFI is pro-trade, with large amounts of intra-firm trade as components produced by units in one set of countries are shipped to units in other countries for assembly, and the assembled final products are shipped to units around the world for sale to final customers.

Trade among parent and affiliates engaged in different stages of production shows that FDI and trade can sometimes be complements. Yet most DFI is not used primarily to locate different stages of production in different countries. Rather, most affiliates largely duplicate the production activities of the parent firm or affiliates located in other countries.

In the case in which foreign affiliates undertake the same kind of production as that of the parent firm or other affiliates, DFI and trade could be substitutes or complements. To some extent they are substitutes. In many industries a firm must find a reasonable trade-off between (1) centralizing production in one or a few locations and exporting to many other countries, to achieve scale economies (recall the discussion of scale economies from Chapter 6), and (2) spreading production to many host countries where the buyers are, to reduce transport costs, to avoid actual or threatened barriers to importing into these countries, or to gain local marketing advantages. When scale economies are less important, or when transport costs and trade barriers are higher, for example, the trade-off would tilt toward DFI—DFI substitutes for trade.

However, the effects of this kind of DFI on trade are actually more complex. To some extent this DFI is also likely to promote trade, for two reasons. First, the affiliates' production of the final product requires components and materials as inputs into production. Often, it is most economic to acquire these components and materials from the parent firm, affiliates in other countries, or independent suppliers in other countries. Although trade in final products may decrease, trade in materials and components increases.

Second, this DFI can increase trade in final products because the affiliate improves the general marketing of the firm's products in the host country. The affiliate provides better information on customers and their needs, the affiliate can better adapt advertising and other aspects of promotion efforts to the local customers, the affiliate and its local production can enhance the image of the multinational firm as a committed and reliable supplier, and the affiliate can provide better after-sales servicing to customers. In many cases the affiliate produces only some of the firm's entire product line locally. Other parts of the product line must be imported from the parent or other affiliates. The affiliate displaces some trade for the specific products that it produces, but it expands trade through better local marketing of other specific products produced by the multinational in other countries.

We have just seen that there are good reasons to think that DFI and trade could be substitutes, and good reasons to think that they could be complements. While each specific instance of DFI has its own outcome, can we say anything about the overall relationship? Most studies conclude that DFI, on net, is somewhat complementary to international trade. For instance, studies of U.S., German, Japanese, and Swedish multinationals find that, controlling for other influences, DFI is associated with higher home exports of products in the same broad industry. The overall complementarity seems to reflect both higher home exports of components used in affiliate production and higher home exports of final goods (the latter applies to many but not all industries). Through better marketing an affiliate increases sales of the specific products that it produces and, often, also increases the sales of other products imported from parent. Some of the multinational's increased sales in the host country come from increasing the country's total demand for the product, while the other part comes from gaining market share at the expense of local firms in the host country and firms based in third countries.

Should the Home Country Restrict DFI Outflow?

To decide whether DFI should be restricted by the home (or source) country is a difficult task. Let's approach it in four steps: (1) surveying the clear and sensible result of standard economic analysis, (2) noting how conclusions about national well-being hinge on how we view the nationality of the multinational firm, (3) noting the special relationship of the multinational firm to international political markets, and (4) considering economic arguments for net national gains from taxing outward DFI.

The best starting point for policy judgments about DFI and multinationals is a static economic analysis that seems to deliver most of the key lessons even though it cannot deal with much of the relevant political and economic dynamics. Look back at Figure 26.1 in Chapter 26, which gives the static-Marshallian portrayal of the effects of international lending. To apply the same framework to direct foreign investment, let the asset (or "wealth") in question become the seldom-measured bundle of managerial and other assets the parent company "invests" in the host-country affiliate. Let the part of the lending country be played by the home country (the country of the parent), and let the part of the borrowing country be played by the host country or countries. The rate of return becomes the rate of earnings (royalties, fees, interest, and profits) on the bundle of productive assets involved in the DFI.

With the framework of Figure 26.1 thus extended to the case of DFI, we get the standard welfare results:

> The home country as a whole gains $(a + b + c)$ because the gains to the investors themselves are greater than the losses to laborers and others in the home country.

and

> The host country as a whole gains $(d + e + f)$ because the gains to laborers and others are greater than the losses to the host-country investors who must compete against the inflow of managerial and other assets from the home country.

The losses to laborers and others in the home country deserve further explanation. Representatives of organized labor in the United States and Canada have fought hard for restrictions on the freedom of companies to set up affiliates producing overseas and in Mexico, arguing that their jobs are being exported. Basically, their protest is correct, even though there are indirect ways in which DFI creates some jobs in the United States and Canada. DFI reduces demand for labor in the home country and tends to lower wages. Organized labor may be especially affected—the freedom to replace home-country production and jobs with production and jobs in other countries is particularly exercised by firms faced with strong labor organizations in the home country. But laborers are not the only ones in home countries who lose from DFI. Taxpayers in general lose because the home country receives little or no taxes from the part of the firms' profits that becomes the profits of their foreign affiliates. Other taxpayers then have the choice of paying more taxes or cutting back on government-financed public programs. The aggrieved taxpayers in this case are analogous to landlords who lose rents because a tenant has emigrated.

Yet for all the losses to laborers and taxpayers in the home country (like those losses to lending-country borrowers in Figure 26.1), the gains to the investors themselves are even greater. If the home country is made up of those laborers, taxpayers, and investors, there is a net gain for the country as a whole.

Here comes the second key step to understanding the welfare effects of DFI, however. To conclude from analysis like that in Figure 26.1 that the home country gains, we had to view the investors as part of the home country. But from many perspectives the nationality of the investors is not clear. They can be investors without a firm political base in any country, just like the disenfranchised migrant laborers of Chapter 25. Suppose that the home country's political debate over DFI denies the investors a voice. They might even be treated as pariahs because of their willingness to "take the money and run," leaving workers and taxpayers behind. The easiest firms to disenfranchise might be the true multinationals, like Royal Dutch/Shell Petroleum, that do not have a home country except as a legal technicality. If the investing firm is viewed by the home country as "them" and not as "us," the exclusively defined home country does indeed lose from free international investment.[5]

Yet, against the possibility that multinational firms are often disenfranchised in national policy debates, we must weigh the frequent reality of the opposite case: the case in which they purchase enough lobbying voice in the political marketplace to distort the foreign policy of the home country to their own ends. Historically, the governments of the United States, Britain, and other investing nations have been involved in costly foreign conflicts in defense of investors' interests that do not align with the interests of other voters. Even though such considerations do not lend themselves to any clear quantitative accounting, the threat of foreign-policy distortion must be weighed as a factor calling for selective restraints on DFI.

There are additional economic arguments for taxing outward-bound DFI. First, a large home country like the United States or Japan might conceivably reap some slight optimal tax gains (à la Figure 26.1) by raising the pretax returns of the restricted outflow of investments, though the power to do so as an individual nation is probably declining. Second, DFI may carry external technological benefits with it. For all the firms' attempts to appropriate all the fruits of their technology, many gains may accrue to others in the place of the investment, through training and imitation. If so, outward DFI takes those external benefits away from the home country. A case can be made for taxing earnings from investments abroad to charge for the externalities, though in practice there is no guarantee that the tax is set at the optimal level.

For the home country, then, a fairly clear set of qualitative results emerges:

1. The direct market effects of DFI are favorable to the home country if the investors are viewed as part of that nation, but

2. This result is reversed if the investors do not count in the home country, and

3. There are political and economic drawbacks to allowing outward DFI, drawbacks that recommend restricting it to some (debatable) degree.

---

[5]In Figure 26.1, these losses can be found, though they are not explicitly identified. The change from no investment to free investment brings the investors the extra return from 2 percent to 5 percent on their entire wealth (W_J). But it costs others in the investing country the trapezoid under the marginal product curve between 2 percent and 5 percent, or $(5\% - 2\%)$ times W_J minus area $(a + b + c)$.

Industrialized countries, the source of most of the world's DFI, actually impose few restrictions on outward-bound DFI. If anything, their policies are somewhat supportive of outbound DFI, because they impose little or no extra tax on affiliates' profits. The multinationals based in a country generally seem to be viewed as part of this home country, so their gains from DFI count politically. In particular, multinationals have been successful in emphasizing the competition among firms from different countries for global market shares and profits. In this competition, using foreign affiliates is often the best way for the multinationals to compete (for instance, through the affiliates' better marketing in the host countries, as we discussed in the previous section). Home-country governments generally refrain from restricting or taxing outward-bound DFI so that firms from the country can better compete globally.

Should the Host Country Restrict DFI?

The effects of DFI on the host country, and the pros and cons of host-country restrictions on it, are symmetrical in form to those facing the home country.

First, as noted above, the standard static analysis of international investment, in the modified version of Figure 26.1 just described, finds that the host country as a whole gains $(d + e + f)$ from the inflow. Laborers and suppliers employed by the new enterprises, along with national and local taxing governments, gain more than competing domestic investors lose.

Second, the host country, like the home country, needs to worry about the troubled relationship of the multinational investor to the political marketplace. Multinationals can enlist the support of powerful home-country governments to pressure the host country in a confrontation. They can also buy host-country politicians and bankroll plots against the government, as International Telephone and Telegraph did against the Allende government in Chile in 1972–73. Such political realities must be weighed in the balance, even though they do not lend themselves to any quantifiable prescription for a tax or other restrictions on DFI.

Again, as with the source country's perspective, the host country must weigh indirect economic effects when deciding whether to tax or subsidize incoming DFI. And again the two main kinds of effects to consider relate to the possibility of an optimal tax and to positive externalities. This time, however, there may be a stronger case for encouraging the investors. As we saw in the section on taxation, host countries already can, and usually do, impose their regular corporate or business income taxes on the affiliates' profits, so some of the returns to the foreign multinationals are shifted to the host-country government. The idea that the host country could charge an even higher optimal tax on DFI inflows (or the private earnings derived from them) is weakened by the fact that few host countries would have the power to get foreign investors to take substantially worse terms when faced with such a high tax. And the possibility that DFI brings technological and other intangible side benefits (training, etc.) wherever it goes argues in favor of *subsidizing* incoming investments to bring the country the side benefits accompanying extra investments.

Thus, the case for taxing or restricting DFI is not strong from the host-country perspective. Although there are political dangers from inviting in large multinationals, there are also static economic gains from direct investment into the country plus the possibility of technological and other side benefits. These advantages increasingly have impressed developing country governments. Since the mid-1970s, they have liberalized their previous restrictions on direct investments into their countries. They have also shifted to competing by offering special tax breaks and other incentives and subsidies in an attempt to woo direct investors.

Summary

Direct foreign investment (DFI) is a flow of a mixture of financial capital and intangible assets like technology, managerial capabilities, and marketing skills and other assets. Its more specific accounting definition is any flow of lending to, or purchase of ownership in, a foreign enterprise that is largely owned by residents of the investing, or home, country. The returns earned by the direct investors are accordingly a mixture of interest, dividends, license fees, and managerial fees.

DFI grew rapidly for several decades after World War II, with the United States being the largest source country. DFI grew more slowly from the mid-1970s to the mid-1980s, but since the mid-1980s, DFI again has grown rapidly. From the mid-1970s to the early 1990s, direct investment flows into developing countries slowed, but these flows have recently increased substantially. Nonetheless, most direct investment is from one industrialized country into another industrialized country. In the 1980s, the United States became an important host country, leaving Japan as the only major home country that is not also a major host to direct investment.

Explaining why DFI occurs requires us to go beyond the simple competitive model. What make direct investment profitable are firm-specific advantages that the firm needs to protect by directly managing production. The firm-specific advantages might be viewed in either of two ways. Hymer's view casts them in shadowy light, as embodiments of imperfect competition trying to protect company secrets and monopoly power. His view helps explain the frequent occurrence of *defensive investment* among multinational firms. Hymer's view implies that the host government should restrict and regulate incoming DFI. An alternative is the *appropriability theory,* which more charitably interprets the firm-specific advantages as productive assets, whose returns can be more effectively captured by the firm if it invests directly. The appropriability theory is the international counterpart to the theory of the size of the firm (i.e., when to control production instead of licensing, when to own instead of lease, etc.). It helps account for the preponderance of technology-intensive lines in DFI, and it implies that the host government can either leave DFI inflows alone or subsidize.

The profits of foreign affiliates are taxed by the host-country government, but generally not taxed or taxed little by the home-country government. When multinationals shop around the globe for the lowest cost sites, they shop for low tax rates. Part of the decision of which country to invest in involves the desire to keep taxes down. In addition, firms can use *transfer pricing* to shift some reported profits to the low-tax countries.

DFI could lead to less international trade in products (substitute for trade) or to more (complement to trade). DFI used to locate different stages of production in different countries increases trade. DFI used to establish affiliate production of final goods for local sales substitutes for imports, and it can be used to reduce transport costs, to avoid import barriers, or to gain local marketing advantages. But better marketing by the affiliate can also expand imports of other final goods produced by the multinational firm in other countries. And affiliate production of final goods often requires use of imported components and materials. Studies of DFI and trade conclude that they are somewhat complementary, on average.

The home (or investing) country gains from the basic market effects of DFI as long as the investors themselves continue to have voices of citizenship. If they do not have such voice, and if we therefore exclude their investment incomes from measures of the national gain, the home country then can be said to lose from DFI. The home country may also have other reasons to tax and restrict outward-bound DFI: the optimal tax argument, the possibility that positive external benefits accompany DFI, and the possibility of foreign-policy distortion from lobbying by multinationals. The actual policies of the industrialized countries (the major home countries) toward outbound DFI are approximately neutral.

The host country has less reason to restrict DFI than does the home country. The possibility of positive external technological and training benefits tips the scales toward subsidizing DFI inflows rather than taxing or restricting them. Political dangers remain, however, in the relationship with major multinational firms.

Suggested Reading

A good collection of articles surveying the economics of multinationals is the set of articles by Little, Vernon, Magee, and Drucker in Adams (1985, Part V). Another good survey, somewhat more technical, is Caves (1996). Hymer's theory is presented in his book (1976). Markusen (1995) discusses how multinational firms can enrich the theories of international trade examined in Part I of this book. Brainard (1997) presents a careful analysis of the trade-off between DFI and trade.

A good survey of research on the determinants of the patterns of DFI is found in United Nations Centre on Transnational Corporations (1992). The annual *World Investment Report*, published by the United Nations Conference on Trade and Development, presents a broad discussion of trends and issues involving DFI and multinational firms.

Graham and Krugman (1995) and Woodward and Nigh (1998) examine direct investments into the United States. Laster and McCauley (1994) analyze the profitability of the U.S. affiliates of foreign firms. U.S. Congress, Office of Technology Assessment (1993), explores how DFI has affected U.S. national interests. Moran (1998) discusses developing countries' policies toward DFI.

Questions and Problems

✦1. "Most DFI is made to gain access to low-wage labor." Do you agree or disagree? Why?

2. "Industrialized countries are the source of most DFI because they have large amounts of financial capital that they must invest somewhere." Do you agree or disagree? Why?

✦3. "Multinational firms often establish affiliates using little of their own financial capital because they want to reduce their exposure to risks." Do you agree or disagree? Why?

4. What might be the reasons that Japan is host to little direct investment?

✦5. Why does much DFI occur in such industries as pharmaceuticals and electronic products while little DFI occurs in such industries as clothing and paper products?

6. Which of the following is direct foreign investment?

   a. A U.S. investor buys 1,000 shares of Daimler Benz, the German company that makes Mercedes-Benz cars.

   b. Procter & Gamble lends $2 million to a firm in Japan that is half-owned by Procter & Gamble and half-owned by a Japanese chemical company.

   c. Mattel, a U.S.-based toy company, buys the 51 percent of its Mexican affiliate that it did not already own.

   d. Intel sets up an affiliate in Brazil using $100,000 of equity capital from Intel and a $1 million loan from a Brazilian bank.

✦7. A firm has affiliates in both a high-tax European country and a low-tax Asian country. The major activity of the Asian affiliate is to produce components that it sells to the European affiliate.

   a. How could the firm use transfer pricing to lower its overall tax payments?

   b. What does each government think of this use of transfer pricing?

8. Labor groups in the United States seek restrictions on the flow of direct investment out of the country. Why? Is their opposition to DFI defending only their special interest, or might it also be in the national interest? Explain.

✦9. What is Hymer's view of why DFI occurs? What implications does it have for countries that are hosts to DFI?

10. A country currently prohibits any DFI into the country. Its government is considering liberalizing this policy. You have been hired as a consultant to a group of foreign firms that wants to see the policy loosened. They ask you to prepare a report on the major arguments for why the country should liberalize its policy. What will your report say?

With each passing year, it gets easier for students in any country to get data on the international economy. One reason is simply that each year adds another year of numbers to the databases that have already been set up around the world. Another is that more countries start supplying fairly reliable numbers. The third and most important source of new convenience for student research is technological progress: the explosion of the Internet complementing cheap photocopying. If you have an idea you'd like to explore about international trade competition, different countries' laws about immigration, the international arms trade, or how hot money moves between countries, rest assured that useful data of some sort are out there waiting for you. To do a good research paper in international economics, you need to have a good idea you really want to pursue, and to think hard about what information you might use to make your argument persuasive. Getting the information is no longer the hardest part.

One way to get quantitative data and other information on many topics is through the World Wide Web. Figure A.1 shows a number of useful Web sites, ranging from those maintained by official global organizations to those maintained by individual experts. You can also use the Internet to look up listings from libraries around the world electronically from your own desk.

In the rest of this appendix, we present information sources that can be found in hard copy in libraries. Some of this information can also be found through the Web. For many research papers, you want to take a close look at the international economic dealings of a single country, perhaps your own. One useful source is usually that country's statistical yearbook, which is likely to be found somewhere in the HA_ range if your library shelves books according to the Library of Congress system. Here are some examples, with the first parts of their typical Library of Congress call numbers in parentheses:

- U.S. Bureau of the Census, *Statistical Abstract of the United States* (HA37.U4).
- Statistics Canada, *Canada Year Book* (HA744.C3).
- Great Britain, Central Statistical Office, *Annual Abstract of Statistics* (HA1122.A33).

- Japan, Statistical Bureau, *Japan Statistical Yearbook* (HA1832.J36).
- Australian Bureau of Statistics, *Year Book Australia* (HA3001.B5).

If you want to compare countries in the same region, you can get numbers for all the countries in the region from such compilations as

- United Nations, Economic Commission for Latin America and the Caribbean, *Statistical Yearbook for Latin America and the Caribbean* (HA751.U49).
- United Nations, *African Statistical Yearbook* (HD1955.U5).
- European Bank for Reconstruction and Development, *Transition Report* (HC331.E2).

For really global coverage of the most often cited national averages and aggregates, see the World Bank's annual *World Tables* (HC59.W669), its *World Development Report* (HC59.7.W659), or its *World Development Indicators* (HC59.15.W656). For most of the main economic aggregates, you can also see the International Monetary Fund's monthly or annual *International Financial Statistics* (HG3881.I626), which covers more than just international finance. Some global volumes cover specific aspects of international economics that are evident from their titles:

- United Nations, *International Trade Statistics Yearbook* (HF91.U5).
- United Nations, *National Accounts Statistics* (HC75.I5.N388).
- International Monetary Fund, *Balance of Payments Yearbook* (HF1014.I512).
- Organisation for Economic Cooperation and Development, *International Direct Investment Statistics Yearbook* (HG4583.I58).
- International Monetary Fund, *Direction of Trade Statistics Yearbook* (HA13.U4).
- International Monetary Fund, *Annual Report on Exchange Arrangements and Exchange Restrictions* (HG3834.I61A3).

FIGURE A.1   *Some Useful Websites*

Creator/Description	Address
Official Multilateral Organizations	
World Trade Organization	www.wto.org
International Monetary Fund	www.imf.org
World Bank	www.worldbank.org
Organization for Economic Cooperation and Development	www.oecd.org
Bank for International Settlements: Information on central banks and international finance, including links to many central bank sites	www.bis.org
International Data Sources	
U.S. Central Intelligence Agency: World Fact Book	www.odci.gov/cia/ publications/factbook
OANDA, the Internet arm of Olsen & Associates, Company: Exchange rate data and news	www.oanda.com
Penn World Tables: Macroeconomic data, including purchasing power parity estimates	www.nber.org/ pwt56.html
National, Regional, and International Data	
U.S. Federal Government: Access to a wide range of data and information	www.fedstats.gov
White House Briefing Room: Data on U.S. economy, including recent news releases	www.whitehouse.gov/ fsbr/esbr.html
St. Louis Federal Reserve Bank: Data on U.S. and other countries (fred), and links to other useful sites	www.stls.frb.org
European Union	www.europa.eu.int
Central Banks	
U.S. Federal Reserve System	www.bog.frb.fed.us
European Central Bank	www.ecb.int
Bank of Japan	www.boj.or.jp/en/ index.htm
Useful Private Sites	
Resources for Economists on the Internet: Links to a broad range of sites with economics information	www.rfe.org
Professor Lloyd Russow: Links to many sites with information on international trade and finance	ib.philacol.edu/ib/ russow.html
University of Kansas: Links to many sites with information on international trade and business	www.ibrc.bschool. ukans.edu
Professor Nouriel Roubini: Links to an immense amount of information on international financial crises	www.stern.nyu.edu/ ~nroubini/asia/ AsiaHomepage.html

Multilateral organizations produce other useful periodic reports, including the World Trade Organization, *Annual Report* (HF1371.A56), the International Monetary Fund, *World Economic Outlook* (HC59.W654), and the Bank for International Settlements, *Annual Report* (HG1997.I6A3).

There are also good global data annuals on topics that are more comparative than international in the sense of dealings between nations, yet still relate to international economics. For environmental data involving issues like those in Chapter 12, see World Resources Institute, *World Resources* (GF1.W667), or United Nations Statistical Commission, *The Environment in Europe and North America: Annotated Statistics.* For military data and the arms trade, see Stockholm International Peace Research Institute, *SIPRI Yearbook: World Armaments and Disarmament* (UA10.I55), or U.S. Arms Control and Disarmament Agency, *World Military Expenditures and Arms Transfers* (UA17.U421).

DERIVING PRODUCTION-POSSIBILITIES CURVES

The shape of the production-possibilities curve used so much in the theory of international trade depends on the factor supplies of the country and on the technology for combining these factors to produce outputs. The usual device for portraying the state of technology is the **production function,** which expresses the output of any one commodity as a function of its inputs. In principle, we can derive the whole shape of the production-possibilities curve just by knowing the total supplies of the factors (or inputs) and the algebraic form of each commodity's production function. In practice, it proves easy to trace out the production-possibilities curve geometrically but often impossible to solve the production-function equations for the trade-offs between one commodity and another (except by approximation or with the help of extra limiting assumptions).

Geometrically, the production function for each commodity can be shown in two dimensions by plotting the various combinations of two factors needed to produce given amounts of the commodity in question. Figure B.1 shows several **production isoquants,** each showing the different combinations of land and labor that could yield a given level of output. The smooth isoquants of Figure B.1A portray a case in which land and labor are partial substitutes for one another in cloth. Starting from a point like W, it would be possible to keep the same cloth output per year (i.e., stay on the isoquant T—T) with less

labor if we used enough more land, as at V. By contrast, in Figure B.1B, the production function has a special form (sometimes called the Leontief production function) in which land and labor are not substitutes at all. Thus, starting from point W, we cannot give up any labor inputs without falling to a lower output isoquant, regardless of how much extra land is added. Thus the isoquant moves vertically up from point W to points like R demanding the same labor inputs. Some industries are thought to resemble this special case, though the factors of production are usually partial substitutes for one another, as in Figure B.1A.

To derive the production-possibilities curve representing the greatest feasible combinations of cloth and wheat output an economy is capable of, we do not need any more economic information than that implicit in the production-function isoquants already sketched. Yet it is useful to pause briefly at this point and remember how the combinations of factors actually used are supposed to relate to factor prices in a competitive economy, since Chapters 3 through 5 make considerable use of this relationship. The relative prices of the two factors are summarized in factor-price slopes like that of lines S—S and S'—S' in Figure B.1A, which are parallel. This slope shows the ratio of the wage rate for labor to the rental rate for land—the number of acres of land use that can be traded for each hour of labor in the marketplace. Given this

FIGURE B.1   A. Production Function for Cloth

B. Production Functions with Fixed Factor Proportions

FIGURE B.2

Edgeworth–Bowley Box Diagram with Fixed Factor Proportions

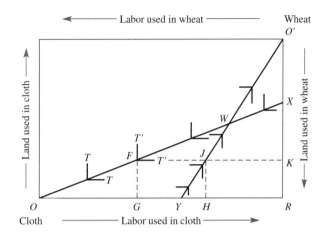

slope, competition would propel firms to produce at points of tangency like *W* since such points maximize output for a given amount spent on inputs. In Figure B.1A, we have shown the often-imagined case in which any expansion of output would be achieved along the *expansion path R,* a straight line from the origin as long as the factor-price ratio is still the slope *S—S.* If land became cheaper relative to labor, with a factor-price slope steeper than *S—S,* firms would tend to substitute some land for labor, shifting to points like *V.* In Figure B.1B, by contrast, the factor proportions would always be fixed, on the more labor-intensive expansion path *X* for cloth and the more land-intensive expansion path *Y* for wheat, regardless of the relative prices of land and labor.

To know the most efficient combinations a nation can produce, we must now combine the technological possibilities represented by the production-function isoquants with the nation's total supplies of land and labor. A handy device for doing this is the so-called **Edgeworth–Bowley box diagram,** in which the dimensions of the box represent the amounts of land and labor in a country, which we shall call Britain. These factor supplies are assumed to be homogeneous in character and fixed in amount. Figure B.2 shows an Edgeworth–Bowley box for production functions with fixed factor proportions and constant returns to scale (so that a proportionate increase in all inputs used to produce a product results in an increase in the product's output by the same proportion). The production function for cloth is drawn with its origin in the lower-left corner of the box at *O,* and with its isoquants, *T—T, T'—T',* and so on, moving out and up to the right. Its expansion path is *OX.* If all the labor in

Britain (*OR*) were used to make cloth, only *RX* of land would be required, and *O'X* of land would be left unemployed. At *X,* the marginal physical product of land would be zero.

The production function for wheat is drawn reversed and upside down, with its origin at *O'* and extending downward and to the left. Its expansion path is *OY.* At *Y,* all the land and *YR* of labor would be employed, but *OY* of labor would be unemployed. *OX* and *O'Y* intersect at *W,* which is the only production point in the box diagram where there can be full employment and positive prices for both factors. At any other point on either expansion path, say, *F* on *OX,* land and labor will be able to produce at *J* on the expansion path for wheat; *OG* of labor will be engaged in cloth, and *HR* in wheat. *RK* of land will be employed in cloth, and *O'K* in wheat. But *GH* of labor will be unemployed.

The curve *OWO',* as in Figure B.2, is in effect a production-possibility curve, showing the various combinations of wheat and cloth that can be produced in Britain, given the factor endowments of the country. The only point providing full employment of the two factors and positive factor prices is *W. OWO'* does not look like a production-possibility curve because it is given in terms of physical units of land and labor, rather than physical units of production. If we remap the *OWO'* curve in Figure B.2 from factor space into commodity space in terms of units of wheat and cloth and turn it right side up, it appears to be a normal production-possibility curve, though kinked at *W,* as in Figure B.3.

If cloth and wheat were produced with fixed factor coefficients, and these were identical, the two expansion

FIGURE B.3

Production-Possibility Curve Derived from Edgeworth–Bowley Box Diagram with Fixed Factor Proportions

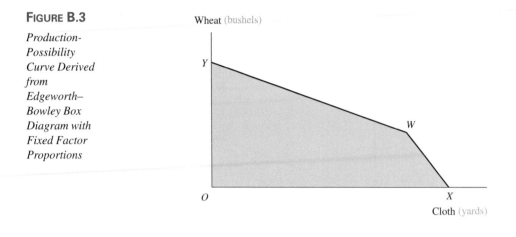

Wheat (bushels)

Cloth (yards)

paths would coincide, as in Figure B.4A. In this case, if production also involves constant returns to scale for both products, then the production-possibility curve becomes a straight line, as in B.4B. Because land and labor are always used in the same combination, they might well be regarded as a single factor. This is equivalent to Ricardo's labor theory of value and its resultant straight-line production-possibility curve. A similar straight-line production-possibility curve would be produced for any economy in which the production functions are constant returns to scale and identical factor-intensity for the two commodities.

When there is the possibility of substitution between factors in the production of a commodity, there is no unique expansion path. Instead, a separate expansion path can be drawn for any given set of factor prices. Or we can draw in the isoquants for both commodities and trace out a locus of points of tangency between them. This locus represents the efficiency path, or the maximum combinations of production of the two goods that can be produced with the existing factor supplies. It is shown in Figure B.5A. To see why it is an efficient path, suppose that production were to take place at *W*, away from the efficiency locus. *W* is on cloth isoquant 7 and on wheat isoquant 5. But there is a point *T*, also on cloth isoquant 7, that is on a higher isoquant (6) of wheat. It would therefore be possible to produce more wheat without giving up any cloth. There is also point *T'* on wheat isoquant 5 that is on cloth isoquant 8. It would be equally possible to produce more cloth and the same amount of wheat. Any point off the

locus of tangencies of isoquants of the two production functions is therefore inefficient, insofar as it would be possible to get more output of one commodity without losing any of the other, by moving to the locus.

When the Edgeworth–Bowley box is used for picturing production, it shows not only the efficient combinations of outputs but also factor combinations and factor prices. If production is at *T*, the factor proportions in cloth are represented by the slope of *OT*, and the factor proportions in wheat by *O'T*. The relative price of land and labor with these outputs is represented by the slope of the tangency to the isoquants at *T*.

If the production function for each product shown in Figure B.5A is constant returns to scale, then the bowed shape of the efficiency locus translates into the bowed-out production-possibilities curve in Figure B.5B. One way to see the basis for this is first to recognize that production along the diagonal of this Edgeworth–Bowley box would result in a straight-line "production-capability" curve. (The logic is essentially the same as that sketched for the case of identical constant-returns-to-scale production functions.) Because moving off the diagonal to produce instead on the efficiency locus increases output for all points except the corners of the box, the actual production-possibilities curve lies outside of this straight line connecting the end points (where the country is completely specialized in producing only one product, corresponding to the corners of the Edgeworth–Bowley box). The resulting production-possibilities curve is bowed out.

FIGURE **B.4**

A. *Constant Opportunity Costs: Identical Fixed Factor Proportions*

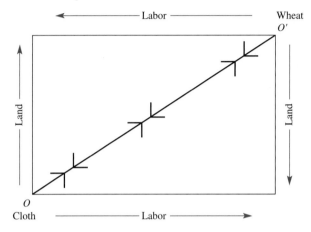

B. *Production-Possibilities Curve Derived from B.4A*

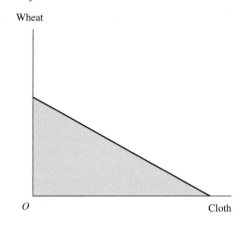

FIGURE **B.5**

A. *Maximum Efficiency Locus Under Variable Factor Proportions*

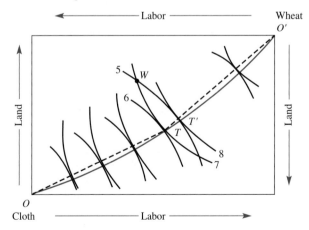

B. *Production-Possibilities Curve Derived from B.5A*

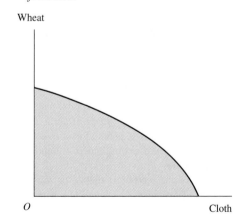

The supply and demand curves used in Chapters 2 and 3 have several advantages. They are familiar, and they offer the easiest way of seeing how to quantify the effects of trade on the well-being of producer and consumer groups in each country. They are also easily extended to the task of analyzing trade effects in many different goods, each taken one at a time. Another geometric device that gives some of the same information is the *offer curve*, which shows how the export and import quantities a nation chooses will vary with the international price ratio. This appendix gives the geometric derivation of the offer curve. Appendix D shows how it can be used in discussing optimal tariff policy.

A region or nation's offer curve is equivalent to both its supply curve for exports and its demand curve for imports. (For examples of the latter two curves, see the center panel of Figure 2.3.) It graphs trade offers as a function of the international price ratio. And it can be derived from the same production-possibilities curves and community indifference curves used extensively in Chapter 3.

Figure C.1 shows the derivation, starting from the usual production and consumption trade-offs. For each international price ratio, the behavior of the United States produces a quantity of exports willingly offered in exchange for imports at that price ratio. At 2 bushels per yard, the United States does not want to trade at all, as shown at S_0. At 1 bushel per yard, the United States would find cloth cheaper, and wheat more valuable, than without trade. It would be willing to export 40 billion bushels and import 40 billion yards, by efficiently producing at S1 and consuming at C_1. A price of 1/2 bushel per yard would again induce the United States to offer 40 billion of wheat exports, but this time in exchange for 80 billion yards of cloth. Each offer of exports for imports is pictured as a trade triangle with corners at the production and consumption points for the price ratio.

Each of these offers is plotted on the lower half of Figure C.1 (as points O, O_1, and O_2), where the axes are

the exports and imports to be exchanged, and the slope of any ray from the origin is a price ratio. The resulting curve O_{US} is the U.S. offer curve. A similar derivation produces the rest of the world's offer curve, O_{RW}. Only at the equilibrium price of 1 bushel per yard, at point O_1, will the United States and the rest of the world be able to agree on how much to trade.

There is another way to derive the same offer curve for a country. We can use *trade indifference curves*, which show the level of well-being attained by a country for different amounts of imports received and exports paid. Imports add to national well-being by expanding consumption while exports detract from well-being because they are not available for local consumption. A trade indifference curve pictures the trade-off that the country would be willing to make while remaining at the same level of overall well-being. The bottom half of Figure C.1 shows two U.S. trade indifference curves: I_2 and I_3.[1] These two trade indifference curves correspond to the levels of U.S. well-being shown by community indifference curves I_2 and I_3 in the top half of the figure. The trade indifference curves have the upward slope and rather peculiar shape for the United States (and I_3 is better than I_2) because more cloth imports are the desirable item, while more exports are undesirable.

We can find a point on the U.S. offer curve by determining the highest trade indifference curve that can be reached if the price ratio is 1 bushel per yard. The highest trade indifference curve, and therefore the highest level of welfare that the United States can reach at this price ratio, is the tangency with trade indifference curve I_2 at point O_1. Thus, O_1 is a point on the U.S. offer curve. For the price ratio of 1/2 bushel per yard, the tangency is with I_3, so O_2 is another point on the U.S. offer curve.

Offer curves can be used to analyze what happens when one of the offer curves shifts. For instance, the implications for the United States of a shift in the offer curve of the rest of the world are straightforward. If it shifts out, the two offer curves' intersection shifts from

---

[1]The trade indifference curves for the country can be derived from its production-possibilities curve and community indifference curves.

FIGURE C.1

*Deriving the
Offer Curve*

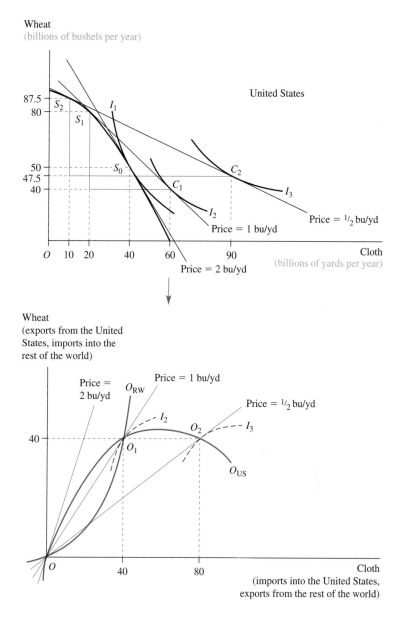

point O_1 to a point like O_2. The extra supply of cloth exports from the rest of the world decreases the relative price of cloth. (The price line becomes flatter.) This represents an improvement in the U.S. terms of trade, and the United States is better off, reaching an indifference curve like I_3 instead of I_2.

Growth of production capabilities in the United States usually shifts the U.S. offer curve. We can use offer curves to show how the international price ratio is affected by this growth. For instance, if the growth increases the willingness to trade (as discussed in Chapter 5), then the U.S. offer curve shifts out (or up), and the relative price of cloth increases in moving to the new equilibrium intersection. The U.S. terms of trade decline.[2]

Holding the country's production capabilities steady, and assuming that the foreign offer curve is also steady, is there anything that a country can do to improve its welfare by moving its own offer curve? Not if the nation consists of large numbers of private individuals competing against each other in production and consumption with no government intervention. Such private competition merely puts us on the offer curve in the first place,

and does not shift the curve. Yet if the nation acted as a single decision-making unit, there is the glimmering of a chance to squeeze more advantage out of trade in Figure C.1. Starting at the free-trade equilibrium O_1, the United States might be able to come up with a way to move a short distance to the southwest along the foreign offer curve O_{RW}, reaching somewhat higher indifference curves than at O_1. How could this be done? Through an optimal tariff of the sort discussed in Appendix D, where the offer curves reappear.

---

[2]We cannot use the original trade indifference curves to analyze the effects of this growth on U.S. well-being because the growth in the U.S. production capabilities means that the United States has a new set of trade indifference curves. Chapter 5 shows how changes in well-being can be examined using production-possibilities curves and community indifference curves once the change in the equilibrium price ratio is determined.

Appendix D
The Nationally Optimal Tariff

Deriving the Optimal Tariff

It is not difficult to derive a basic formula for the tariff level that is nationally optimal for a country that can affect the foreign-supply price of its imports without fear of retaliation, as in the latter part of Chapter 7. This appendix does so using both the demand–supply framework of Part II and the offer-curve framework of Appendix C, showing that similar simple formulas emerge from both. An analogous formula is derived for the optimal export duty, both for a nation and for an international cartel.

We saw in the demand–supply framework in Chapter 7 that a small increase in an import tariff brings an area of gain and an area of loss to the nation. Figure D.1 compares these two areas for a tiny increase in the tariff above its initial absolute level, which is the fraction t times the initial price level, P. The extra gains come from being able to lower the foreign price on continuing imports, gaining the level of imports M times the foreign price drop dP/dt. The extra losses come from losing the extra imports (dM/dt) that were worth tP more per unit to consumers than the price (P) at which foreigners were willing to sell them to us.

The optimal tariff rate is that which just makes the extra losses and extra gains from changing the tariff equal each other. That is, the optimal tariff rate t^* as a share of initial price is the one for which

$$\text{Extra gains} - \text{extra losses} = M\frac{dP}{dt} - t^*P\frac{dM}{dt} = 0$$

so that

$$t^* = \frac{dP/dt}{dM/dt}\frac{M}{P}$$

Since the foreign supply elasticity is defined as $s_m = \dfrac{dM/dt}{dP/dt} \cdot \dfrac{P}{M}$ along the foreign supply curve, the formula for the optimal tariff is simply $t^* = 1/s_m$, as stated in Chapter 7. If the world price is fixed beyond our control, so that $s_m = \infty$, then the optimal tariff rate is zero. The more inelastic the foreign supply, the higher the optimal tariff rate.[1]

Optimal Export Taxes

We can derive the optimal rate of *export* duty in the same way. Just replace all terms referring to imports with terms referring to exports, and redraw Figure D.1 so that the extra gain at the expense of foreign buyers of our exports comes at the top of the tariff gap instead of at the bottom. It turns out, symmetrically, that the optimal export duty equals the absolute value of $1/d_x$, or the reciprocal of the foreign demand elasticity for our exports.

The formula for the optimal export duty can also be used as the optimal rate of markup of an international cartel. Since both the international cartel maximizing joint profits from exports and the single nation optimally taxing its exports are monopolistic profit maximizers, it stands to reason that the formula linking optimal markup to foreign demand elasticity should hold in both cases. So the optimal markup for an international exporting cartel is $t^* = |1/d_c|$, or the absolute value of the reciprocal of the world demand elasticity for the cartel's exports.

We can extend the formula to show how the optimal export markup for cartel members depends on the other elasticities and the market share discussed in Chapter 13's treatment of cartels like OPEC. The formula given

---

[1]Figure D.1 makes it easy to show that the nationally optimal tariff is lower than the tariff rate that would maximize the government's tariff revenue, even when the foreign supply curve slopes upward. The optimal tariff in Figure D.1 is one that equates the "extra gains" area with the "extra losses" area. But at this tariff rate a slight increase in the tariff still brings a net increase in government tariff revenue. By raising the tariff rate slightly, the government collects more duty on the remaining imports, M, while losing the "extra losses" area on the discouraged imports. However, its gain in revenue on M is not just the "extra gains" area already introduced, but this plus the thin unlabeled rectangle above the tP gap, which takes the form of a higher price to consumers importing M. A slight increase in the tariff would still raise revenue even when it brings no further net welfare gains to the nation. It follows that the revenue-maximizing tariff rate is higher than the optimal tariff rate. Thus a country would be charging too high a rate if it tried to find its nationally optimal tariff rate by finding out what rate seemed to maximize tariff revenues.

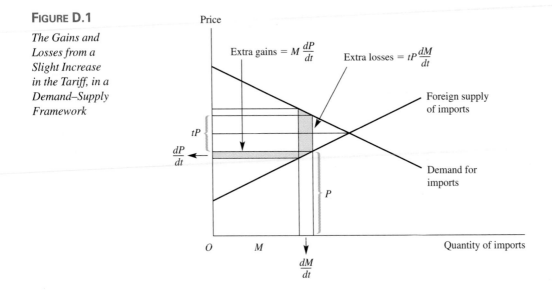

FIGURE D.1

The Gains and Losses from a Slight Increase in the Tariff, in a Demand–Supply Framework

in Chapter 13 can be derived here. We can link the elasticity of demand for the cartel's exports to world demand for the product, the supply of perfect substitutes from other countries, and the cartel's share of the world market by beginning with a simple identity:

$$\text{Cartel exports} = \text{world exports} - \text{other countries' exports}$$

or

$$X_c = X - X_0$$

Differentiating with respect to the cartel price yields

$$\frac{dX_c}{dP} = \frac{dX}{dP} - \frac{dX_0}{dP}$$

This can be reexpressed in ways that arrive at an identity involving elasticities:

$$\frac{dX_c/dP}{X} = \frac{dX/dP}{X} - \frac{dX_0/dP}{X}$$

$$\frac{dX_c}{dP}\frac{P}{X_c}\frac{X_c}{X} = \frac{dX}{dP}\frac{P}{X} - \frac{dX_0}{dP}\frac{P}{X_0}\frac{X_0}{X}$$

The cartel's share of the world market is defined as $c = X_c/X = 1 - (X_0/X)$. The elasticity of demand for the cartel's exports is defined as $d_c = (dX_c/dP)(P/X_c)$; the elasticity of world export demand for the product is $d = (dX/dP)(P/X)$; and the elasticity of noncartel countries' competing

export supply of the product is $s_0 = (dX_0/dP)(P/X_0)$. Substituting these definitions into the equation above yields

$$d_c \cdot c = d - s_0(1 - c)$$

so that

$$d_c = \frac{d - s_0(1 - c)}{c}$$

Now since the optimal markup rate is $t^* = |1/d_c|$, this optimal cartel markup rate is

$$t^* = \frac{c}{|d - s_0(1 - c)|}$$

As noted in Chapter 13, the optimal markup as a share of the (markup-including) price paid by buying countries is greater, the greater the cartel's market share (c), or the lower the absolute value of the world demand elasticity for exports of the product (d), or the lower the elasticity of noncartel countries' export supply (s_0).

The Optimal Tariff Again with Offer Curves

The nationally optimal tariff on imports (or exports) can also be portrayed using the offer-curve framework of Appendix C, though this framework is less convenient for showing the *formula* for the optimal tariff. A trade-taxing country can use the tariff to move its own offer curve until it reaches the point on the foreign offer curve

FIGURE D.2

*An Optimal
Tariff,
Portrayed with
Offer Curves*

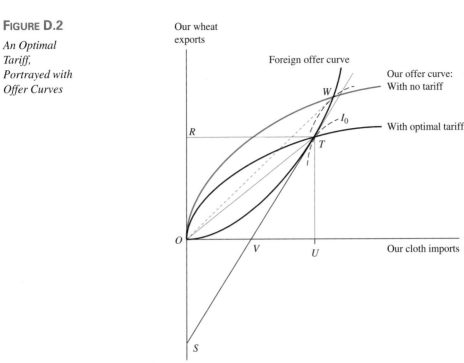

At point *T*, foreign sellers are paid only *OR* of our wheat for *OU* of their cloth. But domestic buyers have to pay the *OR* plus the tariff revenue of *OS* in extra wheat to get that *OU* of cloth. While that is bad for our cloth consumers in their role as cloth consumers, our nation gets to the better trade indifference curve I_0, helped by the fact that foreign suppliers pay some of the tariff, in effect, when they are forced to accept a lower world price (the slope of *OT*) than the price reflected by the slope *OW*, which they would receive for cloth with no tariffs.

that maximizes the country's well-being. Figure D.2 shows this optimal tariff for a wheat-exporting country. Our country, the wheat exporter, has pushed its offer curve to the right by making the price of imported cloth in units of wheat higher within the country than the price received by our foreign cloth suppliers. At point *T* domestic consumers must pay for cloth at the domestic price ratio *SR/RT*, giving up *SR* in wheat for *RT* in cloth. The foreign suppliers receive only *OR* in wheat for their *RT* of cloth. The government has intervened to collect tariff revenue at the tariff rate *SO/OR*.

Figure D.2 shows that this particular tariff rate happens to be optimal, since at point *T* the foreign offer curve is tangent to I_0, the best indifference curve we can reach through trade. The optimal tariff is positive because the foreign offer curve is not infinitely elastic. If

it were infinitely elastic, in the form of a fixed world price line coming out of the origin, our optimal tariff would be zero since no other tariff can put us on as high an indifference curve as we can reach on our free-trade, no-tariff offer curve. The same principle emerges here as in the demand–supply framework: The more elastic the foreign trading curve, the lower is our optimal tariff.

Deriving the formula for the optimal tariff rate is a little more complicated with offer curves than with demand and supply curves. The elasticity of the foreign offer curve is conventionally defined differently from a foreign supply curve, and defined in a way that is hard to identify in the offer-curve diagram itself. Any country's offer-curve elasticity is conventionally defined as the ratio of the percent response of its import demand to a percent change in the relative price of its imports:

$$\text{Offer-curve elasticity } (e) = \frac{-(\% \text{ change in } M)}{[\% \text{ change in } (X/M)]}$$

Since the change in the price ratio X/M is not easy to spot on an offer-curve diagram like Figure D.2, let's convert this definition into a more usable equivalent:

$$e = \frac{-(\% \text{ change in } M)}{(\% \text{ change in } X) - (\% \text{ change in } M)}$$

$$= \frac{-1}{\dfrac{(\% \text{ change in } X)}{(\% \text{ change in } M)} - 1} = \frac{1}{1 - \left(\text{slope } \dfrac{\partial X}{\partial M} \right)(M/X)}$$

This last expression can be translated into a relationship among line segments in Figure D.2. We now take the foreigners' point of view since it is their offer curve we are trying to interpret. The foreigners export cloth and import wheat. Thus the slope showing how a change in cloth exports relates to a change in their wheat imports at point T is the ratio RT/RS, and the ratio (M/X) is OR/RT. Therefore the elasticity of their offer curve becomes

$$e = \frac{1}{1 - \dfrac{RT}{SR} \dfrac{OR}{RT}} = \frac{1}{1 - \dfrac{OR}{SR}} = \frac{SR}{SR - OR} = \frac{SR}{SO}$$

(Some authors derive an equivalent ratio on the cloth axis: $e = UO/VO$.)

We can now see the close link between the optimal tariff rate at point T and the elasticity of the foreign offer curve:

$$t^* = SO/OR = \frac{SO}{SR - SO} = \frac{1}{\dfrac{SR}{SO} - 1}$$

or

$$t^* = \frac{1}{e - 1}$$

This expression seems to differ slightly from the formula relating to the foreign supply elasticity for our imports, derived above. But the difference is only definitional. The elasticity of the foreign offer curve is defined as the elasticity of the foreigners' wheat imports with respect to the world price of wheat, not the elasticity of their cloth exports (supply of our cloth imports) with respect to the world price of cloth. Since the ratio of the foreigners' cloth exports to their wheat imports is just the world price of wheat, the foreign offer-curve elasticity [(percent change in wheat)/(percent change in cloth/wheat)] is equal to one plus their elasticity of supply of our import, cloth. So the above expression is equivalent to the reciprocal of the foreigners' supply elasticity of our import good, as in the demand–supply framework.[2]

---

[2]One word of caution in interpreting the optimal tariff formula relating to the foreign offer curve: The tariff rate can equal the formula $1/(e - 1)$ for *any* tariff rate, not just the optimal one. To know that the rate is optimal, as at point T, you must also know that the foreign offer curve is tangent to our indifference curve.

THE POSSIBLE MONOPOLY EFFECT OF AN IMPORT QUOTA

A significant difference between a tariff and a quota is that the conversion of a tariff into a quota that admits exactly the same volume of imports may convert a potential monopoly into an actual monopoly and reduce well-being even further. Figures E.1 and E.2 give a demonstration.

Figure E.1 returns us to the case of a tariff on a product for which our nation faces a fixed world price, P_0. By raising the domestic price to P_1, the tariff cuts imports to M_1 and causes deadweight welfare losses b and d, just as in Chapter 7. Figure E.1 brings out the point that this is the result of the tariff even if there is only one domestic producer. Though the tariff gives the producer some extra economic rents, represented by area a, it still leaves him a price taker, since any attempt on his part to charge a higher price than P_1 would leave buyers the option of shifting all of their demand to imports. Facing this flat demand curve, he does not charge more than P_1, and society loses only b and d from the tariff.

The quota shown in Figure E.2 is "equivalent" to the tariff in the limited sense that it also allows the same imports of M_1. But it plays into the hands of the sole domestic producer better than the tariff does. It leaves her with a sloping demand curve for her product by sharply limiting buyers' ability to avoid her by buying abroad. Realizing this, the domestic producer will (discreetly) let her price drift up to the higher price that maximizes profit. For such a monopolist, that higher price will lower quantity demanded and output back to where marginal costs and marginal revenues match. That higher price is P_2, and the more restricted domestic production level is S_2. The quota thus makes domestic output lower, and domestic price even higher, than the equivalent tariff does. The output S_2 with the quota and monopoly is lower than the output S_1 with a tariff, and the monopoly price P_2 is greater than P_1.

When a domestic monopoly is created by a quota, the nation as a whole loses the same deadweight loss from the reduction of imports *plus* an extra social waste from the monopoly. In Figure E.2 the reduction of imports costs society areas b and d, as with the tariff, and the new monopoly-power costs are shown by the shaded area. All of these areas represent a lost opportunity to let consumers buy something that costs the nation less to obtain than the extra purchases were worth to consumers. By holding production back at S_2 and imports at M_1, the quota-plus-monopoly keeps consumers from enjoying purchases that they value at more than P_0, even though the marginal costs of obtaining the extra units are as low as the marginal cost curve or the world price, whichever is less.

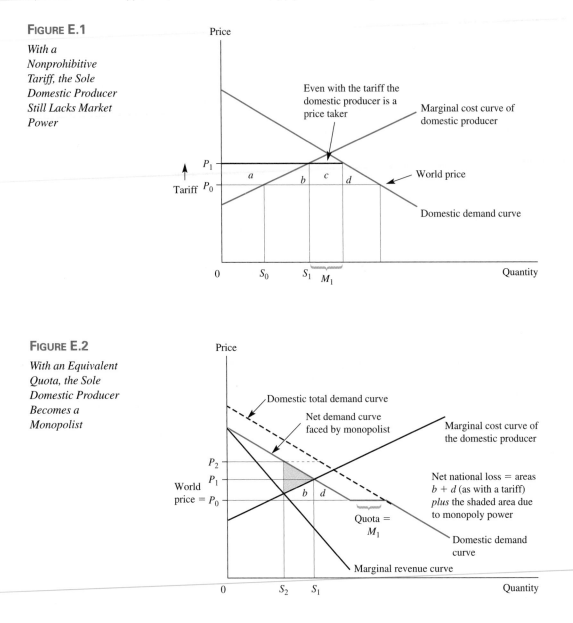

FIGURE E.1

With a Nonprohibitive Tariff, the Sole Domestic Producer Still Lacks Market Power

Even with the tariff the domestic producer is a price taker

Marginal cost curve of domestic producer

World price

Domestic demand curve

FIGURE E.2

With an Equivalent Quota, the Sole Domestic Producer Becomes a Monopolist

Domestic total demand curve

Net demand curve faced by monopolist

Marginal cost curve of the domestic producer

Net national loss = areas $b + d$ (as with a tariff) *plus* the shaded area due to monopoly power

Quota = M_1

Domestic demand curve

Marginal revenue curve

APPENDIX F
MANY PARITIES AT ONCE

In Chapter 17 we introduced two parity conditions relating interest rates in different countries and exchange rates. In Chapter 18 we introduced another parity condition, purchasing power parity, that linked the prices of goods in different countries through exchange rates. These parity conditions are all based on people's ability to arbitrage between countries. As long as there are different ways of starting with one asset or good and ending up with another asset or good, the prices at which the assets or goods can be exchanged will be closely related.

These parity conditions reveal relationships between foreign exchange markets and such macroeconomic phenomena as inflation and real interest rates. To see the relationships, let's think about the fact that investors can move between currencies and goods. To simplify here, let us think about uniform goods that can be bought or sold in either country. In addition to holding currencies today or in the future, you can hold goods today or in the future. Investors must always worry about price trends for goods as well as price trends for currencies. Suppose,

for example, you fear more inflation in the prices of goods in Britain than in America over the next 90 days. How should your decision about where to hold your wealth relate to this fear and to the interest rates and trends in exchange rates? If others share your fear, what will happen to currency and commodity markets?

There are a number of links here, portrayed by Figure F.1. The central rectangle is just the lake diagram of Figure 17.1, revisited. Now, however, there also are ways to buy and sell goods with currencies. You can trade either currency for goods today at the dollar price $P_\$$ or the sterling price $P_£$. If you start with today's dollars, your way of buying goods depends on the relative prices shown at the bottom of Figure F.1. You might just take, say, \$10,000 and buy $10,000/P_\$$ in current goods with it. Or you could take a more roundabout route, using the \$10,000 to buy £$10,000/r_s$ worth of sterling and then using it to buy $10,000/(r_s P_£)$ in goods today. Do whichever is cheaper. That is, you have an incentive to travel the cheaper of the two routes between today's

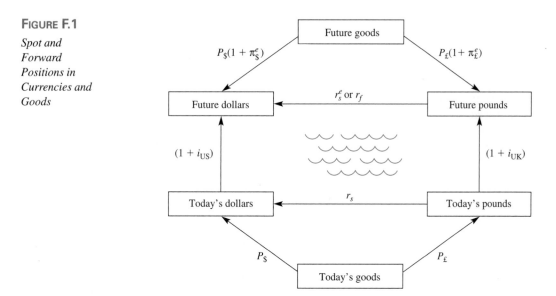

FIGURE F.1

Spot and Forward Positions in Currencies and Goods

Moving with the arrow, multiply the value of your goods or investment by the expression. Moving against the arrow, divide by it.
Symbols: $P_\$$, $P_£$ = today's price level for goods (wheat, soccer balls, etc.) in terms of \$, £; $\pi_\$^e$, $\pi_£^e$, = the expected rate of inflation in the dollar and sterling goods price levels; r_s, r_f = the spot and forward prices of the £ (in \$/£); r_s^e = the expected future level of the spot price of the £ (not to be confused with the present forward price of it); i_{US}, i_{UK} = the interest rates on widely marked assets (e.g., treasury bills) in America and Britain. (Ignore transactions fees and ignore futures markets in goods such as grain futures.)

659

1. **Purchasing power parity (PPP) today:** $r_s P_£ = P_\$$, roughly (see Chapter 18).
2. **Expected future PPP:** $r_s^e P_£(1 + \pi_£^e) = P_\$(1 + \pi_\$^e)$, roughly, so that $r_s^e/r_s = (1 + \pi_\$^e)/(1 + \pi_£^e)$, or, approximately, Expected appreciation of £ = expected \$ inflation – expected £ inflation
3. **Covered interest parity:** $(r_f/r_s) = (1 + i_{US})/(1 + i_{UK})$ definitely.
4. **Speculators' forward equilibrium:** Forward rate measures average expected future spot rate, or $r_s^e = r_f$, we think.
5. **Uncovered interest parity:** $(r_s^e/r_s) = (1 + i_{US})/(1 + i_{UK})$, we think.
   Combining parities 2, 3, and 5, we see that $r_s^e/r_s = r_f/r_s = (1 + i_{US})/(1 + i_{UK}) = (1 + \pi_\$^e)/(1 + \pi_£^e)$, or, approximately,

$$\underset{\text{of £}}{\text{Expected appreciation}} = \underset{\text{forward £}}{\text{premium on}} = \underset{\text{\$ and £ interest rates}}{\text{difference between}} = \underset{\text{between \$ and £ inflation rates}}{\text{expected difference}}$$

   So we expect real interest rates to be roughly equal internationally:
6. **Real interest rate equilibrium:** $(1 + i_{US})/(1 + \pi_\$^e) = (1 + i_{UK})/(1 + \pi_£^e)$
   or, approximately, $(i_{US} - \pi_\$^e) = (i_{UK} - \pi_£^e)$

dollars and today's goods. The availability of this choice means that the two prices will tend to be bid into line: $P_\$ = r_s P_£$. This is the purchasing power parity (PPP) condition discussed in Chapter 18. As argued in that chapter, it is a general tendency that works quite well over decades, but only more roughly over shorter periods, because of trade barriers, the costs of transactions and transportation, and the underlying differences in the goods whose prices are being compared.

A version of purchasing power parity should also hold for the future. If it doesn't, there may be unexploited chances for profitable arbitrage. Buying goods with dollars in the future should look equally cheap whether we expect to buy directly at the future dollar price or at the future pound price of goods times the dollar price of getting each pound. These different prices will depend on how much price inflation people expect between now and the future (say, 90 days from now). If people expect dollar prices to go up by the fraction $\pi_\$^e$ and pound prices to go up by the fraction $\pi_£^e$, then these average expectations should be tied to what future exchange rate people expect (r_s^e). Their expectations should equate the direct and indirect dollar prices of goods shown at the top of Figure F.1, or $P_\$(1 + \pi_\$^e) = r_s^e$ $P_£(1 + \pi_£^e)$. This condition can be called **expected future PPP.** It is only a rough tendency, like today's PPP, when actual changes in prices are used as measures of the expected changes $\pi_\$^e$ and $\pi_£^e$.

The tendencies toward purchasing power parity today and in our expectations about the future provide links between expected price inflation, interest rates, and exchange rates. Recall from Chapter 17 that the forward price of the pound, r_f, should equal r_s^e, the average

expectation about the future value of the spot rate. Combining the equality $r_s^e = r_f$ with the interest parity conditions of Chapter 17 gives further results shown in Figure F.2's summary of key parity conditions.

One result that emerges from all these arbitrage equilibria is that real interest rates should tend to be the same across countries. This is only a rough long-run tendency. In fact, expected real interest rates, as best (such) expectations can be measured, can differ noticeably between countries for years at a stretch. There is nonetheless a tendency toward equality.

Figure F.2 shows some of the intricacy we must expect from increasingly international financial and commodity markets. To illustrate, let us return to a question posed above: What would happen if more inflation in Britain were expected in the near future? If you alone have this new perception of higher British inflation, you can act on it by moving away from sterling into dollars or commodities over any of the routes shown in Figure F.1. As long as your fear is confirmed, you will gain from the eventual general exodus from sterling. If everyone eventually agrees with your quick interpretation of the latest news, then prices and rates must change. The nominal interest rate must rise in Britain and the forward premium on the pound must decline, as the parity conditions in Figure F.2 show.

The moral of Figure F.1 and Figure F.2 is that interest rates, exchange rates, and expected inflation rates are tied together. Whatever affects international differences in one is likely to affect international differences in the other two. It should be stressed, though, that one parity is much more reliable than the others. That one is the covered interest parity condition.

Appendix G
Devaluation and the Current Account Balance

This appendix extends Chapter 22's explorations of the possible effects of a drop in the value of the home currency on the trade balance or the net balance on current account.[1] It derives a general formula for such effects and applies it to some special cases that establish the range of possible results.

Current Account Elasticities

The current account (or trade) balance defined in foreign currency (here, pounds, the foreign currency) is[2]

$$CA_£ = V_x - V_m = P_x^£ X - P_m^£ M \qquad (G.1)$$

where V_x is the value of exports, and V_m is the value of imports. To derive the elasticity of the current account balance with respect to the exchange rate, begin by differentiating the balance:

$$dCA_£ = dV_x - dV_m \qquad (G.2)$$

or

$$dCA_£/V_m = dV_x/V_m - dV_m/V_m \qquad (G.3)$$

Let us define

$$E_{ca} = \frac{dCA_£/V_m}{dr/r} = \text{the elasticity of the current account}$$
balance with respect to r, the exchange rate (or price of the foreign currency, in $/£)

$$E_x = \frac{dV_x/V_x}{dr/r} = \text{the elasticity of the value of exports}$$
with respect to the exchange rate r

$$E_m = \frac{dV_m/V_m}{dr/r} = \text{the elasticity of the value of imports}$$
with respect to the exchange rate r

Then if we divide both sides of (G.3) by the proportion of change in the exchange rate (dr/r), we get

$$E_{ca} = \frac{V_x}{V_m} E_x - E_m \qquad (G.4)$$

Deriving the formula for the effect of the exchange rate on the current account balance amounts to deriving a formula relating E_{ca} to the underlying elasticities of demand and supply for exports and imports.

Export and Import Elasticities

The export (or import) value is defined as the product of a trade price and a traded quantity. We therefore need to derive expressions giving the elasticities of these trade prices and quantities with respect to the exchange rate. Let's do so on the export side. There the supply, which depends on a dollar price ($P_x^\$ = P_x^£ \cdot r$), must be equated with demand, which depends on a pound price. We start with the equilibrium condition in the export market, differentiate it, and keep rearranging terms until the equation takes a form relating elasticities to the change in export prices:

$$X = S_x(P_x^£ r) = D_x(P_x^£) \qquad (G.5)$$

$$dX = \frac{\partial S_x}{\partial P_x^\$}(rdP_x^£ + P_x^£ dr) = \frac{\partial D_x}{\partial P_x^£}dP_x^£ \qquad (G.6)$$

$$dX/X = \frac{\partial S_x}{\partial P_x^\$}\frac{1}{S_x}(rdP_x^£ + P_x^£ dr) = \frac{\partial D_x}{\partial P_x^£}\frac{1}{D_x}dP_x^£ \qquad (G.7)$$

Multiplying within both sides by $P_x^\$/r = P_x^£$ and dividing by dr/r yields

$$\frac{dX/X}{dr/r} = \left[\frac{\partial S_x}{\partial P_x^\$}\frac{P_x^\$}{S_x}\right]\left(\frac{dP_x^£/P_x^£}{dr/r} + 1\right) =$$

$$\left[\frac{\partial D_x}{\partial P_x^£}\frac{P_x^£}{D_x}\right]\frac{dP_x^£/P_x^£}{dr/r} \qquad (G.8)$$

The expressions in brackets on the left and right are the elasticities of export supply (s_x) and demand (d_x), respectively, so that

---

[1]There are other determinants of the current account balance besides the exchange rate, of course. We focus on the role of exchange rate changes.

[2]The derivation follows that given in Jaroslav Vanek (1962).

$$\frac{dX/X}{dr/r} = s_x \left(\frac{dP_x^£/P_x^£}{dr/r} + 1 \right) = d_x \frac{dP_x^£/P_x^£}{dr/r} \qquad (G.9)$$

and the percent response of the pound price of exports to the exchange rate is

$$\frac{dP_x^£/P_x^£}{dr/r} = \frac{s_x}{d_x - s_x} \qquad (G.10)$$

This has to be negative or zero, since d_x is negative or zero and s_x is positive or zero. (The response of the dollar price of exports to the exchange rate equals this same expression plus one.)

Recalling that the value of exports equals the price times the quantity of exports, we can use the fact that any percent change in this export value equals the percent price change plus the percent quantity change:

$$E_x = \frac{dX/X}{dr/r} + \frac{dP_x^£/P_x^£}{dr/r} \qquad (G.11)$$

From (G.9) and (G.10), we get the relationship between the elasticity of the value of exports and the elasticities of demand and supply of exports:

$$E_x = \frac{d_x s_x}{d_x - s_x} + \frac{s_x}{d_x - s_x} = \frac{d_x + 1}{(d_x/s_x) - 1} \qquad (G.12)$$

which can be of any sign.

Going through all the same steps on the imports side yields expressions for the responses of the pound price of imports, the quantity of imports, and the value of imports with respect to the exchange rate:

$$\frac{dP_m^£/P_m^£}{dr/r} = \frac{d_m}{s_m - d_m} \quad (\leq 0) \qquad (G.13)$$

$$\frac{dM/M}{dr/r} = \frac{s_m d_m}{s_m - d_m} \quad (\leq 0) \qquad (G.14)$$

and

$$E_m = \frac{s_m + 1}{(s_m/d_m) - 1} \quad (\leq 0) \qquad (G.15)$$

The General Trade Balance Formula and the Marshall–Lerner Condition

We have now gathered all the materials we need to give the general formula for the elasticity of response of the

current account (or trade) balance to the exchange rate. From (G.4), (G.12), and (G.15), the formula is

The elasticity of the trade balance with respect to the exchange rate =

$$E_{ca} = \frac{V_x}{V_m} \left(\frac{d_x + 1}{(d_x/s_x) - 1} \right) - \frac{s_m + 1}{(s_m/d_m) - 1} \qquad (G.16)$$

By studying this general formula and some of its special cases, we can determine what elasticities are crucial in making the trade balance response stable (i.e., in making E_{ca} positive). It turns out that

> The more elastic are import demand and export demand, the more "stable" (positive) will be the response of the current account balance.

Demand elasticities are crucial, but supply elasticities have no clear general effect on the trade balance response.

These results can be appreciated more easily after we have considered four important special cases listed in Figure G.1. The perverse result of a trade balance that worsens after the domestic currency has been devalued is the *inelastic-demand case,* discussed in Chapter 22. As shown in Figure G.1, this Case 1, in which $d_m = d_x = 0$, yields clear perversity regardless of the initial state of the trade balance. The "J curve" of Chapter 22 is based on the suspicion that this case may sometimes obtain in the short run, before demand elasticities have had a chance to rise.

A second special case, also discussed in Chapter 22, is the *small-country case,* in which both export prices and import prices are fixed in terms of foreign currencies in large outside-world markets. This Case 2 is represented in Figure G.1 by infinite foreign elasticities: $s_m = -d_x = \infty$. In the small-country case, devaluation or depreciation of the home currency definitely improves the current account balance. The small-country case is realistic for so many countries—even many "large" ones are international price-takers—that its result is a main reason for presuming that the current account balance response to an exchange rate change is stable, at least beyond the short run.

Consistent with the emphasis on the importance of demand elasticities is the extreme result for Case 3. With *prices fixed in buyers' currencies,* for example, by infinitely elastic demands for imports both at home and abroad ($d_m = d_x = -\infty$), the general formula yields the most improvement.

FIGURE G.1

Devaluation and the Trade Balance: Applying the General Formula to Special Cases

	Assumed Elasticities	Effect of Devaluation on the Trade Balance
Case 1: Inelastic demands	$d_m = d_x = 0$	Trade balance worsens: $$E_{ca} = -\frac{V_x}{V_m} < 0$$
Case 2: Small country	$s_m = -d_x = \infty$	Trade balance improves: $$E_{ca} = \frac{V_x}{V_m}s_x - d_m > 0$$
Case 3: Prices fixed in buyer's currencies	$d_m = d_x = -\infty$	Trade balance improves: $$E_{ca} = \frac{V_x}{V_m}s_x + s_m + 1 > 0$$
Case 4: Prices fixed in sellers' currencies	$s_x = s_m = \infty$	It depends: $$E_{ca} = \frac{V_x}{V_m}(-d_x - 1) - d_m \overset{>}{\underset{<}{=}} 0$$

In Case 4, if trade was not initially in surplus, the Marshall–Lerner condition is sufficient for improvement: $|d_x + d_m| > 1$.

The fourth special case considered here is one in which *prices are kept fixed in sellers' currencies.* This fits the Keynesian family of macromodels, in which supplies are infinitely elastic and prices are fixed within countries. In Case 4, the net effect of devaluation on the current account balance depends on a famous condition, the **Marshall–Lerner condition,** which says that the absolute values of the two demand elasticities must exceed unity: $|d_x + d_m| > 1$. This is sufficient for a stable result if the current account balance is not initially in surplus (i.e., if $V_x \leq V_m$, as is typical of devaluations). While the Marshall–Lerner condition strictly holds only in a narrow range of models, it is a rougher guide to the likelihood of the stable result, since it reminds us of the overall pattern that higher demand elasticities give more stable results. Authors tend to argue that the Marshall–Lerner condition would be sufficient for devaluation to work as it should, even though this follows only under the assumptions of Case 4.

Chapter 2

1. Consumer surplus is the net gain to consumers from being able to buy a product through a market. It is the difference between the highest price someone is willing to pay for each unit of the product and the actual market price that is paid, summed over all units that are demanded and consumed. The highest price that someone is willing to pay for the unit indicates the value that the buyer attaches to that unit. To measure consumer surplus for a product using real-world data, three major pieces of information are needed: (1) the market price, (2) the quantity demanded, and (3) the slope (or shape) of the demand curve in terms of how quantity demanded would change if the market price increased. Consumer surplus could then be measured as the area below the demand curve and above the market-price line.

3. The country's supply of exports is the amount by which the country's domestic quantity supplied exceeds the country's domestic quantity demanded. The supply-of-exports curve is derived by finding the difference between domestic quantity supplied and domestic quantity demanded for each possible market price for which quantity supplied exceeds quantity demanded. The supply-of-exports curve shows the quantity that the country would want to export for each possible international market price.

5. There is no domestic market for winter coats in this tropical country, but there is a domestic supply curve. If the world price for coats is above the minimum price at which the country would supply any coats (the price at which the supply curve hits the price axis), then in free trade the country would produce and export coats. The country gains from this trade because it creates producer surplus—the area above the supply curve and below the international price line, up to the intersection (which indicates the quantity that the country will produce and export).

7. It is true that opening trade bids prices into equality between countries. With a competitive market this also means that marginal costs are equal between countries. But ongoing trade is necessary to maintain this equilibrium. If trade were to stop, the world would return to the no-trade equilibrium, at which prices would differ, and there would be an incentive for arbitrage. The ongoing trade in the free-trade equilibrium is why prices are equalized—trade is not self-eliminating.

9. The demand curve D_{US} shifts to the right. The U.S. demand-for-imports curve D_m shifts to the right. The equilibrium international price rises above 1,000. It is shown by the intersection of the new U.S. D_m curve and the original S_x curve.

11. a. With no international trade, equilibrium requires that domestic quantity demanded (Q_D) equals domestic quantity supplied (Q_S). Setting the two equations equal to each other, we can find the equilibrium price with no trade:

$$350 - (P/2) = -200 + 5P$$

The equilibrium no-trade price is $P = 100$. Using one of the equations, we find that the no-trade quantity is 300.

b. At a price of 120, Belgium's quantity demanded is 290, and its quantity supplied is 400. In free trade Belgium exports 110 units.

c. Belgian consumer surplus declines. With no trade it is a larger triangle below the demand curve and above the 100 price line. With free trade it is a smaller triangle below the demand curve and above the 120 price line. Belgian producer surplus increases. With no trade it is a smaller triangle above the supply curve and below the 100 price line. With free trade it is a larger triangle above the supply curve and below the 120 price line. The net national gain from trade is the difference between the gain of producer surplus and the loss of consumer surplus. This gain is a triangle whose base is the quantity traded (110) and whose height is the change in price (120 − 100 = 20) so the total gain is 1,100.

Chapter 3

1. Disagree. This statement describes absolute advantage. It would imply that a country that has a higher labor productivity in all goods would export all goods and import nothing. Ricardo instead showed that mutually beneficial trade is based on comparative advantage—trading according to maximum relative advantage. The country will export those goods whose *relative* labor productivity (relative to the other country *and* relative to other goods) is high, and import those other goods whose relative labor productivity is low.

3. Pugelovia has 20 percent of the world's labor [20/(20 + 80)], whereas it has 30 percent [3/(3 + 7)] of the world's land. Pugelovia is land-abundant and labor-scarce relative to the rest of the world. H–O theory predicts that Pugelovia will export the land-intensive good (wheat) and import the labor-intensive good (cloth).

5. To derive the country's cloth demand curve, we need to find the price line for each price ratio, and then find the tangency with a community indifference curve. The tangency indicates the quantity demanded at that price ratio. The price line has the slope indicated by the price ratio, and it is tangent to the country's production-possibilities curve. (This tangency indicates the country's production at this price ratio.) As each price ratio is lower, the tangency with the production-possibilities curve shifts

to the northwest, as shown in the accompanying graph. As the price line shifts and becomes flatter, the tangency with a community indifference curve shifts to the right. Representative numbers are shown, with each decrease of price by 0.5 increasing quantity demanded by 10.

7. a. Lindertania has an absolute disadvantage in both goods. Its labor input per unit of output is higher for both goods, so its labor productivity (output per unit of input) is lower for both goods.

   b. Lindertania has a comparative advantage in producing rice. Its relative disadvantage is lower (75/50 < 100/50).

   c. With no trade, the relative price of rice would be 75/100 = 0.75 yards of cloth per bushel of rice.

   d. With free trade the equilibrium international price ratio will be greater than or equal to 0.75 yard per bushel, and less than or equal to 1.0 yard per bushel (the no-trade price ratio in the rest of the world). Lindertania will export rice and import cloth.

9. a. With no trade, the real wages in the United States are 1/2 = 0.5 bushel per hour and 1/4 = 0.25 yard per hour. The real wages in the rest of the world are 1/1.5 = .67 bushel per hour and 1/1 = 1.0 yard per hour. The absolute advantages (higher labor productivities) in the rest of the world translate into higher real wages in the rest of the world.

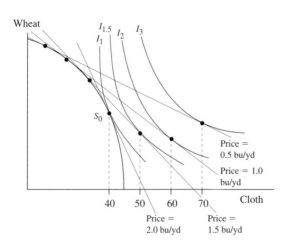

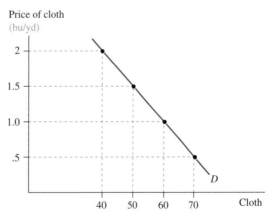

b. With free trade the United States completely specializes in producing wheat. The U.S. real wage with respect to wheat remains 0.5 bushel per hour. Cloth is obtained by trade at a price ratio of one, so the U.S. real wage with respect to cloth is 0.5 yard per hour. The gains from trade for the United States are shown by the higher real wage with respect to cloth (0.5 > 0.25). As long as U.S. labor wants to buy some cloth, the United States gains from trade by gaining greater purchasing power over cloth. With free trade the rest of the world completely specializes in producing cloth. Its real wage with respect to cloth is unchanged at 1.0 yard per hour. Its real wage with respect to wheat rises to 1.0 bushel per hour, because it can trade for wheat at the price ratio of one. The rest of the world gains from greater purchasing power over wheat.

c. The rest of the world still has the higher real wage. Absolute advantage matters—higher labor productivity translates into higher real wages.

11. a. They could make 7 wheat, with no cloth production.

b. They could make 6 cloth, with no wheat production.

c. The ppc is not a straight line between (6 cloth, 0 wheat) and (0 cloth, 7 wheat). Rather it has four parts with different slopes. Here is a tour of the ppc, starting down on the cloth axis (*x* axis). They could produce anything from (6 cloth, 0 wheat) up to (5, 2) by having *A* shift between cloth and wheat while the others make only cloth. Then they could make anything from (5, 2) up to (3, 5) by keeping *A* busy growing wheat and *B* and *C* busy at cloth, while *D* switches between the two tasks. Then they could make anything from (3, 5) up to (2, 6) by choosing how to divide *C*'s time, keeping *B* in wheat making and *A* and *D* in cloth. Finally, they could make anything between (2, 6) and (0, 7) by varying *B*'s tasks while the others make cloth.

   Study this result to see how the right assignments relate to people's comparative advantages. Note that with four different kinds of comparative advantage, there was a convex curve with four slopes. In general, the greater the number of different kinds of individuals, the

smoother and more convex the curve. Therefore, we get an increasing-cost ppc for the nation, even if every individual is a Ricardian constant-cost type.

Chapter 4

1. Mexico is abundant in unskilled labor and scarce in skilled labor relative to the United States or Canada. With freer trade Mexico will export a greater volume of unskilled-labor–intensive products and import a greater volume of skilled-labor–intensive products. According to the Stolper–Samuelson theorem, a shift toward freer trade then will increase the real wage of unskilled labor in Mexico, reduce the real wage of unskilled labor in the United States or Canada, decrease the real wage of skilled labor in Mexico, and increase the real wage of skilled labor in the United States or Canada.

3. Disagree. Opening up free trade does hurt people in import-competing industries in the short run—essentially due to the loss of producer surplus. The long-run effects are different because people and resources can move between industries, but everyone will not gain in the long run. If trade develops according to the Heckscher–Ohlin theory, then the owner of the factors of production that are relatively scarce in the country lose real income. Because the country imports products that are intensive in these factors, trade effectively makes these factors "less scarce" and reduces their returns.

5. Leontief conducted his research shortly after World War II, when it seemed clear that the United States was abundant in capital and scarce in labor, relative to the rest of the world. According to the Heckscher–Ohlin theory, the United States then should export capital-intensive products and import labor-intensive products. But in his empirical work using data on production in the United States and U.S. trade flows, Leontief found that the United States exported relatively labor-intensive products and imported relatively capital-intensive products.

7. a. With prices of 100, the two equations are

$$100 = 60w + 40r$$
$$100 = 75w + 25r$$

   Solving these simultaneously, the equilibrium wage rate is 1 and the equilibrium rental rate is also 1. The labor cost per unit of wheat output is 60 (60 units of labor at a cost of 1 per unit of labor). The labor cost per unit of cloth is 75. The rental cost per unit of wheat is 40. The rental cost per unit of cloth is 25.

b. With the new price of cloth, the two equations are

$$100 = 60w + 40r$$
$$120 = 75w + 25r$$

Solving these simultaneously, the new equilibrium wage rate is about 1.53 and the new equilibrium rental rate is 0.2.

c. The real wage with respect to wheat increases from 0.01 (or 1/100) to about 0.0153 (or 1.53/100). The real wage with respect to cloth increases from 0.01 (or 1/100) to about 0.01275 (or 1.53/120). On average the real wage is higher—labor benefits from the increase in the price of cloth. The real rental rate with respect to wheat decreases from 0.01 (or 1/100) to 0.002 (or 0.2/100). With respect to cloth it decreases from 0.01 (or 1/100) to about 0.0017 (or 0.2/120). On average the real rental rate is lower—landowners lose real income as a result of this increase in the price of cloth.

d. These results are an example of the Stolper–Samuelson theorem. Wheat is relatively intensive in land, and cloth is relatively intensive in labor. The increase in the price of cloth raises the real income of labor (its intensive factor) and lowers the real income of the other factor (land).

9. The total input share of labor in each dollar of cloth output is the sum of the direct use of labor plus the labor that is used to produce the material inputs into cloth production:

$$0.5 + 0.1 \times 0.3 + 0.2 \times 0.6 = 0.65$$

The total input share of capital is calculated in the same way:

$$0.2 + 0.1 \times 0.7 + 0.2 \times 0.4 = 0.35$$

Cloth is labor-intensive relative to the country's import substitutes (0.65 > 0.55). Thus the country's trade pattern is consistent with the Heckscher–Ohlin theory. This labor-abundant country exports the labor-intensive product.

Chapter 5

1. By expanding its export industries, Pugelovia wants to sell more exports to the rest of the world. This increase in export supply tends to lower the international prices of its export products, so the Pugelovian terms of trade (price of exports relative to the price of imports) tend to decline.

3. The drought itself reduces production in these Latin American countries and tends to lower their well-being. (Their production-possibilities curves shrink inward.) But the lower export supply of coffee tends to raise the international price of coffee so the terms of trade of these Latin American countries tend to improve. The improved terms of trade tend to raise well-being. (The purchasing power of their exports rises.) If their terms of trade improve enough, the countries' well-being improves. The greater purchasing power of the remaining exports is a larger effect than the loss of export (and production) volumes. The gain in welfare is more likely (1) if these Latin American countries represent a large part of world coffee supply so that their supply reduction can have a noticeable impact on the world price, (2) if foreign demand for coffee is price-inelastic (as it probably is) so that the coffee price rises by a lot when supply declines, and (3) if exports of coffee are a major part of the countries' economies so that the improvement in the terms of trade can have a noticeable benefit to the countries. (This answer is an example of immiserizing growth "in reverse.")

5. R&D is a production activity that is intensive in the use of highly skilled labor (scientists and engineers) and perhaps also in the use of capital that is willing to take large risks (e.g., venture capital). The industrialized countries are relatively abundant in highly skilled labor and in risk-taking capital. According to Heckscher–Ohlin theory, a production activity tends to locate where the factors that it uses intensively are abundant.

7. a. This is balanced growth through increases in factor endowments. The production-possibilities curve shifts out proportionately so that its relative shape is the same.

b. This is balanced growth through technology improvements of similar magnitude in both industries. The production-possibilities curve shifts out proportionately so that its relative shape is the same.

c. The intercept of the production-possibilities curve with the cloth axis does not change. (If there is no wheat production, then the improved wheat technology does not add to the country's production.) The rest of the production-possibilities curve shifts out. This is growth biased toward wheat production.

9. a. The entire U.S. production-possibilities curve shifts out, with the outward shift relatively larger for the good that is intensive in capital. If the U.S. trade pattern follows the Heckscher–Ohlin theory, then this good is machinery. Growth is biased toward machinery production.

b. According to the Rybczynski theorem, production of machinery increases and production of clothing decreases if the product price ratio is unchanged. The extra capital is employed in producing more machinery, and the machinery industry must also employ some extra labor to use with the extra capital. The extra labor is drawn from the clothing industry, so clothing production declines.

c. The U.S. willingness to trade increases. With growth of production and income, the United States wants to consume more of both goods. Demand for imports of clothing increases because domestic consumption increases while domestic production decreases. (Supply of exports also increases because the increase in domestic production of machinery is larger than the increase in domestic demand.)

d. The increase in demand for imports tends to increase the international equilibrium relative price of clothing. (The increase in supply of exports tends to lower the international equilibrium relative price of machinery.)

e. The change in the international equilibrium price ratio is a decline in the U.S. terms of trade. U.S. well-being could decline—immiserizing growth is possible. If the decline in the terms of trade is large enough, then this negative effect can be larger than the positive effect of growth in production capabilities.

11. a. The U.S. production-possibilities curve shifts out for all points except its intercept with the food axis. This is growth biased toward clothing production.

b. The U.S. willingness to trade probably decreases because the United States is now capable of producing its import good at a lower cost. Although the extra production and income lead to an increase in U.S. demand for clothing, the expansion of the supply of clothing that results from the improved technology is likely to be larger, so U.S. demand for clothing imports probably decreases.

c. The decrease in U.S. demand for imports reduces the equilibrium international relative price of clothing. The U.S. terms of trade improve.

Chapter 6

1. Disagree. The Heckscher–Ohlin theory indicates that countries should export some products (products that are intensive in the country's abundant factors) and import other products (products that are intensive in the country's scarce factors). Heckscher–Ohlin theory predicts the pattern of interindustry trade. It does not predict that countries would engage in a lot of intra-industry trade, which involves both exporting and importing products that are the same (or very similar).

3. There are two major reasons. First, product differentiation can result in intra-industry trade. Imports do not lead to lower domestic output of the product, because exports provide demand for much of the output that previously was sold at home. Output levels do not change much between industries, so there is (1) little shift between industries in factor demand and (2) little pressure on factor prices. There are likely to be fewer losers from Stolper–Samuelson effects. Second, there is a gain from trade that is shared by everyone—the gain from having access to greater product variety through trade. Some groups that otherwise might believe that they are losers because of trade could instead believe that they are winners if they place enough value on this access to greater product variety.

5. a. External economies of scale mean that the average costs of production decline as the size of an industry in a specific geographic area increases. With free trade and external economies, produc-

tion will tend to concentrate in one geographic area to achieve these external economies. Whichever area is able to increase its production can lower its average costs. Lower costs permit firms in this area to lower their prices so that they gain more sales, grow bigger, and achieve lower costs. Eventually production occurs in only one country (or geographic area) that produces with low costs.

b. Both countries gain from trade in products with external economies. The major effect is that the average cost of production declines as production is concentrated in one geographic area. If the industry is competitive, then the product price declines as costs decline. In the importing country, consumers' gains from lower prices more than offset the loss of producer surplus as the local industry ceases to produce the product. In the exporting country, producer surplus may increase as production expands, although this effect is countered by the decrease in the price that producers charge for their products. In the exporting country, consumer surplus increases as the product price declines. Thus the exporting country can gain for two reasons: an increase in producer surplus and an increase in consumer surplus.

7. a. Consumers in Pugelovia are likely to experience two types of effects from the opening of trade. First, consumers gain access to the varieties of products produced by foreign firms, as these varieties can now be imported. Consumers gain from greater product variety. Second, the additional competition from imports can lower the prices of the domestically produced varieties, creating an additional gain for domestic consumers.

b. Producers in Pugelovia also are likely to experience two types of effects from the opening of trade. First, imports add extra competition for domestic sales. As we noted in the answer to part *a*, this is likely to force domestic producers to lower their prices, and some sales will be lost to imports. Second, domestic producers gain access to a new market, the foreign market. They are likely to be able to make additional sales as exports to consumers in the foreign market who prefer these producers' varieties over the ones produced locally there.

9. a.

Product Category	Intra-industry Trade Share	Net Trade as a Percentage of Total Trade
Food, beverages, and tobacco	89.6%	10.4%
Petroleum and other fuels	24.3	75.7
Chemicals	45.9	54.1
Machinery and transport equipment	66.6	33.4
Clothing and footwear	22.7	77.3

b. The product categories with the highest intra-industry trade shares are (1) food, beverages, and tobacco and (2) machinery and transport equipment. Some of this intra-industry trade could result from two-way trade in goods that are very similar but differentiated in the eyes of consumers. This could be true, for instance, for beverages or transport equipment. However, much of the apparent intra-industry trade may simply be the result of adding up different types of products into these broad categories. For instance, industrialized countries' food exports tend to be products that grow in temperate climates, while their food imports are different products that grow in tropical climates.

c. The categories that show substantial net trade are petroleum and other fuels, clothing and footwear, and chemicals. Explanations of net trade between industrialized countries and the rest of the world usually are based on the Heckscher–Ohlin theory. The industrialized countries are substantial importers of oil because they are not blessed with substantial endowments of oil in the ground. They are substantial importers of clothing and footwear because production of these products is intensive in unskilled labor, which is relatively scarce in industrialized countries. They are substantial net exporters of chemicals because production of chemicals is intensive in capital and more skilled labor, factors that are relatively abundant in the industrialized countries.

Chapter 7

1. You could calculate it if you know only the size of the tariff and the amount by which it would reduce imports. (See Figure 7.4.)

3. The production effect of a tariff is the deadweight loss to the nation that occurs because the tariff encourages some high-cost domestic production (production that is inefficient by the world standard of the international price). Producing the extra domestic output that occurs when the tariff is imposed has a domestic resource cost that is higher than the international price that the country would have to pay to the foreign exporters to acquire these units as imports with free trade. The domestic resource cost of each unit produced is shown by the height of the domestic supply curve. Thus, the production effect is the triangle above the free-trade world price line and below the domestic supply curve, for the units between domestic production quantity with free trade and domestic production quantity with the tariff. It can be calculated as one-half of the product of the change in domestic price caused by the tariff and the change in production quantity caused by the tariff.

5. (a) U.S. consumers gain $420 million per year. (b) U.S. producers lose $140 million per year. (c) The U.S. government loses $240 million per year. (d) The United States as a whole gains $40 million a year.

7. (a) U.S. consumers gain $5,125,000. (b) U.S. producers lose $1,875,000. (c) U.S. government loses $6,000,000 in tariff revenue. (d) The United States as a whole loses $2,750,000 each year from removing the tariff. The U.S. national loss stems from the fact that the U.S. tariff removal raises the world price paid on imported motorcycles. In question 5, it was assumed that removing the duty had no effect on the world price (of sugar).

9. The $1.25 is made up of 60 cents of value added, 35 cents of cotton payments, and 30 cents of payments for other fibers. The effective rate is (60¢ − 40¢)/ 40¢ = 50%.

Chapter 8

1. Import quotas are government-decreed quantitative limits on the total quantity of a product that can be imported into the country during a given period of time. Here are three reasons why a government might want to use a quota rather than a tariff: (1) Quotas ensure that imports will not exceed the amount set by the quota. This could be useful if the government wants to assure domestic producers that imports are actually limited. (2) A quota gives government officials greater power and discretion over who gets the valuable right to import. (3) The government may accede to the desires of domestic producers who could have monopoly pricing power if import competition is removed at the margin. For instance, a quota would be preferred by a domestic monopoly, because the monopoly could raise its price with no fear of growing imports as long as a quota limits the quantity imported.

    A quota does not bring a greater national gain. From the point of view of the national interest, a quota is no better than an equivalent tariff, and it may be worse.

3. This would happen if the domestic product market were perfectly competitive, and the import quota rights were auctioned off competitively.

5. The tariff would be less damaging to the United States, because it gives the United States the tariff revenue that instead would be a price markup pocketed by foreign film makers with a VER. Both would bring the same overall loss in world welfare (unless the VER was biased against low-cost foreign producers, in which case the VER would be worse).

7. a. Relative to free trade, the tariff gives the United States a terms-of-trade gain of $180 million and an efficiency loss of $100 million for a net gain of $80 million. In terms of Figure 8.2, this is area *e* minus area (*b* + *d*). The VER costs the United States $300 million (area *c*) plus $100 million (*b* + *d* again) for a loss of $400 million. For the United States, then, the tariff is best and the VER is worst.

    b. If the United States imposes the $80 tariff, Canada loses $180 million (area *e*) and $60 million (area *f*) for a total loss of $240 million. By contrast, if the United States and Canada (Bauer) negotiate a VER arrangement, Canada gains $300 million on price markups (area *c*) and loses $60 million (area *f*) for a net *gain* of $240 million. For Canada, the U.S. tariff is the most harmful, whereas the VER actually brings a net gain.

c. For the world as a whole (United States plus Canada here), either the tariff or the VER brings a net loss of $160 million (areas $b + d$ and f). Free trade is still best for the world as a whole.

9. Before the demand increase, the tariff and the quota are essentially equivalent (domestic price P_1, domestic production quantity S_1, domestic consumption quantity D_1, import quantity $D_1 - S_1$, domestic producer surplus VAP_1, domestic consumer surplus UBP_1, deadweight losses AEC and BGJ, and government tariff revenue or quota import profits $ABGE$). With the increase in demand to D_d', the unchanged tariff and the unchanged quota are no longer equivalent:

	Tariff	Quota
Domestic price	P_1	P_2
Production quantity	S_1	S_2
Consumption quantity	D_3	D_2
Producer surplus	VAP_1	VLP_2
Consumer surplus	TRP_1	TNP_2
Deadweight losses		
Production	AEC	LFC
Consumption	RIK	NHK
Tariff revenue or quota		
import profits	$ARIE$	$LNHF$

After domestic demand increases, with the quota domestic price is higher, domestic quantity produced is higher, domestic quantity consumed is lower, the quantity imported is lower, domestic producer surplus is larger, domestic consumer surplus is smaller, and the deadweight losses are larger.

Chapter 9

1. a. Yes, there are external benefits—a positive spillover effect. The benefits to the entire country are larger than the benefits to the single firm innovating the new technology. Other firms that do not pay anything to this firm receive benefits by learning about and using the new production technology.

    b. The economist would say that the production subsidy is preferable to the tariff. Both can be used to increase domestic production, but the tariff distorts domestic consumption, leading to an unnecessary deadweight loss (the consumption effect).

    c. The economist would use the specificity rule. The actual problem is that innovating firms do not have enough incentives to pursue new production technologies (because other firms get benefits without paying). The economist would recommend some form of subsidy to new production

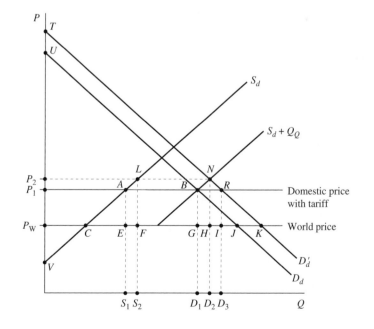

technology as better than a production subsidy or tariff. The technology subsidy could be a subsidy to undertake research and development, or monetary awards or prizes for new technology once it is developed.

3. One such set of conditions described in this chapter is the developing government argument. If the government is so underdeveloped that the gains from starting or expanding public programs exceed the costs of taxing imports, then the import tariff brings net national gains by providing the revenue so badly needed for those programs. Another answer could be: Tax imports if our consumption of the product brings external costs. For example, a country that does not grow tobacco could tax tobacco imports for health reasons.

5. Yes, even though no such case was explicitly introduced in this chapter. Think about incentive distortions, and ask how a nation could have too little private incentive to buy imports. The most likely case is one in which buying and using foreign products could bring new knowledge benefits throughout the importing country, benefits that are not captured by the importers alone. To give them an incentive matching the spillover gains to residents other than the importers, the national government could use an import subsidy.

7. Policy A, the production subsidy, would be the lowest cost to the country. By comparison, the tariff (Policy B) would raise the domestic price of aircraft, which will distort buyer decisions and thwart the growth of the domestic airline industry. The tariff adds a deadweight loss (the consumption effect). Policy C, the import quota, would be the most costly to the country. The sole Australian producer would gain monopoly power, and it will raise the domestic price even higher. The deadweight loss will be larger.

9. In favor: Adjustment assistance is designed to gain the benefits of increased imports by encouraging workers to make a smooth transition out of domestic production of the import-competing good. A key problem is that workers pushed out of import-competing production suffer large declines in earnings when forced to switch to some other industry or occupation. Adjustment assistance can overcome this problem by offering workers retraining, help with relocation, and temporary income support during retraining and relocation. Adjustment assistance represents an application of the specificity rule. It is better than using a tariff or nontariff barrier to limit imports and resist shrinking the domestic industry. And politically, it can reduce the pressure to enact these import barriers.

Opposed: Workers are faced with the need to relocate and develop new skills for a variety of reasons—not only increased imports but also changing consumer demand and changing technologies. There is nothing special about increasing imports, and workers affected by increasing imports deserve no special treatment. In fact, offering adjustment assistance could encourage workers to take jobs in import-competing industries that are shrinking, because they have the social insurance offered by adjustment assistance. In addition, adjustment assistance is not that effective. It does offer temporary income assistance to those who qualify, but it is much less successful at effective retraining and smooth relocation.

Chapter 10

1. One definition of dumping is selling an export at a price lower than the price charged to domestic buyers of the product within the exporting country. This definition emphasizes international price discrimination. The second defintion is selling an export at a price that is lower than the full average cost of the product (including overhead) plus a reasonable profit margin. This definition emphasizes pricing below cost (counting some profit as a cost of capital).

3. Tipper Laurie, because its at-brewery price is lower for exports to the United States than for domestic sales. Bigg Redd, because its at-brewery export price is below average cost.

5. The result would look like the complete round-trip from point *A* back to point *A* in Figure 10.3, with the United States and blue jeans now playing the roles played by Korea and steel.

The United States would lose, because the U.S. government would just pay out a subsidy of $5 on every pair of blue jeans to Canada, and reap no benefits for it. Canada would gain the same $5 on each pair, collected as a tariff, while not feeling any effect on the domestic price or sales volume. The world as a whole would be unaffected, since in this case Canada's gain equals the United States' loss.

7. a. In this case, Airbus would gain by producing even without government intervention. Airbus would gain 5 if Boeing did produce, and 100 if Boeing did not produce. There would be no reason for European governments to subsidize Airbus.

   b. In this case, Boeing is sure to produce since Boeing gains whether or not Airbus produces. The EU should recognize this. With Boeing producing, the net gain for Airbus without government help is zero. If none of Airbus's customers were in Europe, there would be no reason to encourage Airbus to produce. Notice, however, that consumers might be better off if Airbus did produce. You can see this either by noticing that production by Airbus would deprive Boeing of 100 in profits taken from consumers (presumably by charging higher prices), or by reasoning that more competition is always a good thing for consumers. Either way, the EU would have reason to subsidize Airbus if its consumers could reap gains from the competition.

9. One way to build the case is to claim that the industry is a global oligopoly, with substantial scale economies and high profit rates (like the Boeing–Airbus example in this chapter). The nation can gain if the country's firm(s) can establish export capabilities and earn high profits on the exports. Another way to build the case is to claim that this industry is an infant industry (discussed in Chapter 9). If the industry could get some assistance, it can grow up and generate new producer surplus when it is strong enough to export. Of the real-world experiences cited in this chapter, the closest to an example of export-oriented subsidies that probably created gains for the nation is the help that Boeing's exports received from the U.S. government.

Chapter 11

1. A customs union keeps a uniform tariff on any imported good or service, regardless of which member country receives the imports. In this case, there is no need to scrutinize goods that move between countries in the customs union, even if the product might have been imported from outside the union.

   In a free-trade area, by contrast, each country can keep its own import tariff rates. Therefore the free-trade area needs to scrutinize goods that move between countries in the free-trade area to make sure

that they were not imported from outside the area into a low-tariff country and then shipped on to a high-tariff country in an effort to avoid the high tariff.

3. Trade creation is the increase in total imports resulting from the formation of a customs union (or free-trade area). Trade creation occurs because importing from the partner country lowers the price in the importing country, so that some high-cost domestic production is replaced by lower-priced imports from the partner, and because the lower price increases the total quantity demanded in the importing country. Trade diversion is the replacement of imports from lower-cost suppliers outside the customs union with higher-cost imports for the partner. It occurs because the outsider suppliers remain hindered by tariffs, while there is no tariff on imports from the partner. Trade creation creates a gain for the importing country and the world. Trade diversion creates a loss for the importing country and the world. The importing country and the world gain from the customs union if trade creation gains exceed trade diversion losses.

5. (a) 10 million radios times ($110 – 100) = $100 million. (b) To offset this $100 million loss, with linear demand and supply curves, the change in imports, ΔM, would have to be such that the trade-creation gains (area b in Figure 11.2) had an area equal to $100 million. So $1/2 \times (\$130 - \$110) \times \Delta M = \$100$ million requires $\Delta M = 10$ million, or a doubling of Homeland's radio imports.

7. This case resembles that shown in Figure 11.2A, assuming the United States is a price-taking country.

   U.S. consumers would gain, as the domestic price drops from $30 to $25. We cannot quantify the dollar value of their consumer-surplus gain without knowing the level of domestic consumption or production.

   U.S. producers would lose from the same price drop, though again we cannot say how much they lose. (We do know, however, that the consumer gain would exceed this producer loss plus the government revenue loss by the triangular area $(1/2) \times \$5 \times 0.2$ million = $0.5 million.)

   The U.S. government would lose the $10 million it had collected in tariff revenue on the imports from China.

   The world as a whole would gain the triangular area $(1/2) \times \$5 \times 0.2$ million = $0.5 million, but lose the rectangular area ($25 – 20) × 1 million = $5 million because of the diversion of 1.0 million pairs from the lower-cost producer (China) to the higher-cost producer (Mexico). So overall, the world loses $4.5 million.

9. The "most certain" is (a), a countervailing duty, which brings net gains for the world as a whole if it just offsets the foreign export subsidy that provoked it. Whether the world as a whole gains from a customs union depends on whether it brings more trade creation than trade diversion. Whether the world gains from an antidumping duty also depends on the specifics of the case, as explained in Chapter 10.

Chapter 12

1. Water pollution, urban sanitation, and urban particulates all tend to get cleaned up as incomes rise. On the other hand, municipal waste and carbon dioxide emissions build up. The pattern for sulfur dioxide emissions is more complex. Within cities, it gets worse when income rises up toward $5,000 per capita, but then gets much better at higher levels of income. On the other hand, the expansion of the cities themselves means that more area and population are covered by those high (though possibly dropping) urban concentrations of SO_2.

3. Both (b) and (d). For item (b), the WTO is unwilling to let a country use trade limits to punish a foreign country for having environmental standards for production in the foreign country that are different from those of the importing country. For (d), the WTO would consider the pollution issue to be a pretext for unacceptable protectionist import barriers, because the imported products are not the only source of the pollution.

5. While there is some room for interpretation here, the specificity rule definitely prefers (c), followed by (d), then (a), then (b).

   The defeatism of (e) is misplaced. Oil spills are the result of shippers' negligence to a large extent, and not just uncontrollable acts of God.

   One drawback to (a) and (b) is that they force each nation's importers or consumers to pay insurance against shippers' carelessness. The more direct approach is to target the shippers themselves. In addition, many oil spills ruin the coastlines of nations that are not purchasers of the oil being shipped, making it inappropriate to charge them.

   It might seem that the most direct approach, (c), is unrealistic because it is hard to get full damages from the oil-shipping companies in court. Yet it is not difficult to make them pay for most or all of the damages. A key point is that the most damaging spills occur within the 200-mile limit, meaning that they occur in the national waters of the country suffering the damage. Full legal jurisdiction applies. The victimized country can legally seize oil shippers' assets, apply jail sentences, and even demand that a shipping company post bonds in advance of spills in exchange for the right to pass through national waters.

   As for (d), intercepting and taxing all tankers in national waters is a reasonable choice. Its workability depends, however, on the cost of such coast-guard vigilance. If all tankers entering national water must put into port, they could be taxed in port. That is unlikely, however, and it might be costly to pursue them all along the whole 200-mile coast. Furthermore, such a tax, like many insurance schemes, makes the more careful clients (shippers) pay to insure the more reckless.

7. Item (4). This tax would lead to substantial reductions in the use of fossil fuels, the major source of manmade greenhouse gases. The other items would have small effects over the next 20 years.

9. No trade barriers are called for by the information given here. If the wood is in fact grown on plantation land that would have been used for lower-value crops anyway, there is no clear externality, no basis for government intervention. Only if the plantations would have been rain forest and only if there is serious environmental damage (e.g., extinction of species or soil erosion) from the clearing of that rain forest land for plantations would there be a case for Indonesia's restricting the cultivation of jelutong. As for the greenhouse-gas effects of cutting more tropical rain forest, they could easily be outweighed by the longer growing life of cedar trees in the temperate zone.

Chapter 13

1. The four arguments in favor of ISI are the infant-industry argument, the developing-government argument, the chance to improve the terms of

trade for a large importing country, and economizing on market information by focusing on selling in the local market rather than in more uncertain foreign markets. The drawbacks to ISI are the deadweight losses from the inefficiencies of import protection, the danger that government officials directing the policy will try to enrich themselves rather than the country, and the lack of competitive pressure on local firms to "grow up" by reducing costs, improving technology, and raising product quality. The arguments in favor of a policy of promoting manufactured exports are that it encourages use of the country's abundant resources (comparative advantage), that export sales can help to achieve scale economies, and that the drive to succeed in foreign markets creates competitive pressure. A major drawback is that the importing countries may erect trade barriers that limit the exporter's ability to expand its exports of manufactures.

3. The available data do indicate that the relative prices of primary products have declined since 1900, perhaps by as much as 0.8 percent per year. But there are biases in the data. Some of the decline could reflect declining transport costs, some could be offset by the rising quality of manufactured products that is not reflected in the price comparison, and some could be offset because the appearance of new manufactured products also creates a bias in the price comparison. The true trend decline is probably less than 0.8 percent per year, and it may even be no decline.

5. (*a*) An elasticity of demand whose absolute value is 1.5. (*b*) A markup of 2/3, or 66.7 percent.

7. The formula implies that the optimal markup of (price – marginal cost) should be twice the price itself! This should look odd since the marginal cost is not likely to be negative. Behind the oddity of the formula is the idea that a monopolist should go on raising price toward infinity as long as the demand is so inelastic as to raise total revenue in response to price hikes, as is implied by the elasticity of –1/2. No, this elasticity cannot hold at all prices. As the greedy monopolist raises prices toward infinity, the buyers become so impoverished that they must cut their purchases radically, with zero purchases as the limit. In some high price range, sooner or later, the elasticity has to exceed 1 in absolute value.

9. The alternative is strong, rapid reforms of policies ("cold turkey" or "big bang"). There are several arguments in favor of fast reform. First, a quick shift to free trade means that international prices quickly become the signals that guide business and consumer decisions. Efficiency gains from resource reallocations can be large. Second, this quick shift also quickly creates competitive pressure on businesses to improve their productivity and product quality. Third, fast reforms can be accomplished before those interested in maintaining the status quo can marshal their political opposition. Fourth, fast reforms can quickly remove government officials from interfering in business decisions. Finally, the policy of rapid reform appears to be more successful, if we compare the performance of the various transition countries of central and eastern Europe and the former Soviet Union.

Chapter 14

1. None. The loss in consumer loss from imposing a tariff is larger than the gain in producer surplus. (The consumer loss is also larger than the combined gains of producer surplus and government tariff revenue, if the latter has "votes.")

3. Imposing the quota will create one clear winner—domestic baseball bat producers. It will create one clear loser—domestic consumers of baseball bats. And it will create one group that may have mixed feelings—the three import distributors—because they will have a smaller volume of business, but the profit margin on the limited business that they conduct will be very profitable. Baseball bat producers probably will be an effective lobbying group because there are a small number of firms that need to organize to lobby (and they may already have a trade association). Baseball bat consumers are unlikely to be an effective lobbying group because each has a small stake and it would be difficult to organize them into a political group. The three import distributors should be an effective lobbying group if they can agree among themselves whether to favor or oppose the quota.

5. Tariff escalation is that the size of the tariff rate tends to increase with the stage of processing. The tariff rate on final consumer goods is usually higher than it is on intermediate products or raw materials.

Because household consumers are a weak lobbying group, producers of final goods are effective at political action to gain higher tariffs on consumer goods. But for intermediate goods and raw materials, the companies that buy and use these goods can mount effective lobbying efforts to oppose tariffs sought by the firms producing the goods. For the companies buying these goods, a tariff would increase its costs, so there is a clear reason to oppose the tariff, and the buying companies are often already organized into trade associations.

7. The producer subsidy equivalent is the net percentage increase in agricultural income created by the combination of the government's policies (like price supports) that raise agricultural prices, agricultural subsidies and taxes, and government policies that change the prices of inputs (like fertilizer). It is a fairly comprehensive measure of the net effects of a range of government policies toward agriculture. It misses the effects of broader government policies on agricultural incomes, and it misses the effects of government policies on the cost of living for a farm family.

9. If the support price remains at $6.00 per bushel, domestic quantity demanded remains at Q_1 and domestic quantity supplied remains at Q_4. But the welfare effects change because the new free-trade price is $4.00 per bushel, and this creates a new standard for judging opportunity costs. Compared with free trade, U.S. consumers now lose more because of the price support (area *NKFE* instead of area *AGFE*), U.S. producers gain more (area *RJFK* instead of area *BJFG*), and the U.S. government loses more by buying at the support price and exporting at the world price (area *VJEL* instead of area *CJEH*). The net loss to the United States is larger (areas *RVJ* and *NEL* instead of areas *BCJ* and *AEH*).

Chapter 15

1. National saving S equals private saving plus government saving (or dissaving if the government budget is in deficit). For this country, national saving equals $678 billion (or $806 − $128). The current account balance equals the difference between national saving and domestic real investment (I_d). For this country, the current account balance is a deficit of $99 billion (or $678 − $777).

3. Saving can be used to make investments. The country can use its national saving to make domestic real investments in new production capital (buildings and machinery), in new housing, and in additions to inventories, or it can use its national saving to invest in foreign financial assets. If it uses its national saving to make domestic real investments, benefits to the nation include the increases in production capacity and capabilities that result from new production capital and the housing services that flow from a larger stock of housing. If it uses its national saving to make foreign investments, benefits to the nation include the dividends, interest payments, and capital gains that it earns on its foreign investments, which add to the national income of the country in the future.

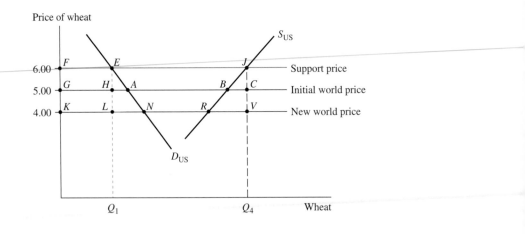

5. Transaction *c* contributes to a surplus in the current account because it is an export of merchandise that is paid for through an item in the capital account. (Transaction *a* leaves the current account unchanged because it is both an export and an import. Transaction *b* contributes to a deficit in the current account because it is an import. Transaction *d* also contributes to a current account deficit because of the outflow as a unilateral transfer. Transaction *e* affects no items in the current account.)

7. a. Credit item in line 3, exports of services. Debit item in line 6, merchandise imports.
   b. Credit item in line 4, income receipts from foreigners (investment income). Debit item in line 14, U.S. investments abroad, in this case a loan.
   c. Credit item in line 16, foreign direct investments in the United States, as the Japanese resident buys a U.S. business (in this case, a football team). Debit item in line 14, U.S. investment abroad (in this case bonds issued by a Japanese city).
   d. Credit item in line 7, services import. Debit item in line 17, foreign investments in the United States, in this case a foreign claim on a U.S. bank.

9. a. The U.S. international investment position declines—an increase in foreign investments in the United States (an increase in what the United States owes to foreigners.)
   b. The U.S. international investment position rises—an increase in private U.S. investment abroad (an increase in U.S. claims on foreigners).
   c. The U.S. international investment position is unchanged. The composition of foreign investments in the United States changes, but the total amount does not change.

Chapter 16

1. *Imports of merchandise and services* result in demand for foreign currency in the foreign exchange market. Domestic buyers often want to pay using domestic currency, while the foreign sellers want to receive payment in their currency. In the process of paying for these imports, domestic currency is exchanged for foreign currency, creating demand for foreign currency. *International capital*

outflows result in a demand for foreign currency in the foreign exchange market. In making investments in foreign financial assets, domestic investors often start with domestic currency and must exchange it for foreign currency before they can buy the foreign assets. The exchange creates demand for foreign currency. Foreign sales of this country's financial assets that the foreigners had previously acquired, and foreign borrowing from this country are other forms of capital outflow that can create demand for foreign currency.

3. a. The value of the dollar decreases. (The SFr increases.)
   b. The value of the dollar decreases. (This is the same change as in part *a*.)
   c. The value of the dollar increases. (The yen decreases.)
   d. The value of the dollar increases. (This is the same change as in part *c*.)

5. The British bank could use the interbank market to find another bank that was willing to buy dollars and sell pounds. The British bank could search directly with other banks for a good exchange rate for the transaction, or it could use a foreign exchange broker to identify a good rate from another bank. The British bank should be able to sell its dollars to another bank quickly and with very low transactions costs.

7. a. Demand for yen. The Japanese firm will sell its dollars to obtain yen.
   b. Demand for yen. The U.S. import company probably begins with dollars, and the Japanese producer probably wants to receive payments in yen. Dollars must be sold to obtain yen.
   c. Supply of yen. The Japanese importer probably begins with yen, and the U.S. cooperative probably wants to receive payment in dollars. Yen must be sold to obtain dollars.
   d. Demand for yen. The U.S. pension fund must sell its dollars to obtain yen, using these yen to buy the Japanese shares.

9. a. Increase in supply of Swiss francs reduces the exchange rate value ($/SFr) of the franc. The dollar appreciates.
   b. Increase in supply of francs reduces the exchange rate value ($/SFr) of the franc. The dollar appreciates.

c. Increase in supply of francs reduces the exchange rate value ($/SFr) of the franc. The dollar appreciates.

d. Decrease in demand for francs reduces the exchange rate value ($/SFr) of the franc. The dollar appreciates.

Chapter 17

1. Agree. As an investor, I think of my wealth and returns from investments in terms of my own currency. When I invest in a foreign-currency–denominated financial asset, I am (actually or effectively) buying both the foreign currency and the asset. Part of my overall return comes from the return of the asset itself—for instance, the yield or rate on interest that it pays. The other part of my return comes from changes in the exchange rate value of the foreign currency. If the foreign currency increases in value (relative to my own currency) while I am holding the foreign asset, the value of my investment (in terms of my own currency) increases, and I have made an additional return on my investment. (Of course, if the exchange rate value of the foreign currency goes down, I make a loss on the currency value, which reduces my overall return.)

3. a. The U.S. firm has an asset position in yen—it has a long position in yen. The risk is that the dollar exchange rate value of the yen in 60 days is uncertain. If the yen depreciates, then the firm will receive fewer dollars.

   b. The student has an asset position in yen—a long position in yen. The risk is that the dollar exchange rate value of the yen in 60 days is uncertain. If the yen depreciates, then the student will receive fewer dollars.

   c. The U.S. firm has a liability position in yen—a short position in yen. The risk is that the dollar exchange rate value of the yen in 60 days is uncertain. If the yen appreciates, then the firm must deliver more dollars to buy the yen to pay off its loan.

5. For forward speculation the relevant comparison is between the current forward exchange rate and the expected future spot exchange rate. Comparing these two rates, we hope to make a profit by buying low and selling high. You expect the Swiss franc to be relatively cheap at the future spot rate ($0.51)

compared with the current forward rate ($0.52). To speculate you should therefore enter into a forward contract today that requires that you sell (or deliver) SFr and buy (or receive) dollars. If the spot rate in 180 days is actually $0.51/SFr, then you can buy SFr at this low spot rate, deliver them into your previously agreed forward contract at the higher forward rate, and pocket the price difference, $0.01, for each franc that you agreed to sell in the forward contract.

7. a. Invest in dollar-denominated asset: $1 \times (1 + 0.0605) = \$1.0605$.
   Invest in yen-denominated asset: $1 \times (1/0.0100) \times (1 + 0.01) \times (0.0105) = \$1.0605$.

   b. Invest in dollar-denominated asset: $1 \times (1 + 0.0605) \times (1/0.0105) = 101$ yen.
   Invest in yen-denominated asset: $1 \times (1/0.0100) \times (1 + 0.01) = 101$ yen.

   c. Invest in dollar-denominated asset: 100 yen $\times (0.01) \times (1 + 0.0605) \times (1/0.0105) = 101$ yen.
   Invest in yen-denominated asset: 100 yen $\times (1 + 0.01) = 101$ yen.

9. a. From the point of view of the U.S.-based investor, the expected uncovered interest differential ("in favor of London") is $[(1 + 0.03) \times 1.77/1.80] - (1 + 0.02) = -0.0072$. Because the differential is negative, the U.S.-based investor should stay at home, investing in dollar-denominated bonds, if he bases his decision on the difference in expected returns. (The approximate formula could also be used to reach this conclusion.)

   b. From the point of view of the U.K.-based investor, the expected uncovered differential ("in favor of New York") is $[(1 + 0.02) \times (1/1.77) \times 1.8] - (1 + 0.03) = 0.0073$. (Note that the position of the interest rates is reversed, and that the exchange rates are inverted so that they are pricing the dollar, which is now the foreign currency. Note also that this differential is approximately equal to the negative of the differential in the other direction, calculated in part *a*.) Because the differential is positive, the U.K.-based investor should undertake an uncovered investment in dollar-denominated bonds, if she bases her decision on the difference in expected returns. (Again, the approximate formula could be used to reach this conclusion.)

c. If there is substantial uncovered investment flowing from Britain to the United States, this increases the supply of pounds in the spot exchange market. There is downward pressure on the spot exchange rate to drop below $1.80/pound. The pound tends to depreciate. (The dollar tends to appreciate.)

Chapter 18

1. The law of one price will hold better for gold. Gold can be traded easily so that any price differences would lead to arbitrage that would tend to push gold prices (stated in a common currency) back close to equality. Big Macs cannot be arbitraged. If price differences exist, there is no arbitrage pressure, so price differences can persist. The prices of Big Macs (stated in a common currency) vary widely around the world.

3. As a tourist, you will be importing services from the country you visit. You would like the currency of this foreign country to be relatively cheap, so you would like it to be undervalued relative to PPP. If it is undervalued, then the current spot exchange rate allows you to buy a lot of this country's currency, relative to the local-currency prices that you must pay for products in the country.

5. According to purchasing power parity, attaining a stable exchange rate between the peso and the dollar requires that the Mexican inflation rate fall so that it is about equal to the 3 percent inflation in the United States. If k is constant, then the rate of growth of the Mexican money supply must fall to about 9 percent (or 6 percent real growth in Y + 3 percent inflation in Mexican prices P).

7. Agree. According to the monetary approach, if real GDP Y falls because of the natural disaster, and the money supply M and the parameter k are steady, then the country's price level P must increase to maintain the equality $M = k \times P \times Y$. To maintain purchasing power parity ($r_s = P/P_f$) when P rises, the nominal exchange rate value of the foreign currency (r_s) will rise. That is, this country's currency will depreciate.

9. a. Using 1975 as a base year, the nominal exchange rate of $1/pnut corresponded to a ratio of U.S. prices to Pugelovian prices of 100/100.

According to PPP, this relationship should be maintained over time. If the price level ratio changes to 260/390 in 2000, then the nominal exchange rate should change to $0.67/pnut. The pnut should depreciate during this time period because of the higher Pugelovian inflation rate (the reason why Pugelovia's price level increased by more than the U.S. price level increased).

b. If the actual exchange rate is $1/pnut in 2000, then the pnut is overvalued. Its exchange rate value is higher than the rate that would be consistent with PPP (using 1975 as a base year).

Chapter 19

1. Disagree. First, exchange rates can be quite variable in the short run. This much variability does not seem to be consistent with the gradual changes in supply and demand for foreign currency that would occur as trade flows changed gradually. Second, the volume of trading in the foreign exchange market is much larger than the volume of international trade in goods and services. Only a small part of total activity in foreign exchange markets is related to payments for exports and imports. Most is related to international financial flows. International financial positioning and repositioning are likely to be quite changeable over short periods of time, explaining the variability of exchange rates in the short run.

3. The first question is whether this decrease in the trade deficit was expected. If it was expected, then there is no true news here, and the effect on the dollar's exchange rate value now should be small. (The effect on the dollar's value would have already occurred as the new expectation of the deficit took hold previously in the market.) If it is unexpected, then this is news, and it can have an impact now on the dollar's value. Most likely, traders and investors will be surprised that the deficit is lower than expected. They are likely to view this as positive for the dollar. If the deficit might continue to be lower, then there will be less demand for foreign currency in paying for the excess imports. If the dollar can be stronger in the future (or, equivalently, the foreign currency can be weaker), then financial investors will tend to bid up the dollar's exchange rate value now in anticipation of the strengthening.

5. a. Sell pesos. Weaker Mexican exports of oil in the future are likely to lower the peso's exchange rate value.

   b. Sell Canadian dollars. The expansion of money and credit is likely to lower the exchange rate value of the Canadian dollar because Canadian interest rates will decline (in the short run) and Canadian inflation rates are likely to be higher (in the long run).

   c. Sell Swiss francs. Foreign investors are likely to pull some investments out of Swiss assets (and to invest less in the future), reducing the exchange rate value of the franc.

7. a. If we use the approximation formula, uncovered interest parity holds (approximately) when the foreign interest rate plus the expected rate of appreciation of the foreign currency equals the domestic interest rate. Using the pound as the foreign currency, it is expected to change (depreciate) at an annual rate of –6% (or (1.98 – 2.00)/2.00 × 360/60 × 100). The uncovered annualized return on a pound-denominated bond is expected to be approximately 11% – 6% = 5%, which equals the annual return of 5% on a dollar-denominated bond. Uncovered interest parity holds approximately. (We could also use the full formula from Chapter 17 to show that the uncovered expected interest differential is approximately zero.)

   b. This shifts the uncovered differential in favor of investing in dollar-denominated bonds. The additional demand for dollars in the foreign exchange market results in an appreciation of the dollar. To reestablish uncovered interest parity with the other rates unchanged, the expected annual rate of change (depreciation) of the pound must be 3 percent so the spot rate now must change to about $1.99/pound. The pound depreciates.

9. If PPP held, the exchange rate r_s should rise steadily by 2 percent per year for five years, ending up 10 percent higher after five years. This matches the path of changes in the domestic price level (relative to the foreign price level) during these five years. PPP does not hold in the short run because the actual exchange rate jumps immediately by more than 10 percent (rather than rising gradually by about 2 percent per year). In the medium run, the actual rate remains above its PPP value, but the two are moving closer together, as the actual rate declines and the PPP rate rises over time. In the long run, PPP holds. According to PPP, the exchange rate eventually should be 10 percent higher, and it actually is 10 percent higher.

Chapter 20

1. In a clean float, the government allows the exchange rate value of its currency to be determined solely by private (or nonofficial) supply and demand in the foreign exchange market. The government takes no direct actions to influence exchange rates. In a managed float, the government is willing and sometimes does take direct actions to attempt to influence the exchange rate value of its currency. For instance, the monetary authorities of the country may sometimes intervene in the market, buying or selling foreign currency (in exchange for domestic currency) in an effort to influence the level or trend of the floating exchange rate.

3. The disequilibrium is the difference between private demand for foreign currency and private supply of foreign currency at the fixed level of the exchange rate. Official intervention by the central bank can be used to defend the fixed exchange rate, selling foreign currency if there is an excess private demand, or buying foreign currency if there is an excess private supply. Another way to see the disequilibrium is that the country's overall payments balance (its official settlements balance) is not zero.

A temporary disequilibrium is one that will disappear within a short period of time, without any need for the country to make any macroeconomic adjustments. If the disequilibrium is temporary, official intervention can usually be used successfully to defend the fixed exchange rate. The country usually will have sufficient official reserve holdings to defend the fixed rate if there is a temporary private excess demand for foreign currency (or a temporary overall payments deficit); the country usually is willing and able to accumulate some additional official reserves if there is a temporary private excess supply of foreign currency (or a temporary overall payments surplus). Indeed, for temporary disequilibriums the well-being of the country can be higher if the government stabilizes the currency by defending the fixed exchange rate through official intervention, as Figure 20.4 shows.

If the disequilibrium is fundamental, then it tends to continue into the future. The country cannot simply use official intervention to defend the fixed exchange rate. The country will run out of official reserves (if its defense involves selling foreign currency), or it will accumulate unacceptably large official reserves (if the defense involves buying foreign currency). Thus, a major adjustment is necessary if the disequilibrium is fundamental. The government may surrender the fixed rate, changing its value or shifting to a floating exchange rate. Or, the government may adjust its macroeconomy to alter private demand and supply for foreign currency.

5. The exchange controls are intended to restrain the excess private demand for foreign currency (the source of the downward pressure on the exchange rate value of the country's currency). Thus, some people who want to obtain foreign currency, and who would be willing to pay more than the current exchange rate, do not get to buy the foreign currency. This creates a loss of well-being for the country as a whole because some net marginal benefits are being lost. Furthermore, these frustrated demanders are likely to turn to other means to obtain foreign currency. They may bribe government officials to obtain the scarce foreign currency. Or they may evade the exchange controls by using an illegal parallel market to obtain foreign currency (typically at a much higher price than the official rate).

7. a. The implied fixed exchange rate is about $4.87/pound (or 20.67/4.2474).
   b. You would engage in triangular arbitrage. If you start with dollars, you buy pounds using the foreign exchange market (because as quoted the pound is cheap). You then use gold to convert these pounds back into dollars. If you start with $4, you can buy one pound. You turn in this one pound at the British central bank, receiving about 0.2354 (or 1/4.2474) ounces of gold. Ship this gold to the United States, and exchange it at the U.S. central bank for about $4.87 (or 0.2354 × 20.67). Your arbitrage gets you (before expenses) about 87 cents for each $4 that you commit.
   c. Buying pounds in the foreign exchange market tends to increase the pound's exchange rate

value so the exchange rate tends to rise above $4.00/pound (and toward $4.87/pound).

9. Key features of the interwar currency experience were that exchange rates were highly variable, especially during the first years after World War I and during the early 1930s. Speculation seemed to add to the instability, and governments sometimes appeared to manipulate the exchange rate values of their currencies to gain competitive advantage. One lesson that policymakers learned from this experience was that fixed exchange rates were desirable to constrain speculation and variability in exchange rates, as well as to constrain governments from manipulating exchange rates. These lessons are now debated because subsequent studies have shown that the experience can be explained or understood in other ways. Exchange rate changes in the years after World War I tended to move in ways consistent with purchasing power parity, which suggests that the fundamental problems were government policies that led to high inflation rates in some countries. The currency instability of the early 1930s seems to be reflecting the large shocks caused by the global depression. Indeed, the research suggests that it may not be possible to keep exchange rates fixed when large shocks hit the system.

11. The Bretton Woods system of fixed exchange rates collapsed largely because of problems with the key currency of the system, the U.S. dollar. The dollar's problems arose partly as a result of the design of the system, and partly as a result of U.S. government policies. As the system evolved, it became a gold-exchange standard in which other countries fixed their currencies to the U.S. dollar, largely held U.S. dollars as their official reserve assets, and intervened to defend the fixed exchange rates using dollars. The United States was obligated to exchange dollars for gold with other central banks at the official gold price. This caused two problems for the system. First, other central banks accumulated dollar official reserves when the United States ran a deficit in its official settlements balance. In the early years of Bretton Woods this was desirable, as other central banks wanted to increase their holdings of official reserves. But in the 1960s, this became undesirable as the U.S. deficits became too large. Expansionary U.S. fiscal and monetary policies led to the large U.S. deficits and also to rising

inflation in the United States. Second, other central banks saw their rising dollar holdings and a declining U.S. gold stock, and they began to question whether the United States could continue to honor the official gold price.

The U.S. government probably could have maintained the system, as least for longer than it actually lasted, if it had been willing to change its domestic policies, tightening up on government spending to contract the economy and cool off its inflation. The United States instead reacted by changing the rules of Bretton Woods, severing the link between the private gold market and the official gold price in 1968, and suspending gold convertibility and forcing other countries to revalue their currencies in 1971. An agreement in late 1971 reestablished fixed exchange rates after a short period in which some currencies floated, but most major currencies shifted to floating in 1973.

Another contributor to the collapse of the system was the ability of investors to take one-way speculative gambles against currencies that were perceived to be candidates for devaluation. The adjustable-peg system gave speculators a bet in which they could gain a lot if the currency was devalued but would lose little if it was not. Most governments did not have large enough holdings of official reserves to defend the fixed exchange rate against a determined speculative attack.

Chapter 21

1. Germany and the United Kingdom. There are two major determinants of how large an impact a change in one country's spending has on the other country. The first is the size of the first country relative to the size of the other. The second is the first country's marginal propensity to import from the other country. A country has a larger effect on the other country if it is larger and if it has a higher propensity to import, strengthening the link between the two countries. The United Kingdom and Germany are both large economies, and they trade a lot with each other (within the European Union).

3. a. The spending multiplier is $1/(0.2 + 0.1) = 3.3$, so domestic product will increase by $3.3 billion.
   b. For a closed economy, the spending multiplier is $1/0.2 = 5$, so domestic product will increase by

$5 billion. This spending multiplier is larger for a closed economy than for a small open economy because there is no import "leakage" for the closed economy. For both economies, as production and income rise following the initial increase in spending, some of the extra income goes into saving (and to pay taxes) so that the next rounds of increases in production and income are smaller. For the open economy, as production and income rise, there is an additional leakage out of the demand stream as some of the country's spending goes to additional imports. Spending on imports does not create extra demand for this country's production. The next rounds of increases in the country's production and income become smaller more quickly, resulting in a smaller multiplier.

5. The intersection of the *IS* and *LM* curves indicates a short-run equilibrium in the country's market for goods and services (the *IS* curve) and a short-run equilibrium in the country's market for money (the *LM* curve). The intersection indicates the equilibrium level of the country's real domestic product and income (its real GDP) and the equilibrium level of its interest rate. We evaluate internal balance by comparing the actual level of domestic product to the level that we estimate the economy is able to produce when it is fully using its supply-side production capabilities. If the short-run equilibrium level of domestic product is too low—less than this "full-employment" level—the country has an internal imbalance that results in high unemployment. If the short-run equilibrium level of domestic product is pushing to be too high—more than its "full-employment" level—the country has an internal imbalance that results in rising inflation (driven by excessive demand).

7. a. A decrease in the money supply tends to raise interest rates (and lower domestic product). Thus, the *LM* curve shifts up (or to the left).
   b. An increase in the interest rate does not shift the *LM* curve. Rather, it results in a movement along the *LM* curve.

9. a. An increase in foreign demand for the country's exports tends to drive the country's overall international payments into surplus. To reestablish payments balance, the country's domestic product and income could be higher (so imports

increase), or the country's interest rates could be lower (to create a capital outflow and reduce the country's capital account balance). Thus, the *FE* curve shifts to the right or down.

b. An increase in the foreign interest rate tends to drive the country's overall international payments into deficit because of capital outflows seeking the higher foreign returns. To reestablish payments balance, the country's domestic product could be lower (to reduce import), or its interest rates could be higher (to reverse the capital outflow). Thus, the *FE* curve shifts to the left or up.

c. An increase in the country's interest rate does not shift the *FE* curve. Rather, it results in a movement along the *FE* curve.

Chapter 22

1. Disagree. The risk is rising unemployment, not rising inflation. The deficit in its overall international payments puts downward pressure on the exchange rate value of the country's currency. The central bank must intervene to defend the fixed exchange rate by buying domestic currency and selling foreign currency in the foreign exchange market. As the central bank buys domestic currency, it reduces the monetary base and the country's money supply falls. The tightening of the domestic money supply puts upward pressure on the country's interest rates. Rising interest rates reduce interest-sensitive spending, lowering aggregate demand, domestic product, and national income. The risk is falling real GDP and rising unemployment.

3. Perfect capital mobility essentially eliminates the country's ability to run an independent monetary policy. The country must direct its monetary policy to keeping its interest rate in line with foreign interest rates. If it tried to tighten monetary policy, its interest rates would start to increase, but this would draw a massive inflow of capital. To defend the fixed exchange rate, the central bank would need to sell domestic currency into the foreign exchange market. This would increase the domestic money supply, forcing the central bank to reverse its tightening. If it tried to loosen monetary policy, interest rates would begin to decline, but the massive capital outflow would require the central bank to defend

the fixed rate by buying domestic currency. The decrease in the domestic money supply forces the central bank to reverse its loosening.

Perfect capital mobility makes fiscal policy powerful in affecting domestic product and income in the short run. For instance, expansionary fiscal policy tends to increase domestic product, but the increase in domestic product could be constrained by the crowding out of interest-sensitive spending as interest rates increase. With perfect capital mobility the domestic interest rate cannot rise if foreign interest rates are steady, so there is no crowding out. Domestic product and income increase by the full value of the spending multiplier.

5. Agree. Consider the value of the country's current account measured in foreign currency (superscript *F*):

$$CA^F = (P_x^F \cdot X) - (P_m^F \cdot M)$$

According to the logic of the J-curve analysis, the price changes resulting from the exchange rate change occur first, and the effects on export and import volumes occur more slowly. The revaluation quickly increases the foreign currency price of the country's exports (because it now takes more foreign currency to yield the same home-currency price). Therefore, the current account improves in the months immediately after the revaluation. (Eventually the revaluation leads to a decrease in export volume, an increase in import volume, and perhaps also an increase in the foreign-currency price of imports, so eventually the current account value is likely to decrease.)

7. a. The FE curve shifts to the right or down.
b. The capital inflows drive the country's overall international payments into surplus. They put upward pressure on the exchange rate value of the country's currency. The central bank must intervene to defend the fixed exchange rate by selling domestic currency in the foreign exchange market.
c. As the central bank intervenes by selling domestic currency in the foreign exchange market, the country's monetary base and its money supply increase. The increase in the money supply lowers domestic interest rates. The lower interest rates encourage interest-sensitive spending, raising aggregate demand, domestic product, and income. External balance is reestablished through

two adjustments. First, domestic product and income are higher so imports increase. Second, the country's interest rates are lower so the capital inflows are discouraged and capital outflows are encouraged.

The increases in the country's domestic product and income alter its internal balance. If the country began with high unemployment, then this would be welcome as a move toward internal balance. If, instead, the country does not have the resources to produce the extra output, the country would develop the internal imbalance of rising inflation as the economy tries to expand and overheats.

In the accompanying IS–LM–FE graph, the increased capital inflows shift the FE curve to the right to FE'. The country's international payments are then in surplus as the intersection of the original IS and LM curves at E_0 is to the left of FE'. The intervention to defend the fixed rate shifts the LM curve down (or to the right). External balance is reestablished at the new triple intersection E_1.

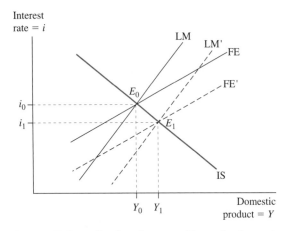

9. a. Tighten fiscal policy to address the internal imbalance of rising inflation, and tighten monetary policy to address the external imbalance of the deficit.
   b. Tighten fiscal policy to address the internal imbalance of rising inflation, and loosen monetary policy to address the external imbalance of the surplus.
   c. Loosen fiscal policy to address the internal imbalance of low demand, and loosen monetary policy to address the external imbalance of the surplus.

Chapter 23

1. Agree. The change in the exchange rate that occurs when there is a change in monetary policy is the basis for the enhanced effectiveness of monetary policy under floating exchange rates. For instance, when monetary policy shifts to be more expansionary, the decrease in the country's interest rate results in a depreciation of the country's currency. This is essentially overshooting (although overshooting also emphasizes that this depreciation is very large). It is overshooting relative to the path of the exchange rate implied by PPP so that the depreciation improves the country's international price competitiveness. The improvement in price competitiveness enhances the effectiveness of the policy. The country exports more and shifts some of its spending from imports to domestic products, further increasing aggregate demand, domestic product, and income.

3. Disagree. Under floating exchange rates the decrease in our exports reduces demand for our currency in the foreign exchange market so our currency depreciates. The depreciation improves our international price competitiveness so exports tend to rebound somewhat, and some spending is shifted from imports to domestic products. This increase in aggregate demand counters the initial drop in demand for our exports, so the adverse effect on our domestic product and income is lessened. This exchange rate adjustment is not possible if the exchange rate is fixed. In addition, with a fixed exchange rate our overall international payments go into deficit when our exports decline. The central bank then intervenes to defend the fixed rate by buying domestic currency. The reduction in the domestic money supply raises our interest rate and makes the decline in our domestic product larger.

5. The tendency for the overall international payments to go into deficit puts downward pressure on the exchange rate value of the country's currency, and it depreciates. This moves the country further from internal balance. The depreciation of the currency tends to increase aggregate demand by making the country's products more price-competitive internationally. The extra demand adds up to the inflationary pressure. In addition, the depreciation raises the domestic-currency price of imports, adding to the inflation pressure.

7. a. The increase in taxes reduces disposable income and reduces aggregate demand. U.S. domestic product and income will fall (or be lower than they otherwise would be). If national income is lower, spending on imports will be lower, so the U.S. current account will improve. The increase in taxes reduces the government budget deficit. The government borrows less, and U.S. interest rates are lower. If international capital flows are mainly responsive to changes in interest differentials, then the lower U.S. interest rates lead to capital outflows (or less capital inflows). The U.S. capital account declines.

b. The pressures on the exchange rate value of the dollar depend on which change is larger: the improvement in the current account or the deterioration in the capital account. If the effect on capital flows is larger, then demand for dollars will decrease (relative to the supply of dollars) in the foreign exchange market so the dollar will depreciate. If the current account change is larger, then the supply of dollars (relative to demand) will decrease, so the dollar will appreciate.

c. If the dollar depreciates, then the United States gains international price competitiveness. U.S. exports increase and imports decrease. The current account improves further. The increase in exports and shift of domestic spending from imports to domestic products add some aggregate demand, so domestic product and income rebound somewhat (or do not decline by as much).

9. a. The FE curve shifts to the right or down.

b. The country's international payments tend toward surplus. The extra demand for the country's currency leads to its appreciation.

c. The appreciation reduces the country's international price competitiveness so the country's exports decrease and its imports increase. The current account worsens, reducing the overall surplus. In addition, the decrease in aggregate demand as the current account worsens reduces domestic product and income. Money demand declines and the country's interest rate declines. The decline in the interest rate discourages some capital inflow or encourages some capital outflow. The capital account worsens, so the overall surplus also falls for this reason. The combined

effects on the current and capital accounts reestablish external balance. The declines in aggregate demand and domestic product affect the county's internal balance. If rising inflation was initially a problem, then this change is desirable. However, the decrease in aggregate demand could instead create or add to an internal imbalance of high unemployment.

In the accompanying IS–LM–FE graph, the increased capital inflows shift the FE curve to the right or down to FE'. The country's currency appreciates so the FE curve shifts back to the left somewhat to FE", and the IS curve shifts to the left to IS" as the country loses international price-competitiveness. The new triple intersection is at point E_2. External balance is reestablished, the interest rate is lower, and domestic product is lower, relative to the initial equilibrium at point E_0.

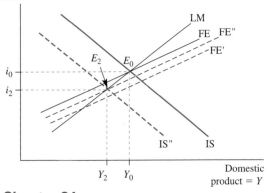

Interest rate = i

Domestic product = Y

Chapter 24

1. Disagree. Countries must follow policies that are not too different if they are to be able to maintain the fixed exchange rates. The policies need not be exactly the same, but the policies must lead to private demand and supply in the foreign exchange market that permits the countries to defend the fixed rates successfully. The most obvious need for consistency is in policies toward inflation rates. For fixed rates to be sustained, inflation rates must be the same or very similar for the countries involved. If inflation rates are the same, then fixed rates are consistent with purchasing power parity over time. If, instead, the inflation rates are different, then with

fixed exchange rates the high-inflation countries will lose price-competitiveness over time. Their international payments will tend toward deficits, and the fixed rates will not be sustainable in the face of the "fundamental disequilibrium." Another need for consistency is in policies that can have a major influence on international capital flows. If policies lead to large capital flows, especially outflows, they may overwhelm the government's ability to defend the fixed exchange rate.

3. A floating exchange rate provides some insulation from foreign business cycles because the rate tends to change in a way that counters the spread of the business cycle through international trade. For instance, when one country goes into recession, its demand for imports declines. This lowers the other country's exports, reducing its aggregate demand, and it also tends to go into recession. With floating exchange rates, the country's international payments tend to go into deficit when the country's exports decline, and the country's currency depreciates. The depreciation improves the country's international price-competitiveness. Its exports rebound somewhat, and it shifts some spending away from imports and toward domestic products. Therefore, aggregate demand rises back up. The tendency toward recession is not so strong, so floating exchange rates provide some insulation from foreign business cycles.

5. Possible criteria include the following. First, if the country wants to shift to a fixed exchange rate to promote international trade by reducing exchange rate risk, then it should consider fixing its exchange rate to the currency of one of its major trading partners. Second, the country should look for a country whose priorities and policies are compatible with its own. For instance, if the country wants to have and maintain a low inflation rate, then it should consider fixing its rate to the currency of a country that has and is likely to maintain policies that result in a low inflation rate. Third, the country should look for a country that is seldom subject to large domestic shocks. With a fixed exchange rate, any economic shocks in the other country will be transmitted to this country. (From this country's point of view, these are external shocks.) The country will lose the ability of floating exchange rates to buffer the disruptiveness of these external shocks, so it should

consider fixing its rate to a country that has a relatively stable domestic economy.

7. a. In the short run the country must implement policies to reduce aggregate demand. The reduction in aggregate demand will create the discipline of weak demand in putting downward pressure on the inflation rate. Tightening up on monetary policy is one way to do this in the short run, and it is crucial to reducing the inflation rate in the long run. In the long run the growth of the money supply is the major policy-controlled determinant of the country's inflation rate. The floating exchange rate can be affected by these policy changes, but the key to reducing the inflation rate is getting domestic policies pointed in the right direction.

   b. The major countries of the world generally have low inflation rates. Adopting a currency board and a fixed exchange rate with one of these currencies may help the country reduce its inflation rate for several reasons. First, the country is accepting the discipline effect of fixed exchange rates. If the country's demand expands too rapidly or its inflation rate is too high, its international payments tend to go into deficit. By intervening to defend the fixed exchange rate, the country's currency board will buy domestic currency. This tends to force a tighter monetary policy on the country. Second, the shift to the currency board and fixed exchange rate can enhance the credibility of the government's policy, signaling that the government is truly serious about reducing the country's inflation rate. Actually reducing the inflation rate is easier if people expect that it is going to decrease. Third, with a fixed exchange rate the local-currency prices of imported goods tend to be steady. The steady prices of imports not only reduce the country's measured inflation rate directly but also put competitive pressure on the prices of domestic products, so these prices do not rise as much.

9. There are several strong arguments. Here are four. First, joining the monetary union and adopting the euro will eliminate the transactions costs of exchanging pounds for euros. Resources used for this purpose can be shifted to other uses. The lower costs will encourage more British trade and invest-

ment with the member countries of the euro-zone. Second, joining the monetary union will eliminate exchange rate risk between the pound and the euro. Again, trade and investment with the euro-zone are encouraged. Third, the risk of rising British inflation is reduced, to the extent that the European Central Bank, with its structure similar to the German central bank, is likely to be better at controlling inflation than the British central bank would be. And finally, the shift to the euro can enhance the role of London as a center of international finance. As long as Britain stays out of the monetary union, European financial activities are likely to drift away from London to other centers (Frankfurt, Paris) where the euro is local currency.

Chapter 25

1. a. A rise in labor demand in the North.
   b. Any "push" factor in the South, such as population pressure or political upheaval.
   c. A drop in the cost or difficulty of migration.

3. The migrants don't gain the full Southern wage markup from $2.00 to $3.20 because some of their extra labor was supplied only at a marginal cost of their own time that rose from $2.00 to $3.20. That's shown in Figure 25.3 by the fact that the curve $S_r + S_{\text{mig}}$ leans further out to the right than does the curve S_r.

   As for the full international wage gain from $2.00 up to $5.00, it is true that the migrants do get paid that full extra $3. However, $1.80 of it is not a real gain in their well-being. It's just compensation for the economic and psychic costs of migrating.

5. She can do so by starting from an above-average income in Country A and moving to a below-average income in Country B. That happens often, and is consistent with her migrating to a higher personal income, as long as the national average income is much higher in B than in A.

7. The greatest net contributors were probably (*b*) electrical engineers arriving around 1970, whose high average salaries made them pay a lot of U.S. taxes and draw few government benefits. As for who contributed least, one could make a case for either (*a*) the political refugees or (*c*) the grandparents. The political refugees, as people who had not

been preparing themselves for life in a new economy until displaced by political events, are generally less well equipped to earn and pay taxes in the economy when they arrive. The grandparents are also likely to pay little taxes and may make some claims on government aid networks, though their qualification for social security is limited.

9. Here are several arguments. First, standard economic analysis shows that there are net economic gains to the Japanese economy, even if the gains to the immigrants are not counted. Japanese employers gain from access to a larger pool of workers, and these gains are larger than any losses to Japanese workers who must compete with the new immigrants (see Figure 25.3). Second, some of the immigrants will take on work that most Japanese shun, such as janitorial work. These immigrants view this work as an opportunity and better than what they had back in their home countries. Third, if immigrants are selectively admitted, the Japanese government can assure that they are net contributors to public finance—that they will pay more in taxes than they add to the costs of running government programs. The Japanese government should favor young adult immigrants, including many with skills that will be valued in the workplace. This effect on public finance is especially important for Japan, because it has a rapidly aging native population, so the costs of providing social security payments to retirees is going to rise quickly in the next decades. Fourth, immigrants bring with them a range of knowledge that can create spillover benefits for Japan. The immigrants bring food recipes, artistic talent, know-how about science and technology, and different ways of doing things. Japan wants to increase the creativity of its people and firms to be more successful in high-tech and information-intensive industries. Immigrants can be a source of creative sparks.

Chapter 26

1. Disagree. Borrowing from foreign lenders provides a net gain to the borrowing country, as long as the money is used wisely. For instance, as long as the money is used to finance new capital investments whose returns are at least as large as the cost of servicing the foreign debt, then the borrowing country

gains well-being. This is the gain of area $(d + e + f)$ in Figure 26.1.

3. The surge in bank lending to developing countries during 1974–1982 had these main causes: (1) a rise in bank funds from the "petrodollar" deposits by newly wealthy oil-exporting governments, (2) bank and investor concerns that investments in industrialized countries would not be profitable, because the oil shocks had created uncertainty about the strength of these economies, (3) developing countries' resistance to direct foreign investment, which led these countries to prefer loans as the way to borrow internationally, and (4) some amount of herding behavior by bank lenders, which built on the momentum of factors (1) through (3) and led to overlending.

5. a. World product without international lending is the shaded area. We first need to calculate the intercepts for the two MPK lines. The negative of the slope of MPK_{Japan} is 1 percent per 600, so the intercept for Japan is 12 percent. The "negative" of the slope of $MPK_{America}$ is also 1 percent per 600, so the intercept for America is about 14.7 percent. Japan's product is the rectangle of income from lending its wealth at 2 percent (120) plus the triangle above it (300), which is income for everyone else in Japan. America's product is the rectangle of income from lending its wealth at 8 percent (320) plus the triangle above it (about 134), which is income to everyone else in America. Adding up these four components, total world product is 874.

   b. Free international lending adds area RST (54), so total world product rises to 928.

   c. The 2 percent tax results in a loss of area TUV (6), so total world product falls to 922.

7. a. A large amount of short-term debt can cause a financial crisis, because lenders can refuse to roll over the debt or refinance it and instead demand immediate repayment. If the borrowing country cannot meet its obligations to repay, default becomes more likely.

   b. Lenders can become concerned that other countries in the region are also likely to be hit with financial crises. This contagion can then become a self-fulfilling panic. If lenders refuse to make new loans and sell off investments, the country

may not be able to meet its obligations to repay, so default becomes more likely. And the prices of the country's stocks and bonds can plummet as investors flee.

9. a. If lenders had detailed, accurate, and timely information on the debt and official reserves of a developing country, they should be able to make better lending and investing decisions, to avoid overlending or too much short-term lending. Better information should also reduce pure contagion, which is often based on vague concerns that other developing countries might be like the initial crisis country. In addition, developing countries that must report such detailed information are more likely to have prudent macroeconomic policies so that they do not have to report poor performance.

   b. Controls on capital inflows can (1) limit total borrowing by the country to reduce the risk of overlending and overborrowing, (2) reduce short-term borrowing if the controls are skewed against this kind of borrowing, and (3) reduce exposure to contagion by reducing the amount of loans and investments that panicked foreign lenders can pull out when a crisis hits some other country.

Chapter 27

1. Disagree. Most DFI goes to industrialized countries, especially the United States and Europe. Wages are not low in these countries. This DFI instead is used to gain access to large markets and to gain the insights and marketing advantages of producing locally in these markets.

3. Agree. One exposure is to exchange rate risk. The home-currency value of the assets of foreign affiliates will vary as exchange rates vary. If foreign-currency borrowings and other liabilities are used to finance the affiliates' assets, they provide a hedge against exchange rate risk by more closely balancing foreign-currency assets and liabilities. Another exposure is to the risk of expropriation. The host government sometimes exercises its power to seize the affiliate of multinational firms. If most of the affiliates' assets are financed by local borrowings and other local liabilities, then the parent firms lose

less because they can refuse to honor the liabilities once the assets are seized.

5. There are inherent disadvantages of DFI arising from lack of knowledge about local customs, practices, laws, and policies, and from the costs of managing across borders. Therefore, firms that undertake DFI successfully generally have some firm-specific advantages that allow them to compete successfully with local firms in the host country. Major types of firm-specific advantages include better technology, managerial and organizational skills, and marketing capabilities. These types of firm-specific advantages are important in industries such as pharmaceuticals and electronic products. The firms that have the advantages can undertake DFI successfully. These types of firm-specific advantages are less important in industries such as clothing and paper products. Fewer firms posses these types of advantages, and there is less DFI in these industries.

7. a. To lower its overall tax payments, the firm should reduce the size of the profits that it shows in its European affiliate and increase the profits shown in its Asian affiliate. It can accomplish this shift using transfer pricing by setting a relatively high price for the components that the Asian affiliate sells to the European affiliate. The higher price increases the profit margin in its Asian affiliate. It lowers the profit margin in its European affiliate (because the price of the components is a cost to the European affiliate as it uses the components to produce finished products).

   b. The government of the Asian country may be pleased with the transfer pricing. More profits are shown in the country, so its tax revenues are higher than they would be if the transfer prices were lower. The government of the European country is likely to be displeased. Its tax revenues are lower. It is likely to police transfer prices to try to ensure that the "correct" prices are used so the "correct" amount of profit is shown in the affiliates in its country.

9. Hymer's view is that DFI occurs so that the firm can protect and exploit the market power that it has as a monopolist or oligopolist. The firm uses firm-specific advantages as a basis for gaining market power, and then uses DFI to defend its market power. Such a view implies that countries that host DFI should view it skeptically. The multinational firm can use its market power to undertake activities and make decisions that are not in the host country's interest. For instance, the firm may limit its affiliates' ability to export to other countries, the firm may charge high prices to exploit its market power, or the firm may use its power to influence local politics, including lobbying for import barriers to shield its local affiliate from outside competition. This view justifies host government policies that restrict or screen DFI into the country, and that regulate the activities of affiliates within the country.

REFERENCES*

Abowd, John M., and Richard B. Freeman, eds. *Immigration, Trade, and the Labor Market.* Chicago: University of Chicago Press for the National Bureau of Economic Research, 1991.

Adams, John, ed. *The Contemporary International Economy: A Reader,* 2d ed. New York: St. Martin's Press, 1985.

Aliber, Robert Z. "Speculation in the Foreign Exchanges: The European Experience, 1919–1926." *Yale Economic Essays* 2 (1962), pp. 171–245.

Allen, Robert C. "International Competition in Iron and Steel, 1850–1913." *Journal of Economic History* 39, no. 4 (December 1979), pp. 911–938.

Amsden, Alice H. *Asia's Next Giant: South Korea and Late Industrialization.* New York: Oxford University Press, 1989.

Anderson, Kym, and Richard Blackhurst, eds. *The Greening of World Trade Issues.* New York: Harvester Wheat-sheaf, 1992.

Anderson, Kym, and Yujiro Hayami, with associates. *The Political Economy of Agricultural Protection.* London: Allen and Unwin, 1986.

Aylward, Lynn, and Rupert Thorne. "Countries' Repayment Performance Vis-à-Vis the IMF." *IMF Staff Papers* 45, no. 4 (December 1998), pp. 595–618.

Balassa, Bela. *The Structure of Protection in Developing Countries.* Baltimore: Johns Hopkins University Press, 1971.

———. *European Economic Integration.* Amsterdam: North-Holland, 1975.

Baldwin, Richard E., and Anthony J. Venables. "Regional Economic Integration." In Grossman and Rogoff (1995).

Baldwin, Robert E. "The Case Against Infant-Industry Protection." *JPE* 77 (1969), pp. 295–305.

———. "Trade Policies in Developed Countries." In Jones and Kenen, eds., *Handbook,* vol. I (1984).

———, and Anne O. Krueger, eds. *The Structure and Evolution of Recent U.S. Trade Policy.* Chicago: University of Chicago Press, 1984.

Bayard, Thomas O., and Kimberly Ann Elliott. *Reciprocity and Retaliation in U.S. Trade Policy.* Washington, DC: Institute for International Economics, 1994.

Beason, Richard, and David Weinstein. "Growth, Economies of Scale, and Targeting in Japan (1955–1990)." *Review of Economics and Statistics* 78, no. 2 (May 1996), pp. 286–295.

Bergsten, C. Fred, ed. *International Adjustment and Financing: The Lessons of 1985–1991.* Washington, DC: Institute for International Economics, 1991.

———, and C. Randall Henning. *Global Economic Leadership and the Group of Seven.* Washington, DC: Institute for International Economics, 1996.

Bhagwati, Jagdish N. "Immiserizing Growth." Reprinted in Caves and Johnson (1968).

———. *Trade, Tariffs and Growth.* Cambridge, MA: MIT Press, 1969.

———. *Anatomy and Consequences of Exchange Control Regimes.* Cambridge, MA: Ballinger, 1978.

———, and Robert E. Hudec, eds. *Fair Trade and Harmonization: Prerequisites for Free Trade? Vol. 1, Economic Analysis.* Cambridge, MA: MIT Press, 1996.

———, and Anne Krueger. A series of volumes on *Foreign Trade Regimes and Economic Development.* New York: Columbia University Press for the National Bureau of Economic Research, 1973–1976.

Binswanger, Hans P., and Pasquale L. Scandizzo. "Patterns in Agricultural Protection." Washington, DC: World Bank, November 1983. *Agricultural Research Unit Discussion Paper* no. 15.

---

*Often-cited journals:

AER = American Economic Review	*JIE = Journal of International Economics*
JEL = Journal of Economic Literature	*JPE = Journal of Political Economy*
JEP = Journal of Economic Perspectives	

Bloom, David E., Gilles Grenier, and Morley Gunderson. "The Changing Labor Market Position of Canadian Immigrants." Working Paper no. 4672. National Bureau of Economic Research, March 1994.

Bloomfield, Arthur I. *Monetary Policy Under the International Gold Standard, 1880–1914.* New York: Federal Reserve Bank of New York, 1959.

Bonner, Raymond. *At the Hand of Man: Peril and Hope for Africa's Wildlife.* New York: Knopf, 1993.

Bordo, Michael D., and Barry Eichengreen, eds. *Retrospective on the Bretton Woods International Monetary System.* Chicago: University of Chicago Press, 1992.

Bordo, Michael D., and Anna J. Schwartz, eds. *A Retrospect on the Classical Gold Standard, 1821–1931.* Chicago: University of Chicago Press, 1984.

Boreman, Stephen M. "Dolphin-Safe Tuna: What's in a Label? The Killing of Dolphins in the Eastern Tropical Pacific and the Case for an International Legal Solution." *Natural Resources Journal* 32, no. 3 (Summer 1992), pp. 425–447.

Borjas, George J. *Friends or Strangers: The Impacts of Immigrants on the U.S. Economy.* New York: Basic Books, 1990.

———. "Immigration and Self-Selection." In Abowd and Freeman (1991), pp. 29–76.

———. "The Economics of Immigration." *JEL* 32, no. 4 (December 1994), pp. 1667–1717.

———. "Immigration and Welfare, 1970–1990." In *Research in Labor Economics,* vol. 14, ed. Solomon W. Polachek. Greenwich, CT: JAI Press, 1995a.

———. "The Economic Benefit from Immigration." *JEP* 9, no. 2 (Spring 1995b), pp. 3–22.

———, Richard B. Freeman, and Laurence F. Katz. "How Much Do Immigration and Trade Affect Labor Market Outcomes?" *Brookings Papers on Economic Activity,* no. 1 (1997), pp. 1–90.

———, and Lynette Hilton. "Immigration and the Welfare State: Immigrant Participation in Means-Tested Entitlement Programs." *Quarterly Journal of Economics* 111, no. 2 (May 1996), pp. 575–604.

Bosworth, Barry P. *Saving and Investment in a Global Economy.* Washington, DC: Brookings Institution, 1993.

Bowen, Harry P., Edward E. Leamer, and Leo Sveikauskas. "Multicountry, Multifactor Tests of the Factor Abundance Theory." *AER* 77, no. 5 (December 1987).

Bowler, Ian A. *Agricultural Under the Common Agricultural Policy.* Manchester: Manchester University Press, 1985.

Brainard, S. Lael. "An Empirical Assessment of the Proximity-Concentration Trade-Off Between Multinational Sales and Trade." *AER* 87, no. 4 (September 1997), pp. 520–544.

Brander, James A. "Strategic Trade Policy." In Grossman and Rogoff (1995).

Brecher, Richard A., and Ehsan U. Choudri. "The Leontief Paradox, Continued." *JPE* 90, no. 4 (August 1982), pp. 820–823.

Breton, Albert. *The Economic Theory of Representative Government.* Chicago: Aldine, 1974.

Brown, Drusilla K., Alan V. Deardorff, and Robert M. Stern. "A North American Free Trade Agreement: Analytical Issues and a Computational Assessment." *World Economy* 15 (January 1992), pp. 11–30.

Bruton, Henry J. "A Reconsideration of Import Substitution." *JEL* 36, no. 2 (June 1998), pp. 903–936.

Bryant, Ralph C. *International Coordination of National Stabilization Policies.* Washington, DC: Brookings Institution, 1995.

Bryant, Ralph, Dale W. Henderson, Gerald Holtman, Peter Hooper, and Steven A. Symansky, eds. *Empirical Macroeconomics for Interdependent Economies.* Washington, DC: Brookings Institution, 1988.

Caves, Richard E. "Economic Models of Political Choice: Canada's Tariff Structure." *Canadian Journal of Economics* 4, no. 2 (May 1976), pp. 278–300.

———. *Multinational Enterprise and Economic Analysis,* 2d ed. New York: Cambridge University Press, 1996.

Cecchini, Paolo. *The European Challenge, 1992: The Benefits of a Single Market.* Aldershot, Hants.: Wildwood House, 1988.

Charnovitz, Steve. "Exploring the Environmental Exceptions in GATT Article XX." *Journal of World Trade* 25, no. 5 (October 1991), pp. 37–56.

Chiswick, Barry R. "Illegal Immigration and Immigration Control." *JEP* 2, 3 (Summer 1988), pp. 101–116.

Choksi, A., et al. *Trade Liberalization Episodes.* Oxford, England: Basil Blackwell, 1991.

Cline, William R. *Exports of Manufactures from Developing Countries.* Washington, DC: Brookings Institution, 1984.

———. *The Economics of Global Warming.* Washington, DC: Institute for International Economics, 1992.

———. *International Debt Reexamined.* Washington, DC: Institute for International Economics, 1995.

———. *Trade and Income Distribution.* Washington, DC: Institute for International Economics, 1997.

Collins, Susan. "Multiple Exchange Rates, Capital Controls, and Commercial Policy." In *Open Economy: Tools for Policy Makers in Developing Countries,* Rudiger Dornbusch, ed. New York: Oxford University Press, 1988.

Coughlin, Cletus C. "U.S. Trade-Remedy Laws: Do They Facilitate or Hinder Free Trade?" *Federal Reserve Bank of St. Louis Review,* July/August 1991, pp. 3–18.

Crystal, Graef. *In Search of Excess.* New York: W. W. Norton, 1991.

Deardorff, Alan V. "Testing Trade Theories and Predicting Trade Flows." In Jones and Kenen, eds., *Handbook,* vol. I, 1984.

Dertouzos, Michael L., Richard K. Lester, and Robert M. Solow. *Made in America.* Cambridge, MA: MIT Press, 1989.

Destler, I. M. *American Trade Politics.* 3d ed. New York and Washington, DC: Institute for International Economics, 1995.

Dixit, Avinash. "Tax Policy in Open Economies." In *Handbook of Public Economics,* eds. Alan Auerbach and Martin Feldstein. New York: North-Holland, 1985.

———, and Victor Norman. *The Theory of International Trade.* Welwyn: James Nisbet, 1980.

Dominguez, Kathryn M., and Jeffrey A. Frankel. *Does Foreign Exchange Market Intervention Work?* Washington, DC: Institute for International Economics, 1993.

Dooley, Michael P. "A Survey of Literature on Controls over International Capital Transactions." *IMF Staff Papers* 43, no. 4 (December 1996), pp. 639–687.

Dornbusch, Rudiger. "Expectations and Exchange Rate Dynamics." *JPE* 84, no. 6 (December 1976), pp. 1161–1176.

Downs, Anthony. *An Economic Theory of Democracy.* New York: Harper & Row, 1957.

Dufey, Gunter, and Ian H. Giddy. *International Money Market,* 2d ed. Englewood Cliffs, NJ: Prentice Hall, 1994.

Duncan, W. *U.S.–Japan Automobile Diplomacy.* Cambridge, MA: Ballinger, 1973.

Edison, Hali. "The Effectiveness of Central Bank Intervention: A Survey of the Post-1982 Literature." *Special Papers on International Economics* 18. Princeton, NJ: Princeton University, July 1993.

———, and Michael Melvin. "The Determinants and Implications of the Choice of an Exchange Rate System." In *Monetary Policy for a Volatile Global Economy,* eds. William Haraf and Thomas D. Willett. Washington, DC: American Enterprise Institute, 1990.

Edwards, Sebastian. "Trade Orientation, Distortions, and Growth in Developing Countries." *Journal of Development Economics* 39 (1992), pp. 31–57.

———. "Openness, Trade Liberalization, and Growth in Developing Countries." *JEL* 31, no. 3 (September 1993), pp. 1358–1394.

———. *Crisis and Reform in Latin America.* New York: Oxford University Press, 1995.

Eichengreen, Barry. "International Competition in the Products of U.S. Basic Industries." In *The United States in the World Economy,* ed. Martin Feldstein. Chicago: University of Chicago Press for the National Bureau of Economic Research, 1988.

———. *Gold Fetters: The Gold Standard and the Great Depression, 1919–1939.* New York: Oxford University Press, 1992.

———. "European Monetary Unification." *JEL* 31, no. 3 (September 1993), pp. 1321–1357.

———. *European Monetary Union: Theory, Practice, and Analysis.* Cambridge, MA: MIT Press, 1997.

———. *Toward a New International Financial Architecture: A Practical Post-Asia Agenda.* Washington, DC: Institute for International Economics, 1999.

———, and Peter H. Lindert, eds. *The International Debt Crisis in Historical Perspective.* Cambridge, MA: MIT Press, 1989.

Eiteman, David K., Arthur I. Stonehill, and Michael H. Moffet. *Multinational Business Finance,* 8th ed. New York: Addison-Wesley, 1998.

Elliott, Kimberly Ann, and J. David Richardson. "Determinants and Effectiveness of 'Aggressively Unilateral' U.S. Trade Actions." In Feenstra (1997).

Enders, Alice, and Amelia Porges. "Successful Conventions and Conventional Success: Saving the Ozone Layer." In Anderson and Blackhurst (1992), pp. 130–144.

Enoch, Charles, and Ann-Marie Gulde. "Are Currency Boards a Cure for All Monetary Problems?" *Finance and Development* 35, no. 4 (December 1998), pp. 40–43.

Espinosa, Marco, and Chong K. Yip. "International Policy Coordination: Can We Have Our Cake and Eat It Too?" *Federal Reserve Bank of Atlanta Economic Review* 78, no. 3 (May/June 1993), pp. 1–12.

Esty, Daniel C. *Greening the GATT: Trade, Environment, and the Future.* Washington, DC: Institute for International Economics, 1994.

Ethier, Wilfred J. "Dumping." *JPE* 90, no. 3 (June 1982), pp. 487–506.

Eun, Cheol S., and Bruce G. Resnick. *International Financial Management.* Burr Ridge, IL: Irwin/McGraw-Hill, 1998.

Feenstra, Robert C. "Estimating the Effects of Trade Policy." In Grossman and Rogoff (1995).

Feenstra, Robert C., ed. *Empirical Methods for International Trade.* Cambridge, MA: MIT Press, 1988.

———. "Auctioning U.S. Import Quotas, Foreign Response and Alternative Policies," *International Trade Journal* 3, no. 3 (Spring 1989), pp. 239–260.

———. "How Costly Is Protectionism?" *JEP* 6, no. 3 (Summer 1992), pp. 159–178.

———, ed. *Effects of U.S. Trade Protection and Promotion Policies.* Chicago: University of Chicago Press, 1997.

Feldstein, Martin, ed. *International Economic Cooperation.* Chicago: University of Chicago Press, 1988.

———. "The Political Economy of the European Economic and Monetary Union: Political Sources of an Economic Liability." *JEP* 11, no. 4 (Fall 1997), pp. 23–42.

———. "Refocusing the IMF." *Foreign Affairs* 77, no. 2 (March/April 1998), pp. 21–33.

Fieleke, Norman S. "The International Monetary Fund 50 Years After Bretton Woods." *New England Economic Review,* September/October 1994, pp. 17–30.

———. "International Capital Movements: How Shocking Are They?" *New England Economic Review* (March/April 1996), pp. 41–60.

Findlay, Ronald, and Harry Grubert. "Factor Intensities, Technological Progress, and the Terms of Trade." *Oxford Economic Papers* 11, no. 1 (February 1959), pp. 111–121.

Finger, J. Michael, ed. *Antidumping: How It Works and Who Gets Hurt.* Ann Arbor: University of Michigan Press, 1993.

Flam, Harry. "Product Markets and 1992: Full Integration, Large Gains?" *JEP* 6, no. 4 (Fall 1992), pp. 7–30.

Flam, Kenneth. *Mismanaged Trade? Strategic Policy and the Semiconductor Industry.* Washington, DC: Brookings Institution Press, 1996.

Fleming, J. Marcus. "Domestic Financial Policies Under Fixed and Floating Exchange Rates." *IMF Staff Papers* 9 (March 1962), pp. 369–377.

Flores, Jr., Renato G. "The Gains from MERCOSUR: A General Equilibrium, Imperfect Competition Evaluation." *Journal of Policy Modeling* 19, no. 1 (February 1997), pp. 1–18.

Frankel, Jeffrey A. "On the Mark: A Theory of Floating Exchange Rates Based on Real Interest Differentials." *AER* 69, no. 4 (September 1979), pp. 610–622.

———, and Andrew K. Rose. "An Empirical Characterization of Nominal Exchange Rates." In Grossman and Rogoff (1995).

Freeman, Richard B. "Are Your Wages Set in Beijing?" *JEP* 9, no. 3 (Summer 1995), pp. 15–32.

Friedberg, Rachel M., and Jennifer Hunt. "The Impact of Immigrants on Host Country Wages, Employment, and Growth." *JEP* 9, no. 2 (Spring 1995), pp. 23–44.

Friedman, Milton. "The Case for Flexible Exchange Rates." In his *Essays in Positive Economics.* Chicago: University of Chicago Press, 1985.

Froot, Kenneth A., and Kenneth Rogoff. "Perspectives on PPP and the Long-Run Real Exchange Rate." In Grossman and Rogoff (1995).

Froot, Kenneth A., and Richard H. Thaler. "Anomalies: Foreign Exchange." *JEP* 4, no. 3 (Summer 1990), pp. 179–192.

Gacs, Janos. "Trade Policy in the Czech and Slovak Republics, Hungary, and Poland in 1989–95—A Comparison." In *Trade and Payments in Central and Eastern Europe's Transforming Economies,* eds. Lucjan T. Orlowski and Dominick Salvatore. Westport, CT: Greenwood Press, 1997.

Gallarotti, Giulio M. "Centralized versus Decentralized International Monetary Systems: The Lesson of the Classical Gold Standard." *Cato Journal,* 1989.

Gardner, Bruce L. *The Economics of Agricultural Policies.* New York: Macmillan, 1988.

Genberg, Hans, and Alexander K. Swoboda. "Policy and Current Account Determination Under Floating Exchange Rates." *IMF Staff Papers* 36, no. 1 (March 1989), pp. 1–30.

Giddy, Ian H. *Global Financial Markets.* Lexington, MA: D. C. Heath, 1994.

Gilbert, Christopher L. "International Commodity Agreements: An Obituary Notice." *World Development* 24, no. 1 (January 1996), pp. 1–19.

Giovannini, Alberto. "How Do Fixed Exchange-Rate Regimes Work: The Evidence from the Gold Standard, Bretton Woods and the EMS." In *Blueprints for Exchange Rate Management,* eds. Marvin Miller, Barry Eichengreen, and Richard Portes. London: Center for Economic Policy Research, 1989.

Goldstein, Morris. *Asian Financial Crisis: Causes, Cures, and Systemic Implications.* Washington, DC: Institute for International Economics, 1998.

Goodfriend, Marvin. "Eurodollars." In *Instruments of the Money Market,* eds. Timothy Q. Cook and Timothy D. Rowe. Richmond, VA: Federal Reserve Bank of Richmond, 1986.

Gordon-Ashworth, Fiona. *International Commodity Cartels: A Contemporary History and Appraisal.* New York: St. Martin's Press, 1984.

Graham, Edward M., and Paul R. Krugman. *Foreign Direct Investment in the United States,* 3d ed. Washington, DC: Institute for International Economics, 1995.

Greenaway, David, and Chris Milner. *The Economics of Intra-Industry Trade.* Oxford, England: Basil Blackwell, 1986.

Greenaway, David, and P. K. M. Tharakan, eds. *Imperfect Competition and International Trade: The Policy Aspects of Intra-Industry Trade.* Atlantic Highlands, NJ: Humanities Press, 1986.

Grilli, Enzo R., and Maw Cheng Yang. "Primary Commodity Prices, Manufactured Goods Prices, and the Terms of Trade of Developing Countries: What the Long Run Shows." *World Bank Economic Review* 2, no. 1 (January 1988), pp. 1–47.

Grossman, Gene M., and Elhanan Helpman. "Technology and Trade." In Grossman and Rogoff (1995).

———, and Kenneth Rogoff. *Handbook of International Economics,* vol. III. New York: North-Holland, 1995.

Grubel, Herbert G., and P. J. Lloyd. *Intra-Industry Trade: The Theory and Measurement of Trade in Differentiated Products.* New York: John Wiley & Sons, 1975.

"Gunboat Diplomacy." *The Economist,* March 12, 1994, pp. 71–73.

Hakkio, Craig S. "Is Purchasing Power Parity a Useful Guide to the Dollar?" *Federal Reserve Bank of Kansas City Economic Review* 77, no. 3 (Third Quarter 1992), pp. 37–51.

Hathaway, Dale E., and Merlinda D. Ingco. "Agricultural Liberalization and the Uruguay Round." In *Uruguay Round and the Developing Countries,* eds. Will Martin and L. Alan Winters. New York: Cambridge University Press, 1996.

Hawkins, William R. "Neomercantilism: Is There a Case for Tariffs?" *National Review* April 6, 1984, pp. 25–45.

Hayes, J. P. *Economic Effects of Sanctions on Southern Africa.* Thames Essay no. 53. Aldershot, Hants.: Gower, 1987.

Heckscher, Eli. "The Effects of Foreign Trade on the Distribution of Income," originally published in 1919. In *Readings in the Theory of International Trade,* eds. Howard S. Ellis and Lloyd M. Metzler. Philadelphia: Blakiston, 1949.

Heliwell, John F., and Tim Padmore. "Empirical Studies of Macroeconomic Interdependence." In Jones and Kenen, eds., *Handbook,* vol. 2, (1984), pp. 1107–1151.

Helleiner, G. K. "The Political Economy of Canada's Tariff Structure: An Alternative Model." *Canadian Journal of Economics* 10, no. 2 (May 1977), pp. 318–326.

Helpman, Elhanan. "Monopolistic Competition in Trade Theory." *Special Papers in International Finance,* no. 16. Princeton, NJ: Princeton University, June 1990.

———, and Paul R. Krugman. *Market Structure and Foreign Trade.* Cambridge, MA: MIT Press, 1985.

Higgins, Bryon. "Was the ERM Crisis Inevitable?" *Federal Reserve Bank of Kansas City Economic Review* 78, no. 4 (Fourth Quarter 1993), pp. 27–40.

Hindley, Brian, and Patrick A. Messerlin. *Antidumping Industrial Policy: Legalized Protectionism in the WTO and What to Do About It.* Washington, DC: AEI Press, 1996.

Hoekman, Bernard, and Michael Kostecki. *Political Economy of the World Trading System: From GATT to WTO.* New York: Oxford University Press, 1996.

Hufbauer, Gary Clyde. "Surveying the Costs of Protection." In *World Trading System: Challenges Ahead,* ed. Jeffrey J. Schott. Washington, DC: Institute for International Economics, 1996.

Hufbauer, Gary Clyde, and Kimberly Ann Elliott. *Measuring the Costs of Protection in the United States.* Washington, DC: Institute for International Economics, 1994.

Hufbauer, Gary C., and J. J. Schott. *Economic Sanctions in Support of Foreign Policy Goals.* Washington, DC: Institute for International Economics, 1983.

———. *Economic Sanctions Reconsidered.* Washington, DC: Institute for International Economics, 1985.

———. *NAFTA: An Assessment,* rev. ed. Washington, DC: Institute for International Economics, 1993.

Humpage, Owen F. "Institutional Aspects of U.S. Intervention." *Federal Reserve Bank of Cleveland Economic Review* 30, no. 1 (Quarter 1, 1994), pp. 2–19.

Hymer, Stephen H. *The International Operation of National Firms: A Study of Direct Foreign Investment.* Cambridge, MA: MIT Press, 1976.

International Monetary Fund. *International Financial Statistics.* Washington, DC: IMF, various months and years.

Irwin, Douglas A. *Against the Tide: An Intellectual History of Free Trade.* Princeton, NJ: Princeton University Press, 1996.

Johnson, Chalmers. *MITI and the Japanese Miracle: The Growth of Industrial Policy, 1925–1975.* Palo Alto, CA: Stanford University Press, 1982.

Johnson, George E. "Changes in Earnings Inequality: The Role of Demand Shifts." *JEP* 11, no. 2 (Spring 1997), pp. 41–54.

Johnson, Harry G. "The Cost of Protection and the Scientific Tariff." *JPE* 68, no. 4 (August 1960), pp. 327–345.

———. "Optimal Trade Policy in the Presence of Domestic Distortions." In *Trade, Growth and the Balance of Payments,* ed. Robert E. Baldwin. Chicago: Rand McNally, 1965.

Jones, Kent A. *Export Restraint and the New Protectionism: The Political Economy of Discriminatory Trade Restrictions.* Ann Arbor: University of Michigan Press, 1994.

Jones, Ronald W., and Peter B. Kenen, eds. *Handbook of International Economics.* Two volumes. New York: North-Holland, 1984.

Kamin, Steven B. "Devaluation, External Balance, and Macroeconomic Performance: A Look at the Numbers." *Princeton Studies in International Finance* no. 62. Princeton, NJ: Princeton University, August 1988.

Koedijk, Kees G., and Mack Ott. "Risk Aversion, Efficient Markets, and the Forward Exchange Rate." *Federal Reserve Bank of St. Louis Review* 69, no. 6 (December 1987), pp. 5–13.

Krueger, Anne O. "The Political Economy of a Rent-Seeking Society." *AER* 64, no. 3 (June 1974), pp. 291–303.

———. *The Benefits and Costs of Import Substitution in India: A Microeconomic Study.* Minneapolis: University of Minnesota Press, 1975.

———. "Trade Policies in Developing Countries." In Jones and Kenen, eds., *Handbook,* vol. I (1984).

———. *Economic Policy at Cross Purposes.* Washington, DC: Brookings Institution, 1993.

———, Maurice Schiff, and Alberto Valdés, eds. *The Political Economy of Agricultural Price Policies.* Oxford, England: Oxford University Press, 1992.

Krugman, Paul R. "Increasing Returns, Monopolistic Competition, and International Trade." *JIE* 9 (1979), pp. 469–479.

————. "New Theories of Trade Among Industrial Countries." *AER* 73, no. 2 (May 1983), pp. 343–347.

————, ed. *Strategic Trade Policy and the New International Economics.* Cambridge, MA: MIT Press, 1986.

Lancaster, Kelvin. "Intra-Industry Trade Under Perfect Monopolistic Competition." *JIE* 10 (1980), pp. 151–175.

Laster, David S., and Robert N. McCauley. "Making Sense of the Profits of Foreign Firms in the United States." *Federal Reserve Bank of New York Quarterly Review* 19, no. 2 (Summer–Fall 1994), pp. 44–73.

Lavergne, Real P. *The Political Economy of U.S. Tariffs.* New York: Academic Press, 1983.

Lawrence, Robert Z. *Single World, Divided Nations? International Trade and OECD Labor Markets.* Washington, DC: Brookings Institution Press, 1996.

Lawrence, Robert Z., and Matthew J. Slaughter. "International Trade and American Wages in the 1980s: Giant Sucking Sound or Small Hiccup?" *Brookings Papers on Economic Activity: Microeconomics* no. 2, 1993, pp. 161–226.

Leahy, Michael P. "The Profitability of U.S. Intervention in the Foreign Exchange Market." *Journal of International Money and Finance* 14, no. 6 (December 1995), pp. 823–844.

Leamer, Edward E. "The Leontief Paradox, Reconsidered." *JPE* 88, no. 3 (June 1980), pp. 495–503.

————. *Sources of International Comparative Advantage: Theory and Evidence.* Cambridge, MA: MIT Press, 1984.

————, and James Levinson. "International Trade Theory: The Evidence." In Grossman and Rogoff (1995).

Leontief, Wassily. "Factor Proportions and the Structure of American Trade: Further Theoretical and Empirical Analysis." *Review of Economics and Statistics* 38, no. 4 (November 1956), pp. 386–407.

————. "Domestic Production and Foreign Trade: The American Capital Position Reexamined." *Economia Internazionale* 7 (February 1954), pp. 3–32.

Levich, Richard M. "Is the Foreign Exchange Market Efficient?" *Oxford Review of Economic Policy* 5, no. 3 (October 1989), pp. 40–60.

————. *International Financial Markets: Prices and Policies.* Burr Ridge, IL: Irwin/McGraw-Hill, 1998.

Lindert, Peter H. *Key Currencies and Gold, 1900–1913.* Princeton, NJ: Princeton University Press, 1969.

————. "Historical Patterns in Agricultural Policy." In *Agriculture and the State: Growth, Employment and Poverty in Developing Countries,* ed. C. Peter Timmer. Ithaca, NY: Cornell University Press, 1990.

————. "Foreign Trade and Trade Policy in the Twentieth Century." In *Cambridge Economic History of the United States,* vol. III, eds. Stanley Engerman and Robert Gallman. New York: Cambridge University Press, forthcoming.

Lipsey, Robert E., and Brigitta Swendenborg. "The High Cost of Eating: Causes of International Differences in Consumer Food Prices." *Review of Income and Wealth* 42, no. 2 (June 1996), pp. 181–194.

Low, Patrick. *Trading Free: The GATT and U.S. Trade Policy.* New York: Twentieth Century Fund, 1993.

Lustig, Nora. *Mexico: The Remaking of an Economy.* Washington, DC: Brookings Institution, 1992.

————, Barry P. Bosworth, and Robert Z. Lawrence, eds. *North American Free Trade: Assessing the Impact.* Washington, DC: Brookings Institution, 1992.

MacDonald, Ronald, and Ian W. Marsh. "On Fundamentals and Exchange Rates: A Casselian Approach." *Review of Economics and Statistics* 79, no. 4 (November 1997), pp. 655–664.

————, and Mark P. Taylor. "Exchange Rate Economics: A Survey." *IMF Staff Papers* 39, no. 1 (March 1992), pp. 1–57.

————. "The Monetary Approach to the Exchange Rate: Rational Expectations, Long-Run Equilibrium, and Forecasting." *IMF Staff Papers* 40, no. 1 (March 1993), pp. 89–107.

————. "The Monetary Model of the Exchange Rate: Long-Run Relationships, Short-Run Dynamics and How to Beat a Random Walk." *Journal of International Money and Finance* 13, no. 3 (June 1994), pp. 276–290.

Magee, Stephen P. "Twenty Paradoxes in International Trade Theory." In *International Trade and Agriculture: Theory and Policy,* eds. Jimmye Hillman and Andrew Schmitz. Boulder, CO: Westview, 1979, pp. 91–116.

————, William Brock, and Leslie Young. *Black Hole Tariffs and Endogenous Policy Theory.* Cambridge, England: Cambridge University Press, 1989.

Mahler, Miles, ed. *Capital Flows and Financial Crises.* Ithaca, NY: Cornell University Press, 1998.

Mark, Nelson C. "Exchange Rates and Fundamentals: Evidence on Long-Horizon Predictability." *AER* 85, no. 1 (March 1995), pp. 201–218.

Markusen, James R. "The Boundaries of Multinational Enterprises and the Theory of International Trade." *JEP* 9, no. 2 (Spring 1995), pp. 169–189.

Marston, Richard C. *International Financial Integration: A Study of Interest Differentials Between the Major Industrial Economies.* New York: Cambridge University Press, 1995.

Maskus, Keith E. "A Test of the Heckscher–Ohlin–Vanek Theorem: The Leontief Commonplace." *JIE* 19, nos. 3/4 (November 1985), pp. 201–212.

Mayer, Thomas, James S. Duesenberry, and Robert Z. Aliber. *Money, Banking, and the Economy,* 4th ed. New York: W. W. Norton, 1990.

McCalla, Alex F., and Timothy E. Josling. *Agricultural Policies and World Markets.* New York: Macmillan, 1985.

McKinnon, Ronald. "Optimum Currency Areas." *AER* 53, no. 1 (March 1963), pp. 717–725.

———. "Monetary and Exchange Rate Policies for International Financial Stability: A Proposal." *JEP* 2, no. 1 (Winter 1988), pp. 83–103.

———. "International Money in Historical Perspective." *JEL* 31, no. 1 (March 1993), pp. 1–44.

———. *Rules of the Game.* Cambridge, MA: MIT Press, 1996.

Meade, James. *Trade and Welfare.* Oxford, England: Oxford University Press, 1955.

Meese, Richard. "Currency Fluctuations in the Post-Bretton Woods Era." *JEP* 4, no. 1 (Winter 1990), pp. 117–134.

———, and Kenneth Rogoff. "Empirical Exchange Rate Models of the Seventies: How Well Do They Fit Out of Sample?" *JIE* 14 (February 1983), pp. 3–24.

Michalopoulos, Constantine, and David Tarr. *Trade Performance and Policy in the New Independent States.* Washington, DC: World Bank, 1996.

Milner, Chris, ed. *Export Promotion Strategies: Theory and Evidence from Developing Countries.* New York: New York University Press, 1990.

Moran, Theodore H. *Foreign Direct Investment and Development.* Washington, DC: Institute for International Economics, 1998.

Morici, Peter. *Making Free Trade Work: The Canada–U.S. Agreement.* New York: Council on Foreign Relations, 1991.

———. *A New Special Relationship: Free Trade and U.S.–Canada Economic Relations in the 1990s.* Ottawa: Center for Trade Policy and Law, 1991.

Morkre, Morris E., and Kenneth H. Kelly. *Effects of Unfair Imports on Domestic Industries: U.S. Antidumping and Countervailing Duty Cases, 1980 to 1988.* U.S. Federal Trade Commission, Bureau of Economics, 1994.

Moyer, H. Wayne, and Timothy E. Josling. *Agricultural Policy Reform.* Ames: Iowa State University Press, 1990.

Mundell, Robert. *International Economics.* New York: Macmillan, 1968.

———. "A Theory of Optimum Currency Areas." *AER* 51, no. 4 (September 1961), pp. 657–665.

Mussa, Michael. "Tariffs and the Distribution of Income." *JPE* 82, no. 6 (December 1974), pp. 1191–1204.

Mutti, John, and Peter Morici. *Changing Patterns of U.S. Industrial Activity and Comparative Advantage.* Washington, DC: National Planning Association, 1983.

Neal, Larry, and Daniel Barbezat. *Economics of the European Union and the Economies of Europe.* New York: Oxford University Press, 1998.

Nurkse, Ragnar. *International Currency Experience: Lessons of the Interwar Period.* Geneva, Switzerland: League of Nations, 1944.

Obstfeld, Maurice. "Europe's Gamble." *Brookings Papers on Economic Activity,* no. 2 (1997), pp. 241–300.

———, and Kenneth Rogoff. "The Mirage of Fixed Exchange Rates." *JEP* 9, no. 4 (Fall 1995), pp. 73–96.

———. "The Global Capital Market: Benefactor or Menace?" *JEP* 12, no. 4 (Fall 1998), pp. 9–30.

Ohlin, Bertil. *International and Interregional Trade.* Cambridge, MA: Harvard University Press, 1933.

Olson, Mancur. *The Logic of Collective Action.* Cambridge, MA: Harvard University Press, 1965.

Organization for Economic Cooperation and Development (OECD). *The Economics of Transfrontier Pollution.* Paris: OECD, 1976.

———. *EMU: Facts, Challenges, and Policies.* Washington, DC: OECD, 1999.

O'Rourke, Kevin, Alan M. Taylor, and Jeffrey G. Williamson. "Land, Labor, and the Wage-Rental Ratio: Factor-Price Convergence in the Late Nineteenth Century." Discussion Paper no. 1629. Cambridge, MA: Harvard Institute of Economic Research, March 1993.

O'Rourke, Kevin, and Jeffrey G. Williamson. "Were Heckscher and Ohlin Right? Factor-Price Convergence in Economic History." *Journal of Economic History* 54, no. 4 (December 1994).

Oswald, Rudy. "Statement of U.S. Aims at the World Trade Ministers' Meeting: A Labor View." In Adams (1985).

Pauls, B. Diane. "U.S. Exchange Rate Policy: Bretton Woods to the Present." *Federal Reserve Bulletin* 76, no. 11 (November 1990), pp. 891–908.

Pigott, Charles A. "International Interest Rate Convergence: A Survey of the Issues and Evidence." *Federal Reserve Bank of New York Quarterly Review* 18, no. 4 (Winter 1993–1994), pp. 24–37.

Pitchford, Ruth, and Adam Cox, eds. *EMU Explained: Markets and Monetary Union,* 2d ed. London: Kegan Paul, 1998.

Pomfret, Richard. *Economics of Regional Trading Arrangements.* Oxford: Clarendon Press, 1997.

Pope, David, and Glenn Withers. "Do Migrants Rob Jobs? Lessons of Australian History, 1861–1991," *Journal of Economic History* 53, no. 4 (December 1993), pp. 719–742.

Postner, Harry. *The Factor Content of Canada's Foreign Trade.* Ottawa: Economic Council of Canada, 1975.

Prestowitz, Clyde. *Trading Places: How We Allowed Japan to Take the Lead.* New York: Basic Books, 1988.

Prusa, Thomas J. "The Trade Effects of U.S. Antidumping Actions." In Feenstra (1997).

Ray, Edward John. "The Determinants of Tariff and Nontariff Trade Restrictions in the United States." *JPE* 89, no. 1 (February 1981), pp. 105–121.

———, and Howard P. Marvel. "The Patterns of Protection in the Industrialized World." *Review of Economics and Statistics* 66, no. 3 (August 1984), pp. 452–458.

Reagan, Ronald. *An American Life.* New York: Simon & Schuster, 1990.

Ricardo, David. *On the Principles of Political Economy and Taxation.* London: John Murray, 1817.

Richardson, J. David. *Sizing Up U.S. Export Disincentives.* Washington, DC: Institute for International Economics, 1993.

Richardson, Pete. "The Structure and Simulation Properties of OECD's Interlink Model." *OECD Economic Studies* 10 (Spring 1988), pp. 57–121.

Rivera-Batiz, Francisco L., and Luis A. Rivera-Batiz. *International Finance and Open Economy Macroeconomics,* 2d ed. New York: Macmillan, 1994.

Rivera-Batiz, Luis A., and Paul M. Romer. "Economic Integration and Endogenous Growth." *Quarterly Journal of Economics* 106, no. 2 (May 1991), pp. 531–556.

Romer, Paul. "New Goods, Old Theory, and the Welfare Cost of Trade Restrictions." *Journal of Development Economics* 43, no. 1 (February 1994), pp. 5–38.

Rueff, Jacques. Translated by Roger Glemet. *The Monetary Sin of the West.* New York: Macmillan, 1972.

Ruffin, Roy J. "The Missing Link: The Ricardian Approach to the Factor Endowments Theory of Trade." *AER* 78, no. 4 (September 1988), pp. 759–772.

Sachs, Jeffrey D., and Andrew M. Warner. "Economic Reform and the Process of Global Integration." *Brookings Papers on Economic Activity,* no. 1 (1995), pp. 1–95.

Samuelson, Paul A. "International Factor-Price Equalization Once Again." *Economic Journal* 59, no. 234 (June 1949), pp. 181–197.

Saunders, R. S. "The Political Economy of Effective Protection in Canada's Manufacturing Sector." *Canadian Journal of Economics* 13, no. 2 (May 1980), pp. 340–348.

Scandizzo, Pasquale L., and Dimitris Diakosawas. *Instability in the Terms of Trade of Primary Commodities, 1900–1982.* Rome: UN, FAO 1987.

Schott, Jeffrey J. *The Uruguay Round: An Assessment.* Washington, DC: Institute for International Economics, 1994.

Simon, Julian L. *The Economic Consequences of Immigration.* Oxford, England: Basil Blackwell, 1989.

Smith, Adam. *Wealth of Nations.* Originally published 1776. New York: Random House (Modern Library edition), 1937.

Smith, James P., and Barry Edmonston, eds. *New Americans: Economic, Demographic, and Fiscal Effects of Immigration.* Washington, DC: National Academy Press, 1997.

Solomon, Robert. *The International Monetary System, 1945–1976.* New York: Harper & Row, 1977.

Stern, J., and D. Chew, eds. *New Developments in International Finance.* Oxford, England: Basil Blackwell, 1988.

Stern, Robert M. *The Balance of Payments.* Chicago: Aldine, 1973.

———, and Keith E. Maskus. "Determinants of the Structure of U.S. Foreign Trade, 1958–76." *JIE* 11, no. 2 (May 1981), pp. 207–224.

Stiglitz, Joseph E. "Dumping on Free Trade: The U.S. Import Trade Laws." *Southern Economic Journal* 64, no. 2 (October 1997), pp. 402–424.

Stolper, Wolfgang F., and Paul A. Samuelson. "Protection and Real Wages." *Review of Economic Studies* 9 (November 1941), pp. 58–73.

Subramanian, Arvind. "Trade Measures for Environmental Regulation: A Nearly Empty Box?" *World Economy,* January 1992, pp. 17–33.

Summers, Robert, and Alan Heston. "A New Set of International Comparisons of Real Product and Price Levels: Estimates for 130 Countries, 1950–1985." *Review of Income and Wealth,* series 34, no. 1 (March 1988), pp. 1–25, and attached diskettes.

Suslow, Valerie Y. "Stability in International Cartels: An Empirical Survey." *Working Paper in Economics* E-88-7. Stanford University, Hoover Institution, February 1988.

Taylor, Dean. "Official Intervention in the Foreign Exchange Market, or, Bet Against the Central Bank." *JPE* 90, no. 2 (April 1982), pp. 356–368.

Taylor, Mark P. "Covered Interest Arbitrage and Market Turbulence." *Economic Journal* 99, no. 396 (June 1989), pp. 376–391.

———. "The Economics of Exchange Rates." *JEL* 33, no. 1 (March 1995), pp. 13–47.

Tharakan, P. K. M. *Policy Implications of Antidumping Measures.* New York: North-Holland, 1991.

———, ed. *Intra-Industry Trade: Empirical and Methodological Aspects.* Amsterdam: North-Holland, 1983.

Tower, Edward, and Thomas D. Willett. "The Theory of Optimum Currency Areas and Exchange Rate Flexibility." *Special Papers in International Economics* no. 11. Princeton, NJ: Princeton University, May 1976.

Trefler, Daniel. "International Factor Price Differences: Leontief Was Right!" *JPE* 101, no. 6 (December 1993), pp. 961–987.

———. "The Case of the Missing Trade and Other Mysteries." *AER* 85, no. 5 (December 1995), pp. 1029–1046.

Triffin, Robert. *Gold and the Dollar Crisis.* New Haven, CT: Yale University Press, 1960.

Tsiang, S. C. "Fluctuating Exchange Rates in Countries with Relatively Stable Economies: Some European Experiences After World War I." *IMF Staff Papers* 7 (October 1959), pp. 244–273.

Tyers, Rodney, and Kym Anderson. *Disarray in World Food Markets.* Cambridge, England: Cambridge University Press for the Trade Policy Research Centre, 1992.

Tyson, Laura D'Andrea. *Who's Bashing Whom? Trade Conflict in High-Technology Industries.* Washington, DC: Institute for International Economics, 1992.

Uimonen, Peter, and John Whalley. *Environmental Issues in the New World Trading System.* New York: St. Martin's Press, 1997.

United Nations Centre on Transnational Corporations. *Determinants of Foreign Direct Investment: A Survey of the Evidence.* New York: United Nations, 1992.

U.S. Congress, Office of Technology Assessment. *U.S.–Mexico Trade: Pulling Together or Pulling Apart?* Washington, DC: U.S. Government Printing Office, 1992.

———. *Multinationals and the National Interest: Playing by Different Rules.* Washington, DC: U.S. Government Printing Office, 1993.

Vanek, Jaroslav. *International Trade: Theory and Economic Policy.* Homewood, IL: Richard D. Irwin, 1962.

Vernon, Raymond G. "International Investment and International Trade in the Product Cycle." *Quarterly Journal of Economics* 80, no. 2 (May 1966), pp. 190–207.

————. "The Product Cycle Hypotheses in a New International Environment." *Oxford Bulletin of Economics and Statistics* 41 (November 1979), pp. 255–267.

Vernon, Raymond G., ed. *The Oil Crisis.* New York: W. W. Norton, 1976.

Vona, Stefano. "Intra-Industry Trade: A Statistical Artifact or a Real Phenomenon?" *Banca Nazionale del Lavorno Quarterly Review* 175 (December 1990), pp. 383–412.

————. "On the Measurement of Intra-Industry Trade: Some Further Thoughts." *Weltwirtschaftliches Archiv.* 127, no. 4 (1991), pp. 678–700.

Weintraub, Sidney. *NAFTA at Three: A Progress Report.* Washington, DC: Center for Strategic and International Studies, 1997.

Whalley, John, and Colleen Hamilton. *Trading System After the Uruguay Round.* Washington, DC: Institute for International Economics, 1996.

Whitt, Joseph A., Jr. "Flexible Exchange Rates: An Idea Whose Time Has Passed?" *Federal Reserve Bank of Atlanta Economic Review* 75, no. 5 (September/October 1990), pp. 2–15.

————. "Monetary Union in Europe." *Federal Reserve Bank of Atlanta Economic Review* 79, no. 1 (January/February 1994), pp. 11–27.

Williamson, John. *Exchange Rate System,* rev. ed. Washington, DC: Institute for International Economics, 1985.

Wonnacott, Paul, and Ronald J. Wonnacott. "Free Trade Between the United States and Canada: Fifteen Years Later." *Canadian Public Policy*, October 1982, supplement.

Wonnacott, Ronald J., and Paul Wonnacott. *Free Trade Between the United States and Canada: The Potential Economic Effects.* Cambridge, MA: Harvard University Press, 1967.

Woo, Wing T. "The Monetary Approach to Exchange Rate Determination Under Rational Expectations: The Dollar–Deutschemark Rate." *JIE* 18 (1985), pp. 1–16.

Woodward, Douglas, and Douglas Nigh, eds. *Foreign Ownership and the Consequences of Direct Investment in the United States: Beyond Us and Them.* Westport, CT: Quorum Books, 1998.

World Bank. *World Development Report 1994.* New York: Oxford University Press, 1994.

World Resource Institute. *World Resources 1992–93.* New York: Oxford University Press, 1992.

Wynne, Mark A. "The European System of Central Banks." *Economic Review, Federal Reserve Bank of Dallas* (First Quarter 1999), pp. 1–14.

Wyplosz, Charles. "EMU: Why and How It Might Happen." *JEP* 11, no. 4 (Fall 1997), pp. 3–21.

Yamamura, Kozo. "Caveat Emptor: The Industrial Policy of Japan." In Krugman (1986).

Yeager, Leland B. "A Rehabilitation of Purchasing-Power-Parity." *JPE* 66, no. 6 (December 1958), pp. 516–530.

————. *International Monetary Relations.* New York: Harper & Row, 1976.

Zeile, William J. "Industrial Targeting, Business Organization, and Industry Productivity Growth in the Republic of Korea, 1972–1985." Unpublished Ph.D. dissertation, University of California–Davis, 1993.

Zimmerman, Klaus F. "Tackling the European Migration Problem." *JEP* 9, no. 2 (Spring 1995), pp. 45–61.